A COMPENDIUM

OF THE

THEOLOGICAL WRITINGS

OF

EMANUEL SWEDENBORG

SAMUEL M. WARREN

PUBLISHED UNDER AUSPICES OF
THE IUNGERICH PUBLICATION FUND

SWEDENBORG FOUNDATION, INC.
NEW YORK

First Edition 1875
Reprinted 1885
,, 1896
,, 1901
,, 1909
,, 1918
,, 1939
,, 1954
,, 1974
,, 1977

Standard Book Number 0-87785-123-9
Library of Congress Catalog Card Number 73-94196

Manufactured in the United States of America

6·10·77 aift to HQ

PREFACE

This volume is constructed on the basis of the "Compendium" compiled by the late Rev. W. H. Fernald, which is long since out of print. The larger proportion of the extracts contained in that volume will be found also in this; together with many new extracts, and a number of new subjects, added by the present compiler; and the whole have been almost entirely rearranged. The book being made up of extracts, the reader will reasonably not expect the same continuity that would be looked for in an original and connected work. A constant effort has been made, however, in the arrangement of the chapters, as well as in the construction of them, to give the volume as much of the character of a continued treatise as was practicable. It is hoped that this object will be found to have been so far attained, that the volume will not be ill adapted to consecutive reading, by those who would obtain, in briefer compass, a general view of the theology and spiritual philosophy embodied in the author's voluminous writings.

The large number of volumes from which the extracts are taken having been translated from the original Latin by different persons, at widely different times, it was deemed important, in such a work, that there should be some attempt at uniformity of style and rendering,—apart from any consideration of the very great and acknowledged imperfections of most of the translations. The translation is therefore for the most part new; and the comparatively small number of extracts that have not been re-translated have been more or less carefully revised.

Some word of apology may be due to the reader who shall make his first acquaintance with the writings of Swedenborg through this volume, for the use of certain unfamiliar terms. The present condition of mankind being such that internal things are but dimly and generally perceived, the mind does not take cognizance of their plurality. It sees as an individual thing what in reality is very multiple. And therefore we have in common use in language only singular terms for many internal things. Thus we commonly speak of good, happiness, etc., which are of the will, and internal, only in the singular number; while to corresponding things that are more external, delights, joys, pleasures, enjoyments, etc., we ascribe plurality, —because we perceive their plurality. This is the reason why, to the unaccustomed mind, there appears a certain oddity of expression in the writings of Swedenborg, where internal things are the constant theme, and are described as they really are, and as they are discerned in heaven,—and, with less fulness, by some on earth. To modify the author's language in order to escape the oddity of unfamiliar expressions, would be to shut out from the reader's mind a large and most valuable part of the spiritual philosophy his writings contain; and would at least endanger his falling into great misapprehensions. The importance of rendering the author into pleasant and popular English *as far as practicable* has, however, not been out of mind; but the translator has not felt at liberty knowingly to sacrifice any shade of the author's meaning on account of it. The writings of Swedenborg embody a system of most profound philosophy, spiritual and natural; and, as with most philosophical writings, and perhaps more than most, it requires for exact expression language in some degree its own; which cannot be changed for more popular and current phraseology without, as was said, the loss of some part of the author's meaning, and while seeming to favour, really hindering the actual apprehension of the profound subjects treated of. What would be the thought of the editor of any of the treatises on which systems of speculative philosophy are founded, if he should undertake to adapt and popularize his author, by doing away with his technical and philosophical terms? But these writings contain a system of philosophy more profound and vast than any and all systems of man's devising. How much less justifiable would it be, then, so to attempt to popularize the standard text of such a system. The place to adapt and apply the teaching of an author, especially such an author, is not in the translation of his writings, but in books and teachings in elucidation and exposition of them.

It may not be out of place to guard the reader against any supposition that the title "Compendium" is intended to involve the idea of condensation, and that the whole substance, or anything more than a general view, and example, of the author's teaching is here given. So far is this from being the case, that there are even very many topics of great interest that could not be included in a volume like this. He who is interested to know the scope and depth of these teachings should study the writings themselves. Nor let him be appalled at the magnitude of the undertaking. For they are as full of varied and most interesting matter everywhere as in the extracts given in this volume; and he will come to rejoice, more and more, that the field is so wide before him.

Samuel M. Warren

KEY TO ABBREVIATIONS
OF SWEDENBORG'S WORKS

A. C.	. . .	ARCANA COELESTIA.
A. E.	. . .	APOCALYPSE EXPLAINED.
A. R.	. . .	APOCALYPSE REVEALED.
Ath. Cr.	. .	ATHANASIAN CREED.
B. E.	. . .	BRIEF EXPOSITION OF THE DOCTRINE OF THE NEW JERUSALEM.
Canons .	. .	CANONS, OR ENTIRE THEOLOGY OF THE NEW CHURCH.
Ch.	. . .	DOCTRINE OF CHARITY.
C. L.	. . .	CONJUGIAL LOVE.
C. L. J. .	. .	CONTINUATION CONCERNING THE LAST JUDGMENT.
Cor.	. . .	CORONIS, OR APPENDIX TO TRUE CHRISTIAN RELIGION.
D. L.	. . .	DIVINE LOVE, APPENDED TO A. E.
D. L. W.	. .	DIVINE LOVE AND WISDOM.
D. P.	. . .	DIVINE PROVIDENCE.
D. W. in A. E.	.	DIVINE WISDOM, APPENDED TO A. E.
E. U.	. . .	EARTHS IN THE UNIVERSE.
F. .	. . .	DOCTRINE OF FAITH.
H. D.	. . .	THE NEW JERUSALEM AND ITS HEAVENLY DOCTRINE.
H. H.	. . .	HEAVEN AND HELL.
I. N. C.	. .	INVITATION TO THE NEW CHURCH.
Inf.	. . .	INTERCOURSE [OR INFLUX] BETWEEN THE SOUL AND THE BODY.
L. .	. . .	DOCTRINE OF THE LORD.
Life	. . .	DOCTRINE OF LIFE.
L. J.	. . .	LAST JUDGMENT.
S. D.	. . .	SPIRITUAL DIARY.
S. D. Minus .	.	THE SMALLER SPIRITUAL DIARY.
S. S.	. . .	DOCTRINE OF THE SACRED SCRIPTURE.
S. S. Post	. .	POSTHUMOUS TRACT ON THE SACRED SCRIPTURE.
Swed. Doc.	. .	DOCUMENTS CONCERNING SWEDENBORG.
T. C. R.	. .	TRUE CHRISTIAN RELIGION.
W. H.	. . .	THE WHITE HORSE.

CONTENTS

SIGNIFICATION OF VARIOUS TERMS AND SUBJECTS IN THE WORD.

BIOGRAPHICAL INTRODUCTION

VISITORS to the cathedral of Uppsala, Sweden, where renowned citizens are interred, may see an impressive red granite sarcophagus on which the name Emanual Swedenborg appears. The sarcophagus contains the remains of one of Sweden's most accomplished sons. As recently as 1910, when belated recognition was extended to this distinguished intellect, Gustav V, King of Sweden, led in paying him national tribute. Resting in public view has been reserved for kings, archbishops, generals, and prominent intellectuals. Only a score of Swedes have earned this distinction.

Who was Emanuel Swedenborg? What historical position did he hold to warrant such honor and attention? What were his major contributions? The great majority of cathedral visitors will doubtless have no idea of the answer to these questions. The flow of persons through the church will include the educated who may possibly remember Swedenborg's scientific and philosophic contributions to eighteenth-century European thought. A scattered few of Swedenborg's followers will look with awe upon the sarcophagus as the final resting place of the man they consider to have been a new prophet of God on earth.

Ancestors endowed this eminent Swede with multiple talents which determined the course and tenor of his life. On his mother's side Swedenborg's relatives had long been prominent in the mining industry; his father was a devout clergyman of intelligence and zeal. Into such a household, marked by a harmonious blending of the secular and the sacred, Emanuel was born on the 29th of January, 1688, in the city of Stockholm. Sara Behm, his mother, died when he was eight years old, but her quiet, benevolent spirit molded the character of her third child and second son. Six other children were born to Jesper and Sara Swedberg before her untimely death in 1696.

His father, professor of theology at the University of Uppsala and dean of the cathedral, later became Bishop of Skara. This post included elevation to the rank of nobleman by Queen Ulrika Eleonora. One result of this honor was the change of the family name from Swedberg to Swedenborg.

The Bishop also served as chaplain to the royal family and thus had an *entrée* into the highest social and political circles of Sweden.

From birth young Swedenborg experienced a family atmosphere characterized by reverence and even religious fervor. The Bishop's children, for the most part, were given scriptural names, to remind them of their duty to God and the church. Emanuel means "God with us" and Swedenborg's early years suited this theme. The family often discussed religious questions at dinner and other gatherings, and the young boy had opportunities to exchange ideas on faith and life with many clergymen. Years later Swedenborg recalled the influence of this early exposure when he wrote: "I was constantly engaged in thought upon God, salvation, and the spiritual sufferings of men . . ."[1]

But theology, while it bulked large in the Swedberg home, did not eliminate all other subjects of conversation. Politics, war, philosophy, technology undoubtedly entered the family dialogues. In June of 1699 intellectual stimulation at home led logically to an early enrollment at Uppsala University. Young Emanuel showed high intellectual promise and a catholic outlook.[2] At the time, the university offered four major fields of study: theology, law, medicine, and philosophy. Although Swedenborg majored in the last, his inquiring mind led him into many other fields as well. The faculty of philosophy then included science and mathematics, but he also took courses in law and, since most instruction at Uppsala was still in Latin, he learned this structured language, adding Greek and Hebrew the following year. Subsequent studies and travels enabled Swedenborg to acquire a knowledge of English, Dutch, French, and Italian in addition to his native Swedish and the scriptural languages. For relaxation he wrote poetry in Latin and studied music. Swedenborg also became sufficiently accomplished on the organ to fill in for the regular accompanist at the church. Versatility and imagination grounded in thoroughness and practicality characterized his academic career.

Upon finishing his formal studies at the university in 1709 he laid plans for an extended period of travel and further study abroad. In 1710, at twenty-two years of age, he went to England for the first time. With the encouragement and financial assistance of his brother-in-law, Eric Benzelius, he

---

[1] Letter to G. A. Beyer, November 14, 1769, in R. L. Tafel, *Documents Concerning Swedenborg* (Swedenborg Society, London, 1875), II, 279-80.

[2] Swedenborg was a lad only eleven years old but entering upon university work at such an age was not unusual for the time.

was able, either under learned individuals or on his own, to study physics, astronomy, and most of the other natural sciences. He also became intensely interested in practical mechanics and learned watchmaking, bookbinding, cabinet work, engraving, and brass instrument construction from skilled English craftsmen. When he went to Holland he studied the technology of lens grinding, then in its early beginnings. His later studies included cosmology, mathematics, anatomy, physiology, politics, economics, metallurgy, mineralogy, geology, mining engineering, and chemistry. In addition he became thoroughly versed in the Bible. Moreover, the avid student-scientist made successful efforts to meet recognized leaders in the world of knowledge. In an age when relatively few men became really learned, Emanuel Swedenborg spent the first thirty-five years of his life in a massive program of formal and self-directed education.

Although he immersed himself in the sciences and other secular pursuits, Swedenborg did not abandon his early religious training. He retained his acceptance of God as the all-pervasive, causal force in the universe. All evidence indicates that he consistently followed the advice which his father gave to him upon leaving Uppsala to accept an appointment in another diocese: "I beg you most earnestly that you fear and love God above all else," the Bishop said, "for without this fear of God all other training, all study, all learning is of no account, indeed quite harmful." [3]

In 1716, even before this period of travel and study ended, Swedenborg began a long career in public service. King Charles XII appointed the talented 28-year-old scientist to the post of Extraordinary Assessor in the Royal College of Mines. The position, though partly honorific, also carried varied duties connected with the supervision and development of mining, one of Sweden's most important industries. For thirty-one years Swedenborg served as a valued member of the Board of Mines. The Board met regularly and made decisions affecting all aspects of the mining industry. Swedenborg sometimes received leaves of absence for travel and study but attended Board meetings faithfully when he was in Sweden.

The post of Assessor became far more than a sinecure. Swedenborg's responsibilities included inspecting mines and rendering detailed reports on the quality and amount of mined ore. He spent most of seven different summers traveling around Sweden on these inspection tours, riding horseback or in carriages through miles of forest, staying at local

[3] Cyriel O. Sigstedt, *The Swedenborg Epic* (New York: Bookman, 1952), p. 11.

inns, going down in all types of safe and unsafe mines. He was involved in personnel and administrative problems, hiring officials, arbitrating labor disputes, and submitting suggestions for improvements. He even had the unpopular responsibility of collecting national taxes levied on mining. His activities on the Board of Mines finally ended when he resigned in 1747 to give full time to more important tasks to which he believed he had been called.

Swedenborg's public career also included some fifty years of service in the House of Nobles, one of the four estates of the Swedish Riksdag or legislature. He first took his seat on the ennoblement of his family in 1719. From that time until a few years prior to his death in 1772, Swedenborg attended most of the sessions of the House of Nobles. Deep dedication to the welfare of Sweden led him to make special efforts to plan his travels abroad during times of legislative adjournment. He usually remained in Sweden when the Riksdag was in session, and though not a ready speaker, he repeatedly wrote pamphlets and resolutions on the important questions of the day. On a number of occasions he expressed views on the nation's economy and tax structure. Foreign policy and matters related to the proper development of Sweden's natural resources also drew his attention.

His most pointed political contest occurred in 1760, during a period of economic stress in Sweden. The Councillor of Commerce, Anders Nordencrantz, became chairman of a special committee on finance. He was authorized to name all the members of his committee, and their report, not surprisingly, reflected Nordencrantz's thinking on the nation's financial crisis which he had detailed earlier in a lengthy published book. The Nordencrantz analysis contained some useful insights, but his proposals for reform threatened to sweep away the entire structure of the government of Sweden; many felt that his recommendations, if adopted, might tear the fabric of society apart.

Swedenborg, while not unmindful of the need for economic improvement, found Nordencrantz's views generally unacceptable. They put the entire blame for the crisis on government officials. Nordencrantz favored replacing all appointees other than those in church and military positions; these, in turn, would be replaced again every second year thereafter. In brief, Nordencrantz argued for reform by means of a continuous turnover of government officials. The most pernicious feature of his plan would have been vastly increased personal power for the King.

Swedenborg's commentary to the Riksdag objecting to the Nordencrantz report argued that Sweden's problems were caused by a variety of factors in both the private and public sectors rather than simply by the corruption and stupidity of officialdom. He underscored the need for a just balance in criticism of the government in the interests of maintaining an effective structure within which social and civil freedom might gradually be expanded. "Mistakes occur in every country," he wrote, "and with every man. But if a government should be regarded simply from its faults, it would be like regarding an individual simply from his failings and deficiencies." [4] In this contest, which he won, Swedenborg showed himself to be a man of moderation willing to work toward practical solutions of real problems.

No summary of Swedenborg's public life would be complete without mention of the many occasions on which he put his mechanical genius to work for his country. King Charles XII asked him to serve as his engineering advisor after the King had been impressed by Swedenborg's contributions as editor of the scientific journal *Daedalus,* the first periodical devoted to the natural sciences ever published in Sweden. In the King's service, Swedenborg acted as construction supervisor on several important public works. His assignments involved creation of a drydock of new design, a canal, machinery for working salt springs, and a system for moving large warships overland. He also showed an inventive imagination in producing feasible sketches of futuristic machines including an airplane, a submarine, a steam engine, an air gun, and a slow-combustion stove.

Although no observer of nature in the 1700's had refined instruments to aid him, leading intellectuals developed the science of the times to a remarkable degree. The limited amount of knowledge made it possible for scholars to be conversant with a broader variety of studies than has been possible since, in the context of the explosion of scientific information during the nineteenth and twentieth centuries. Swedenborg's keen mind coupled with his extensive educational background placed him in the front rank of the learned scientists of the day.

In a century which was ignorant of the existence of oxygen, the circulation of the blood, the composition of water, the makeup of the earth's atmosphere, electricity, spectrum analysis, photography, the concept of the conservation of energy, and the workings of atoms, Swedenborg propounded some impressive theories along with making some incorrect speculations. As his mind developed he became more interested in generalizing from the findings of others rather than conduct-

[4] Tafel, *Documents,* I, 511-15.

ing extensive experiments of his own. His thinking exhibited a philosophic rather than an empirical bent.

Nevertheless, in metallurgy and biology he made experimental discoveries which rank him with the original thinkers of these two disciplines. In metallurgy his conclusions regarding the proper treatment of iron, copper, and brass advanced both the science and the technology involved.

In biology, his studies of the nervous system and the brain earned him credit for supplying the first accurate understanding of the importance of the cerebral cortex, and the respiratory movement of the brain tissues. Modern scholars conclude that Swedenborg's findings pointed the way to ''most of the fundamentals of nerve and sensory physiology.'' [5] He is also praised for his insight into the function and importance of the ductless glands, especially the pituitary.

Had he spent all of his mature years in metallurgy and biology he might have gone considerably farther in these two fields than he did. He refrained from extensive research because he felt that he was not especially gifted in this type of activity. Furthermore, he found that, when he did make a modest experimental discovery, he tended to let it draw him away from philosophical generalizations into one-sided explanations too extensively dependent upon his own observation. He believed that there were two main types of mind; on the one hand, there were those gifted in ''experimental observation, and endowed with a sharper insight than others, as if they possessed naturally a finer acumen: such are Eustachius, Ruysch, Leeuwenhoek, Lancisi, etc.'' And then there were others ''who enjoy a natural faculty for contemplating facts already discovered, and eliciting their causes. Both are peculiar gifts, and are seldom united in the same person.'' [6]

Swedenborg had two central philosophic interests: cosmology and the nature of the human soul. From approximately 1720 until 1745 he studied, wrote, and published on these two subjects. His first significant philosophic work, entitled *Chemistry* and published in 1720, emphasized his developing view that everything in nature could be explained mathematically. He rejected the Newtonian concept of permanent, irreducible particles of matter and suggested that everything material was essentially motion arranged in geometric forms.

During the 1720's he developed his thoughts on the process by which the universe exists and continues. A nearly 600-page manuscript called the *Lesser Principia*, published posthu-

[5] George Gaylord Simpson and William S. Beck, *Life* (New York: Harcourt, 1965), pp. 827-28.

[6] O. M. Ramström, ''Swedenborg on the Cerebral Cortex as the Seat of Physical Activity,'' International Swedenborg Congress, p. 56.

mously, was one product of these efforts, but the great work of his philosophical studies appeared in 1734. It contained three volumes under the general title *Philosophical and Minerological Works*. In Volume One, which he called *The Principia*, according to the habit of eighteenth-century philosophers, he presented his primary cosmological conclusions. He based his explanations of the ''Principles of Natural Things'' on experience, geometry, and reason and postulated the creation of a ''first natural point'' of matter. This first natural point, caused by divine impulse to action, consisted of pure motion. From this point of pure motion a series of finites descended, each series larger and somewhat less active than the preceding finite. Swedenborg's cosmology thus teems with energy from beginning to end. He argued that activity permeated all three natural kingdoms, animal, vegetable, and mineral. Any material substance emanated energy spheres which interacted with surrounding matter. His studies of magnetism, crystallography, phosphorescence, and metallurgy contributed to his belief in an active universe.

Modern experimentation, particularly in the field of atomic energy, has confirmed many of Swedenborg's cosmological speculations. Svante Arrhenius, noted Nobel-Prize chemist and founder of the twentieth-century science of physical chemistry, concluded that Buffon, Kant, Laplace, Wright, and Lambert all propounded systems of creation which had been suggested earlier in Swedenborg's *Principia*.[7] The second volume of the *Philosophical and Mineralogical Works* dealt with iron and steel, and the third with copper and brass. In them Swedenborg treated not only the technology involved in the use of metals, but included further philosophical speculations regarding the makeup and operation of the universe.

Nothing in Swedenborg's *Philosophical and Mineralogical Works* indicated that purely material explanations of the universe satisfied him. His writings rest upon the assumption that divine force underlies all matter and his speculations next turned to the relationship between the finite and the infinite. His book-length essay on the Infinite published in 1734, carried the full title ''Outlines of a Philosophical Argument on the Infinite, and the Final Cause of Creation and on the Mechanism of the Operation of Soul and Body.'' In this and similar studies, Swedenborg judged that although the finite could not know the infinite, reason compelled man to conclude that the human individual was the end of creation. Everything in creation contributed to man's functioning as a thinking being. The soul must be the link between God and

---

[7] Sigstedt, *Swedenborg Epic*, pp. 116-17, and footnotes 170 and 569.

man, the infinite and the finite, even though man could not
see or measure that soul.

Swedenborg developed his search for the soul most comprehensively in a study which he called *The Economy of the Animal Kingdom,* published in two lengthy volumes in 1740 and
1741. As the title implies, he found the kingdom of life to be
a marvelous unity, tautly structured according to some grand
design consistent with the concept of the individual soul as
the center of creation. His speculations, which made use of
the best anatomical knowledge of the day, focused on the blood
as the most likely carrier of the soul. Swedenborg came close
to predicting the manner in which the lungs purify the blood
at a time when the discovery of oxygen was fifty years in the
future. He then drew upon his earlier studies of the brain
and concluded that the operations of the brain and the body,
by means of the blood, depended upon a "spirituous fluid"
which, while it could not be "known" scientifically, must be
the carrier of the soul. He pursued his search for rational
explanations of the workings of the soul in a second book, *The
Animal Kingdom,* and in other works. He hoped to disperse
the "clouds which darken the sacred temple of the mind"
and open a path to faith.[8] Other books from this period,
some published and some left in manuscript, include *The
Brain, The Senses, The Organs of Generation,* and *Rational
Psychology.*

The Economy of the Animal Kingdom drew praise from the
scholars of the day. However, reviewers increasingly ignored
later work in his search for the soul, and his unpublished manuscripts were, of course, unknown outside the circle of Swedenborg's intellectual intimates.

Swedenborg had gone as far as he could go in attempting to
explain the great questions of human existence solely through
the faith into which he was born and which was reinforced by
his own reasoning powers. The results of his search left him
dissatisfied, but a new phase of his life opened and the remaining years of his career must be viewed in a different perspec-
tive.

During 1744 and 1745 he had a number of dreams and visions which moved him profoundly. He sometimes feared and
sometimes felt exhilarated by what he experienced. These
were years of disquiet which he could not explain satisfactorily
and, typically, he kept silent about them to others, although
his *Journal of Dreams* and *Journal of Travel* written during

---

[8] Swedenborg, *The Animal Kingdom* (Newbery: London, 1843; Reprinted Swedenborg Scientific Association: Bryn Athyn, Pa., 1960,
I. 15.)

this period recorded his experiences and emotions. He renewed his study of the Bible and began to write a book entitled *Worship and Love of God.*

A distinguished modern psychologist, Wilson Van Dusen, has concluded that Swedenborg, at this stage in his career stood at the "door to psychology." The discipline was then in its infancy and, according to Van Dusen, Swedenborg's attempts to "describe mental experience directly" were a "great step." Van Dusen observes "he had collected facts from every other area. Why not try to penetrate inwardly and observe the operations of psyche directly? Perhaps he could catch the soul at work. And he did. This method is now called phenomenology. It gathers the raw data of experience itself. It attempts to observe, understand and describe human experience itself. As in many other things he was ahead of his time." [9]

Then in April of 1745 Swedenborg underwent a penetrating experience. In London, while dining alone at an inn, he noted that the room seemed to grow dark. He then saw a vision, and an apparition spoke to him. When the room cleared again Swedenborg went home to his apartment, considerably stirred by his experience. During that night he again saw the vision. A spirit reappeared and spoke with him regarding the need for a human person to serve as the means by which God would further reveal himself to men in somewhat the manner of the biblical visions of the Old Testament. [10]

Swedenborg came to believe that God had called him to bring a new revelation to the world, and from 1745 until his death twenty-seven years later he spent the bulk of his time adding theological works to his already lengthy scientific and philosophical writings. Few transcendent experiences recorded in human history encompass such a sweeping claim.

He spent the two years immediately following his "call" in further close study of the Bible. He wrote some 3,000 folio pages of unpublished commentary and prepared an extended *Bible Index* which he used in all of his further works on theology. He perfected his knowledge of Hebrew and Greek in order to study the Bible in the original texts, and, in effect, made a new translation of many of the books of both the Old and New Testaments. In 1747 he began publication of his

---

[9] Van Dusen, *The Presence of Other Worlds* (New York: Harper & Row, 1974)

[10] Swedenborg's account as related to Carl Robsahm, a Stockholm banker and friend of the Swedenborg family. Tafel, *Documents,* I, 35-36.

most extended theological work, *Arcana Coelestia—Heavenly Secrets*. This study of the books of Genesis and Exodus runs to more than 7,000 pages or about three million words. The subtitle of this multi-volume work asserted that the "heavenly secrets" it contained "are in the Sacred Scripture of the Word of the Lord disclosed" and were presented along with "wonderful things which have been seen in the World of Spirits and in the Heaven of Angels."

Theological writings continued to flow from Swedenborg's pen. He wrote eight volumes explaining the book of Revelation, single volumes entitled *Divine Providence, Divine Love and Wisdom*, and *The Four Doctrines*, i.e., the Lord, the Holy Scripture, Life, and Faith. He presented an account of experiences in the other world in the highly descriptive volume titled *Heaven and Its Wonders and Hell*. In 1768 he published a long volume on the subject of marriage under the title *The Delights of Wisdom Pertaining to Conjugial Love after which follow the Pleasures of Insanity Pertaining to Scortatory Love*. Shorter works dealt with a variety of subjects.[11]

There are several aspects of the theological phase of Swedenborg's career. First, for much of the period, he wrote and published anonymously, and therefore few, even among his close friends, knew the nature of the theological studies as they evolved. Second, he invested a considerable amount of his own funds in the process since none of his theological studies enjoyed any significant circulation. He gave away many copies anonymously, to clergymen, universities, and libraries. Third, he lived a normal though sometimes secluded life during the early theological years. Unmarried, he was much alone with his books, often in a small summerhouse which he built at the back of the garden of his Stockholm property. Fourth, experiences in his last years reversed the anonymous and secluded pattern of his life as his works became widely diffused in learned circles. Finally, he remained convinced that the Lord had commissioned him to bring a new revelation to men. Fulfillment of this commission depended upon a dual existence in both the spiritual and natural worlds alternately, for year upon year as his commentaries multiplied.

Swedenborg made no effort to establish a religious sect or to induce people to form themselves into a church following. In fact, his efforts to remain anonymous with regard to his theological works lasted until 1759. In that year an incident

[11] The contents of the individual theological works by Swedenborg are summarized in the Appendix to this study.

occurred in Sweden which brought him considerable notoriety and which eventually led many to connect Swedenborg for the first time with his unusual theological works, particularly *Heaven and Hell.* In July, in the city of Gothenburg, approximately 300 miles from Stockholm, while he dined with friends at the home of William Castel, a wealthy local merchant, Swedenborg became pale and disturbed, withdrew for a time to the garden, and returned with news that a great fire had broken out in Stockholm not far from his home. He said that the fire was spreading rapidly and he feared that some of his manuscripts would be destroyed. Finally, at 8:00 P.M. he spoke with relief: "Thank God! The fire is extinguished the third door from my house!"

Persons present, disturbed by the incident since some had homes or friends in Stockholm, were impressed by Swedenborg's apparent clairvoyance. The same evening one of them told the story to the provincial governor and he, in turn, requested that Swedenborg render him a full account. The next day, Sunday, Swedenborg gave the governor details regarding the nature and extent of the fire and the means by which it had been extinguished. News of the alleged fire spread widely in the city of Gothenburg and the subject became the general topic of conversation.

Not until Monday evening did a messenger arrive, from the Stockholm Board of Trade, with details on the fire.[12] Since they agreed with those Swedenborg had given, the general curiosity aroused made him a public figure, and not long afterwards his authorship of *Heaven and Hell* and the *Arcana Coelestia* became known. A variety of prominent persons, curious to meet with a man who claimed to be able to see into the spiritual world, began to write accounts of Swedenborg and his habits. Those who had not yet had an opportunity to meet him tended to conclude that Swedenborg had become insane. After meeting and talking with him they found him, on the contrary, to be quite reasonable. They frequently ended in a quandary, not willing to accept his sweeping claims, yet convinced of his sanity.

In the spring of the following year another incident occurred that further revealed Swedenborg's strange powers. The widow of the Dutch ambassador in Stockholm, Mme. de Marteville, became interested in Swedenborg's alleged power to converse with spirits. She hoped that he might be able to help her in a practical matter. A silversmith had presented her with a large bill for a silver service which her husband

---

[12] The many similar accounts of this incident and the two succeeding ones are synthesized and cited in Sigstedt, *Swedenborg Epic*, pp. 269-82.

had purchased before his death. She felt sure that her husband had paid the bill, but could find no receipt. Swedenborg agreed to ask her husband about it if he saw him in the spiritual world. A few days later Swedenborg reported that he had seen her husband and that the ambassador had told him that he would tell his wife where the receipt was hidden. Eight days later Mme. de Marteville dreamed her husband told her to look behind a particular drawer in the desk. She did so and found not only the receipt but a diamond hairpin which had been missing. The next morning, Swedenborg called on the widow, and, before she told him of her dream and discovery, he reported that he had again conversed with her husband the preceding night and that the ambassador had left the conversation to tell his wife of the missing receipt.

An even more striking incident concerned the ''Queen's secret.'' In the fall of 1761, Count Ulric Scheffer invited Swedenborg to go to the court with him to visit Queen Lovisa Ulrika who had become interested in Swedenborg through hearing of his varied abilities. The Queen asked if he would communicate with her late brother Augustus William who had died two years before. Swedenborg agreed to do so and a few days later called at the royal residence, presented the Queen with copies of some of his books, and then in a private audience at the far end of the room told her some secret that caused her to show great amazement. She exclaimed that only her brother could have known what Swedenborg told her. The incident became widely known and discussed in Swedish social circles.

These three examples of Swedenborg's clairvoyant abilities, along with lesser incidents, served to spread his fame. He continued to live and write as before, but curious persons often interrupted his studies; many sought to visit with the man who claimed, in a calm and reasonable way, to be able to converse with angels.

The great German philosopher Immanuel Kant's reaction to Swedenborg's visionary powers is of interest in this connection. Although Kant never met Swedenborg himself, he wrote to him and also sent personal messages through mutual friends. Kant, the great rationalist, tended to discount all stories of mystical experience but the persistent and authoritative reports on Swedenborg's powers gave him repeated pause. At times he wrote favorably; at times quite the reverse. However, Kant's continuing interest is indicated by a variety of evidence. Even his most critical survey, *Dreams of a Spirit-Seer,* published in 1766, in which Kant attempted to denigrate Swedenborg, reveals doubts regarding the basis for his own ridicule. In short, Kant must be numbered

among those intellects of Swedenborg's day who experienced
difficulty explaining satisfactorily the theological phase of
Swedenborg's distinguished career.

During Swedenborg's final years a variety of old friends
and new acquaintances wrote accounts of their impressions of
him. His claims seemed preposterous to many, yet few who
met and talked with him had anything really adverse to say
of him. They were perplexed at his accounts of conversations
with spirits, but found him otherwise tó be a gentle, humorous
man with a relaxed, benign air. Occasionally, when callers
tried to make fun of him, Swedenborg spoke cuttingly, but in
general he was the perfect host.

In 1768, Swedenborg, eighty years of age but in excellent
health and spirits, set out on the next-to-last extensive journey
of his life on earth. Many previous trips had taken him all
over Europe including Italy, France, Germany, Holland, and
England. On this occasion he went first to France and then
to England, where he took lodgings with a young couple in
Wellclose Square, London. During the summer he spent
many hours working on his last great theological work, a
study entitled *True Christian Religion*. He also enjoyed
walking in the nearby parks, talking with acquaintances, and
visiting friends. One associate said of him during this period,
"Someone might think that Assessor Swedenborg was ec-
centric and whimsical; but the very reverse was the case. He
was very easy and pleasant in company, talked on every subject that came up, accommodating himself to the ideas of the
company; and never spoke on his own views unless he was
asked about them."[13]

In 1769 he returned to Sweden, partly to answer charges of
heresy which had been leveled against him by some of the
prelates of the Lutheran state church. He had been informed
by friendly correspondents that his theological writings were
the cause of much controversy in the Lutheran Consistory in
Gothenburg. By this time several of Swedenborg's works had
been translated into Swedish, and followers, both among the
clergy and the laity, spoke out in favor of his theology.

In September, 1768, a country parson precipitated a decisive
debate by introducing a resolution in the Gothenburg Consistory calling for measures to stop the circulation of works at
variance with the dogmas of Lutheranism. The parson ob-
jected particularly to Swedenborg's writings. While some
members of the Consistory insisted that no judgment be
rendered until all members had thoroughly studied the works

[13] Testimony of Arvid Ferelius, Tafel, *Documents*, II, 560.

in question, Dean Ekebom, the ranking prelate, announced that he found Swedenborg's doctrines to be "corrupting, heretical, injurious, and in the highest degree objectionable." Although he confessed that he had not read any works other than the *Apocalypse Revealed* with any care, he concluded that Swedenborg's views on the nature of the Divine, the Bible, the Holy Supper, faith, and other basic teachings should be suppressed as dangerous to established religious concepts. He charged Swedenborg with Socinianism or refusal to accept the divinity of Christ.

On being apprised of these charges Swedenborg wrote vigorously in his own defense. The Socinianism charge particularly upset him, and he wrote, "I look upon the word Socinian as a downright insult and diabolical mockery." One of Swedenborg's most carefully argued lines of theological reasoning directly refutes Socinianism and argues for the acceptance of Christ as God on earth.

The dispute became inflamed and shifted to the political level when the matter was brought up in the national Diet. The Dean's legal advisor and chief prosecutor urged that "the most energetic measures" be taken to "stifle, punish, and utterly eradicate Swedenborgian innovation and downright heresies by which we are encompassed . . . so that the boar which devastates and the wild beast which desolates our country may be driven out with a mighty hand." The Royal Council, appointed through the Diet, finally rendered its report in April, 1770. The anti-Swedenborgians won most of what they were seeking. Swedenborg's clerical supporters were ordered to cease using his teachings, and customs officials were directed to impound his books and stop their circulation in any district unless the nearest consistory granted permission. In its own words, the Royal Council "totally condemned, rejected, and forbade the theological doctrines contained in Swedenborg's writings."

While the dispute dragged on for three more years, Swedenborg continued to protest the decision of the Council and petitioned the King himself. The Royal Council referred the matter to the Götha Court of Appeals, which asked several universities, including Swedenborg's alma mater, Uppsala, to make a thorough study of Swedenborg's ideas. The universities, however, asked to be excused. Their theological faculties found nothing which they felt they should condemn, but, on the other hand, they had no inclination to put bishops and entire consistories on trial for false accusation, the only means by which the anti-Swedenborgian decisions could be reversed. The matter quieted down. Some clergymen preached Swedenborgian ideas; most did not. Emanuel Swedenborg continued to write and speak as he pleased in his few remaining years on earth.[14]

Completion of the crowning work of his theological period engrossed him. Although 82 years of age, he undertook his final, eleventh, foreign journey to promote this effort. Apparently he felt he would not return to Sweden for he made farewell calls on the members of the Board of Mines, supporters, and close friends. He arranged a pension for his faithful housekeeper, made lists of his possessions for estate distribution, and told his long-time friend and neighbor, Carl Robsahm, "Whether I shall return again, I do not know, but . . . this I can assure you, for the Lord has promised it to me, . . . I shall not die until I have received from the press this work . . . now ready to be printed."[15] He referred to the manuscript to be published in 1771 in Holland under the title *True Christian Religion.*

A skeptical but generally friendly observer visited Swedenborg in Amsterdam during the printing of *True Christian Religion* and reported that the seer, in spite of his advanced age, worked "indefatigably" and even "in an astonishing and superhuman way," reading proofs and returning them to the publisher. He found Swedenborg convinced that he served, as the title page stated, in the capacity of "Servant of the Lord Jesus Christ."[16]

When the book was printed Swedenborg left Amsterdam and crossed the Channel to England. He arrived in London in early September of 1771 and again rented quarters with a family named Shearsmith in Great Bath Street. Although his health declined he continued to work at his books. But in December, he suffered a stroke which destroyed his ability to speak and rendered him unconscious for most of three weeks. During January and February he gradually recovered and again talked with visitors.

He wrote to John Wesley, the noted English minister, and told him that he would be happy to discuss religion with him if Wesley could come to London. Swedenborg mentioned that he had learned in the world of spirits that Wesley wanted to talk with him about theology. Wesley expressed his great surprise to friends regarding Swedenborg's invitation because he did not recall having told anyone of his interest in the Swedish seer. Wesley answered Swedenborg's letter with hopes that he would be welcomed upon comple-

---

[14] The best account of the Gothenburg heresy trial is found in Sigstedt, *Swedenborg Epic,* chap. 41.

[15] Tafel, *Documents,* I, 38-39.

[16] Johan Christian Cuneo as quoted in Sigstedt, *Swedenborg Epic,* p. 415.

tion of a six months' journey on which he had just embarked. When he received Wesley's reply Swedenborg remarked that six months would be too long since he, Swedenborg, would permanently enter the world of spirits on the 29th of March, 1772. The maid who attended Baron Swedenborg during his final months also reported that he predicted the exact date of his death.[17]

Several friends visited Swedenborg during March and urged him to make a final statement regarding the truth or falsity of the new revelation which had been flowing from his pen for so many years. Swedenborg answered pointedly: ''I have written nothing but the truth, as you will have more and more confirmed to you all the days of your life, provided you keep close to the Lord and faithfully serve Him alone by shunning evils of all kinds as sins against Him and diligently searching His Word which from beginning to end bears incontestible witness to the truth of the doctrines I have delivered to the world.'' On another occasion, in answer to a similar question, Swedenborg said: ''As truly as you see me before your eyes, so true is everything that I have written; and I could have said more had it been permitted. When you enter eternity you will see everything, and then you and I shall have much to talk about.''[18]

On Sunday, March 29, 1772, Mrs. Shearsmith and Elizabeth Reynolds, the maid, observed Swedenborg, waking from a long sleep. He asked the women to tell him the time of day. They replied that it was five o'clock. ''That is good,'' Swedenborg said. ''I thank you. God bless you.''[19] He then sighed gently and died.

Shortly after Swedenborg's death, an energetic Londoner named Robert Hindmarsh, came upon a copy of *Heaven and Hell*. Upon reading it he became a convert and organized the first group of followers of Swedenborg. Meeting regularly in London, the Hindmarsh circle began to expound the tenets of Swedenborgian theology. Swedish followers organized under the leadership of Johan Rosén and Gabriel A. Beyer, two noted intellectuals who had been reading Swedenborg for some time. James Glen, a sometime member of the Hindmarsh group in England, brought copies of Swedenborg's writings to Philadelphia in 1784, and Swedenborgianism in America dates from Glen's efforts to establish Swedenborgian reading circles in the Quaker city and elsewhere. Although the total number of Swedenborg followers has never grown large, there are active adherent groups all over the world.

[17] Tafel, *Documents* II, 564-65, 546.
[18] Ibid., 579-80, 557-58.
[19] Ibid., II, 578, 568-69.

Swedenborg's teachings exert a clear and direct influence on those who regard themselves as followers of the new faith. Swedenborgians study his theological writings and, like members of other religious sects, they attempt to put the principles expressed into effect in their own lives. The less tangible evidence of Swedenborg's influence—his effect on the mainstream of world thought—remains to be evaluated. Scholars who attempt the task may conclude, with Arthur Conan Doyle, that they have a "mountain peak of mentality" under scrutiny.[20]

Sig Synnestvedt
State University of
New York
Brockport, New York

This biographical introduction is taken from Dr. Synnestvedt's *The Essential Swedenborg* with permission of Twayne Publishers, New York, 1970.

[20] Arthur Conan Doyle, *History of Spiritualism* (New York: Doubleday, 1926), p. 22.

CONCERNING GOD.

THE idea of God enters into all things of the Church, of religion, and of worship. Not only do theological subjects reside above all [others] in the human mind, but supreme therein is the idea of God. If this therefore be false all things which follow derive from the beginning whence they flow, that they are false, or falsified. For the supreme, which also is the inmost, constitutes the very essence of the sequences; and the essence, as a soul, forms them into a body after its own image; and when in its descent it lights upon truths, it infects them also with its own blemish and error. (B. E. n. 40.)

Upon a just idea of God the universal heaven and the Church universal on earth, and in general the whole of religion, are founded; for through this there is conjunction, and through conjunction light, wisdom, and eternal happiness. (Pref. to A. R.)

Of how great importance it is to have a just idea of God may appear from the consideration, that the idea of God forms the inmost of thought with all who have any religion; for all things of religion and all things of worship have relation to God; and as God is in all things of religion and of worship universally and particularly, therefore unless there be a just idea of God there cannot be any communication with the heavens. Hence it is that in the spiritual world every nation is assigned a place according to its conception of God as a Man; for in this, and in no other, there is an idea of the Lord. That man's state of life after death is according to the idea of God confirmed within him clearly appears from its opposite, that the denial of God constitutes hell,—and in Christendom, the denial of the Lord's Divinity. (D. L. W. n. 13.)

God is One.

All the principles of human reason unite and as it were concentre in this, that there is one God, the Creator of the universe. A man who has reason, therefore, from a common attribute of his understanding, does not and cannot think otherwise. Say to any one of sound reason that there are two Creators of the universe, and you will find an aversion to you on account of it—and perhaps from the bare sound of the words in the ear. It is evident from this that all the principles of human reason unite and as it were concentre in the idea that God is one. There are two reasons why this is so. *First*, because the very faculty of thinking rationally, in itself considered, is not man's but is God's in him; upon that faculty human reason, as to the common attribute, depends; and this common attribute causes it to see this, as of itself. *Second*, because by means of that faculty man either is in the light of heaven, or derives thence the common principle of his thought; and the universal principle of the light of heaven is, that God is one. It is otherwise if by that faculty a man has perverted the lower principles of the understanding; he, it is true, has ability by that faculty, but through the intorsion of the lower principles, he turns it in another direction, whereby his reason becomes unsound. (D. L. W. n. 23.)

Who that has sound reason does not perceive that the Divine is not divisible, and that there is not a plurality of Infinite, Uncreate, Omnipotent beings,—and thus, Gods? If another, who has no reason, shall say that several Infinite, Uncreate, Omnipotent beings—therefore Gods,—are possible, if. only they have one and the same essence; and that through this there is one Infinite, Uncreate, Omnipotent being and God:—Is not one and the same essence, the same one? and the same one cannot be several. If it shall be said that one is from the other:—Then he that is from the other is not God in himself; and yet God, from whom all things are, is God in Himself. (*ib.* n. 27.)

He who in faith acknowledges and in heart worships one God is in the communion of saints on earth, and in the communion of angels in the heavens. They are called communions, and are so, because they are in one God and one God is in them. They are also in conjunction with the whole angelic heaven, and I might venture to affirm with all and each of the angels there; for they all are as the children and descendants of one father, whose minds, manners, and faces are resemblant, so that they mutually recognize each other. The angelic heaven is harmoniously arranged in societies, according to all the varieties of the love of good; which varieties all tend to one most universal love, which is love to God. From this love they who in faith acknowledge and in heart worship one God, the Creator of the universe, and at the same time the Redeemer and Regenerator, are all propagated. (T. C. R. n. 15.)

GOD IS VERY MAN.

(handwritten marginal note: Kingdom of Heaven within)

In all the heavens there is no other idea of God than of a Man. The reason is, that heaven is a Man in form, in whole and in part, and the Divine which is with the angels constitutes heaven, and thought proceeds according to the form of heaven. It is therefore impossible for the angels to think otherwise of God. Hence it is that all those in the world who are in conjunction with heaven think of God in like manner, when they think interiorly within themselves, or in their spirit. It is from the fact that God is Man that all angels and all spirits are men in perfect form. The form of heaven effects this, which in its greatest and in its least parts is like itself. It is known from Gen. i. 26, 27, that men were created *after the image and likeness of God;* and also that God was seen as a Man by Abraham and others. (D. L. W. n. 11.)

If any one thinks of the very Divine without the idea of a Divine Man, he thinks indeterminately,—and an indeterminate idea is no idea,—or he forms a conception of the Divine from the visible universe without end, or with an end in darkness, which conception conjoins itself with that of the worshippers of nature,—even falls into nature, and so becomes no conception [of God]. It is evident that thence there would be no conjunction with the Divine, by faith nor by love. All conjunction requires an object; and the conjunction is according to the character of the object. Hence it is that the Lord as to the Divine Human is called the Mediator, and the Intercessor; but He mediates and intercedes with Himself. It is evident from the Lord's words in John that the very Divine cannot by any conception be apprehended:—" *No man hath seen God at any time; the only begotten Son, which is in the bosom of the Father, He hath manifested Him* " (i. 18); and again, "*Ye have neither heard the Father's voice at any time, nor seen His shape*" (v. 37). Yet, which is remarkable, all who think of God from themselves, or from the flesh, think of Him indeterminately, that is, without any definite idea; but those who think of God not from themselves, nor from the flesh, but from the spirit, think of Him determinately; that is, they present to themselves a conception of the Divine under the human form. The angels in heaven thus think of the Divine; and thus the wise Ancients thought,

to whom when the very Divine appeared He appeared as a
Divine Man.   (A. C. n. 8705.)

God is not in Space.

That God, and the Divine which immediately proceeds from
Him, is not in space, although He is omnipresent,—even with
every man in the world, with every angel in heaven, and with
every spirit under heaven,—cannot be comprehended by a
merely natural conception ; but it can be in some measure by a
spiritual conception.   The reason why it cannot be comprehended
by a merely natural conception, is that in this there is space ;
for it is formed from such things as are in the world, in all and
each of which, that appear before the eyes, there is space.   Every
idea of great and small, in the world, is according to space ; all
length, breadth, and height,—in a word, every measure, figure, and
form therein, is of space.   But yet a man may comprehend it by
natural thought if only he admits into it something of spiritual
light.   Something shall therefore first be said concerning a
spiritual conception and thought thence.   A spiritual conception
derives nothing from space, but derives its all from state.   State
is predicated of love, of life, of wisdom, of affections, and of the
joys from these ; in general, of good and of truth.   A truly
spiritual conception of these has nothing in common with space.
It is higher, and sees conceptions derived from space below itself,
as heaven looks down upon the earth.   But as angels and spirits
equally with men see with their eyes, and objects cannot be seen
except in space, therefore in the spiritual world, where spirits
and angels dwell, spaces appear similar to the spaces on earth.
And yet they are not spaces, but appearances ; for they are not
fixed and stated as on earth, but may be lengthened and
shortened, may be changed and varied.   Now because they thus
cannot be determined by measurement, they cannot there be
comprehended by any natural conception, but only by a spiritual
conception ; which conception of distances in space is no other
than as of distances of good, or distances of truth, which are
affinities and likenesses according to their states.   It is evident
from these considerations that by a merely natural conception a
man cannot comprehend that the Divine is everywhere, and yet
not in space ; and that angels and spirits comprehend it clearly :
consequently, that man also can do so, if only he admit something of spiritual light into his thought.   The reason that man
can comprehend it is because it is not his body that thinks but
his spirit, thus not his natural but his spiritual.   And the reason
why many do not comprehend it is that they love the natural,

and are therefore not willing to elevate the thoughts of their understanding above it into spiritual light; and they who will not cannot think even of God except from space, and to think of God from space is to think of the expanse of nature. (D. L. W. n. 7-9.)

An angel of heaven can by no means think otherwise, when he thinks of the divine omnipresence, than that the Divine fills all things without space. What an angel thinks is truth, because the light which enlightens his understanding is divine wisdom. This thought concerning God is fundamental; for without it what is to be said of the creation of the universe from God Man, and of His providence, omnipotence, omnipresence, and omniscience, though it should be understood cannot be retained. Because the merely natural man, when he understands them, relapses yet into his life's love, which is of his will; and this love dissipates, and immerses them in space, in which what he calls his rational light is,—not knowing that in proportion as he denies those things he is irrational. (D. L. W. n. 71, 72.)

THE VERY DIVINE ESSENCE IS LOVE AND WISDOM.

No one can deny that in God love, and at the same time wisdom, is in its very essence; for He loves all from love in Himself, and leads all from wisdom in Himself. The created universe too, viewed in relation to its order, is so full of wisdom from love, that it may be said all things in the complex are wisdom itself; for things innumerable are in such order, successive and simultaneous, that together they constitute one. It is from this, and no otherwise, that they can be held together and perpetually preserved.

It is because the very Divine essence is love and wisdom that man has two faculties of life, from one of which he has his understanding, and from the other his will. The faculty from which he has his understanding derives all that it has from the influx of wisdom from God; and the faculty from which he has his will derives all that it has from the influx of love from God. That man is not justly wise, and does not exercise his love justly, does not take away the faculties, but inwardly closes them. (D. L. W. n. 29, 30.)

THE DIVINE LOVE AND THE DIVINE WISDOM ARE SUBSTANCE AND FORM.

The common idea of men, concerning love and wisdom, is that of a something volatile, and floating in subtile air or ether; or of an exhalation from something of the kind; scarcely any one thinks that they are really and actually substance and form. Those who see that they are substance and form, yet perceive love and wisdom out of their subject, as issuing from it; and that which they perceive out of the subject, as issuing from it, though it is perceived as a something volatile and floating, they also call substance and form; not knowing that love and wisdom are the subject itself, and that what is perceived as a something volatile and floating without it is only an appearance of the state of the subject within itself. The reasons why this has not heretofore been seen are several: one is, that appearances are the first things from which the human mind forms its understanding, and that it cannot shake them off but by an investigation of the cause; and if the cause lies very deep, it cannot investigate it without keeping the understanding, for some time, in spiritual light, in which it cannot keep it long, by reason of the natural light which continually draws it down. The truth however is, that love and wisdom are very and actual substance and form, and constitute the subject itself.

But as this is contrary to appearance, it may seem not to merit belief unless it be shown, and it cannot be shown, except by such things as a man can perceive by his bodily senses; wherefore it shall be shown by them. A man has five senses, which are called feeling, taste, smell, hearing, and sight. The subject of feeling is the skin, with which a man is encompassed, the substance and form of the skin causing it to feel what is applied; the sense of feeling is not in the things which are applied, but in the substance and form of the skin, which is the subject; the sense is only an affection thereof, from the things applied. It is the same with the taste; this sense is only an affection of the substance and form of the tongue; the tongue is the subject. So with the smell; it is well known that odours affect the nose, and are in the nose, and that there is an affection thereof from odoriferous substances touching it. So with the hearing; it appears as if the hearing were in the place where the sound begins; but the hearing is in the ear, and is an affection of its substance and form; that the hearing is at a distance from the ear is an appearance. So also with the sight; it appears, when a man sees objects at a distance, as if the sight were there, but yet it is in the eye, which is the subject, and is, in like manner, an affection thereof; the distance is only from the judgment forming its conclusions of space from intermediate objects, or from the diminution and consequent obscuration of the object, the image of which is produced within the eye according to the angle of incidence. It hence appears that the sight does not go from the eye to the object, but that the image of the object enters the eye, and affects its substance and form. For it is the same with the sight, as with the hearing; the hearing does not go out of the ear to catch the sound, but the sound enters the ear and affects it. It thus appears that the affection of a substance and form, which constitutes sense, is not a thing separate from the subject, but only causes a change in it, the subject remaining the subject then, as before, and after. Hence it follows that sight, hearing, smell, taste, and feeling, are not a something volatile flowing from those organs, but that they are the organs themselves, considered in their substance and form, and that whilst they are affected the sense is produced. It is the same with love and wisdom, with this only difference, that the substances and forms which are love and wisdom are not extant before the eyes, like the organs of the external senses. But still no one can deny that those things of wisdom and love which are called thoughts, perceptions, and affections, are substances and forms, and that they are not volatile entities flowing from nothing, or abstract from that real and actual substance and form which is the subject. For in the brain there are innumerable substances and forms, in which every interior sense that has relation to the understanding and the will, resides. The affections, perceptions, and thoughts there are not all exhalations from the substances, but are actually and really the subjects, which do not emit anything from themselves, but only undergo changes, according to the influences which affect them, as may evidently appear from what has been said above concerning the senses.

Hence it may first be seen that the Divine love and the Divine wisdom in themselves are substance and form, for they are very Being and Existing; and if they were not such a Being and Existing as that they are substance and form, they would be a mere creature of reason which in itself is not anything. (D. L. W. n. 40-43.)

GOD IS LOVE ITSELF AND LIFE ITSELF.

If it is thought that Life itself is God, or that God is Life itself, and there is at the same time no idea of what life is, in that case there is no intelligence of what God is beyond these expressions. The Divine love—which in the Divine wisdom is Life itself, which is God—cannot be conceived of in its essence; for it is infinite, and so transcends human apprehension. But in its appearance it may be conceived of. The Lord appears before the eyes of the angels as a sun, from which heat and light proceed. That sun is the Divine love; the heat is the Divine love going forth, which is called Divine good; and the light is the Divine wisdom going forth, which is called Divine truth. But yet we are not permitted to have an idea of the Life which is God, as of fire, or heat, or light, unless there be in it at the same time an idea of love and wisdom—thus, that the Divine love is as fire, and the Divine wisdom as light; and that the Divine love together with the Divine wisdom is as a bright radiance. For God is perfect Man, in face and in body like Man; there being no difference as to form, but as to essence. His essence is, that He is Love itself and Wisdom itself, and thus Life itself. (Ath. Cr. n. 27. A. E. n. 1124.)

Because God is Life, it follows that He is uncreate. The reason that He is uncreate is that life cannot be created, though it can create. For to be created is to exist from another; and if life existed from another there would be another being that would be life, and this life would be life itself. (Ath. Cr. 29. A. E. n. 1126.)

If one can but think from reason elevated above the sensualities of the body, how plain it is to see that life is not creatable! For what is life but the inmost activity of love and wisdom, which are in God and which are God; which life may also be called the very essential living force. (T. C. R. n. 471.)

Nothing exists, subsists, is acted upon, or moved by itself, but by some other being or agent; whence it follows that everything exists, subsists, is acted upon and moved by the First Being, who has no origin from another, but is in Himself the living force which is life. (Ath. Cr. n. 45. A. E. n. 1146.)

THE NATURE OF THE DIVINE LOVE.

There are two things which constitute the essence of God— love and wisdom. And there are three which constitute the essence of His love—to love others out of Himself; to desire to be one with them; and to make them happy from Himself. The same three constitute the essence of His wisdom; because love and wisdom in God make one, and love wills these things, and wisdom accomplishes them. The first essential—*to love others out of Himself*—is acknowledged to be in God, from His love towards the whole human race. And on their account God loves all things that He has created, because they are means; for whoever loves an end loves also the means. All persons and all things in the universe are out of God, because they are finite and God is infinite. The love of God reaches and extends, not only to men and things that are good, but also to men and things that are evil; consequently, not only to men and things in heaven, but to men and things also in hell; thus not to Michael and Gabriel only, but to the Devil and Satan also. For God is everywhere, and from eternity to eternity the same. He Himself also says, that "*He maketh His sun to rise on the evil and on the good, and sendeth His rain on the just and on the unjust*" (Matt. v. 45). But the reason why evil men and things are still evil, is in the subjects and objects themselves, in that they do not receive the love of God as it is, and as it is inmostly within them, but according to their own qualities or states, as the thorn and the nettle receive the heat of the sun and the rain of heaven. The second essential—*to desire to be one with others*—is also acknowledged, from His conjunction with the angelic heaven, with the Church on earth, with every individual therein, and with every good and truth in man and in the Church. Love indeed in itself regarded is nothing else than an endeavour towards conjunction. Therefore, in order that this essential of love might take effect, God created man in His image and likeness, that thus He might have conjunction with Him. That the Divine love continually intends such conjunction is evident from the Lord's words, expressing His desire *That they may be one, He in them, and they in Him, and that the love of God may be in them* (John xvii. 21-23, 26). The third essential of God's love—*to make others happy from Himself*—is acknowledged, from the gift of eternal life, which is blessedness, satisfaction, and happiness, without end. These He gives to those who receive His love in themselves. For God, as He is love itself, is also blessedness itself; and as all love breathes forth delight from itself, so Divine love breathes forth very blessedness, satisfaction, and happiness to all eternity. Thus God makes angels, and also men after death, happy from Himself; which is effected by conjunction with them.

That such is the nature of the Divine love is apparent from its sphere, which pervades the universe, and affects every one according to his state. This sphere especially affects parents, inspiring them with a tender love for their children, who are out of or without them, and with a desire to be one with them, and to make them happy from themselves. It affects even the evil as well as the good; and not only man, but beasts and birds of every kind. For what is the object of a mother's thoughts when she brings forth her child, but to unite herself, as it were, with it, and to provide for its good? What is a bird's concern when she has hatched her young, but to cherish them under her wings, and with every mark of endearment to feed and nourish them? It is a well-known fact that even serpents and vipers love their offspring. This universal sphere of Divine love affects in a particular manner those who receive within themselves the love of God, as they all do who believe in God and love their neighbour; the charity that reigns within them being the image of that love. Even what is called friendship among men of the world puts on the semblance of that love; for every one when he invites a friend to his table gives him the best that his house affords, receives him with kindness, takes him by the hand, and makes him offers of service. This love is also the cause and only origin of all the sympathies and tendencies of congenial and similar minds towards union with each other. Nay, the same Divine sphere operates even upon the inanimate parts of the creation, as trees and plants. But then it acts through the instrumentality of the natural sun, and its heat and light; for the heat entering into them from without conjoins itself with them, and causes them to bud, and blossom, and bear fruit—which operations may be called their state of bliss. And this is effected by the sun's heat, because it corresponds with spiritual heat, which is love. Representations of the operation of this love are manifested also in various subjects of the mineral kingdom, and their types may be seen in the uses and consequent value to which each is exalted. (T. C. R. n. 43, 44.)

The Infinity and Eternity of God.

The immensity of God has relation to spaces, and His eternity to times. His infinity comprehends both immensity and eternity. But as infinity transcends what is finite, and the knowledge of it, the finite mind, in order to attain some degree of perception of the subject, it must be considered after the following series:—1. God is infinite because He is and exists in Himself, and all things in the universe are and exist from Him. 2. God is infinite because He was before the world, consequently before spaces and times had birth. 3. God, since the world was made, is in space without space, and in time without time. 4. Infinity in relation to spaces is called immensity, and in relation to times eternity; and yet, notwithstanding these relations, there is nothing of space in God's immensity, and nothing of time in His eternity. 5. From very many objects in the world enlightened reason may discover the infinity of God the Creator. 6. Every created thing is finite; and the infinite is in finite things as in its receptacles, and in man as in its images. (T. C. R. n. 27.)

Men cannot but confound the Divine Infinity with infinity of space; and as they cannot conceive of the infinity of space as other than a mere nothing, as it really is, they disbelieve the Divine Infinity. The case is similar in respect to eternity, which men can only conceive of as eternity of time, it being presented to the mind under the idea of time with those who are in time. The true idea of the Divine Infinity is insinuated into the angels by this: that in an instant they are present under the Lord's view, without any intervention of space or time, even from the farthest extremity of the universe. The true idea of the Divine Eternity is insinuated into them by this: that thousands of years do not appear to them as time, but scarcely otherwise than as if they had only lived a minute. Both ideas are insinuated into them by this: that in their NOW they have at once things past and future. Hence they have no solicitude about things to come; nor have they ever any idea of death, but only of life. Thus in all their NOW there is the Eternity and Infinity of the Lord. (A. C. n. 1382.)

THE OMNIPOTENCE OF GOD.

As regards the Divine omnipotence, it does not involve any power of acting contrary to order, but it involves all power of acting according to order; for all order is from the Lord. (A. E. n. 689.)

God is omnipotent because He has all power from Himself, and all others from Him. His power and will are one; and because He wills nothing but what is good, therefore He can do nothing but what is good. In the spiritual world no one can do anything contrary to his own will. This they there derive from God, whose power and will are one. God also is Good itself; while therefore He does good He is in Himself, and He cannot go out of Himself. Hence it appears that His omnipotence proceeds and operates within the sphere of the extension of good, which is infinite. For this sphere, from the inmost, fills the universe and all and everything therein; and from the inmost it governs those things which are without, as far as they conjoin themselves according to their order. And if they do not conjoin themselves, still it sustains them, and with all effort labours to bring them into order, according to the universal order in which God is in His omnipotence; and if this is not effected, they are cast out from Him, where, nevertheless, He sustains them from the inmost. (T. C. R. n. 56.)

That the Lord has infinite power may appear from these considerations: That He is the God of heaven and the God of earth; that He created the universe, full of innumerable stars, which are suns, consequently so many systems and earths in the systems; that they exceed many hundreds of thousands in number; and that He alone continually preserves and sustains them since He created them. Likewise, that as He created the natural worlds, so also He created the spiritual worlds above them, and perpetually fills these with myriads of myriads of angels and spirits; and that He has hidden the hells under them, which are as many in number as the heavens. Moreover, that He alone gives life to all and each of the things which are in the worlds of nature and in the worlds above nature; and as He alone gives life, that no angel, spirit, or man, can move hand or foot except from Him. The quality of the infinite power of the Lord is especially evident from the consideration that He alone receives all that come from so many earths into the spiritual worlds, who are some myriads every week from our earth, and consequently so many myriads from so many thousands of earths in the universe; and not only receives, but also by a thousand mysteries of Divine wisdom leads every one to the place of his life, the faithful to their places in the heavens, and the unfaithful to their places in the hells; and that He everywhere rules the thoughts, intentions, and wills of all, singly as well as universally; and causes all and each one in the heavens to enjoy their felicity, and all and each one in the hells to be held in their bonds, insomuch that not one of them can lift up a hand, much less rise out, to the injury of any angel. Also that all are thus held in order, and in bonds, howsoever the heavens and the hells may be multiplied, to eternity. These and many other things, which from their abundance cannot be enumerated, would be impossible if the Lord had not infinite power. (A. E. n. 726.)

The Omniscience of God.

God perceives, sees, and knows all things, even to the most minute, that are done according to order; because order is universal from things the most single. For the single things taken together are denominated the universal; as the particulars taken together are denominated a general. The universal together with its most single things is a work cohering as one, insomuch that one part cannot be touched and affected without some sense of it being communicated to all the rest. It is from this quality of order in the universe that there is something similar in all created things in the world. But this shall be illustrated by comparisons taken from things that are visible. In the whole man there are things general and particular, and the general things there include the particulars, and adjust themselves by such a connection that one thing is of another. This is effected by the fact that there is a common covering about every member of the body, and that this insinuates itself into the single parts therein, so that they make one in every office and use. For example, the covering of every muscle enters into the single moving fibres therein, and clothes them from itself; in like manner the coverings of the liver, the pancreas, and the spleen, enter into the single things of them that are within; so the covering of the lungs, which is called the pleura, enters into their interiors; likewise the pericardium enters into all and the single things of the heart; and generally the peritonæum, by anastomoses with the coverings of all the viscera; so also the meninges of the brain; these, by fibrils emitted from them, enter into all the glands below, and through these into all the fibres, and through these into all parts of the body. Thence it is that the head, from the brains, governs all and the single things subordinate to itself. These things are adduced merely in order that, from visible things, some idea may be formed as to how God perceives, sees, and knows all things, even to the most minute, which are done according to order.

God, from those things which are according to order, perceives, knows, and sees all and single things, even to the most minute, that are done contrary to order; because God does not hold man in evil, but withholds him from evil; thus does not lead him [in evil] but strives with him. From that perpetual striving, struggling, resistance, repugnance, and reaction of the evil and the false against His good and truth, thus against Himself, He perceives both their quantity and quality. This follows from the omnipresence of God in all and the single things of His order; and at the same time from His omniscience of all and the single things therein; comparatively, as one whose ear is in harmony and accord exactly detects every discordant and inharmonious sound, how much and in what manner it is discordant, as soon as it enters. (T. C. R. n. 60, 61.)

THE OMNIPRESENCE OF GOD.

The Divine omnipresence may be illustrated by the wonderful presence of angels and spirits in the spiritual world. In that world, because there is no space, but only the appearance of space, an angel or a spirit may, in a moment, become present to another, if only he comes into a similar affection of love, and thought from this; for these two cause the appearance of space. That such is the presence of all there, was manifest to me from the fact that I could see Africans and Hindoos there very near me, although they are so many miles distant upon earth; nay, that I could become present to those who are in other planets of this system, and also to those who are in the planets in other systems beyond this solar system. By virtue of this presence, not of place, but of the appearance of place, I have conversed with the Apostles, with departed popes, emperors, and kings; with the founders of the present church—Luther, Calvin, and Melancthon—and with others from different countries. Since such is the presence of angels and spirits, what limits can be set to the Divine presence, which is infinite, in the universe! The reason that angels and spirits have such presence is, because every affection of love, and every thought of the understanding from this, is in space without space, and in time without time. For any one can think of a brother, relation, or friend in the Indies, and have him then as it were present to him; in like manner, he may be affected by their love, from the remembrance of them. By these things, because they are familiar to every one, the Divine omnipresence may, in some degree, be illustrated; and also by human thought, in that when any one recalls to mind what he has seen in travelling in various places, he is as it were present in them. Nay, the sight of the body emulates the same presence. The eye does not perceive distances, except by intermediate objects, which as it were measure them. The sun itself would be near the eye, nay, in the eye, unless intermediate objects discovered that it is so distant. That it is so writers on optics have also observed in their books. Each sight of man, both the intellectual and corporeal, has such presence, because his spirit sees through his eyes. But no beast has similar presence, because they have no spiritual sight. From these things it is evident that God is omnipresent, from the first to the last things of His order. (T. C. R. n. 64.)

KNOWLEDGE RESPECTING GOD ONLY POSSIBLE BY REVELATION.

As to the nature and character of the one God, nations and peoples have strayed and are still straying into diverse opinions; for many reasons. The first is, that there can be no knowledge respecting God, and consequent acknowledgment of God, except by revelation; and no knowledge and consequent acknowledgment of the Lord, that in Him dwells all the fullness of the Godhead bodily, except from the Word, which is the crown of revelations. But by revelation given man can approach and receive influx from God, and so from natural become spiritual; and a primeval revelation pervaded the whole world. But the natural man perverted it, in many ways; whence the differences, dissensions, heresies, and schisms of religions. . . . Human reason, however, if it will, may perceive or conclude that there is a God, and that He is one. This truth it can confirm by innumerable things in the visible world. For the universe is as a theatre on which the testimony that there is a God, and that He is one, is continually set forth. (T. C. R. n. 11, 12.)

CREATION.

EVERY one who thinks with clear reason sees that the universe is not created from nothing, because he sees that it is impossible for anything to be made out of nothing. For nothing is nothing, and to make anything out of nothing is contradictory, and what is contradictory is contrary to the light of truth, which is from the Divine wisdom; and whatever is not from the Divine wisdom is not from the Divine omnipotence. Every one who thinks from clear reason sees also that all things were created of substance which is substance in itself; for this is the very Being from which all things that are can exist. And as God alone is substance in itself, and hence the very Being, it is evident that the existence of things is from no other source. Many have seen this, for reason gives to see it, but have not dared to confirm it; fearing that thereby they might come to think that the created universe is God, because it is from God; or that nature exists from itself, and thus that its inmost is what is called God. Hence, although many have seen that the existence of all things is from no other source than from God and from His Being, yet they dared not proceed beyond the first thought on the subject, lest they should entangle their understanding in a Gordian knot, as it is called, from whence they might not afterwards be able to extricate it. The reason why they might not have been able to extricate their understanding is, that they thought of God, and of the creation of the universe by God, from time and space, which are peculiar to nature; and no one can perceive God and the creation of the universe from nature, but every one whose understanding is in any degree of interior light, may perceive nature and its creation from God, because God is not in time and space. (D. L. W. n. 283.)

The universe in its greatest and least parts, as well as in its first and last principles, is so full of Divine love and Divine wisdom that it may be said to be Divine love and Divine wisdom in an image. That this is so is manifest from the correspondence of all things in the universe with all things in man. Each and all things that exist in the created universe have such correspondence with each and all things of man that it may be said that man also is a kind of universe. There is a correspondence of his affections and of his thoughts from them with all things of the animal kingdom; a correspondence of his will, and of his understanding from this, with all things of the vegetable kingdom; and a correspondence of his ultimate life with all things of the mineral kingdom. It does not appear to any one in the natural world that there is such a correspondence, but it appears to every one who attends to it in the spiritual world. In that world are all things that exist in the natural world, in its three kingdoms; and they are the correspondences of the affections and thoughts—of the affections of the will and the thoughts of the understanding,—as also of the ultimates of the life, of those who dwell there. They appear around them with an aspect like that of the created universe, with the difference that they are in lesser form. From this it is manifest to the angels that the created universe is an image representative of God Man; and it is His love and wisdom that are manifested in the universe in an image. Not that the created universe is God Man, but that it is from Him. For nothing whatever in the created universe is a substance and form in itself, or life in itself, or love and wisdom in itself; yea, neither is man a man in himself; but all is from God, who is Man, wisdom and love, and form and substance, in Himself. That which IS, in itself, is uncreate and infinite; but that which is from this, having nothing about it which is, in itself, is created and finite. And this represents the image of Him from whom it is and exists. (D. L. W. n. 52.)

Two Worlds, the Spiritual and the Natural.

There are two worlds, the spiritual and the natural; and the spiritual world derives nothing from the natural world, nor the natural world from the spiritual world. They are altogether distinct, and communicate only by correspondences. (D. L. W. n. 83.)

Two Suns, by means of which all Things in the two Worlds were created.

There are two suns by which all things were created from the Lord, the sun of the spiritual world and the sun of the natural world. All things were created from the Lord by the sun of the spiritual world, but not by the sun of the natural world; for the latter is far below the former, and in a middle distance. The spiritual world is above and the natural world is beneath it; and the sun of the natural world was created to act as a medium or substitute. (D. L. W. n. 153.)

Spiritual things cannot proceed from any other source than from love; and love cannot proceed from any other source than from Jehovah God, who is love itself. The sun of the spiritual world therefore, from which all spiritual things issue as from their fountain, is pure love, proceeding from Jehovah God, who is in the midst of it. That sun itself is not God, but is from God, and is the proximate sphere about Him from Him. Through this sun the universe was created by Jehovah God. By the universe all the worlds [systems] in one complex are understood, which are as many as the stars in the expanse of our heaven. (Influx, n. 5.)

The centre and the expanse of nature are derived from the centre and expanse of life, and not the contrary. Above the angelic heaven there is a sun, which is pure love, of a fiery appearance like the sun of the world. From the heat proceeding from that sun angels and men derive will and love; and from its light, understanding and wisdom. All things derived from that sun are called spiritual; and all things proceeding from the world's sun are containants or receptacles of life, and are called natural. The expanse of the centre of life is called the spiritual world, which subsists from its sun; and the expanse of the centre of nature is called the natural world, which subsists from its sun. Now, as spaces and times cannot be predicated of love and wisdom, but instead of them states are predicated, it follows that the expanse around the sun of the angelic heaven is not an extense; and yet it is in the extense of the natural sun, and is present there with all living subjects according to their reception; and their reception is according to their forms and states. The fire of the sun of the world is derived from the sun of the angelic heaven; which is not fire, but the Divine love proximately proceeding from God, who is in the midst of it. Love in its essence is spiritual fire; hence fire in the Word, or Holy Scripture, according to its spiritual sense, signifies love. This is the reason why priests, when officiating in the temple, pray that heavenly fire may fill the hearts of those who worship; by which they mean heavenly love. (T. C. R. n. 35.)

The sun of the natural world is pure fire,[1] and therefore dead;

---

[1] In another place the author states, more definitely, that—"The sun of this world consists of created substances the activity of which produces fire." (T. C. R. n. 472.)

and since nature derives its origin from that sun, it also is dead. Creation itself cannot in the least be ascribed to the sun of the natural world, but all to the sun of the spiritual world, because the sun of the natural world is wholly dead; but the sun of the spiritual world is alive, being the first proceeding of the Divine love and the Divine wisdom; and what is dead does not act from itself, but is acted on. Therefore to ascribe to it anything of creation would be like ascribing the work of the artificer to the instrument with which the hand of the artificer operates. . . . The actuality of the sun of the natural world is not from itself, but from the living power proceeding from the sun of the spiritual world. If therefore the living power of the latter sun were withdrawn or taken away the former sun would perish. Hence it is that the worship of the sun is the lowest of all kinds of worship of a God; for it is as dead as the sun itself. And therefore in the Word it is called an abomination. (D. L. W. n. 157.)

ATMOSPHERES, WATERS, AND EARTHS, IN THE SPIRITUAL AND NATURAL WORLDS.

The spiritual world and the natural world are similar, with the only difference that each and everything in the spiritual world is spiritual, and each and everything in the natural world is natural.

These two worlds being alike, therefore in both there are atmospheres, waters, and earths, which are the generals by and from which each and everything exists with infinite variety.

The atmospheres, which are called ethers and air, in the spiritual and natural worlds are alike, only that those in the spiritual world are spiritual and those in the natural world are natural. The former are spiritual because they exist from the sun which is the first proceeding of the Divine love and Divine wisdom of the Lord; and from Him they receive within them Divine fire, which is love, and Divine light, which is wisdom, and convey these two to the heavens, where the angels dwell, and cause the presence of that sun in the greatest and least things there. The spiritual atmospheres are discrete substances, or most minute forms, originating from the sun. And as they severally receive the sun, hence its fire—being divided into so many substances or forms, and as it were covered or enclosed in them, and tempered by these coverings—becomes heat, proportioned finally to the love of the angels in heaven and of spirits under heaven. The same may be said of the light of the sun. The natural atmospheres are similar to the spiritual atmospheres, in being also discrete substances of very minute form, originating from the sun of the natural world. Which sun also they each of them receive; and they treasure up in them its fire, and temper, and convey it as heat to the earth, which is the dwelling-place of men. And in like manner the light.

The difference between the spiritual atmospheres and the natural is, that the spiritual atmospheres are receptacles of Divine fire and Divine light, thus of love and wisdom, for they contain these within them; while the natural atmospheres are not receptacles of Divine fire and Divine light, but of the fire and light of their own sun, which in itself is devoid of life (as was shown above); and therefore they contain nothing from the sun of the spiritual world, but still are surrounded by spiritual atmospheres which come from that sun. That this is the difference between the spiritual atmospheres and the natural is learned from the wisdom of the angels.

The existence of atmospheres in the spiritual world as well as in the natural, is evident from the fact that angels and spirits breathe, speak, and hear equally with men in the natural world; and respiration, speech, and hearing are effected by means of the air or ultimate atmosphere. Also from the fact that angels and spirits see equally with men in the natural world; and sight is not possible but by means of an atmosphere purer than air. From this also, that angels and spirits think and are affected equally with men in the natural world; and thought and affection do not exist but by means of still purer atmospheres. And lastly from the fact, that all things belonging to the bodies of angels and spirits, as well external as internal, are held in proper connection by atmospheres; their externals by an aërial atmosphere, and their internals by ethereal atmospheres. Were it not for the circumpressure and action of these atmospheres, it is evident that the interior and exterior forms of the body would be dissolved. Since the angels are spiritual, and each and all things of their bodies are held in their connection, form, and order, by atmospheres, it follows that those atmospheres also are spiritual; and they are spiritual because they originate from the spiritual sun, which is the first going forth of the Divine love and Divine wisdom of the Lord. (D. L. W. n. 174-176.)

THE ORIGIN OF MATTER.

That substances or matters, such as are on the earth, were produced from the sun by its atmospheres, is affirmed by all who think that there are perpetual mediations from the first to the last; and that nothing can exist but from a prior self, and at length from the First. And the First is the sun of the spiritual world; and the First of that sun is God Man, or the Lord. Now as the atmospheres are the prior things by which that sun presents itself in ultimates, and as those prior things continually decrease in activity and expansion to ultimates, it follows that when their activity and expansion cease in the ultimates they become substances and matters such as are on the earth; which retain from the atmospheres, whence they originated, an effort and endeavour to produce uses. Those who do not evolve the creation of the universe and all things therein by continual mediations from the First, cannot but build hypotheses that are incoherent and disconnected from their causes, which, when examined by a mind that looks interiorly into things, appear not as houses but as heaps of rubbish. (D. L. W. n. 303.)

The origin of earths, treated of in the preceding article, may show that in the substances and matters of which they consist there is nothing of the Divine in itself, but that they are deprived of all that is Divine in itself; being, as was there said, the ends and terminations of the atmospheres, whose heat has ended in cold, whose light in darkness, and whose activity in inertness. But still they have brought with them, by continuation from the substance of the spiritual sun, that which was there from the Divine, which was the sphere surrounding God Man or the Lord. From this sphere, by continuation from the sun, proceeded, by means of the atmospheres, the substances and matters of which the earths consist. (D. L. W. n. 305.)

THE DIVINE OBJECT IN THE CREATION OF THE UNIVERSE.

The end of the creation of the universe is, that there may be an angelic heaven; and as the angelic heaven is the end, so also is man or the human race, because heaven consists of the human race. Hence all things that are created are mediate ends and uses, in the order, degree, and respect that they have relation to man, and by man to the Lord. (D. L. W. n. 329.)

The universal end, which is the end of all things in creation, is, that there may be an eternal conjunction of the Creator with the created universe; and this is impossible unless there be subjects in which His Divine may be, as in Himself, thus in which it may dwell and remain. Such subjects, in order that they may be His habitations and mansions, must be recipients of His love and wisdom as of themselves. They must therefore be such as can, as of themselves, elevate themselves to the Creator, and conjoin themselves with Him. Without this reciprocation no conjunction can be effected. These subjects are men who can, as of themselves, elevate and join themselves. By this conjunction the Lord is present in every work created from Himself; for every created thing is finally for the sake of man. Therefore the uses of all things that are created ascend by degrees from ultimates to man, and through man to God the Creator, from whom they originate.

Creation is in continual progression to this ultimate end, by the three [gradations], end, cause and effect; for these three exist in God the Creator, and the Divine is in all space without space, and is the same in the greatest and least things. Hence it is evident that the created universe, in its general progression to its ultimate end, is relatively the mediate end; for forms of uses are continually raised from the earth by the Lord the Creator, in their order up to man, who as to his body is likewise from the earth. Next, man is elevated by the reception of love and wisdom from the Lord; and all means are provided that he may receive them; and he is made such that he can receive them if he will. (D. L. W. n. 170, 171.)

ALL THINGS OF THE CREATED UNIVERSE, VIEWED FROM USES, REPRESENT MAN IN AN IMAGE.

Man was called a microcosm by the ancients, because he resembled the macrocosm, which is the universe in the whole complex. But at this day it is not known why man was so called by the ancients; for there appears in him nothing more of the universe or the macrocosm than that he is nourished and lives, as to his body, from its animal and vegetable kingdoms, and that he is kept in a living state by its heat, sees by its light, and hears and breathes by its atmospheres. These, however, do not make man a microcosm, as the universe with all things therein is a macrocosm. The ancients called man a microcosm, or little universe, from the knowledge of correspondences which the most ancient people possessed, and from their communication with the angels of heaven; for the angels of heaven know, from the visible things about them, that all things in the universe, viewed as to uses, represent man in an image.

But that man is a microcosm, or little universe, because the created universe viewed as to uses is man in an image, cannot enter the thought and knowledge of any one, except from an idea of the universe as seen in the spiritual world. It cannot therefore be shown but by some angel in the spiritual world, or by some one to whom it has been granted to be in that world, and to see the things therein. As this has been granted to me, I am enabled, by what I have seen there, to reveal this arcanum.

Be it known that the spiritual world, in external appearance, is altogether similar to the natural world. Lands, mountains, hills, valleys, plains, fields, lakes, rivers and fountains appear there, consequently all things of the mineral kingdom; also paradises, gardens, groves, woods, with trees and shrubs of all kinds, fruits and seeds, also plants, flowers, herbs and grasses, thus all things of the vegetable kingdom; and animals, birds, and fishes of all kinds, thus all things of the animal kingdom appear there. Man, there, is an angel and a spirit. This is premised that it may be known that the universe of the spiritual world is altogether similar to the universe of the natural world; only that things there are not fixed and stationary, like those in the natural world, because in the spiritual world nothing is natural, but everything is spiritual.

That the universe of that world resembles a man in image, may be clearly seen from the fact that all the things just mentioned appear to the life, and exist about an angel and about angelic societies, as produced or created from them; they remain about them, and do not go away. That they are as things produced or created from them, is evident from the fact that when an angel goes away, or a society departs to another place, they no longer appear; also, that when other angels come in their place, the face of all things about them changes; the paradises change as to trees and fruits, the gardens as to flowers and seeds, the fields as to herbs and grasses; and the kinds of animals and birds likewise change. Such things exist and so change because all these exist according to the affections and derivative thoughts of the angels; for they are correspondences. And as things which correspond make one with him to whom they correspond, therefore they are a representative image of him. The image does not indeed appear when all these are seen in their forms, but only when they are seen in their uses. It has been given me to see, that the angels, when their eyes have been opened by the Lord, and they have beheld these things from the correspondence of uses, have acknowledged and seen themselves in them.

Now, as the things that exist about the angels according to their affections and thoughts resemble a kind of universe, in the fact that there are earths, vegetables and animals, and these form a representative image of an angel, it is clear whence it was that the ancients called man a microcosm. (D. L. W. n. 319-323.)

Creation began from the highest or inmost, because from the Divine, and went forth to the ultimates or extremes and then first subsisted. The ultimate of the creation is the natural universe; and in it the terraqueous globe and all things thereon. When these were completed man was created, and into him were gathered all things of Divine order, from the first to the last. In his inmost parts were gathered those things which are in the first [degrees] of that order, and in his ultimates those which are in the last. So that man was made Divine order in form. (L. J. n. 9.)

MAN.

ALL men, as to the interiors which belong to their minds, are spirits, clothed in the world with a material body, which is in every case subject to the thought of the spirit, and to the decision of its affection. For the mind, which is spirit, acts, and the body, which is matter, is acted upon. Every spirit, too, after the rejection of the material body, is a man, in a form similar to that which he had while he was a man in the world. (Ath. Cr. n. 41.)

Man is so created as to be, at the same time, in the spiritual world and in the natural. The spiritual world is the abode of angels, and the natural of men; and being so created, he is endowed with an internal and an external—the internal being that by which he is in the spiritual world, and the external that by which he is in the natural world. His internal is what is called the internal man, and his external is what is called the external man. (T. C. R. n. 401.)

Man is not life, but a recipient of life from God. It is generally believed that life is in man, and is his own; consequently that he is not merely a recipient of life, but actually is life. This general belief is founded upon the appearance; for man lives—that is, he feels, thinks, speaks, and acts altogether as of himself. . . . But how is it possible, according to any rational conception, for the Infinite to create anything but what is finite? Can a man, therefore, being finite, be reasonably conceived to be anything but a form, which the Infinite may vivify from the life which He possesses in Himself? (ib. 470.)

Man is an organ of life, and God alone is life. God infuses His life into the organ and all its parts, as the sun infuses its heat into a tree and all its parts. And God grants man a sense that the life in himself is as if it were his own; and is desirous that he should have such a sense of it, to the intent that he may live, as of himself, according to the laws of order—which are as many in number as the precepts of the Word—and may thus dispose himself to receive the love of God. Yet God continually, as it were, with His finger holds the perpendicular tongue that is over the balance, to moderate it; but still He never violates free determination by compulsion. . . . Man's free determination results from the fact that he has a sense that the life he enjoys is his own. (*ib.* n. 504.)

What the Internal and External Man are.

Few, if any, at the present day know what the internal and the external man are. It is generally supposed that they are one and the same; and the reason of this is, that most persons believe that they do good and think truth of themselves, or from their proprium; this being a necessary consequence of sub-mission to its influence. . . . The internal man is as distinct from the external as heaven from earth. Both the learned and the unlearned, when reflecting on the subject, have no other conception of the internal man than that it consists of thought, because it is within; and they believe that the external man is the body, with its sensual and voluptuous principle, because they are without. But thought, which is thus ascribed to the internal man, does not, in fact, belong to it; for in the internal man there are nothing but goods and truths derived from the Lord, conscience being implanted in the interior man by the Lord. For example, the wicked, yea, the very worst of men, and even those who are des-titute of conscience, have a principle of thought; from which it is evident that the faculty of thought does not belong to the internal, but to the external man. That the material body, with its sensual and voluptuous principle, does not constitute the external man, is manifest from the consideration that spirits, who have no material bodies, have an external man as well as men on earth. . . . The internal man is formed of what is celestial and spiri-tual; and the external man of what is sensual—not belonging to the body, but derived from corporeal things; and this is not only so with man, but also with spirits. (A. C. n. 978.)

The very Inmost of Man.

With every angel, and likewise with every man, there is an inmost or supreme degree, or a something inmost and supreme, into which the Divine of the Lord first or proximately flows, and from which it disposes the other interior things in the angel or man, which succeed, according to the degrees of order. This in-most or supreme may be called the Lord's entrance to the angel and to man, and His veriest dwelling-place with them. By virtue of this inmost or supreme man is man, and is distinguished from

The Divine Spirit

brute animals; for these have it not. Hence it is that man, different from animals, as to all the interiors which are of his mind [*mens*] and mind [*animus*] can be elevated by the Lord to Himself, can believe in Him, be affected with love to Him, and thus see Him; and that he can receive intelligence and wisdom, and speak from reason. Hence also it is that he lives to eternity. But what is disposed and provided by the Lord in that inmost does not flow manifestly into the perception of any angel, because it is above his thought, and exceeds his wisdom. (H. H. n. 39, see also p. 57.)

THE LIFE OF MAN.

The very life of man is his love; and such as the love is such is the life, and even such is the whole man. But this is to be understood only of the ruling or governing love; for it is this that determines the quality of the man. This love has many others subordinate to it, which are its derivatives. (T. C. R. n. 399.)

Man knows of the existence, but not the nature, of love. He is aware of its existence from the use of the word in common speech, as when it is said one loves me; the king loves his subjects, and the subjects love their king; the husband loves his wife, and the mother her children, and *vice versa;* or when it is said that one loves his country, his fellow-citizens, or his neighbour; so when it is said of things abstract from person, that we love this or that thing. Yet, though the word love is so universally in the mouths of men, scarcely any one knows what love is. While meditating upon it, since he can form no idea of thought concerning it, one says either that it is nothing real, or that it is merely something that flows in by sight, hearing, feeling, and conversation, and so affects him. Man is quite ignorant of the fact that it is his very life, not merely the common life of his whole body, and the common life of all his thoughts, but the life also of all their particulars. A wise man may perceive this from the following queries: If you take away the affection, which is of love, can you think on any subject? or can you do anything? In proportion as the affection, which is of love, grows cold, do not thought, speech, and action grow cold also? and in proportion as it is warmed, are they not also warmed? But this the wise perceive, not from knowledge that love is the life of man, but from experience of this fact. (D. L. W. n. 1.)

THE ORIGIN OF VITAL HEAT.

It is well known that there is vital heat in man, and in every animal, but its origin is not known. Every one speaks of it from conjecture. Those, therefore, who have no knowledge of the correspondence of natural things with spiritual, have ascribed it either to the heat of the sun, or to the activity of particles, or to life itself; but as they did not know what life is, they proceeded no further than barely to say this. But he who knows that there is a correspondence of love and its affections with the heart and its derivations, may know that love is the origin of vital heat. Love proceeds as heat from the spiritual sun, where the Lord is, and is also felt as heat by the angels. This spiritual heat, which in its essence is love, flows by correspondence into the heart and the blood, and imparts heat to it, and at the same time vivifies it. That a man is heated, and as it were fired, according to his love, and its degree, and grows torpid and cold according to its decrease, is well known, for it is felt and seen; it is felt from the heat of the whole body, and is seen in the redness of the face. And, on the other hand, its extinction is felt from the coldness of the body, and seen from the paleness of the face. (*ib.* n. 379.)

The Primitive Condition of Man.

That man was created a form of Divine order follows from his being created in the image and likeness of God; for since God is order itself, man was therefore created the image and likeness of order. There are two origins from which order exists, and by which it subsists—Divine love and Divine wisdom; and man was created a receptacle of them both. Consequently he was created in the order according to which these two operate in the universe; and particularly into that according to which they operate in the angelic heaven; for by virtue of such operation the whole heaven is a form of Divine order in its largest portraiture, and appears in the sight of God as a single man. (T. C. R. n. 65.)

In the first ages of the world men acknowledged in heart and soul that they received all the good of love, and hence all the truth of wisdom, from God. They were, therefore, called images of God, sons of God, and born of God. (*ib.* n. 692.)

I have been informed that the men of the Most Ancient Church were of so heavenly a character that they conversed with angels, and that they had the power of holding such converse by means of correspondences. From this the state of their wisdom became such that when they looked upon any of the objects of this world they not only thought of them naturally, but also spiritually, thus in conjunction with the angels of heaven. (*ib.* n. 202.)

THE FALL OF MAN.

The Nature of the Fall.

" But of the tree of the knowledge of good and evil thou shalt not eat of it; for in the day that thou eatest thereof thou shalt surely die." These words, together with those just explained, signify that it is allowable to obtain a knowledge of what is true and good by means of every perception derived from the Lord, but not from self and the world; or, that it is unlawful to inquire into the mysteries of faith by means of things of sense and knowledge, by which means his celestial quality is destroyed.

A desire to investigate the mysteries of faith by means of things sensuous and known, was not only the cause of the fall or decline of the Most Ancient Church, in the succeeding generation, but it is the cause of the fall or decline of every church; for hence come not merely false opinions, but evils of life also.

The worldly and corporeal man says in his heart, "If I am not instructed by the senses concerning faith, and the things relating to it, so that I may see them, or by means of knowledge, so that I may understand them, I will not believe;" and he confirms himself in his incredulity by the fact that natural things cannot be contrary to spiritual. Thus he would be instructed in heavenly and Divine subjects by the experience of his senses; which is as impossible as for a camel to go through the eye of a needle. For the more he would grow wise by such a process, the more he blinds himself; till at length he comes to believe nothing, not even the reality of spiritual existences, or of eternal life. This is a necessary consequence of the principle which he lays down. This is to eat of the tree of the knowledge of good and evil; of which the more a man eats the more dead he becomes. But he who would grow wise by wisdom derived from the Lord, and not from the world, says within himself that he ought to believe the Lord, that is, the things which the Lord has spoken in the Word, because they are truths; and according to this principle he regulates his thoughts. Such a person confirms himself in his belief by things of reason and knowledge, sensual and natural; and things which do not confirm he rejects. (A. C. n. 126-128.)

The evil of the Most Ancient Church, which existed before the flood, as well as of the Ancient church founded after that event, of the Jewish church, and subsequently of the new church or church of the Gentiles after the coming of the Lord, and also the evil of the church of the present day is, that instead of believing the Lord, or the Word, they trusted to themselves and the evidence of their senses. Hence faith became annihilated, and when there was no faith there was no love to the neighbour, so that all was evil and falsity.

At this day, however, the evil is much greater than in former times, because men can now confirm the incredulity of the senses by knowledges of which the ancients were ignorant, which have given birth to indescribable darkness, at which mankind would be astonished did they but know how great it is. (*ib.* n. 231, 232.)

LOSS OF INTERNAL PERCEPTION BY THE FALL.

The Most Ancient Church had a perception of what was good and true; the Ancient church had no perception, but in the place of it a different kind of internal dictate, which may be called conscience. But, what has hitherto been unknown to the world, and will perhaps appear incredible, the man of the Most Ancient Church had internal respiration, and none that was externally perceptible. They therefore did not converse so much by words as afterwards, and at the present day, but like the angels, by ideas which they were able to express by innumerable variations of the looks and countenance, and especially of the lips. For in the lips there are innumerable series of muscular fibres which at the present day are not developed, but which, being then unloosed, served so perfectly to set forth, signify, and represent their ideas, that in a minute they could relate what it would now require an hour to express by articulate sounds or words; and that more fully and evidently to the apprehension and understanding of those present, than can ever be by words, and series of combined sounds. This is perhaps incredible, but nevertheless it is true. There are also many others, not inhabitants of this earth, who have conversed and at this day converse in a similar manner. I have, moreover, been informed as to the nature of this internal respiration, and how in the progress of time it became changed. As they breathed like the angels—for they respire in a similar manner—so also they were in profound ideas of thought, and were capable of enjoying such perception as cannot be described; and indeed, were it done the description would be rejected as incredible, because it could not be understood. Among their posterity, however, this internal respiration gradually ceased, and with those who were occupied with direful persuasions and fantasies, it became so changed that they could no longer visibly express any but the most deformed idea of thought; the effect of which was that they could not survive, and therefore became extinct.   (A. C. n. 607.)

THE IMAGE OF GOD NOT ACTUALLY DESTROYED IN MAN.

The image of God and the likeness of God are not destroyed with man, but are as if destroyed; for they remain implanted in his two faculties that are called rationality and liberty. They became as destroyed when man made the receptacle of the Divine love, which is his will, the receptacle of the love of self, and the receptacle of the Divine wisdom, which is his understanding, the receptacle of his own intelligence. Thereby he inverted the image and likeness of God; for he turned away those two receptacles from God, and turned them round to himself. Hence it is that they are closed above and open below, or that they are closed before and open behind, when yet by creation they were open before and closed behind; and when they are opened and closed thus inversely, then the receptacle of love or the will receives influx from hell or from its proprium; in like manner the receptacle of wisdom or the understanding. Hence arose in the churches the worship of men in place of the worship of God, and worship from the doctrines of falsity in place of worship from the doctrines of truth; the latter from their own intelligence, and the former from the love of self. From these things it is manifest, that religion in process of time decreases and is consummated by the inversion of the image of God with man.   (D. P. n. 328.)

EXTERNAL RESPIRATION, AND THE ORIGIN OF VERBAL LANGUAGE BY THE FALL.

As internal respiration ceased, external respiration almost like that of the present day succeeded; and with this came the language of words, or the determination of the ideas of thought into articulate sounds. Thus the state of man became entirely changed, and he became such that he was unable any longer to have that perception enjoyed by the Most Ancient Church. But instead of perception, he had another kind of dictate, which, as it resembled so it may be called *conscience*, although it was intermediate in nature between perception and the conscience known to some in the present day. When the ideas of thought became thus determined into verbal expressions, the capacity of being in-

structed through the internal man, possessed by the most ancient people, ceased, and the external became the inlet to
knowledge. Then, therefore, doctrinals succeeded to the revelations of the Most Ancient Church; which being first apprehended by the external senses were afterwards formed into the
material ideas of the memory, and thence into the ideas of
thought, by which and according to which they were instructed.
Hence it was that this church, which succeeded to the Most
Ancient, was of an entirely different genius; and unless the
Lord had brought the human race to this genius or state, no
man could ever have been saved. (A. C. n. 608.)

The Most Ancient Church, above all churches in the whole
world, was from the Divine; for it was in the good of love to
the Lord. Their voluntary and intellectual faculties made one,
thus one mind. They therefore had a perception of truth from
good; for the Lord flowed in, through an internal way, into the
good of their will, and through this into the good of the understanding or truth. Hence it is that that church in preference
to the others was called Man. But when that generation
expired, another succeeded of a totally different character. Instead of discerning truth by good, or estimating the relations of
faith by love, they acquired a knowledge of what is good by
means of truth, and of love by the knowledges of faith; and with
many among them mere knowledge was the desideratum. Such
was the change made after the flood, to prevent the destruction
of the world. (*ib.* n. 4454, 200.)

The Fall was Gradual and Successive.

From what is here stated respecting the first man, it is
manifest that all the hereditary evil existing at the present day
was not derived from him, as is commonly but erroneously
supposed. . . . With respect to hereditary evil the case is this :
Every one who commits actual sin acquires a nature conformable to it, whence evil is implanted in his children, and
becomes hereditary. Consequently it is derived from each
particular parent, from his father, his grandfather, his great-
grandfather, and their ancestors; and is thus multiplied and
augmented in each descending generation. And it remains
with each, and is increased in each by actual sin; nor does it
ever become dissipated or lose its baneful influence except in
those who are regenerated by the Lord. Every attentive observer
may see evidence of this truth in the fact that the evil inclinations of parents visibly remain in their children; so that a
family, yea, an entire race, may be thereby distinguished from
every other. (A. C. n. 313.)

The Nature and Extent of Hereditary Evil.

Hereditary evil from the father is interior; and hereditary evil from the mother is exterior. The former cannot easily be eradicated, but the latter can be. When man is regenerated, the hereditary evil inrooted from the next parents is extirpated; but it remains with those who are not regenerated, or not capable of being regenerated. This then is hereditary evil. This is evident to every one who reflects; and further, from the fact that every family has some peculiar evil or good by which it is distinguished from other families; and it is known that this is from parents and ancestors. It is so in regard to the Jewish nation which remains at this day; which it is very manifest is distinct and may be known from other nations, not only by their peculiar genius, but also by their manners, speech, and countenance. But few know what hereditary evil is. It is believed to consist in doing evil; but it consists in willing and thence thinking evil. Hereditary evil is in the will itself, and thence in the thought, and is the very tendency which is within it; and even adjoins itself when a man does good. It is known by the delight which arises when evil befalls another. That root lies deeply hidden, for the very interior form recipient of good and truth from heaven, or through heaven from the Lord, is depraved, and so to speak, detorted; so that when good and truth flow in from the Lord they are either turned aside, perverted, or suffocated. Hence it is that there is no perception of good and truth at this day, but instead of it the regenerate conscience, which acknowledges as good and true what is learned from parents and masters. It is of hereditary evil to love self in preference to another; to will evil to another if he does not honour self; to perceive delight in revenge; also to love the world, and all the lusts or evil affections thence derived, more than heaven. Man does not know that such things are in him; and still less that such things are opposite to heavenly affections. But yet in the other life it is manifestly shown how much of hereditary evil every one has attracted to himself by actual life; also how much he has removed himself from heaven by evil affections from it. (A. C. n. 4317.)

Every man is born, of his parents, into the evils of the love of self and of the world. Every evil which by habit has as it were contracted a nature, is derived into the offspring; thus successively from parents, from grandfathers, and from great-grandfathers, in a long series backward. Hence the derivation of evil is at length become so great that all man's own life is nothing else but evil. This continued derived [evil] is not broken and altered except by a life of faith and charity from the Lord. (*ib.* n. 8550.)

THE DOCTRINE OF THE LORD.[1]

THE DIVINE HUMAN FROM ETERNITY.

IN heaven the Divine Human of the Lord is all; the reason is, because no one there, not even an angel of the inmost or third heaven, can have any conception of the Divine itself; according to the Lord's words in John, "*No man hath seen God at any time*" (i. 18). "*Ye have neither heard the voice of the Father at any time, nor seen His shape*" (v. 37). For the angels are finite, and what is finite can have no conception of the infinite. In heaven therefore, if they had not an idea of God in the human shape, they would have no idea, or an unbecoming one; and thus they could not be conjoined with the Divine either by faith or love. This being so, therefore in heaven they perceive the Divine in the human form. Hence it is that in the heavens the Divine Human is the all in their intuitions concerning the Divine; and is thus the all in their faith and love; whence comes conjunction, and by conjunction salvation. (A. C. n. 7211.)

That Jehovah appearing means the appearing of the Lord's Divine in His Human, is evident from this, that His Divine cannot appear to any man, nor even to any angel, except by the Divine Human; and the Divine Human cannot appear but by the Divine Truth which proceeds from Him. (*ib.* n. 6945.)

When Jehovah appeared before the coming of the Lord into the world He appeared in the form of an angel; for when He passed through heaven He clothed Himself with that form, which was the human form. For the universal heaven, by virtue of the Divine there, is as one man, called the Greatest Man. Hence then is the Divine Human; and as Jehovah appeared in the human form as an angel, it is evident that it was still Jehovah himself; and that very form was also His, because it was His Divine in heaven. This was the Lord from eternity. (*ib.* n. 10,579.)

When the Lord made His Human Divine He did this from

---

[1] By the Lord, in the Writings of Swedenborg, the Lord Jesus Christ is always meant, or God incarnate, afterwards glorified. (A. C. n. 14.)

the Divine, by transflux through heaven. Not that heaven contributed anything of itself, but that the very Divine might flow into the human it flowed in through heaven. This transflux was the Divine Human before the coming of the Lord, and was Jehovah Himself in the heavens, or the Lord. (*ib.* n. 6720.)

THE LORD'S APPEARANCE ON EARTH BEFORE THE INCARNATION, AS AN ANGEL.

The angel of Jehovah is often mentioned in the Word, and everywhere, when in a good sense, he represents and signifies some essential appertaining to the Lord, and proceeding from Him. But what is particularly represented and signified may be seen from the series of things treated of. There were angels who were sent to men, and also who spake by the prophets; but what they spake was not from the angels, but by them; for the state they were then in was such that they did not know but they were Jehovah, that is, the Lord. Yet when they had done speaking, they presently returned into their former state, and spake as from themselves. This was the case with the angels who spake the Lord's Word; which it has been given me to know by much similar experience at this day, in the other life. This is the reason why the angels were sometimes called Jehovah, as is very evident from the angel who appeared to Moses in the bush, of whom it is thus written : " *The angel of Jehovah appeared unto him in a flame of fire out of the midst of the bush. . . . And when Jehovah saw that he turned aside to see, God called unto him out of the midst of the bush. . . . God said unto Moses, I am that I am. . . . And God said moreover unto Moses, Thus shalt thou say unto the children of Israel: Jehovah God of your fathers, hath sent me unto you* " (Exod. iii. 2, 4, 14, 15). From these words it is evident that it was an angel who appeared to Moses as a flame in the bush; and that he spake as Jehovah because the Lord, or Jehovah, spake by him. For in order that man may be addressed by vocal expressions, which are articulate sounds in the ultimates of nature, the Lord uses the ministry of angels, by filling them with the Divine spirit or influence, and laying asleep what is of their *proprium*, so that they do not know but that they are Jehovah. Thus the Divine spirit or influence of Jehovah, which is in the highest or inmost, descends into the lowest or outermost things of nature, in which man is as to sight and hearing. It was so with the angel who spake with Gideon, of whom it is thus written in the book of Judges : " *The angel of Jehovah appeared unto him, and said unto him, Jehovah is with thee, thou mighty man of valour. And Gideon said unto him, O my Lord! why hath all this befallen*

*us ? . . . And Jehovah looked at him and said, Go in this thy
might. . . . And Jehovah said unto him, Surely I will be with
thee"* (vi. 12, 13, 16); and afterwards, *" When Gideon perceived that
he was an angel of Jehovah, Gideon said, Alas, O Lord Jehovih !
for because I have seen an angel of Jehovah face to face. And
Jehovah said unto him, Peace be unto thee; fear not"* (ver. 22, 23).
Here, in like manner, it was an angel who appeared to Gideon,
but in such a state that he knew not but that he was Jehovah,
or the Lord. So again in the book of Judges : *" The angel of
Jehovah came up from Gilgal to Bochim, and said, I made you to
go up out of Egypt, and have brought you into the land which I
sware unto your fathers ; and I said I will never break my covenant with you "* (ii. 1) ; where, in like manner, the angel spake
in the name of Jehovah, saying, that he had brought them up
out of the land of Egypt; when yet the angel did not bring
them up, but Jehovah, as it is frequently said in other places.
From this it may be seen how the angels spake by the prophets,
viz., that the Lord Himself spake, though by angels, and that
the angels did not speak at all from themselves. That the
Word is from the Lord appears from many passages ; as from
this in Matthew : *" That it might be fulfilled which was spoken
of the Lord by the prophet, saying, Behold, a virgin shall be with
child, and shall bring forth a Son "* (i. 22, 23) ; not to mention
other passages. It is because the Lord spake by angels when
He spake with man, that throughout the Word He is called an
angel; and in such cases, as observed above, some essential is
signified appertaining to the Lord, and proceeding from the
Lord. (A. C. n. 1925.)

The Israelitish church worshipped Jehovah, who in Himself
is the invisible God, but under a human form, which Jehovah
God put on by means of an angel ; and in this form He was seen
by Abraham, Sarah, Moses, Hagar, Gideon, Joshua, and sometimes by the prophets ; which human form was representative
of the Lord who was to come. (T. C. R. n. 786.)

THE VERY INFINITE CANNOT BE MANIFESTED OTHERWISE THAN BY
THE DIVINE HUMAN.

The very Infinite, which is above all the heavens and above
the inmost things in man, cannot be manifested except by the
Divine Human, which exists with the Lord alone. The communication of the Infinite with the finite is in no other way
possible; which is also the reason why Jehovah, when He
appeared to the men of the Most Ancient Church, and afterwards to those of the Ancient church after the Flood, and also

in succeeding times to Abraham and the prophets, was manifested to them as a man. Hence it may appear that the Infinite Esse never could have been manifested to man except by the Human Essence, consequently by the Lord. (A. C. 1990.)

What proceeds immediately from the very Divine, not even the angels in the inmost heaven can comprehend. The reason is, because it is infinite and thus transcends all, even angelic comprehension. But what proceeds from the Lord's Divine Human, this they can comprehend, for it exhibits God as a Divine Man, of whom some conception can be formed from the Human. (A. C. n. 5321.)

THE INCARNATION.

In the Christian churches at this day, it is believed that God, the Creator of the universe, begat a Son from eternity; and that this Son descended and assumed the Human, to redeem and save men. But this is erroneous, and falls of itself to the ground, when it is considered that God is one, and that it is more than fabulous in the eye of reason, that the one God should have begotten a Son from eternity, and also that God the Father, together with the Son and the Holy Ghost, each of whom singly is God, should be one God. This fabulous representation is entirely dissipated when it is shewn from the Word, that Jehovah God Himself descended and became MAN, and became also the Redeemer. As regards the first—That Jehovah God Himself descended and became Man, is evident from these passages: "*Behold, a virgin shall conceive and bring forth a Son, who shall be called God with us*" (Isaiah vii. 14; Matt. i. 22, 23). "*Unto us a Child is born, unto us a Son is given, and the government shall be upon His shoulder, and His name shall be called Wonderful, God, Hero, the Father of Eternity, the Prince of Peace*" (Isaiah ix. 6). "*It shall be said in that day, Lo, this is our God, whom we have waited for to deliver us; this is Jehovah, whom we have waited for: let us be glad and rejoice in His salvation*" (xxv. 9). "*The voice of one crying in the wilderness, Prepare a way for Jehovah; make smooth in the desert a way for our God; . . . and all flesh shall see together*" (xl. 3, 5). "*Behold, the Lord Jehovah is coming in the mighty one, and His arm shall rule for Him; behold, His reward is with Him, . . . and He shall feed His flock like a shepherd*" (xl. 10, 11). "*Jehovah said, Sing and rejoice, O daughter of Zion; behold, I am coming to dwell in the midst of thee; then many nations shall cleave to Jehovah in that day*" (Zech. ii. 10, 11). "*I Jehovah have called thee in righteousness, . . . and I will give thee for a covenant of the people; . . . I am Jehovah; that is My name, and My glory will I not give to another"* (Isaiah xlii. 6, 8). *"Behold, the days come, when I will raise unto David a righteous branch, who shall reign king, . . . and execute judgment and justice in the earth; and this is His name, . . . Jehovah our Righteousness"* (Jerem. xxiii. 5, 6; xxxiii. 15, 16): besides other passages, where the coming of the Lord is called the day of Jehovah, as Isaiah xiii. 6, 9, 13, 22; Ezek. xxxi. 15; Joel i. 15; ii. 1, 2, 11; iii. 2, 4; iv. 1, 4, 18; Amos v. 13, 18, 20; Zeph. i. 7-18; Zech. xiv. 1, 4-21; and other places. That Jehovah Himself descended and assumed the Human, is very evident in Luke, where are these words: *"Mary said to the angel, How shall this be, since I know not a man?"* To whom the angel replied, *"The Holy Spirit shall come upon thee, and the power of the Most High shall overshadow thee; therefore that Holy Thing that is born of thee, shall be called the Son of God"* (i. 34, 35). And in Matthew: The angel said to Joseph, the bridegroom of Mary, in a dream, *"That which is conceived in her is of the Holy Spirit; . . . and Joseph knew her not, until she brought forth a Son, and he called His name Jesus"* (i. 20, 25). That by the Holy Spirit is meant the Divine which proceeds from Jehovah, will be seen in the third chapter of this work. Who does not know that the child has its soul and life from the father, and that the body is from the soul? What therefore is said more plainly, than that the Lord had his soul and life from Jehovah God? And since the Divine cannot be divided, that the Divine itself was His soul and life? Therefore the Lord so often called Jehovah God His Father, and Jehovah God called him His Son. What then can be heard more preposterous, than that the soul of our Lord was from the mother Mary, as both the Roman Catholics and the Reformed at this day dream, not having as yet been awaked by the Word.

That a Son born from eternity descended and assumed the Human, evidently falls and is dissipated as an error, by the passages in the Word in which Jehovah Himself says that He is the Saviour and the Redeemer; which are the following: *"Am not I Jehovah? and there is no God else besides Me; a just God and a Saviour; there is none besides Me"* (Isaiah xlv. 21, 22). *"I am Jehovah, and besides Me there is no Saviour"* (xliii. 11). *"I am Jehovah thy God, and thou shalt acknowledge no God but Me: there is no Saviour besides Me"* (Hosea xiii. 4). *"That all flesh may know that I Jehovah am thy Saviour and thy Redeemer"* (Isaiah xlix. 26; lx. 16). *"As for our Redeemer, Jehovah of Hosts is His name"* (xlvii. 4). *"Their Redeemer is mighty; Jehovah of Hosts is His name"* (Jerem. l. 34). *"O Jehovah, my rock and my Redeemer"* (Psalm

xix. 14). *"Thus saith Jehovah, thy Redeemer, the Holy One of Israel, I am Jehovah thy God"* (Isaiah xlviii. 17; xliii. 14; xlix. 7). *"Thus saith Jehovah thy Redeemer, . . . I am Jehovah, that maketh all things . . . even alone by Myself"* (xliv. 24). *"Thus saith Jehovah the King of Israel, and His Redeemer, Jehovah of Hosts, I am the First and the Last, and beside Me there is no God"* (xliv. 6). *"Thou, O Jehovah, our Father, our Redeemer from eternity is Thy name"* (lxiii. 16). *"With the mercy of eternity I will have mercy, thus saith Jehovah thy Redeemer"* (liv. 8). *Thou hast redeemed Me, O Jehovah, God of truth"* (Psalm xxxi. 5). *"Let Israel hope in Jehovah, because in Jehovah is mercy, and with Him is plenteous Redemption, and He will redeem Israel from all his iniquities"* (cxxx. 7, 8). *"Jehovah God, and thy Redeemer the Holy One of Israel, the God of the whole earth shall He be called"* (Isaiah liv. 5). From these passages and very many others, every man who has eyes and a mind opened by means of them, may see that God, who is one, descended and became Man, for the purpose of accomplishing the work of redemption. Who cannot see this as in the morning light, when he gives attention to these the very Divine declarations which have been adduced? But those who are in the shade of night, by being confirmed in favour of the birth of another God from eternity, and of His descent and redemption, close their eyes at these Divine declarations; and in that state think how they may apply them to their falsities, and pervert them. (T. C. R. n. 82, 83.)

JEHOVAH GOD DESCENDED AS TO DIVINE TRUTH, AND WAS SAID
TO BE BORN.

All truth is from good, for it is the form of it, and all good is the esse (or inmost being) of truth. Good when it is formed, so as to appear to the mind, and through the mind, in speech, is called truth. (A. E. n. 136.)

Truth is the form of good; that is, when good is formed so that it can be intellectually perceived, then it is called truth. (A. C. n. 3049.)

There are two things which make the essence of God, the Divine Love and the Divine Wisdom; or what is the same the Divine Good and the Divine Truth. These two in the Word are meant also by Jehovah God; by Jehovah, the Divine Love or Divine Good, and by God, the Divine Wisdom or Divine Truth. Thence it is that in the Word they are distinguished in various ways, and sometimes only Jehovah is named, and sometimes only God. For where it treats of the

Divine God = good
Divine Truth = God

Divine Good, there it says Jehovah, and where of the Divine
Truth, God, and where of both, Jehovah God. That Jehovah
God descended as the Divine Truth, which is the Word, is
evident in John, where are these words: "*In the beginning was
the Word, and the Word was with God, and the Word was God.
All things were made by Him, and without Him was not any thing
made that was made. . . . And the Word became flesh, and
dwelt among us*" (i. 1, 3, 14). (T. C. R. n. 85.)

In the Word the Lord is called Jehovah as to Divine Good;
for Divine Good is the very Divine. And the Lord is called
the Son of God as to Divine Truth; for Divine Truth proceeds
from Divine Good, as a son from a father, and also is said to be
born. (A. C. n. 7499.)

YET DID NOT SEPARATE THE DIVINE GOOD.

Lord
Divine Good can in nowise be and exist without Divine
Truth, nor Divine Truth without Divine Good, but one in the
other, mutually and reciprocally. . . . The Divine Good is the
Father, and the Divine Truth the Son. (A. C. n. 2803.)

That God, although He descended as the Divine Truth, still
did not separate the Divine Good, is evident from the conception,
concerning which we read, that *The virtue of the Most High overshadowed Mary* (Luke i. 35); and by the virtue of the Most
High is meant the Divine Good. The same is evident from the
passages where He says, that the Father is in Him, and He in
the Father; that all things of the Father are His; and that the
Father and He are one; besides many other things. By the
Father is meant the Divine Good. (T. C. R. n. 88.)

[NOTE.—To assist the reader to the rationality of the above conception, it may
be briefly stated that, as the Divine Good and Truth from eternity were not separated, so in the Lord Jesus Christ ; although He descended, or came out from
infinity and eternity as Divine *Truth*, yet this is spoken of in reference to manifestation, as He is also called the *Son* of God in reference to His Divine Humanity,
which only can be seen. Good, when it is *formed*, or brought forth so that it can be
intellectually perceived, is called Truth ; for there is but one Divine Essence,
which is Love or Good, of which Wisdom or Truth is the bodily form. But
although the Lord was Divine Good, because He was Jehovah Himself, yet that
whole Good and Truth *appearing*, is called Divine *Truth*. Hence may be comprehended the rationality of the explanation, that, although He descended as to
the Divine Truth, yet he did not separate the Divine Good.—*Fernald.*]

REASONS FOR THE INCARNATION.

After all the celestial in man, that is, all love to God was lost,
so that there remained no longer any will to what was good, the
human race was separated from the Divine, for nothing conjoins

them but love, and when there was no love disjunction took place, the consequence of which is destruction and extirpation. A promise, therefore, was then made concerning the coming of the Lord into the world, who should unite the Human to the Divine, and through this union should effect conjunction of the human race in Himself, by a faith grounded in love and charity. From the time of the first promise (concerning which see Gen. iii. 25), faith grounded in love to the Lord who was to come was effective of conjunction; but when there was no longer any such faith remaining throughout the earth, then the Lord came, and united the Human Essence to the Divine, so that they became entirely one, as He Himself expressly declares. He at the same time taught the way of truth, showing that every one who should believe on Him—that is, should love Him and the things appertaining to Him, and who should be in His love, which is extended towards the whole human race—should be conjoined with Him, and be saved. When the Human was made Divine, and the Divine Human, in the Lord, then the influx of the Infinite or Supreme Divine took place with man, which could never otherwise have come to pass. Hence, also, there was a dispersion of the direful persuasions of falsity, and of the direful lusts of evil, with which the world of spirits was filled and was continually being filled, by souls continually flowing in from the world; and they who were in those evils and falsities were cast into the hells, and thus were separated. Unless such a dispersion had been effected, mankind must have totally perished, for they are governed of the Lord by means of spirits. Nor was there any other method of effecting such dispersion; since there could be no operation of the Divine upon man's internal sensual [principles] through the rational, this being far beneath the Supreme Divine not thus united with the Human. (A. C. n. 2034.)

The reason why it pleased the Lord to be born a man was, that He might actually put on the Human, and might make this Divine, to save the human race. Know, therefore, that the Lord is Jehovah Himself or the Father in a human form. This also the Lord Himself teaches in John, "*I and the Father are one*" (x. 30); again, "*Jesus said, Henceforth ye have known and seen the Father. . . . He that hath seen Me hath seen the Father. . . . Believe Me that I am in the Father and the Father in Me*" (xiv. 7, 9, 11); and again, "*All Mine are thine, and all thine are Mine*" (xvii. 10). This great mystery is described in John in these words: "*In the beginning was the Word, and the Word was with God, and God was the Word; the same was in the beginning with God; all things were made by Him, and without Him was not any thing made that was made. . . . And the Word was made flesh, and dwelt among us, and we beheld His glory, the glory as of the only begotten of the Father. . . . No man hath seen God at any time; the only begotten Son, who is in the bosom of the Father, He hath brought Him forth to view* " (i. 1-3, 14, 18). The Word is the Divine truth which has been revealed to men; and because this could not be revealed except from Jehovah as Man, that is, except from Jehovah in the human form, thus from the Lord, therefore it is said, "*In the beginning was the Word, and the Word was with God, and God was the Word.*" It is known in the church that by the Word the Lord is meant. It is therefore openly said, "*The Word was made flesh, and dwelt among us, and we beheld His glory, the glory as of the only begotten of the Father.*" That the Divine truth could not be revealed to men except from Jehovah in the human form, is also clearly stated: "*No one hath seen God at any time; the only begotten Son, who is in the bosom of the Father, He hath brought Him forth to view.*" From this it is evident that the Lord from eternity was Jehovah or the Father in a human form, but not yet in the flesh; for an angel has not flesh. And as Jehovah, or the Father, willed to put on all the human, for the sake of the salvation of the human race, therefore He also assumed flesh; wherefore it is said, "*God was the Word, . . . and the Word was made flesh;*" and in Luke, "*Behold My hands and My feet, that it is I Myself; handle Me and see, for a spirit hath not flesh and bones, as ye see Me have*" (xxiv. 39). By these words the Lord taught that He was no longer Jehovah under the form of an angel, but that He was Jehovah Man; which also is meant by these words of the Lord, "*I came forth from the Father, and am come into the world; again I leave the world, and go to the Father*" (John xvi. 28). (A. C. n. 9315.)

Man is so natural and sensual that he is quite incapable of any idea of thought concerning things abstract, unless he adjoins something natural which had entered from the world through the sensuals, for without such his thought perishes as in an abyss, and is dissipated. Therefore, lest the Divine should perish with man, entirely immersed in corporeal and earthly things, and in those with whom it remained should be defiled by an impure idea, and with it everything celestial and spiritual from the Divine, it pleased Jehovah to present Himself actually as He is, and as He appears in heaven,—namely, as a Divine Man. For every part of heaven conspires to the human form; as may be seen from what has been shown at the close of the chapters, concerning the correspondence of all things of man with the Greatest Man, which is heaven. This Divine, or this [presence] of Jehovah in heaven is the Lord from eternity. The same also the Lord took upon Him when He glorified or made Divine the human in Himself; which also is very manifest from the form in which He appeared before Peter, James, and John, when He was transfigured (Matt. xvii. 1, 2); and in which He also occasionally appeared to the prophets. Hence it is that now every one is able to think of the very Divine as of a Man, and then of the Lord, in whom is all the Divine, and the perfect Trine. For in the Lord the very Divine is the Father; that Divine in heaven is the Son; and the Divine thence proceeding is the Holy Spirit. And that they are one, as He Himself teaches, is therefore manifest. (A. C. n. 5110.)

Inasmuch as the Lord operates all things from the first by means of the last, and in the last or the ultimates is in His power and in His fulness, therefore it pleased the Lord to take upon Him the Human, and to become Divine truth, that is, the Word; and thereby from Himself to reduce to order all things of heaven, and all things of hell, that is, to execute a last judgment. This the Lord could accomplish from the Divine in Himself, which is in first [principles], by means of His Human, which was in ultimates; and not from His presence or abode in the men of the Church, as formerly; for these had entirely fallen away from the truths and goods of the Word, in which before was the habitation of the Lord with men. This, and also that He might make His Human Divine, was the primary cause of the Lord's advent into the world; for thereby He put Himself in possession of the power to keep all things of heaven and all things of hell in order to eternity. (A. E. n. 1087.)

Before the coming of the Lord into the world, there was with men and with spirits influx of life from Jehovah or the Lord through the celestial kingdom, that is, through the angels who were in that kingdom; hence they then had power. But when the Lord came into the world, and thereby made the human in Himself Divine, He put on that itself which was with the angels of the celestial kingdom, thus that power; for the Divine transflux through that heaven had before been the Human Divine; it also was the Divine Man which was presented when Jehovah so appeared. But this Human Divine ceased when the Lord Himself made the Human in Himself Divine. (A. C. n. 6371.)

The very Divine in heaven, or in the Greatest Man, was the Divine Human, and was Jehovah Himself thus clothed with the human. But when mankind became such that the very Divine clothed as the Divine Human could no longer affect them,—that is, when Jehovah could no longer come to man, because he had so far removed himself,—then Jehovah, who is the Lord as to the Divine Essence, descended and took upon Him a human by conception Divine, and by birth from a virgin like that of another man. But this He expelled, and by Divine means He made Divine the Human that was born, from which all the Holy proceeds. Thus the Divine Human exists, an Essence by itself, which fills the universal heaven, and effects that those should be saved who before could not be saved. This now is the Lord, who, as to the Divine Human, alone is Man, and from whom man derives that he is man. (A. C. n. 3061.)

Let it be well understood that all the correspondence there is with heaven is with the Divine Human of the Lord; since heaven is from Him and He is heaven. For unless the Divine Human flowed into all things of heaven, and according to correspondences into all things of the world, neither angel nor man would exist. From this again it is manifest why the Lord became Man, and clothed His Divine with the Human from first to last; that it was because the Divine Human from which heaven existed before the coming of the Lord, was no longer sufficient to sustain all things; because man, who is the basis of the heavens, subverted and destroyed order. (H. H. n. 101.)

It has been told me from heaven, that in the Lord from eternity, who is Jehovah, before the assumption of the Human in the world, there were the two prior degrees actually, and the third degree in potency, as they are also with the angels; but that after His assumption of the Human in the world He put on also the third or natural degree, and thereby became Man, similar to a man in the world,—save that in Him this degree, like the two prior, is infinite and uncreate, while in angels and men these degrees are finite and created. For the Divine, which filled all space without space, penetrated also to the ultimates of nature. But before the assumption of the Human, the Divine influx into the natural degree was mediate through the angelic heavens; but after the assumption it was immediate from Himself. This is the reason why all the churches in the world before His advent were representative of spiritual and celestial things, but after His coming became spiritual and celestial-natural, and representative worship was abolished; also why the sun of the angelic heaven—which is the proximate proceeding of His Divine love and Divine wisdom—after His assumption of the Human shone with more eminent effulgence and splendour than before the assumption. This is meant by the words of Isaiah: " *In that day, the light of the moon shall be as the light of the sun, and the light of the sun shall be sevenfold, as the light of seven days*" (xxx. 26); which is spoken of the state of heaven and the church, after the Lord's coming into the world. And in the Apocalypse: " *The countenance of the Son of Man was as the sun shineth in his strength*" (i. 16) ; and elsewhere, as in Isaiah lx. 20; 2 Sam. xxiii. 3, 4; Matt. xvii. 1, 2. The mediate enlightenment of men through the angelic heaven, which there was before the Lord's coming, may be compared to the light of the moon, which is the mediate light of the sun; and because this was made immediate after His coming it is said in Isaiah, " *That the light of the moon shall be as the light of the sun ;*" and in David, " *In His days shall the righteous flourish, and abundance of peace, until there is no longer any moon*" (lxxii. 7). This also is spoken of the Lord.

The Lord from eternity or Jehovah put on this third degree, by the assumption of the Human in the world, because He could not enter into this degree except by a nature similar to the human nature; therefore only by conception from His Divine, and by nativity from a virgin. (D. L. W. n. 233, 234.)

It should be known that the Lord is present with men in His Divine natural; with the angels of His spiritual kingdom in His Divine spiritual; and with the angels of His celestial kingdom in His Divine celestial; yet He is not divided, but appears to every one according to his quality. (A. R. n. 466.)

" *Until Shiloh come.*" That this signifies the coming of the Lord, and the tranquillity of peace then, appears from the signification of Shiloh, which is the Lord,—who is called Shiloh from the fact that He calmed and tranquillized all things ; for in the original tongue Shiloh is derived from a word which signifies tranquillity. Why the Lord is here called Shiloh is evident from what was said just above concerning the celestial kingdom and its power; for when the Divine was manifested through that kingdom there was intranquillity; because the things which are in heaven, and those which are in hell, could not be reduced by it to order—inasmuch as the Divine which flowed through that kingdom could not be pure, because heaven is not pure. That kingdom therefore was not so strong that by it all things might be kept in order ; on which account infernal and dia- bolical spirits even issued forth from the hells, and domineered over the souls which came from the world. From which it came to pass that no others than the celestial could thus be saved ; and at length scarcely they, if the Lord had not assumed the human, and thereby made it in Himself Divine. By this the Lord reduced all things to order ; first the things which are in heaven, next those that are in the hells. From this is the tranquillity of peace. (A. C. n. 6373.)

All the churches that existed before His advent were repre- sentative churches, which could not see Divine truth, save as it were in the shade ; but after the advent of the Lord into the world a church was instituted by Him which saw Divine truth, or rather which could see it, in the light. The difference is as that between evening and morning. The state of the church before the Lord's advent is also called evening ; and the state of the church after His advent is called morning. The Lord was indeed present with the men of the church before His

coming into the world, but mediately through angels who represented Him ; but since His advent in the world, He is immediately present with the men of the church.   For in the world He
put on also the Divine Natural, in which He is present with
men.   (T. C. R. n. 109.)

It is frequently said in the Word concerning the Lord, that
He was sent by the Father, as also it is said here (Gen. xix.
13), *" Jehovah hath sent us ;"* and everywhere, to be sent, signifies in the internal sense, to go forth ; as in John : *" They have
received and have known, surely, that I came forth from Thee, and
have believed that Thou hast sent Me"* (xvii. 8).   So in other
places ; as in the same Evangelist : *" God sent not His Son into
the world, to judge the world, but that the world through Him
might be saved"* (iii. 17).   Again : *" He that honoureth not the Son,
honoureth not the Father who sent Him"* (v. 23) ; besides many
other passages.   In like manner it is said of the Holy of the Spirit,
that it is sent ; that is, that it goeth forth from the Divine of the
Lord ; as in John : *" Jesus said, When the Comforter shall come,
whom I will send unto you from the Father, the Spirit of Truth,
which goeth forth from the Father, He shall testify of Me"* (xv. 26).
Again : *" If I go away I will send the Comforter unto you"* (xvi. 7).
Hence the Prophets were called the Sent, because the words which
they spake went forth from the Holy of the Spirit of the Lord.
And because all Divine Truth goes forth from Divine Good, the
expression, to be sent, is properly predicated of Divine Truth.
And what it is to go forth is also evident, namely, that he who
goes forth, or that which goes forth, is of him from whom it goes
forth.   (A. C. n. 2397.)

Why it is said that Jesus proceeded forth and came from God, and was sent.

In the spiritual sense to go forth or to proceed is to present
one's self before another in a form accommodated to him, thus
to present one's self the same only in another form.   In this
sense going forth is predicated of the Lord in John : *" Jesus said
of Himself, I proceeded forth and came from God"* (viii. 42).
*" The Father loveth you, because ye have loved Me, and have believed
that I came forth from God : I came forth from the Father, and
am come into the world ; again I leave the world, and go to the
Father.   The disciples said, . . . We believe that thou camest forth
from God"* (xvi. 27, 28, 30).   *" They have known truly that I
came forth from God"* (xvii. 8).   To illustrate what is meant by
going forth or proceeding, take the following examples :—It is
said of truth, that it goes forth or proceeds from good when truth

is the form of good, or when truth is good in a form which the understanding can apprehend. It may also be said of the understanding that it goes forth or proceeds from the will, when the understanding is the will formed, or when it is the will in a form apperceivable to the internal sight. In like manner of thought which is of the understanding, it may be said to go forth or proceed when it becomes speech; and of the will, when it becomes action. Thought clothes itself in another form when it becomes speech, but it is still the thought which so goes forth or proceeds, for the words and sounds which are put on are nothing but adjuncts, which by accommodation cause the thought to be apperceived. So the will assumes another form when it becomes action, but it is still the will which is presented in such form; the gestures and motions that are put on are nothing but adjuncts, which by accommodation make the will appear and affect the external man. Also it may be said that it goes forth or proceeds from the internal, yea, substantially, because the external man is nothing else than the internal so formed that it may act suitably in the world wherein it is. From all this it may be seen what, to go forth, or proceed, is in the spiritual sense; namely, when predicated of the Lord, that it is the Divine formed as Man, thus accommodated to the perception of the believing; yet both are one. (A. C. n. 5337.)

The Lord's Hereditary Evil.

One may be surprised that it is said there was hereditary evil from the mother with the Lord; but as it is here (Gen. xiii. 7) so manifestly declared, and the internal sense is concerning the Lord, it cannot be doubted that it was so. It is quite impossible for any man to be born of a human parent and not thence derive evil. But there is a difference between hereditary evil which is derived from the father, and that which is derived from the mother. Hereditary evil from the father is more interior, and remains to eternity, for it can never be eradicated. The Lord had no such evil, since He was born of Jehovah as His Father, and thus as to internals was Divine, or Jehovah. But hereditary evil from the mother pertains to the external man: this was with the Lord. Thus the Lord was born as another man, and had infirmities as another man. That He derived hereditary evil from the mother evidently appears from the fact that He suffered temptations; for it is impossible that any one should be tempted who has no evil, evil being that in man which tempts and by which he is tempted. That the Lord was tempted, and that He suffered temptations a thousand times more grievous than any man can ever sustain, and that He endured them alone, and by His own power overcame evil, or the devil and all hell, is also evident. . . . An angel can never be tempted of the devil, because, being in the Lord, evil spirits cannot approach him even distantly. They would instantly be seized with terror and fright. Much less could hell approach to the Lord if He had been born Divine, that is, without an adherence of evil from the mother. That the Lord bore the iniquities and evils of mankind, is a form of speaking common with preachers; but for Him to take upon Himself iniquities and evils otherwise than in the hereditary way, was impossible. The Divine Nature is not susceptible of evil. Wherefore, that He might overcome evil by His own strength, which no man ever could or can do, and might thus alone become righteousness, He was willing to be born as another man. Otherwise there would have been no need that He should be born; for He might have assumed the Human Essence without nativity, as sometimes He had formerly done, when He appeared to those of the Most Ancient Church, and likewise to the prophets. But in order that He might also put on evil, to fight against and conquer it, and might thus at the same time join together in Himself the Divine Essence and the Human Essence, He came into the world. The Lord, however, had no actual evil, or evil that was His own, as He Himself declares in John: " *Which of you convicteth Me of sin ?*" (viii. 46.)   (A. C. n. 1573.)

The Lord made his Human Divine by his own Might.

It is known that the Lord was born as another man, that when an infant He learned to talk as another infant, and that then He grew in knowledge, and in intelligence, and in wisdom. It is evident from this that His human was not Divine from nativity, but that He made it Divine by His own power. It was by His own power, because He was conceived of Jehovah; and hence the inmost of His life was Jehovah Himself. For the inmost of the life of every man, which is called the soul, is from the father; and what that inmost puts on, which is called the body, is from the mother. That the inmost of life, which is from the father, is continually flowing in and operating upon the external which is from the mother, and endeavouring to make this like itself, even in the womb, can be seen from children, in that they are born into the natural qualities of the father; and sometimes grandsons and great-grandsons into the natural qualities of the grandfather and great-grandfather, because the soul, which is from the father, continually wills to make the external, which is from the mother, like itself. Since this is so with man, it is evident that it must have been especially the case with the Lord. His inmost was the very Divine, for it was Jehovah Himself; for He was His only begotten Son. And as the inmost was the very Divine, could not this, more than in the case of any man, make the external which was from the mother an image of itself, that is, like to itself, thus make Divine the human which was external and from the mother? And this by His own power, because the Divine, which was inmost, from which He operated into the human, was His; as the soul of man, which is the inmost, is his. And as the Lord advanced according to Divine order, His Human when He was in the world He made Divine Truth, and afterwards when He was fully glorified He made it Divine Good, thus one with Jehovah. (A. C. n. 6716.)

THE GLORIFICATION.

The Lord successively and continually, even to the last of His life when He was glorified, separated from Himself and put off what was merely human, namely, that which He derived from the mother; until at length He was no longer her Son, but the Son of God, as well in respect to nativity as conception, and was one with the Father, and was Himself Jehovah. (A. C. n. 2649.)

The external man is nothing else than a something instrumental or organic, having no life in itself, but receiving life from the internal man; from which the external man appears to have life of itself. With the Lord, however, after He had expelled the hereditary evil, and thus had purified the organic substances or vessels of the human essence, these also received life; so that as the Lord was life with respect to the internal man, He became life also as to the external man. This is what is signified by glorification in John: "*Jesus said, Now is the Son of Man glorified, and God is glorified in Him. If God be glorified in Him, God shall also glorify Him in Himself, and shall straightway glorify Him*" (xiii. 31, 32). And again: "*Father, the hour is come; glorify Thy Son, that Thy Son also may glorify Thee. . . . And now, O Father, glorify Thou Me with Thine own self, with the glory which I had with Thee before the world was*" (xvii. 1, 5). And again: Jesus said, "*Father, glorify Thy name. Then came there a voice from heaven, saying, I both have glorified it, and will glorify it again*" (xii. 28). (*ib.* n. 1603.)

The Lord, by the most grievous temptation combats, reduced all things in Himself into Divine order; insomuch that there remained nothing at all of the human which He had derived from the mother. So that He was not made new as another man, but altogether Divine. For the man who is made new by regeneration still retains within him an inclination to evil, yea, evil itself, but is withheld from evil by an inflowing of the life of the Lord's love,—and this by exceedingly strong power; but the Lord entirely cast out every evil which was hereditary to Him from the mother, and made Himself Divine even as to the vessels, that is, as to truths. This is what in the Word is called glorification. (*ib.* n. 3318.)

The union of the Lord's Human Essence with His Divine was not effected at once, but successively through the whole course of His life, from infancy to the end of His life in the world. He thus ascended continually to glorification, that is, to union. This is what is said in John: "*Jesus said, Father, glorify Thy name. Then came there a voice from heaven, saying, I both have glorified it, and will glorify it again*" (xii. 28). (*ib.* n. 2033.)

The Glorification was fully completed by the Passion of the Cross.

The reason why the union itself was fully effected by the passion of the cross, is because that was the last temptation which the Lord suffered in the world, and conjunction is effected by temptations. For in temptations man, to appearance, is left to himself alone; and yet he is not left, for God is then most present in His inmost parts, and supports him. When therefore any one conquers in temptation, he is in inmost conjunction with God; and the Lord was then in inmost union with God His Father. That in the passion of the cross the Lord was left to Himself, is evident from this His exclamation upon the cross: "*O God, why hast Thou forsaken Me ?*" and also from these words of the Lord: "*No man taketh life from Me, but I lay it down of Myself; I have power to lay it down, and I have power to take it again ; this commandment have I received from My Father*" (John x. 18). From these passages, now, it is evident that the Lord did not suffer as to the Divine, but as to the Human; and that then an inmost and thus a complete union was effected. (T. C. R. n. 126.)

Of the Glorification, by which is meant the unition of the Divine Human of the Lord with the Divine of the Father, which was fully completed by the passion of the cross, the Lord thus speaks: "*After Judas went out, Jesus said, Now the Son of Man is glorified, and God is glorified in Him; if God be glorified in Him, God will also glorify Him in Himself, and will straightway glorify Him*" (John xiii. 31, 32). Here glorification is predicated both of God the Father and of the Son; for it is said, "*God is glorified in Him, and God will glorify Him in Himself.*" That this is to be united is plain. "*Father, the hour is come, glorify Thy Son, that Thy Son also may glorify Thee*" (xvii. 1, 5). It is thus said because the unition was reciprocal; and so it is said, "*The Father was in Him and He in the Father.*" "*Now My soul is troubled; . . . and He said, Father, glorify Thy name; and a voice came out of heaven, I both have glorified, and will glorify again*" (xii. 27, 28). This was said because the unition was effected successively. "*Ought not Christ to have suffered these things, and to enter into His glory?*" (Luke xxiv. 26.) Glory, in the Word, when it is predicated of the Lord, signifies Divine Truth united to Divine Good. From these passages it is very manifest that the Human of the Lord is Divine. (*ib.* n. 128.)

THE LORD, IN GLORIFICATION, DID NOT TRANSMUTE OR CHANGE HIS HUMAN NATURE INTO DIVINE, BUT PUT OFF THE HUMAN AND PUT ON THE DIVINE.

That the Lord had a Divine and a Human, the Divine from Jehovah as the Father, and the Human from the Virgin Mary, is known. Hence it is that He was God and Man, and so had the very Divine essence and a Human nature, the Divine essence from the Father, and the Human nature from the mother; and therefore He was equal to the Father as to the Divine, and less than the Father as to the Human. But then He did not transmute this Human nature from the mother into the Divine essence, nor commix it therewith, as the doctrine of faith called the *Athanasian Creed* teaches; for the Human nature cannot be transmuted into the Divine essence, nor can it be commixed with it. And yet it is from the same doctrine, that the Divine assumed the Human, that is united itself to it as a soul to its body, so that they were not two but one person. From this it follows, that He put off the Human taken from the mother,—which in itself was like the human of another man, and thus material,—and put on a Human from the Father; which in itself was like His Divine, and thus substantial, by which means the Human also was made Divine. (L. n. 35.)

THE LORD DID NOT ACKNOWLEDGE MARY AS HIS MOTHER, BECAUSE HE PUT OFF THE HUMAN DERIVED FROM HER.

It is believed that the Lord, as to the Human, not only was but also is the Son of Mary; but in this the Christian world is under a delusion. That He was the Son of Mary is true; but that He is so still is not true; for by acts of redemption He put off the Human from the mother, and put on a Human from the

Father. Hence it is that the Human of the Lord is Divine, and that in Him God is Man and Man God. That He put off the Human from the mother, and put on a Human from the Father, which is the Divine Human, may be seen from the fact that He never called Mary His mother, as appears from these passages : *" The mother of Jesus saith unto Him, They have no wine. Jesus saith unto her, Woman, what have I to do with thee ? Mine hour is not yet come"* (John ii. 3, 4); and in another place : From the cross *" Jesus saw His mother and the disciple standing by whom He loved, and saith to His mother, Woman, behold thy son ! Then saith He to the disciple, Behold thy mother !"* (xix. 26, 27): And from the fact that once He did not acknowledge her: *" It was told Jesus by some, saying, Thy mother and Thy brethren are standing without, and desire to see Thee. Jesus answering, said, My mother and My brethren are these who hear the Word of God, and do it"* (Luke viii. 20, 21; Matt. xii. 46-49 ; Mark iii. 31-35). Thus the Lord did not call her "mother," but "woman," and gave her as a mother to John. In other places she is called His mother, but not by His own mouth. This also is confirmed by the fact that He did not acknowledge Himself to be the Son of David ; for it is said in the Evangelists, *" Jesus asked the Pharisees, saying, What think ye of Christ ? Whose Son is He ? They say unto Him, David's. He saith unto them, How then doth David, in spirit, call Him his Lord, saying, The Lord said unto my Lord, Sit Thou on My right hand, until I make Thine enemies Thy footstool. If, then, David calleth Him Lord, how is He his Son ? And no man was able to answer Him a word"* (Matt. xxii. 41-46 ; Mark xii. 35-37 ; Luke xx. 41-44 ; Psalm cx. 1). To the above I shall add this new thing : It was once granted me to speak with Mary the mother. She passed by at one time, and appeared in heaven above my head, in white raiment, as of silk ; and then, pausing a little, she said that she had been the mother of the Lord, who was born of her; but that having become God He put off all the Human derived from her, and she therefore worships Him as her God, and did not wish any one to acknowledge Him as her Son, because all in Him is Divine. From all these things there shines forth this truth: That thus Jehovah is Man, as in first things, so also in the last, according to these words : *" I am the Alpha and the Omega, the Beginning and the Ending, He who is, and who was, and who is to come, the Almighty"* (Rev. i. 8, 11). *When John saw the Son of Man in the midst of the seven candlesticks, he fell at His feet as dead ; and He laid His hand upon him, saying, . . . " I am the First and the Last"* (Rev. i. 13, 17; xxi. 6). *" Behold, I come quickly, . . . that I may give to every one according to his work. I am the Alpha and the Omega, the Beginning and the End, the First and the Last"* (xxii.

12, 13). And in Isaiah : " *Thus said Jehovah, the King of Israel, and His Redeemer, Jehovah of Hosts, I am the First and the Last* " (xliv. 6 ; xlviii. 12). (T. C. R. n. 102.)

The Lord's whole Life was a continual Temptation and Victory.

That the life of the Lord, from His earliest childhood even to the last hour of His life in the world, was a continual temptation and continual victory, appears from many passages in the Word of the Old Testament. And that it did not cease with the temptation in the wilderness is evident from these words in Luke, " *When the Devil had ended all the temptation, he departed from Him for a season* " (iv. 13); also from the fact that He was tempted even to the death of the cross, thus to the last hour of His life in the world. Hence it appears that the Lord's whole life in the world, from His earliest childhood, was a continual temptation and continual victory. The last was when on the cross He prayed for His enemies, thus for all on the face of the whole earth. In the Word of the life of the Lord by the Evangelists, there is no mention of any but His temptation in the wilderness, except the last. Others were not disclosed to the disciples. Those which were disclosed appear, according to the literal sense, so light as scarcely to be any temptation; for so to speak and so to answer is no temptation. And yet it was more grievous than any human mind can ever conceive or believe. No one can know what temptation is unless he has been in it. The temptation which is related in Matt. iv. 1-11, Mark i. 12, 13, Luke iv. 1-13, contains the temptations in a summary; namely, that out of love towards the whole human race, the Lord fought against the loves of self and of the world, with which the hells were filled. All temptation is against the love in which a man is; and the degree of temptation is according to that of the love. If not against the love it is no temptation. To destroy one's love is to destroy his very life, for love is life. The Lord's life was love towards the whole human race; and it was so great, and of such a nature, as to be nothing but pure love. Against this, His life, continual temptations were admitted, as was said, from His earliest childhood to His last hour in the world. . . . In brief, from His earliest childhood to the last hour of His life in the world the Lord was assaulted by all the hells, which were continually overcome, subjugated, and conquered by Him; and this solely out of love towards the human race. And because this love was not human, but Divine, and temptation is great in proportion as the love is great, it is evident how grievous were His combats, and how great the ferocity

on the part of the hells.   That these things were so I know of a
certainty.   (A. C. n. 1690.)

That the Lord suffered and sustained the most grievous temptations, or more grievous than all in the universe, is not so fully
known from the [letter of the] Word ; where it is only mentioned
that He was in the wilderness forty days, and was tempted of the
Devil.   The temptations themselves which He then had are not
described except in a few words ; yet these few involve all.   As
for example it is mentioned in Mark (i. 12, 13), that He was with
the beasts, by which are signified the worst of the infernal crew;
and elsewhere it is related that He was led by the Devil upon a
pinnacle of the Temple, and upon a high mountain, which are
nothing else than representatives of most grievous temptations
which He suffered in the wilderness.   (*ib.* n. 1663.)

THE LORD WAS TEMPTED EVEN BY ANGELS.

That the Lord at the last fought in temptations with the angels
themselves, yea, with the whole angelic heaven, is an arcanum
which has not until now been revealed.   But the case is this :—
The angels are indeed in the highest wisdom and intelligence,
but all their wisdom and intelligence is from the Lord's Divine.
Of themselves, or from what is their own, they have nothing of
wisdom and intelligence ; so far therefore as they are in truths
and goods from the Lord's Divine they are wise and intelligent.
The angels themselves openly confess that they have nothing of
wisdom and intelligence from themselves ; yea, are even indignant if one attributes to them anything of wisdom and intelligence.   For they know and perceive that this would be to
derogate from the Divine that which is Divine, and to claim for
themselves what is not their own, thus to incur the crime of
spiritual theft.   The angels also say, that all their proprium is
evil and false, both from what is hereditary and from actual life
in the world when they were men ; and that what is evil and
false is not separated or wiped away from them, and they thus
justified, but that it all remains with them ; and that they are
withheld from what is evil and false, and kept in good and truth
by the Lord.   These things all angels confess ; nor is any one
admitted into heaven unless he knows and believes them ; for
otherwise they cannot be in the light of wisdom and intelligence
which is from the Lord, and therefore not in good and truth.
Hence also it may be known how it is to be understood,
that heaven is not pure in the eyes of God, as in Job xv.
15.   Because it is so, in order that the Lord might restore the
universal heaven to heavenly order, He even admitted into
Himself temptations from the angels ; who in so far as they

were in what is their own were not in good and truth. These temptations are the inmost of all; for they act only upon ends, and with such subtlety as to escape all observation. But in so far as the angels are not in what is their own they are in good and truth, and cannot tempt. Moreover the angels are continually being perfected by the Lord, and yet can by no means, to eternity, be so far perfected that their wisdom and intelligence can be compared to the Divine wisdom and intelligence of the Lord; for they are finite, and the Lord is infinite, and there is no comparison of the finite with the infinite. (A. C. n. 4295.)

How the Lord bore the Iniquities of All.

It is known in the Church that it is said of the Lord that He carried sins for the human race, but it is yet unknown what is meant by carrying iniquities and sins. By some it is believed it means, that He took upon Himself the sins of the human race, and suffered Himself to be condemned even to the death of the cross ; and that thus, because damnation for sins was cast upon Him, mortals were liberated from damnation; and also that damnation was taken away by the Lord through the fulfilling of the law, since the law would have condemned every one who did not fulfil it. But these things are not meant by carrying iniquity, since every man's deeds remain with him after death, and he is then judged either to life or death according to their quality; and they therefore cannot be taken away by transfer to another who carries them. Hence it is evident that something else is meant by carrying iniquities. And what is meant may be seen from the carrying itself of iniquities or of sins by the Lord; for the Lord carries them when He fights for man against the hells. For man of himself cannot fight against them; but this the Lord alone does, even continually for every man,—but with a difference according to the reception of Divine good and Divine truth. When the Lord was in the world He fought against all the hells, and entirely subdued them. Hence He was also made Justice. He thus redeemed from damnation those who receive Divine good and truth from Him. If this had not been done by the Lord no flesh could have been saved; for the hells are continually with man, and so far as the Lord does not remove them they have dominion over him; and He removes them in proportion as man desists from evils. He who once conquers the hells conquers them to eternity; and that this might be accomplished by the Lord He made His Human Divine. He therefore who alone fights for man against the hells,—or what is the same, against evils and falsities, for these are from the hells,—is said to carry sins, for He alone sustains that burden. By carrying sins is also signified the removal of evils and falsities from those who are in good; because this is a consequence. For so far as the hells are removed from man evils and falsities are removed; for both, as was said, are from the hells. Evils and falsities are sins and iniquities. . . . That by carrying diseases, griefs, and iniquities, and by being thrust through and bruised by them, a state of temptation is signified is evident; for in temptation there are griefs of mind, straitness, and despair, which cause anguish. Such things are induced by the hells; for in temptations they assault the love itself of him against whom they fight. The love of every one is the inmost of his life. The Lord's love was the love of saving the human race; which love was the Being of His life, for the Divine in Himself was that love. It is so described too in Isaiah, where the Lord's combats are spoken of in these words: "*He said, Surely they are My people; . . . therefore He became a Saviour to them; in all their affliction He was afflicted; . . . in His love and His clemency He redeemed them, and took them, and carried them all the days of eternity*" (lxiii. 8, 9). That the Lord endured such temptations when He was in the world, is described in few places in the Evangelists, but in many places in the Prophets, and especially in the Psalms of David. In the Evangelists it is only said that He was led away into the wilderness, and afterwards was tempted of the Devil; and that He was there forty days, and was with the beasts (Mark i. 12, 13; Matt. iv. 1). But that He was in temptations, that is in combats with the hells, from earliest childhood to the end of His life in the world, He did not reveal,— according to these words in Isaiah: "*He was oppressed, and He was afflicted, yet He opened not His mouth; He is led as a lamb to the slaughter, and as a sheep before her shearers is dumb, so He opened not His mouth*" (liii. 7). His last temptation was in Gethsemane (Matt. xxvi.; Mark xiv.), and afterwards the passion of the cross. That by this He fully subdued the hells He Himself teaches in John: "*Father, deliver Me from this hour; but for this* [*cause*] *came I to this hour; Father, glorify Thy name. There came a voice from heaven,* [*saying*] *I have both glorified and will glorify* [*it*]." Then Jesus said, "*Now is the judgment of this world; now shall the prince of this world be cast out*" (xii. 27, 28, 31). The prince of this world is the Devil, thus all hell; to glorify is to make the Human Divine. The reason why only the temptation after forty days in the wilderness is mentioned is, that forty days signify and involve temptations to the full, thus of many years; the wilderness signifies hell; and the beasts with which He fought there, the diabolical crew. (A. C. n. 9937.)

The Use of the Lord's Temptations.

Good cannot be conjoined with truth in the natural man without combats, or what is the same without temptations. But that it may be known how the case is in respect to man, it must be briefly stated:—Man is nothing but an organ, or vessel, which receives life from the Lord; for man does not live of himself. The life which flows in with man from the Lord is from His Divine love. This love, or the life thence, flows in and applies itself to the vessels which are in man's rational [part], and which are in his natural. These vessels in man are in a contrary position with respect to the influent life, in consequence of the hereditary evil into which man is born, and of the actual evil which he himself acquires. But as far as the influent life can dispose the vessels to receive it it does so dispose them. . . . Good itself, which has life from the Lord, or which is life, is what flows in and disposes. When therefore these vessels, which are variable as to forms, are as was said in a contrary position and direction in respect to this life, it is evident that they must be reduced to a position in accordance with the life, or in compliance with it. This can in no wise be effected so long as man is in the state into which he is born and into which he has reduced himself; for the vessels do not yield, because they are obstinately resistant and opposed to heavenly order, according to which the life acts. For the good that moves them, and to which they are compliant, is of the love of self and the world; which good, from the gross heat that is in it, makes them such. Therefore, before they can be rendered compliant, and be made fit to receive anything of the life of the Lord's love, they must be softened. This softening is effected by no other means than by temptations; for temptations remove those things which are of self-love, and contempt of others in comparison with one's self, consequently which are of self-glory, as well as of hatred and revenge on account of them. When therefore the vessels are somewhat tempered and subdued by temptations, they begin to become yielding to and compliant with the life of the Lord's love, which continually flows into man. Hence it is that good now begins to be conjoined to truths, first in the rational man, and afterwards in the natural. . . . This is the reason why man is regenerated, that is made new, by temptations, or what is the same, by spiritual combats, and that he is afterwards gifted with another disposition, being made mild, humble, simple, and contrite in heart. From these considerations it may now be seen what use temptations effect; namely, that good from the Lord can not only flow in, but also dispose the vessels to obedience, and so conjoin itself with them. . . . But as regards the Lord,

He, by the most grievous combats in temptation, reduced all things in Himself to Divine order, even until there remained nothing at all of the human which He had derived from the mother; so that He was made, not new as another man but altogether Divine. For a man who is made new by regeneration still retains in himself an inclination to evil, yea, evil itself, but is withheld from the evil by an influx of the life of the Lord's love, and this by exceedingly strong power. But the Lord entirely cast out every evil which was hereditary to Him from the mother, and made Himself Divine even as to the vessels, that is as to truths. That is what in the Word is called glorification. (A. C. n. 3318.)

As the Lord from the beginning had a human from the mother, and successively put this off, therefore during His abode in the world He passed through two states, one a state of humiliation, or exinanition, and the other a state of glorification, or union with the Divine, which is called the Father. The state of humiliation was at the time and in the degree that He was in the human from the mother; and the state of glorification was at the time and in the degree that He was in the Human from the Father. In the state of humiliation He prayed unto the Father as to one different from Himself; but in the state of glorification He spake with the Father as with Himself. In this latter state He said that the Father was in Him, and He in the Father, and that the Father and He were one; but in the state of humiliation He endured temptations, and suffered the cross, and prayed to the Father that He would not forsake Him. For the Divine could not be tempted; much less could it suffer the cross. From all this, then, it appears that by temptations, and at the same time continual victories, and by the passion of the cross which was the last of the temptations, He entirely conquered the hells and fully glorified the human, as was shown above. That the Lord put off the human from the mother, and put on a Human from the very Divine, which is called the Father, appears also from the fact that so often as the Lord spake by His own mouth unto the mother, He did not call her " mother," but " woman." (L. n. 35.)

It is known from the Word by the Evangelists, that the Lord adored and prayed to Jehovah His Father; and this as from Himself to another, although Jehovah was in Him. But the state in which the Lord then was was His state of humiliation, the nature of which has been described ; namely, that He was then in the infirm human derived from the mother. But in the degree that He put off that human and put on the Divine He was in a different state, which is called His state of glorification. In the former state He adored Jehovah as one different from

Himself, although He was in Him; for, as stated above, His internal was Jehovah. But in the latter state, namely, the state of glorification, He spake with Jehovah as with Himself, for He was Himself Jehovah. But how these things are cannot be apprehended unless it be known what the internal is, and how the internal acts upon the external; and, further, how the internal and external are distinct from each other, and yet conjoined. This however may be illustrated by its like, namely, by the internal in man, and its influx into and operation upon his external. The internal of man is that by which man is man, and by which he is distinguished from the unreasoning animals. By means of this internal he lives after death, and to eternity; and by this he is capable of being elevated by the Lord among the angels. It is the very first form by virtue of which he becomes and is a man. Through this internal the Lord is united to man. The very heaven nearest to the Lord is of these human internals. This however is above the inmost angelic heaven, wherefore these belong to the Lord Himself. . . . These internals of men have not life in themselves, but are forms recipient of the life of the Lord. In proportion then as the man is in evil, whether actual or hereditary, he is as it were separated from this internal which is of the Lord and with the Lord, and therefore in that degree is separated from the Lord; for although this internal is adjoined to man and is inseparable from him, yet, in so far as man recedes from the Lord he as it were separates himself from it. This separation however is not evulsion from it, for then man could no longer live after death; but it is disagreement and dissent from it of his faculties that are beneath it, that is of his rational and external man. In the degree that there is dissent and disagreement he is disjoined; and in the degree that there is not dissent and disagreement he is conjoined by the internal to the Lord. This takes place in proportion as he is in love and charity; for love and charity conjoin. Thus it is in respect to man. But the internal of the Lord, since He was conceived of Jehovah, was Jehovah Himself, who cannot be divided and become another's as in the case of a son conceived of a human father; for the Divine is not like the human divisible, but is and remains one and the same. With this internal the Lord united the Human essence. And because the internal of the Lord was Jehovah it was not a form recipient of life, like the internal of man, but was life itself. His human essence also, by union, in like manner became life. Therefore the Lord so often says that He is life; as in John,—"*As the Father hath life in Himself, so hath He given to the Son to have life in Himself*" (v. 26); besides other passages in the same Evangelist, as i. 4; v. 21; vi. 33, 35, 48; xi. 25. In proportion therefore as the

Lord was in the human which He received hereditarily from the mother, He appeared distinct from Jehovah, and adored Jehovah as one different from Himself; but in proportion as He put off this human the Lord was not distinct from Jehovah, but one with Him. The former state, as has been said, was the Lord's state of humiliation, but this was His state of glorification. (A. C. n. 1999.)

The Lord's Glorification is imaged in Man's Regeneration.

The state of the Lord's glorification may in some manner be apprehended from the state of the regeneration of man; for the regeneration of man is an image of the Lord's glorification. When man is regenerated he is made new, and becomes entirely another man. Therefore when he is regenerated he is said also to be born again, and created anew. Then, although he has a similar face and similar speech yet his mind is not similar. When he is regenerated his mind is open towards heaven, and therein dwell love to the Lord and charity towards the neighbour, with faith. It is the mind which makes him another and a new man. Change of state cannot be apperceived in the body of man, but in his spirit. The body is only the covering of his spirit; and when it is put off his spirit appears, and this in quite another form when he is regenerated. For then it has the form of love and charity, in inexpressible beauty, instead of its previous form, which was that of hatred and cruelty, with a deformity also in~ expressible. From this then it may appear what the regenerate man is, or one who is born again or created anew,—that he is in truth quite another and a new man. From this image it may in some measure be conceived what the glorification of the Lord was. He was not as man is regenerated, but was made Divine; and this from the veriest Divine love, for He became Divine Love itself. What His form then was He made visible to Peter, James, and John, when it was given them to see Him, not with the eyes of the body but with the eyes of the spirit; namely, that "*His face did shine as the sun*" (Matt. xvii. 2). And that this was His Divine Human is clear from the voice which then came out of the cloud, saying, "*This is My beloved Son*" (ver. 5). (A. C. n. 3212.)

The Resurrection.

Since the Human of the Lord was glorified, that is was made Divine, therefore after death He rose again on the third day with His whole body; which does not take place with any man, for man rises again only as to the spirit, but not as to the body. That man might know, and no one should doubt, that the Lord rose again with His whole body, He not only said this by the angels who were in the sepulchre, but He even showed Himself in His human body to the disciples, saying to them, when they believed that they saw a spirit, "*Behold My hands and My feet, that it is I Myself; handle Me, and see, for a spirit hath not flesh and bones, as ye see Me have. And when He had said this, He showed them His hands and His feet*" (Luke xxiv. 39, 40; John xx. 20). And further: "*Jesus said to Thomas, Reach hither thy finger, and behold My hands; and reach hither thy hand, and thrust it into My side, and be not faithless, but believing. Then said Thomas, My Lord and my God*" (John xx. 27, 28). That the Lord might more fully prove to them that He was not a spirit, but a Man, He said to the disciples, "*Have ye here any meat? And they gave Him a piece of broiled fish and of an honeycomb, which He took and ate before them*" (Luke xxiv. 41-43). Since His body now was not material, but substantial and Divine, therefore *He came in to the disciples while the doors were shut* (John xx. 19, 26). And after He had been seen "*He became invisible*" (Luke xxiv. 31). Such now the Lord was taken up and sat at the right hand of God; for it is said in Luke, "*It came to pass while Jesus was blessing the disciples, He departed from them, and was carried up into heaven*" (xxiv. 51). And in Mark: "*After He had spoken to them, He was received up into heaven, and sat at the right hand of God*" (xvi. 19). To sit at the right hand of God signifies Divine Omnipotence. (L. n. 35.)

The Lord made the very corporeal in Himself Divine, both its sensuals and their recipients. He therefore rose again from the sepulchre even with His body, and also after the resurrection said to the disciples, "*Behold My hands and My feet, that it is I Myself; handle Me and see, for a spirit hath not flesh and bones, as ye see Me have*" (Luke xxiv. 39). Very many at this day who are of the Church believe that every one will rise again at the last day, and then with the body. This opinion is so universal that scarcely any one from doctrine believes otherwise. But the opinion has prevailed on account of the fact that the natural man supposes it is the body alone which lives; unless therefore he should believe that the body is to receive life again he would entirely deny the resurrection. But the case is this:—Man rises again immediately after death; and then appears to himself to be in the body, precisely as in the world, with such a face, with such members, arms, hands, feet, breast, belly, loins; yea, when he sees and touches himself, he also says that he is a man, as in the world. But it is not his external which he carried about in the world that he sees and touches, but the internal, which constitutes that

very human that lives, and which had about itself, or outside of
the single things of itself, an external whereby it could be in the
world, and fitly act and perform its functions there. The earthly
corporeal itself is no longer of any use to him. He is in another
world, where there are other functions and other capabilities and
powers, to which such a body as he has there is adapted. This
body he sees with his eyes; not with the eyes that he had in the
world, but those which he has there, which are the eyes of his
internal man, and with which, through the eyes of the body, he
had before seen worldly and terrestrial things. He also feels it
with the touch; not with the hands or sense of touch that he
enjoyed in the world, but with the hands and sense of touch
which he there enjoys,—which is that from which sprang his
sense of touch in the world. Every sense there is also more
exquisite and perfect, because it is the sense of man's internal
set loose from the external; for the internal is in a more perfect
state, inasmuch as it gives the power of sensation to the external.
But when it acts in the external, as it does in the world, the sensation is dulled and obscured; besides, it is the internal which
sensates the internal, and the external which sensates the external. Hence it is that men see each other after death, and are
together in society, according to their interior [states]. That I
might be certain of these things it has even been given me to
touch spirits themselves, and frequently to talk with them on
this subject. Men after death,—who are then called spirits, and
those that have lived in good, angels,—are greatly surprised that
the man of the Church should believe that he is not to see eternal life until a last day when the world is to perish; and that
then he will be clothed again with the dust that has been rejected,—when yet the man of the Church knows that he rises
again after death. For when a man dies, who does not say afterwards that his soul or spirit is in heaven or in hell? And who
does not say of his own infants who are dead, that they are in
heaven? And who does not comfort the sick, or one condemned
to death, by the assurance that he will shortly come into another
life? And he who is in the agony of death, and is prepared,
believes no otherwise. Yea, from that belief also many claim to
themselves power to deliver from places of damnation, and to
introduce into heaven, and to celebrate masses for them. Who
does not know what the Lord said to the thief—" *To-day shalt
thou be with Me in paradise*" (Luke xxiii. 43); and what He said
concerning the rich man and Lazarus, that the former was carried into hell, but the latter by angels into heaven? (Luke xvi. 22,
23.) And who is not acquainted with what the Lord taught
concerning the resurrection, that " *He is not the God of the dead,
but of the living?*" (Luke xx. 38.) Man is acquainted with these

things; and he so thinks and speaks too when he thinks and speaks from the spirit. But when he speaks from doctrinals he says quite the contrary; namely, that he is not to rise again till the last day,—when yet it is the last day with every one when he dies; and then also is his judgment, as many also say. These things are said in order that it may be known that no man rises again in the body with which he was clothed in the world; but that the Lord so arose, and this because He glorified or made His body Divine while He was in the world. (A. C. n. 5078.)

THE REDEMPTION.

Redemption itself was the Subjugation of the Hells, and the establishment of Order in the Heavens, and preparation thereby for a new spiritual church. (T. C. R. n. 115.)

That the Lord while He was in the world fought against the hells, and conquered and subjugated them, and thus brought them under obedience to Him, is evident from many passages in the Word, of which I shall select these few:—In Isaiah: *" Who is this that cometh from Edom, besprinkled as to His garments from Bozrah ? this [that is] honourable in His apparel, travelling in the multitude of His strength ? I that speak in righteousness, mighty to save. Wherefore art Thou red in Thine apparel, and Thy garment as one that treadeth in the wine-press? I have trodden the wine-press alone; and of the people [there was] not a man with Me; therefore I trod them in Mine anger, and trampled them in My wrath; thence their victory is sprinkled upon My garments; . . for the day of vengeance is in Mine heart, and the year of My redeemed is come: . . . Mine arm brought salvation to Me; . . . I made their victory descend to the earth. . . . He said, Behold My people, they are children ; therefore He became to them a Saviour; . . . in His love and in His pity He redeemed them "* (lxiii. 1-9). These things are said of the Lord's conflict against the hells. By the garment in which He was honourable and which was red the Word is meant, to which violence was offered by the Jewish people. The conflict itself against the hells and the victory over them is described by the saying that *He trod them in His anger, and trampled them in His wrath.* That He fought alone and of His own power is described by the words: *" Of the people [there was] not a man with Me; . . . Mine arm brought salvation to Me; I made their victory descend to the earth."* That thereby He saved and redeemed is meant by these : *" Therefore He became to them a Saviour ; in His love and in His pity He redeemed them."* That this was the cause of His coming is meant by the words : *" The day of vengeance is in Mine heart, and the year of My redeemed is come."* Again in Isaiah: " *He saw that there was no man, and wondered that there was no intercessor; therefore His arm brought salvation unto Him, and His righteousness it sustained Him; and He put on righteousness as a breastplate, and the helmet of salvation upon His head; and He put on the garments of vengeance, and covered Himself with zeal as with a cloak. . . . Then cometh the Redeemer to Zion"* (lix. 16, 17, 20). In Jeremiah: " *They were dismayed, . . . their mighty ones were beaten down; they fled apace; they looked not back; this day is to the Lord Jehovah of Hosts a day of vengeance, that He may take vengeance on His enemies; the sword shall devour and be satiated"* (xlvi. 5, 10). Both of these passages relate to the Lord's conflict against the hells, and victory over them. In David: " *Gird Thy sword upon Thy thigh, O Mighty; . . . Thine arrows are sharp; the people shall fall under Thee, from the heart of the King's enemies; Thy throne . . . is for ever and ever. . . . Thou hast loved righteousness, therefore God hath anointed Thee"* (Psa. xlv. 3-7); also in many other places. Since the Lord alone conquered the hells, without help from any angel, therefore He is called a *Hero and a Man of Wars* (Isa. xliv. 15; ix. 6); *The King of Glory, Jehovah the Mighty, the Hero of War* (Psa. xiv. 8, 10); *The Mighty One of Jacob* (cxxxii. 2); and in many places *Jehovah Sabaoth,* that is, *Jehovah of Hosts.* And also His advent is called *the day of Jehovah, terrible, cruel, a day of indignation, of wrath, of anger, of vengeance, of ruin, of war, of a trumpet, of a loud noise, of tumult.* In the Evangelists it is said: " *Now is the judgment of this world: the prince of this world shall be cast out"* (John xii. 31); " *The prince of this world is judged"* (xvi. 11); " *Be assured I have overcome the world"* (xvi. 33); " *I beheld Satan as lightning fall from heaven"* (Luke x. 18). By the world, the prince of the world, Satan, and the Devil, is meant hell. (T. C. R. n. 116.)

It is known in the Church that the Lord is the Saviour and Redeemer of the human race; but how this is to be understood is known by few. They who are in the externals of the Church believe that the Lord redeemed the world, that is the human race, by His blood, by which they understand the passion of the Cross. But those that are in the internal [truths] of the Church know that no one is saved by the Lord's blood, but by a life according to the precepts of faith and charity from the Lord's Word. Those who are in the inmost [truths] of the Church, understand by the Lord's blood the Divine Truth proceeding from Him, and by the passion of the cross they understand the last of the Lord's temptation, by which He entirely subjugated the hells, and at the same time glorified His Human, that is made it Divine; and that thereby He redeemed and saved all who suffer themselves to be regenerated, by a life according to the precepts of faith and charity from His Word. By the Lord's blood also in the internal sense, according to which the angels in the heavens perceive the Word, Divine Truth is meant proceeding from the Lord. But how man was saved and redeemed by the Divine, through the subjugation of the hells and the glorification of His Human, no one can know unless He knows that with every man there are angels from heaven, and spirits from hell, and unless these are present with man continually he cannot think anything, or will anything; and that thus as to his interiors man is either under the dominion of spirits who are from hell, or under the dominion of angels from heaven. When this is first known, then it may be known that unless the Lord had entirely subdued the hells, and reduced all things both there and in the heavens to order, no man could have been saved. So, unless the Lord had made His Human Divine, and had thereby acquired to Himself Divine power over the hells and over the heavens to eternity. For without Divine power neither the hells nor the heavens can be kept in order; since the power by which anything exists must be perpetual in order that it may subsist, for subsistence is perpetual existence. The very Divine, which is called the Father, without the Divine Human, which is called the Son, could not effect this; inasmuch as the very Divine without the Divine Human cannot reach to man, nor even to an angel, when the human race have altogether removed themselves from the Divine,—as was the case in the end of times, when there was no longer any faith nor any charity. For this reason the Lord then came into the world and restored all things, and this by virtue of His Human, and thus saved and redeemed man through faith and love to the Lord from the Lord. For those [that have this faith and love] the Lord can withhold from the hells and from eternal damnation; but not those who reject faith and love from Him to Him, for these reject salvation and redemption. (A. C. n. 10, 152.)

THE LORD THUS REDEEMED NOT ONLY MAN, BUT THE ANGELS.

At the time of the first coming of the Lord, the hells had increased to such a height that they filled all the world of spirits, —which is intermediate between heaven and hell,—and thus not only disordered the heaven which is called the last or lowest, but also assaulted the middle heaven; which they infested in a thousand ways, and which would have gone to destruction if the Lord had not withstood them. Such an insurrection of the hells is meant by the tower built in the land of Shinar, the head of which was to reach even unto heaven; but the design of the builders was frustrated by the confusion of tongues, and they were dispersed, and the city was called Babel (Gen. xi. 1-9). What is there meant by the tower, and the confusion of tongues, is explained in the *Arcana Cœlestia,* published in London. The reason why the hells had grown to such a height was, that at the time when the Lord came into the world the whole earth had completely alienated itself from God, by idolatry and magic ; and the church which had existed among the children of Israel, and afterwards among the Jews, was utterly destroyed through the falsification and adulteration of the Word. And both the former and the latter after death flocked into the world of spirits, where at length they so increased and multiplied, that they could not be expelled but by the descent of God Himself, and then by the strength of His Divine arm. How this was done is described in a little work on the Last Judgment, published at London in the year 1758. This was accomplished by the Lord when He was in the world. A similar judgment has also been accomplished by the Lord at this day, for, as was said above, now is His second coming, which is foretold everywhere in the Apocalypse; and in Matt. xxiv. 3, 30; in Mark xiii. 26; in Luke xxi. 27; also in the Acts of the Apostles i. 11 ; and in other places. The difference is that at His first coming the hells had so increased by idolaters, magicians, and falsifiers of the Word ; but at this second coming by so-called Christians, both those who are steeped in naturalism, and also those who have falsified the Word, by confirmations of their fabulous faith concerning three Divine Persons from eternity, and concerning the passion of the Lord, that it was redemption itself; for it is these who are meant by the dragon and his two beasts in the Revelation xii. and xiii. (T. C. R. n. 121.)

The reason why the angels could not have subsisted in a state of integrity if redemption had not been wrought by the Lord, is that the whole angelic heaven, together with the church on earth, before the Lord is as one man, whose internal constitutes the angelic heaven, and whose external constitutes the church; or more particularly, whose head constitutes the highest heaven, whose breasts and middle region of the body constitute the second and the ultimate heaven, and whose loins and feet constitute the church on earth; and the Lord Himself is the soul and life of this whole man. If therefore the Lord had not wrought redemption this man would have been destroyed,—as to the feet and loins, by the defection of the church on earth; as to the gastric region, by the defection of the lowest heaven; as to the breast, by the defection of the second heaven; and then the head, having no correspondence with the body, would fall into a swoon. (T. C. R. n. 119.)

Without Redemption Wickedness would spread throughout all Christendom in both Worlds.

There are many reasons why without redemption by the Lord iniquity and wickedness would spread through all Christendom, both in the natural and the spiritual worlds; one of which is this:—Every man after death comes into the world of spirits, and then is precisely like himself,—of the same character as before; and upon entrance there no one can be restrained from conversation with departed parents, brothers, relations, and friends; every husband then first seeks his wife, and every wife her husband; and they are introduced by each other into various companies of such as appear like lambs outwardly, but inwardly are as wolves; and even those who have striven after piety are corrupted by them. From this cause, and from abominable arts unknown in the natural world, the world of spirits is as full of the malicious as a green and stagnant pool, of the spawn of frogs. That association with the wicked there produces this result may be rendered obvious by these illustrations:—It is as if one should associate with robbers or pirates,—at length he becomes like them; or as if one should live with adulterers and harlots,—at length he thinks nothing of adulteries; or as if one should mingle with the rebellious,—at length he thinks nothing of doing violence to any one. For all evils are contagious, and may be compared to a pestilence, which an infected person communicates by the breath or by exhalation; or to a cancer or gangrene, which spreads and corrupts the nearer and by degrees the remoter parts, until the whole body perishes. The delights of evil into which every one is born are the cause. From all this then it is evident, that without redemption by the Lord no one could be saved; nor could the angels subsist in a state of integrity. The only refuge from destruction for any one is in the Lord; for He says, "*Abide in Me and I in you; as the branch cannot bear fruit of itself except it abide in the vine, no more can ye except ye abide in Me. I am the vine, ye are the branches: he that abideth in Me, and I in him, the same bringeth forth much fruit; for without Me ye can do nothing. If a man abide not in Me, he is cast forth and is withered, and is cast into the fire and burned*" (John xv. 4-6). (T. C. R. n. 120.)

Redemption could not be effected but by God Incarnate.

The reason why redemption could not have been wrought but by God incarnate, that is made Man, is that Jehovah God as He is in His infinite essence cannot approach hell, much less enter into it; for He is in purest and first [principles]. Wherefore if Jehovah God, such in Himself, should but breathe upon those who are in hell, it would kill them instantly; for He said to Moses, when he wished to see Him, " *Thou canst not see My face, there shall no man see Me and live*" (Exod. xxxiii. 20). Since therefore Moses could not, still less could those who are in hell, where all are in the last and grossest [things], and thus in the most remote; for they are in the lowest degree natural. For this reason, if Jehovah God had not assumed the Human, and thus clothed Himself with a body which is in lowest [principles], it would have been in vain for him to enter upon any work of redemption. . . . It should be known that the conflict of the Lord with the hells was not an oral conflict, as between reasoners and disputants. Such a conflict effects nothing at all in such a case. But it was a spiritual conflict, which is that of Divine truth from Divine good, which is the very vital of the Lord. The influx of this truth by means of sight no one in hell can resist. There is such power in it that the infernal *genii* flee at the mere perception of it, cast themselves down into the deep, and creep into caves that they may hide themselves. This is what is described in Isaiah: " *They shall go into the caves of the rocks, and into clefts of the dust, for fear of Jehovah . . . when He shall arise to terrify the earth*" (ii. 19); and in the Revelation: "*All hid themselves in the dens of the rocks, and in the rocks of the mountains, and said to the mountains and to the rocks, Fall on us, and hide us from the face of Him that sitteth upon the throne, and from the wrath of the Lamb*" (vi. 15-17). (T. C. R. n. 124.)

FALSE VIEWS OF THE ATONEMENT.

It is believed in the church that the Lord was sent by the Father to make an atonement for the human race, and that this was done by the fulfilling of the law and the passion of the cross; and that thus He took away damnation, and made satisfaction; and that without that atonement, satisfaction, and propitiation the human race would have perished in eternal death, —and this from justice, which by some is also called vindictive. (L. n. 18.)

What at this day more fills and crams the books of the orthodox, or what is more zealously taught and inculcated in the schools, and more frequently preached and proclaimed from the pulpits, than that God the Father, being enraged against mankind, not only separated them from Himself, but also sentenced them to universal damnation, and thus excommunicated them; but that because He is gracious, He persuaded or excited His

Son to descend and take upon Himself the determined damnation, and thus appease the anger of His Father; and that thus, and not otherwise, He could look upon man with some favour? Then that this was even done by the Son; so that in taking upon Himself the damnation of the human race, He suffered Himself to be scourged by the Jews, to be spit upon in the face, and afterwards to be crucified as one accursed of God (Deut. xxi. 23); and that after this was done the Father became propitious, and from love towards His Son cancelled the sentence of damnation,—but only in respect to those for whom He should intercede; and that He thus became a Mediator in the presence of His Father for ever. These and similar ideas at this day sound forth in temples and are reverberated from the walls as an echo from the woods, and fill the ears of all there. But cannot any one whose reason is enlightened and made sound by the Word see that God is Mercy and Pity itself, because He is Love itselt and Good itself, and that these are His essence; and therefore that it is a contradiction to say that Mercy itself, or Good itself, can look upon man with anger, and decree his damnation, and yet continue to be His own Divine essence? Such things are scarcely ascribed to an upright man, but rather to one who is not upright; nor to an angel of heaven, but rather to a spirit of hell. It is therefore shocking to attribute them to God! But if one inquires into the cause, it is this:—That men have taken the passion of the cross for redemption itself. From this have these opinions flowed, as from one falsity falsities flow in a continued series. (T. C. R. n. 132.)

THE TRUE MEANING OF MEDIATION, INTERCESSION, ATONEMENT, AND PROPITIATION.

There are four terms expressive of the grace of the one only God in His Humanity. God the Father can never be approached, nor can He come to any man; because He is infinite, and dwells in His own being, which is Jehovah; from which being if He should come to man He would consume or decompose him, as fire consumes wood when it reduces it to ashes. This is evident from what He said to Moses, who desired to see Him:—"*No man shall see Me and live*" (Exod. xxiii. 20). And the Lord says, "*No man hath seen God at any time, save the Son which is in the bosom of the Father*" (John i. 18; Matt. xi. 27); also that *no one hath heard the voice of the Father, nor seen His shape* (John v. 27). It is indeed written that Moses saw Jehovah face to face, and talked with Him, as one man with another; but this was through the medium of an angel, as was also the case with

Abraham and Gideon. Now since such is God the Father in Himself, therefore He was pleased to assume the Humanity, and in this Humanity to admit mankind to Himself, and so to hear and to talk with them; and it is this Humanity which is called the Son of God, and which mediates, intercedes, propitiates, and atones. MEDIATION signifies that the Humanity is the medium by which man may come to God the Father, and God the Father to him; and thus be his teacher and guide unto salvation. INTERCESSION signifies perpetual mediation; for love itself, the qualities of which are mercy, clemency, and grace, perpetually intercedes, that is mediates, for those that do His commandments, and who are thus the objects of His love. ATONEMENT signifies the removal of sins,—into which a man would rush headlong if, in supplication, he were to approach the unveiled Jehovah. PROPITIATION signifies the operation of clemency and grace, to prevent man from falling into damnation by sin, and at the same time to guard against the profanation of what is holy. This was signified by the propitiatory, or mercy-seat, over the ark in the tabernacle. It is acknowledged that God spake in His Word according to appearances; as when it is said that He is angry, that He avenges, that He tempts, that He punishes, that He casts into hell, that He condemns, yea, that He does evil; while the truth is that God is never angry with any one, that He never avenges, tempts, punishes, casts into hell, or condemns. Such things are as far from God, nay infinitely farther, than hell is from heaven. They are forms of speech then, used only according to the appearances. So also, but in a different sense, are the terms atonement, propitiation, intercession, and mediation; for these are forms of speech expressive of the approach which is opened to God by means of His Humanity. These terms being misunderstood men have divided God into three; and upon that division they have grounded all the doctrine of the church, and so have falsified the Word. Hence has arisen THE ABOMINATION OF DESOLATION, foretold by the Lord in Daniel, and again in Matt. xxiv. (T. C. R. n. 135.)

Mediation and intercession is of Divine truth, because this is next to Divine good, which is the Lord Himself. That Divine truth is next to Divine good, which is the Lord, is because it immediately proceeds from Him. Since occasion is given, it shall here be shown how the case is with the Lord's mediation and intercession. They that believe from the literal sense of the Word, that there are three persons who constitute the Divine, and together are called one God, have no other idea of mediation and intercession, than that the Lord sits at the right hand of His Father, and speaks with Him as man with man, brings the supplications of men to the Father, and entreats that for His sake, because He endured the cross for the human race, He will pardon them and be merciful. Such is the idea of intercession and mediation which the simple derive from the literal sense of the Word. But it should be known that the literal sense is adapted to the apprehension of simple men, that they may be introduced into the interior truths themselves; for the simple cannot form any different idea of the heavenly kingdom than such as they have of an earthly kingdom, nor any different idea of the Father than as of a king on earth, nor of the Lord, than as of the son of a king, who is heir of the kingdom. . . . But he who knows the interior [truths] of the Word has an entirely different notion of the Lord's mediation, and of His intercession; namely, that He does not intercede as a son with a father king on earth, but as the Lord of the universe with Himself, and of Himself as God; for the Father and He are not two, but One, as He teaches in John xiv. 8-11. He is called the Mediator and Intercessor because the Son means Divine truth, and the Father Divine good, and mediation is effected by Divine truth, for by it access is given to Divine good. For Divine good cannot be approached, because it is as the fire of the sun; but Divine truth can be, because this is as the light from it which gives passage and approach to man's sight, which is from faith. It can be seen from this what is to be understood by mediation and intercession. Further, it should be stated why it is that the Lord Himself, who is the very Divine good and the very Sun of heaven, is called the Mediator and Intercessor with the Father. The Lord when He was in the world, before He was fully glorified, was Divine truth; for this reason there then was mediation, and He interceded with the Father, that is, with the very Divine good (John xiv. 16, 17; xvii. 9, 15, 17). And after He was glorified as to the Human, He is called the Mediator and Intercessor from the fact that no one can think of the very Divine unless he sets before himself the idea of a Divine Man; still less can any one be conjoined by love to the very Divine except by means of such an idea. . . . It is for this reason that the Lord as to the Divine Human is called the Mediator and Intercessor; but He mediates and intercedes with Himself. (A. C. n. 8705.)

How the Lord fulfilled the whole Law.

It is believed by many at this day that when it is said of the Lord that He fulfilled the law it is meant that He fulfilled all the commandments of the Decalogue, and that thus He became righteousness, and also justified mankind through faith in this. This however is not what is meant, but that He fulfilled all things which are written of Him in the Law and the Prophets, that is in the whole sacred Scripture; for this treats of Him alone. The reason why many have believed otherwise is, that they have not searched the Scriptures and seen what is there meant by the Law. By the Law there, in a strict sense, the Ten Commandments of the Decalogue are meant; in a wider sense, all that was written by Moses in his five books; and in the widest sense, all the Word. (L. n. 8.)

That the Lord fulfilled all things of the Law means that He fulfilled all things of the Word, is manifest from the passages where it is said that by Him the Scripture was fulfilled, and that all things were finished. As from these: "*Jesus went into the synagogue, . . . and stood up to read. There was delivered unto Him the book of the prophet Isaiah; and when He had opened the book, He found the place where it was written, The Spirit of the Lord is upon Me, because He hath anointed Me to preach the gospel to the poor; He hath sent Me to heal the broken-hearted, to preach deliverance to the bound, and sight to the blind; . . . to proclaim the acceptable year of the Lord. And He closed the book and said, This day is this Scripture fulfilled in your ears*" (Luke iv. 16-21). "*Ye search the Scriptures, and they testify of Me*" (John v. 39). "*That the Scripture might be fulfilled, He that eateth bread with Me hath lifted up his heel upon Me*" (John xiii. 18). "*None of them is lost but the son of perdition, that the Scripture might be fulfilled*" (John xvii. 12). "*That the saying might be fulfilled which He spake, Of those whom thou gavest Me I have not lost one*" (John xviii. 9). "*Then said Jesus unto Peter, Put up thy sword into its place; . . . how then should the Scriptures be fulfilled, that thus it must be? . . . But all this was done, that the Scriptures of the Prophets might be fulfilled*" (Matt. xxvi. 52, 54, 56). "*The Son of Man indeed goeth as it is written of Him; . . . that the Scriptures may be fulfilled*" (Mark xiv. 21, 49). "*Thus the Scripture was fulfilled which saith, He was numbered with the wicked*" (Mark xv. 28; Luke xxii. 37). "*That the Scripture might be fulfilled, They parted my raiment among them, and for my vesture they did cast lots*" (John xix. 24). "*After this, Jesus knowing that all things were now consummated, that the Scripture might be fulfilled*" (John xix. 28). "*When Jesus had received the vinegar, He said, It is finished,*" that is, "*it is fulfilled*" (John xix. 30). "*These things were done that the Scripture might be fulfilled, A bone of Him shall not be broken. And again another Scripture saith, They shall look on Him whom they pierced*" (John xix. 36, 37). Besides these, in other places passages of the Prophets are adduced where it is not at the same time said that the Law or the Scripture was fulfilled. That the whole Word was written concerning Him, and that He came into the world to fulfil it, He also taught His disciples before He departed, in these words: "*Jesus said to them, O fools and slow of heart to believe all that the Prophets have spoken. Ought not Christ to have suffered this, and to enter into His glory? And beginning at Moses and all the Prophets, He expounded to them in all the Scriptures the things concerning Himself*" (Luke xxiv. 25-27). Afterwards, Jesus said to His disciples, "*These are the words which I spake unto you whilst I was yet with you, That all things must be fulfilled which were written in the Law of Moses, and in the Prophets, and in the Psalms concerning Me*" (Luke xxiv. 44). That the Lord in the world fulfilled all things of the Word, even to its minutest particulars, is evident from these His words: "*Verily I say unto you, Till heaven and earth pass, one jot or one tittle shall in no wise pass from the Law till all be fulfilled*" (Matt. v. 18). From these now one may clearly see that by the Lord's fulfilling all things of the Law it is not meant that He fulfilled all the commandments of the Decalogue, but all things of the Word. (L. n. 11.)

ALL POWER IN THE HEAVENS AND ON EARTH GIVEN TO THE LORD.

The Lord Himself says, "*All power is given unto Me, in heaven and on earth*" (Matt. xxviii. 18). . . . In respect to all power being given to the Son of Man, both in the heavens and on earth, it should be known that the Lord had power over all things in the heavens and on earth before He came into the world; for He was God from eternity, and Jehovah,—as He Himself plainly says in John: "*And now, O Father, glorify Thou Me with Thine own self, with the glory which I had with Thee before the world was*" (xvii. 5); and again: "*Verily, verily I say unto you, Before Abraham was I am*" (viii. 58). For He was Jehovah and God to the Most Ancient church which was before the flood, and appeared to the men of that church; He was also Jehovah and God to the Ancient church which was after the flood; and He it was whom all the rites of the Jewish church represented, and whom the members of that church worshipped. And the reason why He says that all power was given unto Him in Heaven and on earth, as if it were then first given, is, that by the Son of Man His Human essence is meant, which when united to the Divine was also Jehovah, and at the same time power was given unto Him; which could not be done before He was glorified, that is, before His Human essence by unition with the Divine had life also in itself, and had thus in like manner become Divine, and Jehovah; as He Himself says in John: "*As the Father hath life in Himself, so hath He given to the Son to have life in Himself*" (v. 26). (A. C. n. 1607.)

" *I am the Alpha and the Omega, the Beginning and the End.*"
This signifies that He governs all things from first [principles]
by means of ultimates, and in this manner governs all things in
heaven to eternity. This is evident from the signification of
Alpha and Omega, which is the first and the last, or in first
[principles] and in ultimates; and He who is in first [principles]
and in ultimates also governs things intermediate, and so all.
These things are said of the Lord's Divine Human, for they are
said of Jesus Christ, by which names His Divine Humanity is
meant. By means of this the Lord is in first [principles] and in
ultimates. But that He governs all things from first [principles]
by ultimates is a mystery which until now has not been perceived by man. For man knows nothing of the successive
degrees into which the heavens are distinguished; and into
which also the interiors of man are distinguished; and but little
of the fact that as to his flesh and bones man is in ultimates.
Neither does he perceive how from first [principles] by ultimates
intermediates are governed; and yet in order that He might thus
govern all things the Lord came into the world to assume the
Human and glorify it, or make it Divine, even to the ultimates,
that is even to the flesh and bones. That the Lord put on such
a Human, and took it with Him into heaven, is known in the
church from the fact that He left nothing of His body in the
sepulchre; and also from what He said to His disciples: " *Behold
My hands and My feet that it is I Myself; handle Me and see, for
a spirit hath not flesh and bones as ye see Me have*" (Luke xxiv. 39).
By this Human, therefore, the Lord is in ultimates; and by
making even these ultimates Divine, He clothed Himself with
Divine power to govern all things from first [principles] by means
of ultimates. If the Lord had not done this, the human race on
earth would have perished in eternal death. (A. E. n. 41.)

He who knows what in the Lord the Son of God signifies, and
what in Him the Son of Man signifies, can see many secrets of
the Word; for the Lord calls Himself sometimes the Son of God,
and sometimes the Son of Man—always according to the subject
treated of. When His Divinity is treated of, His unity with the
Father, His Divine power, faith in Him, and life from Him, He
calls Himself the Son, and the Son of God,—as in John v. 17-26,
and elsewhere; but where His passion, the judgment, His coming,

and in general, redemption, salvation, reformation, and regeneration are treated of, He calls Himself the Son of Man. (L. n. 22.)

Various Names of the Lord.

Since the Lord alone reforms and regenerates men, therefore He is called in the Word the Former from the womb, as in Isaiah: *" Jehovah, thy Maker and Former from the womb, helpeth thee"* (xliv. 2, 24); again: *" Jehovah hath called me from the womb, from the bowels of my mother He hath remembered my name. . . . Thus saith Jehovah, my Former from the womb, for his servant, to bring back Jacob unto Himself; and Israel shall be gathered to Him"* (xlix. 1, 5). In many parts of the Word the Lord is called the Creator, Maker, and Former from the womb, and also Redeemer; because He creates man anew, reforms, regenerates and redeems him. It may be supposed that the Lord is so called because He created man, and forms him in the womb; but it is a spiritual creation and formation which is there meant; for the Word is not only natural, but also spiritual. (A. E. n. 710.)

In the Word of the Old Testament, where Jehovah, the Lord Jehovah, Jehovah Zebaoth, Lord, Jehovah God, God, in the plural and singular, the God of Israel, the Holy One of Israel, the King of Israel, Creator, Saviour, Redeemer, Schaddai, Rock, and so on, are mentioned, by all these names not many are meant, but one; for the Lord is thus variously named according to His Divine attributes (*ib.* n. 852).

That the profoundest mysteries lie hidden in the internal sense of the Word very manifestly appears from the internal sense of the two names of our Lord, Jesus Christ. Few have any other idea, when these names are mentioned, than that they are proper names, and almost like the names of another man, but more holy. The more learned indeed know that Jesus signifies Saviour, and Christ, the Anointed, and hence conceive a somewhat more interior idea. But yet these are not the things which the angels in heaven perceive from those names; they are still more Divine. By the name Jesus, when pronounced by man in reading the Word, they perceive the Divine good; and by the name Christ, the Divine truth; and by both, the Divine marriage of good and truth, and of truth and good. (A. C. n. 3004.)

Practical Use of a correct Idea of the Lord.

The first and chief thing of a church is to know and acknowledge its God; for without that knowledge and acknowledgment there is no conjunction; thus there is none in the church without the acknowledgment of the Lord. (H. D. n. 296.)

The very essential of the church is the acknowledgment of the union of the very Divine in the Human of the Lord, and this must be in each and all things of worship. The reason why this is the essential of the church, and hence the essential of worship, is because the salvation of the human race depends solely on that union. (A. C. n. 10370.)

The chief thing of the church is to acknowledge the Lord, His Divine [nature] in the Human, and His omnipotence in saving the human race; for by this acknowledgment man is conjoined to the Divine, since the Divine is nowhere else. Even there is the Father, for the Father is in Him and He is in the Father, as the Lord Himself teaches; they therefore who look to another Divine [being] near Him, or at His side,—as is usual with those who pray to the Father to have mercy on them for the sake of the Son,—turn aside from the way, and adore a Divine elsewhere than in Him. And, moreover, they then think nothing about the Lord's Divine [nature], but only of His Human, which yet cannot be separated; for the Divine and Human are not two but one only Person, conjoined as the soul and the body,—according to the doctrine received by the churches from the faith of Athanasius. Therefore to acknowledge the Divine in the Human [nature] of the Lord, or the Divine Human, is the chief thing of the church, by which conjunction is effected; and as it is the chief it is also the first thing of the church. It was because this is the first thing of the church that the Lord when He was in the world so often asked those whom He healed whether they believed that He was able to do this, and when they answered that they believed, said, "*According to your faith be it unto you.*" This He so often said, in order that they might first believe that He had Divine omnipotence from his Divine Human; for without that faith the church could not have been begun; and without that faith they would not have been conjoined to the Divine, but separated from it, and so could receive nothing of good from Him. Afterwards the Lord taught them how they might be saved, namely, that they should receive Divine truth from Him; and this is received when it is applied, and implanted in the life by doing it. Hence the Lord so often said they should do His words. It is therefore manifest that these two, namely, believing in the Lord and doing His words, make one, and that they can by no means be separated; for he that does not the Lord's words does not believe in Him. And he who imagines that He believes in the Lord, and does not His words, does not believe in Him; for the Lord is in His words, that is in His truths, and from them the Lord gives faith to man. From these few considerations it may be known that conjunction with the Divine is effected by the acknowledgment of the Lord, and by the reception of Divine truth from Him. (A. E. n. 328.)

The Lord is said to be rejected when He is not approached and worshipped; and also when He is approached and worshipped only as to His Human, and not at the same time as to His Divine. He is therefore at this day rejected within the church by those who do not approach and worship Him, but pray to the Father that He will have compassion for the sake of the Son; while yet neither any man nor angel can ever approach the Father, and immediately worship Him; for He is the invisible Divine, with which no one can be conjoined in faith and love; for that which is invisible does not fall into the conception of thought, and therefore not into the affection of the will. (A. E. n. 114.)

In the whole heaven no other one is acknowledged as the God of heaven than the Lord alone. They say there, as He Himself taught, *that He is one with the Father; that the Father is in Him, and He in the Father; and he that seeth Him seeth the Father; and that everything holy proceedeth from Him* (John x. 30, 38; xiv. 10, 11; xvi. 13-15). I have often talked with angels on this subject, and they have constantly said that in heaven they cannot distinguish the Divine into three, since they know and perceive that the Divine is one, and that it is one in the Lord. They said also that those who came from the world, out of the church, with whom there is an idea of three Divine [persons], cannot be admitted into heaven, since their thought wanders from one to another; and one may not there think three and say one, because in heaven every one speaks from the thought, for speech there is cogitative, or thought speaking. Wherefore those who in the world have distinguished the Divine into three, and have acquired a different conception of each, and have not concentrated and made it one in the Lord, cannot be received; for there is communication of all thoughts in heaven. If therefore any one should come thither who thinks three and says one he would immediately be discovered and rejected. But it should be known that all who have not separated truth from good, or faith from love, when instructed in the other life, receive the heavenly idea of the Lord, that He is God of the universe. It is otherwise however with those who have separated faith from life, that is who have not lived according to the precepts of true faith. (H. H. n. 2.)

The Divine under the Human form is the Lord's Divine Human. Because this is the chief [truth] of the church, therefore it continually flows into man from heaven. Hence it is as it were impressed upon every one to think of the Divine [Being] under the human form, and thus inwardly to see within themselves their Divine [Being]—except those who have extinguished this impression within them. (A. E. n. 151.)

The Recognition of the Lord as God sheds Light upon every particular of the Word.

If it be received as doctrine and acknowledged that the Lord is one with the Father, and that His Human is Divine from the Divine in Him, light will be seen in the least particulars of the Word,—for what is received as doctrine, and acknowledged from doctrine, is in the light when the Word is read,—even the Lord, from whom is all light and who has all power, will illuminate them. But, on the other hand, if it be received and acknowledged as doctrine that the Divine of the Father is another, separate from the Divine of the Lord, nothing in the Word will be seen in the light; since the man who is in that doctrine turns himself from one Divine [Being] to another, and from the Divine of the Lord, which he may see,—which is done in thought and faith,—to a Divine which he cannot see; for the Lord says, " *Ye have neither heard the Father's voice at any time, nor seen His shape*" (John v. 37, and also i. 18); and to believe in and love a Divine [Being] which cannot be thought of under any form is impossible. (A. E. n. 200.)

Jehovah Himself, in His Divine Human, is the only Saviour.

" *Thus saith Jehovah thy Creator, O Jacob, and thy Former, O Israel; . . . for I have redeemed thee. . . . I am Jehovah, thy God, the Holy One of Israel, thy Saviour* " (Isaiah xliii. 1, 3). "*Surely God is in Thee, and there is no God else. Verily Thou art a God that hidest Thyself, O God of Israel, the Saviour* " (xlv. 14, 15). . . . " *Thus saith Jehovah, the King of Israel, and His Redeemer, Jehovah of Hosts, . . . Beside Me there is no God*" (xliv. 6). " *I am Jehovah, and beside Me there is no Saviour* " (xliii. 11). " *Am not I Jehovah, and there is no other besides Me; . . . and a Saviour, there is none beside Me* " (xlv. 21). " *I am Jehovah thy God, . . . thou shalt know no God but Me, for there is no Saviour beside Me* " (Hosea xiii. 4). " *Look unto Me, that ye may be saved, all ye ends of the earth; for I am God, and there is none else* " (Isaiah xlv. 22). " *Jehovah of Hosts is His name, and thy Redeemer, the Holy One of Israel, the God of the whole earth shall He be called* " (liv. 5). From these passages it may be seen that the Divine of the Lord,—which is called the Father, and here Jehovah, and God,—and the Divine Human,—which is called the Son, and here the Redeemer, and Saviour, also the Former, that is the Reformer and Regenerator,—are not two, but one. For not only is it said Jehovah God and the Holy One of Israel is the Redeemer and Saviour, but it is also said that Jehovah is the Redeemer and Saviour; yea, it is even said, "I Jehovah am thy Saviour, and there is none beside Me." From which it is very clear that the Divine and Human in the Lord are one person, and that even the Human is Divine; for the Redeemer and Saviour of the world is no other than the Lord as to the Divine Human, which is called the Son. Redemption and salvation, in fact, are the peculiar attribute of His Human which is called merit, and righteousness; for His Human suffered temptations and the passion of the cross, and therefore by the Human He redeemed and saved. (L. n. 34.)

WHY JEHOVAH IS NOWHERE NAMED IN THE WORD OF THE NEW TESTAMENT, BUT THE LORD INSTEAD.

In the Word of the New Testament by the Evangelists, and in the Apocalypse, Jehovah is nowhere named, but for Jehovah it says Lord, and this for hidden reasons, of which presently. That the Word of the New Testament says Lord instead of Jehovah is very evident in Mark: "*Jesus said, The first of all the commandments is, Hear, O Israel! the Lord our God is one Lord; therefore thou shalt love the Lord thy God with all thy heart, and with all thy soul, and with all thy mind, and with all thy strength*" (xii. 29, 30). The same in Moses reads thus: "*Hear, O Israel! Jehovah our God is one Jehovah, and thou shalt love Jehovah thy God with all thy heart, and with all thy soul, and with all thy strength*" (Deut. vi. 4, 5). Here it is plain that the name Lord is used for Jehovah. So in John: "*I saw, . . . and behold a throne was set in heaven, and one sat on the throne; . . . and round about the throne were four animals, full of eyes before and behind; . . . each of them had six wings round about, and within full of eyes; . . . and they said, Holy, holy, holy, Lord God Almighty*" (Apoc. iv. 2, 6, 8). This in Isaiah is thus expressed: "*I saw the Lord sitting upon a throne high and lifted up; . . . the seraphim standing above it; each one had six wings; . . . and one cried unto another, Holy, holy, holy, Jehovah of Hosts*" (vi. 1, 3, 5, 8). Here the name Lord is used for Jehovah, and Lord God Almighty for Jehovah of Hosts. That the four animals are seraphim or cherubim is plain from Ezekiel i. 5, 13-15, 19; x. 15. From many other passages also it appears that in the New Testament the Lord is Jehovah; as in Luke: "*The angel of the Lord appeared to Zacharias*" (i. 11). The angel of the Lord stands for the angel of Jehovah. In the same Evangelist the angel said to Zacharias concerning his son: "*Many of the children of Israel shall he turn to the Lord their God*" (i. 16); to the Lord their God, for to Jehovah God. Again: the angel said to Mary concerning Jesus: "*He shall be great, and shall be called the Son of the Highest, and the Lord God shall give unto Him the throne of . . . David*" (i. 32); the Lord God for Jehovah God. Again: "*Mary said, My soul doth magnify the Lord, and my spirit hath rejoiced over God my Saviour*" (i. 46, 47). Here also the Lord is put for Jehovah. Again: "*Zacharias . . . prophesied, saying, Blessed be the Lord God of Israel*" (i. 67, 68). Here the Lord God, for Jehovah God. Again: "*The angel of the Lord stood near the shepherds, and the glory of the Lord shone round about them*" (ii. 9). The angel of the Lord, and the glory of the Lord, for the angel of Jehovah, and the glory of Jehovah. In Matthew: "*Blessed is He that cometh in the name of the Lord*" (xxi. 9; xxiii. 39; Luke xiii. 35; John xii. 13). In the name of the Lord, for in the name of Jehovah. There are also many other passages, as Luke i. 28; ii. 15,·22-24, 29, 38, 39; v. 17; Mark xii. 10, 11. Among the hidden reasons why they called Jehovah Lord were also these: because if it had been declared at that time that the Lord was the Jehovah so often mentioned in the Old Testament, it would not have been received, for it would not have been believed; and because the Lord was not made Jehovah even as to His Human until He had entirely united the Divine Essence to the Human, and the Human to the Divine. The plenary unition was effected after the last temptation, which was that of the cross; wherefore, after the resurrection, the disciples always called Him Lord (John xx. 2, 13, 15, 18, 20, 25; xxi. 7, 12, 15-17, 20; Mark xvi. 19, 20); and Thomas said, "*My Lord and my God*" (John xx. 28). ·And because the Lord was Jehovah, who is so often mentioned in the Old Testament, therefore also He said to the disciples, "*Ye call Me Master and Lord, and ye say well; for I am*" (John xiii. 13, 14, 16); by which words it is signified that He was Jehovah God. . . . That the Lord was Jehovah is meant also by the words of the angel to the shepherds: "*Unto you is born this day . . . a Saviour, who is Christ the Lord*" (Luke ii. 11); Christ is put for the Messiah, the Anointed, the King, and Lord for Jehovah. They who examine the Word without much attention cannot know this, believing that our Saviour, like others, was called Lord merely from a common form of expressing reverence; but He was so called because He was Jehovah. (A. C. n. 2921.)

That Jehovah in the Old Testament is called the Lord in the New appears from these passages: It is said in Moses, "*Hear, O Israel! Jehovah our God is one Jehovah; and thou shalt love*"

Jehovah thy God with all thy heart and with all thy soul" (Deut. vi. 4, 5); but in Mark: *" The Lord our God is one Lord; and thou shalt love the Lord thy God with all thy heart and with all thy soul"* (xii. 29, 30). Then in Isaiah: *" Prepare ye the way for Jehovah; make straight in the desert a path for our God"* (xl. 3); but in Luke: *" Thou shalt go before the face of the Lord, to prepare the way for Him"* (i. 76); and elsewhere. And also the Lord commanded His disciples to call Him Lord; and therefore He was so called by the Apostles in their Epistles; and afterwards by the Apostolic Church, as appears from its creed, which is called the Apostles' Creed. The reason was that the Jews did not dare to speak the name Jehovah, on account of its sanctity; and also that by Jehovah is meant the Divine Esse, which was from eternity, and the Human which He assumed in time was not that Esse. (T. C. R. n. 81.)

THE REASON WHY THESE THINGS CONCERNING THE LORD ARE NOW FIRST PUBLICLY MADE KNOWN.

The reason why these things respecting the Lord are now for the first time divulged is, that it is foretold in the Revelation (xxi. and xxii.) that a new church would be instituted by the Lord at the end of the former one, in which this should be the primary truth. This church is there meant by the New Jerusalem; into which none can enter but those who acknowledge the Lord alone as the God of heaven and earth. And this I am able to proclaim, that the universal heaven acknowledges the Lord alone; and that whoever does not acknowledge Him is not admitted into heaven. For heaven is heaven from the Lord. This very acknowledgment, from love and faith, causes all there to be in the Lord and the Lord in them; as the Lord Himself teaches in John: *" In that day ye shall know, that I am in My Father, and ye in Me, and I in you"* (xiv. 20). And again: *"Abide in Me, and I in you. . . . I am the vine, ye are the branches; he that abideth in Me, and I in him, the same bringeth forth much fruit; for without Me ye can do nothing. If a man abide not in Me, he is cast out"* (xv. 4-6; xvii. 22, 23). This has not been seen before from the Word, because if seen before it would not have been received. For the last judgment had not yet been accomplished, and before that the power of hell prevailed over the power of heaven, and man is in the midst between heaven and hell; if therefore this doctrine had been seen before, the devil, that is hell, would have plucked it from the hearts of men, nay more, would have profaned it. This state of the power of hell was entirely crushed by the last judgment which has now been accomplished; since that event, that

is now, every man who will may become enlightened and wise.
(L. 61.)

WHY THE LORD WAS BORN ON THIS EARTH.

There are many reasons why it pleased the Lord to be born
and to assume the Human on our earth and not on another, concerning which I have been informed from heaven.

The principal reason was for the sake of the Word, that this
might be written in our earth, and being written might be published throughout the whole earth, and once published might be
preserved to all posterity; and that thus it might be made manifest, even to all in the other life, that God was made Man.

That the principal reason was for the sake of the Word, was
because the Word is the very Divine truth, which teaches man
that there is a God, that there is a heaven, that there is a hell,
that there is a life after death; and teaches moreover how he
ought to live and believe that he may come into heaven and
thus be happy to eternity. All these things without revelation,
—thus on this earth without the Word,—would have been
entirely unknown; and yet man is so created that as to his
internal man he cannot die.

The Word could be written on our earth, because from a very
ancient time the art of writing has existed here, first on tablets
of wood, then on parchments, afterwards on paper, and finally,
[writing came] to be published by types. This was provided
of the Lord for the sake of the Word.

The Word could then be published through all this earth, because here there is communication of all nations by land and
by water with all parts of the globe. The Word once written
could therefore be conveyed from one nation to another, and be
everywhere taught. That there should be such communication
was also provided of the Lord for the sake of the Word.

The Word once written could be preserved to all posterity,
even for thousands and thousands of years; and it is known
that it has been so preserved.

It could thus be made known that God became Man; for this
is the first and most essential thing for which the Word was
given. For no one can believe in a God, and love a God, whom
he cannot have a conception of under some form; wherefore they
who acknowledge what is incomprehensible glide in thought into
nature, and so believe in no God. For this reason it pleased the
Lord to be born here, and to make this evident by the Word; in
order not only that it might be made known on this globe, but
also that thereby it might be made manifest to all in the universe
who from any other earth whatsoever come into heaven; for in
heaven there is a communication of all things.

It should be known that the Word on our earth, given through heaven by the Lord, is the union of heaven and the world,—for which end there is a correspondence of all things in the letter of the Word with Divine things in heaven; and that the Word in its highest and inmost sense treats of the Lord, of His kingdom in the heavens and on the earths, and of love and faith from Him and in Him, therefore of life from Him and in Him. Such things are presented to the angels in heaven, from whatsoever earth they are, when the Word of our earth is read and preached.

In every other earth truth Divine is made known by word of mouth, through spirits and angels, . . . but this is done within families. For in most of the earths mankind dwell apart according to families; and therefore the Divine truth, thus revealed by spirits and angels, is not conveyed far beyond the families; and unless a new revelation constantly succeeds it is either perverted or lost. It is otherwise on our earth, where truth Divine, which is the Word, remains for ever in its integrity.

It should be known that the Lord acknowledges and receives all, from whatsoever earth they are, who acknowledge and worship God under the Human form; since God under the Human form is the Lord. And as the Lord appears to the inhabitants of the earths in an angelic form, which is the human form, therefore when spirits and angels from those earths hear from the spirits and angels of our earth that God is actually Man, they receive that Word, acknowledge it, and rejoice that it is so.

To the reasons which have been already adduced it may be added, that the inhabitants, the spirits, and the angels of our earth relate to the external and corporeal sense in the Greatest Man; and the external and corporeal sense is the ultimate, in which the interiors of life end, and in which they rest, as in their common [receptacle]. So is truth Divine [in its ultimates] in the letter which is called the Word; and on this account too it was given on this earth and not on another. And because the Lord is the Word, and its first and last, that all things might exist according to order He was willing also to be born on this earth, and to become the Word,—according to these words in John: "*In the beginning was the Word, and the Word was with God, and God was the Word. The same was in the beginning with God: all things were made by Him, and without him was not anything made that was made. . . . And the Word was made flesh and dwelt among us, and we beheld His glory, the glory as of the only-begotten of the Father. . . . No man hath seen God at any time; the only-begotten Son, who is in the bosom of the Father, He hath brought Him forth to view*" (i. 1-3, 14, 18). The Word here is Divine truth. But this is a mystery which will be intelligible only to a few. (A. C. n. 9350-9360.)

THE HOLY SPIRIT.

THE Holy Spirit is the Divine truth and also the Divine operation proceeding from the one only God, in whom there is a Divine Trinity, proceeding therefore from the Lord God the Saviour. (T. C. R. n. 138.)

The Divine operation is effected by the Divine truth which proceeds from the Lord; and that which proceeds is of one and the same essence with Him from whom it proceeds. Like these three, the soul, the body, and the proceeding [action], which together make one essence,—with man merely human, but with the Lord Divine and at the same time Human; united after the glorification, just as the prior with its posterior, and as the essence with its form. Thus the three essentials which are called the Father, the Son, and the Holy Spirit, are one in the Lord. (T. C. R. n. 139.)

That the Comforter or Holy Spirit is Divine Truth proceeding from the Lord is very evident, for it is said the Lord Himself told them *the Truth*, and declared that when He should go away He would send the Comforter, *the Spirit of Truth*, who should guide them *into all truth*, and that He would not speak from Himself, but from the Lord. . . . And because Divine Truth proceeds from the Human of the Lord glorified, and not immediately from His very Divine,—inasmuch as this in itself was glorified from eternity,—therefore it is said, " *The Holy Spirit was not yet, because Jesus was not yet glorified* " (John vii. 39). They greatly wonder in heaven that the man of the Church does not know that the Holy Spirit, which is Divine Truth, proceeds from the Human of the Lord and not immediately from His Divine; when yet the doctrine received in the whole Christian world teaches that, " As is the Father, so also is the Son, uncreate, infinite, eternal, omnipotent, God, Lord; neither of them is first or last, nor greatest or least. Christ is God and Man; God from the nature of the Father, and Man from the nature of the mother; but although He is God and Man, yet nevertheless they are not two, but one Christ; He is one, not by changing the divinity into the humanity, but by the divinity receiving to itself the humanity. He is altogether one, not by a commixture of two natures, but one person alone; because as the body and soul are one man, so God and Man is one Christ." This is from the Creed of Athanasius. Now, since the Divine and Human of the Lord are not two, but one only person, and are united as the soul and body, it may be known that the Divine [effluence] which is called the Holy Spirit goes forth and proceeds from His Divine, by the Human, thus from the Divine Human; for nothing whatever can proceed from the body except as from the soul by the body, inasmuch as all the life of the body is from its soul. And because, as is the Father so is the Son, uncreate, infinite, eternal, omnipotent, God and Lord, and neither of them is first or last, nor greatest or least, it follows that the Divine Proceeding which is called the Holy Spirit, goes forth from the very Divine of the Lord by His Human, and not from another Divine which is called the Father; for the Lord teaches that He and the Father are one, and that the Father is in Him, and He in the Father. But that most in the Christian world think otherwise in their hearts, and therefore believe otherwise, the angels have said is from the fact that they think of the Human of the Lord as separate from His Divine; which yet is contrary to the doctrine which teaches that the Divine and Human of the Lord are not two persons, but only one person, and united as soul and body. . . . Since the proceeding Divine which is Divine Truth flows into man both immediately, and mediately through angels and spirits, it is therefore believed that the Holy Spirit is a third person, distinct from the two who are called the Father and the Son; but I am able to assert that no one in heaven knows any other Holy Divine than the Divine Truth proceeding from the Lord. (A. E. n. 183.)

Now, because the Divine Truth is meant by the Holy Spirit, and this was in the Lord, and was the Lord Himself (John xiv. 6), and because it could not therefore proceed from any other source, He said, " *The Holy Spirit was not yet, because Jesus was not yet glorified* " (vii. 39); and after the glorification, "*He breathed on the disciples, and said, Receive ye the Holy Spirit*" (xx. 22). The reason why the Lord breathed upon the disciples and said this was, that breathing upon was an external representative sign of Divine inspiration. But inspiration is insertion into angelic societies. (T. C. R. n. 140.)

The Holy Spirit is called the proceeding Divine, yet no one knows why it is called proceeding. This is not known, because until now it has been unknown that the Lord appears before the angels as a sun, and that heat, which in its essence is Divine love, and light, which in its essence is Divine wisdom, proceeds from that sun. So long as these truths were unknown it could not be known but that the proceeding Divine was a Divine by itself, and as the Athanasian doctrine of the Trinity declares, that there is one person of the Father, another of the Son, and another of the Holy Spirit. But when it is known that the Lord appears as a sun, a just idea can be had of the proceeding Divine, which is called the Holy Spirit; that it is one with the Lord, but proceeds from Him, as heat and light from the sun. (D. L. W. n. 146.)

BLASPHEMY AGAINST THE HOLY SPIRIT.

Jesus said, "*All sin and blasphemy shall be remitted unto men; but blasphemy against the Spirit shall not be remitted unto men: yea, whosoever speaketh a word against the Son of Man, it shall be remitted unto him; but whosoever shall speak against the Holy Spirit, it shall not be remitted unto him, neither in this age nor in that which is to come*" (Matt. xii. 31, 32). "*I say unto you, that all sins shall be remitted unto the sons of man, . . . but whosoever shall have blasphemed against the Spirit, shall not have remission for ever, but shall be liable to eternal judgment*" (Mark iii. 29). "*Whosoever shall speak a word against the Son of Man it shall be remitted unto him; but unto him that shall have blasphemed against the Holy Spirit it shall not be remitted*" (Luke xii. 10). What is signified by sin and blasphemy against the Holy Spirit, and by a word against the Son of Man, has not as yet been known in the church, and this for the reason that it has not been known what is properly meant by the Holy Spirit and by the Son of Man. By the Holy Spirit the Lord is meant as to Divine truth as it is in the heavens, thus the Word as it is in the spiritual sense, for this is the Divine truth in heaven; and by the Son of Man is meant Divine truth as it is on earth, therefore the Word as it is in the natural sense, for this is the Divine truth on earth. When it is known what is meant by the Holy Spirit, and by the Son of Man, it may also be known what is signified by sin and blasphemy against the Holy Spirit, and by a word against the Son of Man; and likewise why a word against the Son of Man can be remitted, but not sin and blasphemy against the Holy Spirit. To deny the Word, or to adulterate the real goods and falsify the real truths of the Word, is sin and blasphemy against the Holy Spirit; and to interpret the natural sense of the Word, which is the sense of the letter, according to appearances is a word against the Son of Man. The reason why to deny the Word is a sin which cannot be remitted, in this age nor in that which is to come, or to eternity, and why he who does it is liable to eternal judgment, is that they who deny the Word deny God, deny the Lord, deny heaven and hell, and deny the church and all things that belong to it; and they who are in such denial are atheists, who though with their lips they attribute the creation of the universe to some supreme Being, or Deity, or God, yet in their hearts ascribe it to nature. Such persons, inasmuch as by denial they have dissolved all bond of conjunction with the Lord, cannot be otherwise than separated from heaven, and conjoined to hell. The reason why to adulterate the real goods and to falsify the real truths of the Word is blasphemy against the Holy Spirit, which cannot be remitted, is because by the Holy Spirit the Lord is meant as to Divine truth as it is in the heavens, thus the Word as it is in the spiritual sense, as was said above. In the spiritual sense are genuine goods and genuine truths; but in the natural sense the same are as it were clothed, and only here and there are naked. They are therefore called goods and truths in appearance, and these are what are adulterated and falsified. And they are said to be adulterated and falsified when they are interpreted contrary to genuine goods and truths, for then heaven removes itself and man is severed from it; because, as was said, genuine goods and truths constitute the spiritual sense of the Word, in which the angels of heaven are:—For example, if the Lord and His Divinity be denied, as was done by the Pharisees, who said that the Lord performed miracles from Beelzebub, and had an unclean spirit; in consequence of which denial they were said to commit sin and blasphemy against the Holy Spirit, because against the Word, as may be seen in the preceding verses of that chapter. Hence also it is that Socinians and Arians, who although they do not deny the Lord yet deny His Divinity, are out of heaven, and cannot be received by any angelic society. Take also for example those who exclude the goods of love and the works of charity from the means of salvation, and assume faith exclusive of them as the one only means, and confirm this not only in doctrine but also in life, saying in their heart,—Good works do not save me, nor evil condemn, because I have faith. These also blaspheme the Holy Spirit, for they falsify the genuine good and truth of the Word, and this in a thousand places where love and charity and deeds and works are mentioned. (A. E. n. 778.)

The Holy Spirit not mentioned in the Old Testament.

In the Word of the Old Testament the Holy Spirit is nowhere mentioned, but the Spirit of holiness,—and only in three places; once in David (Ps. li. 13), and twice in Isaiah (lxiii. 10, 11). But in the Word of the New Testament it is frequently mentioned,—in the Evangelists, as well as in the Acts of the Apostles, and in their Epistles. The reason is, that then—when the Lord came into the world,—there first was the Holy Spirit; for it goes forth out of Him from the Father. (T. C. R. n. 158.)

THE DIVINE TRINITY.

THESE three, the Father, the Son, and the Holy Spirit, are the three essentials of the one God, like the soul, the body, and operation in man. (T. C. R. n. 166.)

At this day human reason is bound, as regards the Divine Trinity, like a man bound with manacles and fetters in prison; and may be compared to a vestal virgin buried in the earth, because she has put out the sacred fire; when yet the Divine Trinity ought to shine as a lamp in the minds of the men of the church, for God in His Trinity and in its unity is the All in all in the sanctities of heaven and the church. (T. C. R. n. 169.)

Every one acknowledges that these three essentials—the soul, the body, and operation, were and are in the Lord God the Saviour. That His soul was from Jehovah the Father can be denied only by Antichrist; for in the Word of both Testaments He is called the Son of Jehovah, the Son of the Most High God, the Only-begotten. The Divine of the Father is therefore, like the soul in man, His first essential. That the Son whom Mary brought forth is the body of that Divine soul, follows from the fact that nothing but the body conceived and derived from the soul is provided in the womb of the mother; this therefore is the second essential. Operations form the third essential, because they proceed from the soul and body together, and the things which proceed are of the same essence with those which produce them. That the three essentials, which are the Father, Son, and Holy Spirit, are one in the Lord, like the soul, body, and operation in man, is very evident from the Lord's words,— that the Father and He are one, and that the Father is in Him and He in the Father; likewise that He and the Holy Spirit are one, since the Holy Spirit is the Divine proceeding out of the Lord from the Father. (T. C. R. n. 167.)

From the Lord's Divine Human itself proceeds the Divine truth which is called the Holy Spirit; and because the Lord was Himself the Divine Truth, when He was in the world He Himself taught the things which were of love and faith, and at that time not by the Holy Spirit; as He Himself teaches in John: "*The Holy Spirit was not yet, because Jesus was not yet glori-*

fied " (vii. 39). But after the Lord even as to the Human was made Jehovah, that is Divine Good,—which was after the re-surrection,—He was then no longer Divine Truth, but this proceeded from His Divine Good. That the Holy Spirit is the Divine truth which proceeds from the Lord's Divine Human, and not any spirit or any spirits from eternity, is very manifest from the Lord's words in the passage cited, that "*the Holy Spirit was not yet.*" And then it is manifest that a spirit himself cannot proceed, but the holy [effluence] of a spirit, that is, the holy [effluence] which proceeds from the Lord, and which a spirit utters. From these considerations now it follows that the whole Trinity is perfect in the Lord, namely, the Father, Son, and Holy Spirit; and thus that there is one God,—and not three, who, distinct as to person, are said to constitute one Divine. The reason why they were called the Father, Son, and Holy Spirit in the Word was that men might acknowledge the Lord, and also the Divine in Him. For man was in so thick darkness,—as he also is at this day,—that otherwise he would not have acknowledged any Divine in the Lord's Human; for this to him would have been above all faith, because entirely incomprehensible. And moreover it is a truth that there is a Trinity; but in one, namely, in the Lord. And it is acknowledged too in the Christian churches that the Trinity dwells perfectly in Him. The Lord also taught plainly that Himself was one with the Father (John xiv. 9-12); and that the holy [truth] which the Holy Spirit speaks is not His, but the Lord's, in John : "*The Comforter, the Spirit of Truth, . . . shall not speak from Himself, but whatsoever He shall hear He shall speak: . . . He shall glorify Me, for He shall take of Mine, and shall proclaim it unto you*" (xvi. 13, 14). That the Comforter is the Holy Spirit is declared in John xiv. 26. (A. C. n. 6993.)

BEFORE THE WORLD WAS CREATED THERE WAS NO TRINITY OF GOD BUT AN IDEAL OR POTENTIAL ONE.

The Sacred Scripture teaches, and reason enlightened therein and therefrom by the Lord sees, that God is one; but that God was triune before the world was created the Sacred Scripture does not teach, and reason enlightened therefrom does not see. What is said in David, "*This day have I begotten Thee,*" is not from eternity, but in the fulness of time; for the future in God is present, thus *to-day.* So likewise this passage in Isaiah: "*Unto us a Child is born, unto us a Son is given, whose name is God, Hero, the Father of eternity.*"

What rational mind, when it hears that before the creation of the world there were three Divine persons, called the Father, the Son, and the Holy Spirit, does not say within itself while thinking on the subject, What is meant by a Son born of God the Father from eternity? How could He be born? And what is the Holy Spirit proceeding from God the Father through the Son from eternity? And how could He proceed and become God by Himself? Or how could a person beget a person from eternity? and both produce a person? Is not a person a person?

The rational mind, in revolving and reflecting upon a Trinity of persons in the Godhead from eternity, might also consider of what use was it for a Son to be born, and for the Holy Spirit to go forth from the Father through the Son, before the world was created? Was there need that three should consult how the universe should be created? And thus that three should create it, when yet the universe was created by one God? Nor was there then occasion that the Son should redeem, since redemption was effected after the world was created, in the fulness of time; nor that the Holy Spirit should sanctify, because as yet there were no men to be sanctified. If then those uses were in the idea of God, yet they did not actually exist before the world, but after it; from which it follows that the Trinity from eternity was not a real Trinity, but ideal; and still more a Trinity of persons.

A Trinity of persons in the Godhead before the world was created, never came into the mind of any one from the time of Adam down to the Lord's advent; as appears from the Word of the Old Testament, and from the histories of the religion of the ancients. Neither did it come into the minds of the Apostles, as is evident from their writings in the Word. And that it did not come into the mind of any one in the Apostolic Church prior to the Council of Nice, is clear from the Apostles' Creed, in which no Son from eternity is mentioned, but a Son born of the Virgin Mary.

The Trinity of God was formed after the world was created, and actually in the fulness of time, and then in God incarnate, who is the Lord the Saviour Jesus Christ. (Canons, pp. 35-37.)

A trinity of Divine persons existing from eternity or before the creation of the world, when conceived in idea, is a trinity of Gods, which cannot be expelled by the oral confession of one God. (T. C. R. n. 172.)

A Memorable Narration concerning the Divine Trinity.

Since it has been granted me by the Lord to see the wonderful things that are in the heavens and beneath the heavens, I must by command relate what has been seen. A magnificent palace was seen, and in the innermost part of it a temple; in the centre of this was a table of gold on which was the Word, at which two angels were standing. Around this were three rows of seats; the seats of the first row were covered with cloth of pure silk of purple colour; the seats of the second row with cloth of pure silk of a blue colour; and the seats of the third row with cloth of white. Under the roof, high above the table, there appeared a broad canopy glittering with precious stones, from the splendour of which light shone forth as a rainbow when the sky is becoming serene after a shower. Then suddenly there were seen sitting upon the seats as many of the clergy [as they would contain], all clothed in the garments of the priestly office. At one side there was a vestry, where an angel custodian was standing; and therein lay splendid garments, in beautiful order. *It was a council called together by the Lord.* And I heard a voice from heaven saying, "*Deliberate.*" They asked, "On what subject?" It was answered, "On *The Lord the Saviour,* and on *The Holy Spirit.*" But when they began to meditate on these subjects they were not in illustration. They therefore prayed, and light then flowed down from heaven, and illuminated first the backs of their heads, afterwards their temples, and finally their faces. And then they began; and, as it was commanded them, *First, on the Lord the Saviour.* The first proposition and subject of investigation was, "*Who assumed the Human in the Virgin Mary?*" And the angel standing at the table on which the Word was, read to them these words from Luke: "*And the angel said unto Mary, Behold, thou shalt conceive in the womb, and shalt bring forth a Son, and shalt call His name Jesus; He shall be great, and shall be called the Son of the Most High. . . . And Mary said to the angel, How shall this be since I know not a man? And the angel, answering, said, The Holy Spirit shall come upon thee, and the Virtue of the Most High shall overshadow thee; wherefore the Holy Thing that is born of thee shall be called the Son of God*" (i. 31, 32, 34, 35). Then he read these also in Matthew: "*The angel said to Joseph in a dream, Joseph, thou son of David, fear not to take unto thee Mary thy wife, for that which is begotten of her is of the Holy Spirit. And Joseph knew her not until she had brought forth her first-born Son; and he called His name Jesus*" (i. 20, 25). And besides these he read many others from the Evangelists, as Matt. iii. 17; xvii. 5; John i. 18; iii. 16; xx. 31; and many in other places, where the Lord, as to His Human, is called *the Son of God,* and where He from His Human calls Jehovah *His Father;* and also from the prophets, where it is foretold that Jehovah Himself was about to come into the world; among which were these two in Isaiah, "*It shall be said in that day, Lo, this is our God, whom we have waited for to deliver us; this is Jehovah, whom we have waited for; we will be glad and rejoice in His salvation*" (xxv. 9). "*The voice of one crying in the wilderness, Prepare ye the way of Jehovah, make straight in the desert a path for our God ; . . . for the Glory of Jehovah shall be revealed ; and all flesh shall see together. . . . Behold, the Lord Jehovah will come in the Mighty One : . . He will feed His flock like a shepherd*" (xl. 3, 5, 10, 11). And the angel said, "Since Jehovah Himself came into the world, and assumed the Human, therefore in the prophets, He is called the *Saviour* and the *Redeemer.*" And then he read to them the following passages: "*Only God is in thee, and there is no God else; verily thou art a God concealed, O God of Israel the Saviour*" (Isaiah xlv. 14, 15). "*Am not I Jehovah? and there is no God else beside Me; a just God and a Saviour there is not beside Me*" (xlv. 21, 22). "*I am Jehovah, and beside Me there is no Saviour*" (xliii. 11). "*I Jehovah am thy God, . . . and thou shalt acknowledge no God but Me, and there is no Saviour beside Me*" (Hosea xiii. 4). "*That all flesh may know that I Jehovah am thy Saviour and thy Redeemer*" (Isaiah xlix. 26; lx. 16). "*As for our Redeemer, Jehovah of Hosts is His name*" (xlvii. 4). "*Their Redeemer is Mighty; Jehovah of Hosts is His name*" (Jer. l. 34). "*Thus saith Jehovah the King of Israel, and His Redeemer, Jehovah of Hosts, I am the First and the Last, and beside Me there is no God*" (Isaiah xliv. 6). "*O Jehovah, my Rock and my Redeemer*" (Psalm xix. 15). "*Thus saith Jehovah thy Redeemer, the Holy One of Israel, I Jehovah am thy God*" (Isaiah xlviii. 17; xliii. 14; xlix. 7; liv. 8). "*Thou O Jehovah art our Father, our Redeemer, Thy name is from everlasting*" (lxiii. 16). "*Thus saith Jehovah thy Redeemer, I am Jehovah that maketh all things, . . . even alone, . . . by Myself*" (xliv. 24). "*Jehovah of hosts is His name, and thy Redeemer, the Holy One of Israel, the God of the whole earth He shall be called*" (liv. 5). "*Behold, the days come, . . . that I will raise unto David a righteous Branch, who shall reign King; . . . and this is His name, . . . Jehovah our Righteousness*" (Jer. xxiii. 5, 6, xxxiii. 15, 16). "*In that day, Jehovah shall be King over all the earth; in that day, Jehovah shall be one, and His name one*" (Zech. xiv. 9). Confirmed by these and the former passages, those who sat on the seats unanimously declared, that Jehovah Himself assumed the Human in order to redeem and save men. But a voice was then heard from Roman Catholics who had concealed themselves behind the altar, saying, "How can Jehovah God become man ? Is He not the Creator of the universe ?" And one of those who sat on the second row of seats turned and said, "Who then ?" And he who was behind the altar, standing now near the altar, replied, "*The Son from eternity.*" But he received the answer, "Is not the Son from eternity, according to your confession, also the Creator of the universe ? And what is a Son and a God born from eternity? And how can the Divine Essence, which is one and indivisible, be separated, and one part of it descend, and not at the same time the whole?"

The second subject of inquiry concerning the Lord was, Whether the Father and He are not therefore one, as the soul and body are one. They said that this followed, because the soul is from the Father. Then one of those who sat upon the third row of seats read from the creed called Athanasian these words: "Although our Lord Jesus Christ, the Son of God, is God and Man, yet they are not two, but one Christ; yea, one altogether; He is one person; for, as the soul and body make one man, so God and Man is one Christ." The creed, said the reader, where these words are found, is received in the whole Christian world, even by the Roman Catholics. And they said, "What need is there for more? 'God the Father and He are one, as the soul and body are one.'" And they added, "Since this is so we see that the Human of the Lord is Divine, because it is the Human of Jehovah; and also that the Lord as to the Divine Human should be approached, and that thus and not otherwise the Divine may be approached which is called the Father." This their conclusion the angel confirmed by many passages from the Word; among which were these: "*Unto us a Child is born, unto us a Son is given, . . . and His name shall be called Wonderful, Counsellor, God, Hero, the Father of Eternity, the Prince of Peace*" (Isa. ix. 6.) "*Abraham doth not know us, and Israel doth not acknowledge us; Thou O Jehovah art our Father, our Redeemer; Thy name is from everlasting*" (lxiii. 16); and in John: "*Jesus said, He that believeth on Me, believeth . . . on Him that sent Me; and he that seeth Me, seeth Him that sent Me*" (xii. 44, 45). "*Philip saith unto Jesus, Show us the Father. . . . Jesus saith unto him, . . . He that seeth Me, seeth the Father; how sayest thou then, Show us the Father? Believest thou not that I am in the Father, and the Father in Me? . . . Believe Me, that I am in the Father, and the Father in Me*" (xiv. 8, 9). "*Jesus said, I and the Father are one*" (x. 30); and also, "*All things that the Father hath are Mine*," and "*all Mine are the Father's*" (xvi. 15; xvii. 10). Lastly, "*Jesus said, I am the Way, the Truth, and the Life; no man cometh unto the Father but by Me*" (xiv. 6). To this the reader added, that similar things to what are here said by the Lord concerning Himself and His Father, may be said also by man concerning himself and his soul. Having heard these things, they all with one voice and one heart said that the Human of the Lord is Divine, and that this must be approached in order to approach the Father; since Jehovah God by means of it sent Himself into the world, and made Himself visible to the eyes of men, and thus accessible. In like manner He made Himself visible and thus accessible in a human form to the ancients; but then by an angel. But because this form was representative of the Lord who was about to come, all things of the church with the ancients were representative."

After this a deliberation followed concerning the Holy Spirit. And there was first disclosed an idea of many concerning God the Father, the Son and the Holy Spirit—that God the Father sits on high, and the Son at His right hand, and that they send forth from them the Holy Spirit, to enlighten, teach, justify, and sanctify men. And then a voice was heard from heaven, saying, " That idea of thought we cannot endure. Who does not know that Jehovah God is omnipresent ? Whoever knows and acknowledges this will acknowledge also that He Himself enlightens, teaches, justifies and saves; and that there is not a mediating God distinct from Him still less distinct from two, as person from person. Therefore let the former idea which is vain be put away, and let this which is just be received, and then you will see this subject clearly." But a voice was then heard from the Roman Catholics, who stood near the altar of the temple, saying, " What then is the Holy Spirit which is mentioned in the Word —in the Evangelists and in Paul—by which so many learned men among the clergy, and especially of our church, say that they are led ? Who in the Christian world at this day denies the Holy Spirit and His operations ?" At these words one of those who sat upon the second row of seats turned and said, " You say that the Holy Spirit is a person by Himself and a God by Himself. But what is a person going forth and proceeding from a person but an outgoing and proceeding operation ? One person cannot go forth and proceed from another, but operation can. Or what is a God going forth and proceeding from God but the outgoing and proceeding Divine ? One God cannot go forth and proceed from another, but the Divine from one God can." Having heard these things, those who sat upon the seats unanimously concluded that " The Holy Spirit is not a person by itself, nor therefore a god by itself, but is the Holy Divine going forth and proceeding from the one only omnipresent God, who is the Lord." To this the angels standing at the golden table upon which the Word was, said, " *Well.* We nowhere read in the Old Covenant that the prophets spoke the Word from the Holy Spirit, but from Jehovah; and where the Holy Spirit is mentioned in the New Testament it means the proceeding Divine, which is the Divine enlightening, teaching, vivifying, reforming, and regenerating." After this followed another inquiry respecting the Holy Spirit; which was,—From whom does the Divine which is meant by the Holy Spirit, proceed ; from the Father or from the Lord ? And while they were investigating this subject a light shone upon them from heaven, by which they saw that the Holy Divine which is meant by the Holy Spirit does not proceed out of the Father through the Lord, but out of the Lord from the Father; comparatively, as in man his activity does not proceed from the soul through the body, but out of the body from the soul. The angel standing near the table confirmed this by the following passages from the Word: "*He whom the Father hath sent speaketh the words of God: He hath given unto Him the Spirit not by measure. The Father loveth the Son, and hath given all things into His hand*" (John iii. 34, 35). "*A Rod shall go forth out of the stem of Jesse, . . . and the Spirit of Jehovah shall rest upon Him, the Spirit of wisdom and understanding, the Spirit of counsel and might*" (Isaiah xi. 1, 2). That the Spirit of Jehovah was bestowed upon Him, and that it was in Him, xlii. 1; lix. 19, 20; lxi. 1; Luke iv. 18. "*When the Holy Spirit shall come, which I will send unto you from the Father*" (John xv. 26). "*He shall glorify Me, because He shall receive of Mine, and make known unto you; all things whatsoever the Father hath are Mine; therefore said I that He shall receive of Mine and make known unto you*" (xvi. 14, 15). "*If I go away I will send the Comforter unto you*" (xvi. 7). That the Comforter is the Holy Spirit, xiv. 26. "*The Holy Spirit was not yet, because Jesus was not yet glorified*" (vii. 39). But after the glorification, "*Jesus breathed upon and said unto the disciples, Receive ye the Holy Spirit*" (xx. 22). And in the Apocalypse, "*Who shall not . . . glorify Thy name, O Lord? for Thou alone art Holy*" (xv. 4). Since the Lord's Divine operation from His Divine omnipresence is meant by the Holy Spirit, therefore when He spoke to the disciples of the Holy Spirit, which He was about to send from the Father, He also said, "*I will not leave you orphans; . . . I go away and come unto you; . . . and in that day ye shall know that I am in My Father, and ye in Me, and I in you*" (xiv. 18, 20, 28). And just before He departed out of the world He said, "*Lo, I am with you all the days, even unto the consummation of the age*" (Matt. xxviii. 20). Having read these passages to them the angel said, "From these and many other passages from the Word, it is plain that the Divine which is called the Holy Spirit proceeds out of the Lord from the Father." To this those who sat upon the seats said, "*This is Divine Truth.*"

Finally, this decree was made:—That from the deliberations in this council we have clearly seen, and therefore acknowledge as holy truth, that the Divine Trinity is in the Lord God the Saviour Jesus Christ; consisting of the Divine from whom [all things are], which is called the Father; the Divine Human, which is called the Son; and the proceeding Divine, which is called the

Holy Spirit; all together exclaiming, " *In Jesus Christ dwelleth all the fulness of the Godhead bodily*" (Coloss. ii. 9). Thus there is one God in the church.

When these deliberations were ended in that magnificent council, they arose, and the angel custodian came from the vestry and brought to each of those who sat upon the seats splendid garments, interwoven here and there with threads of gold, and said, " Receive *the wedding garments.*" And they were conducted in glory into the New Christian Heaven, with which the Lord's church upon earth, which is the New Jerusalem, will be conjoined. (T. C. R. n. 188.)

IMPORTANCE OF A RIGHT IDEA OF THE TRINITY.

Having written of the Triune God, it is important also to treat of the Divine Trinity,—which is known in the Christian world, and yet unknown. For by this alone can a just idea of God be obtained; and a just idea of God in the church is as the sanctuary and altar in the temple, and as the crown upon the head and sceptre in the hand of a king sitting upon his throne. For hereon depends, as a chain upon its first link, the whole body of theology. And, if you will believe it, every one is assigned his place in heaven according to his idea of God; for this is as the touchstone by which is discovered the quality of the gold and silver, that is, the good and truth, in man. For there is no saving good in him, except from God ; nor any truth, that does not derive its quality from out the bosom of good. . . .

But how the things written in the Word respecting the Trinity are to be understood,—whether, that there are three Gods, who in essence and hence in name are one God; or, that there are three objects of one subject, so that they are only qualities or attributes of one God, which are so named, or in another way,—reason left to itself can by no means see. But what counsel is to be offered ? There is no other than that a man shall go to the Lord God the Saviour, and read the Word under His guidance,—for He is the God of the Word,—and he will be enlightened and see truths, which reason also will acknowledge. . . . But to read the Word under guidance of one's own intelligence,—as is done by all who do not acknowledge the Lord as God of heaven and earth, and therefore approach and worship Him alone,—may be likened to children playing, who tie a bandage over the eyes and try to walk in a straight line, and even think they are walking in a straight line, when yet step by step they are turning aside, and at length go in the opposite direction, strike against a stone, and fall. (T. C. R. n. 163, 165.)

THE SACRED SCRIPTURES.

It is in the mouth of all that the Word is from God, is divinely inspired, and therefore holy. But yet it has been unknown hitherto where within it its Divinity resides. For in the letter the Word appears like a common writing, in a foreign style, neither lofty nor luminous as, to appearance, secular writings are. From this it is that the man who worships nature instead of God, or rather than God, and therefore thinks from himself and his *proprium*, and not out of heaven from the Lord, may easily fall into error concerning the Word, and even into contempt for it, and say within himself when he is reading it, What is this? What is that? Is this Divine? Can God, who has infinite wisdom, speak thus? Where and from whence is its holiness but from religious feeling and thence persuasion?

But he who so thinks does not reflect that the Lord Jehovah, who is the God of heaven and earth, spoke the word by Moses and the Prophets, and that therefore it cannot but be Divine Truth; for this is what the Lord Jehovah Himself speaks. Nor does he consider that the Lord the Saviour, who is the same with Jehovah, spoke the Word by the Evangelists, many things from His own mouth, and the rest by the Spirit of His mouth, which is the Holy Spirit, through His twelve Apostles. Hence it is, as He Himself says, that in His words there is spirit and life, that He is the light which enlighteneth, and that He is the Truth. . . .

But still the natural man cannot be persuaded by these considerations that the Word is Divine Truth itself, in which there is Divine Wisdom and Divine Life; for he judges of it by its style, in which he does not see them. Yet the style of the Word is the Divine style itself, with which no other style, however lofty and excellent it may appear, can be compared. Such is the style of the Word that it is holy in every sentence, and in every word, nay, sometimes in the very letters. Therefore the Word conjoins man to the Lord and opens heaven. There are two things that proceed from the Lord, Divine Love and Divine Wisdom, or what is the same, Divine Good and Divine Truth; the Word in its essence is both. And because it conjoins man to the Lord and opens heaven, as has been said, therefore it fills man with the goods of love and the truths of wisdom; his will with the goods of love, and his understanding with the truths of wisdom. Hence man has life through the Word. But it should be well known, that they only obtain life from the Word who read it for the purpose of drawing Divine truths from it, as from their fountain, and for the purpose, at the same time, of applying the Divine truths thence drawn to the life; and that the contrary takes place with those who read the Word for the purpose of acquiring honour and worldly gain. (T. C. R. n. 189-191.)

THERE IS A SPIRITUAL SENSE IN THE WORD HITHERTO UNKNOWN.

No man who does not know that there is any spiritual sense in the Word, like the soul in the body, can judge of the Word otherwise than from its literal sense; when yet this is as a casket containing precious things, which are its spiritual sense. While therefore this internal sense is unknown, a man can only judge of the Divine sanctity of the Word as he might of a precious stone from the matrix which encloses it, and which sometimes appears as a common stone; or as he would judge of a casket made of jasper, lapis-lazuli, amianthus, or mica, or agate, in which lie in their order diamonds, rubies, sardonyxes, oriental topazes, etc. So long as this is not known it is not to be wondered at if this casket should be estimated only according to the value of the material of it which appears to the eye. So is it with the Word as to its literal sense. Lest therefore man should remain in doubt whether the Word is Divine and most holy, its internal sense has been revealed to me by the Lord; which in its essence is spiritual, and which is within the external sense which is natural, as the soul in the body. This sense is the spirit which gives life to the letter. It can therefore testify of the Divinity and holiness of the Word, and convince, if he is willing to be convinced, even the natural man.

Who does not acknowledge and assent when it is said that the Word, because it is Divine, in its bosom is spiritual? But who as yet has known what the spiritual is, and where in the Word it is concealed? The Word in its bosom is spiritual, because it descended from the Lord Jehovah and passed through the angelic heavens; and the very Divine, which in itself is ineffable and imperceptible, in its descent became adapted to the perception of angels, and at last to the perception of men. Hence is the spiritual sense; which is within, in the natural, just as the soul is in man, the thought of the understanding in speech,

and the affection of the will in action. And if it may be compared with such things as appear before the eyes in the natural
world, the spiritual sense is in the natural sense as the whole
brain is within its meninges or *matres,* or as the young shoots of
a tree are within its barks and rinds, nay, as all things for the
generation of the chick are within the shell of the egg, and so
on. But that there is such a spiritual sense of the Word within
its natural sense has been divined by no one hitherto. It is
therefore necessary that the mystery, which is eminent above all
the mysteries yet revealed, should be opened to the understanding. (T. C. R. n. 192, 193.)

Since it was predicted that at the end of this church also
darkness would arise, from the non-recognition and acknowledgment of the Lord as the God of heaven and earth, and from the
separation of faith from charity, therefore, lest through this the
genuine understanding of the Word should perish, it has pleased
the Lord now to reveal the spiritual sense of the Word; and to
make manifest that the Word in that sense, and from that in the
natural sense, treats of the Lord and of the church, yea of these
only; and many other things by which the light of truth from
the Word, almost extinguished, may be restored. That at the
end of the church the light of truth would be almost extinguished is predicted in many places in the Apocalypse; and
is also meant by these words of the Lord in Matthew: "*Immediately after the tribulation of those days shall the sun be
darkened, and the moon shall not give her light, and the stars shall
fall from heaven, and the powers of the heavens shall be shaken;
and then . . . they shall see the Son of Man coming in the clouds
of heaven with power and glory*" (xxiv. 29, 30). By the sun here
the Lord as to love is meant; by the moon, the Lord as to faith;
by the stars, the Lord as to cognitions of good and truth; by the
Son of Man, the Lord as to the Word; by a cloud, the literal
sense of the Word; and by glory, its spiritual sense, and its
shining through the literal sense. (S. S. n. 112.)

What the Spiritual Sense of the Word is.

The spiritual sense of the Word is not that which shines forth
from the literal sense, while one is searching and explaining
the Word to confirm some dogma of the church; this sense may
be called the literal sense of the Word. But the spiritual sense
does not appear in the literal sense; it is interiorly within it, as
the soul is in the body, as the thought of the understanding is
in the eyes, and as the affection of love is in the countenance,
which act together as cause and effect. It is this sense chiefly,
which renders the Word spiritual, not only for men, but also for

angels; therefore the Word by this sense communicates with the heavens. (T. C. R. n. 194.)

From the Lord proceed the CELESTIAL, the SPIRITUAL, and the NATURAL, one after the other. What proceeds from His Divine Love is called CELESTIAL, and is Divine Good; what proceeds from His Divine Wisdom is called SPIRITUAL, and is Divine Truth; the NATURAL is from both, and is their complex in the ultimate. The angels of the Lord's celestial kingdom, who constitute the third or highest heaven, are in the Divine that proceeds from the Lord which is called celestial, for they are in the good of love from the Lord; the angels of the Lord's spiritual kingdom, who constitute the second or intermediate heaven, are in the Divine that proceeds from the Lord which is called spiritual, for they are in the truths of wisdom from the Lord; and the men of the church in the world are in the Divine natural, which also proceeds from the Lord. From this it follows that the Divine going forth from the Lord to its ultimates, descends through three degrees, and is called celestial, spiritual, and natural. The Divine which comes down from the Lord to men descends through these three degrees, and when it has descended it contains these three degrees within it. Such is everything Divine; when, therefore, it is in its ultimate degree it is in its fulness. Such is the Word. This in the ultimate sense is natural, in its interior is spiritual, and in its inmost celestial; and in each it is Divine. That such is the nature of the Word does not appear in the sense of the letter, which is natural, for the reason that heretofore man in the world has not known anything of the heavens, and consequently has not known what the spiritual and the celestial are, nor therefore the distinction between them and the natural.

The distinction between these degrees cannot be known unless correspondence is known; for these three degrees are entirely distinct from each other, like end, cause, and effect, or like what is prior, posterior, and postreme, and yet make one by correspondences; for the natural corresponds to the spiritual, and also to the celestial. (S. S. n. 6, 7.)

The Word was written by Correspondences.

Since then the Word interiorly is spiritual and celestial, therefore it was written by pure correspondences. And what was written by pure correspondences in its ultimate sense is written in such a style as by the Prophets and Evangelists, which, though it appear common, yet conceals within it all Divine and angelic wisdom. (S. S. n. 8.)

Each and all things in nature correspond to spiritual things;

and in like manner each and all things in the human body. But hitherto it has been unknown what correspondence is. Yet it was very well known in the most ancient times; for to those who then lived the knowledge of correspondences was the knowledge of knowledges, and was so universal that all their books and manuscripts were written by correspondences. The Book of Job, which is a book of the Ancient church, is full of correspondences. The hieroglyphics of the Egyptians, and the fabulous stories of highest antiquity, were nothing else. All the ancient churches were churches representative of spiritual things; their ceremonies, and also their statutes, according to which their worship was instituted, consisted of pure correspondences. In like manner all things of the Church among the children of Israel,—their burnt-offerings, sacrifices, meat-offerings, and drink-offerings, with the particulars of them,—were correspondences. Also the tabernacle, with all things therein, as well as their feasts,—such as the feast of unleavened bread, the feast of tabernacles, the feast of first-fruits; and the priesthood of Aaron and the Levites, and their garments of holiness; and besides these all their statutes and judgments, which related to their worship and life, were correspondences. Now since Divine things present themselves in the world by correspondences, therefore the Word was written by pure correspondences; for the same reason the Lord, as He spake from the Divine, spake by correspondences; for whatever is from the Divine this descends into such things in nature as correspond to the Divine, and which then conceal things Divine, which are called celestial and spiritual, in their bosom.

I have been informed that the men of the Most Ancient church, which was before the flood, were of so heavenly a genius that they conversed with the angels of heaven, and that they were enabled to converse with them by means of correspondences; hence their state of wisdom became such, that whatever they saw on earth they not only thought of it naturally, but also at the same time spiritually, thus in conjunction with the angels of heaven. I have moreover been informed that Enoch,— who is mentioned in Genesis, v. 21-24,—with his associates, gathered correspondences from their lips, and transmitted the knowledge of them to their posterity; in consequence of which it came to pass that the knowledge of correspondences was not only known in many kingdoms of Asia, but was also cultivated, especially in the land of Canaan, Egypt, Assyria, Chaldea, Syria, and Arabia, and in Tyre, Sidon, and Nineveh; and that from thence it was conveyed into Greece, where it was turned into fable, as may appear from the most ancient writers of that country. (T. C. R. n. 201, 202.)

Loss of the Knowledge of Correspondences, and Origin of Idolatry.

Because the representative rites of the church, which were correspondences, in process of time began to be converted into things idolatrous and also magical, then that knowledge, by the Divine providence of the Lord, was gradually lost, and among the Israelitish and Jewish people entirely forgotten. The worship of that people consisted indeed of correspondences, and was consequently representative of heavenly things; but yet they did not know what anything signified; for they were merely natural men, and therefore had neither inclination nor ability to know anything of spiritual and heavenly things, nor consequently anything of correspondences; for correspondences are representations of spiritual and heavenly things in natural.

That the idolatries of the nations in ancient times derived their origin from the knowledge of correspondences, was because all things that appear on the earth correspond; thus not only trees and plants, but also beasts and birds of every kind, as well as fishes and all other things. The ancients who were in the knowledge of correspondences made themselves images which corresponded to heavenly things, and took delight in them, because they signified such things as pertained to heaven and the church; and for this reason they not only placed them in their temples, but also in their houses; not to worship them, but to call to mind the heavenly things which they signified. Hence in Egypt and elsewhere there were images of calves, oxen, serpents, and of children, old men, and virgins; because calves and oxen signified the affections and powers of the natural man; serpents, the prudence and also the subtlety of the sensual man; children, innocence and charity; old men, wisdom; and virgins, affections of truth; and so on. Their posterity, when the knowledge of correspondences was forgotten, began to worship as holy, and at length as deities, the images and emblems set up by the ancients, because they found them in and about their temples. Hence with the ancients worship was also in gardens and in groves, according to the kinds of trees in them, and also on mountains and hills; for the gardens and groves signified wisdom and intelligence, and every tree something thereof,—as the olive, the good of love; the vine, truth from that good; the cedar, rational good and truth; a mountain, the highest heaven; a hill, the heaven below it. That the knowledge of correspondences remained with many orientals even to the coming of the Lord, is evident from the wise men of the east who visited the Lord when He was born; wherefore *a star went before them, and they brought with them gifts; gold, frankincense, and myrrh* (Matt. ii. 1, 2, 9-11); for the star which went before them signified cognition from heaven; gold signified celestial good; frankincense, spiritual good; and myrrh, natural good; from which three is all worship.   But still there was no knowledge whatever of correspondences among the Israelitish and Jewish people, although all things of their worship, and all the statutes and judgments given them by Moses, and all things in the Word, were pure correspondences.   The reason was that at heart they were idolaters, and therefore of such a character that they were not even willing to know that anything of their worship signified what is celestial and spiritual, for they believed that all those things were holy in themselves; if there-fore things celestial and spiritual had been laid open to them, they would not only have rejected but even profaned them; for this reason heaven was so closed to them that they scarcely knew that there was an eternal life.   That this was so is evident from the fact that they did not acknowledge the Lord, although the whole Sacred Scripture prophesied of Him and foretold His advent. They rejected Him for the sole reason that He taught them of a heavenly and not of an earthly kingdom; for they wanted a Mes-siah who should exalt them above all the nations in the world, and not any Messiah who should have care for their eternal sal-vation.   (T. C. R. n. 204, 205.)

WHY THE SPIRITUAL SENSE OF THE WORD WAS NOT REVEALED BEFORE.

The knowledge of correspondences through which the spiritual sense of the Word is given was not disclosed after that time, be-cause the Christians in the primitive church were so exceedingly simple that it could not have been disclosed to them; for if it had been disclosed it would have been of no use to them, nor would they have understood it.   After their times darkness arose upon the whole Christian world; first, through the heresies of many that were spread abroad, and immediately afterwards through the counsels and decrees of the Council of Nice con-cerning three Divine Persons from eternity, and concerning the Person of Christ, that He was the Son of Mary and not the Son of Jehovah God.   Thence came forth the present belief in justi-fication, in which they approach three Gods in their order; on which belief each and all things of the present church depend, as the members of the body upon its head.   And as they applied all things in the Word to confirm this erroneous belief, the spiri-tual sense could not be disclosed; for if it had been disclosed they would have applied that sense also to the same purpose, and thereby would have profaned the very holiness of the Word, and so would have entirely closed heaven against themselves, and removed the Lord from the church.

The knowledge of correspondences through which the spiritual sense is given is at this day revealed, because now the Divine truths of the Church are coming forth to light, and it is these of which the internal sense of the Word consists; and while these are in man he cannot pervert the literal sense of the Word. For the literal sense of the Word can be turned hither and thither; but if it is turned to falsity, its internal holiness, and with this its external, is destroyed; and if it be turned to the truth it remains. But of these things more will be said hereafter. That the spiritual sense would be opened at this day is meant by the fact that John saw heaven opened, and then a white horse, and that he saw and heard that an angel standing in the sun called all to a great supper; of which in the Apocalypse, xix. 11-18. But that for a long time this would not be acknowledged is meant by the beast, and by the kings of the earth that were about to make war against Him who sat upon the white horse (Apoc. xix. 19); and also by the dragon, in that it persecuted the woman which brought forth the man-child, even into the desert, and then cast out of his mouth waters as a flood, that he might overwhelm her. (T. C. R. n. 206, 207.)

The Spiritual Sense is in each and all things of the Word.

This cannot be better seen than by examples. For instance, John says in the Apocalypse, "*I saw heaven opened, and behold a white horse, and He that sat upon him was called Faithful and True, and in righteousness He doth judge and make war. His eyes were as a flame of fire; and on His head were many crowns; and He had a name written that no man knew but He Himself. And He was clothed with a vesture dipped in blood; and His name is called the Word of God. And the armies which were in the heavens followed Him upon white horses, clothed in fine linen, white and clean. And He hath on His vesture and on His thigh a name written, King of Kings, and Lord of Lords*" (xix. 11-14, 16). No one can know what these particulars involve except from the internal sense. It is manifest that each is representative and significative of something. For indeed it is said that heaven was opened; that there was a horse which was white; that One sat upon him who in righteousness doth judge and make war; that His eyes were as a flame of fire; that on His head were many crowns; that He had a Name which no man knew but He Himself; that He was clothed with a vesture dipped in blood; that the armies which were in the heavens followed Him upon white horses; that they were clothed in fine linen, white and clean; and that on His vesture and on His thigh He had a Name written. It is plainly said that He is the Word, and that He who is the Word is the Lord; for it is said, "*His name is called the Word of God;*" and afterwards, "*He hath on His vesture and on His thigh a name written, King of Kings, and Lord of Lords.*" From the interpretation of each expression it is clear that the Word is here described as to its spiritual or internal sense. That heaven was opened, represents and signifies that the internal sense of the Word is seen in heaven, and therefore by those to whom heaven is open in the world. The horse, which was white, represents and signifies the understanding of the Word as to its interior truths. That this is the signification of the white horse will be clear from what follows. That He who sat upon him is the Lord as to the Word, therefore the Word, is manifest; for it is said, "*His name is called the Word of God;*" He is called Faithful, and is said to judge in righteousness, from Good; and is called True, and is said in righteousness to make war, from Truth. For the Lord Himself is righteousness. His eyes, as a flame of fire, signify Divine Truth from the Divine Good of His Divine Love. The many crowns upon His head signify all goods and truths of faith. Having a name written, that no man knew but Himself, signifies that what the Word is in the internal sense no one sees but Himself, and him to whom He reveals it. Clothed with a vesture dipped in blood, signifies the Word in the letter, to which violence has been done. The armies in the heavens which followed Him upon white horses signify those who are in the understanding of the Word as to its interior truths. Clothed with fine linen white and clean, signifies the same in truth from good. A name written on His vesture and on His thigh, signifies truth and good and their quality. From these particulars, and from those which precede and follow [in the chapter], it is evident that it is therein foretold that at about the last time of the church the spiritual or internal sense of the Word would be opened. (W. H. n. 1; S. S. n. 9.)

It is written in the Apocalypse, "*I saw a new heaven and a new earth; for the first heaven and the first earth were passed away. . . . And I saw the holy city, New Jerusalem, coming down from God out of heaven, prepared as a bride adorned for her husband. . . . The city had a wall great and high, which had twelve gates, and at the gates twelve angels, and names written thereon, which are the names of the twelve tribes of the children of Israel. . . . And the wall of the city had twelve foundations, and in them the names of the twelve apostles of the Lamb. . . . And the city lieth four square, and the length is as large as the breadth. And he measured the city with the reed, twelve thousand furlongs; and the length, and the breadth, and the height of it were equal.*

And he measured the wall thereof, an hundred and forty and four cubits; the measure of a man, that is, of an angel. And the wall of it was of jasper; but the city itself was pure gold, like unto pure glass; and the foundations of the wall of the city were of every precious stone. . . . And the twelve gates were twelve pearls; . . . and the street of the city was pure gold, as it were transparent glass. . . . The glory of God did lighten it, and the Lamb was the lamp thereof. And the nations of them which are saved shall walk in the light of it, and the kings of the earth shall bring their glory and honour into it " (xxi. 1, 2, 12-24). When a man reads these words he does not understand them otherwise than according to the sense of the letter; he therefore understands that the visible heaven and earth will be dissolved, and a new heaven be created; and that the holy city Jerusalem will descend upon the new earth; and that as to its measure it will be according to the description. But the angels understand these things very differently; that is, the particulars which man understands naturally they understand spiritually. And the things which the angels understand are what they signify, and this is the internal or spiritual sense of the Word. According to this internal or spiritual sense, in which the angels are, by a new heaven and a new earth a new church is meant, both in the heavens and on the earth, each of which shall be spoken of hereafter; by the city Jerusalem descending from God out of heaven its heavenly doctrine is signified; by the length, breadth, and height, which are equal, are signified all the goods and truths of that doctrine in the complex; by its wall are meant the truths which protect it; by the measure of the wall, which is a hundred and forty-four cubits, which is the measure of a man, that is of an angel, all those defending truths in the complex are meant, and their quality; by the twelve gates, which are of pearl, introductive truths are meant,—which are likewise signified by the twelve angels at the gates; by the foundations of the wall, which are of every precious stone, the knowledges are meant whereon that doctrine is founded; by the twelve tribes of Israel, and also by the twelve Apostles, are meant all things of the church in general and in particular; by gold like unto pure glass, whereof the city and its streets were built, the good of love is signified, by which the doctrine and its truths are made transparent; by the nations who are saved, and the kings of the earth who bring glory and honour into the city, are meant all from the church who are in goods and truths; by God and the Lamb the Lord is meant as to the very Divine and the Divine Human. (H. D. n. 1.)

In the Apocalypse, chap. vi., it is said, *That when the Lamb opened the first seal of the book there went forth a white horse, and he who sat thereon had a bow, and a crown was given unto him;*

that when He opened the second seal there went forth a red horse, and unto him who sat thereon there was given a great sword; that when He opened the third seal there went forth a black horse, and he that sat thereon had a pair of balances in his hand; and that when He opened the fourth seal there went forth a pale horse, and the name of him that sat thereon was Death. What these things signify can only be evolved by means of the spiritual sense; and it is fully evolved when it is known what is signified by the opening of the seals, by the horses, and by the other particular things mentioned. By these things the successive states of the church are described as to its understanding of the Word, from its beginning to its end. The opening of the seals of the book by the Lamb signifies the making of those states of the church manifest by the Lord. By a horse the understanding of the Word is signified; the white horse is the understanding of truth from the Word in the first state of the church. The bow of him that sat upon that horse signifies the doctrine of charity and faith contending against falsities; the crown signifies eternal life, the reward of victory. The red horse signifies the understanding of the Word as to good, destroyed in the second state of the church; the great sword is falsity fighting against truth. The black horse signifies the understanding of the Word destroyed, as to truth, in the third state of the church; the pair of balances signifies that the estimation of truth is so little as scarcely to be any. The pale horse signifies the understanding of the Word annihilated, by evils of life and the falsities from them, in the fourth or last state of the church; and death signifies eternal damnation. That such is the signification of these things in the spiritual sense is not apparent in the sense of the letter, or the natural sense; unless therefore the spiritual sense were once opened, the Word, as to this passage and the rest of the Apocalypse, would have been closed entirely so that at length no one would know where the Divine Holiness therein was concealed. It is equally so, in respect to what is signified by the four horses and the four chariots that came forth from between the two mountains of brass, in Zechariah vi. 1-8.

In the Apocalypse, chap. ix., it is written: " *The fifth angel sounded, and I saw a star fall from heaven unto the earth, and to him was given the key of the bottomless pit; and he opened the bottomless pit, and there arose a smoke out of the pit as the smoke of a great furnace; and the sun and the air were darkened by reason of the smoke of the pit; and there came out of the smoke locusts upon the earth, and unto them was given power as the scorpions of the earth have power . . . The shapes of the locusts were like unto horses prepared for battle; and on their heads were as it were crowns like gold; and their faces were as the faces of men, and they had hair as the hair of women, and their teeth were as the teeth of lions; and they had breastplates as of iron; and the sound of their wings was as the sound of many chariots running to battle; and they had tails like unto scorpions, and there were stings in their tails; and their power was to hurt men five months. And they had a king over them, which is the angel of the bottomless pit, whose name in the Hebrew tongue is Abaddon, but in the Greek tongue hath his name Apollyon."* Neither would any one be able to understand these things unless the spiritual sense were laid open to him, for nothing here is uselessly said, but all things, even to the least particulars, have a signification. The subject here treated of is the state of the church when all knowledges of truth from the Word are destroyed, and consequently man, having become sensual, persuades himself that falsities are truths. By a star fallen from heaven are signified the knowledges of truth destroyed; by the sun and air being darkened is signified the light of truth made darkness; by the locusts which came forth out of the smoke of the pit are signified falsities in the extremes,—such as pertain to those who have become sensual, and who see and judge all things from fallacies; by a scorpion is signified their persuasive [power]. That the locusts appeared as horses prepared for battle signifies their ratiocinations, as if from the understanding of truth; that the locusts had crowns like unto gold upon their heads, and faces as the faces of men, signifies that they appeared to themselves as conquerors, and wise; their having hair as the hair of women signifies that they appeared to themselves as if they were in the affection of truth; their having teeth as the teeth of lions signifies that sensual things, which are the ultimates of the natural man, appeared to them as if they had power over all things; their having breastplates as breastplates of iron signifies argumentations grounded in fallacies, by which they fight and prevail; that the sound of their wings was as the sound of chariots running to battle signifies ratiocinations as if from truths of doctrine from the Word, for which they were to contend; their having tails like scorpions signifies persuasions; their having stings in their tails signifies the cunning arts of deceiving thereby; their having power to hurt men five months signifies that they induce a kind of stupor on those who are in the understanding of truth and in the perception of good; their having a king over them, the angel of the bottomless pit, whose name is Abaddon, or Apollyon, signifies that their falsities were from hell, where they are who are merely natural and in self-intelligence. This is the spiritual sense of these words; nothing of which appears in the sense of the letter. There is such a spiritual sense throughout the Apocalypse. (S. S. n. 12, 13.)

That it may be seen that the prophetical parts of the Word of the Old Testament in many places are not intelligible without the spiritual sense, I will adduce only a few passages; as this in Isaiah : " *Then Jehovah of Hosts shall stir up a scourge against Ashur, according to the smiting of Midian at the rock of Oreb; and His rod shall be upon the sea, which He shall lift up after the manner of Egypt. And it shall come to pass in that day, that His burden shall be taken away from off thy shoulder, and His yoke from off thy neck. . . . He shall come against Aiath ; He shall pass to Migron; against Michmash He shall direct His arms ; they shall pass over Mebara ; Gebah shall be a lodging to us; Ramah shall tremble; Gibeah of Saul shall flee. Wail with thy voice, O daughter of Gallim ; hearken, O Laish, O wretched Anathoth. Madmenah shall be a wanderer ; the inhabitants of Gebim shall gather themselves together ; as yet there is not a day to stand in Nob ; the mountain of the daughter of Zion, the hill of Jerusalem, shall shake her hand. . . . Jehovah shall cut down the thickets of the forest with iron, and Lebanon shall fall by the Mighty One* " (x. 26-34). Here mere names occur, from which no meaning can be drawn but by the aid of the spiritual sense ; in which sense all names in the Word signify things pertaining to heaven and the church. From this sense it is gathered that these things signify that the whole church was devastated, by means of sensuous knowledges perverting all truth and confirming all falsity. In another place in the same Prophet it is written : "*In that day . . . the envy also of Ephraim shall depart, and the adversaries of Judah shall be cut off; Ephraim shall not envy Judah, and Judah shall not vex Ephraim ; but they shall fly upon the shoulders of the Philistines towards the west; they shall spoil them of the east together ; they shall lay their hand upon Edom and Moab. . . . Jehovah shall utterly destroy the tongue of the Egyptian sea, and with His mighty wind shall He shake His hand over the river, and shall smite it in the seven streams, and make men go over dryshod ; and there shall be a highway for the remnant of His people which shall be left, from Assyria*" (xi. 11-16). Here also no one can see anything Divine unless he knows what is signified by each particular name ; and yet the subject treated of is the advent of the Lord, and what shall then come to pass, as plainly appears from verses 1-10. Who then without the aid of the spiritual sense would see that these things in their order signify, that they who are in falsities through ignorance, and have not suffered themselves to be seduced by evils, will come to the Lord ; that the Church will then understand the Word ; and that then falsities will be no longer hurtful to them. The case is the same where no names occur ; as in Ezekiel : " *Thus saith the Lord Jehovah : Thou son of man, speak unto every feathered fowl, and to every beast of the field, Assemble yourselves, and come; gather yourselves from every side to My sacrifice that I do sacrifice for you, even a great sacrifice upon the mountains of Israel, that ye may eat flesh and drink blood. Ye shall eat the flesh of the mighty, and drink the blood of the princes of the earth;* . . . *ye shall eat fat till ye be full, and drink blood till ye be drunken, of My sacrifice which I have sacrificed for you. Ye shall be filled at My table with the horse and the chariot, with the mighty man, and with every man of war.* . . . *And I will set My glory among the heathen"* (xxxix. 17-21). He who does not know from the spiritual sense what is signified by sacrifice, what by flesh and blood, what by the horse and the chariot, the mighty man, and the man of war, will understand no otherwise than that such things are to be eaten and drunken; but the spiritual sense teaches that to eat the flesh and drink the blood of the sacrifice which the Lord Jehovah shall offer upon the mountains of Israel, signifies to appropriate Divine Good and Divine Truth from the Word. For the subject referred to is the calling together of all to the Lord's kingdom; and in particular the establishment of the church by the Lord among the Gentiles. Who cannot see that flesh is not here meant by flesh, nor blood by blood?—so that men should drink blood till they are drunken, and that they should be filled with the horse, the chariot, the mighty man, and every man of war? So in a thousand other places in the Prophets.

Without the spiritual sense no one could know why the Prophet Jeremiah was commanded to buy himself a girdle, and put it on his loins; and not to draw it through the waters, but to hide it in the hole of a rock by the Euphrates (Jer. xiii. 1-7); or why the Prophet Isaiah was commanded to loose the sackcloth from off his loins, and to put off the shoe from off his foot, and go naked and barefoot three years (Isaiah xx. 2, 3); or why the Prophet Ezekiel was commanded to pass a razor upon his head, and upon his beard, and afterwards to divide [the hairs of] them, and burn a third part in the midst of the city, smite a third part with the sword, scatter a third part in the wind, and bind a little of them in his skirts, and at last to cast them into the midst of the fire (Ezek. v. 1-4); or why the same prophet was commanded to lie upon his left side three hundred and ninety days, and upon his right side forty days; and to make himself a cake of wheat, and barley, and millet, and fitches, with cows' dung, and eat it; and in the meantime to raise a rampart and a mound against Jerusalem, and besiege it (Ezek. iv. 1-15); or why the Prophet Hosea was twice commanded to take to himself a harlot to wife (Hosea i. 2-9; iii. 2, 3), and many such things. Moreover, who without the spiritual sense would know what is signified by all things belonging to the tabernacle,—by the ark, the mercy seat, the cherubim, the candlestick, the altar of incense, the bread of faces on the table, and its veils and curtains? Or who, without the spiritual sense, would know what is signified by Aaron's garments of holiness,—by his coat, his cloak, the ephod, the Urim and Thummim, the mitre, and other things? Who, without the spiritual sense, would know what is signified by all the things which were enjoined concerning burnt-offerings, sacrifices, meat-offerings, and drink-offerings? concerning Sabbaths also, and feasts? The truth is, that not the least thing of these was enjoined which did not signify something relating to the Lord, to heaven, and to the church. From these few examples it may be clearly seen that there is a spiritual sense in each and all things of the Word. (S. S. n. 15, 16.)

SIX DEGREES OF DIVINE TRUTH, THE LETTER OF THE WORD BEING THE LOWEST.

Truth Divine is not of one degree, but of several: Truth Divine in the first degree, and also in the second, is what immediately proceeds from the Lord; this is above angelic understanding. Truth Divine in the third degree is such as is in the inmost or third heaven; this is such that nothing of it can be apprehended by man. Truth Divine in the fourth degree is such as is in the middle or second heaven; neither is this intelligible to man. Truth Divine in the fifth degree is such as is in the ultimate or first heaven; this may for some little while be perceived by man, but by one enlightened; and yet it is such that a great part of it cannot be uttered by human words; but when it falls into ideas it produces a faculty of perceiving and also of believing that it is so. And Truth Divine in the sixth degree is such as is with man, accommodated to his apperception; thus it is the sense of the letter of the Word. This sense or this truth is represented by a cloud; and the interior truths by the glory in a cloud. Hence it is that Jehovah, that is the Lord, so often appeared to Moses and to the children of Israel in a cloud. (A. C. n. 8443.)

THE LITERAL SENSE OF THE WORD IS THE BASIS, THE CONTAINANT, AND FOUNDATION OF ITS SPIRITUAL AND CELESTIAL SENSES.

In everything Divine there is a first, a mediate, and an ultimate or last; and the first passes through the mediate to the ultimate, and so exists and subsists; the ultimate therefore is the BASIS. Then the first is in the mediate, and by the mediate in the ultimate; so that the ultimate is the CONTAINANT; and since the ultimate is the containant and the basis, it is also the

FOUNDATION. The learned reader will understand that these three may be called the end, the cause, and the effect; and also the Being, Becoming, and Existing; and that the end is Being, the cause Becoming, and the effect Existing; consequently, that in every complete thing there is a trine, which is called the first, the mediate, and the ultimate; also the end, the cause, and the effect. When these points are understood it will also be understood that every Divine work is complete and perfect in the ultimate; and also that all is in the ultimate, because the prior things are together in it. (T. C. n. 210.)

There are three heavens; the highest, the middle, and the lowest. The highest heaven constitutes the Lord's celestial kingdom; the middle heaven forms His spiritual kingdom; and the lowest heaven, His natural kingdom. And just as there are three heavens, there are also three senses of the Word,—the celestial, the spiritual, and the natural; with which also those things coincide which were said above,—that is to say, that the first is in the mediate, and by the mediate in the ultimate; just as the end is in the cause, and by the cause in the effect. From this the nature of the Word is clear,—namely, that within the sense of its letter, which is natural, there is an interior sense which is spiritual, and within this an inmost sense which is celestial; and thus that the ultimate sense, which is natural, and is called the sense of the letter, is the containant, and so the basis and foundation of the two interior senses. (T. C. R. n. 212.)

The Literal Sense of the Word is a Guard to the Truths Concealed within it.

Moreover, it should be known that the literal sense of the Word is a guard to the genuine truths concealed within it; and the guard consists in this, that this sense may be turned in different directions, and explained according to the apprehension, and yet the internal not be hurt and violated by it. For it does no harm that the literal sense of the Word is understood by one differently from another. But it does harm if the Divine Truths which are concealed within are perverted; for thereby violence is done to the Word. Lest this should be, the literal sense guards it, —and it guards it with those who from their religion are in falsities and do not confirm them; for these do no violence. This guard is signified by the cherubim, and is also described by means of them in the Word. This is signified by the cherubim which, after Adam and his wife were cast out of the garden of Eden, were placed at its entrance; of which we read that,—*When Jehovah God had driven out the man, He made cherubim to dwell at the east of the garden of Eden, and the flame of a sword, which turned this way and that way, to keep the way of the tree of life* (Gen. iii. 23, 24). By cherubim a guard is signified; by the way of the tree of life is signified entrance within to the Lord, which men have by means of the Word; by the flame of a sword turning itself this way and that way Divine Truth in its ultimates is signified, which is like the Word in its literal sense, that can thus be turned. (S. S. n. 97.)

In the Literal Sense of the Word Divine Truth is in its Fulness, in its Holiness, and in its Power.

That in the sense of the letter the Word is in its fulness, in its holiness, and in its power, is because the two prior or interior senses, which are called spiritual and celestial, exist simultaneously in the natural sense, which is the sense of the letter, as stated above. But how they are simultaneously in that sense shall be further explained. There is in heaven and in the world a successive order and a simultaneous order. In successive order one thing succeeds and follows another, from the highest down to the lowest; but in simultaneous order one thing is next to another, from the inmost things to the outermost. Successive order is like a column with degrees from the summit to the base; and simultaneous order is like a work coherent with the periphery, from the centre to the outermost surface. It shall now be explained how successive order, in the ultimate becomes simultaneous order. It comes to pass in this manner: The highest [degrees] of successive order become the inmost of simultaneous order; and the lowest [degrees] of successive order become the outermost of simultaneous order; comparatively as a column of degrees subsiding becomes a body coherent in a plain. Thus the simultaneous is formed from the successive, and this in each and all things of the natural world, and in each and all things of the spiritual world; for everywhere there is a first, a mediate, and an ultimate; and the first tends and passes through the mediate to its ultimate. But it should be well understood that there are degrees of purity, according to which each order is produced. Now to the Word:—The celestial, the spiritual, and the natural proceed from the Lord in successive order, and in the last or ultimate they exist in simultaneous order; so then the celestial and spiritual senses of the Word exist simultaneously in its natural sense. When this is comprehended it may be seen how the natural sense of the Word is the containant, the basis, and the foundation of its spiritual and celestial senses; and how Divine good and Divine Truth in the literal sense of the Word are in their fulness, in their holiness, and in their power. It may be seen from all this that the Word is the very Word in its literal sense; for in this interiorly there is spirit and life. This is what the Lord says in John: "*The words that I speak unto you are spirit and life*" (vi. 63); for the Lord spoke His words in the natural sense. The celestial and the spiritual senses are not the Word without the natural sense; for they are like spirit and life without a body; and are as a palace which has no foundation. (T. C. R. n. 214.)

By means of the Literal Sense of the Word Man has Conjunction with the Lord and Consociation with the Angels.

The reason why there is conjunction with the Lord by means of the Word is, that the Word treats of Him alone; and therefore the Lord is the all and all of it, and is called the Word, as has been shown in the Doctrine concerning the Lord. The conjunction is in the literal sense because in this sense the Word is in its fulness, in its holiness, and in its power, as was shown above. The conjunction is not apparent to man, but exists in his affection for truth, and in his perception of it, and thus in the love and faith of Divine truth in Him.

The reason why there is consociation with angels by means of the literal sense is, that the spiritual and celestial senses are within this sense, and the angels are in those senses,—the angels of the spiritual kingdom in the spiritual sense of the Word, and the angels of the celestial kingdom in its celestial sense. Those senses are evolved from the natural sense of the Word, which is the literal sense, when a true man is in this sense. The evolution is instantaneous; and therefore the consociation also.

That the spiritual angels are in the spiritual sense of the Word, and the celestial angels in its celestial sense, has been shown me by much experience. It has been granted me to perceive that when I read the Word in its literal sense communication took place with the heavens,—now with one society of them, now with another; and that the things which I understood according to the natural sense, the spiritual angels understood according to the spiritual sense, and the celestial angels according to the celestial sense, and this in an instant. As this communication has been perceived by me some thousands of times, there remains with me no doubt about it. There are also spirits that are beneath the heavens, who abuse this communication; for they read aloud some passages out of the literal sense of the Word, and immediately observe and mark the society with which communication takes place. This too I have often seen and heard. From these circumstances it is given me to know, by living experience, that the Word, as to its literal sense, is the Divine medium of conjunction with the Lord and with heaven. (S. S. n. 62-64.)

I have been informed from heaven that the most ancient people had immediate revelation, since their interiors were turned to heaven; and that thence there was at that time a conjunction of the Lord with the human race. But that after their times there was not such immediate revelation, but mediate by correspondences; for all their Divine worship consisted of correspondences; and therefore the churches of that time were called representative churches. For they then knew what correspondence and what representation was, and that all things that exist on earth correspond to spiritual things which are in heaven and in the church; or what is the same, represented them. The natural things therefore which constituted the externals of their worship, served them as mediums for thinking spiritually, thus with the angels. After the knowledge of correspondences and representations was lost then the Word was written, in which all the words and the meanings of the words are correspondences; they thus contain a spiritual or internal sense, in which the angels are. When therefore a man reads the Word, and understands it according to the literal or external sense, the angels understand it according to the internal or spiritual sense; for all the thought of angels is spiritual, and the thought of man is natural. These thoughts indeed appear diverse; but still they are one, because they correspond. Hence it is that after man removed himself from heaven, and broke the bond, a medium of conjunction of heaven with man by the Word was provided by the Lord. (H. H. n. 306.)

The Word was thus written in order that it may be a conjunction of heaven with man; and it is a conjunction, because every word therein, and in some places every letter, contains a spiritual sense, in which the angels are; so that when man apprehends the Word according to its appearances of truth, the angels who are around man understand it spiritually; in this way the spiritual of heaven is conjoined with the natural of the world, as to such things as conduce to man's life after death. If the Word had been otherwise written there could have been no conjunction of heaven with man. And because the Word is such in the letter, therefore it is as it were a support for heaven; for all the wisdom of the angels of heaven as to such things as pertain to the Church terminates in the literal sense of the Word, as in its basis, wherefore the Word in the letter may be called the stay of heaven. The literal sense of the Word is therefore most holy; yea, it is even more powerful than its spiritual sense,—which has been made known to me by much experience in the spiritual world. For when spirits quote any part of the Word according to the sense of the letter, they immediately excite some heavenly society to conjunction with them. It is evident from these considerations that all that is of the doctrine of the church must be confirmed from the literal sense of the Word, in order that there may be any sanctity and power in it; and indeed from those books of the Word in which there is a spiritual sense. It also appears from this how dangerous it is to falsify the Word, to the destruction of the Divine truth which is in its spiritual sense, for so heaven is closed to man. (A. E. n. 816.)

THE MARRIAGE OF THE LORD AND THE CHURCH, AND HENCE THE MARRIAGE OF GOOD AND TRUTH, IS IN EVERY PART OF THE WORD.

That the marriage of the Lord and the church, and hence the marriage of good and truth is in all the least parts of the Word, has not hitherto been seen; nor could be seen, because the spiritual sense of the Word was not before revealed, and it can only be seen by means of that sense. For there are two senses in the Word lying concealed within its literal sense, the spiritual and the celestial. In the spiritual sense the things that are in the Word relate chiefly to the church; and in the celestial sense they relate chiefly to the Lord. Then in the spiritual sense they relate to Divine truth, and in the celestial sense to Divine good; hence is that marriage in the literal sense of the Word. But this is not apparent to any but those who, from the spiritual and celestial senses of the Word, know the significations of its words and names; for some words and names are predicted of good and some of truth; and some include both; without this knowledge therefore that marriage in the several particulars of the Word cannot be seen. This is the reason why this arcanum has not before been revealed.

Because there is such a marriage in the least parts of the Word, there are often pairs of expressions in the Word which appear as repetitions of the same thing. They are not repetitions however, but one has relation to good, and the other to truth; and both taken together form a conjunction of good and truth, thus one thing. Hence also is the Divinity of the Word and its sanctity; for in every Divine work there is a conjunction of good with truth, and of truth with good. (S. S. n. 80, 81.)

That there are pairs of expressions in the Word, which appear like repetitions of the same thing, must be seen by readers who give attention to the subject; as brother and companion; poor and needy; wilderness and desert; vacuity and emptiness; foe and enemy; sin and iniquity; anger and wrath; nation and people; joy and gladness; mourning and weeping; justice and judgment; etc. These appear as synonymous words, and yet they are not so. For the words brother, poor, wilderness, vacuity, foe, sin, anger, nation, joy, mourning, and justice, are predicated of good, and in the opposite sense of evil; but companion, needy, desert, emptiness, enemy, iniquity, wrath, people, gladness, weeping, and judgment, are predicated of truth, and in the opposite sense of falsity. And yet it appears to the reader who is not acquainted with this arcanum, that poor and needy, desert and wilderness, vacuity and emptiness, foe and enemy, etc., are one thing, whereas they are not so, but form one thing by conjunction. Many things are also coupled together in the Word; as fire and flame; gold and silver; brass and iron; wood and stone; bread and wine; purple and fine linen; etc.; because fire, gold, brass, wood, bread, and purple, signify good; and flame, silver, iron, stone, water, wine, and fine linen, signify truth. In like manner it is said, that men are to love God with all the heart and with all the soul; and that God will create in man a new heart and a new spirit; for the heart is predicated of the good of love, and the soul of truth from that good. There are also words which because they partake of both, that is of good and of truth, are used alone, not being joined with others. But these, and many other things, appear to the angels only, and to those who while in the natural sense are also in the spiritual sense.

It would be tedious to show from the Word that there are such pairs of expressions therein, which appear like repetitions of the same thing; for it would fill sheets. But that all doubt may be removed I will adduce passages where judgment and justice [or righteousness] are mentioned together; also nation and people; and joy and gladness. The following are passages where judgment and justice are mentioned together: " *The city was full of judgment, justice lodged in it* " (Isa. i. 21). " *Zion shall be redeemed with judgment, and her converts with justice* " (Isa. i. 27). " *Jehovah of hosts shall be exalted in judgment, and God that is holy shall be sanctified in justice* " (Isa. v. 16). " *Let him that glorieth glory in this, that . . . Jehovah exerciseth judgment and justice in the earth* " (Jer. ix. 24). " *Execute ye judgment and justice. . . . Woe unto him that buildeth his house without justice, and his chambers without judgment. . . . Did not thy father . . . do judgment and justice, and then it was well with him?* " (Jer. xxii. 3, 13, 15). " *I will raise unto David a righteous Branch, and a King shall reign, . . . and shall execute judgment and justice in the earth* " (Jer. xxiii. 5; xxxiii. 15). . . . The reason why judgment and justice are so often mentioned is that judgment is predicated of truths, and justice of good; and therefore also to execute judgment and justice means to act from truth and from good. The reason why judgment is predicated of truth, and justice of good, is that the government of the Lord in the spiritual kingdom is called judgment, and the government of the Lord in the celestial kingdom is called justice. . . .

That these repetitions, as it were of the same thing, in the Word, are on account of the marriage of good and truth, may be more clearly seen in places where nations and peoples are mentioned; as in the following: "*Ah! sinful nation, a people laden with iniquity*" (Isa. i. 4). . . . "*Jehovah will destroy . . . the covering over all peoples and the vail over all nations*" (Isa. xxv. 7). "*Come near, ye nations, . . . and hearken, ye people*" (Isa. xxxiv. 1). "*I have called thee, . . . for a covenant of the people, for a light of the nations*" (Isa. xlii. 6). "*Let all the nations be gathered together, and let the people be assembled*" (Isa. xliii. 9). "*Behold, I will lift up my hand to the nations, and set up my standard to the people*" (Isa. xlix. 22). . . . The reason why nations and peoples are mentioned together is that by nations are meant those who are in good, and in the opposite sense those who are in evil, and by people those who are in truths, and in the opposite sense those who are in falsities. For this reason they who are of the Lord's spiritual kingdom are called peoples, and they who are of his celestial kingdom are called nations. For in the spiritual kingdom all are in truths, and thence in wisdom; and in the celestial kingdom all are in good, and thence in love.

It is the same with the other expressions, as that where joy is mentioned, gladness also is mentioned; as in these passages: "*Behold joy and gladness, slay the ox*" (Isa. xxii. 13). "*They shall obtain joy and gladness, and sorrow and sighing shall flee away*" (Isa. xxxv. 10; li. 11). . . . "*Joy and gladness shall be found in Zion, thanksgiving and the voice of melody*" (Isa. li. 3). "*And thou shalt have joy and gladness, and many shall rejoice at His birth*" (Luke i. 14). "*Then will I cause to cease, . . . the voice of joy and the voice of gladness, the voice of the bridegroom and the voice of the bride*" (Jer. vii. 34; xvi. 9; xxv. 10). "*Again there shall be heard in this place . . . the voice of joy and the voice of gladness, the voice of the bridegroom and the voice of the bride*" (Jer. xxxiii. 10, 11). And in other places. Both joy and gladness are spoken of because joy is of good, and gladness of truth; or joy is of love, and gladness of wisdom. For joy is of the heart, and gladness of the spirit; or joy is of the will, and gladness of the understanding. It is also evident that there is a marriage of the Lord and the church in these expressions, from the fact that it is said, "*The voice of joy and the voice of gladness, the voice of the bridegroom and the voice of the bride*" (Jer. vii. 34; xvi. 9; xxv. 10; xxxiii. 10, 11); and the Lord is the Bridegroom, and the church the bride. That the Lord is the Bridegroom may be seen in Matt. ix. 15; Mark ii. 19, 20; Luke v. 35; and that the church is the bride may be seen in Apoc. xxi. 2, 9; xxii. 17. Therefore John the Baptist said of Jesus, "*He that hath the bride is the Bridegroom*" (John iii. 29). (*ib.* n. 84-87.)

Doctrine should be drawn from the Literal Sense of the Word, and confirmed by it.

The reason of this is, that the Lord is present therein, and teaches and enlightens; for the Lord never performs any of His operations except in fulness, and the Word is in its fulness in the literal sense, as was shown above. Hence it is that doctrine should be drawn from the sense of the letter. The doctrine of genuine truth can also be drawn entirely from the literal sense of the Word; for the Word in that sense is as a man clothed, whose face is bare, and whose hands also are bare. All things which concern the faith and life of man and consequently his salvation are naked therein, but the rest are clothed. And in many places where they are clothed they appear through, as objects to a woman through a thin veil of silk before her face. As the truths of the Word are multiplied from the love of them, and as by this they are arranged in order, they also shine and appear more and more clearly.

It may be supposed that the doctrine of genuine truth can be acquired by the spiritual sense of the Word, which is given through the knowledge of correspondences; but doctrine is not acquired, but only illustrated and corroborated by that sense; for, as was said before, by some correspondences that are known a man may falsify the Word, by connecting and applying them to confirm that which inheres in his mind from a principle assumed. Besides, the spiritual sense is not given to any one except by the Lord alone; and it is guarded by Him as the angelic heaven is guarded, for this is within it. (T. C. R. n. 229, 230.)

Appearances of Truth in the Letter of the Word.

Truths Divine themselves are such that they can never be comprehended by any angel, still less by any man; they exceed every faculty of their understanding. Yet that there may be a conjunction of the Lord with men, truths Divine flow in with them into appearances; when they are in appearances they can both be received and acknowledged. This is effected adequately to the comprehension of every one; therefore appearances, that is truths angelic and human, are of a threefold degree. (A. C. n. 3362.)

If man were not instructed by appearances he would never suffer himself to be instructed at all; what is contrary to the appearance he does not believe nor comprehend, unless late in life when his judgment is ripened and he is gifted with the faith of charity. (*ib.* n. 1838.)

Many things in the Word, and more than any one could believe, are spoken according to appearances, and according to the fallacies of the senses; as where it is said that Jehovah is in wrath, anger, and fury, against the wicked; that He rejoices to destroy them and blot them out; yea, that He slays them. But these things were said that persuasions and evil lusts might not be broken, but bent; for to speak otherwise than as man conceives,—that is according to appearances, fallacies, and persuasions,—would have been to sow seed in the water, and to say that which would instantly be rejected. But yet these forms of speech may serve as common vessels within which there are things spiritual and celestial; for it can be insinuated into them that all things are from the Lord; afterwards that the Lord permits, but that all evil is from diabolical spirits; then that the Lord provides and disposes that evils may be turned into good; and finally that nothing but good is from the Lord. Thus the sense of the letter vanishes as it ascends, and the sense becomes spiritual, afterwards celestial, and at last Divine. (*ib.* n. 1874.)

Rational human truth does not comprehend things Divine, because these are above the sphere of its understanding. For this truth communicates with the knowledges that are in the natural man; and in so far as it looks from these at the things above itself it does not acknowledge them. For this truth is in appearances which it cannot put off; and appearances are those [forms] which are from things of sense, which induce a belief as if things Divine themselves were also such,—when yet these are removed from all appearances,—and when they are spoken of this rational truth cannot believe them, because it cannot comprehend them. For example: when it is said that man has no life but what is from the Lord, the rational supposes from appearances that then man cannot live as of himself; when yet he then first truly lives when he perceives that his life is from the Lord. The rational, from appearances, supposes the good that a man does is from himself; when yet there is nothing of good from himself but from the Lord. The rational, from appearances, believes that a man merits salvation when he does good; when yet of himself a man can merit nothing, but all merit is the Lord's. From appearances man supposes that when he is withheld from evil and kept in good by the Lord, there is nothing with him but what is good and just, yea, and holy; when yet in man there is nothing but what is evil, unjust, and profane. From appearances man thinks that when he does good from charity he does it from the voluntary part in him, when yet it is not from his voluntary but from his intellectual part, in which charity has been implanted. From appearances man conceives that there can be no glory without the glory of the world; when yet in the glory of heaven there is nothing at all of the glory of the world. From appearances man believes that no one can love his neighbour more than himself, but that all love begins from himself; when yet in heavenly love there is nothing of the love of self. From appearances man thinks there can be no light but what is from the light of the world; when in the heavens there is nothing of the light of the world, and yet so great light that it exceeds a thousand times the mid-day light of the world. From appearances man thinks the Lord cannot shine as a sun before the universal heaven; when yet all the light of heaven is from Him. From appearances man cannot conceive that there are progressions in the other life; when yet they appear to themselves to progress just as men on earth,—as in their habitations, courts and paradises; still less can he comprehend if it be said that these are changes of state, which so appear. From appearances man cannot conceive that spirits and angels—since they are invisible to the [bodily] eyes—can be seen, nor that they can speak with man; when yet they appear to the internal sight, or the sight of the spirit, more visibly than man to man on earth; and in like manner their speech is also more distinctly heard. Besides thousands of thousands of such things which man's rational [faculty] from its own light (*lumen*), born of sensual things and thereby darkened, can never believe. Yea, even in natural things themselves the rational is dim-sighted; for instance, in that it cannot comprehend how the inhabitants directly opposite to us can stand upon their feet and walk; and in very many other things. What then must it not be in things spiritual and celestial, which are far above the natural? (*ib.* n. 2196.)

There are however degrees of the appearances of truth. Natural appearances of truth are for the most part fallacies, but when they are with those who are in good they ought not to be called fallacies, but appearances, and even in some respect truths; for the good that is in them, and in which the Divine is, effects that they have a different essence. But rational appearances of truth are more and more interior; the heavens are in these appearances,—that is, the angels who are in the heavens. (*ib.* n. 3207.)

There are also some things that appear like contradictions; and yet there is no contradiction in the Word viewed in its own light. (S. S. n. 51.)

GENUINE TRUTH IN THE LITERAL SENSE OF THE WORD, WHICH THE TRUTH OF DOCTRINE MUST BE, APPEARS ONLY TO THOSE WHO ARE IN ENLIGHTENMENT FROM THE LORD.

Enlightenment is from the Lord alone, and is with thosewho love truths because they are truths, and apply them to the uses of life; with others there is no enlightenment in the Word. That enlightenment is from the Lord alone is because the Word is from Him, and therefore He is in it; that it is with those who love truths because they are truths and apply them to the uses of life, is because they are in the Lord and the Lord is in them. For the Lord is the Truth itself; and the Lord is loved when man lives according to His Divine truths; thus when uses are performed from them,—according to these words in John: " *In that day ye shall know that . . . ye are in Me, and I in you. He that hath My commandments, and doeth them, he it is that loveth Me; . . . and I will love Him, and will manifest Myself to him; . . . and I will come unto him, and make an abode with him*" (xiv. 20, 21, 23). These are they who are in enlightenment when they read the Word, and to whom the Word is bright and translucent. The reason why the Word to them is bright and translucent is that in the least parts of the Word there is a spiritual and a celestial sense, and these senses are in the light of heaven; and therefore through these senses and their light the Lord flows in into the natural sense of the Word, and into the light of this with man. Hence, from an interior perception, man acknowledges the truth, and then sees it in his thought; and this as often as he is in the affection of truth for the sake of truth. For perception comes from affection, and thought from perception; and thus the acknowledgment is produced which is called faith. (T. C. R. n. 231.)

Since few know how it is with the influx of Divine truth, and enlightenment thence with man, it is permitted here to say something on these subjects. It is known in the church that the good of love and the truth of faith is all not from man, but is with him out of heaven, from the Divine there; and that they are in enlightenment who receive this. But the influx and enlightenment are effected in this manner: Man is such that as to his interiors, which are of the thought and will, he can look downwards and can look upwards. To look downwards is to look outwards, into the world and to himself; and to look upwards is to look inwards, to heaven and to God. Man looks outwards, which is called downwards, of himself; since when he looks of himself he looks to hell. But man looks inwards not of himself but of the Lord; this is called upwards because as to his interiors which are of the will and the understanding he is then elevated by the Lord to heaven, and so to the Lord. The interiors are in fact actually elevated; and then are actually withdrawn from the body and from the world. When this is effected the interiors of man actually come into heaven, and into its light and heat. Hence he receives influx and enlightenment; the light of heaven illuminates his understanding,—for that light is Divine truth, which proceeds from the Lord as a sun; and the heat of heaven enkindles his will,—for that heat is the good of love, which at the same time proceeds from the Lord as a sun. As man is then among the angels there is communicated to him from them, that is through them from the Lord, the intelligence of truth and the affection of good. It is this communication which is called influx and enlightenment. But it should be known that influx and enlightenment are effected according to the faculty of reception in man; and the faculty of reception is according to his love of truth and of good. They therefore are elevated who are in the love of truth and of good for the sake of truth and good, as ends. (A. C. n. 10,330.)

How Heretical Opinions are derived from the Letter of the Word.

Many things in the Word are appearances of truth, and not naked truths; and many things are written according to the apprehensions of the natural, yea the sensual man, and yet so that the simple can understand them simply, the intelligent intelligently, and the wise wisely. Now such being the Word, appearances of truth, which are truths clothed, may be taken for naked truths; which when they are confirmed become falsities. But this is done by those who believe themselves to be wise above others, when in fact they are not wise; for it is wise to see whether a thing be true before it is confirmed, and not to confirm whatever one pleases. This they do who have a strong inclination for confirming and are in the pride of their own intelligence; but they do the former who love truths and are affected by them because they are truths, and who apply them to the uses of life. For these are enlightened of the Lord, and see truths by their own light; but the others are enlightened from themselves, and see falsities by the light of falsities.

That appearances of truth, which are truths clothed can be

taken for naked truths from the Word, and that when confirmed they become falsities, is evident from the many heresies there have been, and are still in Christendom. Heresies themselves do not condemn men, but an evil life with confirmations of the falsities which are in heresy, from the Word and by reasonings from the natural man, condemn. For every one is born into the religion of his parents, from infancy is initiated into it, and afterwards retains it; nor is he able of his own power, on account of his occupations in the world, to extricate himself from its falsities. But to live wickedly, and to confirm falsities to the destruction of genuine truths, this condemns. For he who remains in his religion and believes in God,—and if within the pale of Christianity believes in the Lord, esteems the Word holy, and from a religious motive lives according to the commandments of the Decalogue, does not bind himself in falsities; and therefore when he hears truths and in his own way perceives them, he can embrace them, and so be withdrawn from falsities. But not so he who has confirmed the falsities of his religion; because falsity confirmed remains, and cannot be extirpated. For falsity after confirmation is as if a man were sworn in it,—especially if it coheres with the love of what is his own, and hence with the pride of his own wisdom. (S. S. n. 91, 92.)

The nature of the power of persuading and of confirming any heresy whatsoever out of the Word is known in the Christian world from the prevalence of so many heresies, every one of which is confirmed and so made persuasive from the literal sense of the Word. The reason is that the literal sense of the Word is accommodated to the apprehension of the simple, and therefore consists in great part of appearances of truth, and appearances of truth are of such a nature that they may be brought to confirm everything that is assumed by any one as a principle of religion, and thence of doctrine, thus even what is false. On this account they who place genuine truth itself in the literal sense of the Word only may fall into many mistakes, if they are not in enlightenment from the Lord and in that enlightenment form doctrine for themselves, which may serve as a lamp to guide them. In the literal sense of the Word there are both naked truths and truths clothed; the latter are appearances of truth, and the appearances cannot otherwise be understood than from those places where naked truths stand forth, from which doctrine may be formed by one enlightened by the Lord, and the rest explained according to it. Hence it is that they who read the Word without doctrine are carried away into manifold errors. (A. E. n. 816.)

No one can know the Divine truths in the literal sense of the Word except by means of doctrine therefrom. If a man has not doctrine for a lamp he is carried away into errors, whithersoever the obscurity of his understanding and the delight of his will leads and draws him. The doctrine which should be for a lamp is what the internal sense teaches;[1] thus it is the internal sense itself, which in some measure lies open to every one who is in the external from the internal, that is, with whom the internal man is open,—although he does not know what the internal sense is ; for heaven, which is in the internal sense of the Word, flows into that man when he reads the Word, enlightens him, and gives him perception, and so teaches him.　(A. C. n. 10,400.)

That doctrinals are derived from the Word does not make them Divine truths; for any doctrinal whatever may be taken out of the literal sense of the Word.　Even such a thing may be seized upon as favours concupiscences, and thus falsity be taken for truth; as in the case of the doctrinals of the Jews, of the Socinians, and of many others.　But not so if the doctrinal be formed from the internal sense.　The internal sense is not only that sense which lies hidden within the external sense ; but also which results from many passages of the literal sense rightly compared with each other ; and is apperceived by those who as to their intellectual [faculty] are enlightened by the Lord.　For the enlightened intellectual [faculty] discerns between apparent truths and real truths, especially between falsities and truths, although it does not judge of real truths in themselves.　But the intellectual [faculty] cannot be enlightened unless it is believed that love to the Lord and charity towards the neighbour are the principal and essential [doctrines] of the church.　He who proceeds from these [doctrines] acknowledged, *if only he be in them,* sees unfolded to him innumerable truths, yea, very many mysteries; and this from interior acknowledgment according to the degree of enlightenment from the Lord.　(*ib.* n. 7233.)

Which are the Books of the Word.

The books of the Word are all those that have an internal sense ; and those that have not are not the Word.　The books of the Word in the Old Testament are the five books of Moses, the book of Joshua, the book of Judges, the two books of Samuel, the two books of the Kings, the Psalms of David, the Prophets, Isaiah, Jeremiah, the Lamentations, Ezekiel, Daniel, Hosea, Joel, Amos,

---

[1] That is, in those parts of the Word where the internal sense is uncovered, and to the enlightened mind appears in the letter, or where the literal sense coincides with and teaches the doctrine of the internal sense.　This teaching is quite consistent with that given elsewhere (p. 117) that "all doctrine ought to be drawn from the letter of the Word, and confirmed by it."　See also note on p. 409.

Obadiah, Jonah, Micah, Nahum, Habakkuk, Zephaniah, Haggai, Zechariah, Malachi; and in the New Testament, the four Evangelists, Matthew, Mark, Luke, John, and the Apocalypse. (A. C. n. 10,325.)

The Character of the Apostolic Writings.

With regard to the writings of St. Paul and the other Apostles, I have not given them a place in my ARCANA CŒLESTIA, because they are dogmatic writings merely, and not written in the style of the Word, like those of the Prophets, of David, of the Evangelists, and the Revelation of St. John. The style of the Word consists throughout of correspondences, and thence effects an immediate communication with heaven; but the style of these dogmatic writings is quite different, having indeed communication with heaven, but only mediate or indirect. The reason why the Apostles wrote in this style was that the Christian church was then to begin through them; and the style that is used in the Word would not have been suitable for such doctrinal tenets, which required plain and simple language, adapted to the capacities of all readers. Nevertheless the writings of the Apostles are excellent books for the church, since they insist on the doctrine of charity, and faith thence; as the Lord Himself has done in the Gospels and in the Revelation of St. John, which will clearly appear to any one who studies these writings with attention. (Letter to Dr. Beyer. Also A. E. n. 815.)

Four Different Styles in the Word.

There are in general four different styles in the Word. The first was that of the Most Ancient Church. Their mode of expression was such that when they mentioned terrestrial and worldly things they thought of the spiritual and celestial things which they represented. They therefore not only expressed themselves by representatives, but also formed them into a certain *quasi* historical series, that they might be the more living, which was to them in the highest degree delightful. This style was meant when Hannah prophesied, saying, " *Speak ye what is high, high, let what is ancient come forth out of your mouth* " (1 Sam. ii. 3). These representatives are called by David " dark sayings of old " (Psalm lxxviii. 2). The particulars concerning the creation, and the garden of Eden, etc., down to the time of Abram, Moses had from the descendants of the Most Ancient Church. The second style is historical, which is found in the books of Moses from the time of Abram, and onwards to Joshua, Judges, Samuel, and the Kings; in which the historical events are precisely as they appear in the sense of the letter, and yet they all and each contain quite other things in the internal sense; of which, by the Divine mercy of the Lord, in their order in the following pages. The third style is prophetical, and was born of the style of the Most Ancient Church, which was greatly revered. But it is not connected and *quasi* historical, like the most ancient, but broken and even scarcely intelligible except in the internal sense; wherein are the pro-foundest mysteries, which follow each other in beautiful con-nected order, and relate to the internal and external man; to the many states of the church; to heaven itself; and in the inmost sense to the Lord. The fourth is that of the Psalms of David; which is intermediate between the prophetical style and that of common speech. The Lord is there treated of in the internal sense under the person of David as a king. (A. C. n. 66.)

The Word of the Old Testament.

No mortal conceives from the letter that the Word of the Old Testament contains the mysteries of heaven; and that all and everything therein relates to the Lord, His heaven, the Church, faith, and things that belong to faith. For from the letter, or the sense of the letter, no one perceives anything but that in general they relate to the externals of the Jewish church; and yet there are everywhere internal things which do not appear at all in the external, save a very few which the Lord revealed and explained to the Apostles; as that the sacrifices are significative of the Lord; and that the land of Canaan and Jerusalem—like-wise Paradise—signify heaven; and therefore they are called the heavenly Canaan and Jerusalem.

But that each and all things, yea, the very least, even to the smallest iota, signify and involve spiritual and celestial things, is to this day profoundly unknown to the Christian world, and therefore it pays little attention to the Old Testament. Yet they might know this from a single consideration; that since the Word is the Lord's and from the Lord, it could not but be that it inwardly contains such things as relate to heaven, to the church, and to faith. Otherwise it could not be called the Word of the Lord, nor be said to have any life within it. For whence is its life, but from those things which are of life? that is, but from the fact that each and all things therein have re-lation to the Lord, who is the veriest Life? Whatever therefore has not regard interiorly to Him has not life. Nay, whatever

expression in the Word does not involve Him, or in its manner
relate to Him, is not Divine. (A. C. n. 1, 2.)

THE APOCALYPSE.

Not a single verse of the Apocalypse could be revealed except
by the Lord. (C. L. n. 532.)

The Apocalypse does not treat of the successive states of the
church, much less of the successive states of kingdoms as some
have hitherto believed, but from beginning to end it treats of
the last state of the church in heaven and on earth; and of
the last judgment; and after this of the New Church which is
the New Jerusalem. (A. R. n. 2.)

" *Things which must shortly come to pass*" (Rev. i. 1), signifies
that they will certainly be, lest the church should perish. By
must shortly come to pass it is not meant that the things foretold
in the Apocalypse will immediately and speedily occur, but certainly; and that unless they do the church must perish. In the
Divine idea, and therefore in the spiritual sense, there is no
time, but instead of time there is state; and as shortly is of
time it signifies certainly, and that it will be before its time.
For the Apocalypse was given in the first century, and seventeen
centuries have now passed; from which it is clear that by shortly
that which corresponds to it must be signified, which is certainly.
Quite the same is also involved in these words of the Lord:
" *Except those days should be shortened, there should no flesh be
saved; but for the elect's sake, those days shall be shortened*" (Matt.
xxiv. 22). By this also it is meant that unless the church should
come to an end before its time it would utterly perish. In that
chapter the consummation of the age and the Lord's coming are
treated of; and by the consummation of the age the last state of
the old church is meant, and by the Lord's coming, the first state
of the new. It was said that in the Divine idea there is no time,
but the presence of all things past and future. Therefore it is
said by David, " *A thousand years in Thy sight are but as yesterday*" (Psalm xc. 4); and again: " *I will declare the decree, Jehovah
hath said unto me, Thou art My Son, this day have I begotten
Thee*" (Psalm ii. 7): " this day" is the presence of the Lord's
advent. Hence it is too that an entire period is called a day in
the Word, and its first state is called the dawning and the morning, and its last evening and night. (*ib.* n. 4.)

" *John to the seven churches*" (ver. 4), signifies, to all who are
in the Christian world where the Word is and by means of it the
Lord is known, and who draw near to the church. Seven
churches are not meant by the seven churches, but all in the

Christian world who are of the church. For numbers in the Word signify things, and seven signify all things and all men [*omnia et omnes*], and therefore also what is full and perfect; and this number occurs in the Word where it treats of a thing that is holy, and in the opposite sense of a thing that is profane. This number therefore involves what is holy, and in the opposite sense what is profane. The reason why numbers signify things, or rather that they are as a kind of adjectives to substantives, denoting some quality in things, is that number in itself is natural; for natural things are determined by numbers, but spiritual by things and their states. He therefore who does not know the signification of numbers in the Word, and especially in the Apocalypse, cannot know many mysteries that are contained therein. Now, as seven signify all things and all men, it is plain that by the seven churches all are meant who are in the Christian world where the Word is, and by means of it the Lord is known. These, if they live according to the Lord's precepts in the Word, constitute the very church.

" *Which are in Asia*" (ver. 4), signifies, to those who are in the light of truth from the Word. Since by all names of persons and places in the Word things of heaven and the church are meant, as was said before, so therefore by Asia, and by the names of the seven churches therein, as will appear from what follows. The reason why those who are in the light of truth from the Word are meant by Asia is, that the Most Ancient Church, and after that the Ancient, and then the Israelitish church, were in Asia; and that the Ancient Word, and afterwards the Israelitish Word, was with them; and all the light of truth is from the Word. (*ib.* n. 10, 11.)

" *I was in the island called Patmos*" (ver. 9), signifies a state and place in which he could be enlightened. The reason why the Revelation to John was made in Patmos was that it was an island of Greece, not very far from the Land of Canaan, and between Asia and Europe; and by islands are signified nations more remote from the worship of God, but yet which will draw near to it, because they are capable of being enlightened. The same is signified by Greece, but the Church itself is signified by the Land of Canaan; by Asia those of the Church who are in the light of truth from the Word; and by Europe those to whom the Word is about to come. Hence it is that by the isle of Patmos is signified a state and place in which he could be enlightened. (*ib.* n. 34.)

" *What thou seest write in a book*" (ver. 11). It is evident without explanation that this signifies that it was revealed for posterity.

" *And send to the churches, to those which are in Asia*," signifies for those in the Christian world who are in the light of truth from the Word. That these are meant by the churches in Asia, see above.

" *Unto Ephesus and Smyrna, and Pergamos and Thyatira, and Sardis and Philadelphia, and Laodicea,*" signifies according to the state of reception of each in particular. For John when this was commanded him was in a spiritual state, and in that state nothing is called by name which does not signify a thing or state. These things which were written by John were therefore not sent to any church in those places, but were told to their angels, by whom are meant those who receive. (*ib.* n. 39-41.)

THE WORD IS IN ALL THE HEAVENS, AND THE WISDOM OF THE ANGELS IS DERIVED FROM IT.

It has been unknown hitherto that the Word is in the heavens, nor could it be made known so long as the church did not know that angels and spirits are men similar to men in the world; and that they have similar attributes to men in every respect, with the only difference that they are spiritual, and that all things with them are from a spiritual origin; while men in the earth are natural, and all things with them are from a natural origin. So long as this knowledge lay concealed it could not be known that the Word is also in the heavens, and that it is read by the angels there, and also by the spirits who are below the heavens. (S. S. n. 70.)

A copy of the Word written by angels inspired by the Lord is kept with every larger society, in its sacred place, lest as to any jot it should be changed elsewhere. (*ib.* n. 72.)

The angels themselves confess that all the wisdom they have is through the Word; for in proportion to their understanding of the Word they are in light. The light of heaven is Divine wisdom, which appears as light before their eyes. In the sacred place where the copy of the Word is kept there is a white and flaming light exceeding every degree of light which is outside of it in heaven. The reason is the same that was mentioned above, that the Lord is in the Word. (*ib.* n. 73).

THE HISTORICAL PARTS OF THE WORD WERE GIVEN ESPECIALLY FOR CHILDREN.

The Word was given that heaven and earth may be united, or angels united with men; on which account it was so written that by the angels it may be apprehended spiritually while by man it is apprehended naturally, and that a holy influence may thus flow in through the angels, by which the union is effected. Such is the Word both in the historical and the prophetical parts; but the internal sense less appears in the historical parts than in the prophetical, because the historical parts are written in another style, but still by significatives. The historical parts were given that children and youth may be initiated thereby into the reading of the Word; for they are delightful to them, and are retained in their minds; and through these communication is thus given them with the heavens, which communication is grateful, because they are in a state of innocence and mutual love. This is the reason that the historical Word was given. (A. C. n. 6333.)

As regards the cognitions of external or corporeal truth which are from collateral good,—and, as was said, contain within them what is Divine, and so can admit genuine goods,—such as are with infant children who are afterwards regenerated, in general they are such as those of the historical portions of the Word; as what is therein said of paradise, of the first man there, of the tree of life in its midst, and of the tree of knowledge where the serpent was that deceived. These are cognitions which have within them what is Divine, and admit into them goods and truths spiritual and celestial, because they represent and signify them. Such cognitions also are the other things in the historical portions of the Word, as what is said of the tabernacle and the temple, and of the construction of them; in like manner what is said of the garments of Aaron and of his sons, and also of the feasts, of tabernacles, of the first-fruits of the harvest, and of unleavened bread, and other such things. When these and such like things are known and thought of by an infant child, then the angels who are with him think of the Divine things which they represent and signify; and as the angels are affected by them their affection is communicated, and causes the delight and pleasure which the child derives from them, and prepares his mind to receive genuine truths and goods. (*ib.* n. 3665.)

DELIGHTFUL PERCEPTION BY ANGELS OF THE INTERNAL SENSE OF THE WORD WHEN DEVOUTLY READ BY MEN.

When the Word of the Lord is read by a man who loves the Word and lives in charity, and even by a man who in simplicity of heart believes what is written, and has formed no principles contrary to the truth of faith which is in the internal sense, it is displayed by the Lord to the angels in such beauty and in such pleasantness—with representatives also, and this with ineffable variety according to their every state in which they then are—that they perceive the least particulars as it were to live. This is the life that is in the Word, and from which the Word had birth when it was sent down from heaven. From this cause the Word of the Lord is such that, though it appears rude in the letter yet within it are stored things spiritual and celestial, which are manifested before good spirits and angels when it is read by man. (A. C. n. 1767.)

And especially when the Word is read by Children.

It may seem a paradox, but yet it is most true, that the angels better and more fully understand the internal sense of the Word when little boys and girls read it, than when it is read by adults who are not in the faith of charity. The reason stated to me is, that little children are in a state of mutual love and innocence, so that their vessels are extremely tender, almost celestial, and merely faculties of reception, which therefore are capable of being disposed by the Lord,—although this does not come to their perception except by a certain delight according to their genius. It is said by the angels that the Word of the Lord is a dead letter, but that in reading it is vivified by the Lord according to the capability of every one, and that it becomes living according to the life of charity and the state of innocence, and this with endless variety. (A. C. n. 1776.)

By means of the Word Light is communicated to the Nations out of the Church.

There can be no conjunction with heaven unless there be somewhere on the earth a church where the Word is and where by means of it the Lord is known, for the Lord is God of heaven and earth, and without Him there is no salvation. It is sufficient that there be a church where the Word is, though it consist of comparatively few. Through this the Lord is yet present everywhere in the whole earth, for thereby heaven is conjoined with the human race.

But it shall be explained how the presence and conjunction of the Lord and of heaven in every land is effected by means of the Word. The universal heaven before the Lord is as one man; so likewise is the church. The church where the Word is read and where thereby the Lord is known is as the heart and as the lungs in that man; the celestial kingdom as the heart, and the spiritual kingdom as the lungs. Just as from these two fountains of life in the human body all the other members and

viscera subsist and live, so also do all those in every part of the
world with whom there is a religion, and who worship one God
and live a good life, and thereby are in that man, and belong to
its members and viscera without the thorax, where the heart
and lungs are, subsist and live from the conjunction of the Lord
and heaven with the church by means of the Word. For the
Word in the church, although it exists with few comparatively, is life from the Lord through heaven to all the rest; just
as the life of the members and viscera of the whole body is from
the heart and lungs. There is also a similar communication.
This too is the reason why the Christians among whom the
Word is read constitute the breast of that man. They are indeed
in the centre of all; and around them are the Papists; and around
these are the Mahometans, who acknowledge the Lord as a very
great prophet and as a son of God. After these come the
Africans; and the nations and peoples in Asia and the Indies
form the outermost circumference. Moreover, all who are in
that man look towards the centre where Christians are.[1]

The greatest light is in the centre, where the Christians are
who are in possession of the Word; for the light in the heavens
is Divine Truth proceeding from the Lord as the sun there; and
because the Word is that Divine Truth the greatest light is with
those who have the Word. From thence as from its centre it diffuses itself around to all the circumferences, even to the outermost; hence the enlightenment of the nations and peoples out of
the church also is by means of the Word. (S. S. n. 104-106.)

The same may be illustrated by this experience. There were
with me certain African spirits from Abyssinia. On a certain
occasion their ears were opened, that they might hear singing in
some church in the world from a Psalm of David. They were
affected by it with such delight that they joined their voices
with those who sung. But presently their ears were closed, so that
they could not hear anything from thence; and then they were
affected with still greater delight because it was spiritual, and
were at the same time filled with intelligence, for that psalm
treated of the Lord and of redemption. The reason of their
increased delight was, that communication was granted them
with the society in heaven which was in conjunction with those
who were singing that psalm in the world. From this and much
other experience it was evident to me that there is communication with the universal heaven through the Word. For this
reason, by the Divine providence of the Lord, there is universal
intercourse of the kingdoms of Europe—especially of those in
which the Word is read—with the nations out of the church.
(*ib.* n. 108.)

---

[1] See note, p. 417.

From all this it may be seen that the Word which is in the church of the Reformed enlightens all nations and peoples through spiritual communication; and that it is provided of the Lord that there shall always be a church on earth where the Word is read and by means of it the Lord is known. When therefore the Word was almost rejected by the Papists, through the Divine providence of the Lord the Reformation took place, and the Word in consequence was again received; and also the Word is accounted holy by a celebrated nation among the Papists. (*ib.* n. 110.)

It has been granted me to know by much experience that man has communication with heaven by means of the Word. While I was reading the Word, from the first chapter of Isaiah to the last of Malachi, and the Psalms of David, it was given me to perceive clearly that each verse communicates with some society in heaven, and that thus the whole Word communicates with the universal heaven. (*ib.* n. 113.)

REVELATION AND INSPIRATION.

All revelation is either from discourse with angels through whom the Lord speaks or from perception. It should be known that they who are in good and thence in truth, especially those that are in the good of love to the Lord, have revelation from perception; but those who are not in good and thence in truth, though they may indeed have revelations, yet not from perception, but by a living voice heard within them, thus by angels from the Lord. This revelation is external, but the former is internal. The angels, especially the celestial angels, have revelation from perception; and so had the men of the Most Ancient Church, and some also of the Ancient Church; but scarcely any one has this at the present day. But very many have had revelations from speech, without perception, even who have not been in good; likewise by visions, or by dreams. Such were most of the revelations of the prophets in the Jewish church; they heard a voice, saw a vision, or dreamed a dream. But as they had no perception the revelations were merely verbal or visual, without discernment of what they signified. For genuine perception comes through heaven from the Lord, and spiritually affects the intellectual faculty, and leads it perceptibly to think just as the thing really is, with an internal assent the source of which he is ignorant of. He supposes it is in itself, and that it flows from the connection of things; but it is a dictate through heaven from the Lord, flowing into the interiors of the thought, concerning such things as are above the natural and the sensual; that is concerning such things as are of the spiritual world, or heaven. From these statements it may be seen what revelation from perception is. (A. C. n. 5121.)

I have been informed how the Lord spake with the prophets through whom the Word was given. He did not speak with them as with the ancients, by an influx into their interiors, but by spirits who were sent to them, whom the Lord filled with His aspect, and thus inspired the words which they dictated to the prophets; so that it was not influx but dictation. And as the words came forth immediately from the Lord they are therefore severally filled with the Divine, and contain within them an internal sense; which is such that the angels of heaven perceive them in a celestial and a spiritual sense, while men understand them in the natural sense. Thus has the Lord conjoined heaven and the world by means of the Word. It has also been shown me how spirits are filled with the Divine from the Lord by aspect. The spirit filled with the Divine from the Lord does not know but that he is the Lord, and that it is the Divine which speaks; and this so long as he is speaking. Afterwards he apperceives and acknowledges that he is a spirit, and that he did not speak from himself but from the Lord. It is because such was the state of the spirits who spoke with the prophets that it is even said by them, that Jehovah spake. The spirits also called themselves Jehovah, as may be seen not only from the prophetical, but also from the historical parts of the Word. (H. H. n. 254.)

The Prophets wrote as the spirit from the Divine dictated; for the very words which they wrote were uttered in their ears. (A. C. n. 7055.)

It is known from the Word that there was an influx from the world of spirits and from heaven into the Prophets, partly by dreams, partly by visions, and partly by speech; and also with some into the speech itself, and into their very gestures, thus into those things which are of the body; and that then they did not speak from themselves nor act from themselves, but from the spirits which then occupied their body. Some of them then acted as if insane; as Saul, in that he lay naked; others, in that they wounded themselves; others, in putting horns upon them; and many such things. (*ib.* n. 6212.)

The world, even the learned, have hitherto considered that the historical parts of the Word are only histories; and that they involve nothing more interior. And yet they say that every jot is Divinely inspired. But they mean nothing more by this than that these histories were revealed, and that something dogmatic applicable to the doctrine of faith may be deduced from them and be of use to those who teach and to those who learn; and that because they are Divinely inspired therefore they have a Divine power over their minds, and are effective of good beyond all other history. But the histories in themselves regarded effect little for the amendment of a man; and nothing for his eternal life. For in the other life the histories are passed into oblivion. For example, of what use would it be there to know that Hagar was a servant maid, and that she was given to Abram by Sarai? to know about Ishmael? or even about Abram? Nothing but the things which are of the Lord and which are from the Lord are necessary for souls, that they may enter into heaven, and rejoice in its joy, that is in eternal life. For these the Word exists; and these are what are contained in its interiors.

Inspiration implies that in the least particulars of the Word, as in the historical so in the other parts, there are celestial things which are of love or good, and spiritual things which are of faith or truth, and therefore things Divine. For what is inspired by the Lord descends from Him; and indeed through the angelic heaven, and so through the world of spirits down to man, to whom it is presented as it is in the letter. But it is entirely different in its first origin. In heaven there is no worldly history, but all is representative of things Divine; nor is anything else perceived there; as may be known, too, from the fact that the things which are there are ineffable. If therefore the historical particulars are not representative of things Divine and thus heavenly, they cannot be Divinely inspired. (*ib.* n. 1886, 1887.)

PREVIOUS TO THE WORD WHICH NOW EXISTS IN THE WORLD THERE WAS A WORD WHICH IS LOST.

It has been told me by the angels of heaven that there was a Word among the ancients written by pure correspondences, but that it was lost. And they said that this Word was still preserved among them; and was in use in that heaven, among the ancients with whom that Word existed when they were in the world. The ancients among whom that Word is still in use in heaven were in part from the land of Canaan and its confines, —Syria, Mesopotamia, Arabia, Chaldea, Assyria, Egypt, Zidon, Tyre, and Nineveh,—the inhabitants of all which kingdoms were in representative worship, and therefore in the knowledge of correspondences. The wisdom of those times was from that knowledge, and through that they had interior perception and communication with the heavens. Those who knew interiorly the correspondences of that Word were called wise and intelligent, and after that diviners and magi. But because that Word was full of such correspondences as remotely signified celestial and spiritual things, and therefore began to be falsified by many, by the Divine providence of the Lord in process of time it disappeared and was finally lost, and another Word was given written by correspondences less remote, and this through the prophets among the children of Israel. In this Word however many names of places are retained which were in the land of Canaan and round about in Asia, which signify similar things as in the ancient Word. It was for this reason that Abraham was commanded to go into that land, and that his posterity from Jacob were led into it.

It is evident too from Moses that there was a Word among the ancients, by whom it is mentioned and some quotation is made from it (Numb. xxi. 14, 15, 27-30); and that the historical parts of that Word were called the *The Wars of Jehovah*, and the prophetical parts *Enunciations*. From the historical parts of that Word Moses has quoted this: " *Wherefore it is said in The book of the Wars of Jehovah, what He did in the Red Sea, and in the brooks of Arnon, and at the stream of the brooks that goeth down to the dwelling of Ar, and lieth upon the border of Moab*" (Numb. xxi. 14, 15). By the wars of Jehovah in that Word, as in ours, are meant and described the Lord's conflicts with the hells and His victories over them when He should come into the world. The same conflicts are also meant and described in many places in the historical parts of our Word, as in the wars of Joshua with the nations of the land of Canaan, and in the wars of the judges and of the kings of Israel. From the prophetical parts of that Word Moses has taken this passage :—" *Wherefore say the Enunciators, Go unto Heshbon; let the city of Sihon be built and strengthened; for a fire is gone out of Heshbon, a flame from the city of Sihon; it hath consumed Ar of Moab, the possessors of the high places of Arnon. Woe unto thee, Moab! thou art undone, O people of Chemosh! He hath given his sons that escaped and his daughters into captivity unto Sihon, king of the Amorites; we have slain them with darts. Heshbon is perished even unto Dibon, and we have laid waste even unto Nophah, which reacheth unto Medebah*" (Numb. xxi. 27-30). The translators render it, *They that speak in Proverbs*, but they should be called *Enunciators*, and their compositions *Prophetical Enunciations;* as it is evident from the signification of the word *Moshalim* in the Hebrew tongue that they were not merely Proverbs, but in truth Prophetical Enunciations; as in Numb. xxiii. 7, 18, xxiv. 3, 15, where it is said that Balaam uttered his *Enunciation*, which was also a prophecy concerning the Lord. His enunciation is called *Moshal*, in the singular number. It may be added that the passages thence quoted by Moses are not proverbs but prophecies. That that Word likewise was Divine or Divinely inspired is plain from a passage in Jeremiah, where we read nearly the same words: "*A fire is gone forth out of Heshbon, and a flame from the midst of Sihon, and shall devour the corner of Moab, and the crown of the head of the sons of tumult. Woe be unto thee, O Moab! The people of Chemosh perisheth, for thy sons are taken away into captivity and thy daughters into captivity*" (xlviii. 45, 46). Besides these a prophetical book of the ancient Word is also mentioned by David and by Joshua, called *The Book of Jasher*, or the book of the Upright. By David: "*David lamented over Saul and over Jonathan; also he bade them teach the children of Judah the bow: behold it is written in The Book of Jasher*" (2 Sam. i. 17, 18). And by Joshua: *Joshua said . . . Sun, stand thou still upon Gibeon, and thou moon in the valley of Ajalon; . . . is not this written in The Book of Jasher?*" (Josh. x. 12, 13). Moreover, it was told me that the first seven chapters of Genesis are extant in that ancient Word, and that not the least word is wanting. (S. S. n. 102, 103.)

That religion has existed from the most ancient times, and that the inhabitants of the globe everywhere know of God, with something about the life after death, has not been from themselves and from their own acuteness, but from the ancient Word mentioned above, and afterwards from the Israelitish Word. From these religious knowledge was diffused into the Indies and their islands; through Egypt and Ethiopia into the kingdoms of Africa; from the maritime parts of Asia into Greece; and from thence into Italy. But as the Word could not be written otherwise than by representatives,—which are such things in the world as correspond to and hence signify heavenly things,—therefore the religious truths of many nations were converted into idolatrous forms, and in Greece into fables; and the Divine attributes and qualities into as many gods, over which they placed one as supreme, whom they called Jove, from Jehovah. It is well known that they had a knowledge of paradise, of the flood, of the sacred fire, and of the four ages—from the first or golden age to the last or iron age—by which the four states of the church are signified in the Word, as in Daniel ii. 31-35. It is also known that the Mahometan religion, which succeeded and destroyed the previous religions of many nations, was taken from the Word of both Testaments. (*ib.* n. 117.)

The Sin of Profaning the Word and the Holy Things of the Church.

Profanation is the conjunction of Divine truth with falsities from evil; and that conjunction which is profanation does not exist with any but those who have first acknowledged those things which are of the church,—and especially who have acknowledged the Lord,—and afterwards deny them. For by the acknowledgment of the truths of the church, and of the Lord, communication with the heavens is effected, and at the same time the opening of the interiors of man towards heaven; and by denial afterwards a conjunction of the same with falsities from evil takes place. For all things which man acknowledges remain implanted, since nothing with man which has entered by acknowledgment perishes. The state of the man in whom there is profanation is, that he has communication with the heavens, and at the same time with the hells; by truths with the heavens, and by the falsities of evil with the hells. (A. C. n. 10,287.)

Those who are within the church can form principles of falsity in opposition to the very truths of faith, and be imbued with them; but those who are without the church cannot do this, because they do not know the truths of faith. Thus the former can profane holy truths, while the latter cannot. (*ib.* n. 2051.)

The Lord by His Divine Providence continually watches and so disposes that evil may be by itself, and good by itself, and thus that they may be separated; but this cannot be effected if a man first acknowledges the truths of faith and lives according to them, and afterwards recedes from and denies them. . . . Whatever a man thinks, speaks, and does from the will, is appropriated to him and remains. . . . Such things are each and all inscribed on his internal memory; and nothing is wanting. This memory is his book of life, which is opened after death, and according to which he is judged. . . . Good and evil moreover are separated by the Lord after death; with those who are inwardly evil and outwardly good the good is taken away, and they are thus left to their evil. The reverse takes place with those who inwardly are good and outwardly like other men have sought after wealth, have striven for dignities, have found delight in various worldly things, and favoured some concupiscences. With these however good and evil were not mixed, but were separated as the internal and the external; thus in the external form they were like the evil in many things, yet not in the internal. On the other hand, the evil too, who in the external form, in piety, in worship, in speech and actions, have appeared as if good, and yet in the internal form were evil,—with them also evil is separated from good. But with those who have first acknowledged the truths of faith and lived according to them, and have afterwards turned away from and rejected them, and especially if they have denied them, goods and evils are no longer separated, but mingled. For such a man has appropriated good to himself, and has also appropriated evil to himself, and so has conjoined and commingled them. He has so far commingled good and evil that they cannot be separated; and if evil cannot be separated from good and good from evil he can neither be in heaven nor in hell. Every man must be either in the one or in the other; he cannot be in both, for thus he would be sometimes in heaven, and sometimes in hell; and while in heaven he would act in favour of hell, and while in hell he would act in favour of heaven. He would thus destroy the life of all around him, heavenly life among the angels, and infernal life among the devils; whereby the life of every one would perish. For the life of every one must be his own; no one lives in another's life, still less in an opposite one. Hence it is that with every man after death when he becomes a spirit or a spiritual man, the Lord separates good from evil, and evil from good; good from evil with those who inwardly are in evil, and evil from good with those who inwardly are in good; which is according to His words, " *To every one that hath shall be given, and he shall have abundance, and from him that hath not shall be taken away even that he hath* " (Matt. xiii. 12; xxv. 29; Mark iv. 25; Luke viii. 18; xix. 26). As good and evil must be separated in every man, and in such a man cannot be separated, therefore as to everything truly human he is destroyed. The truly human in every one exists from rationality; in that he can see and know, if he will, what is true and what is good; and also in that from liberty he can will, think, speak and do it. But this liberty with its rationality is destroyed with those who have commingled good and evil in themselves; for they cannot from good see evil, nor from evil recognize good, because [in them] they make one. They therefore have no longer rationality in capability or in power, nor consequently any liberty. For this reason they are like mere forms of fantastic delirium; and no more appear like men, but as bones with some covering of skin; and therefore when mentioned they are not called he or she, but it. Such a lot have they who in this manner commingle things holy with profane. But there are many kinds of profanation which are yet not of this character.

No man so profanes holy things who does not know them; for he who does not know them cannot acknowledge and then deny them. They therefore who are outside of the Christian world, and do not know anything about the Lord, and about redemption and salvation by Him, do not profane this holy truth when they do not receive it, nor even when they speak against it. Neither do the Jews themselves profane this holy truth, because from infancy they are not willing to receive and acknowledge it. It would be otherwise if they received and acknowledged and afterwards denied, which however is rarely done;

although many of them outwardly acknowledge it and inwardly deny it, and are like hypocrites. But they profane holy things by commingling them with things profane who first receive and acknowledge, and afterwards turn away from and deny them. That they received and acknowledged in infancy and childhood is of no [such] effect,—every Christian does this,—because they do not then receive and acknowledge the things of faith and charity from any rationality and liberty, that is in the understanding from the will, but only from memory and from confidence in a superior; and if they live according to them it is from blind obedience. But when a man comes into the use of his rationality and liberty, which by degrees he does as he grows up and advances to maturity, if then he acknowledges truths and lives according to them and afterwards denies them, he mingles holy things with profane, and from a man becomes a monster, as described above. But if a man is in evil from the time when he comes into the exercise of his own rationality and liberty, that is until he comes to act of his own right in early manhood, and afterwards acknowledges the truths of faith and lives according to them, if only he then remains in them to the end of life he does not mingle them; for the Lord then separates the evils of his former life from the goods of his after life. This takes place with all who repent.

In the most general sense by profanation is meant all impiety; and therefore by profaners all the impious are meant who in heart deny God, the holiness of the Word, and therefore the spiritual things of the church; which are the holy things themselves, of which they even speak impiously. But it is not these that are here treated of. . . . In the impious who deny the Divine and Divine things there is nothing holy which they can profane; they are profaners indeed, but yet not the profane.

The profanation of what is holy is meant in the second commandment of the decalogue by, *Thou shalt not profane the name of thy God;* and that there should not be profanation is meant in the Lord's prayer by, *Hallowed be Thy Name.* . . . The name of God signifies God, with all the Divine that is in Him, and that proceeds from Him; and as the Word is the proceeding Divine that is the name of God; and as all the Divine things which are called the spiritual things of the church are from the Word, they also are the name of God. (D. P. n. 226-230.)

Different Kinds and Degrees of Profanation.

Since by the profanation of what is holy is meant profanation by those who know the truths of faith and the goods of charity from the Word, and also in some manner acknowledge them, and not those who do not know them, nor those who from impiety entirely reject them, therefore what follows is said not of the latter but of the former.   Their profanation is of many kinds, lighter, and more grievous; but they may be reduced to these seven.

The first kind of profanation is by those who jest from the Word and about the Word, or from the Divine things of the church, and about them.   This is done by some from a depraved habit of taking names or forms of speech from the Word, and mixing them up with conversation scarcely becoming, and sometimes filthy; which cannot but be connected with some contempt for the Word.   And yet in each and all things the Word is Divine and Holy; for every word therein conceals in its bosom something Divine, and thereby it has communication with heaven. But this kind of profanation is lighter or more grievous according to the acknowledgment of the holiness of the Word, and the unbecoming character of the discourse in which it is introduced by the jesters.   (D. P. n. 231.)

They who jest from the Word do not esteem it holy; and they who jest about the Word account it of trifling value.   And yet the Word is the very Divine Truth of the Lord with man ; and the Lord is present in the Word, and also heaven; for the least particulars of the Word communicate with heaven, and through heaven with the Lord.   Therefore to jest from the Word, and about the Word, is to strew the dust of the earth upon the sacred things of heaven.   (A. E. n. 1064.)

The second kind of profanation is by those who understand and acknowledge Divine truths, and yet live contrary to them. But they more lightly profane who only understand; and they more grievously who also acknowledge; for the understanding only teaches, scarcely otherwise than as a preacher, and of itself does not conjoin itself with the will; but acknowledgment conjoins itself, for nothing can be acknowledged but with the consent of the will.   But this conjunction is various ; and according to the conjunction is the profanation when the life is contrary to the truths which are acknowledged.   For example, if one acknowledges that revenge and hatred, adultery and fornication, fraud and deceit, blasphemy and lying, are sins against God, and yet commits them, he is in this more grievous kind of profanation; for the Lord says, " *The servant which knoweth his Lord's will, and doeth not His will, shall be beaten with many stripes* " (Luke xii. 47).   And again, " *If ye were blind, ye would not have sin ; but now ye say, We see, therefore your sin remaineth* " (John ix. 41). But it is one thing to acknowledge appearances of truth, and another to acknowledge genuine truths.   They that acknowledge genuine truths and yet do not live according to them, in the spiritual world appear without the light and heat of life in their voice and speech, as if they were mere inactivities.

The third kind of profanation is by those who apply the literal sense of the Word to confirm evil loves and false principles. The reason [why this is profanation] is, that the confirmation of falsity is the denial of the truth, and the confirmation of evil is the rejection of good; and the Word in its bosom is nothing but Divine truth and Divine good; and this in the ultimate sense which is the sense of the letter does not appear in genuine truths, except where it teaches about the Lord and the very way of salvation, but in truths clothed, which are called appearances of truth. This sense therefore can be wrested to confirm many kinds of heresies. But he who confirms evil loves does violence to Divine goods; and he who confirms false principles does violence to Divine truths. This violence is called the falsification of truth; and that the adulteration of good. Both are meant in the Word by blood; for a holy spiritual [principle] which is indeed the Spirit of Truth proceeding from the Lord, is within the least particulars of the literal sense of the Word. This holy [principle] is injured when the Word is falsified and adulterated; that this is profanation is obvious.

The fourth kind of profanation is by those who utter pious and holy things with the mouth, and also simulate the affections of the love of them in tone and gesture, and yet in heart do not believe and love them. The most of these are hypocrites and Pharisees; from whom after death all truth and good is taken away, and then they are sent into outer darkness. Those of this kind who have confirmed themselves against the Divine and against the Word, and therefore also against the spiritual things of the Word, sit in that darkness mute, unable to speak; wishing to babble pious and holy things as in the world, but they cannot. For in the spiritual world every one is constrained to speak as he thinks; but the hypocrite wishes to speak otherwise than as he thinks. Hence arises an opposition in the mouth, from which it is that he can only mutter. But hypocrisies are lighter or more grievous according to confirmations against God and reasonings outwardly in favour of God.

The fifth kind of profanation is by those who attribute Divine things to themselves. It is they who are meant by Lucifer in Isaiah xiv. Lucifer there means Babylon, as may be seen from the 4th and 22nd verses of that chapter, where the lot of such also is described. The same are meant too by the whore sitting upon the scarlet beast, in the Apocalypse, xvii. Babylon and Chaldea are mentioned in many places in the Word; and by Babylon is there meant the profanation of good, and by Chaldea the profanation of truth; both with those who attribute to themselves things Divine.

The sixth kind of profanation is by those who acknowledge the Word, and yet deny the Divinity of the Lord. They are called in the world Socinians, and some of them Arians. The lot of both is that they invoke the Father and not the Lord, and continually pray the Father,—some indeed for the sake of the Son,—that they may be admitted into heaven, but in vain; even until they become without hope of salvation; and then they are let down into hell among those who deny God. It is they who are meant by those that blaspheme the Holy Spirit, to whom it would not be remitted in this age nor in that which is to come (Matt. xii. 32). The reason is that God is one in Person and in Essence, in whom is a Trinity, and that God is the Lord; and as the Lord is also heaven, and hence those who are in heaven are in the Lord, therefore they who deny the Divinity of the Lord cannot be admitted into heaven and be in the Lord.

The seventh kind of profanation is by those who first acknowledge Divine truths and live according to them, and afterwards recede from and deny them. This is the worst kind of profanation, for the reason that they so commingle holy things with profane that they cannot be separated; and yet they must be separated that they may be either in heaven or in hell; and because with them this cannot be done, all the intellectual and voluntary human is eradicated and they become no longer men, as was said before. Nearly the same takes place with those who in heart acknowledge the Divine things of the Word and of the church, and entirely immerse them in their proprium, which is the love of ruling over all things, of which much has been said before; for after death when they become spirits they will not be led by the Lord, but by themselves; and when the rein is given to their love they would not only rule over heaven, but even over the Lord. And because they cannot do this they deny the Lord, and become devils. (D. P. n. 231.)

The Effects of Profanation.

Divine truth cannot be profaned except by those who have first acknowledged it. For they first enter into truth by acknowledgment and belief, and so are initiated into it. When afterwards they recede from it there continually remains a vestige of it inwardly impressed, which is recalled at the same time with falsity and evil; and hence the truth, because it adheres to them, is profaned. They therefore with whom this is the case have continually within them that which condemns, thus their

hell. For when the infernals approach towards the sphere
where good and truth are, they instantly feel their hell; for they
come into that which they hate, consequently into torment.
They therefore who have profaned truth dwell continually with
that which torments them; and this according to the degree of
profanation. Because it is so it is most specially provided by
the Lord that Divine good and truth shall not be profaned.
And it is provided especially by this, that the man who is of
such a character that he cannot but profane is withheld as far
as possible from the acknowledgment and belief of truth and
good; for, as was said, no one can profane but who has first
acknowledged and believed. This was the reason why internal
truths were not made known to the posterity of Jacob, the
Israelites and Jews. Not even was it openly declared that
there was any internal in man, and thus that there was
any internal worship; and scarcely anything of a life after
death, and of the Lord's heavenly kingdom; or of the Messiah
whom they expected. The reason was that they were of such a
character that it was foreseen that if such truths had been
revealed to them they could not but have profaned them; for
they desired only earthly things. And because that generation
was and also is of such a character, it is still permitted that they
should be in a state of entire unbelief; for if they once acknowledged and afterwards receded, they could not but have induced
upon themselves the most grievous of all hells. This also was the
reason why the Lord did not come into the world and reveal the
internal [truths] of the Word until there was no good at all, not
even natural good, remaining with them. (A. C. n. 3398.)

Ideas commingled by profanation remain associated, so that
whenever a holy thought comes into the mind the profane idea
connected with it also enters. The effect of which is that the
man cannot be in any society but that of the damned. The
association of ideas in the mind of every one is exquisitely perceived in the other life, even by spirits in the world of spirits,
and much more so by angelic spirits; so that from a single idea
they know the quality of a man. The separation of profane and
holy ideas, when thus conjoined, cannot be effected except by
such horrible infernal torment that if a man was aware of it
he would guard himself against profanation as against hell
itself. (*ib.* n. 301.)

By the Providence of the Lord care is taken lest man should be
admitted into real acknowledgment and belief of heart farther
than he can afterwards be kept in it, and this on account of the
punishment of profanation, which in hell is most grievous.
It is for this reason that so few at this day are permitted to
believe from the heart that the good of love and charity is heaven

in man, and that all the Divine is in the Lord; for men are in the life of evil. (*ib.* n. 2357.)

The Lord does not admit man interiorly into the truths of wisdom and into the goods of love, except so far as man can be kept in them to the end of life. (D. P. n. 233.)

They who know what the truth and good of faith is and yet do not in heart believe, as is the case with very many at this day, cannot profane; because the intellectual faculty does not receive and imbue itself therewith. (A. C. n. 4601.)

MEMORABILIA RESPECTING THE DIVINE WORD IN THE HEAVENS.

That the Word in the letter conceals such sublime treasures within it, is often visibly shown to spirits or souls that come into the other life; and it has sometimes been granted me to be present when this was done. . . . A certain spirit came to me, not long after his departure from the body,—as I could infer from the fact that as yet he did not know that he was in the other life, but imagined he was still living in the world.   Perceiving that he was given to study, I spoke with him about his studies.   But he was suddenly carried up on high; at which, being surprised, I conjectured that he was one of those who aspire to exalted station,—for such are often elevated to a lofty position; or of those that imagine heaven is on high,—who likewise are taken up, that they may thus know that heaven is not above, but within.   But I soon perceived that he was taken up to the angelic spirits who are before, a little to the right, at the first threshold of heaven.   He afterwards spoke with me from there, saying that he saw sublimer things than human minds can anywise conceive.   When this occurred I was reading the first chapter of Deuteronomy, about the Jewish people, how that some were sent to explore the land of Canaan and what was there.   But as I was reading he said he perceived nothing of the sense of the letter, but the things which are in the spiritual sense, and that these were wonderful,—such as could not be described.   This was at the first threshold of the heaven of angelic spirits.   What would not be perceived then in that heaven itself!   And what, in the heaven of Angels! . . . . After this, on two occasions, I saw others taken up among the angelic spirits in another heaven, and they talked with me from there.   I was then reading the third chapter of Deuteronomy, from the beginning to the end.   They said they were in the interior sense only of the Word, and earnestly declared that there is not even a point in which there is not a spiritual sense, most beautiful, coherent with all the rest; and that the names are significant. (A. C. n. 3473, 3474.)

SIGNIFICATION OF VARIOUS TERMS
AND SUBJECTS IN THE WORD.

THE DAYS OF CREATION.

THE six days or periods, which are so many successive states, of man's regeneration are in general as follows :—

The first state is that which precedes, both from infancy and immediately before regeneration, and is called a *void, emptiness,* and *darkness.* And the first motion, which is the Lord's mercy, is *the Spirit of God moving over the faces of the waters.*

The second state is when there is a division between those things which are the Lord's and those that are man's own. Those which are of the Lord are called in the Word remains [1] (*reliquæ*), and are here especially cognitions of faith acquired from infancy. They are laid up and not manifested until he comes into this state; a state which rarely exists at this day without temptation, misfortune, and sorrow,—which cause the things that are of the body and the world to be quiescent, and as it were dead. The things that are of the external man are thus separated from those that belong to the internal man. In the internal are the *remains* laid up by the Lord to this time, and for this use.

The third is a state of repentance, in which from the internal man he talks piously and devoutly, and brings forth things good, as works of charity; but which are yet inanimate, because he believes them to be from himself. And they are called *the tender herb ;* then, *the herb yielding seed ;* and afterwards, the *tree bearing fruit.*

The fourth state is when he is affected by love, and en-lightened by faith. Before indeed he talked piously, and brought forth things that were good, but from a state of temptation and distress, not from faith and charity. These are therefore now enkindled in the internal man, and are called *two luminaries.*

The fifth state is, that he talks from faith, and confirms him-self thereby in truth and good. The things which he now pro-

---

[1] In the common English version of the Bible the nearly synonymous word "remnant" is used.

duces are animate, and are called *the fishes of the sea,* and *the birds of the heavens.*

The sixth state is when he utters truths and does good deeds from faith, and therefore from love. The things that he now produces are called *the living soul,* and *the beast.* And as he now begins to act at once both from faith and from love, he becomes a spiritual man; who is called an *image.* His spiritual life is delighted, and is sustained, by those things which are of the cognitions of faith and of the works of charity, which are called his *meat;* and his natural life is delighted and supported by those things that belong to the body and the senses; whence a conflict arises, until love reigns, and he becomes a celestial man.

They that are regenerated do not all attain this state. But some,—at this day even the greater part,—only reach the first; some only the second; some the third; the fourth; the fifth,— rarely the sixth; and scarcely any one the seventh. (A. C. n. 6-13.)

ENOCH.

There were those at that time who formed doctrine out of the perceived truths of the Most Ancient and the succeeding churches, that it might serve for a test by which to know what is good and true. Such were called Enoch. This is signified by the words,—*"And Enoch walked with God."* Thus also they named that doctrine; and this [doctrine] too is signified by the name Enoch, which means *to instruct.* The same also appears from the signification of the word *walk,* and from the circumstance that he is said to have walked *with God,* and not with Jehovah. To walk with God is to teach and to live according to the doctrine of faith; but to walk with Jehovah is to live the life of love. To *walk* is a customary form of expression signifying to *live;* as to walk in the law, to walk in the statutes, to walk in the truth. To walk properly has relation to a way, which is of truth, consequently, which is of faith or of the doctrine of faith. (A. C. n. 519.)

" He was not, for God took him," signifies that that doctrine was preserved for the use of their posterity. The fact with regard to Enoch is, as was said, that he reduced to doctrine the perceived truth of the Most Ancient Church. This at that time was not permitted; for it is a very different thing to cognize by perception and to learn from doctrine. They who are in perception have no need to learn to know by the way of formulated doctrine what they have cognizance of; just as, for the sake of illustration, he who knows how to think well has no need to

learn to think artificially, whereby his faculty of thinking well would be destroyed, as with those who cleave to scholastic dust. They who [learn] from perception, to them it is given by the Lord by an internal way to cognize what is good and true; but they who [learn] from doctrine, to them it is given to know by an external way or through the bodily senses. The difference is as between light and darkness. Add to this that the perceptions of the celestial man can in no wise be described; for they enter into the very least and most single particulars, with every variety according to states and circumstances. But as it was foreseen that the perceptive faculty of the Most Ancient Church would be lost, and that afterwards men would learn what is true and good by doctrines, or through darkness come to the light, therefore it is said that *God took him;* that is He preserved [the doctrine] for the use of their posterity. (*ib.* n. 521.)

THE GIANTS.

" *There were giants (Nephilim) in the earth in those days* " (Gen. vi. 4). By *Nephilim* are signified those who from a persuasion of their own eminence and great superiority set at naught all things holy and true. This appears from what precedes and presently follows, namely, that they immersed doctrinal truths in their lusts, which is signified by these words, that " *The sons of God went in unto the daughters of men* " [" sons of God " signifying doctrinal truths of faith, and " the daughters of men " lusts, as shown before, n. 570]; and here that " *they bare unto them.*" The high opinion of themselves and of their own conceits increases,—and that too according to the multitude of the falsities entering into them,—so that at length it becomes indelible; and when doctrinal truths of faith are added, they become so strongly persuaded of their principles that they set at naught all things holy and true, and become *Nephilim.* This race, which lived before the flood, is of such a character, as was said before, that they so deaden and suffocate every spirit with their most horrible conceits, which are poured forth from them like a poisonous and suffocating sphere, that the spirits do not in the least know how to think, and seem to themselves half dead. And if the Lord by His coming into the world had not freed the world of spirits from so malignant a race no one could have existed there; and therefore the human race would have perished, for it is governed by the Lord by means of spirits. . . . Further mention is made of them in the Word; and their posterity are called Anakim and Rephaim. That they are called Anakim appears in Moses :—The explorers of the land of Cannan said,

" *There saw we the Nephilim, the sons of Anak, of the Nephilim ; and we were in our own eyes as grasshoppers, and so were we in their eyes* " (Numb. xiii. 23). That they are called Rephaim appears also in Moses :—" *The Emim dwelt before in the land of Moab, a people great and many, and tall, as the Anakim ; they were also accounted Rephaim (giants) as the Anakim ; and the Moabites called them Emim* " (Deut. ii. 10, 11). The Nephilim are no more mentioned, but the Rephaim, who are described by the Prophets as of such a character as has been stated. Thus in Isaiah :—" *Hell beneath was moved for thee, to meet thee at thy coming ; it hath stirred up the Rephaim for thee* " (xiv. 9). The subject referred to is the hell where such have their abode. In the same :—" *The dead shall not live ; the Rephaim shall not rise ; for that thou hast visited and destroyed them, and made all their memory to perish* " (xxvi. 14). Here also their hell is spoken of, from which they shall no more rise. . . . And in David :—" *Wilt thou show wonders to the dead ? shall the Rephaim arise and praise Thee ?* " (Ps. lxxxviii. 10). This likewise is said of their hell, and signifies that they cannot rise and infest the sphere of the world of spirits with the most direful poison of their persuasions. But it has been provided by the Lord that the human race should no longer be imbued with such dreadful conceits and persuasions. Those that lived before the flood were of such a nature and genius that they could be imbued therewith, for a reason hitherto known to no one, but of which by the Lord's Divine mercy hereafter. (A. C. n. 581.)

Repentance of the Lord.

" *And it repented Jehovah that He had made man on the earth, and it grieved Him at His heart* " (Gen. vi. 6). That Jehovah repented signifies mercy ; that He grieved at heart has a similar signification. *To repent* has relation to wisdom : *to grieve at heart* has relation to love.

That Jehovah repented that He had made man on the earth signifies mercy, and that He grieved at heart also signifies mercy, is evident from the consideration that Jehovah never repents, because He foresees all and every thing from eternity ; and when He made man, that is created him anew, and perfected him till he became celestial, He also foresaw that in process of time he would become such as he now was, and therefore He could not repent. This plainly appears in Samuel. Samuel said, " *The Strength of Israel will not lie, nor repent ; for He is not a man that He should repent* " (1 Sam. xv. 29). And in Moses :—" *God is not a man that He should lie, neither the son of man that He should re-*

pent: hath He said, and shall He not do it? or hath He spoken, and shall He not make it good?" (Numb. xxiii. 19).

But it is said of the Lord that He repents and grieves at heart because such feeling is sure to be in all human mercy, and the expression here, as in many other places in the Word, is according to the appearance. What the mercy of the Lord is no one can know, because it infinitely transcends all understanding of man. But man knows what the mercy of man is,—that it is to repent and grieve; and unless he forms an idea of (Divine) mercy from another affection the quality of which he knows, he could never think anything about it, and therefore could not be instructed. This is the reason why human properties are often predicated of the attributes of Jehovah, or the Lord; as that Jehovah or the Lord punishes, leads into temptation, destroys, and is angry; when yet He never punishes any one, never leads any into temptation, never destroys any, and is never angry. (A. C. n. 586–588.)

THE FLOOD.

By the flood (Gen. vi.) is signified an inundation of evil and falsity. This is evident from what was said above respecting the posterity of the Most Ancient Church: That they were possessed with filthy lusts; had immersed the doctrinal truths of faith in them; and therefore were infected with false persuasions, which extinguished all truth and good, and at the same time so closed up the way against remains that they could not operate; and therefore it could not but be that they destroyed themselves. When the way is closed against remains man is no longer man, because he can no longer be protected by the angels, but is entirely possessed by evil spirits, who seek and desire nothing else than to extinguish man. Hence the death of the antediluvians, which is described by a flood or total inundation. The influx of fantasies and lusts from evil spirits indeed is not unlike a kind of flood, and therefore it is called a flood or inundation in various parts of the Word.

To *" destroy all flesh wherein is the breath of lives from under the heavens,"* signifies that the whole posterity of the Most Ancient Church would destroy themselves. This appears from the description of them already given,—that they successively derived from their parents such an hereditary genius that they beyond others were imbued with so dreadful persuasions; especially for the reason that they immersed the doctrinal truths of faith in their filthy lusts. They who have no doctrinals of faith, but live entirely in ignorance, cannot do so, and therefore cannot profane holy things, and so close the way against remains, and in consequence drive the angels of the Lord away from themselves. Remains, as has been said, are all things of innocence, all things of charity, all things of mercy, and all things of the truth of faith, which man from infancy has had from the Lord, and has learned. Each and all of these are carefully stored up; for if man were not in possession of them there could never be anything of innocence, of charity, and of mercy in his thoughts and actions, and of course nothing of good and of truth, and consequently he would be worse than the wild beasts. So, if he have remains of such things, and by filthy lusts and direful persuasions of falsity should stop the way against them so that they could not operate. Such were the antediluvians who destroyed themselves, who are meant by " all flesh wherein is the breath of lives under the heavens."

" *Everything that is in the earth shall die,*" signifies those who were of that church and had become of such a character. That the earth does not mean the whole terrestrial globe, but only those who were of the church, was shown above. Therefore no flood is here meant, much less a universal flood, but only the extinction or suffocation of those who were of the church, when they were separated from remains and therefore from intellections of truth and volitions of good, and consequently from the heavens. (A. C. n. 660-662.)

" *All the fountains of the great deep were broken up,*" signifies the extreme of temptation as to things of the will. . . . The deep in ancient times signified hell, and fantasies and false persuasions were likened to waters and streams, as well as to the vapour from them. So also some of the hells actually appear as deeps and as seas. Thence come the evil spirits who devastate and also who tempt man, and the fantasies they infuse and the desires with which they inflame him are like inundations and exhalations from thence; for, as was said, by evil spirits man is conjoined with hell, and by angels with heaven. Such things are therefore signified when all the fountains of the great deep are said to be broken up. That hell is called the deep, and the filthy things thence issuing, streams, appears from Ezekiel: " *Thus saith the Lord Jehovah: In the day when he went down to hell I caused to mourn; I covered the deep above him, and I restrained the rivers thereof, and the great waters were stayed*" (xxxi. 15). Hell is also called an abyss in John (Rev. ix. 1, 2, 11; xi. 7; xvii. 8; xx. 1, 3).

" *The flood-gates of heaven were opened,*" signifies the extreme of temptation as to things of the understanding. (*ib.* n. 756, 757.)

" *And the waters were strengthened exceedingly exceedingly upon the earth,*" signifies that false persuasions so increased. This appears from what has been said and shown before respecting the waters; namely, that the waters of the flood or the inundating waters signify falsities. Here, because there were still greater falsities or persuasions of the false, it is said that "the waters were strengthened exceedingly exceedingly," which is the superlative form in the original tongue. Falsities are principles of what is false and persuasions of what is false, and that these immensely increased among the antediluvians is evident from what has been said above concerning them. Persuasions of what is false increase immensely when men immerse truths in their lusts, or cause them to favour self-love and the love of the world; for then they pervert them, and in a thousand ways force them into agreement.

"*All the high mountains that were under the whole heaven were covered*," signifies that all the goods of charity were extinguished. This appears from the signification of mountains among the most ancient people. With them mountains represented the Lord, because they worshipped Him upon mountains, for the reason that they are the most elevated parts of the earth. Mountains therefore signified things celestial,—which they also called the highest,—consequently love and charity, and therefore the goods of love and charity, which are celestial. . . . What is signified by the waters with which the mountains were covered is therefore plain; namely, that they were persuasions of what is false, which extinguish all the good of charity. (*ib.* n. 794-797.)

It has been granted me to learn by experience what an inundation or flood is in the spiritual sense. This inundation is twofold; one is of lusts and the other of falsities. That which is of lusts is an inundation of the voluntary part, and of the right part of the brain; and that which is of falsities is an inundation of the intellectual part, in which is the left part of the brain. When a man who had lived in good is remitted into his proprium, thus into the sphere of his very own life, there appears as it were an inundation; while he is in that inundation he is indignant, is angry, thinks restlessly, desires vehemently; in one way when the left part of the brain is inundated, where falsities are, and in another way when the right is inundated, where evils are. But when the man is kept in the sphere of life which he had received from the Lord by regeneration, he is entirely beyond such an inundation, and is as it were in serenity and sunshine, and in joy and happiness; and therefore far from indignation, anger, restlessness, lust, and the like. This is the morning or spring of spirits, the other state is the evening or autumn. It has been given me to perceive that I was out of the inundation, and this for a considerable length of time, while I saw that other spirits were in it; but afterwards I was immersed, and then apperceived the similitude of an inundation. They who are in temptations are in such an inundation. By this experience I was also instructed as to what is signified in the Word by the flood; namely, that the last posterity of the most ancient people who were of the Lord's celestial church entirely were inundated by evils and falsities, and so perished. (*ib.* n. 5725.)

The Resting of the Ark upon the Mountains of Ararat.

"*And the ark rested in the seventh month, on the seventeenth day of the month, upon the mountains of Ararat*" (Gen. viii. 4). "The ark rested" signifies regeneration. This may be seen from the consideration that the ark signifies the man of that church [the new church represented by Noah, which succeeded the Most Ancient Church]. All things within the ark signify whatever appertained to that man. When therefore the ark is said to rest, it signifies the regeneration of that man. . . .

"The seventh month" signifies what is holy. This holiness corresponds to what was said of the celestial man (ch. ii. 3), where it is written that the seventh day was sanctified because *God rested* thereon.

"The seventeenth day" signifies a new [state]. This appears from what was said respecting this number in the preceding chapter (vii. 11), where it signifies a beginning; for every beginning is a new [state].

"The mountains of Ararat" signify light [*lumen*]. This may appear from the signification of a mountain, which is the good of love and charity; and from the signification of Ararat, which is light, and indeed the light of one who is regenerate. The new light or first light of the regenerate never springs from cognitions of the truths of faith, but from charity. For truths of faith are as the rays of light, and love, or charity, as the flame. The light in one who is being regenerated is not from the truths of faith but from charity; the truths of faith are the rays themselves of light from it. It thus appears that the mountains of Ararat signify such light. This light is the first light after temptation; which because it is the first is obscure, and is called *lumen*, not *lux*.[1]

From all this now it may be seen what the words of this verse signify in the internal sense; namely, that the spiritual man is a holy rest, from new intellectual light, which is the light of charity. With such wonderful variety and in so delightful order are these things perceived by the angels, that if a man could only enter into one such conception there would be

---

[1] *Lux* is used by the author to designate the light of the spiritual man; and *lumen* to denote the light of the natural man, and of man in the earlier stages of regeneration.

thousands and thousands of things, in multiplying series, which would penetrate and affect him; yea indeed such things as can never be described. Such is the Lord's Word everywhere in the internal sense; although it appears in the literal sense as a rude history, like these words,—which signify these things,—that " the ark rested in the seventh month, on the seventeenth day of the month, upon the mountains of Ararat." (A. C. n. 850-855.)

The Bow in the Cloud.

" *I have set my bow in the cloud,*" signifies the state of the regenerate spiritual man, which is like the rainbow. It may be wondered that the bow in the cloud, or the rainbow, should be taken as the token of the covenant in the Word,—when the rainbow is nothing more than a certain appearance arising from the modification of the rays of light from the sun then falling upon the drops of rain; and—unlike the other signs of the covenant in the Church just referred to—only a natural phenomenon. But that the bow in the cloud represents regeneration, and signifies the state of the regenerate spiritual man, no one can know unless it be given him to see and therefore to know how it is:—When the spiritual angels, who were all regenerate men of the spiritual church, are so presented to view in the other life, there appears as it were a rainbow about the head. But the rainbows which appear are entirely according to their state; and their quality is discerned from them in heaven and the world of spirits. The reason why the resemblance of a rainbow appears, is that their natural [truths] corresponding to their spiritual present such an appearance. It is a modification of spiritual light from the Lord in their natural [truths]. These angels are those who are said to be born again of water and of the Spirit; but the celestial angels are those regenerated by fire. . . . It is because natural things correspond to spiritual that when what is around the regenerate spiritual man is thus presented to view it appears like a bow in the cloud; which bow is a representation of spiritual things in his natural. The regenerate spiritual man has a *proprium* of the understanding into which the Lord insinuates innocence, charity, and mercy; and according to the reception of these gifts by a man is the appearance of his rainbow when it is presented to view,—more beautiful the more the *proprium* of the man's will is removed, subdued, and reduced to obedience. (A. C. n. 1042.)

Ham.

Those who are in faith separated from charity are described

by Ham; in that he observed the nakedness of his father, that is his errors and perversities. They who are of such a character see nothing else in a man. But it is different with those who are in the faith of charity; they observe the good, and if they see anything evil and false they excuse it, and if they can, endeavour to amend it in him,—as it is here related of Shem and Japheth. Where there is no charity there is self-love, consequently hatred towards all who do not favour themselves. Hence it is that such men see nothing in their neighbour but his evil, and if they see what is good they regard it as nothing, or construe it into evil. . . . With such there dwells a continual contempt of others, or a continual derision of others ; and as occasion offers they publish their errors. . . . With those who are in charity it is quite otherwise. Hereby are these two kinds of men distinguished, especially when they come into the other life. With those who are in no charity the spirit of hatred is then manifest in every least thing. They desire to examine every one, yea, to judge every one, and wish nothing more earnestly than to discover evil,—continually purposing in mind to condemn, punish, and torment. But those who are in charity hardly see another's evil, but observe all that is good and true in him, and what is evil and false they construe into good. Such are all the angels; and this they have from the Lord, who turns all evil into good. (A. C. n. 1079, 1080.)

ISHMAEL.

" *And he shall be a wild-ass man; his hand shall be against all, and the hand of all against him; and he shall dwell over against the face of all his brethren* " (Gen. xvi. 12). The rational part of man consists of good and truth, that is, of those things which are of charity and those that belong to faith. Rational truth is what is signified by the wild-ass. It is this then that is represented by Ishmael, and is described in this verse. No one can believe that rational truth separate from rational good is of such a nature; nor should I have known it to be such, but that I have been convinced by living experience. It is the same whether we speak of rational truth, or of a man whose rational mind is of the nature here described. A man whose rational is such that he is only in truth, although in the truth of faith, and not at the same time in the good of charity, is entirely of such a character. He is morose, impatient, opposed to all, viewing every one as in falsity, instantly rebuking, castigating and punishing, is without pity, and does not apply himself or endeavour to bend the minds and affections of others; for he regards everything from the truth and nothing from good.

Every genuine rational consists of good and truth, that is of what is celestial and spiritual. Good or the celestial is its very soul or life; truth or the spiritual is what thence receives its life. The rational without life from celestial good is as is here described; it fights against all, and all fight against it. Rational good never fights, howsoever assaulted, because it is meek and gentle, patient and pliable; for its attributes are those of love and mercy. And although it does not fight yet it conquers all, nor ever thinks of combat, or boasts of victory; and this because it is Divine and is protected by the Divine itself. For no evil can attack good, nor even stay in the sphere where good is; when it only approaches, the evil withdraws of itself and retreats; for evil is infernal, and good is heavenly. It is nearly the same with the celestial-spiritual, that is with truth from a celestial origin, or with truth which is from good; for this truth is truth formed by good, so that it may be called the form of good. But truth separate from good, which is here represented by Ishmael and is described in this verse, is entirely different; for indeed it is like a wild ass, and fights against all, and all against it. Nay, it thinks and breathes scarcely anything but combats; its common delight or governing affection is to conquer, and when it conquers it boasts of victory. For this reason it is described by the wild ass, or the mule of the wilderness or ass of the forest, which cannot abide with others. Such a life is the life of truth without good, yea the life of faith without charity.

In the other life such truth is representatively manifested in various ways, and is always exhibited as strong, powerful, and hard, so that it cannot possibly be resisted. When spirits only think of such truth there arises something of terror; because its nature is such that it never yields, and therefore never withdraws; from all which it may appear what is also meant by his dwelling over against the face of all his brethren. Every one must see that some mystery lies hidden in this description; but what it is has hitherto been unknown. (A. C. n. 1949-1951.)

LAUGHTER.

"*And Abraham fell upon his face and laughed.*" To fall upon the face signifies to adore, "and laughed" signifies an affection of truth. This may be seen from the origin and essence of laughter. It has no other origin than an affection of truth or an affection of falsity. Hence comes the joy and the hilarity that expresses itself in the face by laughter. It is plain then that the essence of laughter is no other [than this affection]. Laughter indeed is something external which is of the body, for it appears in the face; but in the Word interior things are expressed and signified by exterior; as all interior affections of mind and soul by the face, interior hearing and obedience by the ear, internal sight or understanding by the eye, power and strength by the hand and arm. And so an affection of truth is expressed and signified by laughter. In the rational part of man is truth, which is the chief thing, and within this is the affection of good; but this is within the very affection of truth as its soul. The affection of good which is in the rational does not express itself by laughter, but by a kind of joy, and an agreeable [sensation] of pleasure therefrom which does not laugh; for in laughter there is commonly something also which is not so good. . . . That laughter here signifies an affection of truth is evident from the fact that it is here mentioned that Abraham laughed, and likewise Sarah, both before Isaac was born and after he was born; and also from the fact that Isaac was named from laughter, for the word Isaac signifies laughter. If such things were not involved in laughing, and in the name of Isaac which signifies laughter, these circumstances would never have been mentioned in the Word.

Laughter is an affection of the rational mind, and in truth an affection either of the true or the false in the rational; all laughter comes from this. So long as such an affection is in the rational as expresses itself by laughter, so long there is something corporeal or worldly, thus merely human. Celestial and spiritual good does not laugh, but expresses its delight and cheerfulness in another way; in the countenance, in the speech, and in the gestures. For there are very many things in laughter; for the most part something of contempt, which although it does not appear yet underlies it, and is easily distinguished from cheerfulness of mind which also produces something like laughter. (A. C. n. 2071, 2072, 2216.)

BORROWING FROM AND SPOILING THE EGYPTIANS.

As these two verses (Exod. iii. 21, 22) relate to the spoiling of the Egyptians, by the women of Israel borrowing from the Egyptian women silver, gold, and raiment; and as no one can know how the matter is to be understood except by a revelation concerning things which are done in the other life,—for the internal sense involves such things as are done among angels and spirits,—therefore something is to be told on the subject. Before the Lord's coming the lower part of heaven was occupied by evil genii and spirits; and after that they were expelled from thence, and that region was given to those who are of the spiritual

Church. So long as the evil genii and spirits were there, they were under the continual view of the angels of the higher heaven; hence they were restrained from doing evils openly. At this day also some who are more deceitful than others,—since they deceive by simulating innocence and charity,—are under the view of the celestials, and for so long are withheld from their wicked deceits. From these circumstances it has been granted me to know what was the state of the evil genii and spirits who before the coming of the Lord occupied the lower region of heaven; namely, that at that time they were withheld by the angels of the higher heaven from the open commission of evils. And it has also been granted me to know how they were withheld from the open commission of evils. They were kept under external restraints; namely, in fear of the loss of honour and reputation, and in fear lest they should be deprived of possessions in that region of heaven, and be thrust down to hell. And then there were adjoined to them simple good spirits; as is the case with men in the world who, although inwardly devils, are yet kept by these external restraints in honesty and justice and well-doing; and that they may be so kept there are adjoined to them spirits who are in simple good. Thus it was with the evil who were in the lower region of heaven before the Lord's coming. And then too they could be constrained to speak the truth and do good by their own loves. Just as evil priests, yea even the worst who inwardly are devils, can preach the doctrinals of their church with such ardour and simulated zeal as to move the hearts of their hearers to piety, yet at the same time are in the love of self and of the world. For the thought of honour and gain universally rules in them, and from that fire they are excited thus to preach. There are evil spirits with them who are in similar love and therefore in similar thought, who lead them; and to these simple good spirits are adjoined. From these statements it may be seen what was the state of heaven before the Lord's coming. But after His coming the states of heaven and hell were entirely changed; for then the evil genii and spirits who occupied the lower region of heaven were cast down, and in their place those who were of the spiritual church were elevated thither. The evil who were cast down were then deprived of external restraints; which, as was said above, were fear of the loss of honour and reputation, and of the deprivation of possessions in that region. They were thus left to their interiors, which were merely diabolical and infernal, and so were consigned to the hells. The deprivation of external restraints is effected in the other life by the removal of the good spirits who were adjoined to them. When these are removed they can no longer be in any simulation of what is good, just, and honest, but are such as they inwardly were in the world; that is such as they were in thought and will, which they had there concealed from others; and then they desire nothing else than to do 'evil. The simple good spirits who were removed from them were given or adjoined to those who were of the spiritual church, to whom that region of heaven was given for a possession. Thus it is that these latter were enriched with truths and goods which were before in the possession of the evil genii and spirits; for enrichment in truths and goods in the other life is effected by the adjunction of spirits who are in truth and good, because through them communication is opened. These are the things which are signified by the children of Israel not going empty from Egypt, and by a woman borrowing of her neighbour, and of her that sojourned in her house, vessels of silver, and vessels of gold, and raiment, and thus spoiling the Egyptians. Every one may see that if such things had not been represented the Divine [being] would never have commanded that the children of Israel should use such artifice against the Egyptians; for every such thing is at the farthest distance from the Divine. But as that people was entirely representative it was permitted by the Divine [being] that they should do so, because it was thus done with the evil in the other life. It should be known that very many things which were commanded by Jehovah, or the Lord, in the internal sense do not signify that they were commanded, but that they were permitted. (A. C. n. 6914.)

The Anger of the Lord.

" *And the anger of Jehovah was kindled against Moses*" (Exod. iv. 14). This signifies clemency. . . . That Jehovah has no anger, is evident from the consideration that He is love itself, good itself, and mercy itself; and anger is the opposite, and is also an infirmity, which cannot be imputed to God. When therefore anger is predicated of Jehovah or the Lord in the Word, the angels do not perceive anger, but either mercy, or the removal of evil from heaven. . . . Anger is attributed to Jehovah or the Lord in the Word because it is a most general truth that all things come from God, thus both the evil and the good; but this most general truth, which children and the simple must receive, ought afterwards to be illustrated; namely, by teaching that evils are from man, but that they appear as from God, and that it is so said to the intent that they may learn to fear God, lest they should perish by the evils which they themselves do. And afterwards they can love Him; for fear precedes love, that in love there may be holy fear. For when fear is insinuated into love, it becomes holy from the holiness of love; and then it is not fear lest the Lord should be angry and punish, but lest they should act against Good itself, because this will torment the conscience. . . . The reason why clemency and mercy are meant by anger is this: All the punishments of the evil arise out of the Lord's mercy to the good, lest they should be injured by the evil. But the Lord does not inflict punishments upon them, but they inflict them upon themselves; for evils and punishments are connected in the other life. The evil inflict punishments on themselves especially when the Lord does mercy to the good; for then their evils increase, and therefore their punishments. Hence it is that for the anger of Jehovah, by which the punishments of the evil are signified, mercy is understood by the angels. From all this it is evident what the quality of the Word is in the sense of the letter, and what truth Divine is in its most general sense; namely, that it is according to appearances, for the reason that man is such that when he sees and apprehends from his sensual he believes, and what he does not see nor apprehend from his sensual he does not believe, and therefore does not receive. Hence it is that the Word in the sense of the letter is according to the things which appear; yet in its interior bosom it contains a store of genuine truths, and in its inmost bosom the very truth Divine which proceeds immediately from the Lord, and therefore also Divine Good, that is, the Lord Himself. (A. C. n. 6997.)

"*Cursed be Canaan.*" To be cursed is to avert one's-self from the Lord. The Lord is as far from cursing and being angry as heaven is from earth. Who can believe that the Lord, who is omniscient and omnipotent, and by His wisdom governs the universe and thus is infinitely above all infirmities, can be angry with dust so miserable, that is, with men, who scarcely know anything that they do, and can do nothing of themselves but what is evil? It is therefore not in the Lord to be angry, but to be merciful. (A. C. n. 1093.)

THE FROGS OF EGYPT.

Frogs signify reasonings from falsities. This is not from their croaking only, but also from their abiding in marshy and putrid lakes, by which infernal falsities are signified; for they who reason from falsities against Divine truths have their abode in hells which appear like marshes, and stagnant, fœtid waters; and those who are there when seen in the light of heaven appear like frogs, some in larger and some in smaller form, according to their elation of mind from reasonings more or less acute; they are also more and less unclean, according as their reasonings against Divine truth are more or less interior and dignified.

That frogs signify reasonings from mere falsities against Divine truths, may appear from the miracle of the frogs in Egypt; for by all the miracles there performed, the plagues or evils are signified with which they are afflicted after death, who by the knowledges of the natural man contend against spiritual goods and truths, and endeavour to destroy them. That by frogs are there signified reasonings of the natural man from falsities against the truths of the spiritual man, is evident from the description of that miracle in Moses: " *He caused the river to bring forth frogs abundantly, and they went up and came into the house of Pharaoh, and into his bed-chamber, and upon his bed, and into the house of his servants, and of his people, and into the ovens and the kneading-troughs. . . . And after they were dead, they were gathered into heaps, and the land stank*" (Exod. viii. 3, 13, 14). Likewise in David: " *He turned their waters into blood, and slew their fish; He caused frogs to come forth upon their lands, into the chambers of their kings*" (Psalm cv. 29, 30); referring to the plagues in Egypt. The waters turned into blood signify truths falsified; the fish that were slain signify knowledges and cognitions of the natural man, that they perished; the frogs coming forth upon the land signify the reasonings of the natural man from falsities; the chambers of the kings signify interior truths, which they perverted by such reasonings,—chambers are the interiors, and kings truths. Similar things are signified by the frogs coming up into the house of Pharaoh, into his bed-chamber, and upon his bed. From these explanations it is plain what is signified by the three unclean spirits like frogs, which came forth out of the mouth of the dragon, of the beast, and of the false prophet (Rev. xvi. 13, 14). (A. E. n. 1000.)

Apparent Contradiction as to the Number of Years which the Israelites dwelt in Egypt.

It is said that " *The sojourning of the children of Israel, which they sojourned in Egypt, was thirty years and four hundred years;*" and further, that " *At the end of the thirty years and four hundred years, in this same day, all the armies of Jehovah went forth from the land of Egypt*" (Exod. xii. 40-42). And yet the sojourn of the children of Israel, from the going down of Jacob into Egypt to the departure of his posterity at this time, was not more than half that time, namely, 215 years; as is very manifest from the chronology of the Sacred Scriptures. For Moses was born of Amram, Amram of Kohath, and Kohath of Levi; and Kohath, together with his father Levi went into Egypt (Gen. xlvi. 11). The period of the life of Kohath was a hundred and thirty-three years (Exod. vi. 18); and the period of the life of Amram, from whom came Aaron and Moses, was 137 years (*ib.* ver. 20); and Moses was a man of eighty years when he stood before Pharaoh (Exod. vii. 7). It is not mentioned in what year of the age of Kohath Amram was born, nor in what year of the age of Amram Moses was born; but that there were not 430 years is manifest, for the years of their ages do not amount to 430, but to 350. This will be seen, if the years of the age of Kohath, 133, be added to the years of the age of Amram, 137, and these to the 80 years of Moses when he stood before Pharaoh. It is less if the years are added from their nativities; it may be seen from the chronology that they were 215 years. But from the descent of Abraham into Egypt to the departure of the children of Israel were four hundred and thirty years; see also the chronology. It is plain therefore that by 430 years the entire period of time from Abraham is here meant, and not from Jacob. That these years were taken, and called the years of the sojourn of the children of Israel in Egypt, was on account of the internal sense, in which they signify the full state and duration of the vastation of those who were of the spiritual church; and who were detained in the lower earth until the Lord's coming, and then liberated. (A. C. n. 7985.)

DIVINE TRUTH PACIFIC AND TUMULTUOUS.

"*And there was the voice of a trumpet, going and strengthening itself exceedingly*" (Exod. xix. 19). This signifies the general [truth] of revelation through the angelic heaven. This appears from the signification of the voice of a trumpet, which is heavenly or angelic truth conjoined with Divine, thus the general truth of revelation. For truth Divine is revelation; and that which is manifested through the medium of heaven is general relatively to the very truth Divine in heaven; for it is without or around, and what is around and without is general relatively to that which is in the midst or which is within. It appears also from the signification of going and strengthening itself, which is its increase. For the case is like that of sound at a high elevation where the atmosphere is purer, which is tacit; but when it descends to lower altitudes where the atmosphere is denser it becomes louder and more sonorous. So is it with Divine truth and Divine good, which in their supremest heights are pacific and entirely without commotion; but as they pass down to lower heights, by degrees they become impacific, and at length tumultuous. These things were thus described by the Lord to Elijah when he was in Horeb, in the first book of the Kings: "*Go forth*

*and stand upon the mountain before Jehovah. Behold Jehovah
passed by; so that a great and strong wind rent asunder the
mountains, and brake in pieces the rocks before Jehovah: Jehovah
was not in the wind; and after the wind an earthquake; yet
Jehovah was not in the earthquake; after the earthquake a fire;
Jehovah was not in the fire; and after the fire a still small voice"*
(xix. 11, 12).   (A. C. n. 8823.)

BORING THE EAR WITH AN AWL.

" *Then his master shall bring him to God, and shall bring him
to a door or to a post, and his master shall bore his ear with an
awl; and he shall serve him for ever"* (Exod. xxi. 6). Who cannot
see that this ritual concerning men-servants who were to remain
contains within it a mystery ? and indeed a Divine mystery, for
it was dictated and commanded by Jehovah from Mount Sinai.
They who do not believe that there is anything more holy or
Divine in the Word than what appears in the letter, must wonder
that these and many other things contained in this and the following chapters were dictated *viva voce* by Jehovah; for they
appear in the letter to be just such things as are contained in
the laws of nations.   Thus this law concerning men-servants,
that such of them as were not willing to go forth from service
should be brought to a door or to a post, and should have an ear
bored through with an awl by their master; in the sense of the
letter this does not savour of the Divine, and yet it is most
Divine.   But this does not appear except by the internal sense.
The internal sense is, that they who are in truths alone and not
in corresponding good, but yet are in the delight of the remembrance of spiritual goods, have some communication and conjunction with spiritual good.   This was represented by the ear
of the man-servant being bored through at a door or a post by
his master; for a door is communication; a post is conjunction;
the ear is obedience; and to bore it through with an awl is
representative of the state in which he was to remain.   Thus the
angels who are with man while he reads this Word perceive
these things. For the angels do not think of a door, or of a post,
or of an ear and of its being bored, or even of a man-servant; but
instead of these they think of the aforesaid communication and
conjunction.   For the angels are intelligent in such things,
because they are in the light; and they only occur to their
minds as spiritual and celestial, and not as natural and worldly,
which the things in the literal sense of the Word are.   For
the literal sense of the Word is natural and worldly, and its
internal sense is spiritual and celestial.   That is for men; this

for angels; and hence there is communication and conjunction of heaven with man by means of the Word. That the mysteries involved in this procedure with men-servants remaining with their master may be further laid open, it must be told whence it is that a door and post signify communication and conjunction. Angels and spirits have habitations which appear quite like those that are in the world; and what is a mystery, each and all things that appear in their habitations are significative of spiritual things. They flow forth also from the spiritual things that are in heaven, and which are from heaven in their minds. Communications of truth with good are represented there by doors, and conjunctions by posts; and other things by the rooms themselves, by the courts, by the windows, and by the various decorations. That this is so men at this day cannot believe, especially those who are merely natural; because such things do not lie open to their bodily senses. And yet it is evident from the Word that such things were seen by the prophets when their interiors were open into heaven; they have also been apperceived and seen by me a thousand times. I have frequently heard them say, too, that the doors of their apartments were open when their thoughts were communicated to me, and that they were shut when they were not communicated. Hence it is that doors are mentioned in the Word where it speaks of communication, as in Isaiah: " *Go away, My people, enter into thy chambers, and shut thy door after thee, hide thyself as it were for a little moment, until the anger be overpast*" (xxvi. 20). To shut the door after them until anger is overpast denotes non-communication with the evils which are [meant by] anger. . . . And in John: " *Verily, verily, I say unto you, He that entereth not by the door into the sheepfold, but climbeth up some other way, the same is a thief and a robber; but he that entereth in by the door is the shepherd of the sheep. . . . I am the door; by Me if any man enter in he shall be saved*" (x. 1, 2, 9). To enter in by the door is to enter in by the truth which is of faith to the good of charity and love, and so to the Lord; for the Lord is Good itself. He is likewise the Truth which leads in; so also the door, for faith is from Him. That communication is signified by a door appears like a metaphorical way of speaking, or comparison; but there are no metaphors or comparisons in the Word, but actual correspondences. Even the comparisons therein are made with such things as correspond. This is evident from what has been said of a door; namely, that doors actually appear in heaven to angels and spirits, and the opening and shutting of them is according to communications. So too with other things.

" *And his master shall bore through his ear with an awl,*" signifies a representative of obedience. This appears from the signification of the ear, which is obedience; and from the signification of the boring through with an awl,—that is, at a door or at a post,—which is to attach; here, because it concerns obedience, it signifies to devote [*i.e.* to service]. The injunction follows therefore that " he shall serve him," that is, obey, " for ever." From this it is plain that boring through the ear of the servant with an awl at a door or at a post by his master, is a representative of obedience. How these things are may be seen from what has preceded; namely, that those who are in truths only and not in corresponding good, that is who are in faith and not in charity, are not free but servants. On the other hand, those who act from good or charity are free, since they act from themselves; for to act from good or charity is to act from the heart, that is from the will, and thus from what is man's own. For that which is of the will is of the man; and what is done from the will is said to go forth from the heart. But those who are only in truths of faith, and not in the good of charity, are relatively servants; for they do not act from themselves,—because they have not the good within themselves from which to act, but out of themselves; and they do it as often as they think of it. Those who remain such to the end of life continue in that state after death; nor can they be brought to such a state that they may act from an affection of charity, thus from good; but they act from obedience. . . . They who actually, that is in very life, put the doctrine of faith in the first place and charity in the second, are Hebrew servants in the representative sense. . . . That the boring of the ear with an awl by his master is representative of obedience, is evident too from the consideration that to fix the ear to a door was to effect that attention should be paid to those things which his master who is in the chamber commands; thus to cause to hear continually, and accordingly obey; here, in the spiritual sense, to cause to obey the things which good wills and commands, for by the lord of the servant spiritual good is represented. As the ear signifies the hearing which is of obedience, therefore from an origin out of the spiritual world there has passed into human speech the expression to pull the ear, for to make to give heed and to remember;[1] and likewise the words hear and hearken in the sense of to obey. For the interior sense of very many expressions has flowed from correspondences from the spiritual world; as when we speak of spiritual light, and of sight from it, which are things belonging to faith; also of spiritual fire and of life therefrom, which things pertain to love.

"*And he shall serve him for ever.*" . . . In the literal sense

[1] This expression, though not unknown in English parlance, is less common than perhaps in some of the other modern languages, and than it appears to have been anciently, at least in the spoken Latin language. (Virg. Ecl. vi. 3.)

for ever here signifies service with his master to the end of his life. But in the internal or spiritual sense it signifies to eternity, because it refers to the state after death. It is said to eternity, for the reason that they who do good from the obedience of faith, and not from an affection of charity,—who are represented by men-servants,—can never be brought to a state of good, that is to such a state that they act from good, in the other life. For the life of every one remains after death. Such as a man is when he dies, such he remains; according to the common saying, " As the tree falleth so it lies." Not that he is such as he was about the hour of death; but such as from the whole course of his life he is when he dies. They therefore who during their life in the world have been accustomed to do good only from obedience, and not from charity, remain so to eternity. These are perfected indeed in respect to obedience, but do not attain to anything of charity. (A. C. n. 8989-8991.)

The Urim and Thummim.

The breastplate of Aaron, which was called the Urim and Thummim, was composed of twelve precious stones, on which were engraven the names of the twelve tribes, or of the twelve sons of Israel (Exod. xxviii. 15-30; xxxix. 8-29). It is well known that responses from heaven were given by this, but from what origin has not as yet been revealed. It shall therefore now be told. All light in the angelic heaven proceeds from the Lord as a sun; that light therefore in its essence is Divine truth, from which comes all the intelligence and wisdom of the angels, and also of men, in spiritual things. This light in heaven is modified into various colours, according to the truths from good which are received; hence it is that colours in the Word, from their correspondence, signify truths from good. And by this means the responses were given, through a resplendency from the colours of the stones which were in the Urim and Thummim, and then at the same time either by a living voice or by a tacit perception, corresponding to the resplendence. (A. E. n. 431.)

The Breaking of the Tables of the Decalogue by Moses, and his Hewing out other Tables.

" *And Moses' anger waxed hot, and he cast the tables out of his hands, and brake them beneath the mount* " (Exod. xxxii. 19). The external of the Word is its literal sense. This sense is signified by the tables, because this sense is as a table, or as a plane, on which the internal sense is inscribed. That the tables which were the work of God were broken by Moses when he saw the calf and the dances, and that at the command of Jehovah other tables were hewn out by Moses, and on them were afterwards inscribed the same words, and thus that the tables were no longer the work of God, but the work of Moses, while the writing was still the writing of God, involves a mystery as yet unknown. The mystery is, that the literal sense of the Word would have been different if the Word had been written among another people, or if this people had not been of such a character. For, because the Word was written among them the literal sense of the Word is concerning that people, as is plain both from the historical and the prophetical parts of the Word; and that people were in evil, because in heart they were idolators. And yet, that the internal and external sense might agree, this people was to be commended, and to be called the people of God, a holy nation, and peculiar. The simple therefore who were to be instructed by the external sense of the Word were to believe that such was the character of that nation, as that nation also itself believes, and likewise the greater part of the Christian world at this day. And besides, many things were permitted them on account of the hardness of their heart, which stand forth in the external sense of the Word, and constitute it. As for example what is mentioned in Matt. xix. 8, and other things also which are here passed by. Since therefore the literal sense of the Word was made such for the sake of that people, those tables which were the work of God were broken, and by command of Jehovah others were hewn out by Moses. But as the same holy Divine was still within, therefore the same words which were upon the former tables were inscribed by Jehovah upon these, as is plain from these words in Moses: "*Jehovah said unto Moses, Hew thee out two tables of stones, like unto the first, that I may write upon the tables the words that were on the former tables, which thou hast broken: And Jehovah wrote upon those tables the words of the covenant, ten words*" (Exod. xxxiv. 1, 4, 28). (A. C. n. 10,453.)

To make this subject more clear, it may be here explained how the external or literal sense was changed for the sake of that nation. For the sake of that nation altars, burnt-offerings, sacrifices, meat-offerings, and libations were commanded; and on this account, both in the historical and prophetical Word, these are mentioned as the most holy things of worship, when in fact they were merely allowed because they were first instituted by Eber. But in the Ancient representative church they were entirely unknown. For the sake of that nation also it came to pass that Divine worship was performed in Jerusalem alone, and that on this account that city was esteemed holy, and was also called holy, both in the historical and prophetical Word. The reason was because that nation was in heart idolatrous; and therefore unless they had all met together at that city on each festival, every one in his own place would have worshipped some god of the Gentiles, or some graven and molten thing. For the sake of that nation too it was forbidden to celebrate holy worship on mountains and in groves, as the ancients had done. This was done lest they should place idols there, and should worship the very trees. For the sake of that nation also it was permitted to marry several wives; which was a thing entirely unknown in ancient times; and likewise to put away their wives for various causes. Hence laws were enacted concerning such marriages and divorces which otherwise would not have entered the external of the Word. This external is therefore called by the Lord that of Moses, and is said to have been "*suffered for the hardness of their heart*" (Matt. xix. 8). It was for the sake of that nation that Jacob, and also the twelve sons of Israel, were so often mentioned as the only elect and heirs; as in the Apocalypse, vii. 4-8, and elsewhere,—although their character was such as is described in the song of Moses (Deut. xxxii. 15-43), and in the prophets also throughout, and by the Lord Himself. Besides other things of which the external of the Word was composed for the sake of that nation. It is this external which is signified by the two tables hewed out by Moses. That within this external there is yet the Divine internal, unchanged, is signified by Jehovah writing on these tables the same words which were on the former tables. (*ib.* n. 10,603.)

SIGNIFICATION OF THE JEWISH SACRIFICES.

The animals which were offered up in the sacrifices and burnt-offerings were oxen, bullocks, he-goats, rams, she-goats, he-kids; and he-lambs, ewe-lambs, and kids of the she-goats. He who does not know what these animals signify cannot know at all what is signified in particular by the sacrifices and burnt-offerings of them. It should be known that all the animals on earth signify such things as pertain to man; which in general refer to the affections which are of his will, and to the thoughts which are of his understanding, and therefore to goods and truths; for goods are of the will, and truths are of the understanding. And as they refer to goods and truths, they also refer to love and faith; for all things that pertain to love are called goods, and all things that pertain to faith are called truths. The fact that animals of different kinds have such a signification has its cause in representatives in the other life; for animals of many kinds, and of innumerable species, appear there. Such animals there are appearances, exactly to the life, corresponding to the affections and the thoughts in spirits and angels. That this is so is in fact evident from the prophetic visions in the Word throughout; for the things seen by the prophets were all such as appear in heaven before the angels. It is for this reason that beasts are so frequently mentioned in the Word; and by every one of them something is signified which relates to such things in man as are spoken of above. Nor is man anything but an animal as to his external man; but he is distinguished by the internal, by which both that and this can be elevated towards heaven and to God, and thence receive faith and love. Hence it is that beasts were devoted to sacrifices and burnt-offerings. He who does not know these things cannot know at all why it was commanded at one time to offer bullocks, rams, and he-lambs; at another, oxen, she-goats, and ewe-lambs; and at another time, he-goats, he-kids, and kids of the she-goats; for otherwise to what purpose would be such distinctions? . . . The sacrifices and burnt-offerings, in general, signified the regeneration of man, and in the highest sense the glorification of the Lord's Humanity. The whole of worship was also represented by the sacrifices and burnt-offerings, according to the various things pertaining to it, thus with every variety; and therefore were the various kinds of animals commanded. . . . That the sacrifices and burnt-offerings, in general, signified the regeneration of man by the truths of faith and the goods of love to the Lord from the Lord, is evident from this fact, that all things of worship have reference to purification from evils and falsities; to the implantation of truth and good; and to their conjunction,—and so to regeneration; for by these three things man is regenerated. Hence it is that sacrifices and burnt-offerings were offered for every sin and for all guilt; and when they were offered it is said that expiation was made, and that it was pardoned (Lev. iv. 20, 26, 31, 35; v. 6, 10, 13, 16, 18; vi. 7; vii. 7; x. 17; xiv. 18, 19; xv. 30, 31; xvi. 6, 24; xvii. 11). The pardon of sins, expiation, propitiation, and redemption, are nothing else than purification from evils and falsities, the implantation of good and truth, and their conjunction, thus regeneration. The whole process of regeneration is also described by the particular rituals of each sacrifice and burnt-offering, and is explained when the representatives are unfolded by the internal sense. . . . By the sacrifices and burnt-offerings of the bullock, the ox, and the he-goat, the purification and regeneration of the external or natural man was represented; by those of the ram, the she-goat, and the he-kid, the purification and regeneration of the internal or spiritual man was represented; and by those of the he-lamb, the ewe-lamb, and the kid of the she-goats was represented the purification or regeneration of the inmost or celestial man. Because there are three degrees in man in succession [from this inmost], the celestial, the spiritual, and the natural; and because, in order that he may be regenerated, man must be regenerated both as to internals and as to externals. . . . The reason why in the highest sense the sacrifices and burnt-offerings signify the glorification of the Lord's Humanity is that all the rituals of the worship instituted among the Israelitish and Jewish nation had reference to the Lord alone; and so the sacrifices and burnt-offerings by which in general the whole of worship was represented, referred principally to Him. And besides, the regeneration of man is from no other source than the Lord: and therefore, wherever in the Word the regeneration of man is referred to, in the highest sense it refers to the glorification of the Lord's Humanity. For man's regeneration is an image of the Lord's glorification. To glorify the Human was to make it Divine; and to regenerate man is to make him heavenly, that the Divine of the Lord may dwell in him. (A. C. n. 10,042).

BALAAM'S ASS SPEAKING.

The mystery of the ass upon which Balaam rode, which turned three times out of the way on seeing an angel with a drawn sword, and the circumstance of its speaking to Balaam, I will here briefly explain. While Balaam was riding upon the ass he continually meditated sorcery against the children of Israel. The gain with which he should be honoured was in his mind; as appears from these words concerning him: "*He went not as at other times to seek for enchantments*" (Numb. xxiv. 1). He was in truth a soothsayer in heart; and therefore he thought of nothing else when he thought from himself. By the ass upon which he rode is signified, in the spiritual sense of the Word, an enlightened intellectual [faculty]. Therefore to ride upon an ass or mule was among the insignia of a chief judge and of a king. The angel with the drawn sword signifies Divine Truth enlightened, and contending against what is false. Hence by the ass turning three times out of the way, it is signified that the understanding when enlightened did not agree with the thought of the sorcerer; and this also is meant by what the angel said unto Balaam: "*Behold, I went out to withstand thee, because thy way is perverse before me*" (Numb. xxii. 32). By a way in the spiritual sense of the Word, that which a man thinks from his intention is signified. It is evident too from what the angel said to him that he was withheld from the thought and intention of using sorceries by the fear of death: " *Unless the ass had turned from me, surely now also I had slain thee*" (Numb. xxii. 33). It sounded in the ears of Balaam as if the ass spoke to him ; and yet she did not speak, but the speech was heard as if proceeding from her. That this is so has often been shown me by living experience. It has been given me to hear horses as it were speaking; and yet the speech was not from them, but as if from them. This was actually the case with Balaam ; to the intent that that history might be described in the Word, for the sake of the internal sense which every single expression of it contains. In that sense it is described how the Lord defends those who are in truths and goods, lest they should be injured by those who speak as if from enlightenment, and yet have the disposition and intention to lead astray. (A. E. n. 140.)

THE SUN AND MOON STANDING STILL AT THE COMMAND OF JOSHUA.

It is written in Joshua : "*Then spake Joshua to Jehovah in the day when Jehovah delivered up the Amorites before the children of Israel, and he said in the sight of Israel, Sun, stand thou still upon Gibeon ; and thou, moon, in the valley of Ajalon. And the sun stood still, and the moon stayed, until the nation was avenged upon its enemies. Is not this written in the book of Jasher ? So the sun stood still in the midst of heaven, and hasted not to go down about a whole day*" (x. 12, 13). The saying that the sun stood still upon Gibeon and the moon in the valley of Ajalon, signified that the church was entirely vastated as to all good and truth. For a battle was then fought against the king of Jerusalem and the kings of the Amorites ; and by the king of Jerusalem the truth of the church entirely vastated by falsities is signified, and by the kings of the Amorites is signified the good of the church vastated by evils. Therefore those kings were smitten with hailstones, by which were signified the horrible falsities of evil. It is said that the sun stood still and the moon stayed, that is in the sight of the children of Israel, that they might see their enemies ; but this was prophetical, although historically related; as may appear from the circumstance that it is said, " *Is not this written in the book of Jasher ?*" which was a prophetical book, out of which these words were taken. From this same book therefore it is said too, " *until the nation was avenged upon its enemies,*" and not " until the children of Israel were avenged upon their enemies ;" for the word " nation" is said prophetically. The same is evident moreover from the consideration that this miracle, if it had been just so accomplished, would have inverted the whole order of nature ; which the other miracles in the Word would not have done. That it might be known therefore that this was said prophetically, it is added, " *Is not this written in the book of Jasher ?*" But yet that there was a light to them out of heaven, like the light of the sun in Gibeon, and a light as of the moon in the valley of Ajalon, is not to be doubted. (A. E. n. 401.)

Magic Sorcery and Enchantments.

By the Egyptians the representatives and significatives of the Ancient church, which church had also existed among them, were turned into magic. For by the representatives and significatives of the church at that time there was communication with heaven ; which communication was among those who lived in the good of charity, and with some of them was open. But with those who did not live in the good of charity, but in the opposites of charity, there was sometimes open communication with evil spirits, who perverted all the truths, and destroyed together with them the goods of the church. Thence magic originated. This may even be seen from the hieroglyphics of the Egyptians, which they also employed in sacred things ; for they signified spiritual things by them, and perverted Divine order. Magic is nothing else than a perversion of order ; especially it is the abuse of correspondences. (A. C. n. 6692.)

In ancient times many kinds of infernal arts called magic were practised, of which some are enumerated in the Word ; as in Deut. xviii. 9-11. There were also enchantments among them, whereby they induced affections and pleasures which another could not resist. This was effected by sounds and secret voices, which they either produced or murmured, and which by analogous correspondences had communication with the will of another, and excited his affection and fascinated him to will, think, and act in a certain manner and not otherwise. Such enchantments indeed the prophets had a knowledge of, and also practised, and excited good affections, hearing, and obedience, by them ; and these enchantments in a good sense are mentioned in the Word by Isaiah iii. 1-3, 20 ; xxvi. 16 ; Jer. viii. 17 ; and by David, in Psalm lviii. 4, 5. But because by such speakings and murmurings evil affections were excited by the evil, and enchantments thus became magical, they also are enumerated among the magical arts, and severely prohibited ; as in Deut. xviii. 9-11 ; Isaiah xlvii. 9, 12 ; Rev. xviii. 23 ; xxii. 15. (A. E. n. 590.)

Sorcerers are those who pervert Divine order, that is the laws of order. Sorcery and magic are nothing else, as is evident from sorcerers ; and especially in the other life, where they abound. For they who have practised cunning in the life of the

body, and have contrived various arts of defrauding others, and
at length, in consequence of success, have attributed all things to
their own prudence, in the other life learn in addition magical
arts, which are nothing else than abuses of Divine order, especially
of correspondences.   For it is according to Divine order that each
and all things correspond.   As for example, the hands, the arms,
and the shoulders, correspond to power; and thence a staff also
has the same correspondence.   Therefore they form to themselves
staffs, and also representatively present shoulders, arms, and
hands, and thereby exercise magical power.   So in a thousand
and a thousand other ways.   The abuse of order and of correspondences is when those things which are of order are not
applied to good ends, but to evil ends; and to the 'end of ruling
over others, and to the end of destroying; for the end of order is
salvation, thus to do good to all.

Where sorceries and enchantments are mentioned in the Word
they signify also the art of so presenting falsities that they appear as truths, and of so presenting truths that they appear as
falsities; which is done chiefly by fallacies. . . . Such is the
signification of enchantments in this passage, "*By thy enchantments were all nations seduced*" (Rev. xviii. 23); which is said of
Babylon. . . . From this it may now be known what is signified
by the sorceries which were to be cut off out of the hand, in
Micah v. 12; namely, the arts of presenting truths as falsities,
and falsities as truths.   These arts also correspond to the fantasies by which the evil in the other life present beautiful things
before the eyes as ugly, and ugly things as beautiful; which
fantasies are in truth a species of sorcery, for they also are
abuses and perversions of Divine order.   (A. C. n. 7296,
7297.)

By witchcraft in the Word nearly the same is signified as by
enchantment, and enchantment signifies such persuasion that a
man does not at all perceive but that the thing is so.   Such a kind
of persuasion exists with certain spirits that they as it were obstruct the understanding of another, and suffocate the faculty of
perceiving.   And as the upright men in the Babylonish nation [1]
are compelled and persuaded to believe and to do what the monks
say, therefore it is said they are seduced by their enchantments
(Rev. xviii. 23).   The enchantments mentioned by Isaiah, xlvii.
9, 12, where also Babylon is treated of, have a similar signification.   So by David in Psalm lviii. 5, 6.   Enchantment is also
among the arts approximating to magic which were prohibited
to the children of Israel (Deut. xviii. 10, 11).   (A. E. n. 1191.)

---

[1] That is, the Papal Church.   Babylon is the Scriptural type of that spiritual
dominion which in the Christian age has had its most remarkable and characteristic embodiment in that religion.

DESTRUCTION OF CHILDREN BY THE BEARS.

" *When Elisha went up into Bethel, as he was going up on the way, there came forth little children out of the city and mocked him, and said unto him, Go up thou bald head! Go up thou bald head! And he looked back behind him, and saw them, and cursed them in the name of Jehovah. And there came forth two she bears out of the wood, and tare in pieces forty and two children of them* " (2 Kings ii. 23, 24). It cannot be known why the little children were cursed by Elisha, and therefore torn in pieces by two bears because they called him bald head, unless it be known what Elisha represented, and what a bald head signifies, and also what is signified by the bears. That this was not done by Elisha from immoderate anger and without just cause might appear from the consideration, that he could not be so cruel to little children for only saying, " Go up thou bald head." It was indeed an offence against the prophet; but not such that they should be torn in pieces by bears on account of it. But it thus came to pass because Elisha represented the Lord as to the Word, and so the Word which is from the Lord. By a bald head the Word deprived of the natural sense was signified, which is the sense of the letter; and by the bears out of the wood was signified power from the natural or literal sense of the Word; and by those children they were signified who blaspheme the Word on account of its natural sense, because it is such as it is; by forty-two blasphemy is signified. Hence now it is plain that the punishment of blaspheming the Word was represented, and therefore signified, by these things. For all the power and holiness of the Word resides concentrated in its literal sense. Indeed if this sense were not there would be no Word; for without this the Word would be like a house without foundation, which would tremble in the air, and then fall to the ground and go to pieces; and it would be like a man without the skin which envelopes and holds together the included viscera in their position and order. And because such a condition is signified by a bald head, and the Word was represented by Elisha, for this reason the children were torn in pieces by bears ; which signified power from the natural sense of the Word, which is the literal sense, both with the good and with the evil. From all this, moreover, it is clear that the historical particulars of the Word equally with its prophetical contain a spiritual sense. (A. E. n. 781.)

SPIRITUAL DRUNKENNESS.

They are called drunkards who believe nothing but what they comprehend, and therefore inquire into the mysteries of faith;

for, as this is done by means of things sensual, known, or philosophical, man is so constituted that he cannot but fall into errors. The thought of man is merely worldly, corporeal, and material; because it is from worldly, corporeal, and material things, which continually cleave to it, and upon which the ideas of his thought are founded and in which they are terminated. To think and reason therefore from these concerning things Divine is to rush into errors and perversions; and it is as impossible for a man thence to obtain faith as it is for a camel to go through the eye of a needle. The error and unsoundness of mind that come from this are called in the Word drunkenness. Indeed souls or spirits in the other life who argue about the truths of faith and against them even become as drunkards, and act like them. . . . Spirits who are in the faith of charity are clearly distinguished from those who are not. Those that are in the faith of charity do not argue about the truths of faith, but say that they are thus; and they also confirm them as far as they can by matters of sense, of knowledge, and the analysis of reason. But as soon as anything obscure arises which they do not understand they set it aside, nor do they ever suffer it to bring them into doubt; saying that there are very few things which they comprehend, and therefore to think a thing is not true because they do not comprehend it would be insane. These are they who are in charity. But those on the contrary who are not in the faith of charity desire nothing but to argue whether it is so, and to know how it is; saying that unless they know how it is they cannot believe it is so. From this merely it is instantly known that they have no faith; and the indication of it is that they not only doubt about everything, but in their heart deny; and when instructed how things are they still persist, and move all manner of scruples against them, and are never at rest, even though it were to eternity. It is these, or such as these, who in the Word are said to be drunk with wine or strong drink. As in Isaiah: "*They also have erred through wine, and through strong drink have gone out of the way; the priest and the prophet have erred through strong drink; they are swallowed up of wine, they are out of the way through strong drink, they err in vision. . . . All tables are full of vomit of filthiness. . . . Whom shall He teach knowledge? And whom shall He make to understand what is heard? Them that are weaned from the milk, and torn away from the breast*" (xxviii. 7-9). Again in the same prophet: "*How say ye unto Pharaoh, I am the son of the wise, the son of ancient kings? . . . Where now are thy wise men? and let them tell thee now. . . . Jehovah hath mingled a spirit of perversities in the midst thereof, and they have caused Egypt to err in every work thereof, as a drunken man staggereth in his vomit*" (xix. 11, 12, 14). A drunken man here stands for those who desire by means of knowledges to search into things spiritual and celestial. Egypt signifies knowledges, and therefore he calls himself the son of the wise. . . . They who believe nothing but what they comprehend by things sensual and things known were also called "mighty to drink;" as in Isaiah: "*Woe unto them that are wise in their own eyes, and intelligent in their own sight! Woe unto them that are mighty to drink wine, and men of strength to mingle strong drink!*" (v. 21, 22.) They are said to be wise in their own eyes and intelligent in their own sight, because those that argue against the truths of faith deem themselves wiser than others. But those that care nothing for the Word and the truths of faith, and thus have no desire to know anything about faith, denying its principles, are called "drunken without wine;" as in Isaiah: "*They are drunken, but not with wine, they stagger, but not with strong drink; for Jehovah hath poured out upon you the spirit of deep sleep, and hath closed your eyes*" (xxix. 9, 10). (A. C. n. 1072.)

MIRACLES.

As regards prodigies and signs, it should be known that they were produced among such as were in external worship and did not desire to know anything of internal; for those who were in such worship were to be constrained by external means. Hence it is that miracles were performed among the Israelitish and Jewish people. For they were solely in external worship, and in no internal; and external worship was also what they ought to be in when they were not willing to be in internal worship,— to the intent that in externals they might represent holy things, and that so communication might be given with heaven, as by something of a church; for correspondences, representatives, and significatives conjoin the natural world to the spiritual. It was then for this reason that so many miracles were performed among that nation. But miracles were not performed among those who were in internal worship, that is in charity and faith; for they are hurtful to them, since miracles compel belief, and what is of compulsion does not remain, but is dissipated. The internal things of worship, which are faith and charity, are to be implanted in a state of freedom; for then they are appropriated, and things which are so appropriated remain. But things which are implanted in a state of compulsion remain outside of the internal man in the external; for nothing enters into the internal man but by means of intellectual ideas, which are reasons, for the ground which receives there is an enlightened rational. Hence it is that no miracles are wrought at this day. That they are also hurtful is therefore evident; for they compel belief, and fix in the external man the idea that it is so; if afterwards the internal man denies what miracles have confirmed, there arises an opposition and collision between the internal and external of man; and at length, when the ideas derived from miracles are dissipated, a conjunction of the false and the true takes place, which is profanation. Hence it appears how hurtful are miracles at this day in the church, when the internals of worship are made known. These things are signified too by the Lord's words to Thomas, " *Thomas, because thou hast seen Me, thou hast believed; blessed are they that do not see, and yet believe* " (John xx. 29). So also they are blessed who believe and not by miracles. But miracles are not hurtful to those who are in external worship without internal, for with such there is no opposition between the internal and external of man; therefore no collision, and so no profanation. That miracles do not contribute anything to faith is sufficiently manifest from the miracles wrought among the people of Israel in Egypt and in the wilderness; in that they had no effect at all upon them. For that people, although a little time before they had seen so many miracles in Egypt, and afterwards the Red Sea divided and the Egyptians overwhelmed, the pillar of cloud going before them by day and the pillar of fire by night, and the manna daily showering down from heaven; and although they had seen Mount Sinai in smoke, and heard Jehovah speaking thence, besides other miracles, yet even in the midst of such things that people declined from all faith, and from the worship of Jehovah to the worship of a calf (Exod. xxxii.). It is evident from this what is the effect of miracles. They would be of still less effect at this day, when it is not acknowledged that anything exists from the spiritual world, and when everything of the kind that takes place, and is not attributed to nature, is denied. For there universally reigns a spirit of denial against the Divine influx and government in the earth. Therefore, if at this day the man of the church were to see the veriest Divine miracles, he would first drag them down into nature and defile them there, and then reject them as phantasms, and finally would laugh at all who attributed them to the Divine and not to nature. That miracles are of no effect is also evident from the Lord's words in Luke: " *If they hear not Moses and the prophets, neither will they be persuaded though one rose from the dead* " (xvi. 31). (A. C. n. 7290.)

It should be known that all the miracles which were wrought by the Lord always involved, and therefore signified, such things as are meant by the blind, the lame, the leprous, the deaf, the dead, and the poor, in the internal sense. The miracles of the Lord were therefore Divine; as were also those wrought in Egypt and in the wilderness, and others recorded in the Word. (A. C. n. 2383.)

Why Fishermen were chosen to be the Lord's Disciples.

There was a diligent inquiry among spirits respecting the disciples,—that they might instruct those who were from the earth Jupiter,—for what reason men of inferior condition like fishermen were chosen, and not any from among the learned: and as I heard them, it may here be related that very many [at that time] were steeped in vanities and the like, so that they could not receive those things which belong to faith, like the unlearned who more easily received and believed them. Therefore they in preference to the learned were chosen. (S. D. n. 1216.)

Love to Enemies.

Internal men, such as the angels of heaven are, do not desire the retaliation of evil for evil; but from heavenly charity forgive. For they know that the Lord protects all who are in good against the evil, and that He protects according to the good that is in them; and that He would not protect if they were inflamed with enmity, hatred, and revenge, on account of evil done to them; for these avert protection. (A. E. n. 556.)

Spiritual Fermentations.

Spiritual fermentations take place in many ways, both in the heavens and on earth; but in the world it is not known what they are, and how they are effected. There are in truth evils and attendant falsities, which admitted into societies act as the ferments put into meal and new wine; by which heterogeneous things are separated and the homogeneous are united, and it becomes pure and clear. These are the fermentations which are meant by these words of the Lord: " *The kingdom of the heavens is like unto leaven which a woman took and hid in three measures of meal, till the whole was leavened* " (Matt. xiii. 33; Luke xiii. 21). (D. P. n. 25.)

Prayer and Worship.

" *All things whatsoever ye shall ask in prayer believing ye shall receive* " (Matt. xxi. 22.) By these words the power is described of those who are in the Lord. They desire nothing, and so ask nothing but from the Lord, and whatsoever they from the Lord desire and ask the same is done; for the Lord says, " *Without Me ye can do nothing ; . . . abide in Me and I in you.*" The angels in heaven have such power that if they only desire a thing they obtain it; but they do not desire anything but what is of use, and they desire it as if of themselves but yet from the Lord.   (A. R. n. 951.)

Prayer in itself considered is discourse with God ; and there is then a certain internal intuition of those things which are objects of prayer, corresponding to which there is a something like influx into the perception or thought of the mind of him who prays; so that there is a kind of opening of man's interiors towards God.   But this with a difference according to the man's state, and according to the essence of the thing which is the object of prayer.   If it be from love and faith, and only for celestial and spiritual things that he prays, then there exists a something resembling revelation in the prayer, which is manifested in the affection of him who prays, in respect to hope, consolation, or some internal joy.   Hence it is that prayer in the internal sense signifies revelation.   (A. C. n. 2535.)

By alms [in the Word], in the universal sense, all the good is meant that a man wills and does; and by prayer, in the same sense, is meant all the truth that a man speaks and utters. . . . They that do good and speak truth not for the sake of themselves and the world, but for the sake of good itself and of truth itself, are meant by those that do alms in secret and pray in secret; for such act and pray from love or affection, and so from the Lord.   This then is to love good and truth for the sake of good and truth.   It is therefore said of them that *their Father in the heavens will reward them openly* (Matt. vi. 4-6).   (A. E. n. 695.)

Worship does not consist in prayers and in outward devotion, but in a life of charity.   Prayers are only its externals, for they proceed out of the man by his mouth, and are therefore such as the character of the man is in respect to his life.   It matters not that he assumes a humble deportment, and kneels and sighs when he prays; these are outward things, and unless outward things proceed from inward they are but gestures and sounds without life.   In all that a man utters there is an affection, and every man spirit and angel is his own affection, for their affection is their life.   It is the affection itself that speaks, and not the man without it.   Wherefore, according to the quality of the affection, such is the prayer.   Spiritual affection is what is called charity towards the neighbour.   True worship is to be in this affection ; prayer is its going forth.   It is plain then that the essential of worship is a life of charity, and that its instrumental is gesture and prayer; or that the primary part of worship is a life of charity, and its secondary is praying. From which it is clear that they who place all Divine worship in oral piety and not in actual piety err exceedingly. Actual piety is to act in every work and in every function from sincerity and rectitude, and according to what is just and equitable, and this because it is commanded by the Lord in the Word; for thus in every work man looks to heaven and to the Lord with whom he is thus conjoined. . . . It is written in David:—"*I cried unto God with my mouth. . . . If I regard iniquity in my heart the Lord will not hear. Verily God hath heard; He hath attended to the voice of my prayer*" (Psa. lxvi. 17-19). It is said, "If I regard iniquity in my heart the Lord will not hear," because the quality of prayer is according to that of the man's heart, and therefore they are not prayers of any worship if the heart is evil. The heart of man is his love, and the love of man is his very life; consequently his prayers have the quality of his love or the quality of his life. It follows therefore that the prayers signify the life of his love and charity, or that his life is meant by prayers in the spiritual sense. . . . Moreover, when a man is in the life of charity he continually prays, though not with the mouth yet with the heart; for that which is of the love is continually in the thought, even when he is unconscious of it. (*ib.* n. 325.)

But a man ought not while he lives in the world to omit the practice of external worship also, for by external worship internal things are awakened; and external things are kept by external worship in a state of sanctity, so that the internal can flow in. Besides which a man is thus caused to imbibe knowledge, and prepared to receive celestial things, that he may be endued also with states of sanctity of which he is unconscious; which states of sanctity are preserved to him by the Lord, for the use of eternal life. For in the other life all man's states of life return. (A. C. n. 1618.)

In all worship there must be humiliation. If there is no humiliation there is nothing of adoration, and therefore nothing of worship. That a state of humiliation is essential to worship is 'for this reason, that in the degree that the heart is humbled in the same degree self-love and every evil therefore ceases, and so far as this ceases good and truth, that is charity and faith, flow in from the Lord. For self-love is what chiefly opposes the reception of these, because in this there is contempt of others in comparison of one's self, together with hatred and revenge if he is not worshipped. (*ib.* n. 2327.)

By worship according to the order of heaven is meant all practice of good according to the Lord's precepts. The worship of God at this day means principally the worship of the lips in a temple morning and evening. But the worship of God does not consist essentially in this, but in a life of uses. This is worship according to the order of heaven. The worship of the lips also is worship, but it is entirely without avail unless there be worship of the life; for this worship is of the heart, and that, in order that it may become worship, must proceed from this. (*ib.* n. 7884.)

The man who is in the course of purification from evils and falsities, and in good and truth, is in genuine worship. For purification from evils and falsities consists in desisting from them, and in shunning them and holding them in aversion; and the implantation of good and truth consists in thinking and purposing what is good and true and speaking and doing them. And the conjunction of the two is life from them; for when good and truth are conjoined in a man he has a new will and a new understanding, and therefore new life. When a man becomes of such a character, in every work that he does there is Divine worship; for he then looks to the Divine [Being] in everything, venerates Him, loves Him, and accordingly worships Him. This is genuine Divine worship. (*ib.* n. 10,143.)

It is believed by those who do not know the mysteries of heaven that worship is from man, because it goes forth from the thought and from the affection that are in him. But the worship which is from man is not worship, consequently the confessions, adorations, and prayers which are from man are not confessions, adorations, and prayers which are heard and received by the Lord. But they must be from the Lord Himself in man. The church knows that this is so; for she teaches that no good proceeds from man, but that all good is from heaven, that is from the Divine there. Therefore all good is worship also, and worship without good is not worship. The Church, accordingly, when she is in a holy [state], prays that God may be present and lead their thoughts and discourse. The case is this: When man is in genuine worship the Lord flows into the goods and truths that are in him, and He raises them up to him, and with them raises the man according to the degree and manner that he is in them. This elevation does not appear to a man unless he is in the genuine affection of truth and good, and in the knowledge, acknowledgment, and faith that all good comes from above, from the Lord. That this is so may be apprehended even by those who are wise from the world; for they know from their erudition that there is not natural influx, which is called by them physical influx, but spiritual influx; that is, that nothing can flow in from the natural world into heaven, but the reverse. From these considerations it may appear how it is to be understood that the influx and operation of the Divine of the Lord is into all and everything of worship. That in truth it is so it has been granted me frequently to experience; for I was permitted to perceive the very influx, the calling forth of the truths which were with me, the application to the objects of prayer, the affection of good adjoined, and the elevation itself. But although this is so, yet a man ought not to hang down his hands and wait for influx, for this would be to act the part of an image without life. He ought still to think, to purpose, and to act, as if from himself, and yet ascribe to the Lord every thought of truth and every effort of good; thereby there is implanted in him by the Lord the capability of receiving Him and influx from Him. (*ib.* n. 10,299.)

Why it is the Lord's will to be Worshipped.

The essence of spiritual love is to do good to others, not for the sake of self, but for their sake. Infinitely more is this the essence of Divine love. It is like the love of parents for their children, in that they do them good from love to them, not for the sake of themselves, but for their sakes. This is plainly seen in the love of a mother towards infants. Because the Lord is to be adored, worshipped, and glorified, it is believed that He loves adoration, worship, and glory, for His own sake; but He loves them for man's sake, because by means of them man comes into such a state that the Divine can flow into him and be perceived; for by means of them man removes his own [*proprium*] which prevents the influx and reception; for what is his own, which is the love of himself, hardens and closes the heart. This is removed by the acknowledgment that nothing but evil comes from himself, and nothing but good from the Lord. Hence comes a softening of the heart and humiliation, from which flow forth adoration and worship. It follows from this that the uses which the Lord renders to Himself through man are in order that He may do good to him from love; and as it is His love [to do this], reception [by man] is the joy of His love. Let no one therefore believe that the Lord is with those who adore Him merely; but that He is with those that do His commandments, thus who perform uses. He has His abode with these, but not with those. (D. L. W. n. 335.)

The Lord's Prayer.

In the Word those things which precede govern in those that follow, and so in a series. This is evident from everything that the Lord spake; and especially from His prayer, which is called the Lord's Prayer. In this prayer all things follow in such a series that they constitute as it were a column increasing from the highest part to the lowest.   In the interiors of this are those things which precede in the series; what is first [or highest] is inmost, and what follows in order adds itself in succession to the inmost, and thus it increases.   What is inmost governs universally in those things which are round about it, that is in each and all things, for hence is the essential of the existence of all. (A. C. 8864.)

That there are innumerable things within the ideas of thought, and that they are within them in order from the interiors, has been evident to me when in the morning and evening I have been reading the Lord's Prayer.   The ideas of my thought were then constantly opened towards heaven, and innumerable things flowed in, so that I clearly observed that the ideas of thought received from the contents of the Prayer were made full from heaven.   And such things were poured in, too, as cannot be uttered, and such also as I cannot comprehend; I was only sensible of the general affection thence resulting.   And it is wonderful that the things which flowed in were varied every day.   From this it was given me to know that there are more things in the contents of that Prayer than the universal heaven has capacity to comprehend; and that to man there are more things in it in proportion as his thought is more opened towards heaven; and on the other hand that there are fewer things in it in proportion as his thought is more closed.   To those indeed whose thought is closed nothing more appears therein than the sense of the letter, or the sense which is nearest to the words.   (*ib.* n. 6619.)

The Lord's Prayer is daily read in heaven, as it is by men on earth.   And the angels do not then think of God the Father, because He is invisible; but they think of Him in His Divine Human, because in this He is visible.   And in this Human He is not called by them Christ, but Lord; and thus the Lord is their Father in heaven. . . . In that prayer it is said, "*Hallowed be Thy name*" and "*Thy kingdom come.*"   The name of the Father is His Divine Human; and the Kingdom of the Father comes when the Lord is immediately approached, and by no means when God the Father is approached immediately.   (A. R. n. 839.)

THE TRANSFIGURATION; AND THE PARTING OF THE LORD'S RAIMENT.

Concerning the Lord's transfiguration, we read: "*Jesus taketh Peter, James, and John his brother, and bringeth them up into an high mountain apart, and was transfigured before them; and His face did shine as the sun, and His raiment was white as the light.*

And behold there appeared unto them Moses and Elias talking with Him. . . . *And behold a bright cloud overshadowed them, and behold a voice out of the cloud, which said, This is My beloved Son, in whom I am well pleased; hear ye Him"* (Matt. xvii. 1-5; Mark ix. 2-8; Luke ix. 28-36.) The reason why the Lord took Peter, James, and John, was because the church was represented by them in respect to faith, charity, and the works of charity; that He took them into a high mountain was because by a mountain heaven was signified; that His face did shine as the sun was because the face signifies the interiors,—it shone as the sun because His interiors were Divine, for the sun is Divine love; His raiment was white as the light, because raiment signifies Divine truth proceeding from Him; the same is signified, too, by light. The reason why Moses and Elias appeared was because they both signify the Word, Moses the historical Word, and Elias the prophetical Word; a bright cloud overshadowed them, because a bright cloud signifies the Word in the letter within which is the internal sense; the voice out of the cloud said, " This is my beloved Son, in whom I am well pleased; hear ye Him," because a voice out of the cloud signifies Divine truth from the Word, and beloved Son, the Lord's Divine Human. And because Divine truth is from Him, and hence all the truth of the church, it was said out of the cloud, " In whom I am well pleased; hear ye Him." It is clear that the Divine Human of the Lord was thus seen, because the very Divine cannot appear to any one except by the Divine Human. This indeed the Lord teaches in John: *"No man hath seen God at any time; the only-begotten Son, who is in the bosom of the Father, He hath manifested Him"* (i. 18). And in another place: " *Ye have neither heard His voice at any time, nor seen His shape"* (John v. 37). . . . From the fact that the Lord's garments signify Divine truth it may be known what is signified by the soldiers dividing the Lord's garments among them, and casting lots upon His vesture; of which it is thus written in John: " *The soldiers took His garments, and made four parts, to each soldier a part, and also His coat; now the coat was without seam, woven from the top throughout. They said therefore among themselves, Let us not rend it, but cast lots for it, whose it shall be. That the scripture might be fulfilled, which saith, They parted My raiment among them, and for My vesture they did cast lots. These things therefore the soldiers did"* (xix. 23, 24). He who does not know that in every particular of the Word there is an internal sense which is spiritual, cannot see any mystery in these things. He knows only that the soldiers divided the garments and not the coat, and perceives nothing more than this; and yet there is a Divine secret not only in this circumstance, but also in every least particular of the things recorded concerning the Lord's passion.

The secret in this circumstance is, that the garments of the Lord signified Divine truth, and so the Word, because the Word is Divine truth; the garments which they divided signified the Word in the letter; and the coat, the Word in the internal sense. To divide them signifies to disperse and falsify; and the soldiers signify those that are of the church who fight for Divine truth; for this reason it is said, "These things therefore the soldiers did." It is plain then that the meaning of these words in the spiritual sense is that the Jewish church dispersed the Divine truth which is in the sense of the letter; but that they could not disperse the Divine truth which is in the internal sense. (A. E. n. 64.)

TEARS.

"*And God shall wipe away all tears from their eyes*" (Rev. vii. 17). This signifies a state of beatitude from the affection of truth after falsities are removed by temptations; as appears from the signification of to wipe away tears from the eyes, which is to take away grief of mind on account of falsities and arising from falsities. And because on the cessation of that grief, after the temptations which they have undergone, beatitude succeeds by means of truths from good, this also is therefore signified; for all the beatitude which the angels enjoy is through truth from good, or through the spiritual affection of truth. The spiritual affection of truth is derived from good, for good causes it. That all the beatitude of the angels comes from this is because Divine truth proceeding from the Lord is what constitutes heaven in general and in particular, and therefore those who are in Divine truths are in the life of heaven, and of course in eternal beatitude. The reason why tears from the eyes signify grief of mind on account of falsities and arising from falsities, is that by the eye the understanding of truth is signified; and therefore tears from the eyes signify grief on account of the non-understanding of truth, that is on account of falsities. The same is also signified by tears in the following passage in Isaiah: "*He will swallow up death in victory, and the Lord Jehovah will wipe away tears from off all faces*" (xxv. 8). This signifies that the Lord by His coming shall remove evils and falsities from those who live from Him, so that there shall be no grief of mind on account of them or from them. Death signifies evil, because evil is the cause of spiritual death; and tears are predicated of what is false. It is to be observed that shedding tears and weeping signify grief on account of falsities and from falsities; but shedding tears signifies grief of mind, and weeping grief of heart on account of them.[1] Grief of mind is grief of the thought and understanding, which are of truth; and grief of heart is grief of the affection and will, which are of good; and because there is everywhere in the word a marriage of truth and good, therefore both weeping and tears are mentioned in the Word when grief is expressed on account of falsities of doctrine or of religion. That weeping is grief of heart may appear from the consideration that it bursts forth from the heart, and breaks out into lamentation through the mouth ; and that shedding tears is grief of mind may appear from the fact that it issues forth from the thought through the eyes. In both weeping and shedding tears water comes forth, but bitter and astringent; which is occasioned by influx into the grief of man from the spiritual world, where bitter water corresponds to defect of truth because of falsities, and to grief on account of them. (A. E. n. 484.)

THE DRAGON.

By the dragon in general they are meant who are more or less natural, and yet in the knowledge of things spiritual from the Word. The reason is that serpents in general signify the sensual things of man, and thence sensual men ; and therefore the dragon which is a flying serpent signifies the sensual man, who though sensual yet flies towards heaven, in that he speaks and thinks from the Word, or from doctrine derived from the Word. (A. E. n. 714.)

THE SPIRITUAL SENSE OF NUMBERS.

Number and measure are mentioned in many places in the Word, and it is supposed that in either case number and measure is meant; but by number and measure in the spiritual sense the quality is meant of the thing treated of. The very quality is determined by the numbers which are expressed. . . . The reason why number signifies the quality of the thing treated of

---

[1] In modern usage "weeping" has become synonymous with "shedding tears;" but the original and more exact meaning of "weep" is to bewail, or to express sorrow, grief, or anguish by outcry or other manifest outward sign. It is necessary to mark this distinction here, for a proper understanding of the author's language. Weeping in this sense it is true is generally accompanied by the shedding of tears, because the understanding acts in sympathy and unison with the will ; but according to the author the tears even then proceed from and therefore correspond relatively to the action of the thought, and the weeping or bewailing to that of the affection. A good example of this distinction between the terms occurs in the passage, "Refrain thy *voice* from weeping and thine *eyes* from shedding tears" (Jer. xxxi. 16).

is that the Word is spiritual, and therefore each and all things therein contained are spiritual; and spiritual things are not numbered and measured, and yet they fall into numbers and measures as they descend out of the spiritual world, or out of heaven where angels are into the natural world or the earth where men are. And in like manner when they descend out of the spiritual sense of the Word, in which the angels are, into the natural sense of the Word in which men are. (The natural sense of the Word is the sense of its letter.) This is the reason why there are numbers in this sense, and why they signify things spiritual, or such things as relate to heaven and the church. That the spiritual things of heaven, and such things also as angels think and say, fall into numbers has been often shown to me. When they have been talking with each other their conversation has been determined into mere numbers, which were seen upon paper; and they afterwards said it was their conversation determined into numbers, and that those numbers contained in a series all that they had said. I was also told what they signified, and how they were to be understood.

There are simple numbers which are significative above others, and from which the greater numbers derive their significations; namely, the numbers two, three, five, and seven. The number two signifies union, and is predicated of good; the number three signifies full, and is predicated of truths; the number five signifies much and some; and the number seven signifies what is holy. From the number two arise the numbers 4, 8, 16, 400, 800, 1600, 4000, 8000, 16,000; which numbers have a similar signification to that of the number two, because they arise from the simple number multiplied into itself, and by multiplication by 10. From the number three arise 6, 12, 24, 72, 144, 1440, 144,000; which numbers also have a similar signification to that of the number three, because they arise from this simple number by multiplication. From the number five arise 10, 50, 100, 1000, 10,000, 100,000; which numbers also have a similar signification to that of the number five, because they arise from it by multiplication. From the number seven arise 14, 70, 700, 7000, 70,000; which numbers have a similar signification too with seven, because they arise out of it. Since the number three signifies full, and full denotes all, from this the number twelve derives its signification of all things and all persons. It is predicated of truths from good; because it arises out of 3 multiplied into 4, and the number 3 is predicated of truths, and 4 of good, as was said above. He who does not know that the number twelve signifies all things, and that the numbers multiplied from it have a similar signification; and who does not know that each tribe signifies some universal and essential of the church, cannot but understand that only 12,000 out of every tribe of Israel were sealed, that is were received or were to be received into heaven, when yet the 12,000 there mentioned do not mean 12,000, nor the tribes there named the tribes of Israel; but by 12,000 all are meant, and by the tribes of Israel those that are in truths from good, and thus all, wheresoever on earth they are, who constitute the church of the Lord. (A. E. n. 429, 430.)

As respects numbers in the Word, the half and the double involve a similar signification; as for instance that of twenty is similar to ten, and that of four to two, that of six to three, of twenty-four to twelve, and so on. So also numbers further multiplied are similar in signification, as a hundred and also a thousand is similar to ten, and seventy-two, and a hundred and forty-four are similar to twelve. What therefore the compound numbers involve may be known from the simple numbers from which and with which they are multiplied. What the more simple numbers involve may also be known from the integral numbers; as what five involves may be known from ten, and what two and a half involves may be known from five, and so on. It should be known in general that numbers multiplied involve the same as the simple numbers, but more full; and that numbers divided involve the same, but not so full. As regards five specifically, this number has a double signification. It signifies a little and hence some; and it signifies remains. It signifies a little from its relation to those numbers which signify much; namely, to a thousand, and to a hundred, and therefore also to ten. When it has relation to ten, five signifies remains; for ten signifies remains. He who does not know that there is any internal sense of the Word which does not appear in the letter, will be quite amazed that even numbers in the Word signify things; especially, because he can form no spiritual idea from numbers; but yet numbers flow from the spiritual ideas which the angels have. What the ideas are, and what the things are to which numbers correspond, may indeed be known; but whence that correspondence is, still lies hidden. As for instance, whence is the correspondence of twelve with all things of faith; and the correspondence of seven with things that are holy; and the correspondence of ten, and likewise of five, with goods and truths stored up in the interior man by the Lord, and so on. But yet it is enough to know that there is a correspondence, and that from such correspondence all the numbers in the Word signify something in the spiritual world; consequently also that the Divine inspired into them lies stored up therein. For example, in the following passages where five is mentioned: In the Lord's parable concerning the man who " *went into a far country, and delivered to his servants his goods, to one five talents, to another two, and to another one; . . . and he that received five talents, traded with the same and gained other five talents; and likewise he that had received two, gained other two; but he that received one, hid his Lord's silver in the earth"* (Matt. xxv. 14, and following verses).   One who does not think beyond the literal sense cannot know but that these numbers, five, two, and one, were assumed merely for composing the story of the parable, and involve nothing further; and yet even in these numbers themselves there is an arcanum.   For by the servant who received five talents, they are signified who have admitted goods and truths from the Lord, that is who have received remains; by him who received two, they are signified who in advanced age have adjoined charity to faith; and by him who received one they who have received faith only, without charity, are signified.   Of this one it is said that he hid his Lord's silver in the earth; for the silver, which is mentioned in connection with him in the internal sense signifies truth which is of faith; and faith without charity cannot make gain, or bear fruit.   Such things are contained in these numbers. So in the other parables. . . .   Likewise in these words of the Lord, " *Think ye that I am come to give peace on the earth?   I tell you nay, but rather division.   For from henceforth there shall be five in one house divided, three against two, and two against three*" (Luke xii. 51, 52).   And also in these actual historical incidents, that *the Lord fed five thousand men with five loaves and two fishes; and that at that time He commanded them to sit down by hundreds and by fifties; and that after they had eaten, they gathered of the fragments twelve baskets* (Matt. xiv. 15-21; Mark vi. 38, and following verses; Luke ix. 12-17; John vi. 5-13). Because these incidents are historical it can scarcely be believed that the numbers in them are significative; as the number five thousand, which was that of the men; the number five, which was that of the loaves; and two, which was that of the fishes; and also the number a hundred, and the number fifty, which were those of the companies that sat down; and lastly twelve, which was that of the baskets containing the fragments.   And yet in each number there is an arcanum; for each particular circumstance took place of Providence, to the end that Divine things might be represented.   That the number five contains within it a heavenly mystery, and similar to that in the number ten, is plain from the cherubim of which we read in the first book of the Kings: " *Within the oracle Solomon made two cherubim of olive wood; the height of each was ten cubits; five cubits was the wing of one cherub, and five cubits was the wing of the other cherub: it was ten cubits from the extremities of its wings to the extremities of its wings; thus ten cubits was the cherub; both cherubim had one measure and one proportion*" (vi. 23-25). It is also evident from the lavers about the temple, and from the candlesticks, of which we read in the same book that "*five bases of the lavers were set near the shoulder of the house to the right, and five near the shoulder of the house to the left*" . . . and that "*five candlesticks were set on the right, and five on the left, before the holy place*" (vii. 39, 49). That "*the brazen sea was ten cubits from brim to brim, and five cubits in height, and thirty cubits in circumference*" (vii. 23), was that holy things might be signified both by the numbers ten and five, and by thirty; which number of the circumference in fact does not geometrically answer to the diameter, but it spiritually involves that which is signified by the compass of that vessel. That all numbers signify things in the spiritual world, is very evident from the numbers in Ezekiel where the new earth, the new city, and the new temple are treated of, which the angel measured as to all its particulars (see chapters xl. xli. xlii. xliii. xlv. xlvi. xlvii. xlviii. xlix.). A description of almost all the holy things therein is exhibited by numbers; and therefore one who does not know what those numbers involve can know scarcely anything of the arcana contained therein. The number ten and the number five occur there (xl. 7, 11, 48; xli. 2, 9, 11, 12; xlii. 4; xlv. 11, 14), besides the multiplied numbers; namely, twenty-five, fifty, five hundred, five thousand. It is manifest from the particulars that the new earth, the new city, and the new temple there signify the Lord's kingdom in the heavens, and His church therefrom on the earth. (A. C. n. 5291.)

A greater and lesser number, or a multiplied and divided number, involves a similar signification to that of the simple numbers from which it is derived. This is very manifest from the number twelve, which has a similar signification, whether it be divided into six or multiplied into seventy-two or into 144; that is twelve into twelve, or into 12,000, or into 144,000. As for instance 144,000 in the Apocalypse: "*I heard the number of them that were sealed, a hundred forty-four thousand, they were sealed out of every tribe of Israel; out of each tribe twelve thousand*" (vii. 4, 5, and following verses). In this passage the sons of Israel are not meant by the sons of Israel; nor the tribes by the tribes, nor number by number, but such things as are in the internal sense are meant; namely, all things of faith and charity; and so by each tribe specifically one genus or one class, as has been explained at Genesis xxix. and xxx. So again in the Apocalypse: "*Lo, a Lamb standing upon mount Zion, and with Him 144,000 having His Father's name written upon their foreheads. . . . They sung a new song before the throne, . . . and no one could learn the song but the 144,000 bought from the earth. . . .*"

These are they that follow the Lamb whithersoever He goeth. These were bought from among men, the first-fruits to God and the Lamb" (xiv. 1, 3, 4). It is evident from this description, that they who are in charity are meant by the 144,000 ; and it is also evident that that number merely designates their state and quality. For that number denotes the same as twelve, since it arises from 12,000 and 12 multiplied into each other ; in like manner as the lesser number 144, which is twelve times twelve, in the same book, " *He measured the wall of the Holy Jerusalem coming down from God out of heaven, 144 cubits, which is the measure of a man, that is of an angel"* (Apoc. xxi. 2, 17). In the spiritual sense the wall of the Holy Jerusalem is not a wall, but the truth of faith defending the things which are of the church ; for this reason too it is said that it was 144 cubits. It is very plain that this is so, for it is said that it is the measure of a man, that is, of an angel. By a man and by an angel, all of the truth and good of faith is signified. And it is plain also from the twelve precious stones which formed the foundation of the wall, and from the twelve gates, each of which was one pearl (ver. 19-21); for by precious stones truths of faith which are from the good of charity are signified ; likewise by a gate, and also by a pearl. Hence now it is evident, that a lesser and greater number involves a similar signification to that of the simple number from which it is formed. From all this it may now be seen that the number of six hundred thousand men going forth out of Egypt also signifies such things. Scarcely any one can believe that this number has such a signification, because it is an historical fact, and everything historical keeps the mind continually in the external sense, and withdraws it from the internal sense. But this number, too, has such a signification ; for there is not even the least word, nay not one jot nor a single point in' the Word which is not in itself holy, because it involves within it what is holy. That in the historical fact alone there is nothing holy every one must see. (*ib.* n. 7973. See also p. 127.)

MEASURES AND WEIGHTS.

" *And he that sat on him had a pair of balances in his hand"* (Rev. vi. 5). This signifies the estimation of good and truth, of what kind it was with those referred to. The estimation of good and truth is signified by the balances in his hand ; for all measures as well as weights, in the Word, signify estimation of the thing treated of. That measures and weights have such a signification is plain from the following in Daniel : " *There was a handwriting before Belshazzar the king of Babylon, when he was drinking wine out of the vessels of gold and of silver which were taken out of the temple in Jerusalem, ' Mene, mene, tekel, upharsin,' which is, numbered, weighed, and divided; wherefore this is the interpretation; 'mene, God hath numbered thy kingdom and finished it; tekel, thou art weighed in the balance and found wanting; peres, thy kingdom is divided and given to the Medes and Persians'"* (v. 1, 2, 26-28). By drinking out of the vessels of gold and silver of the temple in Jerusalem, and at the same time worshipping other gods, the profanation of good and truth is signified; so also by Babel; mene, or to number, signifies to know his quality as to truth; tekel, or to weigh, signifies to know his quality as to good; peres, or to divide, signifies to disperse. That the quality of truth and good is signified by measures and balances in the Word, is evident in Isaiah: " *Who hath measured the waters in the hollow of His hand, and meted out the heavens with the span, and comprehended the dust of the earth in a measure, and weighed the mountains in scales and the hills in a balance?*" (xl. 12). And in the Apocalypse: " *The angel measured the wall of the Holy Jerusalem, an hundred and forty and four cubits, which is the measure of a man, that is of an angel*" (xxi. 17). (A. R. n. 313.)

Alpha and Omega.

The Lord is called the Alpha and the Omega, because Alpha is the first and Omega the last letter in the Greek alphabet, and from this circumstance signify all things in the complex; the reason is that each letter of the alphabet in the spiritual world signifies something; and a vowel, because it is used for sound, signifies something of affection or love. From this origin is spiritual and angelic language, and also that of the Scriptures. But this is an arcanum hitherto unknown. . . . The Lord describes His Divinity and infinity by Alpha and Omega; which signify that He is the All in all of heaven and the church. Because in the spiritual world, and therefore in angelic language, each letter of the alphabet signifies something, David wrote the 119th Psalm, in order according to the letters of the alphabet, beginning with Aleph and ending with Thau, as may be seen from the initials of the verses. Something similar to this appears in Psalm cxi., but not so evidently. On this account also Abram was called Abraham, and Sarai was called Sarah. This was done in order that in heaven not they but the Divine should be understood by Abraham and Sarah. And it is so understood; for the letter H involves infinity, because it is only an aspirate. (A. R. n. 29, 38.)

THE TEN COMMANDMENTS.

THERE is not a nation in the whole world which does not know that it is evil to kill, to commit adultery, to steal, and to testify falsely; and that if these evils were not guarded against by laws, the kingdom, republic, or established order of society of whatever form would perish. Who then can conceive that the Israelitish nation was so senseless beyond others that it did not know that those things were evil? One may therefore wonder that these laws, universally known in the world, should be so miraculously promulgated from mount Sinai by Jehovah Himself. But listen: they were thus miraculously promulgated, that they might know these laws are not only civil and moral laws, but also Divine laws; and that to act contrary to them is not only to do evil against the neighbour, that is against the citizen and against society, but is also to sin against God. Therefore these laws, by their promulgation from mount Sinai by Jehovah, were made also laws of religion. It is evident that whatever Jehovah commands, He commands that it be a matter of religion, and thus that it be done for the sake of salvation. But before the commandments are explained something shall be premised concerning their holiness, that it may be manifest that religion is in them.

Because the commandments of the decalogue were the first-fruits of the Word,[1] and therefore the first-fruits of the church that was about to be established with the Israelitish nation, and because they were in a brief summary a complex of all things of religion, by which the conjunction is effected of God with man and of man with God, therefore they were so holy that there is nothing holier. That they are most holy is evidently manifest from the following facts: That the Lord Jehovah Himself descended upon Mount Sinai in fire and with angels, and therefrom promulgated them by the living voice, and that the mountain was hedged about lest any should draw near and die. That neither the priests nor the elders approached, but Moses only. That these commandments were written upon two tables of stone by the finger of God. That when Moses brought the tables down the second time his face shone. That the tables

[1] See note, p. 257.

were afterwards deposited in the ark, and this in the inmost of the tabernacle, and over it was placed the propitiatory, and over this were placed the cherubim of gold; that this inmost of the tabernacle, where the ark was, was called the holy of holies. That without the veil within which was the ark, various things were arranged which represented the holy things of heaven and the church; which were the table overlaid with gold on which was the bread of faces; the golden altar on which incense was burned; and the golden candlestick with seven lamps; also the curtains round about, of fine linen, purple, and scarlet. The holiness of this whole tabernacle arose from nothing else than the law which was in the ark. On account of the holiness of the tabernacle from the law in the ark, all the people of Israel by command encamped around it, in order according to the tribes, and marched in order after it; and then a cloud was over it by day and a fire by night. On account of the holiness of that law, and the presence of Jehovah therein, Jehovah talked with Moses over the propitiatory between the cherubim, and the ark was called Jehovah There; but it was not lawful for Aaron to enter within the veil except with sacrifices and incense, lest he should die. On account of the presence of Jehovah in and about that law miracles also were wrought through the ark which contained the law. Thus the waters of the Jordan were divided, and so long as the ark rested in the middle of it the people passed over on dry ground; the walls of Jericho fell down by the ark being carried around them; Dagon the god of the Philistines fell on his face before it, and afterwards, severed from the head, lay with the two palms of the hands upon the threshold of the temple; the Bethshemites were smitten on account of it to the number of several thousands; and Uzzah died because he touched it. And the ark was introduced by David into Zion, with sacrifice and jubilation; and afterwards by Solomon into the temple at Jerusalem, where it became its sanctuary. Besides many other facts, from all which it is plain that the decalogue was holiness itself in the Israelitish church. (T. C. R. n. 282, 283.)

In the spiritual and celestial senses the decalogue contains universally all the precepts of doctrine and of life, thus all things of faith and charity. This is because the Word in the sense of the letter, in all and the least things of it, or in the whole and in every part, contains two interior senses; one which is called spiritual and another which is called celestial; and because in these senses Divine truth is in its light and Divine goodness in its heat. Now the Word being of such a nature in the whole and in every part, it is necessary that the ten commandments of the decalogue should be explained according to the three senses, called natural, spiritual, and celestial. (T. C. R. n. 289.)

The laws of spiritual life, the laws of civil life, and the laws of moral life also, are delivered in the ten precepts of the decalogue ; in the first three the laws of spiritual life, in the following four the laws of civil life, and in the last three the laws of moral life. (H. H. n. 531.)

The First Commandment.

" *Thou shalt have no other God before my faces.*" These are the words of the first commandment (Exod. xx. 3 ; Deut. v. 7). In the natural sense, which is the sense of the letter, its most obvious meaning is that idols must not be worshipped ; for it follows :—" *Thou shalt not make unto thee any graven image, or any likeness [of any thing] that is in the heavens above, or that is in the earth beneath, or that is in the waters under the earth. Thou shalt not bow down thyself to them, and shalt not serve them ; for I am Jehovah thy God, a jealous God*" (ver. 4, 5). The reason why this commandment most obviously means that idols must not be worshipped was, that before that time, and after it down to the Lord's advent, there was idolatrous worship in much of the Asiatic world. . . . The Israelitish nation also was in such worship when in Egypt, as may appear from the golden calf which they worshipped in the wilderness instead of Jehovah ; and it appears from many places in the Word, both historical and prophetical, that they were not afterwards alienated from that worship.

This commandment, " *Thou shalt have no other God before my faces,*" also means in the natural sense that no man, dead or alive, shall be worshipped as God ; which also was done in the Asiatic world, and in various neighbouring regions. Many gods of the Gentiles were no other than men ; as Baal, Ashtaroth, Chemosh, Milcom, Beelzebub ; and at Athens and Rome, Saturn, Jupiter, Neptune, Pluto, Apollo, Pallas, etc. Some of these they at first worshipped as saints, afterwards as powers (*numina*), and finally as gods. That they also worshipped living men as gods is evident from the edict of Darius the Mede, that for thirty days no man should ask anything of God, but only of the king, or otherwise he should be cast into a den of lions (Dan. vi. 8 to the end).

In the natural sense, which is that of the letter, this commandment also means that no one but God, and nothing but that which proceeds from God, is to be loved above all things ; which is also according to the Lord's words in Matt.

xxii. 35-37, and Luke x. 25-28. For to him who loves any person or thing above all things that person or thing is God, and is Divine. For example, to him who loves himself or the world above all things himself or the world is his God. This is the reason why such do not in heart acknowledge any God. They are conjoined with their like in hell, where all are collected who love themselves and the world above all things.

The spiritual sense of this commandment is that no other God than the Lord Jesus Christ is to be worshipped ; because He is Jehovah who came into the world and wrought the redemption without which no man nor any angel could have been saved.

The celestial sense of this commandment is that Jehovah the Lord is Infinite, Immense, and Eternal; that He is Omnipotent, Omniscient, and Omnipresent ; that He is the First and the Last, the Beginning and the End ; who Was, Is, and Will Be ; that He is Love itself and Wisdom itself, or Good itself and Truth itself, consequently Life itself; thus the Only One, from whom all things are. (T. C. R. n. 291-295.)

THE SECOND COMMANDMENT.

" *Thou shalt not take the name of Jehovah thy God in vain ; for Jehovah will not hold him guiltless that taketh His name in vain.*" In the natural sense this means the name itself, and the abuse of it in various kinds of conversation; especially in speaking falsely or lying, and in oaths without cause, and for the purpose of exculpation in one's evil intentions (which are cursings), and in sorceries and enchantments. But to swear by God and His Holiness, the Word, and the Evangelists, in coronations, in inaugurations into the priesthood, and inductions into offices of trust, is not taking the name of God in vain, unless the swearer afterwards casts aside his solemn promises as vain. And the name of God, because it is Holiness itself, must continually be used in the holy things pertaining to the church ; as in prayers, psalms, and in all worship ; and also in preaching, and in writing on ecclesiastical subjects.' For God is in all things pertaining to religion, and when rightly invoked by His name He is present and hears. In these things the name of God is hallowed. . . . The name Jesus is likewise holy, as is known from the saying of the Apostle, that at that name every knee should bow, in heaven and on earth ; and moreover from the fact that no devil in hell can speak that name. The names of God are many, which must not be taken in vain; as Jehovah, Jehovah God, Jehovah of Hosts, the Holy One of Israel, Jesus, and Christ, and the Holy Spirit.

In the spiritual sense, the name of God means all that the church teaches from the Word, and through which the Lord is invoked and worshipped. All these things in the complex are the name of God. To take the name of God in vain means to take anything therefrom in frivolous conversation, in speaking falsely, in lying, imprecations, sorceries, and enchantments; for to do this also is to revile and blaspheme God, thus His name.

In the celestial sense, to take the name of God in vain means what the Lord said to the Pharisees, that "*All sin and blasphemy shall be remitted unto man, but the blasphemy of the Spirit shall not be remitted*" (Matt. xii. 31, 32). By blasphemy of the Spirit is meant blasphemy against the Divinity of the Lord's Humanity, and against the holiness of the Word. (T. C. R. n. 297-299. See also p. 84.)

Since the name of God means that which is from God and which is God, and this is called Divine truth, and with us the Word, this because it is in itself Divine, and Most Holy is not to be profaned; and it is profaned when its Holiness is denied, as is done when it is contemned, rejected, and opprobriously treated. When this is done heaven is closed and man is left to hell; for the Word is the only medium of conjunction of heaven with the church, and therefore when from the heart it is rejected that conjunction is broken, and man being then left to hell no longer acknowledges any truth of the church. There are two things by which heaven is closed to the men of the church; one is the denial of the Lord's Divinity, and the other the denial of the Holiness of the Word. The reason is, that the Lord's Divinity is the all of heaven; and Divine truth, which is the Word in the spiritual sense, makes heaven. Hence it is evident that he who denies either the one or the other denies that which is the all of heaven, and from which heaven is and exists; and that he thereby deprives himself of all communication, and hence of conjunction, with heaven. To profane the Word is the same as the blasphemy of the Holy Spirit, which is not remitted to any one; and therefore it is said in this commandment also, that he shall not be left unpunished who profanes the name of God. (A. E. n. 960.)

Because by the name of God Divine truth or the Word is meant, and the profanation of it means the denial of its sanctity, and therefore contempt, rejection, and blasphemy, it follows that the name of God is inwardly profaned by a life against the commandments of the decalogue. For there is profanation which is inward and not outward; and there is profanation that is inward and at the same time outward; and there may also be something of outward profanation and not at the same time inward. Inward profanation is caused by the life; outward, by the speech. Inward profanation which is by life is outward also, or by speech, after death; for then every one thinks and purposes, and as far as he is permitted speaks and acts, according to his life, thus not as in the world. In the world man is accustomed to speak and act otherwise than as he thinks and purposes, on account of the world, and to acquire fame. For this reason it is said there is inward profanation and not at the same time outward. That there may also be something of outward profanation and not at the same time inward, is in consequence of the style of the Word; which is not at all a style of the world, and may therefore be somewhat contemned from ignorance of its inward sanctity.

Whoever abstains from profaning the name of God, that is from profaning the sanctity of the Word, by contempt, rejection, or any kind of blasphemy, has religion; and his religion is according to the quality of his abstention. For no one can have religion except from revelation, and revelation with us is the Word. The abstention from profaning the sanctity of the Word must be from the heart, and not from the lips only. They that abstain from the heart live from religion; but they that abstain only with the lips do not live from religion, for they abstain either for the sake of self, or for the sake of the world,—because the Word serves them as a means of acquiring honour and gain,—or they abstain from some motive of fear. But many of these are hypocrites, who have no religion. (*ib.* n. 962, 963.)

THE THIRD COMMANDMENT.

"*Remember the Sabbath-day, to keep it holy; six days thou shalt labour and do all thy work; but the seventh day is a Sabbath to Jehovah thy God.*" In the natural sense, which is that of the letter, this means that the six days are for man and his labours, and the seventh for the Lord and for man's rest from Him. The word Sabbath in the original tongue signifies Rest. The Sabbath among the children of Israel was the sanctity of sanctities, because it represented the Lord; the six days represented His labours and conflicts with the hells; and the seventh, his victory over them, and therefore rest; and it was holiness itself, because that day was representative of the close of the Lord's whole work of redemption. But when the Lord came into the world, and the representations of Him therefore ceased, that day became a day of instruction in Divine things; and thus too a day of rest from labours, and of meditation on such things as relate to salvation and eternal life; as also a day of love towards the neighbour.

By this commandment, in the spiritual sense, the reformation and regeneration of man by the Lord is signified; the six days of labour signify his warfare against the flesh and its concupiscences, and at the same time against the evils and falsities that are in him from hell; and the seventh day signifies his conjunction with the Lord, and regeneration thereby. Man's reformation and regeneration are signified by this commandment, in the spiritual sense, because they coincide with the Lord's labours and conflicts with the hells, and with His victory over them, and the rest after victory; for the Lord reforms and regenerates man, and renders him spiritual, in the same manner that He glorified His Human and made it Divine.

In the celestial sense conjunction with the Lord is meant by this commandment, and then peace, because protection from hell; for rest is signified by the Sabbath, and in this highest sense, peace. (T. C. R. n. 301-303.)

The third and fourth commandments of the decalogue contain the things which are to be done: they enjoin that the Sabbath is to be kept holy, and that parents are to be honoured. The rest of the commandments contain what are not to be done; namely, that other gods are not to be worshipped, that the name of God is not to be profaned, that man is not to steal, nor to kill, nor to commit adulteries, nor to bear false witness, nor to covet the goods of others. The reason why these two commandments are to be done is that the keeping of the rest of the commandments depends upon them; for the Sabbath signifies the union of the very Divine and the Divine Human in the Lord, likewise His conjunction with heaven and the church, and therefore the marriage of good and truth with the man who is regenerated. Because the Sabbath signifies these things it was the chief representative of all things pertaining to worship in the Israelitish church; as is evident in Jer. xvii. 20-27, and elsewhere. The reason of its being the principal representative of all things pertaining to worship was, that the first of all things of worship is the acknowledgment of the Divine in the Lord's Human; for without that acknowledgment man cannot believe and act except from himself; and to believe from himself is to believe falsities, and to act from himself is to do evils, as is evident from the words of the Lord Himself in John: " *Then said they unto Him, What shall we do that we might work the works of God? Jesus said, This is the work of God, that ye believe on Him whom God hath sent*" (vi. 28, 29); and again: " *He that abideth in Me, and I in Him, the same bringeth forth much fruit, for without Me ye can do nothing*" (xv. 3). (A. E. n. 965.)

The Fourth Commandment.

"·Honour thy father and thy mother, that thy days may be pro-longed, and that it may be well with thee upon the earth." To honour thy father and thy mother in the natural sense, which is the sense of the letter, means, to honour parents, to obey them, to be attentive to them, and to show gratitude to them for the benefits they confer; which are, that they feed and clothe their children, and introduce them into the world, that they may act in it the part of civil and moral beings, and also into heaven by the precepts of religion, and thus consult their temporal pros-perity, and also their eternal felicity; and all these things they do from the love in which they are from the Lord, in whose stead they act. In an adapted sense, if the parents are dead, the honour of guardians by their wards is meant. In a wider sense, to honour the king and the magistracy is meant by this com-mandment; since they exercise the care over things necessary to all in common which parents do in particular. In the widest sense this commandment means that men should love their country, because it sustains them and protects them; it is there-fore called father-land (*patria*), from father (*pater*). But to their country and to the king and magistracy the honours must be paid by parents, and be implanted by them in their children.

In the spiritual sense, to honour father and mother means to adore and love God and the church. In this sense by father God is meant, who is the Father of all; and by mother, the church. Infants in the heavens and angels know no other father and no other mother, since they are there born anew of the Lord by the church. The Lord therefore says, " *Call no man your father on the earth; for one is your Father, who is in the heavens*" (Matt. xxiii. 9). These words were spoken for children and angels in heaven, but not for children and men on earth. The Lord teaches the same in the common prayer of the Christian churches: " *Our Father, who art in the heavens, hallowed be Thy name.*" That the church is meant by mother, in the spiritual sense, is because just as a mother on earth feeds her children with natural food the church feeds them with spiritual food; and for this reason the church is frequently called mother in the Word; as in Hosea: " *Plead with your mother . . . . ; she is not my wife, neither am I her husband*" (ii. 2, 5); in Isaiah : " *Where is the bill of your mother's divorcement, whom I have put away ?*" (l. 1; and Ezek. xvi. 45; xix. 10). And in the Evangelists : " *Jesus, stretch-ing out His hand to the disciples, said, My mother and My brethren are those who hear the Word of God and do it*" (Matt. xii. 48, 49; Luke viii. 21 ; Mark iii. 33-35; John xix. 25-27.

In the celestial sense, our Lord Jesus Christ is meant by father; and by mother the communion of saints, by which His church is meant, scattered over the whole world. (T. C. R. n. 305-307.)

The Fifth Commandment.

"*Thou shalt not kill.*" This commandment not to kill, in the natural sense means not to kill man, and not to inflict upon him any wound of which he may die, and also not to mutilate his body; and it means, moreover, not to bring any deadly evil upon his name and fame, since with many fame and life go hand in hand. In a wider natural sense murder means enmity, hatred, and revenge, which breathe the spirit of murder; for murder lies concealed within them, as fire in wood beneath the ashes. Infernal fire is nothing else; hence one is said to be inflamed with hatred, and to burn with revenge. These are murders in intention and not in act; and if the fear of the law and of retaliation and revenge were taken away from them, they would burst forth into act; especially if there be treachery or ferocity in the intention. That hatred is murder is evident from these words of the Lord: "*Ye have heard, that it was said by them of old time, Thou shalt not kill; and whosoever shall kill, shall be in danger of the judgment. But I say unto you, that whosoever is rashly angry with his brother, shall be in danger of hell-fire*" (Matt. v. 21, 22). This is because all that is of the intention is also of the will, and thus in itself is of the act.

In the spiritual sense murder means all modes of killing and destroying the souls of men, which are various and manifold; as turning them away from God, religion, and Divine worship, by throwing out scandals against them, and by persuading to such things as excite aversion and also abhorrence.

In the celestial sense, to kill means to be rashly angry with the Lord, to hate Him, and wish to blot out His name. It is those who do this of whom it is said that they crucify Him; which they would even do, as did the Jews, if as before He were to come into the world. This is meant by "*the Lamb standing as it had been slain*" in Rev. v. 6, xiii. 8; and by "*the crucified*" in Rev. xi. 8; Heb. vi. 6; Gal. iii. 1. (T. C. R. n. 309-311.)

Since all who are in hell are in hatred against the Lord, and therefore in hatred against heaven,—for they are against goods and truths,—therefore hell is the very murderer, or the state whence murder itself proceeds. The reason is that man is man from the Lord, by virtue of the reception of good and truth, and therefore, to destroy good and truth is to destroy the very human, and thus to kill man. That those who are in hell are of such a character was not yet so well known in the world; for the reason that there does not then appear any hatred against good and truth, nor against heaven, and still less against the Lord, with those who are of hell and therefore come into hell after death. For every one while he lives in the world is in externals, which from infancy are taught and accustomed to feign such things as are honest and decorous, and just and equitable, and good and true; and yet hatred lies concealed in their spirit, and this in proportion to the evil of their life; and as hatred is in the spirit, therefore it breaks forth when the externals are put off, as is the case after death. This infernal hatred against all who are in good is deadly hatred, because it is hatred against the Lord. This is especially evident from their delight in doing evil, which is such as to exceed in degree every other delight; for it is a fire burning with the lust of destroying souls. It has in fact been proved that this delight is not from hatred against those whom they attempt to destroy, but from hatred against the Lord Himself. Now since man is man from the Lord, and the human which is from the Lord is good and truth; and since those who are in hell, from hatred against the Lord lust to kill the human, which is good and truth; it follows that it is hell from whence murder itself proceeds. (A. E. n. 1013.)

When a man abstains from hatred, and holds it in aversion and shuns it as diabolical, then charity, mercy, and clemency flow in through heaven from the Lord; and then first are the works that he does works of love and charity. The works that he did before, however good they might appear in the external form, were all works of the love of self and of the world, in which there lay concealed hatred if they were not rewarded. So long as hatred is not removed so long man is merely natural, and a merely natural man remains in all his hereditary evil; nor can he become spiritual until hatred, with its root, which is the love of ruling over all, is removed; for the fire of heaven, which is spiritual love, cannot flow in so long as the fire of hell, which is hatred, opposes and precludes it. (*ib.* n. 1017.)

The Sixth Commandment.

" *Thou shalt not commit adultery.*" In the natural sense this commandment not only forbids to commit adultery, but also to purpose and to do obscene acts, and therefore to think and speak of lascivious things. That merely to lust is to commit adultery is known from these words of the Lord: " *Ye have heard that it was said by them of old time, Thou shalt not commit adultery. But I say unto you, that whosoever looketh on the woman of another to lust after her, hath committed adultery with her already in his heart"* (Matt. v. 27, 28).

In the spiritual sense, to commit adultery means to adulterate the goods of the Word, and to falsify its truths. (T. C. R. n. 313, 314.)

Scarcely any one at this present day knows that these things are signified in the spiritual sense by committing adultery and whoredom, because at this day few within the church know what the spiritual is, and in what respect it differs from the natural; and scarcely any one knows that there is a correspondence of each with the other,—and in truth of such a nature that the image of the one is presented in the other, that is the spiritual is represented in the natural; consequently that the spiritual is as the soul and the natural as its body, and that thus by influx and by conjunction thence they constitute one,—just as in the regenerate man his internal man, which also is called spiritual, and his external, which also is called natural, make one. Since such things are unknown at this day it cannot therefore be known what to commit adultery signifies further, than that it is to be illegitimately conjoined as to the body. Because these things, as was said, are at this day unknown, it is permitted to declare the reason why in the spiritual sense to commit adultery signifies to pervert those things which are of the doctrine of faith and charity, and so to adulterate goods and falsify truths. The reason (which at this day is an arcanum) is, that conjugial love descends from the marriage of good and truth, which is called the heavenly marriage; the love that exists between good and truth in heaven, which flows in from the Lord, is turned into conjugial love on earth, and this by correspondence. Hence it is that in the internal sense the falsification of truth is fornication, and the perversion of good is adulteration. Hence also it is that they who are not in the good and truth of faith cannot be in genuine conjugial love; and that they who find the delight of their life in adulteries can no longer receive anything of faith. I have heard it said by the angels that as soon as any one commits adultery on earth, and takes delight in it, heaven is closed to him; that is he refuses any longer to receive thence anything of faith and charity. The reason why adulteries are made light of by very many at this day in the kingdoms where the church exists is because the church is at its end, so that there is no longer any faith, because there is no charity. For the one corresponds to the other; where there is no faith falsity is in the place of truth, and evil in the place of good; and it flows therefrom that adulteries are no more reputed as crimes; for when heaven is closed in man such things flow in from hell. That in the internal or spiritual sense to commit whoredom and adultery is to falsify and pervert the truths and goods of faith and charity, consequently also to confirm what is false and evil by perverse applications of the Word, may appear from the several passages in the Word where the commission of adultery, whoredom, and fornication is mentioned. This will be very plain from the following in Ezekiel: " *Son of man, make Jerusalem to know her abominations.* . . . *Thou didst play the harlot because of thy renown, and didst pour out thy fornication on every one that passed by. Thou didst take of thy garments and didst make to thyself variegated high places, and didst play the harlot upon them. Thou hast also taken the implements of thine adorning, of My gold and of My silver, which I had given thee, and didst make to thyself images of a male, and didst commit fornication with them.* . . . *Thou hast taken thy sons and thy daughters whom thou hast borne unto Me, and hast sacrificed them. Is this, concerning thy fornications, a small thing?* . . . *Thou hast committed fornication with the sons of Egypt thy neighbours, great of flesh, and hast multiplied thy fornications, to provoke Me to anger.* . . . *And thou didst commit whoredom with the sons of Ashur, when thou wast not satiated with whom thou didst also commit whoredom, and yet wast not satisfied. And thou didst multiply thy fornication* . . . *even to Chaldea, the land of merchandise; and yet in this thou wast not satisfied.* . . . *An adulterous woman, under her husband, hath received strangers. They give a gift to all whores; but thou givest thy gifts to all thy lovers, and dost remunerate them, that they may come to thee from every side to thy fornications.* . . . *Wherefore, O harlot, hear the word of Jehovah,* . . . *I will judge thee with the judgments of adulterous [women] and of them that shed blood*" (xvi. 1, 15-17, 20, 26, 28, 29, 32, 33, 35, 38). Who does not see that falsifications of truth and adulterations of good are meant here by fornications? And who can understand a single word here unless he knows that fornication has such a signification, and also knows what is meant by the sons of Egypt, the sons of Ashur, and Chaldea, with whom Jerusalem is said to have committed fornication? That she did not commit fornication with those people themselves is evident. (A. C. n. 8904.)

Because Babylon[1] adulterates and falsifies the Word beyond others she is called THE GREAT WHORE, and these words are spoken of her in the Revelation: "*Babylon hath made all nations drink of the wine of the wrath of her fornication*" (xiv. 8). The angel said, "*I will show thee the judgment of the great Whore* . . . *with whom the kings of the earth have committed fornication*" (xvii. 1, 2). "*He hath judged the great Whore, which did corrupt the earth with her fornication*" (xix. 2). Because the Jewish nation had falsified the Word, it was called by the Lord, "*an*

[1] See note, p. 172.

adulterous generation" (Matt. xii. 39; xvi. 4; Mark viii. 38), and
"the seed of the adulterer" (Isa. lvii. 3). Besides which there are
many other places where by adulteries and whoredoms adulterations and falsifications of the Word are meant.

In the celestial sense, to commit adultery means to deny the
holiness of the Word, and to profane it. That this is meant in
this sense follows from the former, the spiritual sense, which is
to adulterate its goods and to falsify its truths. They deny and
profane the holiness of the Word who in heart laugh at everything of the church and of religion; for all things of the church
and of religion in the Christian world are from the Word. (T.
C. R. n. 314, 315.)

Who at this day can suppose that the love of adultery is the
fundamental love of all diabolical and infernal loves? and that
the chaste love of marriage is the fundamental love of all
heavenly and Divine loves? and consequently that in proportion
as a man is in the love of adultery in the same proportion he is in
every evil love, if not in act yet in disposition? and on the other
hand that in proportion as a man is in the chaste love of marriage
in the same proportion he is in every good love, if not in act yet
in disposition? Who at this day can think that he who is in
the love of adultery does not believe anything of the Word, nor
therefore anything of the church? nay, that in his heart he
denies God? and on the other hand, that he who is in the chaste
love of marriage is in charity, and in faith, and in love to God?
and that the chastity of marriage makes one with religion, and
the lasciviousness of adultery makes one with naturalism? The
reason that these things are unknown at this day is because the
church is at its end, and is devastated as to truth and as to
good; and when the church is in such a condition the man of
the church, by influx from hell, comes into the persuasion that
adulteries are not detestable, nor abominations. And therefore he
also comes into the belief that marriages and adulteries do not
differ in their essence, but only in respect to order; when yet
the difference between them is such as that between heaven and
hell. That there is this difference between them will be seen in
what follows. Hence now it is that in the Word, in the spiritual
sense, heaven and the church are meant by nuptials and marriages; and that hell and the rejection of all things of heaven
and the church are meant by adulteries and fornications. (A.
E. n. 981.)

That adultery is hell, and therefore an abomination, any one
may conceive from the idea of a commixture of diverse semen in
the womb of one woman; for it is the semen of man in which
lies hidden the inmost of his life, and therefore the rudiment of

a new life; and on this account it is holy. To make this common with others' inmosts and rudiments, as is done in adulteries, is profane. Hence it is that adultery is hell; and hell in general is called adultery. Because nothing but corruption can come of such commixture—also from a spiritual origin—it follows that adultery is an abomination. Accordingly in the brothels that are in hell foulnesses of every kind appear; and when light from heaven is admitted into them, adulteresses with adulterers are seen like swine, lying in very filth, and what is marvellous, like swine they are in their delight when in the midst of filth. But these brothels are kept closed, because when they are opened a stench is exhaled from them which excites vomiting. In chaste marriages it is different. In these the life of the man adds itself by the semen to the life of the wife; whence springs the intimate conjunction by which they become not two but one flesh; and according to the conjunction thereby conjugial love increases, and with this every good of heaven. (*ib.* n. 1005.)

The Future State of Adulterers.

Because adulteries are contrary to conjugial love it is impossible for adulterers to be with the angels in heaven; and because also they are in the opposites to good and truth. And so it is impossible that they should be in the heavenly marriage; for the reason, too, that they have none but impure ideas of marriage. When marriage is but named or the idea of it occurs, there instantly enter into their ideas lascivious, obscene, yea, abominable things. So when the angels converse respecting good and truth adulterers think contrary to them; for with man after death all affections, and the thoughts from them, continue such as they were in the world. Adulterers are in the disposition to destroy societies; thus in heart they are opposed to charity and mercy, laughing at the miseries of others; they desire to deprive every one of his own, and do it as far as they dare; and it is a pleasure to them to destroy friendships and stir up enmities. Their religion is, that they say they acknowledge a Creator of the universe, and a Providence,—but only universal, and salvation by faith, and that worse cannot be done to them than to others. But when they are explored as to what they are at heart,—which is done in the other life,—they do not in fact believe these things; but think of universal nature as Creator of the universe, instead of a universal Providence believe in none, and think nothing of faith. All these things because adulteries are entirely opposed to good and truth. How then adulterers can come into heaven any one may judge. (A. C. n. 2747.)

From the goods enumerated and described which come of chaste marriages, it may be concluded what the evils are which follow from adulteries; for these evils are the opposites of those goods. That is, instead of the spiritual and celestial loves which are in those who live in chaste marriages, there are infernal and diabolical loves with those who are in adulteries; in place of the intelligence and wisdom which they possess who live chastely in marriages, there are insanities and follies with those who are in adulteries; in place of the innocence and peace which they enjoy who live in chaste marriages, there are guile and no peace with those who are in adulteries; in place of the power and the protection against the hells which they possess who live chastely in marriages, asmodean and infernal demons themselves are with those who live in adulteries; and in place of the beauty of those who live chastely in marriages, there is deformity with those who live in adulteries,—which is monstrous according to the quality of their adulteries. The final lot of adulterers is that from extreme impotence to which they at length reduce themselves, they become void of all the fire and light of life, and dwell by themselves in wildernesses, as inert, and weary of their very life. (A. E. n. 1003.)

I have been informed by the angels that when any one commits adultery on earth heaven is instantly closed to him, and that afterwards he lives only in worldly and corporeal things. And that then though he hears about matters of love and faith they do not penetrate to his interiors; and what he himself says about them does not come from his interiors, but only from his memory and his mouth under the impulse of conceit or the love of gain. For the interiors are closed, and cannot be opened but by earnest repentance. (A. C. n. 2750.)

He who abstains from adulteries for any other reason than because they are sins, and against God, is still an adulterer. For example, if one abstains from them for fear of the civil law and its punishment; for fear of the loss of reputation, and thence of honour; for fear of the diseases arising from them; for fear of upbraidings from his wife at home, and thence of intranquillity of life; for fear of chastisements from the servants of the injured husband; on account of poverty, or of avarice; on account of any infirmity arising from abuse, or from age, or from impotence, or from disease. Nay, if he abstain from them on account of any natural or moral law, and does not at the same time abstain from them on account of the Divine law, he is yet inwardly unchaste and an adulterer; for he none the less believes that they are not sins, and in his spirit declares them lawful, and so commits them in spirit though not in the body. Therefore after death when he becomes a spirit, he openly speaks in favour of them, and commits them without shame. It has been given me to see virgins in the spiritual world who accounted fornication as abominable because against the Divine law; and also virgins who did not account them abominable, but yet abstained from them because they were disreputable and would turn away their suitors. These virgins I saw encompassed with a dusky cloud in their descent to the abodes below; and the former I saw surrounded with a bright light in their ascent to the abodes above. (A. E. n. 1009.)

All who regard adulteries as of no consequence, that is who believe that they are not sins, and from this confirmed belief, and purposely, commit them, are evil doers and impious in heart; for the conjugial human [principle] and religion go together at every pace; and every step and every advance by religion and in religion, is also a step and advance by and in the conjugial [principle] which is peculiar and proper to a Christian man. (C. L. n. 80.)

The Seventh Commandment.

" *Thou shalt not steal.*" In the natural sense this commandment means according to the letter, not to steal, rob, or commit piracy in time of peace; and in general not to take from any one his goods, secretly, or under any pretext. It also extends itself to all impostures, illegitimate gains, usuries, and exactions; and also to fraudulent practices in paying duties and taxes, and in discharging debts. Workmen offend against this commandment who do their work unfaithfully and dishonestly; merchants who deceive in merchandise, in weight, in measure, and in accounts; officers who deprive the soldiers of their just wages; and judges who give judgment for friendship, bribes, relationship, or for other reasons by perverting the laws or the judicial investigations, and who thus deprive others of their goods which they should rightfully possess.

In the spiritual sense to steal means to deprive others of the truths of their faith, which is done by falsities and heresies. Priests who minister only for the sake of gain or worldly honour, and teach such things as they see or may see from the Word are not true, are spiritual thieves; since they take away from the people the means of salvation, which are the truths of faith.

In the celestial sense by thieves are meant those who take away Divine power from the Lord; and also those who claim for themselves His merit and righteousness. These, though they adore God, yet do not trust in Him, but themselves; and they also do not believe in God, but in themselves. (T. C. R. n. 317-319.)

He who abstains from thefts understood in the wide sense, nay, who even shuns them, for any other reason than on account of his religion and for eternal life, is not purified from them; for no other motive opens heaven. For the Lord removes the evils in man by means of heaven, as by heaven he removes the hells. For example, administrators of goods, higher and lower, merchants, judges, officers of every kind, and labourers; if they abstain from thefts, that is from unlawful gains and usuries, and even shun them, for the acquisition of a good name, and thereby of honour and gain, or on account of civil and moral laws,—in a word from any natural love or any natural fear, thus on account of outward restraints alone and not from religion, their interiors are yet full of thefts and robbery. And when outward restraints are taken away from them, as is the case with every one after death, they break forth. The apparent sincerity and rectitude of such is only a mask, pretence, and cunning.

Now in proportion as the different kinds and species of thefts are removed, and the more they are removed, the different kinds and species of good to which they oppositely correspond, and which in general relate to what is sincere, right, and just, enter in and occupy their place. For when a man is averse to and shuns unlawful gains acquired by fraud and cunning, in so far he purposes what is sincere, right, and just; and at length begins to love what is sincere because it is sincere, what is right because it is right, and what is just because it is just. He begins to love them because they are from the Lord and the love of the Lord is in them. For to love the Lord is not merely to love His person, but to love those things that come from the Lord; for these are the Lord with man. Thus it is also to love sincerity itself, right itself, justice itself; and as these are the Lord, therefore in the degree that a man loves them, and so acts from them, in that degree he acts from the Lord. And in that degree the Lord removes insincerity and injustice as to the very intentions and purposes wherein their roots are; and every time with less resistance and conflict, thus with easier labour, than in the beginnings. Thus a man thinks from conscience, and acts from integrity; not the man indeed of himself, but as if from himself; for he then acknowledges, from faith as well as from perception, that it appears indeed as if he thought and did these things from himself, when yet they are not from himself but from the Lord. (A. E. n. 972, 973.)

Take for example administrators of the goods of others, higher and lower: If they deprive their king, their country, or their master of his goods, clandestinely or by artifice, or under fair pretence by fraud, they have no religion and no conscience; for they hold in contempt and render null the Divine law concern-

ing theft. Though they frequent temples, are devout in listening
to sermons, attend the Sacrament of the Supper, pray morning
and evening, and talk piously from the Word, yet nothing flows
in and is present from heaven in their worship, piety, and speech,
because their interior minds are full of thefts, robberies, knav-
ishness, and injustice; and so long as these are within, the way
into them from heaven is closed. Therefore the works that they
do are all evil. But on the other hand administrators of goods
who shun unlawful gains and fraudulent transactions, because
they are contrary to the Divine law of theft, have religion, and
consequently conscience also. And the works that they do are
good works; they act from sincerity for the sake of sincerity,
and from justice for the sake of justice. And moreover they are
content with their own, and are of cheerful mind and joyful heart
as often as it occurs that they have not defrauded.

Take merchants also for example: Their works are all evil so
long as they do not regard as sins, and for that reason shun, all unlawful gains and illicit usuries, and frauds and craft; for such works
cannot be done from the Lord, but are from man himself. And
their works are worse by so much as from the internal they
know how, more skilfully and subtlely, to fabricate deceptions
and circumvent their companions; and their works are yet worse
the more skill they have in bringing such things into effect
under the guise of sincerity, justice, and piety. The more delight
a merchant takes in such things, the more the origin of his
works is derived from hell. And if he acts sincerely and justly
in order to acquire reputation, and by reputation wealth,—even
so far as to appear to act from the love of sincerity and justice,—
and does not act sincerely and justly from affection or from
obedience to the Divine law, he is yet inwardly insincere and
unjust, and his works are thefts; for under the guise of sincerity
and justice he is disposed to steal. That this is so is made
manifest after death, when man acts from his interior will and
love, and not from the exterior. He then thinks and contrives
nothing but crafty tricks and robberies; and he withdraws
himself from the sincere, and betakes himself either to forests
or to deserts, where he devotes himself to his insidious wiles.
In a word, they become robbers. But it is otherwise with those
merchants who shun all kinds of theft as sins, especially the
interior and more hidden thefts which are accomplished by acts
of cunning and deceit. Their works are all good, because they
are from the Lord; for the influx from heaven, that is through
heaven from the Lord, for effecting them is not intercepted by
the evils above mentioned. Riches do no harm to them, because
wealth is to them the means of use. Mercantile transactions with
them are uses whereby they serve their country and their fellow-

citzens; and they are also placed by their wealth in a position to perform any uses to which the affection of good leads them.

From what has been said it may now be seen what is meant in the Word by good works; namely, all the works that are done by man while evils are being removed as sins. For the works that are afterwards done are not done by the man otherwise than as by him; they are in truth done by the Lord; and works that are done by the Lord are all good, and are called goods of life, goods of charity, and good works. For example, all the judgments of a judge who has justice for his end and venerates and loves this as Divine, while he detests adjudications for the sake of reward, for friendship, or from favour, as flagitious; for so he consults the good of his country, by causing justice and judgment to reign therein as in heaven, and so he consults the peace of every harmless citizen, and protects him from the violence of evil-doers; all which are good works. The offices of administrators also and the dealings of merchants are all good works when they shun illicit gains as sins against the Divine laws. While man is shunning evils as sins he daily learns what a good work is, and the affection of doing good increases with him, and the affection of knowing truths for the sake of good; for the more truths he knows the more fully and wisely he can act, and therefore the more truly good his works become. Cease therefore to inquire in thyself what are the good works that I may do, or what good shall I do that I may receive eternal life. Only abstain from evils as sins, and look to the Lord, and the Lord will teach and lead thee. (A. E. n. 977-979.)

THE EIGHTH COMMANDMENT.

" *Thou shalt not bear false witness against thy neighbour.*" To bear false witness against the neighbour, or testify falsely, in the natural sense most obviously means to act the part of a false witness before a judge, or before others out of a court of justice, against any one who is inconsiderately accused of any evil, and to asseverate this by the name of God or anything holy, or by himself and such things of himself as are of some repute. In a wider natural sense this commandment forbids lies of every kind, and artful hypocrisies which regard an evil end; and also to traduce and defame the neighbour, so that his honour, name, and fame, on which the character of the whole man depends, are injured. In the widest natural sense it forbids plots, deceits, and premeditated evils against any one, from various motives, as from enmity, hatred, revenge, envy, rivalry, etc.; for these evils conceal within them the testifying to what is false.

In the spiritual sense, to bear false witness means to persuade that falsity is truth in a matter of faith, and that evil is good in a matter of life, and the reverse; but it is to do these of purpose, and not from ignorance, that is, to do them after one knows what is true and good, and not before.

In the celestial sense, to bear false witness means to blaspheme the Lord and the Word, and so to banish the very truth from the church; for the Lord is the Truth itself, and also the Word. On the other hand, in this sense to witness means to utter truth; and testimony means the truth itself. Hence the Decalogue is also called the Testimony. (T. C. R. n. 321-323.)

In the inmost sense this commandment forbids to falsify the truth and good of the Word; and on the other hand to establish falsity of doctrine as true by confirming it by fallacies, appearances, fictions, knowledges falsely applied, and sophistries, and the like. The very confirmations and the persuasions from them are false witness, for they are false testimonies. (A. E. n. 1019.)

THE NINTH AND TENTH COMMANDMENTS.

" *Thou shalt not covet thy neighbour's house; thou shalt not covet thy neighbour's wife, nor his man-servant, nor his maid-servant, nor his ox, nor his ass, nor anything that is thy neighbour's.*" These two commandments look to the commandments which precede, and teach and enjoin that as evils must not be done, they also must not be lusted after; consequently that they are not of the external man only, but of the internal also; for he who does not commit evils, and yet lusts to commit them, even does commit them. For the Lord says, " *Whosoever lusteth after the wife of another hath already committed adultery with her in his heart*" (Matt. v. 28); and the external man does not become internal, or act as one with the internal, until lusts are put away. This also the Lord teaches, saying, " *Woe unto you, Scribes and Pharisees, . . . for ye make clean the outside of the cup and of the platter, but within they are full of extortion and excess. Thou blind Pharisee, cleanse first the inside of the cup and platter, that the outside of them may be clean also*" (Matt. xxiii. 25, 26). And moreover, in that whole chapter the internals which are Pharisaical are lusts after those things which are commanded not to be done in the first, second, fifth, sixth, seventh, and eighth commandments. . . . That these two commandments might look to all those which precede, that [the evils prohibited] should not be lusted after, therefore the house is first named, afterwards the wife, and then the man-servant, the maid-servant, the ox and the ass, and lastly, all that is the neighbour's. For the house involves all things that follow; for it contains the husband, the wife, the man-servant, the maid-servant, the ox, and the ass. The wife, who is afterwards named, involves again the things which follow; for she is the mistress, as the husband is the master, in the house; the man-servant and maid-servant are under them, and the oxen and asses under them; and lastly come all things that are below or without, in that it is said, "anything that is thy neighbour's." From which it is plain that these two commandments have reference to all the preceding in general and in particular, in a wide and in a restricted sense.

In the spiritual sense these commandments prohibit all lusts which are contrary to the spirit, thus which are contrary to the spiritual things of the church, which relate chiefly to faith and charity; for unless lusts are subdued, the flesh with its liberty would rush into all wickedness. For it is known from Paul, that " *The flesh lusteth against the spirit, and the spirit against the flesh* " (Gal. v. 17). In short, these two commandments, understood in the spiritual sense, regard all things that have before been presented in the spiritual sense, and forbid to lust after them; and likewise all that have before been presented in the celestial sense. But to repeat them is unnecessary. (T. C. R. n. 326, 327.)

The ten commandments of the decalogue contain all things which are of love to God, and all that are of love to the neighbour.

In eight precepts, the first, second, fifth, sixth, seventh, eighth, ninth and tenth, there is nothing said of love to God and of love towards the neighbour; for it is not said that God should be loved, nor that the name of God should be hallowed, nor that the neighbour should be loved, nor therefore that he should be dealt with sincerely and uprightly; but only that Thou shalt have no other God before My face; Thou shalt not take the name of God in vain; Thou shalt not kill; Thou shalt not commit adultery; Thou shalt not steal; Thou shalt not bare false witness; Thou shalt not covet the things that are thy neighbour's. That is, in general, that evil ought not to be purposed, meditated, or done, either against God or against the neighbour. But the reason why such things as relate directly to love and charity are not commanded, but that it is only commanded that such things as are opposed to them should not be done, is that in so far as a man shuns evils as sins in so far he purposes the goods which are of love and charity. The first thing of love to the Lord and love towards the neighbour is to do no evil; and the second is to do good.

It was said that in so far as a man shuns evils he desires to do good ; the reason is that evils and goods are opposites, for evils are from hell and goods from heaven. So far therefore as hell, that is evil, is removed heaven draws near and the man looks to good. That it is so is very manifest from the above eight commandments of the decalogue thus viewed. Thus, I. In so far as any one does not worship other gods, in so far he worships the true God. II. In so far as any one does not take the name of God in vain, in so far he loves the things which are from God. III. In so far as any one is not willing to kill, and to act from hatred and revenge, in so far he wishes well to the neighbour. IV. In so far as any one is not willing to commit adultery, in so far he desires to live chastely with a wife. V. In so far as any one is not willing to steal, in so far he practises sincerity. VI. In so far as any one is not willing to bear false witness, in so far he is willing to think and speak the truth. VII. and VIII. In so far as any one does not covet the things that are the neighbour's, in so far he is willing that the neighbour should enjoy his own. Hence it is evident that the commandments of the decalogue contain all things which are of love to God, and of love towards the neighbour. Therefore Paul says, " *He that loveth another hath fulfilled the law. For this, Thou shalt not commit adultery, Thou shalt not kill, Thou shalt not steal, Thou shalt not bear false witness, Thou shalt not covet ; and if there be any other commandment, it is comprehended in this saying, Thou shalt love thy neighbour as thyself. Charity worketh no evil to the neighbour ; therefore charity is the fulfilment of the law* " (Rom. xiii. 8-10). (T. C. R. n. 329, 330.)

Offending in One Commandment Offending in All.

It is affirmed that no one can fulfil the law, and the less because he who offends against one commandment of the decalogue offends against all. But this form of speech is not just as it sounds. For it is to be understood in this manner ; that he who of purpose or determination acts contrary to one commandment, acts contrary to the rest ; since to act from purpose and determination is entirely to deny that it is a sin, and if he is told that it is sin, to reject the admonition as of no moment. He who thus denies, and makes a sin a matter of no concern, makes light of everything that is called sin. (T. C. R. n. 523.)

FAITH.

WHAT FAITH IS.

FAITH is an internal acknowledgment of truth. They who are in the spiritual affection of truth have an internal acknowledgment of it. As the angels are in that affection they totally reject the tenet that the understanding ought to be kept in subjection to faith; for they say, "How can you believe a thing when you do not see whether it is true?" And if any one affirms that what he advances must be believed for all that, they reply, "Dost thou think thyself a God, that I am to believe thee? or that I am mad, that I should believe an assertion in which I do not see any truth? If I must believe it, cause me to see it." The dogmatizer is thus constrained to retire. Indeed, the wisdom of the angels consists solely in this, that they see and comprehend what they think.

There is a spiritual conception, of which few have any cognizance, which enters by influx into the minds of those who are in the affection of truth, and interiorly dictates that the thing which they are hearing or reading is true or not true. In this conception they are who read the Word in enlightenment from the Lord. To be in enlightenment is nothing else than to be in the perception, and thence in an internal acknowledgment, that this or that is true. It is they who are in this enlightenment that are said to be taught of Jehovah, in Isaiah liv. 13; John vi. 45; and of whom it is said in Jeremiah, "*Behold, the days come, . . . that I will make a new covenant; . . . this shall be the covenant; . . . I will put My law in their inward parts, and write it in their hearts: . . . and they shall no more teach every man his neighbour, and every man his brother, saying, Know ye Jehovah; for they shall all know Me*" (xxxi. 31, 33, 34).

From these considerations it is plain that faith and truth are a one. This also is the reason why the ancients, who were accustomed to think of truth from affection much more than we, used the word truth instead of faith; and for the same reason in the Hebrew language truth and faith are expressed by one word, which is Amuna, or Amen. (F. n. 1, 4-6.)

The angels who are in celestial love will not hear anything of faith, saying, "What is faith? Is it not wisdom? And what is charity? Is it not to do?" And when they are told that faith consists in believing what is not understood they turn away, saying, "He is out of his senses." It is these who are in the third heaven, and are the wisest of all. Such have they become who in the world applied the Divine truths which they heard immediately to the life, turning away from evils as infernal, and worshipping the Lord alone.

The angels also who are in spiritual love do not know what faith is. If it be mentioned they understand truth, and if charity be mentioned they understand doing the truth; and when they are told they must believe they call it a vain saying, and add, "Who does not believe truth?" They say this because in the light of their heaven they see truth; and to believe what they do not see they call either simplicity or foolishness. (D. L. W. n. 427, 428.)

The veriest faith, which saves, is trust; but there can never be this trust save in the good of life. Without the good of life there is no reception; and where there is no reception there is no trust,—unless sometimes a certain apparent trust, in disordered states of mind or body, when the lusts of the love of self and of the world are quiescent. But with those who are in evil of life, when this crisis passes or is changed, this deceptive trust entirely vanishes. For there is a trust even with the wicked. But he who would know the quality of his trust, let him examine within himself his affections, and ends, as well as the actions of his life. (A. C. n. 2982.)

The Essence of Faith is Charity.

It should be known that charity and faith form one, as the will and understanding; because charity belongs to the will, and faith to the understanding. In like manner charity and faith form one like affection and thought; because affection belongs to the will, and thought to the understanding. So again charity and faith form one like good and truth; because good has relation to affection which belongs to the will, and truth has relation to thought which belongs to the understanding. In a word, charity and faith constitute one like essence and form; for the essence of faith is charity, and the form of charity is faith. Hence it is evident that faith without charity is like a form without an essence, which is nothing; and that charity without faith is like an essence without a form, which likewise is nothing.

It is with charity and faith in man just as with the motion of the heart, which is called its systole and diastole, and the motion of the lungs, which is called respiration. There is also an entire correspondence of these with the will and understanding of man, and of course with charity and faith; for which reason the will and its affection are meant by the heart when mentioned in the Word, and the understanding and its thought by the soul, and also by the spirit. Hence, to yield the breath (or soul) is to retain animation no longer; and to give up the ghost (or spirit) is to respire no longer. Hence it follows that there can be no faith without charity, nor charity without faith; and that faith without charity is like respiration of the lungs without a heart, which cannot take place in any living thing, but only in an automaton; and that charity without faith is like a heart without lungs, in which case there can be no sense of life; consequently, that charity accomplishes uses by faith, as the heart by the lungs accomplishes actions. So great indeed is the similitude between the heart and charity, and between the lungs and faith, that in the spiritual world it is known by a person's breathing what is the nature of his faith, and by his pulse what is the nature of his charity. For angels and spirits as well as men live by the pulsation of the heart and by respiration; hence it is that they, as well as men in this world, feel, think, act, and speak. (F. n. 18, 19.)

There are many who have not an internal acknowledgment of truth, and yet have the faith of charity. They are such as have had respect to the Lord in their life, and from a principle of religion have avoided evils, but who have been kept from thinking of truths by cares and business in the world, and also from a want of truth in their teachers. Yet interiorly or in their spirit, these are in the acknowledgment of truth, because they are in the affection of it; and therefore after death, when they become spirits and are instructed by the angels, they acknowledge truths and receive them with joy. But it is otherwise with those who in their life have not looked to the Lord, and have not avoided evils from a principle of religion. These inwardly or in their spirit are not in any affection of truth, and consequently are not in any acknowledgment of it; after death therefore, when they become spirits and are instructed by the angels, they are unwilling to acknowledge truths, and of course do not receive them. For evil that is of the life interiorly hates truths; but good that is of the life interiorly loves truths. (*ib.* n. 30.)

Cognitions [1] of Truth and Good are not of Faith until a Man is in Charity.

The cognitions of truth and good which precede faith appear to some as if they were of faith; and yet they are not. Men do not therefore believe because they think and say they believe. And these [truths] are not of faith; for it is only cognized that they are *so*, and not internally acknowledged that they are truths. And faith that they are truths while it is not known that they are, is a species of persuasion remote from internal acknowledgment. But as soon as charity is implanted they become cognitions of faith, yet only so far as there is charity within it. (F. n. 31.)

The Truths of Faith are first in Time, but Charity is first in End.

Faith, by which also truth is meant, is first in time; and charity, by which good also is meant, is first in end. And that which is first in end is actually the first, because it is primary, and so is also the first-born; but that which is first in time is not actually first, but apparently. But that this may be comprehended it shall be illustrated by comparisons; as with the creation of a temple, and of a house, the formation of a garden, and the preparation of a field. In the erection of a temple, the first thing in point of time is to lay the foundation, to build the walls, to put on the roof, and then to put in the altar, and rear the pulpit; but the first thing in end for the sake of which these things are done is the worship of God in it. In the building of a house, the first thing in time is to build its outer parts, and to furnish it with various articles of necessity; but the first thing in end is a suitable-dwelling for one's self and for the others who shall be in the house. In the formation of a garden, the first thing in time is to level the ground, and prepare the soil, and plant trees, and sow the seeds of such things as will be of use; but the first thing in end is the use of their fruits. In the preparation of a field, the first thing in time is to clear the land, to plough, to harrow, and then to sow the seeds; but the first thing in end is the harvest, and so also the use. From these comparisons any one may conclude which in itself is first; for does not every one, when he would build a temple or a house, or make a garden or cultivate a field, first purpose a use, and constantly keep and turn this over in his mind while he is procuring the means to it? We conclude then that the truth of faith is first in time, but that the good of charity is first in end; and that this

[1] See note p. 284.

therefore because it is primary is actually the first-begotten in the mind. (T. C. R. n. 336.)

Faith never becomes Faith till the Truths of it are willed and done.

All the things of faith which are signified by the first-born of sons are those which are from the good of charity; for faith exists from this good. For truths, whether taken from the Word or from the doctrine of the church, can in no wise become truths of faith unless there be good in which they may be implanted. The reason is that the intellectual [faculty] is what first receives truths, since it sees them and introduces them to the will; and when they are in the will they are in the man, for the will is the man himself. He therefore who supposes that faith is faith with man before he wills these truths, and from willing does them, is exceedingly deceived; the very truths of faith have no life before. All that is of the will is called good, because it is loved; and so truth becomes good, or faith becomes charity, in the will. . . . That the man of the church has been in obscurity on these subjects is because he has not perceived that all things in the universe relate to truth and good, and that they must have relation to both in order that anything may exist; and has not perceived that in man there are two faculties, the understanding and the will, and that truth has relation to the understanding and good to the will, and that if there is not the relation to each nothing is appropriated to man. Inasmuch as these things have been in obscurity, and yet the ideas of man's thought are founded on such things [according to his conception of them] therefore the error could not be made manifest to the natural man. And yet if it had once been made manifest the man of the church would have seen as in clear light from the Word, that the Lord Himself has spoken innumerable things of the good of charity, and that this is the chief thing of the church; and that faith is nowhere but in that good. The good of charity consists in doing good from purposing good. (A. C. n. 9224.)

In so far as any one shuns Evils as Sins he has Faith.

Evil which is of the life destroys the truth of faith; because evil of life belongs to the will and the truth of faith to the understanding; and the will leads the understanding and causes it to act in unity with itself. If therefore there be any truth in the understanding which does not agree with the will, when a man is left to himself, or thinks under the influence of his evil and the love of it, he either casts out such truth, or by falsification forces it into unity. It is otherwise with those who are in good which is of the life; for when left to themselves they think under the influence of good, and love the truth which is in the understanding because it agrees therewith. Thus a conjunction of faith and of life is effected like the conjunction of truth and good, each resembling the conjunction of the understanding and the will.

Hence then it follows that in the degree that a man shuns evils as sins, in the same degree he has faith, because in the same degree he is in good. This is confirmed also by its contrary, that whosoever does not shun evils as sins has not faith, because he is in evil and evil has an inward hatred against truth. Outwardly indeed it can put on a friendly appearance, and endure, yea love that truth should be in the understanding; but when the outward is put off, as is the case after death, the truth which was thus for worldly reasons received in a friendly manner is first cast off, afterwards is denied to be truth, and finally is held in aversion. (Life, n. 44, 45.)

Faith is the first Principle of the Church in appearance, but Charity is actually the first.

There are two things which constitute the church; namely, charity and faith. Charity is of affection, and faith is of thought thence derived. The very essence of the thought is the affection; for without an affection no one can think, everything of life which is in the thought being from affection. It is therefore evident that the first principle of the church is affection, which is of charity or love; and the reason why faith is called the first principle of the church is because it first appears. For what a man believes, that he thinks and in thought sees; while that by which a man is spiritually affected he does not think, nor therefore see it in thought, but he perceives it by a certain sense which has no reference to sight, but to another sensitive principle which is called the sensitive principle of delight. And since this delight is spiritual and above the sense of natural delight, man does not perceive it except when he has become spiritual, that is when he is regenerated by the Lord. Hence it is that those things which belong to faith, and so to sight, are believed to be the first things of the church, although they are so only in appearance. This therefore is called the beginning of the creation of God (Rev. iii. 14), because in the letter, the Word is written according to the appearance. For the appearance in the letter is for the simple; but spiritual men like the angels are elevated above appearances, and perceive the Word as it is in its internal sense; consequently they perceive that charity is the first principle of the church, and that faith is from charity; for faith which is not from charity and which is not of charity is not faith. Even from ancient times it has been a matter of controversy what is the first principle of the church, whether faith or charity. And they who did not know the nature of charity have said that faith is first; but those who knew the nature of charity have affirmed that charity is first, and that faith is charity as to its appearance,—since the affection of charity appearing to the sight in thought is faith; for the delight of an affection when it passes from the will into thought forms itself, and in various forms renders itself visible. This was unknown to the simple, and therefore they took that to be the first principle of the church which appeared before the sight of their thought; and as the Word in the letter is written according to appearances this is there called the first, the beginning, and the first-born. For this reason Peter, by whom the faith of the church was represented, is said to be the first of the apostles; when yet John was the first, since John represented the good of charity. That John and not Peter was the first of the apostles is evident from the circumstance that John leaned on the Lord's breast, and that he and not Peter followed the Lord (John xxi. 20-22). For the same reason, too, Reuben represented faith, because he was the first-born of Jacob, and it was believed that the tribe which had its name from him was the first; and yet that tribe was not the first but the tribe of Levi, because Levi represented the good of charity. And for that reason this tribe was appointed to the priesthood, and the priesthood is the first order of the church. For the same reason also in the first chapter of Genesis, —where in the literal sense it speaks of the creation of heaven and earth, but in the internal sense of the new creation or regeneration of the man of the church at that time,—it is said that the light was first made, and afterwards the sun and the moon, as may be seen in verses 3-5, and 14-19, of that chapter, when yet the sun is first, and light is from the sun. The reason why light was said to be the first of creation, was that light signifies the truth of faith, and the sun and moon the good of love and of charity. From these considerations it is evident what is signified by the beginning of the creation of God; namely, faith from the Lord, which is the first principle of the church as to the appearance. (A. E. n. 229.)

Since man does not see good in his thought,—for good as has been said is only felt, and is felt under the manifold form of delight,—and as man does not attend to the things that he feels in thought, but to those that he sees in it, therefore he calls all that which he feels with delight good; and he feels evil with delight, because this is innate from his birth, and proceeds from the love of self and of the world. This is the reason why it is not known that the good of love is the all of heaven and of the church; and that this is only from the Lord in man; and that it does not flow from the Lord into any but such as shun evils and the delights thereof as sins. This is what is meant by the Lord's words, that the law and the prophets hang upon these two commandments, *Thou shalt love God above all things, and thy neighbour as thyself* (Matt. xxii. 35-38). And I can aver that there is not in man a grain of truth which is truth in itself except so far as it is from the good of love from the Lord; and therefore that there is not a grain of faith which is faith in itself, that is which is living, salutary, and spiritual, except so far as it is from charity which is from the Lord. Since the good of love is the all of heaven and the church, therefore the universal heaven and the church universal are arranged in order by the Lord according to the affections of love, and not according to anything of thought separated from them; for thought is affection in form, just as speech is sound in form. (A. R. n. 908.)

How Faith is formed from Charity.

It shall also be explained how faith from charity is formed. Every man has a natural mind and a spiritual mind; a natural mind for the world, and a spiritual mind for heaven. As to his understanding man is in both worlds; but not as to his will until he shuns and turns away from evils as sins. When he does this his spiritual mind also is open in respect to the will; and then spiritual heat flows thence into the natural mind from heaven,—which heat in its essence is charity,—and gives life to the knowledges of truth and good that are therein, and out of them forms faith. It is the same as with a tree, which does not receive vegetative life until heat flows from the sun and conjoins itself with the light, as it does in the time of spring. There is moreover a full parallelism between the quickening of man with life and the vegetation of a tree, in this respect, that the one is effected by the heat of this world and the other by the heat of heaven; which is the reason why man is so often likened to a tree by the Lord. (F. n. 32.)

Truth rooted in the Mind by doing it.

All truth is sown in the internal man, and rooted in the external; unless therefore the truth which is inseminated takes root in the external man,—which is effected by doing it,—it becomes like a tree set not in the ground but upon it, which on exposure to the heat of the sun withers. The man who has done the truth takes this root with him after death; but not the man who has only known and acknowledged it. (A. R. n. 17.)

Faith Alone, or Faith without Charity.

With those who are in the doctrine of faith alone there is in truth no faith, that is no spiritual faith, or no faith of the church. But they have a natural faith, which is also called persuasive faith; for they believe that the Word is Divine, they believe in eternal life, they believe also in the remission of sins, and in many other things. But with those who are without charity such faith is merely a persuasive faith; which in itself considered does not differ from faith in things unknown that are heard from others in the world, and are believed though neither seen nor understood because they are said by some one whom they think worthy of confidence; thus it is only the faith of another in themselves, and not their own. And this faith which is not made their own by sight and understanding, is not unlike the faith of one born blind to colours and objects of sight in the world, whose sense of touch also is dull; of which he has a strange idea which no one knows but himself. This is what is called historical faith, and is by no means a spiritual faith, such as the faith of the church ought to be. Spiritual faith or faith of the church is all from charity, so that in its essence it is charity; the spiritual things which are believed indeed appear in light to those who are in charity. This I say from experience; for in the other life every one who has lived in charity during his abode in the world sees his truth which he believes, while there they who have been in faith alone see nothing at all. Yet historical faith only, by means of thought concerning God, concerning heaven, and eternal life, has some conjunction with heaven; but only by obscure thought, and not by the affection of charity, for this affection it has not. By the affection therefore which they have,—which is affection of the love of self and of the world,—they are conjoined to hell. Hence it may appear that they are between heaven and hell, inasmuch as they look with their eyes towards heaven while their heart is inclined to hell. To do this is to profane, and the lot of profaners in the other life is of all others the worst. To profane is to believe in God, the Word, eternal life, and many things which are taught in the literal sense of the Word, and yet live contrary to them. Hence then it is that it is said, " *I would thou wert cold or hot* "

(Rev. iii. 15); for he who is cold, that is who is without faith, does not profane; neither does he who is hot, that is who has charity alone. (A. E. n. 232.)

THE INVENTED MODES OF CONNECTING GOOD WORKS WITH FAITH ALONE.

Some examples shall be adduced of the methods of connecting good works with faith, invented by those who have believed themselves more acute and sagacious than others, and endowed at the same time with so ingenious talent that by reasonings from fallacies they can induce upon any falsity the appearance of truth. That they may be examined, apprehended, and then enlarged upon, I will here recount some connections of good works with faith, by which it appears as if the discordance with the Word was removed,—some of them believed by the simple, and some invented by the learned. 1. The most simple know no otherwise than that faith alone is to believe the things which are in the Word, and which the doctrine of the church thence teaches. 2. The less simple do not know what faith alone is, but think that faith is to believe what is to be done; few of them distinguish between believing and doing. 3. Others indeed suppose that faith produces good works, but do not think how it produces them. 4. Others think that faith in all cases precedes, and that goods are thence produced, or come as fruit from a tree. 5. Some believe that this is effected through co-operation by man, and some that it is effected without co-operation. 6. But as the doctrinal tenet dictates that faith alone saves without good works, therefore some make no account of good works, saying in their hearts that all things that they do in the sight of God are good, and that evils are not seen by God. 7. But as deeds and works and doing and working are frequently mentioned in the Word, therefore from the necessity of reconciling the Word with the dogma they devise connections of different kinds, which yet are such that faith is by itself and works by themselves, so that salvation may be in faith and nothing of it in works. 8. Some connect faith with an endeavour to do good with those who have arrived to the last degree of justification; but with an endeavour which derives nothing from the voluntary part of man, but is solely from influx or inspiration, because good from the voluntary part of man in itself is not good. 9. Some connect faith with the Lord's merit, saying that this is operative in all things of man's life, while he is ignorant of it. 10. Some connect faith with moral and civil good,—which goods are to be done for the sake of man's life in the world, but not for the sake of eternal life,—and affirm that these goods are meant by the deeds and works and doing and working mentioned in the Word; and that for the sake of uses in the world good works are to be taught and preached to the laity, because they do not know these mysteries concerning the connection of faith and works, and some cannot comprehend them. 11. Many of the learned suppose that the conjunction of all things is in faith alone, namely, that therein is love to God, charity towards the neighbour, the good of life, works, the Lord's merit, and God; besides, that man himself thinks somewhat concerning these things, and wills and does from himself. 12. It must be known that there are yet many other methods of connection invented, and still more by the same class in the spiritual world; for spiritual thought can extend into innumerable things into which natural thought cannot go. It was given me to see a certain person in the spiritual world devise more than a hundred methods of such connection, and in every one there was a progression of thought from the beginning through the means to the end; but when he was in the end and believed that he now saw the connection he was enlightened, and noticed that the more interiorly he thought upon the subject the more he separated faith from good works instead of conjoining them. From all this the nature may appear of the modes of connection which the learned especially have invented, whereby the disagreement of the dogma of faith alone with the Word appears to be removed; which is understood by the wound of death of the beast being healed (Rev. xiii. 3). (A. E. n. 786.)

The Errors and Blindness of those who are in Faith Alone.

They who place salvation in faith alone and not at the same time in the life of faith, that is in the life of charity, believe that any one can come into heaven, and to the Lord, however he may have lived. For they do not know what the life of man is, and because they do not know this, they suppose the life is nothing. If therefore they are asked whether an evil person can be among the good, they say that through the mercy of God he can, because it is a work of Omnipotence. Nay, if asked whether a devil can become an angel of heaven they answer in the affirmative, if only he be willing to receive faith; for they have no doubt about his power to receive. And if they are told that evil cannot be turned into good, thus hell into heaven with man, and that this is impossible because contrary to order, therefore contrary to Divine Truth, and so contrary to God Himself, who is order, they respond to this that such things are reasonings about salvation, with which they have nothing to do. From these, and innumerable other illustrations, it may be seen into what blindness concerning salvation and eternal life the doctrine of faith alone leads. (A. C. n. 8765.)

They who place salvation in faith alone, when they read the Word, attend not at all to the things which are said therein concerning love and charity; indeed they do not see them, for these things fall into the shade of vision, as things that are quite aside, or as things which are behind. (*ib.* n. 8780.)

The Lord's Providence over those who are taught the Doctrine of Faith alone.

The greater part of those that are born within the churches where the doctrine of faith alone and of justification thereby is received, do not know what faith alone is, nor what is meant by justification. When therefore they hear these things from their teachers, they think that a life according to God's commandments in the Word is thereby meant; for they believe this to be faith and also justification, not entering more deeply into the mysteries of doctrine. They also, when instructed concerning faith alone and justification by faith, believe no otherwise than that faith alone is to think of God and of salvation, and how they ought to live; and that justification is to live before God. All who are saved within the church are kept by the Lord in this state of thought and faith; and after their departure from the world they are instructed in truths, because they can receive instruction. But those who have lived according to the doctrine of faith alone and of justification by faith are blinded; for faith alone is not faith, and therefore justification by faith alone is a nonentity. . . . It should however be known that there are very few who thus live from doctrine, although it is believed by the preachers that all who hear their preachings are under their influence. It is in truth of the Lord's Divine Providence that there are very few such. (A. E. n. 233.)

That the Divine Providence of the Lord is continually operating in order that they may be saved with whom faith separate from charity has become [the faith] of religion, shall now be shown: It is of the Lord's Divine Providence that although that faith has become [the faith] of religion, every one may yet know that that faith does not save, but a life of charity with which faith acts as one. For in all the churches where that religion is received it is taught that there is no salvation unless a man examines himself, sees his sins, acknowledges them, repents, desists from them, and enters on a new life. This is read with much zeal before all who approach the Holy Supper; and it is added

that unless they do this they will mix holy things with profane,
and cast themselves into eternal damnation; yea, in England,
that unless they do this the devil will enter into them, as he
entered into Judas, and destroy them as to body and soul.   It
is evident from this that in the churches where faith alone is
received, every one yet is taught that evils are to be shunned as
sins.   Further, every one who is born a Christian knows that
evils are to be shunned as sins, from the fact too that the
decalogue is put into the hands of every boy and every girl, and
is taught by parents and masters.   And all the citizens of the
kingdom, especially the common people, are examined by the
priest out of the decalogue alone, repeated from memory, as to
what they know of the Christian religion; and they are also
admonished that they should do the things which it contains.
It is never said then by any bishop that they are not under the
yoke of that law, nor that they cannot do those things because
there is no good from themselves.   The Athanasian Creed is also
received in the whole Christian world, and that also which is last
said in it is acknowledged, that the Lord will come to judge the
living and the dead, and then they that have done good will
enter into eternal life, and they that have done evil into eternal
fire.   In Sweden, where the religion of faith alone is received, it
is also taught openly that there is no faith separate from charity,
or without good works. This is inserted in a kind of admonitory
Appendix to all the books of Psalms, which is called Hin-
drances or Stumbling-blocks of the Impenitent (*Obotferdigas Foer-
hinder*), wherein are these words: " They who are rich in good
works show thereby that they are rich in faith; since when
faith is saving it operates by charity ; for justifying faith never
exists alone and separate from good works, as a good tree does
not exist without fruit, nor the sun without light and heat, nor
water without moisture." These few facts are adduced to show
that although the religion of faith alone is received, yet the
goods of charity which are good works are everywhere taught,
and that this is of the Lord's Divine Providence, lest the common
people should be misled by it.   I have heard Luther (with
whom I have several times spoken in the spiritual world) exe-
crate faith alone, and say that when he established it he was
admonished by an angel of the Lord not to do it; but that he
thought within him that if he did not reject works a separation
from the Catholic religion would not be effected.   Contrary
therefore to the admonition he confirmed that faith.   (D. P.
n. 258.)

Many of the Learned who were in Truths of Doctrine are in Hell, while others who were in Falsities are in Heaven.

There are some who are in genuine truths, some who are in truths not genuine, and some who are in falsities; and yet those who are in genuine truths are often damned, and those who are in truths not genuine, and also those who are in falsities, are often saved. This to most will seem a paradox, but still it is a truth; experience itself has confirmed it. For there have been seen in hell those who were more learned than others, in truths from the Word and from the doctrine of their church, dignitaries as well as others; and on the other hand, there have been seen in heaven those who were not in truths, and also those who were in falsities, both Christians and Gentiles. The reason why the former were in hell was indeed because they were in truths as to doctrine, but in evils as to life; and the reason why the latter were in heaven was that though they were not in truths as to doctrine, they were yet in good as to life. Some newly arrived spirits with whom it was granted me to speak expressed their surprise that those who had been distinguished for learning, in the Word and in the doctrine of their church, were among the damned; of whom they had yet believed that they would become luminaries in heaven, according to the words in Daniel: "*The intelligent shall shine as the brightness of the firmament, and they that justify many as the stars, for ever and ever*" (xii. 3). But they were told that the intelligent are those that are in truth and teach truths, and they that justify are those who are in good and lead to good; and that therefore the Lord said, "*The just shall shine as the sun in the kingdom of their Father*" (Matt. xiii. 43). They were further told that those that are learned as to doctrine, but evil as to life, are the ones who are meant by the Lord in Matthew: "*Many shall say to Me in that day, Lord, Lord, have we not prophesied in Thy name, and in Thy name have cast out devils, and in Thy name have done many wonderful works? But then will I confess unto them, I know you not: depart from Me, ye workers of iniquity!*" (vii. 22, 23); and in Luke: "*Then shall ye begin to say, We have eaten and drunk in Thy presence, and Thou hast taught in our streets; but He shall say, I tell you, I know you not, whence ye are; depart from Me, all ye workers of iniquity*" (xiii. 26, 27); and that they were also meant by the foolish virgins who had no oil in their lamps, of whom it is thus written in Matthew: "*Afterward came also the other virgins, saying, Lord, Lord, open to us; but He answering, said, Verily I say unto you, I know you not*" (xxv. 11, 12). To have oil in the lamps is to have good in the truths which are of the faith of the church. And they were told that those who are not in truths, yea, who from ignorance are in falsities, and yet in good and thence in the affection of knowing truth, were meant by the Lord in Matthew : " *I say unto you, that many shall come from the east and west, and shall sit down with Abraham, and Isaac, and Jacob, in the kingdom of the heavens ; but the children of the kingdom shall be cast out into outer darkness* " (viii. 11, 12) ; and in Luke : " *They shall come from the east and the west, and from the north and the south, and shall recline in the kingdom of God ; and behold there are last which shall be first, and there are first which shall be last* " (xiii. 29, 30). They who are in evil as to life, although they are in truths as to doctrine, are yet in the falsities of their evil. That this is so clearly manifests itself in the other life ; when they are left to themselves they think from evil against the truths which they have known and professed, and so think falsities. They likewise do the same in the world, when being left to themselves they think ; for they then either pervert truths or deny truths to defend the evils of their life. But those who are in good and yet not in truths, yea, who from ignorance are in falsities,—as many are within the church, and many also out of the church, who are called Gentiles,—regard their own falsities indeed as truths ; but as those falsities come from good they bend them to good ; there is therefore nothing of malignity in them, as there is in falsities which are from evil. And as the falsities are on this account mild and flexible they are capable of receiving truths, and also do receive them when instructed by the angels. (A. C. n. 9192.)

Of Intellectual Faith.

What intellectual faith is shall be explained. In the spiritual sense the Word treats in many places of the understanding of Divine truth in the Word ; and where it refers to the desolation of the Church it treats also of its understanding of Divine truths from the Word being destroyed. And from the passages on this subject, taken collectively and examined as to their interior sense, it is plain that in so far as the understanding of truth perishes in the church, the church perishes. The understanding of the Word is signified too in many passages by Egypt, Ashur, Israel, and Ephraim ; and by Egypt the natural understanding of it is signified, by Ashur the rational understanding of it, by Israel the spiritual understanding of it, and by Ephraim the understanding itself of the Word in the church. But these three degrees of understanding, namely, the natural, rational, and spiritual, must exist together in order that man by enlightenment may see and perceive the genuine truths of the Word ; for the natural understanding, which is the lowest, cannot be illuminated by its own light (*lumen*), but must be illuminated by the light (*lux*) of the rational man, which is intermediate, and this from spiritual light. For the spiritual understanding is in the light of heaven, and sees by that light; and the rational is intermediate between the spiritual and the natural, and receives spiritual light which it transmits into the natural and enlightens it. It is therefore plain that the natural understanding without light through the rational from the spiritual is not properly understanding, being without light from heaven; and the truths of the church, which are also the truths of heaven, can by no means be seen except in the light of heaven. The reason is that Divine truth proceeding from the Lord as a sun is the light of heaven, and the Lord alone by His own light, which is spiritual light, enlightens man. From these considerations it is evident that the Lord wills that man may not only know the truths of His church, but also understand them; not however from natural light separated from spiritual light, for natural light separated from spiritual light, in the things of heaven or spiritual things, is not light but thick darkness. For from natural light thus separated man looks at the things of the church from himself, and not from the Lord; he therefore cannot see them otherwise than from appearances and fallacies, and to see them thus is to see falsities for truths and evils for goods. The fire which propagates and also enkindles that light is the love of self and the conceit therefrom of his own intelligence. When a man thinks from that fire and its light, in so far as he excels in ingenuity, and therefore in the ability to confirm anything that he pleases, he is able to confirm even falsities and evils, and make them appear as truths and goods; nay, he can exhibit falsities and evils in a shining natural light, which yet is a delusive light augmented by the artful contriver. But to embrace the things of the church from this light is not to understand them, but rather not to understand; for from this light alone man sees truths as falsities, and falsities as truths. This is especially so when any received dogma is assumed as the very truth, without being previously examined as to whether it is true or not, except in the way of confirmation by reasonings from the natural man, or by confirmations from particular passages in the Word not understood. A man who looks at all the dogmas of his religion in this manner may assume as a principle whatever he pleases, and by the light of confirmation cause it to appear as if it were a truth from heaven, although it be a falsity from hell. From what has been said it may be concluded that by the understanding of the truths of the church the understanding of them illuminated by the light of heaven is meant, thus by the Lord. A man who is in such enlightenment is thereby enabled to see the truths of the church rationally in the world, and spiritually after death. But to enter into the things of the church, which inwardly are spiritual and celestial, from natural light (*lumen*) separated from spiritual light, which is the light of heaven from the Lord, is to proceed in inverted order; for what is natural cannot enter into what is spiritual, but what is spiritual can enter into what is natural. For with man there is no natural influx,—which is also called physical influx,—into the thoughts and intentions of his spirit; but there is spiritual influx, that is to say influx of the thoughts and intentions of the spirit into the body, and into its actions and sensations. (A. E. n. 846.)

Of Persuasive Faith.

With evil of life there is persuasive faith, but not saving faith; for persuasive faith is the persuasion that all things which are of the doctrine of the church are true, not for the sake of truth, nor for the sake of life, nor even for the sake of salvation,—for this latter they scarcely believe,—but for the sake of gain; that is for the sake of hunting after honours and wealth, and for the sake of reputation on account of them. With a view to obtain such things they learn doctrinals; thus not to the end that they may serve the church and promote the salvation of souls, but that they may serve themselves and their connections. It is therefore the same to them whether the doctrinals be true or false. This they are not concerned about, still less inquire into, for they are in no affection of truth for the sake of truth; but they confirm them whatsoever their quality, and when they have confirmed them they persuade themselves that they are true; not considering that falsities may be confirmed as well as truths. (A. C. n. 8148.)

They who in the world aspire after greatness, and covet many things, are more strongly in the persuasion that truth is what the doctrine of the church teaches than those that do not aspire after greatness and covet many things. The reason is that the doctrine of the church is to the former only a means of attaining their own ends; and in the degree that the ends are desired the means are loved and are also believed.

But the case in itself is this: In so far as men are in the fire of the loves of self and of the world, and from that fire talk, preach, and act, in so far they are in that persuasive faith, and then do not see otherwise than that it is so. But when they are not in the fire of those loves they believe nothing, and many of them deny. Hence it is evident that persuasive faith is a faith of the mouth and not of the heart; thus that in itself it is not faith.

They who are in a persuasive faith do not know from any internal enlightenment whether what they teach is true or false, nor indeed do they care about it if only they are believed by the people; for they are in no affection of truth for the sake of truth. They also more than others defend faith alone; and make account of the good of faith, which is charity, in proportion as they can gain by it.

Those who are in a persuasive faith abandon faith if they are deprived of honours and gains, provided their reputation is not imperilled; for a persuasive faith is not interiorly within a man, but stands without in the memory only, from which it is brought forth when it is taught. After death therefore that faith with its truths vanishes away; for then there remains only so much of faith as is interiorly within.a man; that is which is enrooted in good, thus which has become of the life. (*ib.* n. 9365-9368.)

No one ought to be persuaded instantaneously of the Truth.

It is according to the laws of order that no one should be instantaneously persuaded of truth, that is that truth should instantaneously be so confirmed as to leave no doubt at all about it. The reason is that the truth which is so impressed becomes persuasive truth and is without any extension, and is also unyielding. Such truth is represented in the other life as hard, and as of such a quality as not to admit good into it, that it may become applicable. Hence it is that as soon as any truth is presented before good spirits in the other life by manifest experience, there is presently afterwards presented some opposite which causes doubt. Thus it is given them to think and consider whether it be so, and to gather reasons, and so bring that truth rationally into their mind. By this the spiritual sight has extension as to that truth even to the opposites. It therefore sees and perceives in the understanding every quality of truth; and hence can admit influx from heaven according to the states of things, for truths receive various forms according to circumstances. This also is the reason why it was permitted the magicians to do the like to what Aaron did; for thereby doubt was excited among the children of Israel concerning the miracle, as to whether it was Divine; and thus opportunity was given them to think and consider whether it was Divine, and at length to confirm in themselves a conviction that it was so. (A. C. n. 7298.)

The Source of Spiritual Light.

Every man has exterior and interior thought; interior thought is in the light of heaven, and is called perception, and exterior thought is in the light of the world. And the understanding of every man is so constituted that it can be elevated even into the light of heaven, and also is elevated if from any delight he desires to see the truth. It has been given me to know that this is so from much experience; concerning which wonderful things may be seen in *The Wisdom of Angels concerning the Divine Providence;* and still more in *The Wisdom of Angels concerning the Divine Love and the Divine Wisdom.* For the delight of love and wisdom elevates the thought, enabling it to see as in the light that a thing is so, although the man had never heard of it before. This light which illuminates the mind, flows from no other source than out of heaven from the Lord; and as those who will be of the New Jerusalem are to approach the Lord directly, that light will flow in in the way of order, which is through the love of the will, into the perception of the understanding. But those who have confirmed themselves in the dogma that the understanding is to see nothing in theological subjects, but that men ought blindly to believe what the church teaches, cannot see any truth in the light; for they have obstructed the way of light into themselves. (A. R. n. 914.)

It is known that one man excels another in the faculty of understanding and of perceiving what is honest in moral life, what is just in civil life, and what is good in spiritual life. The reason consists in the elevation of the thought to the things which are of heaven; thereby the thought is withdrawn from the outward things of sense. For those who think only from the things of sense cannot at all see what is honest, just, and good; they therefore trust to others and speak much from the memory, and thereby appear to themselves wiser than others. But those who are able to think above the things of sense, if the things that are in the memory are in orderly arrangement, are in a superior faculty of understanding and perceiving, and this according to the degree in which they view things from the interior. (A. C. n. 6598.)

Every Man may see Spiritual Truth who desires it.

Every man whose soul desires it is capable of seeing the truths of the Word in the light. No animal exists which does not know the food proper to its life, when it sees it; and man is a rational and spiritual animal, who sees the food of his life, not that of his body but of his soul, which is the truth of faith,—if he hunger after it, and seek it from the Lord. (A. R. n. 224.)

Why Saving Faith is in the Lord Jesus Christ.

The reason why men ought to believe, that is to have faith, in God the Saviour Jesus Christ, is that it is faith in a visible God, in whom is the invisible ; and faith in a visible God, who is Man and at the same time God, enters into man. For in its essence faith is spiritual, but in its form it is natural; with man therefore it becomes spiritual-natural; for everything spiritual is received in the natural, in order that it may be a reality to man. The naked spiritual indeed enters into man, but it is not received ; it is like the ether which flows in and flows out without effect; for in order to effect there must be perception, and thus reception,—each in man's mind ; and this cannot be with man except in his natural. But on the other hand a merely natural faith or faith devoid of spiritual essence is not faith, but only persuasion or knowledge. Persuasion emulates faith in externals, but because there is nothing spiritual in its internals there is therefore nothing saving. Such is the faith of all who deny the Divinity of the Lord's Human ; such was the Arian faith, and such also is the Socinian faith, because both reject the Divinity of the Lord. What is faith without a definite object ? Is it not like a look into the universe, which falls as it were into an empty void and is lost ? And it is like a bird flying above the atmosphere into the ether, where it expires as in a vacuum. The abode of this faith in the mind of man may be compared to the dwelling of the winds in the wings of Æolus. And to the habitation of light in a falling star ; it comes forth like a comet, with a long tail, but it also passes away like a comet and disappears. In a word, faith in an invisible God is actually blind, because the human mind does not see its God. And the light of this faith, because it is not spiritual-natural, is a fatuous light ; and this light is like that of the glowworm, and like the light in marshes, or on sulphurous glebes at night, and like the light of rotten wood. Nothing arises from this light but what is of the nature of fantasy, in which an appearance is seen as if it were a reality, and yet it is not. Faith in an invisible God shines with no other light ; and especially when it is thought that God is a spirit, and a spirit is thought of as like the ether. What follows from this, but that man looks upon God as he looks upon the ether ? And so he seeks Him in the universe ; and when he does not find Him there, he believes nature to be the God of the uni-

verse. The naturalism reigning at this day is from this origin.
Did not the Lord say, that " *No man hath heard the voice of the
Father at any time, nor seen His shape* "? (John v. 37). And also,
that " *No man hath seen God at any time* "? And that " *The only-
begotten Son which is in the bosom of the Father, He hath revealed
[Him]* "? (i. 18). And " *No one hath seen the Father, but He who
is with the Father ; He hath seen the Father* "? (vi. 46). Also
that no one cometh to the Father, but through Him ? (xiv. 6).
And further, *that the man who seeth and knoweth Him seeth and
knoweth the Father* ? (xiv. 7, and the following verses). But faith
in the Lord God the Saviour, who since He is God and Man can
be approached and seen in thought, is different. It is not an
indeterminate faith, but has an object from whence it proceeds
and to whom it is directed (*habet terminum a quo et ad quem*).
And when once received it remains,—just as when one has seen
an emperor or a king, as often as he is reminded of it, their image
returns. The sight of that faith is as if one should see a bright
cloud and an angel in the midst of it who invites man to him,
that he may be elevated into heaven. Thus the Lord appears to
those who have faith in Him ; and He draws near to every one
just as he recognises and acknowledges Him. This is done as
he knows and does His commandments, which are to shun evils
and do good ; and at length the Lord comes into his house, and
together with the Father who is in Him makes His abode with
him ; according to these words in John : " *Jesus said, He that hath
My commandments, and doeth them, he it is that loveth Me ; and he
that loveth Me shall be loved of My Father, and I will love him, and
will manifest Myself to him ; . . . and We will come unto him, and
make our abode with him*" (John xiv. 21, 23). These things were
written in the presence of the twelve apostles of the Lord, who
were sent to me by the Lord while I was writing them.   (T. C. R.
n. 339.)

OF THE FAITH BY WHICH DISEASES WERE HEALED BY THE LORD.

There were three reasons why faith in the Lord healed the
sick. The first was that they acknowledged His Divine omnipotence, and that He was God. The second was that acknowledgment is faith, and from acknowledgment comes the looking
up to Him,—and all direction of the mind to another from
acknowledgment causes him to be present ; which in the spiritual
world is a common thing. And so here the looking up to Him
was from the acknowledgment of the Lord's omnipotence ; which
was the acknowledgment from which they were first to regard
the Lord when a new church was about to be established by

Him. It may hence appear what in those miracles is meant by faith. The third reason was that all the diseases which the Lord healed represented and therefore signified the spiritual diseases corresponding to those natural diseases ; and spiritual diseases can only be healed by the Lord, and indeed through looking up to His Divine omnipotence, and through repentance of life; and therefore He also said at different times, " Thy sins are remitted thee; go and sin no more." This faith too was represented and signified by that miraculous faith. But the faith by which spiritual diseases are healed by the Lord cannot be given otherwise than by truths from the Word and a life according to them; the very truths and life according to them constitute the nature of the faith ; but upon this subject more will be said in what follows. . . . When the disciples could not heal the lunatic, " *Jesus said unto them, O faithless and perverse generation, how long shall I be with you ?* " and Jesus healed him ; and said to the disciples, that they could not heal him because of their unbelief (Matt. xvii. 14-20). " *When Jesus came into His own country, . . . and they were offended in Him, He said, A prophet is not without honour save in his own country, and in his own house. And He did not many mighty works there because of their unbelief* " (Matt. xiii. 57, 58). The reason why the Lord called the disciples men of little faith when they could not do miracles in His name, and why He could not do miracles in His own country on account of their unbelief, was that although the disciples did indeed believe the Lord to be the Messiah or Christ and also the Son of God, and the Prophet of whom it was written in the Word, they did not yet believe Him to be very God Omnipotent, and that Jehovah the Father was in Him ; and in so far as they believed Him to be a man and not at the same time God, His Divine, to which omnipotence belongs, could not become present with them by faith. For faith makes the Lord present, as was said above; but faith in Him as a man only, does not bring his Divine omnipotence present. This also is the reason why they cannot be saved in the world at this day who look to His Human and not at the same time to His Divine, as is the case with Socinians and Arians. It was for the same reason that the Lord could not do miracles in His own country ; for there they had seen Him from infancy as another man, and could not therefore add to this idea the idea of His Divinity ; and though the Lord is indeed present in man when this idea is not present, yet not with Divine omnipotence ; for faith causes the Lord to be present in man according to the nature of the perception of Him. (A. E. n. 815.)

Confirmations.

That the natural man can confirm whatever he will is manifest from the numerous heresies in the Christian world, each of which is confirmed by its adherents. Who does not know that evils and falsities of every kind may be confirmed? It is possible to confirm, and the wicked actually do confirm, that there is no God, and that nature is everything, and is self-created; that religion is only a means whereby simple minds may be held under restraint; that human prudence does everything, and Divine Providence nothing, except that it maintains the universe in the order in which it was created; also that murder, adultery, theft, fraud, and revenge are allowable, according to Machiavelli and his followers. The natural man can confirm these and such like things, yea can fill books with the confirmations; and when these falsities are confirmed they appear in an infatuating light, and truths in such obscurity that they cannot be seen but as spectres at night. In a word, take the falsest thing and form it into a proposition, and tell an ingenious person to confirm it, and he will confirm it, to the complete extinction of the light of truth. But put aside his confirmations, return, and look at the proposition itself from your own rationality, and you will see its falsity in all its deformity. (D. L. W. n. 267.)

They who by various considerations can confirm a dogma once received whatever its quality, and by various reasonings make it appear like the truth, believe themselves wiser than others. But this is very far from the part of a wise man; any one can do this who is distinguished by some ingenuity, and the wicked more skilfully than the well-disposed. For it is not of the rational man to do this, inasmuch as the rational man can see as from a superior [light] whether what is confirmed be true or false. And seeing this, he makes no account of things confirmative of falsity, and in his own mind regards such things but as ridiculous and vain, however another may believe them chosen from the school of wisdom itself. In a word, nothing is less the part of a wise man, yea nothing is less rational, than to be able to confirm falsities; for it is the part of a wise man and is rational first to see that a thing is true, and next to confirm it; inasmuch as to see what is true is to see from the light of heaven, which is from the Lord, whereas to see the false as true is to see from a delusive light which is from hell. (A. C. n. 4741.)

Difficulty of Extirpating Falsities that have been Confirmed by Evil Life.

Those who have confirmed themselves against the truths and goods of faith, as all do who live wickedly, close the internal man above within them, and open it beneath; so that their internal man looks only to the things that are beneath, that is, looks into the external or natural man, and through that into the things that are in the world, and into the things that are about its body, and which are upon the earth. And when this is so they look downwards, which is towards hell. With such the internal man cannot be opened towards heaven, unless the things negative of truth or affirmative of falsity which have closed it are first shaken off, and they must be shaken off while in the world; which cannot be done except by a total inversion of the life, thus in the course of several years. For falsities arrange themselves in series, and form a continual connection between each other, and give shape to the natural mind itself, and its view as to the things which are of the church and heaven. Hence it is that all things of faith and charity, that is of the doctrine of the church or of the Word,—in general all things heavenly and Divine are to them thick darkness; and on the other hand worldly and terrestrial things are light to them. It is therefore evident that to destroy the falsities with such is to destroy life itself; and that if they are to have a new [principle] of life, falsities must be successively extirpated, and in their place truths and goods implanted, which in like manner shall form a continual connection with each other, and be arranged in series. This is meant by the total inversion of the life, which can only be effected in the course of several years. (A. C. n. 9256.)

Man cannot search into the Mysteries of Faith by things known.

By things known to explore the mysteries of faith is as impossible as for a camel to pass through the eye of needle, or for a rib to govern the purest fibrils of the chest and heart;—so gross, yea much more gross, is the sensual and knowing relatively to the spiritual and celestial. He who would investigate only the secrets of nature, which are innumerable, with difficulty discovers one; and as is known, he falls into errors while investigating. What then if he would investigate the secrets of spiritual and celestial life, where there are myriads of things for one that is invisible in nature! For the sake of illustration take only this example:—Of himself man cannot act otherwise than wickedly, and so turn away from the Lord; yet the man does not act but evil spirits who are with him; nor do the evil spirits, but evil itself which they have appropriated; and yet man does evil, and turns himself away, and is in fault; and yet he lives only from the Lord. On the other hand, man of himself cannot do good and turn to the Lord but by the angels; nor can the angels but by the Lord only; and yet man can as of himself do good, and turn to the Lord. That this is so can neither be comprehended by the senses, nor by knowledge and philosophy. They would, if consulted, utterly deny these things, although in themselves they are true. So in all other things. From this it is evident that they who consult things sensual and things known about matters of faith, not only cast themselves into doubt, but also into denial, that is into darkness; and when in darkness into all cupidities. For while they believe falsity they also do falsity. And while they believe there is no spiritual and celestial, they believe there is only what is corporeal and worldly. Thus they love whatever is of themselves and the world, therefore lusts and evils, from falsity. (A. C. n. 233.)

Of the False Assumption that Nothing is to be Believed until it is Understood.

Every one may see that a man is governed by the principles he adopts, be they ever so false, and that all his knowledge and reasoning favour his principles; for innumerable considerations tending to support them readily present themselves to his mind, and thus he is confirmed in falsities. He therefore who assumes as a principle that nothing is to be believed until it is seen and understood can never believe; for spiritual and celestial things are neither seen with the eyes nor grasped by the imagination. But the true order is that a man should have wisdom from the Lord, that is from His Word; then all things follow in their order, and he is enlightened even in matters of reason and knowledge. For man is by no means forbidden to acquire knowledges, —they are both serviceable to life and delightful, nor is it denied to one who is in faith to think and speak as the learned in the world. But it should be from this principle; that he believes the Lord's Word, and confirms spiritual and celestial truths by natural truths, in terms familiar to the learned world, as far as lies in his power. His principle of belief will therefore be from the Lord and not from himself. The former is life and the latter death. (A. C. n. 129.)

So long as men continue in dispute as to whether a thing

exist, and whether it be so, they can never advance into anything of wisdom; for in the thing itself about which they dispute there are innumerable particulars, which they can never see so long as they do not acknowledge the thing; because each and all its particulars are at once unknown. The learning of this day scarcely advances beyond these limits; namely, the inquiry whether a thing exists, and whether it be so; and therefore they stand excluded from the discernment of truth. For example, he who merely contends whether there is an internal sense of the Word can never see the innumerable, yea, indefinite things which are in the internal sense. Just so he who disputes whether charity is anything in the church, and whether or not all things of the church are matters of faith, cannot know the innumerable, yea, indefinite things that are in charity, but remains altogether in ignorance as to what is charity. And so with the life after death, the resurrection of the dead, the last judgment, and with heaven, and hell; they who only dispute as to whether such things exist stand the while outside the doors of wisdom, and are like persons who but knock at the door, and cannot even look into wisdom's magnificent palaces. And what is surprising, those who are of this description think themselves wiser than others, and the more wise the better they are able to discuss whether a thing is so, and the more to confirm that it is not so; when yet the simple, who are in good and whom they despise, can perceive in a moment without any dispute, not to say without learned controversy, both the existence of the thing and its nature. They have a general sense of apperception of truth; while the former have extinguished this sense by such dispositions, which determine first to discuss whether a thing exists. The Lord speaks of these two classes when He says, *"that things are hidden from the wise and intelligent, and are revealed unto babes"* (Matt. xi. 25; Luke x. 21). (*ib.* n. 3428.)

It is one thing to believe *from* the rational, the known, and the sensual, or to consult them that one may believe; and another to confirm and corroborate what is believed by matters of reason and knowledge and of sense. (*ib.* n. 2538. See also p. 173.)

Affirmative and Negative States of Mind.

There are two principles, òne of which leads to all folly and madness, the other to all intelligence and wisdom. The former principle is to deny all things, or to say in one's heart that he cannot believe them, until he is convinced by what he can comprehend or be sensible of; this principle is what leads to all folly and madness, and may be called the negative principle.

The other principle is to affirm the things which are of doctrine from the Word, or to think and believe within one's self that they are true, because the Lord has said it; this principle is what leads to all intelligence and wisdom, and may be called the affirmative principle. Those who think from the negative principle, the more they take counsel of matters of reason, of knowledge, and of philosophy, the more they plunge themselves into darkness, until at length they come to deny all things. The reason is that from things inferior no one comprehends things superior, that is things spiritual and celestial,—still less things Divine, because they transcend all understanding; and besides, everything is then involved in negatives from the beginning. But on the contrary they who think from the affirmative principle may confirm themselves in things spiritual and celestial by whatever rational considerations, by whatever matters of knowledge, yea, and of philosophy, they are able; for all such things were given them for confirmation, and afford them a fuller idea of a subject. Moreover there are some who are in doubt before they deny; and others who are in doubt before they affirm. They who are in doubt before they deny are those that incline to a life of evil, and in so far as this life carries them away, as often as they think of things spiritual and celestial they deny. But they who are in doubt before they affirm are those that incline to a life of good, and in so far as they suffer themselves to be turned to this life by the Lord, as often as they think of these things they affirm them. (A. C. n. 2568.)

But let this be illustrated by examples: According to the doctrine of the Word, the first and principal thing of doctrine is love to the Lord and charity towards the neighbour. They who are in the affirmative in respect to this, may enter into whatever considerations of reason and knowledge, yea, and of sense they please, every one according to his gift, his knowledge, and his experience; indeed the more they enter the more they are confirmed, for universal nature is full of confirmation. But they who deny this first and chief matter of doctrine, and wish first to be convinced that it is so by matters of knowledge and of reason, never suffer themselves to be convinced, because they deny it in heart, and continually insist on some other principle which they believe essential; at length, by confirmations of their own principle, they so blind themselves that they cannot even know what is love to the Lord and what is love towards the neighbour. And because they confirm themselves in things contrary to them, they at length confirm themselves also in the belief that there is no other love attended with delight but the love of self and of the world; and this to such a degree that, if not in doctrine yet in life, they embrace infernal love instead of heavenly love.

Take also another example: it is one of the primary points of the doctrine of faith that all good is from the Lord, and all evil from man or from self. They who are in the affirmative respecting this may confirm themselves by many considerations both of reason and knowledge; as that no good can flow into man from any other source than from Good itself, that is from the fountain of good and therefore from the Lord; and that there can be no beginning of good from elsewhere they may illustrate to themselves by what is truly good in themselves, in others, in the community, yea, in the created universe. But those who are in the negative principle confirm themselves in the contrary conclusion by all things that ever come under their consideration; insomuch that at length they do not know what is good, but dispute with each other as to what is the highest good,—in profound ignorance of the truth that celestial and spiritual good, which is from the Lord, is that good; by which every lower good is vivified, and that from this delight is truly delightful. Some even conceive that good cannot be from any other source than themselves. Again, take for example the truth that they who are in love to the Lord and in charity towards the neighbour can receive the truths of doctrine, and have faith from the Word, and not those that are in the life of self-love and of the love of the world; or what is the same, that they who are in good can believe, but not those who are in evil. They who are in the affirmative principle can confirm this by innumerable evidences both of reason and of knowledge; of reason by the consideration that truth and good agree together, but not truth and evil; and that as in evil so also from evil everything is false, and that if in some there be yet truth, it is upon the lips and not in the heart; of knowledge, by many things, as that truths shun evils, and that evils spew out truths. But they who are in the negative principle confirm themselves in the belief that every one, of whatever character, even though he live in continual hatred, in the delights of revenge, and in deceits, is capable of believing like others; and this until they entirely reject from doctrine the good of life,—which being rejected they believe nothing. To make it still more plain, take another example, respecting the Word. They who are in the affirmative, that the Word was so written that it has an internal sense, which does not appear in the letter, may confirm themselves by many rational considerations; as that by the Word man has connection with heaven; that there are correspondences of natural things with spiritual, and that these latter do not so much appear; that the ideas of interior thought are entirely different from material ideas which fall into expressions of speech; that during his abode in the world man may also be in heaven (inasmuch as he was born to live in both), by means of the Word which is for both; that with some a certain Divine light flows in into their intellectual operations and into their affections while the Word is being read; that it was necessary that something which descended from heaven should be written, and that in its origin it could not be such as it is in the letter; that nothing can be holy but by virtue of a holiness which is within. They may also confirm themselves by things known; as that in old time men were in representatives, and that the writings of the ancient church were of such a character; that therefore the writings of many even among the Gentiles were also of a similar character; and that for this reason the style was venerated in the churches as holy, and among the Gentiles as learned; several books may likewise be mentioned (as instances of this kind of writing). But they who are in the negative principle, if they do not deny all this, yet do not believe it; and they persuade themselves that the Word is such as it is in the letter, appearing indeed worldly, but yet that it is spiritual,—but where the spiritual is concealed does not concern them, though for manifold reasons they are willing to assert it,—and this they can confirm by many arguments. In order that this subject may be presented even to the apprehension of the simple, it may be expedient to illustrate it scientifically by the following example. They who are in the affirmative in respect to the truth that sight is not of the eye but is of the spirit, which by the eye as by an organ of its body sees things that are in the world, may confirm themselves by many things; as from speech, in that when it is heard it reports itself to a certain interior sight and is transmuted into it,—which could not be the case if there did not exist an interior sight or vision; also that whatever is thought of is seen by an interior sight, by some more clearly, by others more obscurely; moreover that things of the imagination present themselves in a manner not unlike the objects of sight; and further, that unless the spirit which is in the body saw that which the eye as an organ takes in, the spirit in the other life could see nothing; when yet it must needs be that it will there see numberless astonishing things which the eye of the body can never see. They may likewise reflect on dreams, especially those of the Prophets, in which many things were equally well seen and yet not by the eyes; lastly, if they have a taste for philosophical contemplations, they may confirm themselves by the consideration that exterior things cannot enter into interior; as things compound cannot enter into things simple, so the things of the body cannot enter into those which are of the spirit, but the reverse;—besides very many other considerations; till at length they are persuaded that sight belongs to the spirit, and not to the eye except from the spirit. But they who

are in the negative either call these things all natural, or fantasies; and when they are told that a spirit exercises and enjoys
a more perfect sight than a man does in the body, they ridicule
and make light of it,—believing that they shall live in darkness
when they are deprived of the sight of the eye; when exactly the
contrary is true, that they will then be in light. From these
examples it may be seen what it is to enter from truths into
reasonings and knowledges, and what to enter from reasonings
and knowledges into truths ; namely, that the former is according to order, but the latter contrary to order; and that when it
is done according to order man is enlightened, but when contrary
to order he is made blind. It is clear then of how much concern
it is that truths should be known and believed; for by truths
man is enlightened, while by falsities he is blinded. By truths
an immense and almost unbounded plain is opened to the rational
faculty ; but by falsities almost none comparatively, although it
appears otherwise. Hence the angels have so great wisdom, because they are in truths; for truth is the very light of heaven. . . .
Those who have blinded themselves by their unwillingness to
believe anything that they do not comprehend by the senses, in
the other life are readily distinguished from other spirits by this,—
that concerning everything that relates to faith they reason whether
it be so; and though it be shown them a thousand and a thousand
times that it is so, they still raise negative doubts against every
confirming proof; and this they would do to eternity. They are
consequently blinded to such a degree that they have not common sense; that is, they cannot comprehend what is good and
true. And yet every one of them supposes that he is wise beyond all in the universe ; placing their wisdom in this,—the conceit that they are able to make null that which is Divine, and
deduce it from the natural. Many who have been accounted
wise in the world are of this character beyond others; for in
proportion as any one excels in the gift of talent and in knowledge, if at the same time he is in the negative principle, he is
more insane than others; but in proportion as he excels in the
gift of talent and in knowledge, and is in the affirmative principle,
he is capable of becoming more wise than others. To cultivate
the rational by knowledge is in nowise forbidden; but it is forbidden to fortify one's self against the truths of faith, which are
of the Word. (A. C. n. 2588.)

NATURE AND SPIRITUAL USE OF OUTWARD ACQUISITIONS OF KNOW-LEDGE.

Truth known is one thing, rational truth is another, and intellectual truth another; they succeed each other. Truth known

is a matter of knowledge; rational truth is truth known confirmed by reason; intellectual truth is conjoined with an internal perception that it is so. (A. C. n. 1496.)

Knowledges are procured in childhood with no other purpose than for the sake of knowing. . . . The knowledges which are procured in childhood are very many, but are disposed by the Lord in order, so that they may be subservient to use; first, that he may be able to think; afterwards that by means of thought they may be used; and finally, that he may bring them into effect, that is that his very life may consist in use, and be a life of uses. These are the offices of the knowledges which he imbibes in childhood. Without these his external man cannot be conjoined with the internal, and together with it become a use. When man becomes a use, that is, when he thinks of all things from a purpose of use, and does all things for the sake of use (if not by manifest yet by tacit reflection, from a disposition thus acquired), then the knowledges which had subserved the first use, that he might become rational, are destroyed, because they are no longer serviceable; and so on. (*ib.* n. 1487.)

Genuine reasonings concerning spiritual things spring from an influx of heaven into the spiritual man, and thence through the rational into the knowledges and cognitions which are in the natural man, by which the spiritual man confirms himself. This way of reasoning concerning spiritual things is according to order. But reasonings about spiritual things which proceed from the natural man, still more those that proceed from the sensual man, are entirely contrary to order; for the natural man,—and still less the sensual man,—cannot flow into the spiritual, and from himself see anything there, since there is no physical influx; but the spiritual man can flow into the natural, and thence into the sensual, for there is spiritual influx. (A. E. n. 569.)

So far as a man has become rational in the world by means of languages and knowledges, he is rational after death; but not at all in proportion as he is skilled in languages and knowledges. I have talked with many whom they in the world believed to be learned, from the fact that they were acquainted with ancient languages, such as Hebrew, Greek, and Latin, but who had not cultivated their rational by the things that are written in them. Some of these appeared as simple as those who knew nothing of those languages; some appeared stupid; and yet there remained with them a pride as if they were wiser than others. I have conversed with some who in the world believed that a man is wise in proportion to the capacity of his memory, and who had also enriched their memory with many things; and they spoke also from it alone, thus not from themselves but from others, and had nowise perfected the rational by the things of memory. Some of these were stupid, some foolish, not at all comprehending any truth, as to whether it is a truth or not, but seizing all falsities that were commended as truths by those who call themselves learned; for of themselves they cannot see whether anything be so or not so; and therefore they can see nothing rationally when they listen to others. I have also conversed with some who had written much in the world, and indeed on matters of knowledge of every kind, and had thereby acquired an extensive reputation for learning. Some of these, indeed, could reason about truths as to whether they are truths or not; some when they turned to those who were in the light of truth understood that they were truths; and yet they did not desire to understand them, and therefore denied them when they returned into their own falsities, and so into themselves; others had no more discernment than the unlearned vulgar. Thus each was differently affected, according as he had cultivated his rational by the matters of knowledge he had written and copied. But those who were opposed to the truths of the church, and thought from their acquisitions of knowledges, and confirmed themselves thereby in falsities, did not cultivate their rational, but only the faculty of arguing, which in the world is believed to be rationality. But it is a faculty different from rationality; it is the faculty of confirming whatever one pleases, and, from assumed principles and from fallacies, of seeing falsities and not truths. Such can never be brought to acknowledge truths, since truths cannot be seen from falsities. But falsities can be seen from truths. The rational of man is like a garden and floretum, and as land newly ploughed; the memory is the ground, truths known and cognitions are seeds, the light and heat of heaven cause them to spring forth; without these there is no germination. So it is also if the light of heaven, which is Divine truth, and the heat of heaven, which is Divine love, are not admitted; from these alone the rational exists. The angels very much grieve that the learned in great part ascribe all things to nature, and that they have thus so shut the interiors of their minds that they can see nothing of truth by the light of truth, which is the light of heaven. Therefore in the other life they are deprived of the faculty of arguing, lest by argumentations they should disseminate falsities among and seduce the simple good; and they are sent into desert places. (H. H. n. 464.)

Memorabilia concerning Faith.

One morning being awaked from sleep I saw two angels descending from heaven, one from the south of heaven and the other from the east of heaven, both in chariots, to which white horses were attached. The chariot in which the angel from the south of heaven was carried shone as with silver, and the chariot in which the angel from the east of heaven was carried shone as with gold, and the reins which they held in their hands glittered as from the flamy light of the morning. Thus did those two angels appear to me at a distance; but when they came near they did not appear in a chariot, but in their angelic form, which is human. The one who came from the east of heaven was dressed in raiment of shining purple, and the one that came from the south of heaven in raiment of violet blue. When they reached the lower region below the heavens they ran to each other, as if they were striving to see which would be first, and mutually embraced and kissed each other. I heard that those two angels while they lived in the world were joined in interior friendship; but now one was in the eastern heaven and the other in the southern heaven. In the eastern heaven are those who are in love from the Lord; and in the southern heaven are those who are in wisdom from the Lord. When they had conversed together for some time concerning the magnificent things in their heavens, their conversation turned upon this subject: "Whether heaven in its essence is love, or wisdom." They agreed immediately that one is of the other; but they discussed the question, which was the original. The angel who was from the heaven of wisdom asked the other, "What is love?" And he answered, "Love originating from the Lord as a sun is the heat of the life of angels and men; thus the *esse* of their life; and the derivations of love are called affections, and by these perceptions are produced, and thus thoughts. Whence it follows, that wisdom in its origin is love; consequently that thought in its origin is the affection of that love; and it may be seen from the derivations viewed in their order that thought is nothing else than the form of affection. This is not known, because the thoughts are in light, and the affections in heat; and therefore one reflects upon thoughts, but not upon affections. That thought is nothing else than the form of the affection of some love, may also be illustrated by speech, in that this is nothing else than the form of sound. It also is similar, because sound corresponds to affection and speech to thought; wherefore affection sounds and thought speaks. This indeed may be made obvious if it is asked, Take away sound from speech, and is there anything of speech? So take away affection from thought, and is there anything of thought? From this now it is manifest that love is the all of wisdom; and therefore, that the essence of the heavens is love, and that their existence is wisdom; or what is the same, that the heavens are from the Divine love, and exist from the Divine love by the Divine wisdom. Wherefore as was said before the one is of the other." There was a novitiate spirit with me, who hearing this asked whether it is the same with charity and faith, because charity is of affection, and faith is of thought. And the angel replied, " It is quite the same. Faith is nothing but the form of charity, just as speech is the form of sound; faith also is formed by charity, as speech is formed by sound. We in heaven know also the manner of formation, but there is not time to explain it here." He added, " By faith I mean spiritual faith, in which alone there is spirit and life from the Lord through charity; for this is spiritual, and by it faith becomes so. Faith therefore without charity is merely natural faith, and this faith is dead; it also conjoins itself with merely natural affection, which is no other than concupiscence." The angels spoke of these things spiritually; and spiritual language embraces thousands of things which natural language cannot express; and, what is wonderful, which cannot even fall into the ideas of natural thought. After the angels had conversed on these subjects they departed; and as they returned each to his own heaven there appeared stars about their heads; and as the distance from me increased they appeared again in chariots as before.

After these two angels were out of my sight I saw on the right a garden, in which were olives, fig trees, laurels, and palms, arranged in order according to correspondences. I looked thitherward and saw angels and spirits walking and talking together among the trees. And then one of the angelic spirits looked at me (they are called angelic spirits who are in the world of spirits preparing for heaven). He came to me from the garden and said, " If you will come with me into our paradise you will hear and see wonderful things ? " And I went with him. And he then said to me, " These whom you see (for there were many) are all in the love of truth, and thence in the light of wisdom. There is also a palace here which we call the TEMPLE OF WISDOM. But no one can see it who believes himself to be very wise; still less one who believes himself to be wise enough; and least of all one who believes that he is wise from himself. The reason is that they are not in the reception of the light of heaven, from the love of genuine wisdom. It is genuine wisdom for a man to see from the light of heaven that what he knows, understands, and appropriates (*sapit*), is as little compared with what he does not know, understand, and appropriate, as a drop of water to the ocean; or scarcely anything. Every one who is in this paradisiacal garden, and from perception and sight within himself acknowledges that he has comparatively so little wisdom, sees that TEMPLE OF WISDOM; for the interior light in the mind of man enables him to see it, but not his exterior light without that. Now as I have often thought, and from knowledge, and then from perception, and at last from interior light have acknowledged that man has so little wisdom, lo, it was granted me to see that temple. As to form it was wonderful. It was very lofty above the ground, quadrangular, with walls of crystal, a gracefully curved roof of transparent jasper, and a foundation of various precious stones. The steps by which they ascended to it were of polished alabaster; at the sides of the steps there appeared, as it were, lions with whelps. And then I asked whether it was allowable to enter; and was told that it was. I therefore ascended; and when I entered I saw as it were cherubim flying under the roof, but presently vanishing. The floor upon which we walked was of cedar; and the whole temple, by the transparency of the roof and walls, was constructed for a form of light. The angelic spirit entered with me, and I related to him what I had heard from the two angels concerning LOVE and WISDOM, and concerning charity and faith; and he then said, "Did they not speak also of a third?" I answered, "What third?" He replied, "THE GOOD OF USE. Love and wisdom are nothing without the good of use. They are but ideal entities; nor do they become real until they exist in use. For love, wisdom, and use, are three things that cannot be separated; if they are separated neither is anything. Love is not anything without wisdom; but in wisdom it is formed to something. This something into which it is formed is use; therefore when love by wisdom is in use then it really is, because it actually exists. They are precisely like end, cause, and effect; the end is not anything unless through the cause it exists in an effect; if one of the three is dispersed the whole is dispersed and becomes as nothing. It is the same with charity, faith, and works. Charity is nothing without faith, neither is faith anything without charity, nor charity and faith without works; but in works they are something, and a something of the same nature as the use of the works. It is the same with affection, thought, and operation. And it is the same with the will, the understanding, and action; for the will without the understanding is like the eye without sight; and both without action are as a mind without a body. It may be clearly seen that it is so in this temple; because the light in which we are here is a light which enlightens the interiors of the mind. And geometry also teaches that there is nothing complete and perfect unless it is a trine; for a line is nothing unless it becomes a surface, nor is a surface anything unless it becomes a body; one therefore is drawn into another that they may exist, and they coexist in the third. As in this, so it is also in each and all created things, which are all terminated in a third. This now is the reason why in the Word the number three signifies what is complete and entire. Since this is so I cannot but wonder that some profess faith alone, some charity alone, and some works alone; when yet one without another of them, or even one with another without the third is nothing." But then I asked, "Cannot a man have charity and faith and yet not works? Cannot a man be in the love of a certain object, and in thought about it, and yet not in the performance of it?" And the angel answered me, "He can ideally only; but not really. He must yet be in the endeavour or will to perform; and the will or endeavour is the act in itself; because it is the continual effort to act, which, adding determination, becomes action in externals. Endeavour and will are therefore accepted by every wise man as an internal act; because they are accepted by God, precisely as an external act,—if only it does not fail when opportunity is given." (T. C. R. n. 386, 387.)

The Fruits of Faith, and Capability of receiving Faith in the other Life.

The fruits of faith are none other than a life according to the precepts of faith. A life according to these precepts is therefore saving; but not faith without the life. For a man carries all the states of his life with him after death, so that he is such as his character had been in the body. For example, he who had despised others in comparison with himself in the life of the body, in the other life also despises others in comparison with himself; he who had indulged in hatred to his neighbour in the life of the body, bears hatred to his neighbour in the other life also; he who had dealt deceitfully with his associates in the life of the body, is deceitful to his associates also in the other life; and so on. Every one retains in the other life the nature he had acquired in the life of the body; and it is known that the nature cannot be put away, and that if put away nothing of life would remain. Hence it is that only works of charity are mentioned by the Lord; for he who is in works of charity, or what is the same, in the life of faith, has the capability of receiving faith, if not in the body yet in the other life; but he who is not in works of charity, or in the life of faith, has by no means any capability of receiving faith, either in the body or in the other life. For evil never harmonizes with truth, but the one rejects the other; and if they who are in evil speak truths they say them from the mouth and not from the heart. And so evil and truth are very far apart. (A. C. n. 4663.)

CHARITY AND GOOD WORKS.

Who is the Neighbour.

It shall first be shown what the neighbour is; for it is the neighbour who is to be loved, and towards whom charity is to be exercised. For unless it be known what the neighbour is charity may be exercised, without distinction, in the same manner towards the evil as towards the good, whereby charity ceases to be charity; for the evil do evil to the neighbour from the benefactions conferred on them, but the good do good.

It is a common opinion at this day that every man is equally the neighbour, and that benefits are to be conferred on every one who needs assistance: but it concerns Christian prudence to look well to the quality of a man's life, and to exercise charity towards him accordingly. The man of the internal church exercises his charity with discrimination, and therefore with intelligence; but the man of the external church, because he cannot so well discern things, does it indiscriminately.

The distinctions of neighbour, which the man of the church ought well to know, depend upon the good that is in every one. And because every good proceeds from the Lord, therefore the neighbour in the highest sense and in a supereminent degree is the Lord, from whom is the origin [of the relationship]. Hence it follows that in so far as any one is receptive of the Lord in that degree he is our neighbour; and since no one receives the Lord, that is good from Him, in the same manner as another, therefore no one is our neighbour in the same manner as another. For all who are in the heavens and all the good that are on earth differ in good; no two ever receive good that is exactly one and the same. It must be different that each may subsist by itself. But all these varieties, —that is all the distinctions of neighbour which depend on the reception of the Lord, or, on the reception of good from Him,— can never be known by any man; nor indeed by any angel except in general, or as to their genera and species. And the Lord does not require more of the man of the church than to live according to what he knows.

Since the good with every one is different, it follows that the quality of his good determines in what degree and in what respect any one is our neighbour. That this is so is plain from the Lord's parable concerning him who fell among thieves, whom half dead the priest passed by, and also the Levite; but the Samaritan, after he had bound up his wounds and poured in oil and wine, took him upon his own beast, and led him to an inn, and ordered that care should be taken of him. Because he exercised the good of charity he is called the neighbour (Luke x. 29-37). It may be known from this that they who are in good are our neighbour. The oil and wine moreover which the Samaritan poured into the wounds signify good and its truth.

It is plain from what has now been said that in the universal sense good is the neighbour; inasmuch as a man is neighbour according to the quality of the good that is in him from the Lord. And as good is the neighbour so is love, for all good is of love; therefore every man is our neighbour according to the quality of the love which he possesses from the Lord. (H. D. n. 84-88.)

Good is the neighbour because good is of the will, and the will is the being of a man's life. The truth of the understanding is also the neighbour, but in so far as it proceeds from the good of the will; for the good of the will forms itself in the understanding, and there makes itself visible in the light of reason. That good is the neighbour is evident from all experience. Who loves a person except for the quality of his will and understanding, that is for what is good and just in him? For example, who loves a king, a prince, a duke, a governor, a consul, or the person of any magistrate, or any judge, but for the discretion from which they act and speak? Who loves a primate, or any minister or canon of the church, but for his learning, uprightness of life, and zeal for the salvation of souls? Who loves the general of an army, or any officer under him, but for his courage, and at the same time prudence? Who loves a merchant but for his sincerity? Who loves a workman or a servant but for his fidelity? Nay, who likes a tree but for its fruit? or ground but for its fertility? or a stone but for its preciousness? &c. And what is remarkable, not only does an upright man love what is good and just in another, but a man who is not upright also does; because with him he is in no fear of the loss of fame, honour, or wealth. But with one who is not upright the love of good is not love of the neighbour; for he does not inwardly love the other, except in so far as he is of service to him. But to love the good in another from good in one's self is genuine love towards the neighbour; for then the goods mutually kiss and are united with each other. (T. C. R. n. 418.)

The Degrees of the Relationship of Neighbour.

Not only is man individually the neighbour, but also man collectively; for indeed a smaller and larger society, our country, the church, the Lord's kingdom, and above all the Lord Himself, is the neighbour. These are the neighbour to which good is to be done from love. These are also the ascending degrees of neighbour. For a society consisting of many is neighbour in a higher degree than an individual man; in a still higher degree our country; in a degree yet higher the church; and in a degree higher still the Lord's kingdom; but in the highest degree the Lord is the neighbour. These ascending degrees are as the steps of a ladder, at the top of which is the Lord.

A society is our neighbour more than an individual man, because it consists of many. Charity is to be exercised towards it as towards man individually, that is, according to the quality of good that is in it; and therefore in an entirely different manner towards a society of well-disposed than towards a society of evil-disposed persons. A society is loved when its good is consulted from the love of good.

Our country is our neighbour more than a society, because it is as a parent; for there a man is born, and it fosters him and protects him from injuries. Good is to be done to our country from love according to its necessities, which have regard especially to its sustenance, and the civil life and spiritual life of those that are therein. He who loves his country and does good to it from good will, in the other life loves the Lord's kingdom; for there the Lord's kingdom is his country. And he who loves the Lord's kingdom loves the Lord, for the Lord is all in all in His kingdom.

The church is the neighbour more than our country; for he who cares for the church cares for the souls and eternal life of the men who dwell in his country. And therefore he who from love cares for the church loves his neighbour in a superior degree; for he desires and wills for others heaven and happiness of life to eternity.

The Lord's kingdom is the neighbour in a still higher degree, because the Lord's kingdom consists of all who are in good, both those who are on earth as those that are in the heavens. Thus the Lord's kingdom is good with its every quality in the complex; when this is loved the individuals who are in good are loved.

These are the degrees of the neighbour, and with those who are in love towards their neighbour the love ascends according to these degrees. But these degrees are degrees in successive order, in which what is prior or superior must be preferred to what is posterior or inferior; and as the Lord is in the supreme degree, and He is to be regarded in each degree as the end to which it looks, therefore He is to be loved above all men and above all things. From all this now it may be seen how love to the Lord conjoins itself with love towards the neighbour. (H. D. n. 91-96.)

The kind of neighbour is according to the kind of good in a man; or, the neighbour is such as the quality of the man is. That every man is not alike the neighbour the Lord's parable of the man wounded by robbers teaches, where it is said that he was the neighbour "*who showed mercy on him.*" Whoever does not distinguish the neighbour according to the kind of good and truth in him may be deceived in a thousand instances, and his charity become confounded and at length annulled. A man-devil may exclaim, "I am the neighbour: do good to me." And if you do good to him he may kill you or others. You are placing a knife or sword in his hand. Simple persons act thus. They say that every man is equally the neighbour; and that therefore they consider they have no business to examine into his quality. But God regards this as merely aid to a wild beast as the neighbour. And this is not to love the neighbour. He who loves the neighbour from genuine charity inquires what the man is, and discretely does him good according to the quality of his good. Such simple ones are withdrawn and separated in the other life; for if they come among diabolical spirits they are allured to act favourably to them, and to wrong the good. For the evil cry out, "Set me free! Help me!" This is the chief [source of] the strength that the evil acquire. Without the help of, and as it were conjunction with them, they are utterly powerless; but with those whom they have deceived under the name of neighbour they are strong. Charity really genuine is prudent and wise. Other charity is spurious; because it is merely voluntary or of good, and not at the same time intellectual or of truth. (Ch. n. 21.)

In regard to mere person one man is not more a neighbour than another; but only in regard to the good which gives him his peculiar nature. For there are as many differences of neighbour as there are differences of good; and the differences of good are infinite. It is commonly believed that a brother, a kinsman, or relation, is more the neighbour than a stranger, and that our fellow-countryman is more the neighbour than a foreigner; and yet every one is the neighbour according to his good, be he Greek or be he Gentile; for every one is the neighbour according to spiritual affinity and relationship. This may be seen from the fact that every man after death comes among his own whom he is similar to in good, or what is the same thing, in affection; and that natural affinities vanish after death, and are succeeded by spiritual affinities, because in the newly-entered heavenly society one man knows another, and they are consociated, by being in similar good. Of ten who are brothers in the world, five may be in hell, and five in heaven, and these five in different societies; and when they meet they do not know each other. Thus they are all in the society of their own affection. It is therefore plain that every man is a neighbour according to the quality of his good. This is especially the case with spiritual goods; and charity has primary regard to them. (*ib.* n. 26.)

What Charity is.

It is believed by many that love to the neighbour consists in giving to the poor, in assisting the needy, and in doing good to every one; but charity consists in acting prudently, and to the end that good may result. He who assists a poor or needy villain does evil to his neighbour through him; for through the assistance which he renders he confirms him in evil, and supplies him with the means of doing evil to others. It is otherwise with him who gives support to the good.

But charity extends itself much more widely than to the poor and needy; for charity consists in doing what is right in every work, and our duty in every office. If a judge administers justice for the sake of justice he exercises charity; if he punishes the guilty and absolves the innocent he exercises charity; for thus he consults the welfare of his fellow-citizens and of his country. The priest who teaches truth and leads to good, for the sake of truth and good, exercises charity. But he who does such things for the sake of self and the world does not exercise charity; because he does not love his neighbour, but himself.

It is the same in other things, whether men are in any office or not; as with children toward their parents, and parents toward their children; with servants toward their masters, and with masters toward their servants; with subjects toward their king, and with a king toward his subjects. Whoever of these does his duty from a sense of duty, and what is just from a sense of justice, exercises charity.

That these things are of love to the neighbour or charity is because as was said above every man is a neighbour, but in a different manner. A smaller and a larger society is more the neighbour; our country is still more the neighbour; the Lord's kingdom yet more; and the Lord above all. And in the universal sense good, which proceeds from the Lord, is the neighbour; consequently sincerity and justice too are so. He therefore who does any good for the sake of good, and who acts sincerely and justly for the sake of sincerity and justice, loves his neighbour and exercises charity; for he does so from the love of what is good, sincere, and just, and consequently from the love of those in whom good, sincerity, and justice are.

Charity is therefore an internal affection from which man wills to do good, and this without remuneration. The delight of his life consists in doing it. With those who do good from an internal affection there is charity in everything that they think and say, and that they will and do. It may be said that a man or an angel as to his interiors is charity, when good is his neighbour. So widely does charity extend itself.

They who have the love of self and of the world for an end can in nowise be in charity. They do not even know what charity is, and cannot at all comprehend that to will and do good to the neighbour without reward, as an end, is heaven in man; and that there is in that affection a happiness as great as that of the angels of heaven, which is ineffable. For they believe that if they are deprived of the joy from the glory of honour and riches, there can be nothing of joy any longer; and yet it is then that heavenly joy, which infinitely transcends the other, first begins. (H. D. n. 100-105.)

The first part of charity consists in looking to the Lord, and shunning evils because they are sins. . . . Who does not see that an impenitent man is a wicked man? And who does not see that a wicked man has no charity? And who does not see that the man who has no charity cannot do charity. Charity comes from charity within a man. (Ch. n. 7, 8.)

The second part of charity consists in doing goods because they are uses. . . . But yet they are goods only in so far as the doer of them shuns evils as sins. If they are done before evils are shunned as sins they are external, nay, meritorious. For they flow forth from an impure fountain, and the things which flow from such a fountain are inwardly evils; for the man is in them, and the world is in them. It is known that doing Christian good is a part of charity; and it is believed by many that good destroys evil, and that thus the evils in a man either cease to exist or are not regarded. But good does not destroy evil if a man does not think about the evils in himself, and actually repent of them. There are many who have thus believed, and have thought that evil had no existence in them, who on examination have confessed themselves full of evils, and that unless they were detained in their externals they could not be saved. (*ib.* n. 10, 12.)

That to do good and to shun evil are two distinct things is plain; for there are men who do every good of charity, from piety and from thought of eternal life, and who yet do not know that to hate and revenge, to commit fornication, to rob, and injure, to vilify and consequently bear false witness, and many more things, are evils. There are judges who lead pious lives and yet think it no sin to adjudicate from friendship, from relationship, and respect to honour and gain; nay, if they know that these thing are sins they confirm in themselves that they are not. The same applies to others. In a word, shunning evils as sins and doing Christian goods are two distinct things. He who shuns evils as sins does Christian goods. But he that does good and does not shun evils as sins is not a doer of Christian good; for evil is against charity, and must therefore be abolished before the good that he does is with, that is of, charity. No man can do good and at the same time will to do evil, or will both good and evil. Every good which is such in itself proceeds from the interior will. Evil is removed from this will by repentance; for there the evil into which man is born resides. And therefore unless a man repents the evil remains in his interior will, and good proceeds from his exterior will; and thus his state is perverted. The inward qualifies the outward, and not the outward the inward. The Lord says, " *Cleanse first the inside of the cup and of the platter.*" Man has a twofold will; an interior one, and an exterior. The interior will is purified by repentance; the exterior then does good from the interior. But exterior good does not remove the evil of concupiscence, or the root of evil. (*ib.* n. 13.)

Good is civil, moral, and spiritual. The good done before a man shuns evils as sins is civil and moral good; but as soon as he shuns evils as sins the good becomes spiritual too, as well as civil and moral, and not before. [Before this] concupiscence lurks within him, and the delight of concupiscence without; and therefore in thinking from concupiscence and its delight he either confirms evil and believes it allowable, or else he takes no thought of any evil in himself, and thus believes he is whole. It is true that a man should confess himself a sinner, and unsound from the head to the sole of the foot. This he can say, that is, say it with outward earnestness; but yet he cannot inwardly believe it unless he knows it by examination. Then he can truly say, and then for the first time he perceives, that there is no soundness in him. Thus, and in no other manner, is the ulcer opened and healed ; otherwise it is merely palliative. Did not the Lord, and the disciples, and John the Baptist, preach repentance ? Isaiah declares that evils must first be desisted from, and that then a man learns to do good. Until this is the case he knows nothing either of the nature or quality of good. Evil is ignorant of good, but good has the power of discerning evil. (*ib.* n. 14.)

Since it is necessary that evil should first be known in order that it may be removed, therefore was the Decalogue the first [*primum*] of the Word,[1] and also in the whole of Christendom is the first of church doctrine. All are initiated into the church by knowing evil and refusing to do it, because it is against God; and therefore was this first so holy, for the reason that no one can do Christian good before. (*ib.* n. 15.)

The Delights of Charity are according to the greatness and importance of the Use performed.

As regards use, they who are in charity, that is in love towards the neighbour,—which imparts a living delight to their pleasure,—look for the fruition of no pleasure but in the performance of uses; for charity is nothing unless it manifests itself in works of charity, since it consists in exercise or use. He who loves his neighbour as himself never perceives the delight of charity except in its exercise; a life of charity therefore is a life of uses. Such is the life of the universal heaven; for the Lord's kingdom, being a kingdom of mutual love, is a kingdom of uses. Therefore every pleasure derived from charity receives its delight from use, and the more exalted the use the greater the delight; hence the angels receive happiness from the Lord according to the essence and quality of the use which they perform. And so it is with every pleasure; the more distinguished its use the greater is its delight. Thus, for example only, conjugial love, because from thence is the seminary of human society and from this is formed the Lord's kingdom in the heavens, which is the greatest of all uses, is therefore attended with so great delight that, as has been said, it is heavenly happiness. So in respect to other pleasures, but with a difference according to the excellence of uses,—which are so numerous that they can scarcely be divided

---

[1] The author's meaning here is well explained in the following passage, from A. E. n. 939 :—" Because evils must be removed before good [deeds] can become [really] good, therefore were the Ten Commandments the first [*primum*] of the Word ; for they were promulgated from Mount Sinai before the Word was written by Moses and the Prophets ; and in them are contained, not the good [deeds] that are to be done, but the evils that are to be shunned. And therefore these Commandments are first taught in the churches ; for they are taught to boys and girls, in order that man may begin his Christian life from them, and by no means forget them when he grows up,—as however he does." In other places, for the same reason, the author calls the Decalogue the " first-fruits" (*primitiæ*) of the Word and of the church (see p. 192). He teaches that the command of the Lord to Moses, " *Be ready for the morning, and* . . . . *come up unto Mount Sinai, and present thyself there to Me on the top of the mount*" (Ex. xxxiv. 2), signifies " *a new rising of revelation* of Divine truth, from the inmost heaven" (A. C. n. 10,606). And speaking elsewhere of the promulgation of the Decalogue from Mount Sinai, he says, " It was the beginning of revelation ; for the rest of the things that are in the Word were written afterwards" (*ib.* n. 9414 ; and n. 10,632. See also A. R. n. 623).

into genera and species; all of which regard the Lord's kingdom, or the Lord, some more nearly and directly, others more remotely and indirectly.   Hence it may be seen that all pleasures are allowed to man for the sake of use only; and that by virtue of their use, with a difference according to its degree, they participate in and live from heavenly felicity.   (A. C. n. 997.)

A MAN IS NOT OF SOUND MIND UNLESS USE BE HIS AFFECTION OR, OCCUPATION.

Man has external thought, and also internal thought.   He is in external thought when in company, whether he then listens, or speaks, or teaches, or acts; and also when he writes.   But the mind is in internal thought when he is at home, and gives place to his own interior affection; this is the proper thought of his spirit in itself, but the former is the proper thought of his spirit in the body.   Each remains with a man after death; and it is not known what the quality of the man is until external thought is taken away, for the thought then speaks and acts from its affection.   A man who is of sound mind will then see and hear wonderful things.   For he will then hear and see that many who in the world have talked wisely, have preached cleverly, have taught learnedly, have written skilfully, and have also acted discretely, as soon as the external of their mind is taken away begin instantly to think insanely, and to speak and act as wildly as lunatics in the world; and, what is strange, they then believe themselves to be wiser than others.   But to prevent the continuance of their insanity they are remitted by turns into their externals, and thereby into the civil and moral life which they lived in the world, when in company and in public assembly there; and there is given a recollection of their insanities, and then they see and confess that they have talked insanely and acted foolishly.   Yet in the very instant of their being remitted into their interiors, or the things proper to their spirits, they are insane as before.   Their insanities are many, which may be reduced to these, that they desire to have dominion, to steal, to commit adultery, to blaspheme, to do hurt, to despise, reject, or sneer at probity, justice, sincerity, and every truth and good of the church and of heaven.   And what is more, they love this state of their spirit; for the experiment has been made with many, whether they desire rather to think sanely or insanely, and it has been found that they prefer to think insanely.   The reason why they are of such a character has been made known; namely, that they loved themselves and the world above all things, that they did not apply their minds to uses, except for the sake of honour and gain, and that they preferred the delights of the body to the delights of the soul. Such was their character in the world that they never thought sanely within themselves, except when in the presence of other men. There is this only cure of their insanity, they are sent into employments under a judgment in hell; and so long as they are in those employments they are not insane, for the employments in which they are occupied keep the mind as in a prison and in bonds, to prevent its wandering into the deliriums of its lusts. There they work for food, clothing, and lodging; thus unwillingly, from necessity, and not freely from affection. But on the other hand all those in the world who have loved uses, and from the love of them have performed them, think sanely in their spirit, and their spirit thinks sanely in their body; for that interior thought is also exterior, and by and from this is their speech and also their action. The affection of use keeps their mind in itself, not suffering it to wander into vanities, into lasciviousness and filthiness, into insanity and deceit, into the unreal delights of various concupiscences. They become of similar character after death; their minds are in themselves angelic, and when the exterior thought is taken away they become spiritual, and angels, thus recipient of heavenly wisdom from the Lord. From all this now it is evident that no man is of sound mind unless use be his affection or occupation. (D. L. n. 15.)

The Delight of doing Good without a Recompense.

Very few at this day know that there is heavenly happiness in doing good without a view to recompense. For men do not know that there is any other happiness than to be advanced to honours, to be served by others, to abound in wealth, and to live in pleasures. They are profoundly ignorant of the fact that above these there is a happiness which affects the interiors of a man; that is, that there is a heavenly happiness, and that this happiness is the happiness of genuine charity. Inquire of the wise at this day, whether they know that this is heavenly happiness. It is on this account indeed that many reject good works, believing that they cannot be done by any one without a view to merit by them. For they do not know that those who are led of the Lord desire nothing more than to do good works; and that they think of nothing less than of merit by them. For this is of the new will which is given by the Lord to those who are regenerated. That will is indeed the Lord's in man. (A. C. n. 6392.)

Those who are in genuine mutual love in heaven are in such

joy and happiness when they perform uses and do good to others, that they seem to themselves then first to be in heaven.   This is given them by the Lord, to each according to the use.   But this happiness vanishes as soon as they think of recompense ; for the thought of recompense while yet they are in the recompense itself renders that love impure and perverts it.   The reason is that then they think of themselves and not of the neighbour; that is, that they may render themselves happy and not others, except so far as themselves.   They thus convert love towards the neighbour into love towards themselves ; and in so far as they do this joy and happiness from heaven cannot be communicated to them; for they concentrate the influx of what is happy from heaven in themselves, and do not transmit it to others; and are like objects which do not remit the rays of light, but absorb them.   Objects which reflect the rays of light appear in light and glow; but those which absorb them are dark and do not glow at all.   They therefore who are of this description are separated from angelic society, as those that have nothing in common with heaven.   (*ib.* n. 6388.)

When an angel does good to any one he also communicates to him his own good, satisfaction, and blessedness; and this with the feeling that he would give to the other everything, and retain nothing.   When he is in such communication good flows into him with much greater satisfaction and blessedness than he gives, and this continually with increase.   But as soon as a thought enters, that he will communicate his own to the intent that he may maintain that influx of satisfaction and blessedness into himself, the influx is dissipated; and still more if there comes in any thought of recompense from him to whom he communicates his good.   This it has been given to know from much experience. From this too it may be seen that in the least things [of heaven] the Lord is present.   For the Lord is such that He wills to give Himself to all ; and therefore satisfaction and blessedness are increased with those who are images and likenesses of Him. (*ib.* n. 6478.)

The blessedness of heavenly affections, which are affections of love to the Lord and charity towards the neighbour, cannot easily be described, because it is internal and rarely manifests itself with any one in the body,—that is rarely to the sense.   For during his life in the body man has a distinct sensation of the things which arise in the body, but a very obscure sensation of those that arise in his spirit, because while he is in the body worldly cares are an impediment. The blessedness of the affections cannot flow down into the sense of the body unless natural and sensual things are reduced to agreement with interior things; and not even then except obscurely, as a certain tranquillity from the fact that he is contented in mind. But after death it manifests itself, and is perceived as blessed and happy; and then it affects both the interiors and exteriors. (A. C. n. 6408.)

The Angels appear in Heaven as Forms of Charity.

In heaven an angel appears as charity in form. The quality of his charity is apparent in the face, and audible in the tone of voice; for after death a man becomes his own love, that is the affection of his own love. A spirit or an angel is nothing else. Nay, the spirit or angel even is himself a form of charity as to his whole body. Some have seen an angel, and what is wonderful have discerned the form of charity in all the members of his body. In the world man is not charity in form as regards his face, body, and voice; but yet he may be as to his mind; and after death his mind is a spirit in the human form. But still a sincere man who has no thought contrary to charity may be recognised as such by the face and voice; and yet with difficulty, for there are such hypocrites as can feign to the life, yea put on, the sincerity of charity. But if an angel beholds his face and hears his voice he discerns the nature of the man, because he does not see the materiality which overveils him; and which, however, the material man attends to. (Ch. n. 37.)

The Criterion of Character.

All spirits are distinguished in the other life by this: Those who desire evil against others are infernal or diabolical spirits; but they who wish good to others are good and angelic spirits. A man may know which he is among, whether among the infernal spirits or the angelic. If he intends evil to his neighbour, thinks nothing but evil of him, and also actually does evil when he can, and finds delight in it, he is among the infernals, and even becomes an infernal in the other life; but if he intends good to his neighbour, and thinks nothing but good of him, and actually does good when he can, he is among the angelic, and becomes an angel too in the other life. This is the criterion. Let every one examine himself by it. It is nothing that a man does not do evil when he either cannot or dare not; nor that he does good from some selfish reason. These are external motives which are removed in the other life. There a man is as he thinks and intends. There are many who, from habit acquired in the world, can speak fairly; but it is instantly perceived whether the mind or intention is in harmony with what is said. If not, the man is cast out among the infernals of his own kind and species. (A. C. n. 1680.)

Every one may see what the quality of his life is, if he will but search out the nature of the end that he regards. Not the nature of the ends, for these are innumerable, being as many as his intentions, and nearly as many as the judgments and conclusions of his thoughts. These are intermediate ends, which are variously derived from the principal end, or tend to promote it. But let him search out the end which he regards in preference to all the rest, and in respect to which the rest are as nothing; and if he has himself and the world for an end, he may know that he is infernal; but if he has for his end the good of the neighbour, the common good, the Lord's kingdom, and especially the Lord Himself, he may know that his life is heavenly. (A. C. n. 1909.)

In the further course of conversation with him [Swedenborg] on the principles of religion advocated and explained by him, I took an opportunity of asking him, How a man, who was confident that he was serious in his duty towards God and his neighbour, could be certain whether or not he was in the right road to salvation? I was answered, That this was very easy; and that such a man need only examine himself and his own thoughts according to the Ten Commandments; as, for instance, whether he loves and fears God; whether he is happy in seeing the welfare of others, and does not envy them; whether, on having received a great injury from others which may have excited him to anger and to meditate revenge, he afterwards changes his sentiments, because GOD has said that vengeance belongs to Him, and so on; then he may rest assured that he is on the road to heaven. But when he discovers himself to be actuated by contrary sentiments, he is on the road to hell. (General Tuxon, *in Sw. Doc.* p. 61.)

A MAN HAS NEITHER FAITH NOR CHARITY BEFORE THEY EXIST IN WORKS.

Hitherto no one has taken cognizance of the fact that all things of a man's life are in his works; for the reason that they appear only as motions, which, because with man they are living, are called actions, and those that are produced by the motions of the mouth, the tongue, and the larynx, are called speech. And yet these are the things which not only manifest the charity and faith in a man, but also complete and perfect them; and this because there is neither faith nor charity in man before they actually exist, and they actually exist in works. That all things of the charity and faith in a man are in his works, is because works are the activities arising from his will and thought, and all of these send and pour themselves forth in works, just as all things of a cause are in the effect, and all things of a seed and tree in its fruit; for works are their complements. It does not appear before the eyes of men that this is so, but it perceptibly appears before the angels. When a man is in the exercise of charity, the sphere of all his affections and thence thoughts appears about him as a watery vapour, and sometimes as a cloud either bright or obscure, which sphere contains all things of his mind in the complex; from which the quality of the man is cognized by the angels as to all things that belong to him. The reason is, that every man is his own love, and works from this make the love active, and while it is active, it pours itself around him. The same spiritual sphere not only manifests itself to the sight as by an undulation, but also to the sight in various representative forms; and this in such a manner that from these representatives the man, spirit, or angel, appears just such as he is. Another reason why the works contain within them all things of the mind, is because all things successive, which proceed in their order from the highest to the lowest, or from the first to the ultimates, form in the lowest or in ultimates the simultaneous in which all things higher or prior coexist; and works are the ultimates of man, derived from his interiors which are in successive order. From all this it is clear that in them all things of the will and thought of man, therefore all things of his love and faith, coexist. (A. E. n. 822.)

Love, Life, and Works, with every Man, make One.

From what has been said above concerning faith and works, I will make the following conclusion, that love, life, and works, with every man, make one, so that whether you say love, or life, or works, it is the same. It was shown above that love constitutes the life of man, and that his life is such as his love; not only the life of the mind, but at the same time also the life of the body; and as that which a man loves in mind he also wills, and in the body does, it follows that love and actions or works make one. It can be shown by many considerations that the works proceed from the life of a man, both internal and external;

and that they are the activities of the sphere of his affections and thence thoughts surrounding him; and that there is no communication of a man's life and love unless the surrounding sphere which is of his life is made active by doing. Therefore as the life, or the love, or the works are with man, so are all things of which that sphere is composed; consequently his faith also. If then the works are evil, it follows that there is no faith of truth, but a faith of falsity; for evil and falsity cohere, but not evil and truth. But if the works are good, it follows that there is a faith of truth, for good and truth mutually love each other and conjoin. But if a man's works in the external form appear good and yet he is interiorly evil, it follows that his is a faith of falsity however with his mouth he may speak truth,—but truth that is contaminated with evil from his interior; his deeds are therefore according to the description of them by the Lord: "*As a cup and platter made clean on the outside, but within full of extortion and excess. And are as whited sepulchres, which appear beautiful without, but inwardly are full of bones of the dead and all uncleanness*" (Matt. xxiii. 25, 27, 28). (A. E. n. 842.)

Love to the Lord and Love to the Neighbour distinguished.

The Divine abiding with those who have faith in the Lord is love and charity: and by love is meant love to the Lord; and by charity love towards the neighbour. Love to the Lord cannot be separated from love towards the neighbour; for the Lord's love is towards the whole human race, which He desires to save eternally, and to adjoin entirely to Himself, so that none of them may perish. Whoever therefore has love to the Lord has the Lord's love, and so cannot but love his neighbour. But they who are in love towards the neighbour are not all therefore in love to the Lord; as upright Gentiles who are in ignorance concerning the Lord,—with whom yet the Lord is present in charity; and others also within the church. For love to the Lord is love in a higher degree. Those who have love to the Lord are celestial men; and those that have love towards the neighbour or charity are spiritual men. The Most Ancient church, which was before the flood and was celestial, was in love to the Lord; but the Ancient church, which was after the flood and was spiritual, was in love towards the neighbour or in charity. (A. C. n. 2023.)

Love the Foundation of all Harmony and Order.

That love is the fundamental principle from and by which heaven exists is evident from this: that there must be such harmony and unanimity, and hence universal consociation, in order that the whole heaven and the whole world of spirits, that is the whole human race from its creation, should form one,—as each and all things in man, where they are indefinite, constitute one body and thus one man ; which body, if any part in it should prefer itself to another part, and not love another rather than itself, could not subsist. For in another he who is in genuine love has an idea to the good of the common and universal man, in respect to which every individual man should be as nothing, as is known. Unless therefore he is associated in idea with his fellow, so that he esteems himself as nothing in respect to the common good, and so loves his neighbour rather than himself, he cannot be in the unanimous body; but in so far as he is distant from that love he of necessity expels himself. (S. D. n. 4046.)

Love to Enemies.

Internal men, such as the angels of heaven are, do not desire retaliation of evil for evil, but from heavenly charity freely forgive ; for they know that the Lord defends all who are in good against the evil, and that He defends according to the good in them ; and that He would not defend if on account of evil done them they should be inflamed with enmity, hatred, and revenge, for these avert protection. (A. C. n. 556.)

The Presence of the Lord with Man is according to Neighbourly Love or Charity.

The presence of the Lord is according to the state of love to the neighbour and of faith in which a man is. The Lord is present in love to the neighbour, because in all good. Not so in faith, as it is called, without love; for faith without love and charity is a thing separate or disjoined. Wherever there is conjunction there must be a conjoining medium, which only is love and charity. This may appear to every one from the consideration that the Lord is merciful to all, and loves every one, and desires to make every one happy to eternity ; whoever therefore is not in such love that he is merciful towards others, loves others, and desires to make others happy, cannot be conjoined to the Lord, because of his dissimilitude and his utter destitution of the image of the Lord. For a man to look up to the Lord by faith, as it is said, and hate his neighbour, is not only to stand afar off from Him, but also to have an infernal gulf between himself and the Lord, into which he would fall were he to approach more nearly; for hatred against the neighbour is the infernal gulf which is interposed. The presence of the Lord with man is first vouchsafed when he loves his neighbour; for the Lord is in love, and so far as man is in love the Lord is present; and in the degree in which the Lord is present He speaks with man. (A. C. n. 904.)

Self-Love and mutual Love contrasted.

There is something inflammatory in self-love, and its lusts; and a delight therefrom, which so affects the life, that one scarcely knows but that eternal happiness itself consists in it. And therefore many make eternal happiness to consist in becoming great after the life of the body, and being served by others, even by angels; while they are willing to serve no one except with a secret view to themselves, that they may be served. When they say that they shall then be willing to serve the Lord alone, it is false; for those who cherish self-love would have even the Lord Himself serve them; and so far as He does not, they draw back. Thus the desire of their hearts is that they themselves may be lord, and rule over the universe. Any one may imagine what sort of government this would be, when there are many, nay when all are such. Would it not be an infernal government, where every one loves himself above others? This lies concealed in self-love. From this the nature of self-love may be seen; also from the consideration that there lurks within it hatred against all who do not subject themselves to it as slaves; and because hatred, therefore revenge, cruelty, deceit, and many atrocities. But mutual love, which alone is heavenly, consists in this: that one not only says, but acknowledges and believes, that he is most unworthy, and that [in himself] he is a vile and unclean thing; and that the Lord out of infinite mercy is continually drawing and keeping him out of hell, into which he is continually attempting, nay desiring, to plunge himself. That he acknowledges and believes this is true because it is true. Not that the Lord, nor any angel, desires that he shall acknowledge and believe this for the sake of humbling himself; but lest he should be puffed up, when yet such is his nature. As if refuse should say that it is pure gold! Or a fly of the dunghill that it is a bird of paradise! In so far then as a man acknowledges and believes that his nature is such as it is, he withdraws from self-love and its lusts, and abhors himself; and in the degree that this is done he receives heavenly love, that is mutual love, from the Lord, which is a desire to serve all others. These are they who are understood by the least who become greatest in the kingdom of God (Matt. xviii. 1-4, xx. 26-28; Luke ix. 46-48). (A. C. n. 1594.)

They who are in the loves of self and of the world can by no means believe that they are in such filthiness and impurity as they actually are; for there is a certain pleasurableness and delight which soothes, favours, and flatters them, and makes them love that life and prefer it to every other; and so they think there is no evil in it. For whatever favours the love and therefore the life of any one is believed to be good. Hence also the rational consents and suggests falsities which confirm; and which causes such blindness that they see nothing of the nature of heavenly love, or if they see they say in their heart that it is something miserable, or a thing of nought, or something like fantasy, which keeps the mind in a state of disease. But every one may see that the life of the love of self and the world with its pleasures and delights is filthy and impure, if he will but think according to the rational faculty with which he is endowed. It is the love of self from which all evils come that destroy civil society. From this, as from a foul pit, stream forth all kinds of hatred, all kinds of revenge, all cruelties, yea all adulteries. For whoever loves himself either contemns, or disparages, or hates, all others who are not subservient to him, or do not show respect to, or favour him; and as he entertains hatred he breathes out revenge and cruelty, and this in proportion as he loves himself. Thus that love is destructive of society and of the human race. (*ib.* n. 2045.)

Mutual love in heaven consists in this, that they love the neighbour more than themselves. Hence the whole heaven presents as it were a single man; for they are all thus consociated by mutual love from the Lord. Hence it is that the happinesses of all are communicated to each, and those of each to all. The heavenly form itself is therefore such that every one is as it were a kind of centre; thus a centre of communication and therefore of happiness from all; and this according to all the diversities of that love, which are innumerable. And as they who are in that love perceive the highest happiness in the fact that they can communicate to others what flows into themselves, and this from the heart, the communication is thereby made perpetual and eternal. From this cause, as the Lord's kingdom increases the happiness of every individual increases. As the angels dwell in distinct societies and mansions, they do not think of this; but the Lord so disposes each and all things. Such is the kingdom of the Lord in the heavens. (*ib.* n. 2057.)

FREE WILL.

MAN cannot be reformed unless he has freedom, because he is born into evils of every kind, which yet must be removed in order that he may be saved; and they cannot be removed unless he sees them in himself, and acknowledges them, and afterwards ceases to purpose them, and at length holds them in aversion. Then first they are removed. This cannot be effected unless a man be in good as well as in evil; for from good he can see evils, but cannot from evil see goods. The spiritual goods which a man is able to think of, he learns from childhood by reading the Word, and from preaching; and the moral and civil goods he learns from a life in the world. This is the primary reason why man ought to be in freedom. Another reason is that nothing is appropriated to man but what is done from an affection, which is of the love. Other things indeed may enter, but no farther than into the thought, and not into the will; and what does not enter even into the will of a man does not become his; for the thought derives all that it has from the memory, but the will from the very life. No action is ever free which is not from the will, or what is the same from an affection which is of the love; for whatever a man wills or loves this he freely does. Hence it is that the freedom of man and the affection which is of his love or will are one. Man therefore has freedom in order that he may be affected by truth and good, or love them, and that thus they may become as his own. In a word, whatever does not enter in freedom into man does not remain; because it is not of his love or will, and the things which are not of a man's love or will are not of his spirit; for the being [esse] of man's spirit is the love or will. It is said the love or will because what a man loves that he wills. This then is the reason why a man cannot be reformed except in freedom. (H. H. n. 598.)

He who does not know that no conjunction of good and truth, that is no appropriation of them, and therefore no regeneration can be effected except in man's freedom, only casts himself into darkness and into grievous errors when he reasons about the Lord's providence, about the salvation of man, and about the damnation of many. For he thinks that if the Lord will He can save every one, and this by innumerable means; as by miracles, by the dead who shall rise again, by immediate revelations, by angels who shall withhold from evils and impel by strong manifest power to good, and by many states into which when man is led he will repent; and by many other means. But he does not consider that all these means are compulsory, and that by them a man cannot be reformed. For whatever compels a man does not impart to him any affection; and if it be of a nature to impart it binds itself to an affection of evil. For it appears as if it infused and indeed does infuse a holy [feeling]; but yet when the state is changed the man returns to his former affections, that is to evils and falsities; and then that holy [feeling] conjoins itself with evils and falsities and becomes profane, and such that it leads into the most grievous hell of all. For he first acknowledges and believes, and is also affected by what is holy, and afterwards denies, yea turns away from it. Hence at this day manifest miracles are not wrought, but miracles that are not obvious or manifest, which are of such a nature that they do not inspire a holy [feeling] nor take away man's freedom; and therefore the dead do not rise again, and man is not withheld from evils by immediate revelations and by angels, and forced on to good by strong manifest power. It is man's freedom upon which the Lord operates and by which He bends him; for all freedom is of the love or its affection, and therefore of his will. If he does not receive good and truth in freedom it cannot be appropriated to him, or become his. For that to which he is compelled is not his, but is of him who compels; since he does not do it of himself, although it is done by himself. (A. C. n. 4031.)

If men had not free will in spiritual things, all the inhabitants of the world might within a day be brought to believe in the Lord; but this cannot be done, for the reason that what is not received by man from a free will does not remain. (T. C. R. n. 500.)

WHAT FREE WILL IS.

That it may be known what free will is, and the nature of it, it is necessary that it should be known whence it is; from the recognition of its origin especially it is known not only that it is, but also what it is. Its origin is from the spiritual world, where the mind of man is kept by the Lord. The mind of man is his spirit, which lives after death. And his spirit is continually in company with its like in that world; and through the material body with which it is encompassed, his spirit is with men in the natural world. The reason why a man does not know that as to his mind he is in the midst of spirits is, that the spirits with whom he is consociated in the spiritual world think and speak spiritually, but the spirit of the man, while he is the material body, thinks and speaks naturally : and spiritual thought and speech cannot be understood or perceived by the natural man, nor the reverse; nor therefore can they be seen. But when the spirit of a man is in association with spirits in their world, then he is also with them in spiritual thought and speech, because his mind is inwardly spiritual but outwardly natural; and therefore by its interiors it communicates with them and by its exteriors with men. Through this communication man has a perception of things, and thinks about them analytically. If man had not this he would think no more nor otherwise than a beast. So also if all intercourse with spirits should be taken away from him he would instantly die. But that it may be comprehended how man can be kept in a middle state between heaven and hell, and thereby in the spiritual equilibrium whence he has free will, it shall be briefly explained:—The spiritual world consists of heaven and hell. Heaven is over head, and hell is beneath the feet there; not however in the centre of the earth inhabited by men, but beneath the earth of that world,—which is also of spiritual origin, and therefore has not extension, but the appearance of extension. Between heaven and hell there is a great interval, which to those who are there appears as an entire world. Into this interval evil from hell is exhaled in all abundance; and on the other hand, from heaven good also flows in there in all abundance. It was this interval of which Abraham said to the rich man in hell—"*Between us and you there is a great gulf fixed; so that those who would pass over from hence to you cannot; neither can they who are there pass over to us*" (Luke xvi. 26). Every man as to his spirit is in the midst of this interval, in order, solely, that he may be in free will. (T. C. R. n. 475.)

The spiritual equilibrium which is free will may be compared to a balance, in each scale of which equal weights are placed; if then a little be added to the scale of one side the tongue of the balance above vibrates. It is also similar to a carrying pole, or a large beam balanced upon its support. All and each of the things that are within man, as the heart, the lungs, the stomach, the liver, the pancreas, the spleen, the intestines, and the other organs, are in such an equilibrium. Hence it is that each one in the greatest quietness can perform its functions. So with all the muscles; without such an equilibrium of the muscles all action and reaction would cease, and man would no longer act as a man. Since then all things in the body are in such an equilibrium, all things in the brain also are in the same condition; consequently all things that are in the mind therein, which relate to the will and the understanding. (*ib.* n. 478.)

A SOMETHING ANALOGOUS TO FREE WILL IN ALL CREATED THINGS.

Unless there had been a certain free will in all created things, both animate and inanimate, there could have been no creation. For as regards beasts, without free will in natural things there would be no choice of food conducive to their nourishment, nor any procreation and preservation of offspring, thus no beast. If there were not such freedom with the fishes of the sea, and the shellfish at the bottom of the sea, there would be no fish and shellfish. So unless it were in every little insect there would be no silkworm producing silk, no bee furnishing wax and honey, nor any butterfly sporting with its consort in the air and nourishing itself with the juices of the flowers, and representing the happy state of man in the heavenly aura after he has cast off his exuviæ like the worm. Unless there were something analogous to free will in the soil of the earth, in the seed cast into it, in all parts of the tree springing from it, and in its fruits, and again in new seeds, there would be no vegetation. If there were not something analogous to free will in every metal and in every stone, common and precious, there would be neither metal nor stone, yea, nor even a grain of sand; for this freely absorbs the ether, emits its natural exhalation, rejects its disused elements, and restores itself with new. Hence is the magnetic sphere about the magnet, a sphere of iron about iron, of copper about copper, of silver about silver, of gold about gold, of stone about stone, of nitre about nitre, of sulphur about sulphur, and a different sphere about all the dust of earth, from which sphere the inmost of every seed is impregnated, and its prolific principle vegetates; for without such an exhalation from every particle of the dust of the earth there would be no beginning, and hence no continuance of germination. How otherwise than by what is exhaled from it could the earth penetrate with its dust and water into the inmost centre of a seed sown, as into " *a grain of mustard seed, which is the least of all seeds, but when it is grown it is the greatest among herbs, and becometh a great tree*"? (Matt. xiii. 32; Mark iv. 30-32). Since then freedom has been granted to all created subjects, to each according to its nature, why not free will to man according to his nature, which is that he may be spiritual? It is for this that free will in spiritual things has been given to man from the womb to the end of his life in the world, and afterwards to eternity. (T. C. R. n. 499.)

How Man is in Freedom from the Lord alone.

The case with man as to his affections and as to his thoughts is this: No one, whatever he be, whether man, or spirit, or angel, can will or think from himself, but does so from others; nor can these others from themselves, but all from others again, and so on; and so each wills and thinks from the First of life, which is the Lord. What is unconnected does not exist. Evils and falsities have connection with the hells, whence comes the power of those who are in them to will and think; whence also comes their love, affection, and delight, and therefore their freedom. But goods and truths have connection with heaven, whence comes the power of those who are in them to will and think; and also their love, affection, and delight, and therefore their freedom. Hence it may appear whence is the one freedom and the other freedom. That such is the case is perfectly well known in the other life, but at this day is quite unknown in the world. (A. C. n. 2886.)

In regard to the life of every one, whether man, spirit, or angel, the truth is that it flows in from the Lord alone, who is Life itself; and this diffuses itself through the universal heaven, also through hell, and thus into every individual therein; and in an order and through series that are incomprehensible. But the life which flows in is received by every one according to his character; good and truth are received as good and truth by the good; while by the evil good and truth are received as evil and falsity, and are even changed into evil and falsity in them. It is comparatively as the light of the sun; which diffuses itself into all objects on the earth, but is received according to the quality of each object, and becomes of a beautiful colour in beautiful forms, and of an ugly colour in ugly forms. This is an arcanum in the world, but in the other life nothing is better known. That I might know that there is such influx, it was granted me to converse with the spirits and angels who were with me, and even to feel and perceive the influx; and this so often that I am not able to determine the number of times. But I know the fallacy will prevail with many that they will of themselves, and think of themselves, and so of themselves have life, when yet nothing is less true. (*ib.* n. 2888.)

Why in Freedom Man feels and wills as of himself, when it is not of himself.

Man is an organ of life, and God alone is life; and God infuses his life into the organ and all its parts, as the sun infuses its heat into a tree and all its parts. And God grants man to feel that life in himself as his own; and God wills that he should so feel it, to the intent that man may live as of himself according to the laws of order,—which are as many as the precepts in the Word,—and dispose himself for the reception of God's love. But still God continually holds with His finger the perpendicular over the balance, and moderates but never violates free will by compulsion. A tree cannot receive anything which the heat of the sun brings through the root unless it is warmed and heated in its single fibres; nor can the elements rise up through its root unless its single fibres from the heat received also give out heat, and thus contribute to their passage. So man, from the heat of life received from God. But he, unlike a tree, feels it as his own, although it is not his; and in so far as he *believes* that it is his and not God's he receives the light of life from God and not the heat of love, but the heat of love from hell; which being gross obstructs and closes the purer branchlets of the organism, as impure blood closes the capillary vessels of the body; and so from spiritual man makes himself merely natural. Man's free will arises from the fact that he feels the life in himself as his own, and that God leaves him so to feel in order that conjunction may be effected,—which is not possible unless it be reciprocal, and it becomes reciprocal when man acts from freedom altogether as from himself. If God had not left this to man he would not be man, neither would he have eternal life; for reciprocal conjunction with God causes man to be man and not a beast, and also causes him to live after death to eternity. Free will in spiritual things effects this. (T. C. R. n. 504.)

MAN OUGHT TO COMPEL HIMSELF, AND IN THIS COMPULSION IS THE HIGHEST FREEDOM.

That man ought to compel himself to do good, to obey the things which the Lord has commanded, and to speak truths,— which is to humble himself beneath the Lord's hands, or to submit himself under the power of Divine good and truth,— implies and involves more arcana than it is possible to unfold in a few words. There are certain spirits who held as a principle while they lived in the world,—because they heard that all good was from the Lord, and that man could do no good of himself,— that they were not to compel themselves to anything, but to resign themselves; believing that because it is so all effort would be vain. They therefore waited for immediate influx into their will's endeavour, and did not compel themselves to do any good;

yea to such a degree that when any evil crept in, because they felt no resistance from within, they gave themselves up to it, thinking it to have been so permitted. But such is their character that they are as it were without any mind of their own [*absque proprio*], and thus have no resolution. They are therefore among the more useless; for they suffer themselves to be led alike by the wicked and by the good, and endure much from the wicked. But they that have compelled themselves to act against evil and falsity, although at first they thought that this was done from themselves, or of their own power, yet,—being afterwards enlightened to see that their effort was from the Lord, yea even the least of all things pertaining to the effort,—they cannot be led by evil spirits in the other life, but are among the happy. It is evident then that a man ought to force himself to do good, and to speak truth. The arcanum herein concealed is this: That man is hereby gifted of the Lord with a heavenly *proprium*.[1] Man's heavenly *proprium* is formed in the thought's endeavour; and if he does not obtain it by compelling himself, as the appearance is, he never does by not compelling himself. To make it plain how this is; in all self-compulsion to good there is a certain freedom, which is not so much apperceived while in the act of compulsion, yet still it is within. Just as when one determines to subject himself to the hazard of losing life with a view to some end, or determines to undergo a painful operation for the recovery of his health; there is a certain willingness, and therefore liberty, from which he acts in those determinations, although the hazards and the pains while he is in them take away the perception of such willingness or freedom. So it is with those who compel themselves to good. There is within a willingness and therefore freedom, from which and for the sake of that to which they compel themselves; namely, for the sake of obedience to those things which the Lord has commanded, and for the sake of the salvation of their souls after death. And within these is a still interior motive which a man is not cognizant of, that of regard for the Lord's kingdom, yea for the Lord Himself. This occurs especially in temptations, in which, when man compels himself in opposition to the evil and falsity which are infused and suggested by evil spirits, there is more of freedom than ever in any state out of temptations, although man cannot then conceive of it. It is an interior freedom, from which he determines to subdue the evil; and so strongly as to be equal in force and resoluteness to the evil which assaults him; otherwise he would never engage in the contest. This freedom is of the Lord, who insinuates it into man's

[1] *Proprium*,—for which we have no equivalent word in our language,—is literally that which is man's own, or which constitutes his distinctive individuality.

conscience, and thereby causes him to conquer the evil as if by his own [power]. Through this freedom man receives a *proprium* in which good can be wrought by the Lord. Without a something of his own [*absque proprio*] acquired, that is given through freedom, no man can be reformed, because he cannot receive the new will which is conscience. Freedom thus bestowed is the very plane into which the influx of good and truth from the Lord descends. Hence it is that they that do not resist in temptations from this willingness or freedom are over- come. In all freedom there is the life of man, because this is his love ; whatever a man does from love appears free to him. And in that freedom in which a man compels himself in opposition to evil and falsity, and to do good, there is heavenly love; which the Lord then insinuates, and by which he creates his *proprium*. Therefore the Lord wills that this should appear to man as his, although it is not his. This *proprium* which he thus receives, by apparent compulsion in the life of the body, is filled by the Lord in the other life with indefinite delights and happinesses. They who receive this are by degrees enlightened, yea confirmed, in the truth that they have compelled themselves not in the least from themselves, but that every slightest effort of their will was from the Lord ; and that the purpose of its appearing to be from themselves was, that a new will might be given them by the Lord as theirs, and that thus the life of heavenly love might be appropriated to them. For the Lord desires to communicate to every one what is His, that is what is heavenly, so that it may appear as his own, and in him, although it is not his. The angels are in such a *proprium ;* and so far as they are in the truth that all good and truth is from the Lord, they are in the delight and happiness of that *proprium*. But they who despise and reject all that is good and true, and are unwilling to believe anything which is repugnant to their lusts and reasonings, cannot compel them- selves, and therefore cannot receive this *proprium* of conscience, or new will. From what has been said above it is also plain that to compel one's self is not to be compelled ; for no good ever comes of being compelled, as when a man is compelled by another man to do good. But that in this matter to compel himself is to act from a certain freedom unrecognised by him ; for there is never anything compulsory from the Lord. Hence it is a universal law, that all good and truth is implanted in freedom ; otherwise the ground is not at all recipient and nutritive of good, nay, there is no ground in which the seed can grow. (A. C. 1937.)

HEAVENLY FREEDOM AND INFERNAL FREEDOM.

Heavenly freedom is that which is from the Lord, and all the angels in the heavens are in this freedom. It is, as was said, the freedom of love to the Lord and mutual love, that is of the affection of good and truth. The quality of this freedom may appear from the fact that from an inmost affection every one who is in it communicates his own blessedness and happiness to others, and that it is a blessedness and happiness to him to be able to communicate. And as such is the universal heaven, therefore every one is a centre of the blessednesses and happinesses of all, and all are at the same time the centre of that of the individuals. This communication is effected by the Lord, by marvellous influxes, in the incomprehensible form which is the form of heaven. From this it may be seen what heavenly freedom is, and that it is from the Lord alone.

How far distant the heavenly freedom which comes from an affection of good and truth is, from the infernal freedom which is from an affection of evil and falsity, may appear from the fact that the angels in the heavens, if only they think of such freedom as is from an affection of evil and falsity,—or what is the same, from the lusts of the love of self and of the world,—are instantly seized with internal pain; and on the other hand, when evil spirits only think of the freedom which is from the affection of good and truth,—or what is the same, from the desires of mutual love,—they instantly fall into agonies. And what is wonderful, so opposite is the one freedom to the other, that to good spirits the freedom of the love of self and of the world is hell; and on the other hand, to evil spirits the freedom of love to the Lord and mutual love is hell. Hence all are distinguished in the other life according to their freedom, or what is the same, according to their loves and affections ; and consequently according to the delights of their life, which is the same as according to their lives. For lives are nothing else than delights, and these are nothing else than the affections of loves. (A. C. n. 2872, 2873.)

To do evil from the delight of love appears like freedom ; but it is servitude, because it is from hell. To do good from the delight of love appears like freedom, and also is freedom, because it is from the Lord. Servitude consists therefore in being led of hell, and freedom in being led of the Lord. This the Lord thus teaches in John : " *Whosoever committeth sin is the servant of sin. The servant abideth not in the house for ever ; the Son abideth for ever. If the Son shall make you free, ye shall be free indeed* " (viii. 34-36).

The Lord keeps man in freedom of thought, and in so far as external restraints do not hinder,—which are the fear of the law and of life, and the fear of the loss of reputation, of honour, and of gain,—He keeps him in freedom of action. But by freedom He turns him away from evil, and by freedom inclines him to good, —so gently and so tacitly leading, that the man does not know but that all proceeds from himself. Thus in freedom the Lord implants and inroots good into the very life of man; and it remains to eternity. The Lord thus teaches this in Mark: "*The kingdom of God is as a man who casteth seed into the earth,* . . . *and the seed springeth and groweth up while he knoweth not. The earth bringeth forth fruit of herself*" (iv. 26-28). (*ib.* n. 9586, 9587.)

The evil spirits that are with man, whereby he communicates with hell, regard him but as a vile slave; for they infuse into him their own lusts and persuasions, and thus lead him whithersoever they desire. But the angels, by whom man communicates with heaven, regard him as a brother, and insinuate into him affections of good, and of truth; and they thus lead him by freedom, not whither they desire, but whither the Lord pleases. From this it may be seen what the quality is of the one and of the other; and that to be led of the devil is slavery, but to be led of the Lord is freedom.

Spirits newly arrived are much perplexed to conceive how no one can do good from himself, nor think truth from himself, but from the Lord; believing that they should thus be like machines without any self-determination; and if so, that they must hold down their hands and suffer themselves to be acted upon. But they are told that they ought entirely of themselves to think, will, and do good, and that otherwise they cannot receive a heavenly *proprium*, and heavenly freedom; but that still they ought to acknowledge that good and truth are not from them, but from the Lord. And they are taught that all the angels are in such acknowledgment, yea, in the perception that it is so; and the more exquisitely they perceive themselves to be led of the Lord, and thereby to be in the Lord, the more they are in freedom.

Whoever lives in good, and believes that the Lord governs the universe, and that from Him alone comes all the good of love and charity and all the truth of faith, yea, that life comes from Him, and therefore that from Him we live, move, and have our being, is in such a state that he can be gifted with heavenly freedom, and with this also peace; for then he trusts only in the Lord, and counts other things of no concern, and is certain that then all things tend to his good, blessedness, and happiness to eternity. But he who believes that he governs himself, is in continual disquietude, being borne away into passionate desires, into solicitude about things to come, and thus into manifold anxieties. And because he so believes, the lusts of evil and the persuasions of falsity also adhere to him. (*ib.* n. 2890-2892.)

The presence of the Lord implies liberty, the one follows the other; for the more intimately present the Lord is, the more free is man; that is, in proportion as he is in the love of good and truth he acts freely. Such is the nature of the Lord's influx by means of angels. But on the other hand the influx of hell is effected by evil spirits, and is attended with the violence and impetuosity of domination,—their ruling desire being to subdue man to such a degree that he may be as nothing and they everything; and then he becomes one of them,—and scarcely one, being as nobody in their eyes. Hence, when the Lord delivers man from their yoke and dominion there arises a conflict. But when he is liberated, or in other words regenerated, he is so gently led of the Lord by angels that there is not the least appearance of bondage or authority; he is led by what is delightful and happy, and is loved and esteemed,—as the Lord teaches in Matthew: "*My yoke is easy, and My burden is light*" (xi. 30). It has been given me to know by much experience that it is exactly the contrary with evil spirits; by whom, as was said, man is regarded as nothing, and who, were it in their power, would torment him every moment. (*ib.* n. 905.)

WHY THE LORD LEADS MAN BY AFFECTIONS AND NOT BY THOUGHTS.

While man is led of the Lord by affections he can be led according to all the laws of His Divine Providence, but not if led by thoughts. Affections do not manifest themselves before a man, but thoughts manifest themselves. Then affections produce thoughts, but thoughts do not produce affections; it appears as if they produced them, but it is a fallacy. And when affections produce thoughts they also produce all things of the man, because they are his life. This indeed is known in the world. For if you hold a man by his affection you keep him bound, and lead him whithersoever you will, and then one reason goes as far as a thousand; but if you have not hold of a man's affection reasons are of no avail, for the affection not being in accord either perverts, or rejects, or extinguishes them. So would it be if the Lord should lead man by thoughts immediately, and not by affections. (A. E. n. 1175.)

REPENTANCE, REFORMATION, AND REGENERATION.

REPENTANCE.

HE who would be saved must confess his sins, and do the work of repentance.

To confess sins is to recognize evils; to see them within himself; to acknowledge them; to make himself guilty and condemn himself on account of them. This when it is done before God is the confession of sins.

To do the work of repentance is, after he has thus confessed his sins, and from an humble heart has made supplication for remission, to desist from them and lead a new life according to the precepts of faith.

He who only acknowledges generally that he is a sinner, and makes himself guilty of all evils, and does not explore himself, that is see his own sins, makes confession, but not the confession of repentance; for he afterwards lives as before.

He who lives the life of faith daily does the work of repentance; for he reflects upon the evils that are within him, and acknowledges them, guards himself against them, and supplicates the Lord for aid. For of himself man is continually lapsing; but is continually raised up by the Lord. Of himself he lapses when he thinks to will evil; and is raised up by the Lord when he resists evil, and therefore does not do it. Such is the state of all who are in good. But they who are in evil lapse continually, and also are continually elevated by the Lord; but it is lest they fall into the hell of all the basest evils, whither of themselves they tend with all their effort, and to restrain them to a milder hell.

The work of repentance which is done in a state of freedom avails, but that which is done in a state of compulsion is of no avail. A state of compulsion is a state of sickness, a state of dejection of mind on account of misfortunes; a state of imminent death; in a word, every state of fear which takes away the use of sound reason. He who is evil, and promises repentance and also does good in a state of compulsion, when he comes into a state of freedom returns into his former life of evil. It is different with a good man; these states to him are states of temptation, in which he conquers.

Repentance of the mouth and not of the life is not repentance; sins are not remitted by repentance of the mouth, but by repentance of the life. Sins are remitted to man continually by the Lord, for He is mercy itself; but the sins adhere to the man howsoever he supposes they are remitted, nor are they removed from him but by a life according to the precepts of faith. So far as he lives according to these precepts his sins are removed, and in so far as they are removed they are remitted. For man is withheld by the Lord from evil, and is held in good; and he can be withheld from evil in the other life in so far as he had resisted evil in the life of the body; and he can then be held in good in so far as he had done good from affection in the life of the body. From this it may be seen what the remission of sins is, and from whence it is. He who believes that sins are remitted in any other way is much deceived.

After a man has examined himself, and acknowledged his sins, and done the work of repentance, he must remain constant in good to the end of life. And if afterwards he relapses to the former life of evil and embraces it, he commits profanation; for then he conjoins evil with good; and therefore his latter state is worse than the first, according to the Lord's words: " *When the unclean spirit is gone out of a man, he walketh through dry places, seeking rest, but doth not find; then he saith, I will return into my house from whence I came out; and when he is come, and findeth it empty, and swept, and garnished for himself, then he goeth away and taketh with himself seven other spirits more wicked than himself, and they enter in and dwell there; and the last state of that man becomes worse than the first*" (Matt. xii. 43-45). (A. C. 8387-8394.)

The Nature of Man before Regeneration, or as to what is properly his own (*proprium*).

The *proprium*[1] of man is all the evil and falsity that stream forth from the love of self and the world; whereby men are inclined to believe in themselves and not in the Lord and the Word, and to think that what they cannot comprehend sensually or by knowledge has no existence. Hence they become altogether evil and false, and therefore see all things perversely. Evil appears to them as good, and good as evil; falsity as truth, and truth as falsity; realities as nothing, and nothing as every-

[1] See note, p. 274.

thing; hatred they call love, darkness light, death life, and *vice versa*. Such in the Word are called the lame and the blind. This then is the *proprium* of man, which in itself is infernal and accursed. (A. C. n. 210.)

The *proprium* of man is in itself a thing merely dead, although it appears a reality, yea, everything to him. Whatever lives in him is from the Lord's life ; and if this were taken away, he would fall dead like a stone. For man is only an organ of life, and the state of the life is according to the nature of the organ. Only the Lord has [an actual or living] *proprium*. From His *proprium* He redeemed mankind, and from His *proprium* He saves them. The Lord's *proprium* is life; and from His *proprium* the *proprium* of man, which in itself is dead, is vivified. (*ib.* n. 149.)

The *proprium* of man is nothing but evil, and the falsity therefrom; the will *proprium* is evil, and the intellectual *proprium* is falsity therefrom. And this *proprium* a man derives principally from his parents, grandfathers, and great-grandfathers, back through a long series; so that finally the hereditary nature which constitutes his *proprium* is nothing but evil successively accumulated and condensed. For every man is born into two diabolical loves; namely, the love of self and the love of the world. From these loves stream forth all evils and falsities, as from their own fountains ; and as man is born into these loves he is born also into evils of every kind. Because as to his *proprium* man is of such a nature, the Lord in His Divine mercy has provided means by which he can be removed from his *proprium*. These means are given in the Word ; and when man co-operates with the means, that is when he thinks and speaks, wills and acts, from the Divine Word, he is kept by the Lord in things Divine, and thus is withheld from his *proprium*. And as he perseveres in this a new *proprium* as it were, both voluntary and intellectual, is formed in him by the Lord, which is entirely separate from his own *proprium*. Man is thus as it were created anew; and this is what is called his reformation and regeneration by truths from the Word, and by a life according to them. (A. E. n. 585.)

Man's great tendency to Evil.

Few, if any, know that all men, how many soever they are, are withheld from evils by the Lord, and this with greater might than man can by any means conceive. For there is in every man a perpetual active impulse [*conatus*] to evil, both from the hereditary evil into which he is born, and from actual evil which he has acquired,—so strong, that unless he were withheld by the Lord he would every moment rush headlong towards the lowest hell. But so great is the Lord's mercy that every moment, yea, every least part of a moment, he is lifted up and withheld from rushing thither. This is the case even with the good; but with a difference according to their life of charity and faith. Thus the Lord continually fights with man and for man against hell; although it does not so appear to man. That it is so it has been given me to know by much experience. (A. C. n. 2406.)

Why Man is born in Ignorance.

If man were imbued with no hereditary evil the rational would be born immediately from the marriage of the celestial things of the internal man with its spiritual things; and through the rational the knowing [faculty] would be born, so that man would have within him all the rational, and all the knowing [faculty], at the moment of his coming into the world. For this would be according to the order of influx; as may be concluded from the fact that all animals whatsoever are born into all the knowing faculty which is necessary and conducive to their sustenance, their protection, their habitation, and their procreation; because their nature is in accordance with order. Why not then man, if order had not been destroyed in him? For he alone is born into no knowledge! The cause of his being so born is hereditary evil, derived from father and mother; in consequence of which all his faculties are in a contrary direction relative to what is true and good, and cannot be brought into forms corresponding to them by immediate influx of what is celestial and spiritual from the Lord. This is the reason why the rational of man must be formed in a way or a manner altogether different; namely, by knowledges and cognitions insinuated through the senses, thus flowing in by an external way, and therefore in inverted order. Man is thus miraculously rendered rational by the Lord. (A. C. n. 1902.)

Reformation and Regeneration.

There are two states into and through which a man must pass while from natural he is becoming spiritual. The first state is called Reformation; and the second Regeneration. In the first state man looks from his natural condition to a spiritual, and desires it; in the second state he becomes spiritual-natural. The first state is formed by means of truths,—which will become truths of faith,—through which he looks to charity; the second is formed by means of the goods of charity, and by these he enters into the truths of faith. Or what is the same, the first is a state of thought from the understanding; and the second of love from the will. When this latter state begins, and while it is progressing, a change takes place in the mind. For a reversal is effected; because now the love of the will flows into the understanding, and actuates and leads it to think in harmony and agreement with its love. Wherefore, so far as the good of love now acts the first part, and the truths of faith the second, man is spiritual and is a new creature. And then he acts from charity and speaks from faith, and feels the good of charity and perceives the truth of faith; and he is then in the Lord, and in peace, and thus is regenerate. A man who in the world has entered the first state, after death can be introduced into the second; but he who in the world has not entered into the first state cannot be introduced into the second after death, thus cannot be regenerated. (T. C. R. n. 571.)

Reformation is ascribed to the understanding, and regeneration to the will. . . . The evils into which man is born are generated in the will of the natural man; and it has been shown that the will brings the understanding to favour itself by thinking in agreement with it. Therefore, in order that man may be regenerated, it is necessary that it be done by means of the understanding as a mediate cause; and this is done through information which the understanding receives, first from parents and masters, afterwards from the reading of the Word, from preaching, books, and conversation. The things that the understanding receives from these sources are called truths; it is the same therefore whether it be said that reformation is effected by means of the understanding, or that it is effected by means of the truths which the understanding receives. For truths teach man in whom and what he should believe, and what he should do, and therefore what he should purpose; for whatever any one does he does from his will according to his understanding. Since therefore the will itself of man is evil by birth, and since the understanding teaches what evil and good are, and he is able to purpose the one and not purpose the other, it follows that man is to be reformed by the understanding. And so long as any one sees and acknowledges in his mind that evil is evil and good is good, and thinks that good is to be chosen, so long he is in the state that is called reformation; but when he wills to shun evil and do good the state of regeneration begins. (*ib.* n. 587.)

But yet no one can be said to be reformed by the mere cognition of truths; for a man can apprehend them, and also talk about, teach, and preach them, from the faculty of elevating the understanding above the love of the will. But he is reformed who is in the affection of truth for the sake of truth; for this affection conjoins itself with the will, and if it goes on conjoins the will to the understanding, and then regeneration begins. (*ib.* n. 589.)

A Sign of Reformation and Non-Reformation.

The Lord continually flows into man with good, and into good with truth; and man either receives it or does not receive it. If he receives it, it is well with him; but if he does not receive it, it is ill with him. If when he does not receive he feels something of anxiety, there is hope that he may be reformed; but if he does not feel anything of anxiety, the hope vanishes. For with every man there are two spirits from hell, and two angels from heaven; for, because man is born into sin, he can in nowise live unless on the one hand he communicates with hell, and on the other with heaven; all his life is therefrom. When a man is grown up, and begins to govern himself from himself,—that is, when he appears to himself to will and to act from his own judgment, and to think and form conclusions concerning matters of faith from his own understanding,—if then he betakes himself to evils the two spirits from hell approach, and the two angels from heaven withdraw a little; and if he turns himself to good, the two angels from heaven draw near, and the two spirits from hell are removed. When therefore a man betakes himself to evils, as is the case with most in youth, if any anxiety is felt when he reflects upon the wrong he has done, it is a sign that he will still receive influx through the angels from heaven, and also a sign that he will afterwards suffer himself to be reformed; but if nothing of anxiety is felt when he reflects upon the wrong he has done, it is a sign that he is no longer willing to receive influx through the angels from heaven, and a sign also that he will not afterwards suffer himself to be reformed. (A. C. n. 5470.)

The Course of Regeneration and of Progress to true Wisdom.

Few, if any, know how man is brought to true wisdom. Intelligence is not wisdom, but leads to wisdom; for to understand what is true and good is not to be true and good, but to be wise is so. Wisdom is predicated only of the life, and means that such is the character of the man. He is introduced to wisdom or life by knowing and cognizing [truth] or by knowledges and cognitions.[1] Every man has two parts, the will and the under-

---

[1] By the terms *scire* and *noscere* (or *nosse*) and *cognoscere*, the author throughout his writings expresses an important distinction in the process of the acquisition of truth, which it is difficult to convey by words in common use in our language,

standing; the will is the primary and the understanding the secondary part. Man's life after death is according to his will-part, not according to his intellectual. The will in man is formed by the Lord from infancy to childhood. It is done by insinuating innocence and love towards parents, nurses, and children of like age, and by many other things which are celestial that man is ignorant of. If these celestial things were not first insinuated into man, while he is an infant and child, he could by no means become a man. *Thus the first plane is formed.* But as man is not man unless he is also endowed with understanding (for the will alone does not constitute man, but understanding with the will); and as understanding cannot be acquired except by means of knowledges and cognitions, therefore from the period of child-hood by degrees he is filled with these. *Thus a second plane is formed.* When the intellectual part is furnished with knowledges and cognitions, especially with cognitions of truth and good, then the man is first capable of being regenerated. And while he is being regenerated, truths and goods from the Lord are implanted by means of cognitions in the celestial things with which he was gifted by the Lord from infancy, so that his intellectual attain-ments form one with his celestial. When the Lord has so con-joined them he is gifted with charity, and begins to act from it, which is as a principle of conscience. He thus first receives new life, and this by degrees. The light of this new life is called wis-dom, which then takes the first place, and is exalted above intel-ligence. *Thus a third plane is formed.* When a man has become such in the life of the body, he is continually perfected in the other life. From this it may be seen what the light of intelligence is, and what the light of wisdom. (A. C. n. 1555.)

THE SIX STATES OF REGENERATION.

(See " The Days of Creation," p. 145.)

REGENERATION PROGRESSES THROUGH SUCCESSIVE CYCLES.

The states of the re-birth of everything sensual and of every-

---

without circumlocution. By *scire* (to know), and the corresponding *scientia* (know-ledge), he refers to the mere outward acquisition of knowledge, or knowledge as facts or truths in the outer memory, acquired by means of the senses,—whether from the Word, or from the world and nature. By *noscere* and *cognoscere* (to be-come acquainted with), and the corresponding *cognitio*, he designates the higher and more interior and real knowledge that is attained when these facts or truths are taken up and actually seen in the light of reason. For the expression of this idea the words *cognize* and *cognition* are warranted,—if any warrant is needed for a necessary term,—by the usage of some of the recent speculative philosophers. Know-ledges may be considered as the means or materials of cognitions.

thing in the natural, and also in the rational, have their progressions from a beginning to an end; and when at the end, they then commence from a kind of new beginning, namely, from that end to which they tended in the former state, to a further end, and so on; and at length the order is inverted, and what was last then becomes first. As, for instance, while man is being regenerated, both as to the rational and as to the natural, then the periods of the first state are from truths, which are of faith, to goods which are of charity; and the truths of faith then apparently act the first part, and the goods of charity the second, for the truths of faith look to the goods of charity as an end; these periods continue until the man is regenerated. Afterwards charity, which was the end, becomes the beginning; and from this new states begin, which proceed both ways, namely, more towards interior things, but also towards exterior things; towards interior things up to love to the Lord, and towards exterior things to the truths of faith, and even to natural truths, and to sensual truths,—which are then successively brought into correspondence with the goods of charity and love in the rational, and so into heavenly order. These are what are meant by progressions and derivations continued even to the last. Such progressions and derivations are perpetual with the man who is being regenerated, from his infancy to the end of his life in the world; and afterwards also to eternity. And yet he can never be so regenerated that it can be said he is in any wise perfect; for there are things innumerable, yea, indefinite in number, which are to be regenerated, both in the rational and in the natural; and every one of them has offshoots indefinite in number, that is, progressions and derivations towards things interior and things exterior. This is entirely unknown to man, but the Lord takes cognizance of each and all things, and provides for every moment. If only for the least moment He were to intermit His providence, all progressions would be disturbed; for what is prior looks to what follows, in a continual series, and produces successive series of consequences to eternity. Whence it is evident that the Divine foresight and providence is in the most single things; and unless it were so, or if it were only universal, the human race would perish. (A. C. n. 5122.)

With respect to the regeneration of the spiritual man, the case is this: He is first instructed in the truths which belong to faith, and is then kept by the Lord in an affection for truth. The good of faith, which is charity towards the neighbour, is at the same time insinuated into him, but so that he scarcely knows it, for it lies concealed in the affection for truth; and this to the end that the truth which is of faith may be conjoined with the good which is of charity. In process of time his affection for the truth of faith increases, and truth is regarded for the sake of the end; namely, for the sake of good, or what is the same, for the sake of life,—and this more and more. Truth is thus insinuated into good; and when this is so man imbibes the good of life according to the truth which was insinuated and thus acts or seems to himself to act from good. Before this time the principal thing to him was truth, which is of faith; but afterwards it becomes good, which is of the life. When this comes to pass man is regenerated; but he is regenerated according to the quantity and quality of the truth which is insinuated into good, and when truth and good act as one according to the quality and quantity of good. Thus it is with all regeneration. (*ib.* n. 2979.)

The Cycles of Regeneration are one with the Cycles of Man's Life.

It is known that the things seen by the eyes and heard by the ears are apperceived by man inwardly, and as it were pass from the world through the eyes or through the ears into the thought, and so into the understanding; for thought is of the understanding. And if they are such things as are loved they pass thence into the will; and afterwards from the will by an intellectual way into the speech of the mouth, and also into the act of the body. Such is the cycle of things from the world through the natural man into his spiritual, and from this again into the world. But it should be known that this cycle is set in operation from the will, which is the inmost of man's life; and that it begins there, and from thence is carried to completion. And the will of the man who is in good is governed from heaven by the Lord, although it appears otherwise. For there is an influx from the spiritual world into the natural, thus through the internal man into his external, but not the reverse; for the internal man is in heaven, and the external in the world. As this cycle is the cycle of man's life, therefore while man is being regenerated he is regenerated along the same cycle; and when he is regenerated, through the same he lives and acts. For this reason, during man's regeneration the truths which will become truths of faith are insinuated through the hearing and sight; and they are implanted in the memory of his natural man. From this memory they are elevated into the thought, which is of the understanding; and those that are loved become of the will. And so far as they become of the will they become of the life; for the will of man is his very life. And so far as they become of the life they become of his affection, thus of charity in the will, and of faith in the understanding. Afterwards the man speaks and acts from that life, which is the life of charity and faith; from charity which is of the will goes forth the speech of the mouth and also the acts of the body, each by an intellectual way, that is by the way of faith. From these things it is evident that the cycle of man's regeneration is like the cycle of his life in general; and that in like manner it is begun in the will, by influx out of heaven from the Lord. (A. C. n. 10,057.)

Understanding separate from the Will is given to Man that he may be regenerated.

The faculty of understanding what is good and true although he does not will it, is given to man in order that he may be reformed and regenerated; and therefore this faculty exists with the evil as well as with the good, yea, sometimes more acutely with the evil; but with this difference, that with the evil there is no affection of truth for the sake of life, that is for the good of life from truth, and therefore they cannot be reformed; but with the good there is an affection of truth for the sake of life, that is for the good of life, and they therefore can be reformed. But the first state of their reformation is, that truth of doctrine appears to them to be in the first place, and the good of life in the second; for they do good from truth; and their second state is, that the good of life is in the first place, and the truth of doctrine in the second; for they do good from good, that is from the will of good; and when this is the case, because the will is conjoined to the understanding as in a marriage, man is regenerated. (A. C. n. 3539.)

Correspondence of Natural Birth to Spiritual Birth.

It is known that the soul of man has its beginning in an ovum of the mother, is afterwards perfected in her womb, and is there encompassed with a tender body, of such a nature that the soul may suitably act by means of it in the world into which it is born. The case is similar when man is born again, that is when he is regenerated. The new soul which he then receives is a purpose of good, which has its beginning in the rational, at first as it were in an ovum there, and afterwards is there perfected as in a womb; the tender body with which this soul is encompassed is the natural [degree] and the good therein, which becomes such that it acts obediently to the purposes of the soul; the truths therein are like the fibres in the body, for truths are formed from good. Hence it appears that an image of the reformation cf man is presented in his formation in the womb; and if you will believe it, it is celestial good and spiritual truth which come from the Lord that form him, and then give him ability successively to receive each; and this in such manner and in the degree that he as a man regards the ends of heaven, and not, as a brute animal, the ends of the world. (A. C. n. 3570.)

DURING REGENERATION THE LORD GOVERNS MAN BY MEANS OF ANGELS.

While man is being regenerated, which is effected in adult age (because before that he does not think from himself about the truths of faith), he is governed by the Lord through angels by this means; that he is kept in the truths which he has impressed upon himself are truths, and by means of these is kept in the affection with which they are conjoined; and as that affection, namely the affection of truth, is from good, he is thus led by degrees to good. That this is so is evident to me from much experience; for when evil spirits have suggested evils and falsities, I have apperceived that angels from the Lord then kept me in the truths which had been implanted, and so withheld me from evils and falsities. From this it was also clear that the truths of faith, inrooted by means of the affection of truth, are the plane in which angels operate. They therefore who have not this plane cannot be led by the angels, but suffer themselves to be led by hell; for then the operation of the angels can be nowhere fixed, but flows through. And this plane cannot be acquired unless the truths of faith are suffered to go into act, and so are implanted in the will, and through the will in the life. It is also worthy of remark that the operation of angels upon the truths of faith in man rarely becomes manifest, that is, so that thought is excited concerning that truth; but there is produced, with an affection, a general idea of such things as agree with that truth. For this operation is effected by imperceptible influx; which when presented to the sight appears as light flowing in, which light consists of innumerable truths in good. These truths encompass some single thing in man, and keep that, while in truth, in the love also which is of that truth. Thus the angels elevate the mind of man from falsities and defend from evils. But these things are entirely unknown to a man. (A. C. n. 5893.)

REGENERATION IS FORESEEN AND PROVIDED FOR FROM ETERNITY.

With those who are being regenerated interior and exterior things are arranged in order by the Lord for all following states, insomuch that things present involve things future, and things future when they become present do the same, and this to eternity; for the Lord foresees all things and provides all things, and His foresight and providence is to eternity, and so eternal. For the Divine which alone is His in itself is infinite, and what is infinite in respect to duration is eternal. Hence it is that whatever the Lord disposes and ordains is eternal. Thus is it done with those whom the Lord regenerates; the regeneration of man begins in the world, and continues to eternity; for man is always being perfected when he becomes an angel. There are in man things external, internal, and inmost; these are all disposed and arranged in order, together and successively, for the reception of things that follow to eternity. (A. C. n. 10,048.)

Regeneration is effected by means of Remains.

Man is called a living soul from a living principle that is within him. No man can live at all, still less live as a man, if he have not something living within him; that is, unless he has something of innocence, charity, and mercy, or something therefrom that is similar to or emulative of them. This [germ] of innocence, charity, and mercy, man receives from the Lord during infancy and childhood; as may be seen from the state of infancy and also from the state of childhood. What man then receives is treasured up within him, and is called in the Word remains;[1] which are of the Lord alone in man, and furnish him with the capacity of becoming truly man on his arrival at adult age. That the states of innocence, charity, and mercy which man has in infancy and during the years of childhood, enable him to become man, is evident from the consideration that, unlike the brutes, he is not born into any exercise of life, but has everything to learn; and what he learns becomes by use habitual, and thus as it were natural to him. He cannot even walk or speak without being taught; and so with all the other actions which habit renders as it were natural to him. So it is also with the states of innocence, charity, and mercy, with which likewise he becomes imbued in infancy; and unless they were present with him he would be much viler than a brute. But these are states which a man does not learn, but receives as a gift from the Lord, and which the Lord preserves in him; and these together with the truths of faith are what are called remains, and are of the Lord alone. In proportion as in adult age a man extinguishes these states he becomes dead; and when he is regenerated these are the beginnings of regeneration. In these he is led; for the

---

[1] See note, p. 145.

Lord, as was said, operates by means of remains. (A. C. n. 1050.)

Remains are all the states of affection for good and truth with which man is gifted by the Lord, from earliest infancy to the end of life; which states are stored for his use in the life after death. For all the states of his life successively return in the other life, and then are tempered by the states of good and of truth with which he had been gifted by the Lord. In proportion therefore as he has received more of remains in the life of the body, or more of good and truth, the more joyous and the more fair do the rest of his states appear when they return. That this is so may be seen by any one if he reflects. At his birth man has not of himself the least of good, but is totally defiled with hereditary evil; and all the good that he has, such as love for parents, nurses, and little companions, enters by influx and this from innocence. These are goods which flow in from the Lord through the heaven of innocence and peace, which is the inmost heaven; and so man is imbued with them during his infancy. Afterwards, as he grows up, little by little this innocent and peaceful infantile good recedes; and in proportion as he is introduced into the world he enters into the pleasures derived from it, and into lusts and so into evils, and in the same proportion the celestial things or goods of his infantile age begin to disappear. But yet they remain, and by them the states are tempered which the man afterwards puts on and acquires. Without these a man can by no means be a man; for his states of lusts or of evil, if not attempered by states of affection of good, would be fiercer than those of any animal. These states of good are what are called remains; which are given and implanted in his disposition by the Lord, and this when man is unconscious of it. In the subsequent period of life he is also gifted with new states; but these are not so much states of good as of truth; for while he is growing up he is imbued with truths, and these likewise are stored up within him in his interior man. By these remains which are remains of truth, born of influx of things spiritual from the Lord, man has power to think and also to understand what the good and truth of civil and moral life are; and likewise to receive spiritual truth or the truth of faith,—but this he cannot do except through the remains of good which he has received in infancy. Man is not at all aware that there are remains, and that they are stored up in man in his interior rational; for the reason that he does not imagine that anything enters by influx, but that it is all a something natural inborn in him, so that everything is in him when an infant. But the fact is quite otherwise. Remains are spoken of here and there in the Word; and they signify those states by which man becomes man, and this from the Lord alone. (*ib.* r. 1906.)

Remains are not only the goods and truths which a man even from his infancy acquires from the Lord's Word, and which are thus impressed upon his memory, but they are also all the states derived therefrom ; as states of innocence from infancy ; of love towards parents, brothers, teachers, and friends ; of charity towards the neighbour; and of compassion also towards the poor and needy ; in a word, all states of good and truth. These states, with the goods and truths impressed upon the memory, are called remains ; and are preserved in man by the Lord, and entirely unconsciously to him are stored up in his internal man, and carefully separated from those things which belong to his *proprium*, or from evils and falsities. All these states are so carefully preserved in man by the Lord that not the least of them is lost ; which it was given me to know by the fact that every state of man, from infancy even to extreme old age, not only remains in the other life but also returns, and this exactly as they were while he lived in the world. Not only the goods and truths of the memory thus remain and return, but also all states of innocence and charity ; and when states of evil and of falsity or of wickedness and phantasy recur,—which also each and all as to every least circumstance remain and return,—then these states are attempered by the Lord, by means of those. It is therefore evident that if man had no remains he could by no means avoid eternal condemnation. (*ib.* n. 561.)

From earliest infancy up to the first period of childhood man is introduced by the Lord into heaven, and indeed among celestial angels ; by whom he is kept in a state of innocence, which it is known is the state of infants until the first period of childhood. When the age of childhood begins he by degrees puts off the state of innocence, but is still kept in a state of charity, by the affection of mutual charity towards his like; which state continues with many until youth. He then is among spiritual angels. Because he then begins to think and accordingly to act by himself, he can no longer be kept as before in charity ; for he then calls forth hereditary evils, by which he suffers himself to be led. When this state arrives the goods of charity and innocence which he had before received, in the degree that he meditates evils and confirms them by act, are exterminated ; and yet are not exterminated, but are withdrawn by the Lord towards the interiors, and there stored up again. But as he has not yet cognized[1] truths, the goods of innocence and charity which he had received in those two states are therefore not yet qualified; for truths give quality to good, and good gives essence to truths. From that age he is therefore imbued with truths,—by instruction, and especially by his own thoughts, and confirmations thereby. In

[1] See note, p. 284.

so far then as he is now in the affection of good, truths are conjoined by the Lord to the good in him, and are stored up for use.
This state is what is signified by the seven years of abundance
of provision [in Gen. xli. 47-49]. These truths adjoined to good
are what in the proper sense are called remains. In the degree
therefore that a man suffers himself to be regenerated the remains
are devoted to their use; for in that degree the Lord draws out
from and lets them into the natural, that a correspondence of the
exteriors with the interiors, or of the natural things with the
spiritual, may be produced. This is effected in the state which
is signified by the seven years of famine. (*ib.* n. 5342.)

In process of time the church decreases, and at last remains
with a few. Those few with whom it remained at the time of
the deluge were called Noah. That the true church decreases
and remains with a few is evident from the other churches which
have thus decreased. Those that are left are called in the Word a
remnant,[1] and the left, or residue, and indeed in the midst or middle
of the land. As it is in the universal, so it is in the particular; or
as it is in the church, so is it in individuals. Unless the Lord
preserved remains in every one, he must perish in eternal death;
for spiritual and celestial life is in remains. In like manner in
the general or universal; unless there were always some with
whom the true church or true faith remained, the human race
would perish. For on account of some few, as is well known, a
city, nay, a whole kingdom, is preserved. They are like the
heart in man : so long as the heart is sound the neighbouring
viscera can live; but when this becomes feeble wasting seizes
upon all, and the man dies. The last remains are what are
signified by Noah; for otherwise the whole earth was corrupt,
as is declared in Gen. vi. 12. These remains in every man, and
in the church, are mentioned in different places in the prophets;
as in Isaiah: "*He that is left in Zion, and he that remaineth in
Jerusalem, shall be called holy, even every one that is written among
the living in Jerusalem : When the Lord shall have washed away
the filth of the daughters of Zion, and shall have purged the blood
of Jerusalem from the midst thereof*" (iv. 3, 4). Here holiness is
predicated of the remnant,—by which the remains of the church
are signified, and also of the man of the church; for those that
were left in Zion and Jerusalem could not therefore be holy
because they were left. Again: "*It shall come to pass in that
day that the remnant of Israel, and such as are escaped of the
house of Jacob, shall no more again stay upon him that smote them,
but shall stay upon Jehovah, the Holy One of Israel, in truth. The
remnant shall return, the remnant of Jacob, unto the mighty God*"
(x. 20, 21). In Jeremiah: "*In those days and in that time, saith*

---

[1] See note, p. 145.

Jehovah, the iniquity of Israel shall be sought for, and there shall be none ; and the sins of Judah, and they shall not be found ; for I will pardon them whom I shall make a remnant" (l. 20). In Micah: *"The remnant of Jacob shall be in the midst of many people as the .dew from Jehovah, as the showers upon the grass"* (v. 7). The remnant or remains of man, or of the church, were also represented by the tenths (tithes), which were holy. Hence too the number ten is holy; and therefore ten is predicated of remains. As in Isaiah, where the remnant is called "the seed of holiness:" *"Jehovah shall remove man, and the many things left in the midst of the land ; and yet in it shall be a tenth, and it shall return, and shall be for extermination, as an oak and a holm-oak when the stem is cast forth from them : the seed of holiness is the stem thereof"* (vi. 12, 13). And in Amos: *"Thus saith the Lord Jehovah, The city that went out a thousand shall leave an hundred, and that which went forth an hundred shall leave ten to the house of Israel"* (v. 3). In these and in many other places, in the internal sense, the remains of which we have been speaking are signified. (*ib.* n. 468.)

When the way for remains is closed up a man is no longer man, because he can no longer be protected by the angels, but is entirely possessed of evil spirits, who seek and desire nothing else than to extinguish him as man. (*ib.* n. 660.)

REGENERATION CANNOT BE EFFECTED SUDDENLY.

When man is born, as to hereditary evils he is a hell in the least form ; and in so far as he takes from his hereditary evils and superadds to them his own he also becomes a hell. Hence it is that from birth and from actual life the order of his life is opposite to the order of heaven; for, of his own, man loves himself more than the Lord, and the world more than heaven; when yet the life of heaven consists in loving the Lord above all things and the neighbour as one's self. It is therefore evident that the former life which is of hell must be entirely destroyed; that is, evils and falsities must be removed, to the intent that a new life which is the life of heaven may be implanted. This can in nowise be done hastily; for every evil enrooted with its falsities has connection with all evils and their falsities ; and such evils and falsities are innumerable, and their connection is so manifold that it cannot be comprehended, not even by the angels, but only by the Lord. From this it is plain that the life of hell in man cannot be suddenly destroyed, for if it were suddenly done he would straightway expire; and that the life of heaven cannot be suddenly implanted, for if this were done suddenly he would also expire. There are thousands and thousands of mysteries, of which scarcely one is known to man, whereby man is led of the Lord, when he is led from the life of hell to the life of heaven. It has been given me to know from heaven that this is so; and it has likewise been confirmed by many things which have come to my apperception. Since man knows scarcely anything about these mysteries, many have fallen into errors concerning man's liberation from evils and falsities, or concerning the remission of sins,—believing that, through mercy, in a moment the life of hell in man can be changed into the life of heaven in him; when yet the whole act of regeneration is mercy, and no others are regenerated but those who in the world receive the mercy of the Lord in faith and life. (A. C. n. 9336.)

EVERY ONE MAY BE REGENERATED, BUT EACH DIFFERENTLY.

Every one can be regenerated, but each according to his state. For the simple and the learned are regenerated differently; yet differently those who are in different studies, and also in different occupations; those who are inquisitive about the externals of the Word, differently from those who inquire about its internals; those who from parents are in natural good, differently from those who are in evil; those who from early childhood have entered into the vanities of the world, differently from those who earlier or later have withdrawn from them; in a word, those who constitute the external church of the Lord, differently from those who constitute the internal. This variety like that of faces and dispositions is infinite; but yet every one, according to his state, can be regenerated and saved. That is is so may be seen from the heavens into which all the regenerate come, in that they are three, a highest, a middle, and lowest; and they come into the highest who by regeneration receive love to the Lord; they come into the middle who receive love towards the neighbour; they into the last who only practise external charity; and all at the same time acknowledge the Lord as God the Redeemer and Saviour. All these are saved, but in different ways. That all may be regenerated and thus saved is because the Lord with His Divine good and truth is present with every man; from this is the life of every one, and from this is the faculty of understanding and willing; and from this they have free agency in spiritual things. These are wanting to no man. And means are also given; to Christians in the Word; and to Gentiles in the religion of every one, which teaches that there is a God, and teaches precepts concerning good and evil. From all this it follows that every one may be saved; consequently, that if he is not saved the Lord is not in fault but man; and man is in fault in that he does not co-operate. (T. C. R. n. 580.)

IN ORDER TO REGENERATION THE NATURAL MUST BE ENTIRELY SUBDUED.

That man may become spiritual it is necessary that his natural should become as nothing, that is, should have no power at all of itself; for in so far as the natural has power of itself the spiritual has not power; for from infancy the natural is imbued with nothing but things which are of the lusts of self and the world and therefore contrary to charity. These evils effect that good cannot flow in through the internal man from the Lord; for whatever flows in is turned in the natural into evil. The natural is the plane in which influx terminates; wherefore unless the natural, that is the evil and the false which had formed the natural, become as nothing, good can by no means flow in from the Lord through heaven. It has no abiding-place, but is dissipated; for it cannot dwell in the evil and false. Hence it is that in so far as the natural does not become as nothing the internal is closed. This is known too in the church, from the doctrinal truth that the old man must be put off, that the new man may be put on. Regeneration is for nothing else than that the natural may be subjugated, and the spiritual obtain dominion; and the natural is subjugated when it is brought into correspondence. And when the natural is brought into correspondence it no longer resists but acts as it is commanded, and follows the behest of the spiritual,—scarcely otherwise than as the acts of the body obey the dictates of the will, and as the speech with the countenance is in accordance with the influx of thought. It is therefore plain that in order that man may become spiritual, the natural, in respect to willing, ought to become entirely as nothing. But it should be known that it is the old natural which must become as nothing, because this is formed of evils and falsities; and when it has become as nothing man is gifted with a new natural, which is called spiritual natural. It is called spiritual from the fact that it is the spiritual which acts by it, and manifests itself by it, just as the cause by the effect. It is known that the cause is all of the effect; the new natural therefore as to thinking, willing, and producing effect, is nothing but the representative of the spiritual. When this comes to pass man receives good from the Lord; and when he receives good he is gifted with truths; and when he is gifted with truths he is perfected in intelligence and wisdom; and when he is per-

fected in intelligence and wisdom he is blessed with happiness to
eternity.   (A. C. n. 5651.)

Even the Sensual in Man must be Regenerated.

The things in man which flow in through heaven from the
Lord flow into his interior, and pass on to the ultimates or extremes, and are there sensibly presented to man.   They consequently flow even into the sensual [degree], and through this
into the things that pertain to the body.   If the sensual is sur-
charged with fantasies arising from fallacies and appearances,
and especially if from falsities, the truths that flow in are there
turned into likeness to them; for they are received there according to the form induced.   And besides, in so far as truths are
turned into falsities, the interiors through which the passage is
are closed; and at length are only so far open that there passes
through merely so much as may afford a faculty of reasoning,
and of confirming evils by falsities.   This being the case with
man, it is necessary when he is regenerated that his natural
[degree] should be regenerated even to the sensual; for if it be
not regenerated there is no reception of truth and good,—since,
as was said above, the inflowing truth is there perverted, and
then the interiors are closed.   Therefore when the exteriors are
regenerated the whole man is regenerated.   This was signified
by the Lord's words to Peter when He washed his feet: "*Simon
Peter saith unto Him, Lord, thou shalt wash not my feet only, but
also my hands and my head: Jesus saith unto him, He that is
washed needeth not save to wash his feet, and is clean every whit*"
(John xiii. 9, 10).   By the feet things natural are signified; by
washing is signified to purify; by the hands are signified the interiors of the natural; and by the head spiritual things.   From
this it is plain what is meant by "He that is washed needeth
not save to wash his feet, and is clean every whit;" namely, that
man is regenerated, when he is regenerated even as to the exteriors which are of the natural.   When therefore a man is
regenerated as to the natural, all things therein are subordinated
to the interiors; and then, when interior things flow into the
natural, they flow as into their general [receptacles], by which
they sensibly present themselves to man.   When this is the case
with man, there is felt by him an affection for the truth which
is of faith, and an affection for the good which is of charity.
But the very sensual, which is the ultimate of the natural, can
with difficulty be regenerated; for the reason that it is entirely
filled with material ideas arising from things terrestrial, corporeal, and worldly.   Therefore the man who is regenerated, at

the present day especially, is not regenerated as to the sensual, but as to the natural which is next above the sensual; to which he is elevated from the sensual by the Lord when he meditates upon the truths and goods of faith. The capability of being elevated out of the sensual is what the man is gifted with who is regenerated by the Lord. (A. C. n. 7442.)

ALL THINGS IN NATURE REPRESENT REGENERATION.

Regeneration is represented by various things in the world; as by the blossoming of all things on the earth in the time of spring, and by their successive growth to the production of fruit; by the growth likewise of every tree, shrub, and flower, from the first month of heat to the last. It is represented also by the progressive ripening of all fruits, from the first setting to their full maturity. It is represented again by morning and evening showers, and by dews, at the coming of which the flowers open, while at the darkness of night they close again; by the fragrance from gardens and fields; and by the rainbow in the cloud (Gen. ix. 14-17). So also by the resplendent colours of the dawn; and in general by the continual renovation of all things in the body, by the chyle, and the animal spirit, and hence by the blood,— whose purification from disused substances and renovation, and as it were regeneration, is perpetual. If the attention is directed to the commonest things on earth, an image of regeneration is presented; in the wonderful transformation of silkworms and many worms into nymphs and butterflies; and of other insects which in time are furnished with wings. To which yet more trifling things may be added; it is represented by the desire of certain birds to plunge into the water to wash and cleanse themselves,— after which, like the nightingales, they return to their songs. In a word, the whole world, from its first things to its last, is full of representations and types of regeneration. (T. C. R. n. 687.)

REGENERATION IS EFFECTED BY COMBATS IN TEMPTATION.

They who have not been instructed concerning the regeneration of man think that man can be regenerated without temptation; and some that he is regenerated when he has undergone one temptation. But it is to be known that no one is regenerated without temptation; and that many temptations succeed, one after another. The reason is that regeneration is effected for an end; in order that the life of the old man may die, and the new life which is heavenly be insinuated. It is evident therefore that there must certainly be a conflict; for the life of the old man resists and determines not to be extinguished; and the life of the new man can only enter where the life of the old is extinct. It is plain then that there is a conflict on both sides; and an ardent conflict, because it is for life. Whoever thinks from an enlightened rational, may see and perceive from this that a man cannot be regenerated without combat, that is without spiritual temptations; and further, that he is not regenerated by one temptation, but by many. For there are very many kinds of evil which formed the delight of his former life, that is of the old life. These evils cannot all be subdued at once and together; for they cleave tenaciously, since they have been inrooted in the parents for many ages back, and are therefore innate in man, and are confirmed by actual evils from himself from infancy. All these evils are diametrically opposite to the celestial good that is to be insinuated, and which is to constitute the new life. (A. C. n. 8403.)

COMBAT MAY BE WAGED EVEN FROM TRUTH NOT GENUINE.

While man is being regenerated he is let into contests against falsities, and is then kept by the Lord in truth,—but in that truth which he had persuaded himself was truth; and from that truth he fights against falsity. He can fight even from truth not genuine if only it be such that it can be conjoined by any means with good; and it is conjoined with good by innocence, for innocence is the medium of conjunction. Hence it is that men can be regenerated within the church from any doctrine whatever; but they before others who are in genuine truths. (A. C. n. 6765.)

THE USE OF TEMPTATIONS.

It should be known that with those who are regenerated a turning is effected; namely, that by truth they are led to good, and afterwards from good they are led to truth. When this turning takes place, or when the state is changed and becomes inverse to the prior state, there is mourning; for then they are let into temptation, by which those things that are their own are weakened and enfeebled, and good is insinuated, and with the good a new will, and with this a new freedom, thus a new *proprium.* (A. C. n. 5773.)

They are evil spirits which excite evils and falsities; and unless they are excited, man scarcely cognizes that there are evils and falsities; but they are then made manifest. And the longer the temptation combats continue, the more manifest do they become, until at length evils and falsities are regarded with horror. (*ib.* n. 1740.)

He who is in the combats of temptation, and conquers, acquires to himself more and more power over evil spirits, or over the diabolical crew, till at length they dare not assail him; but as often as he obtains a victory so often the Lord reduces to order the goods and truths by which he combated, and so often purifies them; and in proportion as they are purified the celestial things of love are insinuated into the exterior man, and it becomes correspondent. (*ib.* n. 1717.)

The Lord permits the infernals in the other life to lead the good into temptation, consequently to infuse evils and falsities; which they also do with all their might; for when they are doing this they are in their life, and in the delight of life. But then the Lord Himself immediately, and mediately through the angels, is present with those who are in temptation, and resists, by refuting the falsities of the infernal spirits, and by dissipating their evil; thence come refreshment, hope, and victory. Thus the truths of faith and the goods of charity, with those who are in the truths of good, are more inwardly implanted and more strongly confirmed; this is the means whereby spiritual life is bestowed.

.   .   .   .

The infernal spirits to whom it is permitted thus to tease the good intend nothing but evil; for they desire with all their power to draw them down from heaven, and plunge them into hell. For to destroy any one as to his soul, thus to eternity, is the very delight of their life. But not the least is permitted them by the Lord but for the end that good may come out of it, namely, that truth and good may be formed and strengthened with those who are in temptation. In the whole spiritual world the end that proceeds from the Lord reigns, which is, that nothing at all, not even the least thing, shall exist except that good may come from it. Therefore the Lord's kingdom is called a kingdom of ends and uses. (*ib.* n. 6574.)

I have talked with spirits about the changes in the state of man's life, in that it is inconstant, and is borne upwards and downwards, namely, towards heaven and towards hell. But they who suffer themselves to be regenerated are carried continually upwards, and thus always into more interior heavenly societies. An extension of sphere into those societies is given by the Lord to those who are regenerated,—principally by temptations, in which there is resistance to evils and falsities; for then the Lord by means of the angels fights against evils and falsities. And so man is introduced into the societies of those angels who are more interior. And into whatever societies he has once been introduced, there he remains; and thence also he receives a more extended and more elevated faculty of perception. (*ib.* n. 6611.)

How Temptations are excited by Evil Spirits.

Scarcely any one in the Christian world at this day knows whence temptations arise. He who undergoes them believes no otherwise than that they are torments arising from the evils which are interiorly within man, and which render him first unquiet, then anxious, and finally torment him; and he is not at all aware that they are effected by evil spirits who are with him. He is unaware of this fact because he does not believe that he is in fellowship with spirits while he lives in the world, and scarcely that there is any spirit with him; when yet as to his interiors man is continually in the society of spirits and angels. As regards temptations, they take place when a man is in the process of regeneration; for no one can be regenerated unless he also undergoes temptations. And they then arise through evil spirits who are about him; for man is then let into the state of evil in which he is,—that is, in which that which constitutes his very *proprium* is,—and when he comes into this state evil or infernal spirits encompass him; and when they apperceive that he is interiorly protected by angels the evil spirits excite the falsities which he had thought, and the evils that he had done; but the angels from within defend him. It is this combat which is perceived in man as [temptation; but so obscurely that he scarcely knows but that it is merely an anxiety. For man, especially one who believes nothing about influx, is in a state entirely unenlightened, and scarcely apperceives a thousandth part of the things concerning which the evil spirits and angels contend; and yet at that time a contest is being waged concerning the man, and concerning his eternal salvation; and it is waged from the man, that is, from the things and concerning the things that are in the man. That this is the case it has been given me most certainly to know. I have heard the combat; I have perceived the influx; I have seen the spirits and the angels; and then and afterwards have talked with them even on that subject. Temptations, as was said, arise chiefly when a man is becoming spiritual; for then he spiritually apprehends the truths of doctrine. The man is often ignorant of this, and yet the angels with him see the spiritual things in his natural; for his interiors are then open towards heaven. And hence it is that the man who is regenerated, after his life in the world is among the angels, and there both sees and perceives the spiritual things which before appeared to him as natural. When therefore a man is such he can be defended by angels in temptation, when assaulted by evil spirits; for the angels have then a plane in which they may operate, for they flow in into the spiritual in him, and through the spiritual into the natural. (A. C. n. 5036.)

As few know the nature of temptations, it may here be briefly explained: Evil spirits never make assault against anything but what a man loves; and they assail it the more violently in proportion as he loves it more ardently. Evil genii are those who assail what has relation to the affection for good, and evil spirits are those who assail what has relation to the affection for truth. As soon as they observe the least thing that a man loves, or perceive as it were by the smell what is delightful and dear to him, they assail and endeavour to destroy it. They thus endeavour to destroy the whole man; for his life consists in his loves. Nothing is more delightful to them than thus to destroy man; nor do they ever desist, were it even to eternity, unless repelled by the Lord. Those that are malignant and cunning insinuate themselves into the very loves, by flattering them; and so they lead man into them, and presently when they have thus drawn him in they try to destroy the loves, and so to kill the man; and this in a thousand ways which are incomprehensible. Nor do they combat merely by reasoning against goods and truths. Such combats are nothing. For if defeated a thousand times they still persist; since such subtle reasonings against goods and truths can never be wanting. But they pervert goods and truths, and enkindle a sort of fire of lust and persuasion, so that the man does not know but that he is in such lust and persuasion; and these at the same time they inflame with a delight which they snatch from the man's delight from another source, and thus most deceitfully they infect and infest; and this so artfully, by hasting from one thing to another, that if the Lord did not bring help, the man could by no means know but that it is so. In like manner they act against the affections for truth which form man's conscience. As soon as they perceive anything whatever of conscience, they form to themselves an affection out of the falsities and infirmities in man, and by this affection they over-shadow the light of truth, and so pervert it, or induce anxiety and torment him. Besides which, they tenaciously keep the thought on one thing, and so fill it with fantasies, and then at the same time clandestinely involve lusts into the fantasies. Together with innumerable other artifices, which can by no means be described to the apprehension. (*ib.* n. 1820.)

EVIL IS NOT EXTERMINATED BY REGENERATION, BUT ONLY SEPARATED TO THE CIRCUMFERENCES, AND REMAINS TO ETERNITY.

The evil in the man who is regenerated, either actual or hereditary, is not exterminated, so that it passes away or becomes none, but is only separated, and through disposition by the Lord is cast out into the circumferences. It thus remains with him, and this to eternity; but he is withheld by the Lord from the evil, and is kept in good. When this is the case it appears as if the evils were rejected and the man purified from them, or as they say, justified. The angels of heaven all confess that what is in them so far as it is from themselves is nothing but evil and the falsity therefrom, but so far as it is from the Lord it is good and truth from good. They who have conceived another opinion on this subject, and when they lived in the world confirmed in themselves, from their doctrinal, [a belief], that they are justified and are then without sins, and thus that they are holy, are remitted into the state of evils from the actual and the hereditary [in them], and are kept in it until they know by living experience that of themselves they are nothing but evil; and that the good in which they had seemed to themselves to be was from the Lord, and therefore was not theirs but the Lord's. So it is with the angels, and so with the regenerate among men. (A. C. n. 4564.)

There are some men who after death are elevated by the Lord into heaven, because they have lived well, but who yet have carried with them the belief that they are clean and pure from sins, and that therefore they are not chargeable with any guilt. They are at first clothed in white raiment according to their belief; for white garments signify a state purified from evils. But afterwards they begin to think as in the world that they are as it were washed from all evil, and to glory therefore in the idea that they are no longer sinners like others,—which can hardly be separated from some elation of mind, and some contempt of others in comparison with themselves. In order therefore that they may be withdrawn from their imaginary belief, they are then sent away from heaven, and remitted into their evils which they had contracted in the world; and at the same time it is shown them that they are also in hereditary evils, of which they had before known nothing. And after they have thus been compelled to acknowledge that their evils are not separated from them, but only removed; that therefore of themselves they are impure, yea nothing but evil; that they are withheld from evils and kept in goods by the Lord; and that this [only] appears to them as if it were of themselves; they are again elevated by the Lord into heaven. (D. P. n. 279.)

Temporary Quiescence of Evils.

There are two loves, so called, and their desires which obstruct the influx of heavenly love from the Lord; for while they reign in the inner and outer man, and hold possession of him, they either cast back or suffocate, and also pervert and defile, the inflowing heavenly love; because they are utterly opposed to it. But in proportion as they are removed, the heavenly love flowing in from the Lord begins to appear, aye, to dawn upon his inner man; and he begins to see that he is in evil and falsity; and then indeed that he is in uncleanness and defilement; and at last, that this is his very *proprium.* These are they who are regenerated with whom those loves are removed. This may also be apperceived by the unregenerate; while the desires of those loves in them are quiescent,—as they are sometimes when they are in pious meditation, or while those loves are asleep, as is the case when men are in misfortunes, in sorrows and in sickness, and especially at the moment of death,—then, because corporeal and worldly things are asleep, and as it were dead, they apperceive somewhat of heavenly light and comfort from this influx. But with them there is no removal, but only a torpidity of those desires; for when they return to their former state they instantly relapse into them. (A. C. n. 2041.)

Difference between the Regenerate and the Unregenerate.

With the regenerate man there is a conscience of what is good and true, and from conscience he does good and thinks truth; the good that he does is the good of charity, and the truth that he thinks is the truth of faith. The unregenerate man has no conscience; or if any it is not a conscience of doing good from charity and of thinking truth from faith, but from some love regarding himself or the world. It is therefore a spurious or false conscience. With the regenerate man there is joy when he acts according to conscience, and anxiety when he is constrained to do anything or to think against conscience. But with the unregenerate it is not so; very many do not know what conscience is, much less what it is to do anything according to conscience or against conscience; but they act according to what favours their loves, while to act against them gives them anxiety. With the regenerate man there is a new will and a new understanding; and the new will and new understanding are his conscience, that is, they are in his conscience, by which the Lord operates the good of charity and the truth of faith. With the unregenerate man there is no will, but in place of will there is lust, and therefore a proneness to every evil; and there is no understanding, but subtle reasoning, and accordingly an easy gliding into every falsity. With the regenerate man there is celestial and spiritual life; but with the unregenerate man there is only corporeal and worldly life. That he can think and understand what is good and true is from the Lord's life, through the remains mentioned above, from which he has the capability of reflecting. With the regenerate the internal man has dominion, and the external is compliant; but with the unregenerate the external man has dominion, and the internal is dormant,—as if it were none. The regenerate man cognizes, or if he reflects can cognize what the internal man is, and what the external; but the unregenerate man knows nothing at all of them, and cannot know although he reflects, for he does not know what the good and truth of faith from charity are. From these considerations it may be seen what the quality of the regenerate man is, and of the unregenerate; and that the difference is as between summer and winter, and between light and darkness. The regenerate is therefore a living man; and the unregenerate is a dead man. (A. C. n. 977.)

What the Heavenly Proprium is,

As regards the heavenly *proprium*, it arises out of the new will which is given by the Lord, and differs from the *proprium* of man in this; that men no longer regard themselves in all and every thing that they do, and in all and every thing that they learn and teach; but they then regard the neighbour, the public, the church, the kingdom of the Lord, and so the Lord Himself. The ends of life are what are changed; the ends regarding lower things, namely, the world, and self, are removed, and ends regarding higher things are substituted in their place. The ends of life are nothing else than the very life of man; for his ends are the very will of a man, and his very loves; for what a man loves that he wills and has for an end. He who is gifted with a heavenly *proprium* is also in tranquillity, and in peace; for he trusts in the Lord, and believes that nothing of evil befalls him, and is conscious that concupiscences do not infest him. And moreover they who are in a heavenly *proprium* are in very freedom; for to be led of the Lord is freedom, because it is to be led in good, from good to good. It is therefore evident that they are in blessedness and happiness, for there is nothing that disturbs,—nothing of self-love, consequently nothing of enmity, of hatred, of revenge; nor anything of the love of the world, and therefore nothing of fraud, of fear, of restlessness. (A. C. n. 5660.)

All that is good which comes of genuine charity towards the neighbour. But no one of himself can be in this good; for it is the very celestial which flows in from the Lord. This celestial continually flows in, but evils and falsities oppose its reception; that it may be received therefore it is necessary that man should remove evils, and as far as he is able falsities also, and so dispose himself to receive the influx. When, evils being removed, man receives the influx, he then receives a new voluntary and a new intellectual [faculty]; and from the new voluntary he feels delight in doing good to his neighbour for no selfish end, and from the new intellectual he apperceives delight in learning what is good and true for the sake of good and truth, and for the sake of life. Since this new intellectual and new voluntary exists by influx from the Lord, therefore he who is regenerated acknowledges and believes that the good and the truth with which he is affected are not from himself, but from the Lord; and that whatever is from himself, or from his *proprium*, is nothing but evil. From this it is evident what it is to be born again; and what the new voluntary and the new intellectual are. (*ib.* n. 5354.)

Goodness of disposition manifests itself by gentleness and sweetness; by gentleness, in that it is afraid to do harm, and by sweetness, in that it loves to do good. (E. U. n. 50.)

MAN IS FIRST IN TRUE FREEDOM WHEN HE BECOMES REGENERATE.

When a man becomes regenerate he then first enters upon a state of freedom; before he was in a state of bondage. It is bondage when lusts and falsities have dominion; it is freedom when affections of good and truth bear sway. A man never perceives in any degree how the case is so long as he remains in the state of bondage; but first does so when he enters into the state of freedom. While he is in the state of bondage, that is while lusts and falsities rule, the man who is subjugated by them supposes that he is in a state of freedom; but it is a gross falsity, for at the very time he is carried along by the delight of his lusts and of the pleasures derived from them,—that is, by the delight of his loves; and because it is by a delight it appears to him as free. Every one thinks himself free while he is being led by some love, —so long as he follows whithersoever it leads; but there are diabolical spirits, in whose society and as it were torrent he is, who bear him onward. This the man imagines to be most free; and to such a degree that he even believes if he should be deprived of this state he would come into a miserable life, yea, that he would be in no life. And this he believes, not only because he does not know that there is any other life, but also from the fact that he has received the impression that no one can come into heaven but through miseries, poverty, and deprivation of pleasures. But it has been given me to know by much experience that this is false; of which experience, by the Lord's Divine mercy, hereafter. A man never comes into a state of freedom until he is regenerated, and is led of the Lord by the love of good and truth. When he is in this state he is for the first time able to know what freedom is; for he then knows what life is, and what the true delight of life is, and what happiness is. Before he did not even know what good is; he sometimes called that the highest good which is the deepest evil. They who from the Lord are in this state of freedom, when they see, and still more when they feel, the life of lusts and falsities, abhor it as those who see hell open before their eyes. But since to very many it is profoundly unknown what the life of freedom is, it is permitted in these few words to say what it is; namely, that the life of freedom is to be led only of the Lord. (A. C. n. 892.)

IGNORANCE OF THE CHURCH AT THE PRESENT DAY CONCERNING REGENERATION.

They who are of the church at this day know so little of any thing relating to regeneration that it is almost nothing. They do not even know this; that regeneration goes on through the whole course of life of him who is regenerated, and that it is continued in the other life; and that the mysteries of regeneration are so innumerable that they can scarcely be known as to a ten thousandth part by the angels, and that those which the angels know are what constitute their intelligence and wisdom. The reason why those who are of the church at the present day know so little concerning regeneration is, that they talk so much about the remission of sins, and about justification; and because they believe that sins are remitted in a moment, and some that they are wiped away, as filth from the body by water; and that by faith alone, or by the confidence of a single moment, a man is justified. The men of the church so believe because they do not know what sin or evil is; if they knew this they would know that sins cannot be wiped away from any one, but that they are separated or cast aside, that they may not rise up when man is kept good by the Lord; and that this cannot be effected unless evil be continually cast out, and this by means which are indefinite in number, and for the most part ineffable. They who have brought this opinion with them into the other life,— that by faith man is justified in a moment, and washed altogether from his sins,—are amazed when they apperceive that regeneration is effected by means indefinite in number, and ineffable; and smile at their own ignorance which they cherished in the world,—which they even call insanity,—concerning the instantaneous remission of sins, and concerning justification. They are sometimes told that the Lord remits sins to every one who from his heart desires it; but yet that they are not therefore separated from the diabolical crew to which they are fast bound by the evils that follow the life which all have with them. They afterwards learn from experience that to be separated from the hells is to be separated from sins; and that this can in no wise be effected but by the thousand and thousand means known to the Lord only,—and this, if you will believe it, in continual succession to eternity. For so great is evil that a man cannot be entirely delivered even from one sin to eternity; and only by the Lord's mercy, if he shall have received it, can he be withheld from sin and kept in good. How therefore man receives new life and is regenerated is contained in the sanctuary of the Word; that is in its internal sense,—to the intent especially, that from the Word when it is read by man the angels may be in their happiness of wisdom, and at the same time also in the delight of serving as mediums. (A. C. n. 5398.)

It is not Difficult to Live a Good Life.

Some believe that it is difficult to live a life that leads to heaven, which is called a spiritual life; because they have heard that a man must renounce the world, and deprive himself of what are called the lusts of the body and the flesh, and that he must live spiritually. Which they understand no otherwise than that they must reject worldly things, which are chiefly riches and honours; that they must walk continually in pious meditation about God, salvation, and eternal life; and must spend their life in prayers, and in reading the Word and pious books. This they conceive to be renouncing the world, and living after the spirit and not after the flesh. But it has been given me to know by much experience, and from conversation with the angels, that the fact is quite otherwise; nay, that they who renounce the world and live after the spirit in this manner acquire a sorrowful life, which is not receptive of heavenly joy; for with every one his own life remains. But in order that a man may receive the life of heaven it is altogether necessary that he live in the world, and engage in its duties and occupations; and then by moral and civil life he may receive spiritual life. And in no other way can spiritual life be formed in a man, or his spirit be prepared for heaven; for to live an internal life and not at the same time an external is like dwelling in a house that has no foundation, which gradually sinks, or cracks and yawns with crevices, or totters till it falls. (H. H. n. 528.)

That it is not so difficult to live the life of heaven as is believed is evident from this: that when anything presents itself that one knows to be insincere and unjust, to which his mind is disposed, he need only think that it ought not to be done because it is contrary to the Divine commands. If a man accustoms himself so to think, and from custom derives the habit, he is then by degrees conjoined to heaven; and in so far as he is conjoined to heaven, the higher degrees of his mind are opened; and in so far as these are opened he sees what is insincere and unjust; and in so far as he sees these evils they can be shaken off,—for it is impossible that any evil can be shaken off until it is seen. This is a state into which a man may enter from freedom; for who is not capable from freedom of thinking in this manner? But when he has made a beginning all goods are wrought in him by the Lord, and He causes him not only to see evils, but also not to will them, and finally to become averse to them. This is meant by the Lord's words, " *My yoke is easy and my burden is light*" (Matt. xi. 30). But it should be known that the difficulty of so thinking, and likewise of resisting evils, increases in proportion as a man from the will commits evils; for in so far he becomes accustomed to them, until at length he does not see them, and afterwards loves them, and from the delight of love excuses them, and by all kinds of fallacies confirms them, and declares that they are allowable and good. But this occurs with those who in the age of adolescence plunge into evils as if without restraint, and at the same time reject Divine things from the heart.

There was once represented to me the way which leads to heaven, and that which leads to hell. There was a broad way tending to the left, or towards the north; and many spirits appeared walking in it. But at a distance a stone was seen of considerable magnitude, where the broad way terminated. From that stone there went afterwards two ways, one to the left, and one in a contrary direction, to the right. The way which tended to the left was narrow or strait, leading by the west to the south, and thus into the light of heaven; the way which tended to the right was broad and spacious, leading obliquely downwards towards hell. At first all seemed to go the same way, until they came to the great stone at the head of the two ways; but when they arrived there they separated. The good turned to the left, and entered the strait way which led to heaven; but the evil did not see the stone at the head of the two ways, and fell upon it and were hurt; and when they rose up they ran on in the broad way to the right, which tended towards hell. It was afterwards explained to me what all these things signified. By the first way, which was broad, in which many both good and evil walked together, and talked with each other as friends,—because no difference between them was apparent to the sight,—they were represented who in externals alike live sincerely and justly, and are not visibly distinguished. The stone at the head of the two ways, or at the corner, upon which the evil stumbled, and from which afterwards they ran into the way leading to hell, represented Divine truth, which is denied by those who look towards hell; in the highest sense the same stone signified the Divine Human of the Lord. But they who acknowledged Divine truth, and at the same time the Divine of the Lord, were conveyed by the way which led to heaven. By these representations it was again made evident that in externals the wicked lead the same kind of life or walk in the same way as the good, thus one as easily as the other; and yet that they who from the heart acknowledge the Divine, especially those within the church who acknowledge the Divine of the Lord, are led to heaven, and those that do not acknowledge are borne onwards to hell. The thoughts of a man which proceed from the intention or will are represented in the other life by ways. The ways there presented to appearance are indeed exactly in accordance with the thoughts from intention; and every one also walks according to his thoughts which proceed from his intention. Hence it is that the character of spirits, and of their thoughts, is known from their ways. It was likewise evident from these things what is meant by the Lord's words, " *Enter ye in through the strait gate ; for wide is the gate and broad is the way that leadeth to destruction, and many there be which go in thereat ; strait is the gate and narrow is the way which leadeth unto life, and few there be that find it*" (Matt. vii. 13, 14). That the way is narrow which leads to life is not because it is difficult, but because, as it is said, there are few that find it. From that stone seen at the corner where the broad and common way terminated, and from which two ways were seen to tend in opposite directions, it was made evident what is signified by these words of the Lord; " *Have ye not read what is written, The stone which the builders rejected is become the head of the corner ? Whosoever shall fall upon that stone shall be broken*" (Luke. xx. 17, 18). A stone signifies Divine truth; and the Stone (Rock) of Israel, the Lord as to the Divine Human; the builders are they who are of the church; the head of the corner is where the two ways meet; to fall and be broken is to deny and perish. (H. H. n. 533, 534.)

It has been granted me to converse with some in the other life who had separated themselves from worldly affairs, that they might live a pious and holy life; and also with some who had afflicted themselves in various ways, because they believed that this was to renounce the world and subdue the concupiscences of the flesh. But most of them—inasmuch as they had thereby contracted a sorrowful life, and removed themselves from the life of charity, which life can only be lived in the world—cannot be consociated with angels; for the life of angels is a life of gladness from bliss, and consists in doing the goods which are works of charity. . . . These things are related that it may be known that the life which leads to heaven is not a life of retirement from the world, but a life in the world; and that a life of piety without the life of charity, which can only be lived in the world, does not lead to heaven. But a life of charity does,—which consists in acting sincerely and justly in every occupation, in every transaction, and in every work, from an interior, that is from a heavenly origin; and this origin is in that life when a man acts sincerely and justly because it is according to the Divine laws. Such a life is not difficult; but a life of piety separate from a life of charity is difficult; which yet leads as much away from heaven as it is believed to lead to heaven. (H. H. n. 535.)

A Man's Life and Actions are Governed by the End proposed.

Whatever has supreme rule in the mind conforms to itself all the thoughts, yea, the minutest particulars of the thoughts.

However man's thoughts and actions may be varied, which they are in innumerable ways, if only the end proposed be good they are all good; but if the end be evil they are all evil. The end proposed is what governs in every particular thing that a man thinks and does. The angels attendant on man, because they are angels of the Lord, govern only his ends; when they govern these they govern also his thoughts and actions, since these all belong to the end. The end proposed by a man is his very life, and all that he thinks and does derives life from it; because, as was said, they belong to the end. Therefore such as is the character of the end proposed, such is the life of a man. The end is nothing but the love; for it is not possible that man should regard anything as an end but what he loves. He whose thoughts and actions are at variance yet has for his end that which he loves; and even in his hypocrisy and deceit there is an end proposed,—which is self-love, or the love of the world, and the delight of life therefrom. Hence every one may conclude that such as a man's love is such is his life. (A. C. n. 1317.)

IMPUTATION.

The imputation which is a part of the faith of the present day is twofold, one of the merit of Christ, and the other of salvation thereby. It is taught in the whole Christian church that justification, and therefore salvation, is effected by God the Father through the imputation of the merit of Christ His Son; and that imputation is of grace, *when and where He will*, thus arbitrary; and that they to whom the merit of Christ is imputed are adopted into the number of the children of God. And because the leaders of the church have not moved a step beyond that imputation, or elevated their minds above it,—owing to their having decreed that God's election is merely arbitrary,—they have fallen into enormous and fanatical errors, and at length into the detestable error of predestination; and also into this abominable error,—that God does not heed the doings of a man's life, but only the faith inscribed on the interiors of his mind. Wherefore unless the error concerning imputation were abolished atheism would invade all Christendom, and then the king of the abyss would reign over them, "*whose name in Hebrew is Abaddon, and in Greek hath the name Apollyon*" (Rev. ix. 11). By Abaddon and Apollyon is signified a destroyer of the church by falsities; and by the abyss is signified the abode of those falsities. See *The Apocalypse Revealed*, n. 421, 440, 442, where it is made manifest that this falsity, and the falsities following from this, in an extended series, are the things over which that destroyer reigns; for, as was said above, the whole theological system of the present day depends on this imputation, as a long chain on a fixed hook, and as man with all his members on the head. And because that imputation everywhere reigns it is, as says Isaiah: "*Jehovah will cut off from Israel head and tail; . . . the honourable he is the head, and the teacher of lies is the tail*" (ix. 14, 15). (T. C. R. n. 628.)

As regards the first part of this twofold imputation concerning the salvation of man, which is the arbitrary imputation of Christ's merit and the imputation of salvation thereby, the dogmatists differ; some teach that this imputation is absolute, of free power, and is offered to those whose external or internal form is well-pleasing; others that the imputation is from foreknowledge to those into whom grace is infused, and to whom this faith can be applied. But yet these two opinions aim at one point, and are like two eyes which have for their object one stone, or two ears which have for their object one song. At first sight it appears as if they went away from each other, but in the end they unite and play together. For since on both sides entire impotence in spiritual things is taught, and everything of man is excluded from faith, it follows that this grace receptive of faith, being infused arbitrarily or of foreknowledge, is a similar election; for if that grace which is called preventive grace were universal, man's application of it from some power of his own would occur, which however is rejected as a leprosy. Hence it is that no one knows any more than a stock or a stone,—such as he was when it was infused,—whether that faith of grace has been given to him or not; for there is no sign testifying it, when charity, piety, the desire of a new life, and the free faculty of doing good as well as evil, are denied to man. The signs which are said to testify to that faith in man are all ludicrous, and are not different from the auguries of the ancients by the flight of birds, or the prognostications of astrologers by the stars, or of players by dice. Things of this kind, and still more ludicrous, follow from the dogma of the imputed righteousness of the Lord, which,—together with the faith which is called that righteousness,—is communicated to the man who is elect. (*ib.* n. 631.)

The Origin of the Doctrine of Imputation.

The faith which is imputative of the merit and righteousness of Christ the Redeemer first arose from the decrees of the council of Nice concerning three Divine persons from eternity; which faith, from that time to the present, has been received by the whole Christian world. As regards the Nicene council itself, it was held by the Emperor Constantine the Great in his palace at Nice, a city of Bithynia, by the advice of Alexander, Bishop of Alexandria; all the bishops in Asia, Africa, and Europe being convoked, in order that the heresy of Arius, a presbyter of Alexandria, might be refuted from the Sacred Scriptures and condemned. This was done in the year of our Lord 325. Those who were called together decided that there were from eternity three Divine persons, the Father, the Son, and the Holy Ghost,—as may be seen especially from the two creeds called the Nicene and Athanasian. In the Nicene Creed it is said,

"*I believe in one God, the Father Almighty, Maker of heaven and earth ; and in one Lord, Jesus Christ, the Son of God, the Only-begotten of the Father, born before all ages, God of God, of the same substance with the Father, who came down from heaven, and became incarnate by the Holy Ghost from the Virgin Mary ; and in the Holy Ghost, the Lord and Giver of life, who proceeds from the Father and the Son, who, together with the Father and the Son, is worshipped and glorified.*" In the Athanasian Creed are these words : " *The Catholic faith is this :— That we worship one God in trinity, and the trinity in unity ; neither confounding the persons, nor dividing the substance. . . . But whereas we are compelled by the Christian verity to acknowledge each person by himself to be God and Lord, so we are forbidden by the Catholic religion to say there be three Gods or three Lords.*" That is, it is lawful to acknowledge but not to say three Gods and three Lords ; and the one is not lawful because religion forbids it, but the other is because the truth dictates it. This Athanasian Creed was written soon after the council of Nice was held, by one or more who had been present at the council; and it also was accepted as œcumenical or catholic. From these it is manifest that it was then decreed that three Divine Persons from eternity ought to be acknowledged ; and, that although each person singly, by Himself, is God, yet that they are not to be called three Gods and Lords, but One. (T. C. R. n. 632.)

IMPUTATION NOT KNOWN IN THE APOSTOLIC CHURCH.

The faith imputative of the merit of Christ was not known in the Apostolic church, which preceded; and is nowhere meant in the Word. The church which preceded the Nicene council is called the Apostolic church. That it was a great church, and extended into the three parts of the globe, Asia, Africa, and Europe, is evident from the fact that the Emperor Constantine the Great was a Christian, and a zealot for religion ; and from his dominion over not only the region afterwards divided into the many kingdoms of Europe, but also over the neighbouring regions out of Europe. Wherefore, as was said before, he convoked the bishops of Asia, Africa, and Europe at his palace at Nice, a city of Bithynia, that he might banish from his empire the scandalous dogma of Arius. This was done of the Lord's Divine Providence; since if the Divinity of the Lord is denied the Christian church dies, and becomes as a sepulchre inscribed with the epitaph—" *Here lies.*" The church that existed before that time is called Apostolic ; and the eminent writers of that church are called the Fathers, and the true Christians at their side, brethren. That this church did not acknowledge three Divine Persons, nor therefore a Son of God from eternity, but only the Son of God born in time, is evident from the creed which from their church is called Apostolic, where we read these words : *" I believe in God the Father Almighty, Creator of heaven and earth; and in Jesus Christ, His only Son our Lord, who was conceived by the Holy Ghost, born of the Virgin Mary. . . . I believe in the Holy Ghost; the holy Catholic church; the communion of saints."* From which it is plain, that they acknowledged no other Son of God than the one conceived of the Holy Spirit and born of the virgin Mary, and by no means any Son of God born from eternity. This creed, like the two others, has been acknowledged as genuinely Catholic, by the whole Christian church to this day. . . . That in that primeval time all in the then Christian world acknowledged that the Lord Jesus Christ was God, to whom was given all power in heaven and on earth, and power over all flesh, according to His very words (Matt. xxviii. 18 ; John xvii. 2), and that they believed in Him, according to His command from God the Father (John iii. 15, 16, 36 ; vi. 40; xi. 25, 26), is also very manifest from the convocation of all the bishops by the Emperor Constantine the Great, for the purpose of convicting and condemning, from the sacred Scriptures, Arius and his followers, who denied the Divinity of the Lord the Saviour born of the virgin Mary. This indeed was done ; but in avoiding the wolf they fell upon a lion ; or, as it is said in the proverb, eager to avoid Charybdis, they fell upon Scylla,—by inventing a Son of God from eternity, who descended and assumed the Human; believing that they should thus vindicate and restore Divinity to the Lord. Not knowing that God Himself the Creator of the universe descended, that He might become the Redeemer, and thus the Creator anew,—according to these plain declarations in the Old Testament; Isaiah xxv. 9 ; xl. 3, 5, 10, 11 ; xliii. 14; xliv. 6, 24; xlvii. 4 ; xlviii. 17; xlix. 7, 26 ; lx. 16 ; lxiii. 16; Jer. l. 34; Hos. xiii. 4; Psa. xix. 14. To these add John i. 14. (T. C. R. n. 636, 637.)

That no faith imputative of the merit of Christ is meant in the Word, clearly appears from the fact that that faith was not known in the church until after the Nicene council introduced the three Divine Persons from eternity; and when this faith had been introduced and pervaded the whole Christian world, every other faith was cast into the shade. (*ib.* n. 639.)

IMPUTATION OF THE MERITS AND RIGHTEOUSNESS OF CHRIST IMPOSSIBLE.

That it may be known that the imputation of the merit and righteousness of Jesus Christ is impossible, it is necessary to understand what His merit and righteousness are. The merit of the Lord our Saviour is redemption, and what this was may be seen above in its appropriate chapter. It is there described that it was the subjugation of the hells, the establishment of order in the heavens, and afterwards the institution of a church; and thus that redemption was a work purely Divine. It was also there shown that by redemption the Lord put Himself in power to regenerate and save the men who believe in Him and do His commandments; and that without that redemption no flesh could have been saved. Since then redemption was a work purely Divine, and of the Lord alone, and this is His merit, it follows that this cannot be applied, ascribed, and imputed to any man, —any more than the creation and preservation of the universe. (T. C. R. n. 640.)

As the merit and righteousness of the Lord are therefore purely Divine, and things purely Divine are such that if they were applied and ascribed to man he would instantly die, and, like a stock cast into the naked sun, would be consumed, so that scarce an ember of him would remain; for this reason the Lord with His Divine draws near to angels and men by light attempered and accommodated to the capacity and quality of every one, thus by light that is adequate and adapted; and in like manner by heat. In the spiritual world there is a sun, in the midst of which the Lord is; from that sun He flows in by means of light and heat into the whole spiritual world, and into all who are there; all the light and all the heat there are from this source. From that sun the Lord also flows in with the same light and the same heat into the souls and minds of men. That heat in its essence is His Divine love, and that light in its essence is His Divine wisdom. This light and this heat the Lord adapts to the capacity and quality of the recipient angel and man; which is done by means of spiritual auras or atmospheres which convey and transfer them. The Divine itself immediately encompassing the Lord constitutes that sun. This sun is distant from the angels,—as the sun of the natural world is from men,—in order that it may not come into naked and therefore immediate contact with them; for thus they would be consumed, as was said, like a stock cast into the naked sun. From these considerations it must be evident that the merit and righteousness of the Lord, since they are purely Divine, cannot possibly be induced by imputation upon any angel or man; nay, if any the least thereof should touch them, not being thus modified as was said, they would instantly writhe as if struggling with death, and with feet cramped and eyes distended would expire. This was made known in the Israelitish church, by the declaration that no one can see God and live. The sun of the spiritual world, as it is since

Jehovah God assumed the Human, and to this added redemption and new righteousness, is indeed described by these words in Isaiah: " *The light of the sun shall be sevenfold, as the light of seven days, in the day that Jehovah shall bind up the breach of His people"* (xxx. 26). This chapter, from beginning to end, relates to the Lord's advent. It is also described what would be if the Lord should descend and draw near to any wicked man, by these words in the Revelation: " *They hid themselves in the dens and in the rocks of the mountains, and said to the mountains and rocks, . . . Hide us from the face of Him that sitteth on the throne, and from the wrath of the Lamb"* (vi. 15). It is said the wrath of the Lamb, because the terror and torment when the Lord draws near so appear to them. This may, moreover, be manifestly concluded from the fact that if any wicked person is introduced into heaven, where charity and faith in the Lord reign, darkness comes over his eyes, giddiness and insanity over his mind, pain and torment into his body, and he becomes like one dead. What then if the Lord Himself with His Divine merit, which is redemption, and His Divine righteousness, should enter into man? The apostle John himself could not endure the presence of the Lord; for we read that *when he saw the Son of Man in the midst of the seven candlesticks, he fell at his feet as dead"* (Rev. i. 17). (*ib.* n. 641.)

It is said in the decrees of the councils, and in the articles of the confessions to which the Reformed swear, that by the merit of Christ infused God justifies the wicked; when yet not the good of any angel can even be communicated to a wicked man, still less conjoined with him, but it is rejected and rebounds like an elastic ball thrown against the wall. (*ib.* n. 642.)

The True Doctrine of Imputation.

Since the fulfilling of the law, and the passion of the cross, have hitherto been understood by many in no other sense than that the Lord did by these two make satisfaction for the human race, and remove from them a foreseen or appointed damnation; from the connection [between them], and at the same time from the principle that man is saved by a mere belief that it is so, has followed the dogma of the imputation of the Lord's merit,—these two, which were of the Lord's merit, being accepted as a satisfaction. But this falls to the ground after what has been said of the fulfilling of the law by the Lord, and of His passion of the cross. And then at the same time it may be seen that imputation of merit is an expression without meaning, unless the remission of sins after repentance is meant by it. For nothing of the Lord can be imputed to man; but salvation may be awarded by the Lord, after a man has repented,—that is, after he has seen and acknowledged his sins, and then desists from them, and this from the Lord. Then salvation is awarded him, in this way; that the man is saved, not by his own merit and his own righteousness, but by the Lord,—who alone has fought and conquered the hells, and who alone afterwards fights also for man, and conquers the hells for him. These are the merit and righteousness of the Lord; and these can never be imputed to man; for if they were imputed the merit and righteousness of the Lord would be appropriated to man as his, and this never is and never can be done. If imputation were possible an impenitent and wicked man might impute to himself the merit of the Lord, and think himself justified by it; which yet would be to defile what is holy with things that are profane, and to profane the name of the Lord. For it would be to keep the thought fixed on the Lord, and the will in hell; and yet the will is the all of man. There is a faith which is of God, and a faith which is of man. They that repent have the faith of God; and they that do not repent, but think continually of imputation, have the faith of man. (L. n. 18.)

To every one after death the evil in which he is is imputed, and likewise the good. That this subject may be presented with some clearness, it shall be considered in the following order: 1. That every one has a life of his own. 2. That with every one his life remains after death. 3. That the evil of his life is then imputed to the evil, and the good of his life is imputed to the good. FIRST:—*Every one has a life of his own,* thus a life distinct from that of another. This is well known; for there is perpetual variety, and no one thing is the same as another; hence there is to each one what is peculiarly his own. This plainly appears from the faces of men; in that there is not one face exactly like another, nor ever can be to eternity,—because there are not two minds alike, and the face is from the mind. For the face, as it is said, is the type of the mind; and the mind derives its origin and form from the life. If man had not a life of his own, as he has a mind and a face of his own, he would have no life after death distinct from that of another; nay, heaven could not exist, for this consists of those who are perpetually different. Its form is solely from the variety of souls and minds, disposed in such order that they make one; and they make one from the One whose Life is in all and in every individual there, as the soul is in man. If this were not so heaven would be dispersed, because its form would be dissolved. The One from whom the life of all and every one is derived, and by virtue of whom that form coheres, is the Lord. SECOND:—*With every one his life remains after death.* This is known in the church from the Word, and in particular from these passages there: "*The Son of Man shall come, . . . and then He shall render unto every one according to his deeds*" (Matt. xvi. 27). "*I saw, . . . and the books were opened, . . . and all were judged, . . . according to their works*" (Apoc. xxi. 12, 13). "*In the day of judgment God will render unto every one according to his deeds*" (Rom. ii. 5, 6; 2 Corinth. v. 10). The works according to which it shall be rendered unto every one are the life; for the life does them, and they are according to the life. Since it has been granted me during many years to be in company with the angels, and to converse with those who have come from the world, I can certainly testify that every one there is explored as to what the quality of his life has been; and that the life which he had contracted in the world abides with him to eternity. I have talked with those who lived ages ago, whose life was known to me from history, and have recognized their likeness to the description. And I have heard from the angels that the life of any one cannot be changed after death, because it is organized according to his love and faith, and his works therefrom; and that if it were changed the organization would be destroyed, which never can take place; moreover, that a change of organization can only take place in the material body, and by no means in the spiritual body after the former is rejected. THIRD :—*The evil of his life is then imputed to the evil, and the good of his life is imputed to the good.* The imputation of evil after death does not consist in accusation, blame, censure, and judgment, as in the world; but the evil itself effects this. For the wicked of their own accord separate themselves from the good, because they cannot be together. The delights of the love of evil are averse to the delights of the love of good,—and their delights exhale from every one, as the odours from every plant on the earth; for they are not absorbed and concealed by the material body, as before, but freely flow forth from their loves into the spiritual air. And as evil is there perceived as it were in respect to its odour, it is this which accuses, blames, and judges,—not before any judge, but before every one who is in good; and this is what is meant by imputation. The imputation of good is effected in a similar manner. This takes place with those who in the world acknowledged that every good in them was and is from the Lord, and nothing of it from themselves. After being prepared they are let into the interior delights of their good; and then a way is opened for them to a society in heaven whose delights are homogeneous. This is done by the Lord. (B. E. n. 110.)

THE CHURCH.

The church of the Lord is scattered over the whole terrestrial globe, and thus is universal. All they are in it who have lived in the good of charity according to their religious belief. (H. H. n. 328.)

As regards the Lord's spiritual church, it should be known that it is throughout the whole terrestrial globe. For it is not limited to those that have the Word, and from this have obtained a knowledge of the Lord, and some truths of faith; but it is also with those who have not the Word, and are therefore entirely ignorant of the Lord, and consequently do not know any truths of faith (for all truths of faith refer to the Lord); that is, with the Gentiles remote from the church. For there are many among them who from rational light have come to know that there is one God; that He created all things, and that He preserves all things; as well as that all good, consequently all truth is from Him, and that similitude with Him makes man blessed; and who live, moreover, according to their religious belief, in love to God and in charity towards the neighbour; who from the affection of good do the works of charity, and from the affection of truth worship the Supreme. It is those that are of such a character among the Gentiles who are in the Lord's spiritual church. And although ignorant of the Lord while they are in the world, yet they have within them the worship and tacit acknowledgment of Him, when they are in good; for in all good the Lord is present. (A. C. n. 3263.)

The Specific Church, and its relation to the Church Universal.

It is called the church where the Lord is acknowledged and where the Word is. For the essentials of the church are love and faith in the Lord from the Lord; and the Word teaches how a man must live in order that he may receive love and faith from the Lord. (H. D. n. 242.)

They that are without the church, and acknowledge one God, and live in a certain charity towards the neighbour according to their religious belief, are in communion with those that are of the church; for no one who believes in God and lives well is condemned. It is therefore clear that the church of the Lord is everywhere in the whole world, although specifically it is where the Lord is acknowledged, and where the Word is. (*ib.* n. 244.)

By means of the Word there is conjunction of heaven with those also who are out of the church, where the Word is not; for the Lord's church is universal, and with all who acknowledge a Divine [Being] and live in charity. And furthermore, after death they are instructed by the angels and receive Divine truths. The church universal on earth is in the sight of the Lord as one man, just as heaven is; and the church where the Word is, and where by means of this the Lord is known, is as the heart and lungs in that man. (H. H. n. 308.)

By means of the church they are saved who are out of the church. None but those that are within the church are in the faith of charity; for the faith of charity is truth of doctrine adjoined to the good of life. For the case is this: The Lord's kingdom on earth consists of all that are in good; who although scattered over the whole earth are yet one, and as members constitute one body. . . . The church on the earth is like the heart and lungs; and they that are without the church are as the parts of the body which are sustained and kept alive by the heart and lungs. It is clear from this that without a church somewhere on earth the human race could not subsist; just as the body cannot without the heart and lungs within it. (A. C. n. 2853.)

Unless there exists somewhere on earth a church where the Word is, and where by means of it the Lord is known, there cannot be conjunction with heaven; for the Lord is God of heaven and earth, and without the Lord there is no salvation. It suffices that there be a church where the Word is, although it consist of a few comparatively; through this the Lord is yet present everywhere throughout the whole earth, for through this heaven is conjoined with the human race. (S. S. n. 104.)

It is known that [the character of] a church is according to its doctrine; and that doctrine is from the Word. But yet doctrine does not establish a church; but the integrity and purity of the doctrine, consequently the understanding of the Word. (T. C. R. n. 245.)

The Lord is present with man through the reading of the Word; but He is conjoined to him by means of and according to his understanding of truth from the Word. And in proportion as the Lord is conjoined to man, the church is in him. (S. S. n. 78.)

Where the Specific Church is.

The church is nowhere else than where the Word is rightly understood; and such as is the understanding of the Word among those who are in the church, such is the church. (S. S. n. 79.)

That there may be a church there must be doctrine from the Word; because without doctrine the Word is not understood. Yet doctrine alone does not constitute the church with man, but a life according to doctrine. From this it follows that faith alone does not constitute the church, but the life of faith, which is charity. Genuine doctrine is the doctrine of charity and of faith together, and not the doctrine of faith without the other; for the doctrine of charity and of faith together is the doctrine of life, but not the doctrine of faith without the doctrine of charity. (H. D. n. 243.)

Who Constitute the Specific Church.

It is one thing for the church to be *with* a nation, and another for the church to be *in* a nation. As for example, the Christian church is *with* those who have the Word, and from doctrine preach the Lord; but yet there is nothing of the church in them unless they are in the marriage of good and truth; that is unless they are in charity towards the neighbour, and thence in faith; or unless the internals of the church are within the externals. (A. C. n. 4899.)

He who is not in spiritual good, that is in the good of charity, and in spiritual truths, that is in truths of faith, is not of the church although he was born within the church. . . . They that do not live according to the Word, or according to doctrine from the Word, so that it is the rule of life, are not of the church, but are out of it; and those who live in evil, thus who live contrary to doctrine, are farther out of the church than the Gentiles who know nothing at all of the Word, of the Lord, and of the Sacraments. For, since they know the goods and truths of the church they extinguish the church within them; which the Gentiles cannot do because they do no not know them. (A. C. n. 6637.)

The Church is one thing and Religion another.

The church is one thing and religion another. The church is called a church from doctrine; and religion is called religion from life according to doctrine. All doctrine is called truth; and its good also is truth, because it only teaches it. But everything of life according to those things which doctrine teaches is called good; doing the truths of doctrine likewise is good. Thus is the church distinguished from religion. But where there is doctrine and not life it cannot be said that there is either a church or religion; because doctrine looks to life, as one with itself,—just as do truth and good, faith and charity, wisdom and love, understanding and will. There is therefore no church where there is doctrine and not life. (A. R. n. 923.)

Who are meant by Gentiles?

In many places the Word refers to those that are in darkness, in the shadow of death, and in thick darkness, whose eyes the Lord will open; and by them the Gentiles are meant, who have been in good works but not in any truths, because they have not known the Lord, neither were in possession of the Word. Precisely similar to these are they in the Christian world who are in works alone, and in no truths of doctrine. They know of the Lord it is true, but yet do not approach Him; and they possess the Word, but do not search after the truths therein. (A. R. n. 110.)

The Good and Truth among the Gentiles is not constituent of the Church.

That the good of life may be [constituent] of the church there must be doctrinals from the Word which are implanted in that good. Without doctrinals it is indeed the good of life, but not yet good [constituent] of the church; thus not yet truly spiritual, save only as to its capacity to become so. Such is the good of life among the Gentiles who have not the Word, and therefore do not know of the Lord. (A. C. n. 3310.)

The Gentiles who are out of the church can be in truths, but not in truths of faith. . . . Truths of faith are all doctrinals concerning the life eternal, concerning the Lord's kingdom, and concerning the Lord. These cannot be known to them, because they have not the Word. (*ib.* n. 2049.)

The Necessity that there should always be a Church.

The human race, even those who are out of the church, derive life from the church of the Lord on earth. The reason is entirely unknown to any one. But that something may be known of it, it may be stated that the whole human race on earth is like the body with its parts, in which the church is as the heart; and unless there were a church, with which as with a kind of heart the Lord might be united, through heaven and the world of spirits, there would be a disjunction; and if there were a disjunction of the human race from the Lord it would instantly perish. This is the reason why from the first creation of man there has always been some church; and that as often as the church began to perish it still remained with some. This also was the reason of the Lord's advent into the world. Unless in His Divine mercy He had come the whole human race on this earth would have perished; for the church was then at the point of destruction, so that there was scarcely any surviving good and truth. The reason why the human race cannot live unless it is conjoined with the Lord, through heaven and the world of spirits, is because in himself regarded man is far viler than the brutes. If he were left to himself he would rush headlong to his own destruction, and that of all others; for he desires nothing but the ruin of them and himself. His order of life should be that one should love another as himself; but now, each loves himself more than others, and consequently hates all others. With the unreasoning animals it is quite different. It is their order, according to which they live. Thus they live entirely in agreement with the order in which they exist; but man altogether contrary to his order. Unless therefore the Lord should have compassion upon him, and conjoin him to Himself by the angels, he would not be able to live a moment. Man does not know this. (A. C. n. 637.)

The Church in Heaven could not subsist without a Church on the Earth.

It should be known that there is a church in the heavens as well as on earth; for the Word is there; there are temples, and preachings in them; there are ministerial and priestly offices. For all the angels there were men; and their departure out of the world was only a continuation of their life. They also are therefore perfected in love and wisdom, every one according to the degree of affection for truth and good which he took with him from the world. The church among them is meant here (Rev. xii. 1) by the woman clothed with the sun, who had upon her head a crown of twelve stars. And because the church in the heavens cannot subsist unless there is also a church on earth, which is in concordant love and wisdom, and because this was about to be, therefore the moon was seen under the feet of the woman; by which here in particular a faith is signified,—of such quality as it is at the present day,—by which there is no con-junction. The reason why the church in the heavens cannot subsist unless there is a church on earth, in conjunction with it, is that heaven where the angels are and the church where men are act as one, like the internal and external in man. And the internal in man cannot subsist in its state unless an external is conjoined with it; for the internal without the external is as a house without a foundation; or as seed upon the ground and not in the ground; and so like anything without a foothold; in a word as a cause without an effect in which it may exist. From these considerations it may appear how absolutely necessary it is that there should be a church somewhere in the world, where the Word is, and by means of it the Lord is known. (A. R. n. 533.)

WHEN THE CHURCH IS NEAR ITS END A NEW CHURCH IS ALWAYS RAISED UP.

When the end of the church is at hand, it is provided by the Lord that a new church shall succeed; because without a church in which the Word is, and in which the Lord is known, the world cannot subsist. For without the Word, and the knowledge and acknowledgment therefrom of the Lord, heaven cannot be con-joined to the human race; nor therefore can Divine truth pro-ceeding from the Lord flow in with new life; and without conjunction with heaven, and thereby with the Lord, man would not be man, but a beast. Hence it is that a new church is always provided by the Lord when an old church comes to its end. (A. E. n. 665.)[1]

THERE HAVE BEEN IN GENERAL FOUR CHURCHES ON THE EARTH.

That there have been four churches in general on this earth since its creation, one succeeding another, can be seen both from the historical and prophetical Word; especially in Daniel, where these four churches are described by the image seen by Nebu-chadnezzar in a dream (chap. ii.), and afterwards by the four beasts coming up out of the sea (chap. vii.). The first church, which is to be called the Most Ancient, existed before the flood; the consummation or end of this is described by the flood. The second church, which is to be called the Ancient, was in Asia, and in part in Africa; this was consummated and destroyed by idolatries. The third church was the Israelitish, which began with the promulgation of the decalogue upon Mount Sinai, and continued through the Word written by Moses and the prophets, and was consummated or ended by the profanation of the Word; the fulness of which profanation was at the time when the Lord

---

[1] The church cannot be raised up anew in any nation until it is en-tirely vastated. (See page 745.)

came into the world,—and therefore Him who was the Word they crucified. The fourth church is the Christian, established by the Lord through the evangelists and apostles. Of this there have been two epochs; one from the time of the Lord to the council of Nice, and the other from that council to the present day. But in its progress this church was divided into three parts, the Greek, the Roman Catholic, and the Reformed. They are all however called Christian. Besides, within each general church there have been several particular churches, which, although they have withdrawn have yet retained the name of the general; as the heresies in the Christian church. (T. C. R. n. 760.)

General Character of these four Churches.

In the most ancient times men were informed concerning heavenly things, or the things which relate to eternal life, by immediate intercourse with the angels of heaven. For heaven then acted as one with the man of the church, for it flowed in through the internal man into their external; whence they had not only enlightenment and perception, but also converse with the angels. This time was called the golden age, from the fact that men were then in the good of love to the Lord; for gold signifies that good. These things are also described by the Garden of Eden in the Word. Afterwards information concerning heavenly things, and concerning the things that relate to eternal life, was given by such things as are called correspondences and representations; the knowledge of which was derived from the most ancient men, who had immediate intercourse with the angels of heaven. Heaven then flowed into these things with them and enlightened them; for correspondences and representations are external forms of heavenly things. And men were then enlightened in proportion as they were in the good of love and charity; for all Divine influx out of heaven is into the good in man, and through the good into truths. And because the man of the church at that time was in spiritual good, which good in its essence is truth, those times were called the silver age; for silver signifies such good. But when the knowledge of correspondences and representations was turned into magic, that church perished; and a third succeeded, in which all worship was indeed performed by things almost similar, but yet it was unknown what they signified. This church was established among the Israelitish and Jewish nation. But as information concerning heavenly things, or the things which relate to eternal life, could not be communicated to them by influx into their interiors, and thus by enlightenment, therefore angels from heaven spoke by the living voice with some of them, and instructed them concerning external things; and little concerning internal things, because they could not comprehend them. Those who were in natural good received these things devoutly; and those times were therefore called the brazen age, for brass signifies such good. But when not even natural good remained with the man of the church, the Lord came into the world and reduced all things in the heavens and in the hells to order; to the end that man may receive influx from Him out of heaven, and be enlightened, and that the hells should not prevent and let in thick darkness. Then a fourth church began which is called Christian. In this church information concerning heavenly things, or concerning the things that relate to eternal life, is communicated solely by means of the Word; through this man has influx and enlightenment. For the Word was written by pure correspondences and pure representatives, which signify heavenly things,—into which the angels of heaven come when man reads the Word. Hence by means of the Word a conjunction of heaven with the church is effected, or of the angels of heaven with the men of the church; but only with those therein who are in the good of love and of charity. But because the man of this church has even extinguished this good, he cannot therefore be informed by any influx, and by enlightenment from the Word,—except concerning some truths which are not connected with good. Hence these times are what are called the iron age; for iron denotes truth in the ultimate of order. But when truth is such it is of the quality described in Daniel: " *Thou sawest iron mixed with miry clay; they shall mingle themselves by the seed of man, but they shall not cleave one to another, even as iron is not mixed with clay*" (ii. 43). From these facts it may be seen how revelations have succeeded, from the most ancient times down to the present; and that at this day revelation is only given through the Word. But genuine revelation is with those who are in the love of truth for the sake of truth, and not with those who are in the love of truth for the sake of honour and gain as ends. For, if you will believe it, the Lord is the Word itself, since the Word is Divine truth, and Divine truth, because from the Lord, is the Lord in heaven. They therefore who love Divine truth for the sake of Divine truth love the Lord; and heaven flows in with those who love the Lord, and enlightens them. But they that love Divine truth for the sake of honour and gain as ends, turn themselves away from the Lord to themselves and to the world; and therefore with them there can be no influx and enlightenment. They also, because in the sense of the letter they keep their minds fixed upon themselves and upon their own fame and glory, interpret that sense in conformity with such things as favour their loves. (A. C. n. 10,355.)

THE FIRST OR MOST ANCIENT CHURCH.

THIS church above all the churches on the whole globe was from the Divine; for it was in the good of love to the Lord. Their voluntary and intellectual part made one, thus one mind. They therefore had a perception of truth from good; for the Lord flowed in through an internal way into the good of their will, and through this into the good of the understanding or truth. Hence it is that that church in preference to the others was called Man[1] (Adam), and also a likeness of God. (A. C. n. 4454.)

The Most Ancient church had immediate revelation from the Lord through their fellowship with spirits and angels; and also by means of visions and dreams,—from which it was given them, in a general way, to know what was good and true. And when they knew generally, then by means of perceptions they confirmed these general goods and truths as principles, by innumerable other things, which were the particulars or single things of the generals to which they related. General [perceptions] were thus daily confirmed as principles. Whatever was not in agreement with general principles they perceived was not true, and whatever was accordant with them they perceived to be true. Such also is the state of the celestial angels. In the Most Ancient church the generals which were as principles were celestial and eternal verities; as, that the Lord governs the universe; that all good and truth are from the Lord; that all life is from the Lord; that man's *proprium* is nothing but evil; and that in itself it is dead; with other like things. They received from the Lord a perception of innumerable things confirming, and harmonizing with them. Love, with them, was the principal of faith; and through love it was given them of the Lord to perceive whatever was of faith; and therefore faith with them was love, as was said before. (*ib.* n. 597.)

The Word in the Most Ancient church, which was before the flood, was not a written Word, but was revealed to every one who was of the church; for they were celestial men, and so were in the perception of good and truth, like the angels, with whom

[1] The word *Adam* אָדָם is the Hebrew generic word for man; corresponding with the Latin *homo*, and with our word *man* in the sense of mankind.

also they had fellowship. They thus had the Word inscribed on their hearts. (*ib.* n. 2896.)

THE WORSHIP OF THE MOST ANCIENT CHURCH.

The man of the Most Ancient church had no other than internal worship, such as there is in heaven; for with them heaven so communicated with man that they made one. This communication was the perception of which so much has been said above. And being thus angelic they were internal men; sensible indeed of the external things relating to their bodies and the world, but not caring for them; perceiving in all objects of sense something Divine and heavenly. Thus, for example, when they saw any high mountain, they did not receive the idea of a mountain, but of height, and from height they had a perception of heaven and of the Lord. Hence it came to pass that the Lord was said to dwell on high; and that He Himself was called the Highest, and the Most Exalted; and that the worship of the Lord was afterwards offered up on mountains. And so in other things. Thus, when they perceived the morning, they did not perceive the morning itself of the day, but the heavenly state which was like the morning and day-dawn in their minds. Hence the Lord was called the Morning, the East (*Oriens*), and the Day-Spring. So when they beheld a tree, and its fruit and leaves, their attention was not occupied with these, but they saw in them as it were man represented,—in the fruit, love and charity; in the leaves, faith. Hence too the man of the church was not only compared to a tree and so to a paradise, and what was in him to fruit and leaves, but they were even so called. Such are they who are in heavenly and angelic ideas. Every one can recognise the fact that the general idea governs all particulars,—thus, all the objects of sense, both those that they see and those that they hear; and even so that they pay no attention to the objects, except in so far as they flow in with one's general idea. Thus, to him who is of joyful mind all things that he sees and hears appear as it were smiling and joyful; and to him who is of sorrowful mind, all things that he sees and hears appear as if sad and sorrowful. So with all other things. For the general affection is in the particular things, and makes one see and hear particular things in the general affection. Otherwise they do not even appear, but are as if they were absent, or as nothing. Thus it was with the man of the Most Ancient church; whatever he saw with his eyes was to him heavenly; and thus with him each and all things were as if alive. From this it is evident what the nature of his Divine worship was; that it was internal, and in no respect external. (A. C. n. 920.)

The reason why a tent is taken in the Word to represent the celestial and holy things of love is, that in ancient times they performed holy worship in their tents. But when they began to profane tents by unholy worship the tabernacle was built, and afterwards the temple; and therefore what the tabernacle and afterwards the temple represented was also signified by tents. For the same reason a holy man was called a tent, and a tabernacle, and also a temple of the Lord. That a tent, a tabernacle, and a temple have the same signification is evident in David: " *One thing have I desired of Jehovah, that will I seek after; that I may dwell in the house of Jehovah all the days of my life, to behold the beauty of Jehovah, and to inquire in His temple; for in the time of trouble He shall hide me in His tabernacle; in the secret of His tent shall He hide me; He shall set me up upon a rock. And now shall mine head be lifted up above mine enemies round about me, and I will offer in His tent sacrifices of shouting* " (Psalm xxvii. 4-6). In the highest sense the Lord as to His Human essence is the tent, the tabernacle, and the temple. Hence every celestial man is so called; and everything celestial and holy. And because the Most Ancient church was more beloved of the Lord than any which succeeded, and they then lived apart or in their own families, and celebrated so holy worship in their tents, therefore tents were accounted more holy than the temple which was profaned. In remembrance thereof the feast of tabernacles was instituted, when they gathered the increase of the land; during which they dwelt in tabernacles, like the most ancients (Levit. xxiii. 39-44; Deut. xvi. 13; Hosea xii. 9). (A. C. n. 414.)

By the names which follow, as Seth, Enos, Cainan, Mahalaleel, Jared, Enoch, Methuselah, Lamech, and Noah, so many churches are meant, of which the first and principal was the one called Man.[1] Of these churches the chief characteristic was perception; and therefore the differences of the churches of that time were chiefly differences of perception. Concerning perception it may here be mentioned that in the universal heaven there prevails only perception of good and truth; and it is such that

---

[1] See note p. 328. For a full account of the successive propagations of the Most Ancient church, indicated by the various names in Genesis, from Adam to Lamech, or to near the time of the deluge, see A. C. 468-536. F.

it cannot be described,—with innumerable differences, so that one society has not the same perception as another. There are genera and species of perceptions there, and the genera are innumerable, and the species of each genus are likewise innumerable; of which by the Divine mercy of the Lord hereafter. Since there are innumerable genera, and innumerable species of each genus, and still more innumerable varieties in each species, it can be seen how little,—almost nothing,—the world knows at this day about spiritual and celestial things, when it does not even know what perception is, and if told does not believe that it exists. And so with other things. The Most Ancient church represented the celestial kingdom of the Lord, even as to the generic and specific differences of perception. But as what perception is, in its most general character, is at this day utterly unknown, if the genera and species of the perceptions of these churches were described, nothing but strange and unaccountable things would be told. They were for that reason distinguished into houses, families, and tribes, and contracted marriages within the houses and families,—in order that genera and species of perceptions might exist, and be derived no otherwise than according to propagations of native qualities from parents. Those who were of the Most Ancient church therefore dwell together also in heaven. (A. C. n. 483.)

These three churches, Man, Seth, and Enos, constitute the Most Ancient church; yet with a difference of perfection as to their perceptions. The perceptive faculty of the first church here and there diminished in the succeeding churches, and became more general. Perfection consists in the faculty of perceiving distinctly; which is diminished when the perception becomes not so distinct and more general. Then in place of the clearer perception an obscurer succeeds; and so it begins to pass away. (*ib.* n. 502.)

Enos, as was said, is the third church,—one of the Most Ancient, but less celestial and consequently less perceptive than the church Seth; and this was not so celestial and perceptive as the parent church called Man. These three, which constitute the Most Ancient church, relatively to those that follow, are as it were the kernel of the fruits or seeds; and the following compare, relatively, to their investing membrane. (*ib.* n. 505.)

PERCEPTION IN THE MOST ANCIENT CHURCH.

With the man of the Most Ancient church there was ground in his will, in which the Lord inseminated goods; in consequence of which he was enabled to know and perceive what was true, or by love to obtain faith; but were this the case now man must necessarily perish eternally, since his will is altogether corrupt. Hence it may be seen how insemination into the will and understanding of man is effected. The man of the Most Ancient church had revelations, by which from infancy he was initiated into the perception of goods and truths; and as these were inseminated into his will, he had a perception of innumerable others without fresh instruction; so that from one general truth he became acquainted with particulars and least particulars from the Lord,—which man must now learn, and thus know. It is scarcely possible, however, now to acquire a thousandth part of the knowledge which they possessed; for the man of the spiritual church knows only what he learns, and what he thus knows he retains and believes to be true. Yea, if he learns what is false, and this is impressed upon him as if it were true, he believes this also; for he has no other perception than that it is so because he has been so persuaded. (A. C. n. 895.)

DIGNITIES AND RICHES AMONG THE MOST ANCIENT MEN.

Dignities and riches in the most ancient times were entirely different from what they gradually became afterwards. In the most ancient times dignities were none other than such as there are among parents and children; which were dignities of love, full of respect and veneration,—not on account of their birth from them, but because of instruction and wisdom received from them, which is a second birth, in itself spiritual, because it was of their spirit. This in the most ancient times was the only dignity; because tribes, families, and houses then dwelt separately, and not as at this day under empires. It was the father of the family in whom this dignity resided. Those times were called by the ancients the golden age. But after those times the love of rule from the mere delight of that love gradually entered; and because there entered at the same time enmity and hostility against those who would not submit, then of necessity tribes, families, and houses gathered themselves into communities, and set over them one whom in the beginning they called a judge, afterwards a prince, and finally a king, and emperor. And then they began also to protect themselves by towers and bulwarks and walls. From the judge, prince, king, and emperor, as from the head into the body, the lust of ruling entered into many like a contagion. Hence arose degrees of dignity, and also honours according to them; and with them the love of self, and pride in their own prudence. Something similar took place with respect to the love of riches. In the most ancient times, when tribes and families dwelt separately from each other, there was no other love of riches than that they might possess the necessaries of life; which they procured for themselves by flocks and herds, and by fields, pastures, and gardens, which furnished them with food. Among the necessaries of their life were also suitable houses, furnished with all kinds of useful things; and also clothing. The parents, children, men-servants, and maid-servants in the house, were occupied in the care and service of all these things. But after the love of ruling entered, and destroyed this commonweal, the love of possessing riches beyond their necessities also entered, and rose to such a height that it desired to possess the wealth of all. These two loves are like kindred; for they who desire to rule over all things desire also to possess all things; for thus all become servants, and they alone masters. (D. P. n. 215.)

THE FOOD OF THE MOST ANCIENT MEN.

Eating the flesh of animals, considered in itself, is somewhat profane; for in the most ancient times they never ate the flesh of any beast or bird, but only grain,—especially bread made of wheat,—the fruits of trees, vegetables, milks, and such things as are made from them, as butter, etc. To kill animals and eat their flesh was to them unlawful, being regarded as something bestial. They only took from them uses and services, as is evident from Gen. i. 29, 30. But in the course of time, when mankind became cruel like wild beasts, yea, more cruel, then first they began to kill animals and eat their flesh. And because man had acquired such a nature the killing and eating of animals was permitted, and is permitted at the present day. (A. C. n. 1002.)

A REMNANT OF THE MOST ANCIENT CHURCH IN THE LAND OF CANAAN.

Remains of the Most Ancient Church, which was Celestial, were still in the land of Canaan [when the Israelites took possession]; and especially among those there who were called Hittites and Hivites. That they were not elsewhere was because the Most Ancient Church, which was called Man or Adam, was in the land of Canaan; and therefore the garden of Eden was there, by which the intelligence and wisdom of that church were signified. (A. C. n. 4447.)

THE SECOND OR ANCIENT CHURCH.

NOAH signifies a new church, which must be called the Ancient church,—to distinguish between the Most Ancient, which was before the flood, and that which existed after the flood. The states of those churches were entirely different. The characteristic of the Most Ancient church was, that they had a perception of good and thence of truth from the Lord; the characteristic of the Ancient church, or Noah, was that they possessed a conscience of what is good and true. Such as the difference is between having perception and having conscience, such was the difference of state between the Most Ancient church and the Ancient church. Perception is not conscience. The celestial have perception; the spiritual have conscience. The Most Ancient church was celestial; but the Ancient was spiritual. (A. C. n. 597. See also p. 293.)

The Most Ancient church from love had cognizance of whatever was of faith; or what is the same, from a will for good they had an understanding of truth. But their descendants derived,—from what was hereditary too,—that lusts which are of the will dominated among them; in which they even immersed the doctrinal truths of faith. . . . When therefore the Lord foresaw that if man remained so constituted he would perish eternally, it was provided of the Lord that the will should be separated from the understanding; and that man should be formed, not as before by a will for good, but that through the understanding of truth charity should be given him, which appears as if it were a will for good. This new church which is called Noah was so constituted; and was therefore of an entirely different character from the Most Ancient church. (*ib.* n. 640.)

The Ancient church, as was said before, was of a different character from the Most Ancient; for it was spiritual, which is such that a man is born again by means of the doctrinal truths of faith. When these are implanted, a conscience is insinuated into him that he may not act contrary to the truth and good of faith; and thus he is endowed with charity, which governs his conscience, and from which he begins to act. Hence it is evident that a spiritual man is not one who believes that faith is saving without charity, but who makes charity the essential of faith, and acts from it. (*ib.* n. 765.)

The state of the Most Ancient church was such that they had internal communication with heaven, and so through heaven with the Lord; they were in love to the Lord,—and all who are in love to the Lord are as angels, only with the difference that they are clothed with a material body,—and their interiors were opened, and continued open even from the Lord. But it was otherwise with this new church, which was not in love to the Lord but in faith, and by faith in charity towards the neighbour. They could not, like the most ancients, have internal communication with heaven, but only external. But to describe the nature of these two kinds of communication would be prolix. All men,—even the wicked have communication with heaven, through the angels who are with them; but with a difference as to degree, in that it is nearer or more remote. Otherwise man could not exist. The degrees of communication are indefinite. The spiritual man can never have such communication as the celestial man ; for the reason that the Lord dwells in love, and not so much in faith. . . . Since those times heaven has never been open, as it was to the man of the Most Ancient church. After that it is true many talked with spirits and angels,—Moses, Aaron, and others,—but in quite another manner; of which, by the Divine mercy of the Lord, hereafter. (*ib.* n. 784.)

The Ancient church, which was established by the Lord after the flood, was a representative church ; which was such that each and all of its externals of worship represented celestial and spiritual things which are of the Lord's kingdom, and in the highest sense Divine things themselves of the Lord ; and its internals of worship each and all had reference to charity. That church was spread throughout much of the Asiatic world, and over many kingdoms there ; and although they differed as to doctrinals of faith, yet it was one church, because they all everywhere made charity the essential of the church. (*ib.* n. 4680.)

Noah, Shem, Ham, and Japheth, although four, yet constitute one. In Noah, by whom the Ancient church in general is meant, are contained as in the parent, or seed, the churches derived from it. . . . All these churches, called Shem, Ham, and Japheth, together constitute the church which is called the Ancient church. (*ib.* n. 773.)

THE ANCIENT CHURCH WAS IN REPRESENTATIVES AND SIGNIFICATIVES.

The truths possessed by the ancients are at this day entirely forgotten ; insomuch that scarcely any one knows that they ever were, and that they could be other than what are taught at this day. But they were quite different. They had representatives and significatives of the celestial and spiritual things of the Lord's kingdom; and so of the Lord Himself. And those that understood such representatives and significatives were called wise; and they also were wise, for they were thus able to talk with spirits and angels. For angelic speech,—which is incomprehensible to man, because it is spiritual and celestial,—when it descends to man, who is in the natural sphere, falls into representatives and significatives such as are in the Word. Hence it is that the Word is a holy book; for the Divine cannot otherwise be presented before the natural man so that there may be full correspondence. And as the ancients were in representatives and significatives of the Lord's kingdom, in which there is nothing but celestial and spiritual love, they also had doctrinals which related only to love to God and charity towards the neighbour; from which doctrinals also they were called wise. From these doctrinals they knew that the Lord would come into the world; and that Jehovah would be in Him; and that He would make the human in Himself Divine, and would thus save the human race. From these doctrinals they also knew what charity is,—namely, an affection for serving others without any view to recompense; and what the neighbour is towards whom charity should be exercised,—namely, all in the universe, but yet to each with discrimination. These doctrinals at this day are entirely lost; and in place of them are doctrinals of faith, which the ancients accounted as relatively nothing. (A. C. n. 3419.)

THE WORSHIP OF THE ANCIENT CHURCH.

The most ancient people who were before the flood saw in each and all things,—as in mountains, hills, plains, valleys, in gardens, groves, and forests, in rivers and waters, in fields and growing crops, in trees of every kind, in animals also of every kind, and in the luminaries of heaven,—something representative and significative of the Lord's kingdom. Their eyes, however,—still less their minds,—did not dwell upon the visible objects; but to them they were the means of thought concerning things celestial and spiritual in the Lord's kingdom; and this to such a degree that there was nothing in universal nature that did not serve them as means. It is indeed true in itself that each and all things in nature are representative; which at this day is a mystery, and scarcely believed by any one. But after the celestial which is of love to the Lord perished, mankind were no longer in that state; that is, in a state to see the celestial and spiritual things of the Lord's kingdom by outward objects as means. But yet the ancients after the flood, from traditions and the collections of some, knew that they were significative; and because they were significative they accounted them holy. Hence the representative worship of the Ancient church; which church, as it was spiritual, was not in the perception but in the cognition that it was so; for it was in a state relatively dim. Still, however, that church did not worship external things, but by external things were reminded of internal; and hence, when they were in those representatives and significatives they were in holy worship. They indeed could be so because they were in spiritual love, that is in charity,—which they made the essential of worship ; and therefore what is holy from the Lord could flow into their worship. (A. C. n. 2722.)

The doctrinals of the Ancient church,—collected from men of the Most Ancient church,—consisted solely of things significative, and so, as it were, enigmatical; namely, of what the things on earth signified,—as that mountains, the morning, and the east signified things celestial, and the Lord; and trees of different kinds with their fruits, man and what is heavenly in him; and so with other things. Of such things did the doctrinals consist which were collected from the significatives of the Most Ancient church; and therefore their writings also were of a similar character. And because in such things they admired and seemed to themselves to behold what is Divine and heavenly,—and also because they admired what was ancient,— their worship from similar things was begun and permitted. Hence their worship upon mountains, and in groves in the midst of trees; hence their statues under the open sky; and at length their altars and burnt-offerings,—which afterwards became the principal things in all worship. (*ib.* n. 920.)

The Ancient Style of Writing.

The most ancient manner of writing was representative of things, by persons and by words whereby they meant entirely different matters from what were apparently expressed. Then profane writers thus joined their histories together, even matters of civil and moral life; and in fact so that nothing was precisely as it was written, as regards the letter, but under these things there was another meaning. To such a degree was this the case that they presented all affections as gods and goddesses; to whom the heathen afterwards instituted Divine worship. That this was so must be known to every man of letters; for such ancient books are still extant. This method of writing they derived from the most ancient people, who lived before the flood; and who represented to themselves things heavenly and Divine by the things that were visible on earth and in the world; and thus filled their minds and souls with joyous and delightful perceptions, when they beheld the objects of the universe,— especially such as were beautiful on account of their form and order. Therefore all books of the church in those times were thus written. Such is the book of Job; in imitation of them, such is Solomon's Song; and such were the two books mentioned by Moses in Numb. xxi. 14, 27; besides many which have been lost. This style of writing was thereafter venerated, both among the Gentiles and among the descendants of Jacob, on account of its antiquity; insomuch that whatever was not so written they did not reverence as Divine. And therefore when they were acted on by the prophetic spirit,—as was Jacob (Gen. xlix. 3-17); Moses (Exod. xv. 1-21; Deut. xxxiii. 2 to the end); Balaam, who was of the sons of the east from Syria, where the Ancient church then was (Numb. xxiii. 7-10, 19-24; xxiv. 5-9, 17-24); and as were Deborah and Barak (Judges v. 2 to the end); Hannah (1 Sam. ii. 2-10), and many others,—they spoke in a similar manner, and this for several hidden reasons. And although they did not understand them, and but very few knew that they signified heavenly things of the Lord's kingdom and church, yet, touched and filled with awe, they were sensible of the presence of what was Divine and holy in them. But that the historical parts of the Word are similar,—namely, representative and significative of the celestial and spiritual things of the Lord's kingdom, as to every single name and word,—has not yet been recognized by the learned world; only that the Word as to the least jot was inspired, and that there are heavenly arcana in each and all things therein. (A. C. n. 1756.)

The Decline of the Ancient Church.

With the churches after the flood the case was this:—There were three churches which are specially mentioned in the Word; namely, the first Ancient church, which was named from Noah; the second Ancient church, which was named from Eber; and the third Ancient church, which was named from Jacob, and afterwards from Judah and Israel. As regards the first church, that which was called Noah, it was as the parent of those that followed; and, as is usual with churches in their beginnings, it was more spotless and innocent; as appears too from the first verse of this chapter (Gen. xi.), where it is said that it had one lip, that is one doctrine,—namely, charity in all things,—as essential. But this church also, as is usual with churches, in process of time began to fall away; and this chiefly from the fact that many of them began to divert worship to themselves, that thus they might be distinguished above others : " *For they said, Let us build us a city and a tower, and the head thereof in heaven; and let us make us a name* " (ver. 4). Such could not be otherwise than as a kind of leaven in the church, or as a firebrand producing a conflagration. When consequently the danger of profanation of what is holy was imminent, the state of this church, of the Lord's providence, was changed, so that its internal worship perished and the external remained. This is here (ver. 7-9) signified by Jehovah confounding the lip of the whole earth. From this also it appears that such worship, which is called Babel, did not prevail in the first Ancient church; but in succeeding churches, when men began to be worshipped as gods, especially after death,—whence came so many gods of the Gentiles. (A. C. n. 1327.)

They who at the time of the Ancient church separated faith from charity, and made faith the essential of the church, were called Ham.[1] But in process of time this church turned away to idolatrous, and in Egypt, Babel, and elsewhere, to magical [practices] ; for they began to worship external things without internal,—and as they thus departed from charity heaven receded from them, and in its place came spirits from hell who led them. (*ib.* n. 4680.)

The Second Ancient Church, called Eber, and origin of Sacrificial Worship.

The first Ancient church, signified by Noah and his sons, was not confined to a few, as is evident from the nations mentioned,[2] but extended over many kingdoms ; certainly over Assyria, Mesopotamia, Syria, Ethiopia, Arabia, Libya, Egypt, Philistia, as

[1] See p. 153.

[2] The author teaches that the most ancient of the four styles in which the Word is written (see p. 124),—consisting not of actual but of composed historical narratives,—continues down to the mention of Eber, in the eleventh chapter of Genesis, where true history in the letter of the Word begins (A. C. n. 1403-1407). But in the tenth chapter, and the eleventh to that point, he states, the style becomes intermediate between that of composed and of actual history (*ib.* n. 1140) ; and the names in the genealogies of Noah and his sons,—though not names of persons, for such persons never existed,—were the names of nations among whom the Ancient church was spread, and to whom it descended in its successive decline, as by spiritual generations (*ib.*). The successive generations mark the actual downward steps of this declension ; and the several names in each generation, the distinguishing characteristics of the several branches of the church, among the different peoples with whom the church existed, in each general stage of its declension.

far as Tyre and Sidon, and over the whole land of Canaan, on this and on the other side Jordan. But a kind of external worship afterwards began in Syria, which in process of time became widely spread,—and in fact over many countries, especially in the land of Canaan,—-which was different from the worship of the Ancient church. And as somewhat of a church thence arose which was separate from the Ancient church, there sprung therefrom a *quasi* new church, which may therefore be called a second Ancient church. The first institutor of it was Eber; for which reason that church was named from Eber. At that time, as has been said before, all were distinguished into houses, families, and nations. One nation acknowledged one father, from whom it also derived its name; and thus the nation which acknowledged Eber as its father was called the Hebrew nation. (A. C. n. 1238.) [This form of society had continued down to them from the most ancient times.[1] *ib.* n. 470, 471.]

As regards Eber being the first founder of a second Ancient church, by whom that church is signified (Gen. x. 24, 25; xi. 14, *seq.*), the case is this:—The first Ancient church, so widely extended as was said over especially the Asiatic world, in the course of time,—as all churches everywhere are wont,—degenerated, and was corrupted by innovators, both as to its external and internal worship; and this in various places. Especially by the fact that all the significatives and representatives which the Ancient church received orally from the Most Ancient church,—all which had reference to the Lord and His kingdom,—were turned to idolatrous and among some nations to magical [purposes]. That the universal church might not perish, it was permitted by the Lord that significative and representative worship should be somewhere restored; which was done by Eber. This worship consisted chiefly in things external. The externals of worship were high places, groves, statues, anointings,—besides priestly offices and things belonging to the priestly functions, and many other things which were called statutes. The internals of worship were doctrinals, from the antediluvian period,—especially from those who were called Enoch,[2] who gathered together the perceived truths of the Most Ancient church and formed doctrinals from them. These were their Word. Of these externals and internals did the worship established by Eber consist,—but increased, and also changed. Especially they began to prefer sacrifices to other rituals,—which in the true Ancient church were unknown; except that they were permitted among some descendants of Ham and Canaan therein, who were idolaters, lest they should sacrifice their sons and daughters. (*ib.* n. 1241.)

[1] See p. 332. [2] See p. 146.

The kind of new church begun by Eber, called the Hebrew church, was in Syria and Mesopotamia, and also among some nations in the land of Canaan; but it differed from the Ancient church in that it placed the essential of external worship in sacrifices. It acknowledged indeed that the internal of worship was charity, but not so much in heart as the Ancient church. (*ib.* n. 4680.)

The Most Ancient church, which was before the flood, never knew anything of sacrifices; nor did it ever come into their minds that they should worship the Lord by the immolation of animals. The Ancient church, which was after the flood, was also ignorant of them. This church indeed was in representatives, but they had no sacrifices.[1] They were in fact first instituted in the succeeding which was called the Hebrew church, and from thence went forth to the nations; from thence also they descended to Abraham, Isaac, and Jacob, and so to his posterity. (*ib.* n. 2180.)

SACRIFICES WERE AT FIRST OFFERED TO JEHOVAH, AND AFTERWARDS BECAME IDOLATROUS.

Their worship was such as was afterwards restored among the posterity of Jacob; and its chief characteristic consisted in the fact that they called Jehovah their God, and offered sacrifices. The Most Ancient church with one mind acknowledged the Lord, and called Him Jehovah,—as appears from the first chapters of Genesis, and also from other parts of the Word. The Ancient church, that is the church after the flood, also acknowledged the Lord and called Him Jehovah,—especially those who had internal worship, and were called sons of Shem; but the others, too, who were in external worship, acknowledged Jehovah and worshipped Him. But when internal worship became external, and when it became even idolatrous, and when each nation began to have its own god which it worshipped, the Hebrew nation retained the name of Jehovah, and called Jehovah its God; and in this they were distinguished from other nations (*ib.* n. 1343). But this church also became idolatrous; and at length it pleased the Lord to establish a new

---

[1] It should be noted that the account of the offerings of Cain and Abel (Gen. iv. 3-5), and of Noah's sacrifice, is in the part of the Word which the author states is not actual history. Of the latter in particular he says,—"What is said of Noah (Gen. viii. 20), that he offered burnt-offerings to Jehovah, is not actual history; but was made historical, because by burnt-offerings the holiness of worship was signified,—as may there be seen" (A. C. n. 1343). Such composed historical narrations, which were not actual facts but mere representative descriptions, appear to have been the mental types which the gross sensualism of the church in its last decline realized, or rather materialized in outward sacrifices.

church among the posterity of Abraham by Jacob, and to introduce among that nation the external worship of the Ancient church. But that nation was such that it could not receive any internal of the church; because at heart they were entirely opposed to charity. (*ib.* n. 4680.)

All the Nations which adopted Sacrificial Worship were called Hebrews.

From the nation which derived its name from Eber as its father, all were called Hebrews who were in similar worship; because there the new worship began. . . . That the posterity of Jacob was not the only Hebrew nation, but that all who had such worship were called Hebrews, is evident from the fact that the land of Canaan was called the land of the Hebrews even in the time of Joseph: "*Joseph said, I was stolen out of the land of the Hebrews*" (Gen. xl. 15). That there were sacrifices among the idolaters in the land of Canaan is abundantly evident; for they sacrificed to their gods,—to Baal and others. It appears, moreover, that Balaam,—who was from Syria where Eber dwelt, and whence the Hebrew nation came,—not only offered sacrifices before the posterity of Jacob came into the land of Canaan, but also called Jehovah his God. That Balaam was from Syria, whence came the Hebrew nation, may be seen in Numb. xxii. 39; xxiii. 1-3, 14, 29; that he called Jehovah his God in chap. xxii. 18, *seq.* (A. C. n. 1343.)

Worship was signified by the altar, because it was signified by the burnt-offerings and sacrifices that were offered upon it,— in many passages of the Word, too numerous to be cited. And because idolatrous worship was signified by the altars of the nations, it was commanded that they should be everywhere destroyed (Deut. vii. 5; xii. 3; Judges ii. 2; and elsewhere). Hence it appears that altars were in use among all the posterity of Eber, and so among those who were called Hebrews,—who for the most part were in the land of Canaan and immediately around it, and also in Syria, whence Abram came. (A. E. n. 391.)

Others of the Ancient Church abominated Sacrifices, and abominated the Hebrews on account of them.

That there were altars in the land of Canaan and immediately around it, is certain from the altars that are mentioned there, and which were destroyed. That they existed also in Syria is clear from the altars erected by Balaam, who was from Syria (Numb. xxiii. 1), and from the altar in Damascus (2 Kings xvi.

10-15); and from the fact that the Egyptians abominated the Hebrews on account of their sacrifices (Exod. viii. 22), even to such a degree that they would not eat bread with them (Gen. xliii. 32). The reason was, that the Ancient church,—which was a representative church, and extended over a great part of the Asiatic world,—had no knowledge of sacrifices, and, when they were instituted by Eber, looked upon them as abominable, in that they would propitiate God by the slaughter of various animals, and thus by blood. The Egyptians were also among those who were of the Ancient church; but that church became extinct among them, because they applied representatives to magical purposes. The reason why they would not eat bread with the Hebrews was, that spiritual consociation was at that time represented, and therefore signified, by dinners and suppers,—which is consociation and conjunction by things that appertain to the church; and by bread in general all spiritual food was signified, and therefore by dining and supping all spiritual conjunction. (A. E. n. 391; see also A. C. n. 1343, *et al.*)

That sacrifices, in which the Hebrew church made its worship chiefly to consist, were an abomination to the Egyptians appears in Moses:—"*Pharaoh said, Go ye, sacrifice, . . . in the land. But Moses said, It is not meet so to do; for we shall sacrifice the abomination of the Egyptians to Jehovah our God. Lo, if we sacrifice the abomination of the Egyptians, in their eyes, will they not stone us?*" (Exod. viii. 25, 26.) (A. C. n. 5702.)

Gradual Descent of the Hebrew Church to Idolatry.

Eber was a nation,—called the Hebrew nation, from Eber as its father,—by which is signified the worship of the second Ancient church in general. (A. C. n. 1342.)

This Second Ancient church, from a kind of internal worship, degenerated and was corrupted until at last it became idolatrous, —as churches are wont to do, in that they pass from their internal things to external, and end at last in mere externals,[1] internal things being blotted out of remembrance. (*ib.* n. 1356.)

The kind of new church begun by Eber, . . . though it differed from the Ancient church in that it placed the essential of external worship in sacrifices, yet acknowledged that the internal of worship is charity; but not so much in heart as the Ancient church. (*ib.* n. 4680.)

---

[1] The author teaches (A. C. n. 4825, *et al.*) that the *principle* of idolatry does not consist in the worship of idols and graven images, but in external worship without internal.

Peleg [the first in descent from Eber] was a nation so called, from him as its father, by which external worship is signified. . . . Reu [son of Peleg, and second in descent from Eber] was a nation so called, from him as its father, which signified worship still more external. . . . Serug [son of Reu, the third in descent] was a nation so named, from him as its father, by which is signified worship in the externals. . . . Nahor [son of Serug, the fourth in descent] was a nation so named, from him as its father, by which is signified worship verging upon idolatrous. . . . Terah [son of Nahor, and father of Abram, Nahor, and Haran,— the fifth in descent from Eber] was a nation so named, from him as its father, by which idolatrous worship is signified. . . . Abram, Nahor, and Haran were persons, from whom also nations were named which were idolaters. (*ib.* n. 1345-1355.)

That this church degenerated to such a degree that a large part of them did not acknowledge Jehovah as God, but worshipped other gods, is evident in Joshua:—"*Joshua said unto all the people, Thus saith Jehovah the God of Israel, Your fathers dwelt on the other side of the river in old time, even Terah the father of Abram and the father of Nahor, and they served other gods. . . . Now therefore fear Jehovah, and serve Him in sincerity and in truth; and put away the gods which your fathers served beyond the river, and in Egypt, and serve ye Jehovah. And if it seem evil in your eyes to serve Jehovah, choose ye this day whom ye will serve; whether the gods which your fathers served who were beyond the river, or the gods of the Amorites*" (xxiv. 2, 14, 15). It is here very manifest that Terah, Abram, and Nahor were idolaters. That Nahor was a nation, in which there was idolatrous worship, is evident also from Laban the Syrian, who dwelt in the city of Nahor,[1] and worshipped images, or teraphim, which Rachel took away (Gen. xxiv. 10; xxxi. 19, 26, 32, 34). And it appears from Gen. xxxi. 53, that there was one god of Abraham, another god of Nahor, and another of their father Terah. It is therefore evident how much this church declined among this nation into idolatrous worship. (*ib.* n. 1356.)

IDOLATRY OF THE HOUSE OF TERAH, WHILE THERE WERE OTHER HEBREW NATIONS THAT RETAINED THE WORSHIP OF JEHOVAH.

In Syria whence Abram came there lingered remains of the Ancient church, and many families there retained the worship of that church,—which is evident from Eber, who was of that country, from whom the Hebrew nation descended; and they likewise retained the name of Jehovah, as has already been

---

[1] "Cities," the Author states, "were but families which dwelt together; and many families constituted a nation." (A. C. n. 1358.)

clearly shown, and as appears from Balaam, who was from Syria, and offered sacrifices, and called Jehovah his God.[1] But it was not so with the house of Terah, the father of Abram and Nahor. This was one among the families of nations there which had not only lost the name of Jehovah, but also served other gods; and in place of Jehovah they worshipped Shaddai, whom they called their god. It is expressly declared concerning Abram that Jehovah was not known to him; and that instead of Jehovah they worshipped Shaddai, whom they called their god:—"*I appeared unto Abraham, unto Isaac, and unto Jacob, in God Shaddai; but by My name Jehovah was I not known to them*" (Exod. vi. 3). (A. C. n. 1992, 1356.)

The ancients designated the one only God by various names, according to His attributes, and according to the various things that are from Him; and as they believed that temptations too are from Him, in time of temptation they called God, Shaddai. Yet by this name they did not mean another god, but the one only God with respect to temptations. But when the Ancient church declined they began to worship as many gods as there were names of the one God, and also of themselves added many more. This at length so prevailed that every family had its god, and distinguished it entirely from the rest that were worshipped by others. The family of Terah, from whom Abram came, worshipped Shaddai for its god. Hence not only Abraham but Jacob also, and in the land of Canaan too, acknowledged him as their god. But this was permitted them, that they might not be forced from their religion; for no one is forced from what he regards as holy. But as the ancients meant by Shaddai Jehovah Himself, or the Lord,—who was so called when they were suffering temptations,—therefore Jehovah or the Lord took this name with Abraham (as appears from Gen. xvii. 1), and also with Jacob (xxxv. 11). That not only temptation, but also consolation was signified by Shaddai, is because consolation follows after all spiritual temptations. (*ib.* n. 5628, 3667.)

Hence it appears that in his youth Abram was, like other Gentiles, an idolater; and that up to this time (Gen. xvii. 1), while he was in the land of Canaan, he had not rejected from his mind the god Shaddai,—by which, in the literal sense, the name of the god of Abram is denoted. And that the Lord was first represented before them by this name,—that is before Abram, Isaac, and Jacob,—appears from the passage just cited (Exod. vi. 3). The reason why the Lord was willing first to be represented before them by the name Shaddai was, that the Lord

[1] That he was of Syria, see Numb. xxiii. 7; that he offered sacrifices, xxii. 39, 40; xxiii. 1-3, 14, 29; that he called Jehovah his God, xxii. 8, 13, 18, 31; xxiii. 8, 12, 16.

is never willing suddenly, much less in a moment, to destroy the worship inseminated from infancy; for this would be to pluck up the root, and so to destroy the holy [principle] of adoration and worship, which the Lord never breaks but bends. The holy [principle] of worship inrooted from infancy is of such a nature that it does not endure violence, but slow and gentle bending. The same takes place with Gentiles who in the life of the body worshipped idols and yet lived in mutual charity; in the other life the holy [principle] of their worship, being inrooted from their infancy, is not taken away in a moment, but gradually. For the goods and truths of faith can easily be implanted in those who have lived in mutual charity,—which they afterwards receive with joy; for charity is the very ground. Thus it came to pass with Abraham, Isaac, and Jacob; the Lord suffered them to retain the name of the god Shaddai,—insomuch that He said He was God Shaddai,—and this on account of its signification. Some interpreters render Shaddai, the *Almighty;* others, the *Thunderer;* but it properly signifies the *Tempter,* and after temptations, the *Benefactor,*—as is evident from Job, who so often mentions him, because he was in temptations. . . . That such is its signification may also appear from the word Shaddai itself, which means *devastation,* thus temptation; for temptation is a species of devastation. . . . As he was thus held to be the god of truth,—for devastation, temptation, chastisement, and rebuke are never from good, but from truth,—and as the Lord was represented by him to Abraham, Isaac, and Jacob, therefore the name was retained in the prophets also; but Shaddai there signifies truth. (*ib.* n. 1992.)

"*And He said, I am God, the God of thy father*" (Gen. xlvi. 3). . . . In the original language God is here named in the first place in the singular, and in the second place in the plural; that is, He is first called *El,* and then *Elohim.* The reason is that by God in the first place it is signified that He is One and alone; and in the second place, that He has many attributes. Hence comes the word *Elohim,* or God in the plural,—as almost everywhere in the Word. As there are many attributes, and the Ancient church gave to each a name, their posterity,—among whom the knowledge of such things was lost,—believed there were many gods, and each family chose one of them for its god; as for example, Abram chose Shaddai; Isaac, the god who was called Pachad, or Dread (Gen. xxxi. 42, 53). And because the god of each was one of the Divine attributes the Lord said to Abram, "*I am God Shaddai*" (Gen. xvii. 1), and here, to Jacob, "*I am the God of thy father.*" (*ib.* n. 6003.)

"*And offered sacrifices unto the God of his father Isaac*" (xlvi. 1). . . . That Jacob sacrificed to the God of his father Isaac indicates the character of the fathers of the Israelitish and Jewish nation; namely, that each of them worshipped his own god. That the God of Isaac was another god than his own is plain from the fact that he sacrificed to him [as the God of Isaac], and that in the visions of the night it was said to him, "*I am God, the God of thy father;*" and also from the fact that he sware by the same,—of which in Gen. xxxi. 53 :—"*The God of Abraham, and the God of Nahor, judge between us, the God of their father. Then Jacob sware by the Dread*[1] *of his father Isaac.*" And it is also evident that Jacob did not acknowledge Jehovah at the beginning, for he said :—"*If God will be with me, and will keep me, in this way that I go, and will give me bread to eat and raiment to put on, and I return in peace to my father's house, then shall Jehovah be my God*" (xxviii. 20, 21). Thus he acknowledged Jehovah conditionally.

It was their custom to acknowledge the gods of their fathers, but each his own in particular. This they derived from their fathers in Syria; for Terah the father of Abram, and also Abram himself when in Syria, worshipped other gods than Jehovah. Hence their posterity, who were called Jacob and Israel, were such that in heart they worshipped the gods of the Gentiles, and Jehovah only with the mouth, and as to name merely. The reason why they were so was, that they were only in externals, without any internal ; and such cannot but believe that worship consists merely in calling upon the name of God, and saying that He is their God,—this, so long as He is favourable,—and that nothing of worship consists in the life of charity and faith. (*ib.* n. 5998.)

It was enjoined upon the family of Abraham to acknowledge Jehovah as their God ; but yet they did not acknowledge Him, except as another god, by whom they might distinguish themselves from the nations,—thus only in name. And therefore did they so often turn aside also to other gods ; as appears in the historical parts of the Word. (*ib.* n. 4208.)

The Name and Worship of Jehovah again lost by the Posterity of Jacob in Egypt.

The posterity of Jacob in Egypt, together with the external worship of Jehovah, lost also the knowledge that their God was called Jehovah. For this reason they were first of all instructed (Exod. iii.) that Jehovah was the God of the Hebrews, and the God of Abraham, of Isaac, and of Jacob. . . . That they had lost both the name and worship of Jehovah appears from these

[1] That is, the object of dread.

words in Moses :—"*Moses said unto. God, Behold, when I come unto the children of Israel, and shall say unto them, The God of your father hath sent me unto you, and they shall say unto me, What is His name? what shall I say unto them? And God said unto Moses, I* AM WHO I AM; *and He said, Thou shalt say unto the children of Israel, I* AM *hath sent me unto you. And God said moreover unto Moses, Thus shalt thou say unto the children of Israel, Jehovah the God of your fathers, the God of Abraham, the God of Isaac, and the God of Jacob, hath sent me unto you. This is My name for ever*" (Exod. iii. 13-15). From this it is plain that even Moses did not know Him, and did not know that they were to be distinguished from others by the name of Jehovah, the God of the Hebrews. (A. C. n. 1343.)

"*And [when] they shall say unto me, What is His name? what shall I say unto them?*" What the posterity of Jacob was, appears from this question that Moses asked ; namely, that they not only had forgotten the name of Jehovah, but also acknowledged a plurality of gods, of whom one was greater than another. Hence it was that they wished to know His name ; and they believed it was enough to acknowledge God as to His name. The reason why they were such was, that they were in externals alone, without internal [principles], and they who are without internal [principles] cannot otherwise think of God, because they can receive nothing of the light of heaven, which may enlighten their interior [minds]. To the intent therefore that they might acknowledge Jehovah, it was told them that the God of their fathers, the God of Abraham, the God of Isaac, and the God of Jacob, was seen, and that He sent. Thus they were induced to acknowledge Jehovah from a blind veneration for their fathers, and not from any internal perception. It was indeed sufficient for that people to worship Jehovah only as to name, because they were incapable of receiving anything but the external of a church, thus that which only represented its internal. This, too, was established among them, for the purpose that what they represented might be caused to appear in internal form in heaven, and that there might thus still be some conjunction of heaven with man. (*ib.* n. 6877.)

WHY SACRIFICIAL WORSHIP, IN ITSELF NOT ACCEPTABLE TO THE LORD, WAS YET COMMANDED TO THE CHILDREN OF ISRAEL.

It has been shown that the [Hebrew] nations were in sacrificial worship. And it is evident from Exod. v. 3; x. 25, 26; xviii. 12; xxiv. 4, 5, that the posterity of Jacob were so before they departed out of Egypt, thus before sacrifices were commanded through Moses on mount Sinai.

This is especially evident from their idolatrous worship before the golden calf; of which it is thus written in Moses :—"*Aaron built an altar before the calf; and Aaron made proclamation and said, To-morrow is a feast to Jehovah. And they rose up early on the morrow, and offered burnt-offerings, and brought peace-offerings; and the people sat down to eat and to drink, and rose up to play*" (Exod. xxxii. 5, 6). This took place while Moses was on mount Sinai, and thus before the command concerning the altar and sacrifices came to them. That command was given for the reason that sacrificial worship with them, as among the Gentiles, had become idolatrous, and they could not be withdrawn from that worship because they believed there was especial holiness in it; and what is once implanted from infancy as holy,—the more if from forefathers and it is thus inrooted,—this, unless it be directly against order, the Lord never breaks but bends. This is the reason why it was prescribed that sacrifices should be so instituted as is written in the books of Moses. But it is very manifest from the prophets that sacrifices were never acceptable to Jehovah, and therefore were only permitted and tolerated for the reason mentioned. It is thus written of them in Jeremiah :—*Thus saith Jehovah of Hosts, the God of Israel : Put your burnt-offerings unto your sacrifices, and eat flesh. For I spake not unto your fathers, nor commanded them, in the day that I brought them out of the land of Egypt, concerning the matter of burnt-offerings and sacrifices : But this word I commanded them, saying, Obey My voice, and I will be your God*" (vii. 21-23). In David :—" *Sacrifice and offering Thou didst not desire, burnt-offering and sacrifices for sin hast Thou not required. . . . I have desired to do Thy will, O my God*" (Psalm xl. 6, 8). In the same :—" *I will take no bullock out of thy house, nor he-goats out of thy folds. . . . Offer unto God the sacrifice of thanksgiving*" (l. 9, 14). And again :—". *Thou delightest not in sacrifice, that I should give it; Thou acceptest not burnt-offering. The sacrifices of God are a broken spirit*" (li. 16, 17; cvii. 22 ; cvi. 17). In Hosea :—" *I desire mercy, and not sacrifice; and the knowledge of God more than burnt-offerings*" (vi. 6). Samuel said to Saul, " *Hath Jehovah delight in burnt-offerings and sacrifices? . . . Behold to obey is better than sacrifice, and to hearken than the fat of rams*" (1 Sam. xv. 22). And in Micah :—" *Wherewith shall I come before Jehovah, and bow myself before the high God? Shall I come before Him with burnt-offerings, with calves the sons of a year? Will Jehovah have pleasure in thousands of rams, in ten thousands of rivers of oil? . . . He hath showed thee, O man, what is good; and what doth Jehovah require of thee but to do justly, and to love mercy, and to humble thyself to walk with God?*" (vi. 7, 8). Hence now it is plain that sacrifices were not commanded, but permitted; and that nothing was regarded in sacrifices but the internal; and that it was the internal and not the external that was pleasing. And indeed for this reason the Lord abrogated them; as was foretold by Daniel, in these words, referring to the Lord's coming:—"*In the midst of the week He shall cause the sacrifice and the oblation to cease.*" (A. C. n. 2180.)

The Externals of the Ancient Churches were restored in the Israelitish Church.

The rituals and statutes which were commanded through Moses to the posterity of Jacob were not new, but existed before, in the Ancient churches, and were only restored among the children of Jacob. They were restored because among other nations they became idolatrous, and in Egypt and in Babel were turned into magic. (A. C. n. 6846.)

As regards the fact that the new church which was established among the posterity of Jacob appears in external form like the Ancient, it should be known that the statutes, judgments, and laws commanded through Moses to the Israelitish and Jewish nation were not different from those that existed in the Ancient church,—as those concerning betrothals and marriages, concerning servants, concerning animals which were fit and unfit for food, concerning cleansings, concerning feasts, tabernacles, the perpetual fire, and many other things; also concerning the altars, burnt-offerings, sacrifices, and libations, which were received in the second Ancient church, instituted by Eber. That these were known before they were commanded to that nation is very plain from the historical parts of the Word. To show only that altars, burnt-offerings, and sacrifices were known: It is related of Balaam that he required that seven altars should be built, and that burnt-offerings and sacrifices of bullocks and rams should be offered upon them (Numb. xxiii. 1, 2, 14, 15, 29); and moreover it is said of the nations in many places that their altars were destroyed; and also of the prophets of Baal whom Elijah slew, that they offered sacrifices. It is therefore evident that the sacrifices commanded to the people of Jacob were not new. So neither were the other statutes, judgments, and laws. But because these things among the nations had become idolatrous, —especially through the fact that by means of such things they worshipped some profane god, and so turned to infernal what represented things Divine, in addition to which they had added many things,—therefore, in order that the representative worship which was of the Ancient church might be restored, the same were recalled [to the service of Jehovah]. Hence it appears that the new church which was instituted among the posterity of Jacob appeared in external form like the Ancient church. (*ib.* n. 4449.)

The representatives instituted among the posterity of Jacob were not exactly similar to those that were in the Ancient church. They were for the most part similar to those that existed in the church instituted by Eber, which was called the Hebrew church. In this there were many new [ceremonials] of worship,—such as burnt-offerings and sacrifices, besides others, —which were unknown in the Ancient church. The internal of the church was not so much conjoined with these representatives as with the representatives of the Ancient church. (*ib.* n. 4874.)

When the Children of Israel first Constituted a Church.

The sons of Jacob themselves did not constitute any church, but their posterity; and this not until after they departed out of Egypt; and not actually until they came into the land of Canaan. (A. C. n. 4430.)

Egyptian Hieroglyphics were perverted Representatives of the Ancient Church.

"*And Pharaoh said, . . . I know not Jehovah*" (Exod. v. 2). . . . In the ancient time the Egyptians knew Jehovah; for the Ancient church was also in Egypt,—as may be clearly seen from the fact that they had among them the representatives and significatives of that church. The Egyptian hieroglyphics were nothing else; for spiritual things were signified by them. They also knew that they actually corresponded. And as they began to make use of such things in their sacred worship, and to worship them, and at length also to turn them into magical appliances, and so to be associated with the diabolical crew in hell, by this means they entirely destroyed the Ancient church among them. Hence it is that by the Egyptians, in the Word, perverted knowledges of the church are signified, and falsities which are contrary to the truths of the church. When Divine worship was thus perverted in Egypt, then also it was no longer permitted them to worship Jehovah, and at length not even to know that Jehovah was the God of the Ancient church; and this in order that they might not profane the name of Jehovah. (A. C. n. 7097. See also p. 171.)

THE THIRD OR ISRAELITISH CHURCH.

THE third church was the Israelitish. It was begun by the promulgation of the Decalogue upon Mount Sinai; was continued through the Word written by Moses and the Prophets; and was consummated, or ended, by the profanation of the Word. The fulness of this profanation was at the time when the Lord came into the world; wherefore He who was the Word was crucified. (T. C. R. n. 760.)

The Israelitish Church worshipped Jehovah, who in Himself is an invisible God (Exod. xxxiii. 18-23), but under a human form, which Jehovah God put on by means of an angel; in which form He appeared to Moses, Abraham, Sarah, Hagar, Gideon, Joshua, and sometimes to the Prophets. This human form was representative of the Lord who was to come; and because this was representative, each and all things of their church also were made representative. It is known that the sacrifices and other things of their worship represented the Lord who was to come, and that when He came they were abrogated. (*ib.* n. 786.)

THIS WAS NOT A TRUE CHURCH, BUT MERELY REPRESENTATIVE, OR THE REPRESENTATIVE OF A CHURCH.

A church merely representative is the resemblance of a church; it is not a church. (A. C. n. 3480.)

The church instituted among the Jews, as regards them, was not a church, but only the representative of a church; for, that there may be a church there must be in the man of the church faith in the Lord, and also love to Him, as well as love towards the neighbour. These constitute the church. But these were not in the people who were called Jacob. For they did not acknowledge the Lord, and therefore were not willing to hear of faith in Him,—still less of love towards Him; and not even of love towards the neighbour. For they were in self-love, and in the love of the world; which loves are entirely opposite to love to the Lord and love towards the neighbour. Such a character was in-rooted in that people from their first parents. Hence it is that no church could be instituted, but that the things of the church could only be represented, among that people. The church is represented when man places worship in externals,—but in such externals as correspond to heavenly things. Then internal things are represented by the external; and the internal are open to heaven, with which there is thus conjunction. Therefore, in order that the Israelitish people might be able to represent, when their interiors were without the faith and love of heaven,—even full of the love of self and the world,—those interiors were over-veiled. The externals could thus communicate with spirits, and by them with angels, without internals; whereas if the internals had not been overveiled they would have been open, and then the representative would have been destroyed, because things abominable would have burst forth and contaminated. That people more than others could be thus overveiled, because they adored the externals [of worship] more than others, and sup-posed the holy, yea, the Divine to be in them. (*ib.* n. 8788.)

The Difference between a Representative Church and the Representative of a Church.

A church is representative when there is internal worship in the external; but the representative of a church is when there is no internal worship, and yet there is external. In each case there are nearly similar external rituals,—namely, similar statutes, similar laws, and similar precepts; but in a representative church the externals so correspond with internals as to make one, while in the representative of a church there is no correspondence, because the externals are either without internals, or at variance with them. In a representative church celestial and spiritual love is principal; while in the representative of a church cor-poreal and worldly love is principal. Celestial and spiritual love is the internal itself; and where there is no celestial and spiritual, but only corporeal and worldly love, the external is with-out an internal. The Ancient church which existed after the flood was a representative church; but that which was estab-lished among the posterity of Jacob was merely the representa-tive of a church. But that the distinction may appear more evident, let it be illustrated by examples:—In the representative church the Divine worship was upon mountains, because moun-tains signified celestial love, and in the highest sense the Lord; and when they were holding their worship on mountains they were in its holiness, because they were then at the same time in celestial love. In the representative church Divine worship was also in groves, because groves signified spiritual love, and in the highest sense the Lord in respect to that love; and when they were having their worship in groves they were in its holiness, because at the same time in spiritual love. In the representative church, when they celebrated Divine worship they turned their faces to the rising of the sun, because the rising sun also signified celestial love. And when they gazed upon the moon they were filled likewise with a certain holy veneration, because the moon signified spiritual love; so when they looked up to the starry heaven, because this signified the angelic heaven, or the Lord's kingdom. In the representative church they had tents or tabernacles, and Divine woship in them; and it was holy because tents or tabernacles signified the holiness of love and worship. So in numberless other things. In the representative of a church, in the beginning Divine worship was indeed in like manner on mountains, and also in groves; they looked likewise toward the rising of the sun; and also to the moon, and to the stars; and moreover worship was in tents or tabernacles. But because they were in external worship without internal, or in corporeal and worldly love, and not in celestial and spiritual love, and so worshipped the mountains and groves themselves, and also the sun, the moon, and the stars, as well as their tents or tabernacles, and thereby made those rituals idolatrous which in the Ancient church were holy, therefore they were restricted to one common mountain, namely, to the mountain where Jerusalem was, and where at length Zion was; and to the rising of the sun [as seen] therefrom and from the temple; and also to one common tent, which was called the tent of the congregation; and finally to the ark in the temple. And this was done to the intent that the representative of a church might exist when they were in a holy external; otherwise they would have profaned holy things. From this it may be seen what the distinction is between a representative church and the representative of a church. In general, that they who were of the representative church, as to their interiors, communicated with the three heavens, to which the externals served as a plane; whereas they who were in the representative of a church did not communicate with the heavens as to their interiors,—but yet the externals in which they were held could serve as a plane; and this miraculously, of the Lord's Providence, to the intent that something of communication might exist between heaven and man by a certain semblance of a church. For without communication of heaven with man by something of a church the race would perish. (A. C. n. 4288.)

THE REPRESENTATIVE OF A CHURCH COULD NOT BE ESTABLISHED TILL
ALL KNOWLEDGE OF INTERNAL THINGS HAD BEEN LOST.

The representative of a church could not be established among
the Jews until the time when they were altogether vastated,
that is, when they had no knowledge of the internal things [of
worship]; for if they had had a knowledge of internal things,
they might have been affected by them, and thus might have
profaned them. For holy things, that is internal truths and
goods, may be profaned by those who know and acknowledge
them, and still more by those who are affected by them; but not
by those who do not acknowledge. Worship is made external
to prevent the violation of the internal. On this account internal
truths were not made known to the Jews. It was therefore provided of the Lord that the genuine representative of the church,
that is the internal, should depart from the posterity of Jacob
before they came into the representatives of the land of Canaan,
insomuch that they did not know anything at all of the Lord.
They indeed expected that the Messiah would come into the
world; but to the intent that He might raise them to glory and
eminence above all the nations of the earth, not that He might
save their souls to eternity. Nay, they knew nothing whatever
of a heavenly kingdom, nor of a life after death, nor even of
charity and faith. That they might be reduced to this ignorance
they were kept for several hundred years in Egypt; and when
they were called out thence, they were ignorant of the very name
of Jehovah (Exod. iii. 12-14). And moreover they lost all the
worship of the representative church; insomuch that after the
precepts of the decalogue had been promulgated in their presence
from Mount Sinai, within a month of days they relapsed to
Egyptian worship, which was that of a golden calf (Exod. xxxii.).
And because that nation which was brought forth out of Egypt
was of such a character, they all perished in the wilderness. Nothing more indeed was required of them than to keep the statutes
and commandments in external form, inasmuch as this was to do
what was representative of the church; but those who had
grown up to mature age in Egypt could not be brought to this.
Their children however could be, although with difficulty,—
in the beginning by miracles, and afterwards by fears and captivities; as appears from the books of Joshua and Judges.
Hence it appears that every genuine or internal representative
of the church departed from them before they came into the land
of Canaan, where the external representative of a church was
begun among them in full form. For the land of Canaan was
the very land itself where representatives of the church could be

presented, inasmuch as all places and all boundaries there were representative from ancient times. (A. C. n. 4289.)

THE JEWISH CHURCH, WITH ALL THINGS APPERTAINING TO IT, WAS REPRESENTATIVE OF ALL THINGS OF THE CHURCH IN HEAVEN AND ON EARTH.

That from being idolatrous the church became representative no one can know unless he knows what a representative is. The things which were represented in the Jewish church, and in the Word, are the Lord and His kingdom; consequently the celestial things of love, and the spiritual things of faith. These are what are represented, besides many things which pertain to them; as for instance all things belonging to the church. The things representing are either persons or things, in the world or on earth; in a word, all things which are objects of sense,—insomuch that there is scarcely any object that may not be a representative. But it is a general law of representation that nothing turns upon the person or upon the thing which represents, but upon that itself which is represented. As for example: Every king, whoever he was, in Judah and Israel, yea, in Egypt and elsewhere, could represent the Lord; the regal function of kings itself is representative. So could the worst of all kings,— as Pharaoh, who exalted Joseph over the land of Egypt, Nebuchadnezzar in Babylon (Dan. ii. 37, 38), Saul, and the other kings of Judah and Israel, of whatever character they were. The anointing itself involved this; whence they were called the anointed of Jehovah. In like manner all priests, how many soever they were, represented the Lord; the priestly function itself is representative. Priests likewise who were evil and impure; because in representatives nothing turns upon the character of the person. Nor did men only represent, but also beasts: As all those which were offered in sacrifice; lambs and sheep represented things celestial; doves and turtles things spiritual; likewise rams, goats, bullocks, and oxen,—but lower celestial and spiritual things. Nor, as was said, did things animate alone represent, but also inanimate things: As the altar, yea, the stones of the altar; and the ark and tabernacle, with all that was in them; and also the temple, with all things therein, as every one may know,—thus the lamps, the bread, and Aaron's garments. Nor were these only representative, but all the rites too that were observed in the Jewish church. In the Ancient churches representatives extended to all objects of the senses; as to mountains and hills; valleys, plains, rivers, brooks, fountains, and pools; to groves, and to trees in general, and each species of tree in particular,—insomuch that every tree had some certain signification; all which afterwards, when the significative church ceased, became representative. From all this it may be seen what is meant by representatives. And as things celestial and spiritual, that is the things of the Lord's kingdom in the heavens and of the Lord's kingdom on earth, could be represented not only by men, whoever and whatever they were, but also by beasts and even by things inanimate, it is evident what a representative church is. The representatives had this effect: That all the things that were done according to the rites commanded appeared holy before the sight of spirits and angels; as when the high priest washed himself with water; when he ministered, clothed in his pontifical garments; when he stood before the lighted candles;—whatever he was, even though most impure and in his heart an idolater. So also the other priests. For, as was said, in representatives nothing turned upon the person, but upon that itself which was represented, quite apart from the person,—just as it was apart from the oxen, bullocks, and lambs that were sacrificed; or from the blood which was poured out around the altar; as also apart from the altar itself, and so on. After all internal worship was lost, and when worship had become not only merely external but also idolatrous, this representative church was instituted; in order that there might be some conjunction of heaven with earth, or of the Lord through heaven with man, even after the conjunction by the internals of worship had ceased. (A. C. n. 1361.)

That the representative of a church might exist among them, such statutes and such laws were given them as were entirely representative, by manifest revelation. So long therefore as they were in them and strictly observed them so long they could represent; but when they turned away from them,—as to the statutes and laws of other nations, and especially to the worship of another god,—they deprived themselves of the capability of representing. For this reason they were driven to laws and to statutes truly representative by external means,—which were captivities, scourges, threats, and miracles,—and were not brought to them by internal means, as they are who have internal worship in the external. (*ib.* n. 4281.)

No one who thinks soundly can believe that the different animals which were sacrificed had no other signification than sacrifices; or that an ox and young bullock or calf signified the same as a sheep, a kid, and a she-goat; and these the same as a lamb; and that the same was signified by turtle-doves and young pigeons. In truth each animal had its special signification; as may sufficiently appear from the fact that one was never offered in the place of another; and that those were expressly named which should be offered in the daily burnt-offerings and sacrifices, in those of the Sabbaths and feasts, in the freewill offerings, in the offerings of vows and of thanksgivings, in the trespass and sin offerings, and which were to be used in offerings for purification. This would never have been unless some special thing were represented and signified by each animal. But what each in particular signified it would be too prolix here to explain. It is sufficient here to know that things celestial are what are signified by the animals, and things spiritual by the birds; and that by each individual one some special celestial or spiritual reality is signified. The Jewish church itself, and all things pertaining to that church, were representative of such realities as are of the Lord's kingdom; where there is nothing but what is celestial and spiritual, that is, nothing but what is of love and faith. This too is evident enough from the signification of the clean and useful beasts; which, because in the Most Ancient churches they signified celestial goods, afterwards,—when worship merely external, and this representative, was held in esteem and acknowledged,—became representative. (*ib.* n. 1823.)

ILLUSTRATION OF WHAT A REPRESENTATIVE CHURCH IS, AND WHY IT IS.

There are three heavens, the inmost or third, the middle or second, and the ultimate or first. In the inmost heaven the good of love to the Lord reigns; in the middle heaven the good of charity towards the neighbour reigns; and in the ultimate heaven those things are represented which are thought and said, and which exist, in the middle and inmost heaven. The representatives which exist there are innumerable,—such as paradises, gardens, forests, fields and plains; cities, palaces and houses; as well as flocks and herds, and animals and birds of many kinds, and innumerable other things. These appear before the eyes of angelic spirits there more clearly than similar things in the light of mid-day on earth; and what is wonderful, what they signify is also apperceived. Such things likewise appeared to the prophets, when their interior sight was opened, which is the sight of the spirit; as horses to Zechariah (vi. 1-9); animals, which were cherubim, and afterwards the New Temple with all things appertaining to it, to Ezekiel (i. ix. x. xl. xlviii.); a candlestick, thrones, animals, which also were cherubim, horses, the New Jerusalem, and many other things, to John,—of which in the Apocalypse; and horses and chariots of fire to the boy of Elisha (2 Kings vi. 17). Similar things appear continually in heaven, before the eyes of spirits and angels, and are the natural forms in which the internal things of heaven terminate, and in which they are figured; and which are thus visibly presented before the very eyes. These are representations. The church therefore is representative when the internal holy things which are of love and faith, from the Lord and to the Lord, are presented by forms visible in the world; as in this chapter and the following (Exod. xxv. xxvi.) by the ark, the propitiatory, and the cherubim, by the tables therein, by the candlestick, and by the other things of the tabernacle. For that tabernacle was so constructed that it should represent the three heavens, and all things that are therein; and the ark, in which was the testimony, represented the inmost heaven, and the Lord Himself there. For this reason the form of it was shown to Moses in the mount, Jehovah then saying, " *That they should make for Him a sanctuary, and He would dwell in the midst of them*" (ver. 8). Every one who is gifted with any faculty of interior thought may perceive that Jehovah could not dwell in a tent, but that He dwells in heaven; and that that tent could not be called a sanctuary unless it had reference to heaven, and to the celestial and spiritual things which are there. Let every one think within himself what it would be for Jehovah, the Creator of heaven and earth, to dwell in a small habitation made of wood overlaid with gold, and compassed about with curtains, unless heaven and the things of heaven had been represented therein in form. For the things which are represented in form really appear in similar form in the ultimate or first heaven, before the spirits who are there; but in the higher heavens the internal things which are represented are perceived,—which, as was said, are the celestial things which are of love to the Lord, and the spiritual things which are of faith in the Lord. Such were the things which filled heaven when Moses and the people were in a holy external, and reverenced the tabernacle as the habitation of Jehovah Himself. It is plain from this what a representative is, and that by means of representatives heaven, and so the Lord, could be present with man. Therefore, when the Ancient church came to its end a representative church was established, among the Israelitish people, that by such means there might be a conjunction of heaven, and so of the Lord, with the human race; for without conjunction with the Lord through heaven mankind would perish, for man derives his life from that conjunction. But those representatives were only the external means of conjunction, with which the Lord conjoined heaven miraculously. And when conjunction by these also perished the Lord came into the world, and opened the internal things themselves which were represented,—which are the things of love and of faith in Him. Now, these conjoin. But yet the sole medium of conjunction at this day is the Word; since this is so written that all and the single things therein correspond, and therefore represent and signify Divine things which are in the heavens.   (A. C. n. 9457.)

What it is for the Lord to be present Representatively.

What it is to be present representatively may be briefly explained.   A man who is in corporeal and worldly love, and not at the same time in spiritual or celestial love, has none but evil spirits present with him,—even when he is in a holy external; for good spirits can by no means be present with such a man, since they perceive immediately what is the quality of a man's love.   It is the sphere which is exhaled from his interiors that spirits so manifestly perceive, just as a man perceives by smell fetid and offensive substances which float about him in the air.   That nation [the Jewish], which is here treated of, as regards good and truth or love and faith was in such a state. Yet in order that they might act as the representatives of a church, it was miraculously provided of the Lord that when they were in a holy external, although surrounded at the same time with evil spirits, the holy [sphere] in which they were might nevertheless be elevated into heaven; and this by good spirits and angels,—not within them, but without them, for within them was nothing but emptiness or uncleanness.   Communication was not therefore given with the very man, but with that holy [external] itself in which they were when they performed the statutes and precepts which were all representative of the spiritual and celestial things of the Lord's kingdom.   This is what is meant by the Lord being representatively present with that nation.   But the Lord is differently present with those within the church who are in spiritual love and thence in faith. With these there are good spirits and angels present, not in external worship only but also at the same time in internal. With these therefore there is communication of heaven with themselves; for the Lord flows in through heaven by their internals into their externals.   To them the holy [external] of worship is of benefit in the other life, but not to the former.   It is the same with priests and presbyters who preach what is holy and yet live wickedly and believe wickedly.   Good spirits are not present with them, but evil, even when they are in worship apparently holy in its external form.   For it is the love of self and of the world, or the love of securing honours and acquiring gain and reputation for their sake, which inflames them, and raises an affection of what is holy,—sometimes to such a degree that nothing of simulation is apperceived, and then is not credited by themselves; when yet they are in the midst of evil spirits, who are then in a similar state and draw near and inspire them. (That evil spirits can be in such a state, and are so when they are in externals, and are inflated with the love of self or of the world, it has been given me to know from manifold experience, of which, by the Divine mercy of the Lord, in the narrations which follow at the end of the chapters.) These have no communication with heaven in themselves; but they have who hear and receive the words from their mouth, if they are in a pious and holy internal. For it matters not from whom the voice of good and truth goes forth if only their life be not openly wicked, for this scandalizes. That such was the nation descended from Jacob, namely, that it was encompassed with evil spirits, and yet the Lord was representatively present with them, may be seen from many passages in the Word. There was indeed nothing which at heart they worshipped less than Jehovah; for as often as miracles ceased they immediately turned to other gods and became idolaters; which was a manifest indication that at heart they worshipped other gods, and only confessed Jehovah with the mouth,—and in fact merely to the end that they might be the greatest, and pre-eminent over all the nations round about. That at heart this people, and among them Aaron himself, worshipped an Egyptian idol, and only with the mouth confessed Jehovah, on account of His miracles, is clearly evident from the golden calf which Aaron made for them,—and this but a month of days after they had seen so great miracles on Mount Sinai, besides what they saw in Egypt,—of which in Exod. xxxii. That Aaron also was of such a character is distinctly related in the same chapter (vers. 2-5, and especially ver. 35). Besides many other passages concerning them in the books of Moses, in the book of Judges, in the books of Samuel, and in the books of the Kings. That they were only in external worship, and not in any internal worship, is evident also from the fact that they were forbidden to come near to Mount Sinai when the law was promulgated, and that if they touched the mountain dying they would die (Exod. xix. 11-13 ; xx. 19). The reason was that their internal man was unclean. Again, it is said, " *That Jehovah dwelt with them in the midst of their uncleannesses;*" (Levit. xvi. 16). The character of that nation appears also from the song of Moses (Deut. xxxii. 15-43), and from many passages in the prophets. It may be known from all this that there was no church with that nation, but only the representative of a church; and that the Lord was present with it only representatively. (A. C. n. 4311.)

What the Kingdoms of Judges, Priests, and Kings signified, and why the Jews were divided into two Kingdoms.

In the representative church among the posterity of Jacob there was first a kingdom of judges, afterwards a kingdom of priests, and finally a kingdom of kings; and by the kingdom of judges Divine truth from Divine good was represented; by the kingdom of priests, who were also judges, Divine good was represented from which Divine truth is derived; and by the kingdom of kings Divine truth was represented without Divine good. But when to the regal office something of the priesthood too was adjoined, by the kings was then represented also Divine truth in which there was so much of good as there was of the priesthood attached to the regal office. All these things in the Jewish church were instituted in order that the states of heaven might be represented by them; for in heaven there are two kingdoms, one which is called the celestial kingdom, and another which is called the spiritual kingdom. The celestial kingdom is what is called the priesthood, and the spiritual kingdom is what is called the royalty of the Lord. In the latter Divine truth reigns, in the former Divine good. And because the representative of the celestial kingdom began to be destroyed when they sought a king, therefore, in order that the representative of the Lord's kingdom in the heavens might still be continued, the Jews were separated from the Israelites, and the celestial kingdom of the Lord was represented by the Jewish kingdom, and His spiritual kingdom by the Israelitish kingdom. Those who know these things may know the reasons why the forms of government among the descendants of Jacob were successively changed; why also when they asked a king it was said to them of Jehovah by Samuel, that by so doing they rejected Jehovah, that He should not reign over them (1 Sam. viii. 7); and that then the right of a king was declared to them (ver. 11 *seq.*), by which Divine truth without good is described. Those who know the things above mentioned may also know why something of the priesthood was granted to David; and also why after the time of Solomon the kingdom was divided into two, the Jewish and the Israelitish kingdoms. (A. C. n. 8770.)

Why the Jews above all others could act as a representative Church.

The nature of their fantasies and lusts no one can know unless he has had some intercourse with them in the other life; and this was granted me in order that I might know ; for at different times I have there conversed with them. They love themselves and love worldly wealth more than all others ; and besides, above all others they fear the loss of honour, and also the loss of gain. And therefore at this day, as formerly, they despise others in comparison with themselves ; and also with intensest application they acquire to themselves wealth. And they are moreover timid. Because such from ancient times had been the character of that nation, therefore they could above other nations be held in a holy external without any holy internal ; and thus could represent in an external form the things which are of the church. These fantasies and these lusts are what caused such contumacy. This also appears from many things that are related of them in the historical parts of the Word. After they were punished they could be in such external humiliation as no other nation ; for whole days they could lie prostrate on the ground and roll themselves in the dust, and not rise up until the third day ; for many days they could bewail, go in sackloth, in tattered garments, with dust or ashes sprinkled on their heads ; could fast continually for many days, and meanwhile burst forth in bitter weeping ; and this merely from corporeal and earthly love, and from fear of the loss of pre-eminence and worldly wealth. It certainly was not anything internal which affected them, for they did not know at all, or indeed wish to know, what was internal,—as for example that there is a life after death, and that there is eternal salvation. It is therefore evident that, such being their character, it could not but be that they were deprived of every holy internal ; for this character in no wise agrees with such a holy external ; they are in fact entirely contrary. It is also evident that they beyond others could act as the representative of a church ; that is to say, could represent holy things in an external form without any holy internal ; and so that by that nation there could be something of communication with the heavens. (A. C. n. 4293.)

Representative Divine worship was yet instituted with that nation ; for representative worship could be instituted with any nation that had holy externals of worship, and worshipped almost idolatrously. For what is representative has no reference to the person, but to the thing ; and the inclination of that people above every other was absolutely to worship external things as holy and Divine, without any internal ; as for instance to adore their fathers, Abraham, Isaac, and Jacob, and afterwards Moses and David, as deities ; and likewise to account as holy and Divine and to worship every stone and every [piece of] wood that was inaugurated into their Divine worship,—as the ark, the tables therein, the lamp, the altar, the garments of Aaron, the urim and thummim, and afterwards the temple. By means of such things at that time there was granted, of the Lord's Providence, a communication of the angels of heaven with man; for there must somewhere be a church, or the representative of a church, in order that there may be communication of heaven with the human race. And because they above every other nation could place Divine worship in external things, and thus act as the representative of a church, that nation was adopted. (A. C. n. 8588.)

Why it is believed that the Jews were chosen above others for their Goodness.

They that know nothing of the internal sense of the Word cannot believe otherwise than that the Israelitish and Jewish nation was elected above every other nation, and therefore that they were more excellent,—as they themselves also believed. And what is extraordinary, not only that nation itself believes this, but Christians also believe it; although they know that nation is in filthy loves, in sordid avarice, in hatred, and in arrogance ; and besides, that they make light of and even hold in aversion the internal things which relate to charity and faith, and which relate to the Lord. That even Christians believe that nation was elected above others is because they believe that the election and salvation of man is of mercy, however a man lives, and thus that the wicked can be received into heaven equally with the pious and the good,—not considering that election is universal, namely, of all who live in good; and that the mercy of the Lord is towards every man who abstains from evil, and wills to live in good, and thus who suffers himself to be led of the Lord, and to be regenerated,—which is effected by the continuance of his life. Hence it is that very many even in the Christian world too believe that that nation will be again elected, and will then be brought back again into the land of Canaan; and this also according to the sense of the letter. (A. C. n. 7051.)

The children of Israel are called the people of Jehovah, not because they were better than other nations, but because they represented the people of Jehovah, that is, those who are of the Lord's spiritual kingdom. That they were not better than other nations is evident from their life in the wilderness, in that they did not believe at all in Jehovah, but in heart believed in the gods of the Egyptians; which is manifest from the golden calf that they made for themselves, and which they called their gods that brought them forth out of the land of Egypt (Exod. xxxii. 8). It is evident also from their life afterwards in the land of

Canaan, of which we read in the historical parts of the Word; and from what is said of them too in the prophetical parts of the Word, and finally by the Lord. Hence also it is that few of them are in heaven, for they have received a lot in the other life according to their life. Be not therefore willing to believe that they before others were elected for heaven. Those who so believe do not believe that the life of every one remains; nor believe that man must be prepared for heaven by his whole life in the world, and that this is done of the Lord's mercy,—and that they are not admitted into heaven of mercy alone, howsoever they have lived in the world. To such an opinion of heaven and of the Lord's mercy the doctrine of faith alone leads, and of salvation by that faith without good works. For they who are in this doctrine are not concerned about the life. Hence they even believe that evils can be wiped away, as filth with water; and thus that a man can be transmitted into the life of good and consequently admitted into heaven in a moment; not knowing that if the life of evil were taken away from the evil they would have nothing of life at all; and that if they who are in the life of evil were admitted into heaven they would feel hell within them, and the more grievous the more interiorly they were in heaven. From all this now it may be seen that the Israelites and Jews were not elected at all, but only accepted to represent the things which are of heaven; and that it was expedient that this should be done in the land of Canaan, because the church of the Lord had been there from the most ancient times, and all places there were therefore become representative of things celestial and Divine. Thus also a Word could be written there wherein the names would signify such things as are of the Lord and of His kingdom. (A. C. n. 7439.)

THE JEWS WERE NOT CHOSEN, BUT WERE URGENT TO BE A CHURCH, FROM THE LOVE OF PRE-EMINENCE.

That the descendants of Jacob were not chosen, but were solicitous that there might be a church with them, appears in many passages of the Word, from its internal historical sense; and plainly in the following: "*Jehovah said unto Moses, Go up hence, thou and the people, which thou hast caused to go up out of the land of Egypt, unto the land which I sware unto Abraham, Isaac, and Jacob, saying, Unto thy seed will I give it. . . . I will not go up in the midst of thee, for thou art a stiff-necked people; lest I consume thee in the way. When the people heard this evil word they mourned, and they put every one his adornment from upon him. . . . And Moses took the tent, and stretched it for himself without the camp, by removing far from the camp; and Moses said unto Jehovah, See, Thou sayest unto me, Cause this people to go up, when Thou hast not made known to me whom Thou wilt send with me. . . . Now, therefore, I pray Thee, if I have found grace in Thine eyes, make known to me, I pray Thee, Thy way, that I may know of Thee, that I have found grace in Thine eyes; and see that this nation is Thy people. He said therefore, My faces shall go until I shall give thee rest*" (Exod. xxxiii.). It is here said that Moses caused the people to go up out of the land of Egypt; and afterwards that they laid aside their adornment, and mourned; and that Moses stretched his tent without the camp, and so Jehovah assented; thus clearly, that they themselves were urgent. Again: "*Jehovah said unto Moses, How long will this people provoke Me? and how long will they not believe in Me, for all the signs which I have shewed in the midst of them? I will smite them with pestilence, and extinguish them, and will make thee into a greater nation and mightier than they.*" But Moses supplicated, and Jehovah being entreated said, "*I will be propitious according to Thy word; nevertheless I live, and the whole earth shall be filled with the glory of Jehovah. For as to all these men who have seen My glory, and My miracles, which I did in Egypt, and in the wilderness, and yet have tempted Me these ten times, and have not obeyed My voice, if they shall see the land which I sware unto their fathers, all that have provoked Me shall not see it; . . . in this wilderness shall their . carcases fall together; . . . but their children I will bring in*" (Numb. xiv.). From this also it appears that Jehovah purposed to extinguish them, consequently not to establish a church among them, but that they were urgent, and therefore it was done. (A. C. n. 4290.)

They were urgent that a church should be instituted among them; but this was for no other end than that they might be distinguished above all nations on the whole globe. For beyond others they were in the love of self, and they could not be exalted to eminence over them by other means than that Jehovah, and thus the church also, should be among them; for where Jehovah is, that is the Lord, there is the church. That this was the end is evident from many passages in the Word; as from these words also in this chapter (Exod. xxxiii.): "*Moses said, Wherein shall it become known here that I have found favour in Thine eyes, I and Thy people? Is it not in Thy going with us, and our being rendered excellent, I and Thy people, above all the people that are on the faces of the earth?*" (ver. 16.) (*ib.* n. 10,535.)

Why the Jews are called in the Word a Holy People.

The reason why that people is called in the Word the people of Jehovah, the chosen and beloved nation, is that by Judah there the celestial church is meant, by Israel the spiritual church, and something of the church by all the sons of Jacob; and by Abraham, Isaac, and Jacob, the Lord Himself also is meant, as well as by Moses, Aaron, and David. (A. C. n. 10,396.)

The Erroneous Belief that the Jews are again to be Chosen.

The character of that nation is such, that above all other nations they adore external things, thus idols; and that they wish to know nothing at all about internal things. For of all nations they are the most avaricious; and avarice such as theirs, by which gold and silver are loved for the sake of gold and silver, and not for the sake of any use, is an affection the most earthly, and draws the mind down entirely into and immerses it in the body, and so closes the interiors that nothing at all of faith and love from heaven can enter. It is therefore plain how much they err who believe that nation will again be chosen, or that the Lord's church will pass again to them, others being rejected, —when yet you shall convert stones to faith in the Lord before them. It is believed the church will pass again to them, because in many places in the prophetical parts of the Word it is said that they are to return; and it is not known that by Judah, by Jacob, and by Israel there, that nation is not meant, but those with whom the church exists. (A. C. n. 8301.)

In Jeremiah it is written: "*Behold, the days come, saith Jehovah, that I will sow the house of Israel and the house of Judah with the seed of man, and with the seed of beast. . . . Behold, the days come, saith Jehovah, that I will make a new covenant with the house of Israel, and with the house of Judah. . . . But this shall be the covenant that I will make with the house of Israel. After those days, saith Jehovah, I will put My law in their inward parts, and write it upon their hearts, and will be their God, and they shall be My people*" (xxxi. 27, 31, 33). By the coming days here the advent of the Lord is meant; and therefore it is not meant that a new covenant would then be made with the house of Israel and with the house of Judah, but with a new church that was to be established by the Lord,—which is meant by the house of Israel and by the house of Judah in whose inward parts the law would be put, and upon whose hearts it would be written. It is well known that this did not take place with the house of

Israel and with the house of Judah; for they entirely rejected
any covenant with the Lord, and in like manner they reject
it also at this day. A covenant signifies conjunction with the
Lord by love to Him; by which conjunction the law or Divine
truth is put in them, both in doctrine and in life,—which is the
law in their inward parts, and written upon their hearts. To
sow the house of Israel and the house of Judah with the seed of
man, and with the seed of beast, signifies to reform those who
are of the new church, by means of the truths and goods which
are of intelligence and affection; seed is truth; man is intelligence; and beast is the good of affection. That beast
signifies this, will be shown hereafter. Again, in Zechariah:
" *Yea, many people and strong nations shall come to seek Jehovah
of Hosts in Jerusalem, and to pray before Jehovah. Thus saith
Jehovah of Hosts, In those days ten men shall take hold, out of all
languages of the nations, even shall take hold of the skirt of him that
is a Jew, saying, We will go with you; for we have heard that God
is with you*" (viii. 22, 23). Those who do not know that by a
Jew they are meant who are in love to the Lord and thence in
truths of doctrine, may easily be led to believe that these things
are said of the Jews, and of their introduction into the land of
Canaan; and that all others who desire to be saved shall then
take hold of the skirt of their garment praying that they may be
permitted to go with them. But when it is known that these
things are not said of any introduction into the land of Canaan
and to Jerusalem there, and that by a Jew they are not meant
who are of that nation; but that by Jerusalem the new church
is meant that would be established by the Lord, and by a Jew
every one who is in the good of love to the Lord, and by the
skirt of a Jew truth from that good, then it may be understood
what all things in this chapter and these words in particular
signify. For the subject here spoken of is the calling together
and accession of the Gentiles to the Church; and by a Jew they
are meant who acknowledge the Lord and love Him; by the
taking hold of his skirt is signified the desire of knowing truth
from him; and by ten men out of all the languages of the
nations all are meant of whatever religion. Ten men signify all;
and the languages of all nations, their religious principles. From
all this it may be seen how far they wander who believe that at
the end of times the Jews will be converted to the Lord, and introduced into the land of Canaan. They are those who believe
that by the land, by Jerusalem, by Israel, and by Judah, in the
Word, are meant the land of Canaan, the city of Jerusalem, the
Israelitish people, and the Jewish nation. But those who
hitherto have so believed are to be excused; because they knew
nothing of the spiritual sense of the Word, and therefore did not

know that by the land of Canaan the church is signified; by Jerusalem, the same as to doctrine; by Israel, those that are of the spiritual church; and by Judah, those that are of the celestial church; and that where their introduction into the land of Canaan is referred to by the prophets, the introduction of the faithful into heaven and into the church is meant. This introduction even took place when the Lord came into the world; for then all those who lived in the good of charity, and worshipped God under the human form, were introduced into heaven,—who were reserved under heaven until the Lord's coming, and introduced after He had glorified His Human. These are they who are meant, in many places in the prophetic Word, where the captivity of the children of Israel and Judah and the bringing of them back into the land are spoken of. They also are meant who were to be introduced from the earth into the church, and thence into heaven, after the coming of the Lord; not only where the Christian religion is received, but also everywhere else.

The two following passages may be taken as an example of those from which the Jews persuade themselves, and also Christians believe, that the Jewish nation will return into the land of Canaan, and be saved in preference to others. In Isaiah: "*Then they shall bring all your brethren out of all nations for an offering unto Jehovah, upon horses, and in chariots, and in carriages, and upon mules, and upon swift beasts, to My holy mountain Jerusalem, saith Jehovah, as the children of Israel bring an offering in a clean vessel into the house of Jehovah. . . . For as the new heavens and the new earth which I will make shall remain before Me, saith Jehovah, so shall your seed and your name remain*" (lxvi. 20, 22). By the new heaven and the new earth are meant the heaven and the church from those who would be saved by the Lord after the glorification of His Human. In the same prophet: "*I will lift up Mine hand to the Gentiles, and set up My standard to the people: and they shall bring thy sons in their bosom, and thy daughters they shall carry upon the shoulders. And kings shall be thy nursing fathers, and their queens thy nursing mothers: they shall bow down to thee with their face toward the earth, and lick up the dust of thy feet*" (xlix. 22, 23). This whole chapter relates to the coming of the Lord, and to the salvation of those who receive Him,—as is very manifest from verses 6-9; and therefore not to the salvation of the Jews, still less to their restoration to the land of Canaan. That the Jewish nation was not meant in the passages adduced is evident also from the fact that it was the worst nation at heart, and was idolatrous; and that they were not led into the land of Canaan on account of any goodness and uprightness of heart, but because of the promise made to their fathers; that there were with them no truths and goods of the church, but only falsities and evils; and that therefore they were rejected and expelled from the land of Canaan, as is evident from all the passages in the Word where that nation is described. (A. E. n. 433.)

Why the Jews have been Preserved unto this Day.

Because the tribe of Judah, more than the other tribes, was of this character [that they could be in a holy external, and so keep holy the rituals whereby the heavenly things of the Lord's kingdom were represented], and at this day, as formerly, keep holy the rituals which can be observed out of Jerusalem, and also have a sacred veneration for their fathers, and an especial reverence for the Word of the Old Testament, and it was foreseen that Christians would almost reject it, and would likewise defile its internals with things profane, therefore that nation has been hitherto preserved,—according to the Lord's words in Matthew (xxiv. 34). It would have been otherwise if Christians, as they were acquainted with internal things, had also lived as internal men. If this had been so, that nation, like other nations, before many ages would have been cut off. (A. C. n. 3479.)

The Land of Canaan, in respect to the Churches there.

The Most Ancient church, which was celestial, and before the flood, was in the land of Canaan; and the Ancient church which was after the flood was also there, and in many countries besides. Hence the origin of the fact that all the nations there, and also all the lands, and all the rivers there were clothed with representatives; for the most ancients, who were celestial men, perceived through all the objects that they saw such things as belong to the Lord's kingdom; and so through the countries too and the rivers of the land. Those representatives, and also the representatives of the places there, remained in the Ancient church. The Word in the Ancient church had also representative names of places therefrom; as also the Word after their time, which is called Moses and the Prophets; and because it was so Abraham was commanded to go thither, and a promise was made to him that his posterity should possess that land. And this not for the reason that they were better than other nations,—for they were among the worst of all,—but that by them a representative church might be instituted, in which nothing should turn upon person or upon place, but upon the things which were represented; and thus the names too of the Most Ancient and of the Ancient church were retained. (A. C. n. 3686.)

There was a church in the land of Canaan from the most ancient times; whence it came to pass that all places there, and which were circumjacent in whatever direction, with the mountains·and rivers, that are mentioned in the Word, became representative and significative of such things as constitute the internals of the church, which are what are called its spiritual things. (H. D. n. 5.)

Why the Israelites were Expelled from the Land of Canaan.

As the Israelitish nation were in externals, without internals, and yet something of the church was to be established among them, it was provided of the Lord that communication with heaven might still be effected, through the representatives which constituted the externals of worship with that nation. This communication, however, was effected miraculously. But, that this might be, two things were requisite; one, that the internal within them should be entirely closed; and the other, that they might be in a holy external while engaged in worship. For, when the internal is entirely closed, then the internal of the church and of worship is neither denied nor acknowledged; it is as if there were none; and then there can be a holy external, and it can even be exalted, because nothing opposes and prevents. This nation was therefore also in entire ignorance of internal things,—which are the things pertaining to love and faith towards the Lord, and to eternal life by means of them. But as soon as the Lord came into the world and revealed Himself, and taught love and faith in Himself, then that nation as they heard these things began to deny them, and so could no longer be kept in such ignorance as before. Therefore they were then driven out of the land of Canaan; that they might not defile and profane internal things, by denial, in that land where, from the most ancient times, all places were made representative of such things as pertain to heaven and the church. (A. C. n. 10,500.)

THE FOURTH, OR FIRST CHRISTIAN CHURCH.

THE Christian church in its essence is the same with the representative church as to its internal form. But the representatives and significatives of that church were abrogated after the Lord came into the world, because each and all of them represented Him, and consequently the things which are of His kingdom; for these are from Him, and so to speak are Himself. But between the Most Ancient church and the Christian the difference is as between the light of the sun by day and the light of the moon and stars by night; for, to see goods by an internal or prior way is like seeing in the day by the light of the sun, while to see by an external or posterior way is like seeing in the night by the light of the moon or stars. There was almost the same difference between the Most Ancient church and the Ancient; only that they of the Christian church were capable of being in fuller light, if they had acknowledged internal things, or had believed and done the truths and goods which the Lord taught. The good itself is the same to each, but the difference is in seeing it clearly or dimly. They who see clearly see innumerable arcana almost as the angels in heaven, and are also affected by what they see; but they that see dimly scarcely see anything without doubt, and the things which they see also mix themselves with the shades of night, that is, with falsities; nor can they be interiorly affected by them. (A. C. n. 4489.)

The externals of the Ancient church were all representative of the Lord and of the celestial and spiritual things of His kingdom; that is of love and charity and of faith thence, consequently of such things as are of the Christian church. Hence it is that when the externals which belonged to the Ancient and also to the Jewish church are unfolded, and as it were unswathed, the Christian church appears. This was signified by the rending asunder of the veil in the temple (Matt. xxvii. 51). (*ib.* n. 4772.)

The Lord abolished the representatives themselves of the Jewish church because the greatest part of them referred to Him; for the shadow vanishes when the form itself appears.

He established therefore a new church, which should not like the former be led by representatives to things internal, but which should know them without representatives. And in place of those representatives He enjoined certain external things only, namely Baptism and the Holy Supper; Baptism, that by it they might remember regeneration; and the Holy Supper, that they might thereby remember the Lord and His love towards the whole human race, and the reciprocal [love] of man to Him. (*ib.* n. 4904.)

In the end of the church, when there is no faith because there is no charity, the interior [truths] of the Word are made known which are to serve the new church for doctrine and life. This was effected by the Lord Himself when the end of the Jewish church was at hand; for then the Lord Himself came into the world and opened the interiors of the Word, especially those concerning Himself, concerning love to Him, concerning love towards the neighbour; and concerning faith in Him,—which before lay hidden in the interiors of the Word, being in its representatives, and thence in the single things of the church and of worship. The truths therefore which the Lord unfolded were the interior truths—and in themselves spiritual—which afterwards served the new church for doctrine and life, according to what was just said above. But yet those truths were not immediately received, nor till after a considerable lapse of time, as is well known from ecclesiastical history. The reason was that they could not be received until all things in the spiritual world were reduced to order; for with men the spiritual world is conjoined to the natural world. Therefore unless that world had first been reduced to order the goods of love and truths of doctrine could not be understood nor perceived by men in the natural world. This was the reason why so long a time intervened before the Christian church was universally established in the European world; for all the effects which exist in the natural world derive their origin from causes in the spiritual world, especially those that concern the things of the church. (A. E. n. 670.)

THE PRIMITIVE CONDITION AND SUBSEQUENT DEGENERATION OF THIS CHRISTIAN CHURCH.

The Christian church, from the time of the Lord, has passed through the several periods from infancy to extreme old age. Its infancy was during the time in which the Apostles lived, and preached to the whole world repentance and faith in the Lord God the Saviour. That they preached these two is evident from these words in the Acts of the Apostles :—" *Paul testified to the Jews, and also to the Greeks, repentance toward God, and faith in our Lord Jesus Christ* " (ch. xx. 21). . . . The church established by the Lord through them is at this day so nearly consummated that scarcely any remnant of it is left; and this has come to pass because they have divided the Trinity into three persons, each of which is God and Lord. And from this a sort of a frenzy has been diffused into all theology, and so into the church which from the name of the Lord is called Christian. It is called frenzy, because the minds of men have been driven by it to such distraction that they do not know whether God is one, or whether there are three. He is one in the word of the mouth, but three in the thought of the mind. The mind is therefore at variance with its mouth, or the thought with its utterance; from which variance it results that there is no God. The prevailing naturalism of the day is from no other source. Consider, if you please, when the mouth says one and the mind thinks three, whether within, where they meet (*in media via*), the one does not in turn destroy the other. Consequently a man scarcely hinks of God, if he does think, otherwise than from the bare vord, without any sense which involves a cognition of it. T. C. R. n. 4.)

In the primitive church, after the Lord's advent, all the members of the church lived as brethren among one another, and also called each other brethren, and mutually loved one another. But afterwards, in the course of time, charity diminished and vanished away. As charity vanished, evils succeeded ; and with evils falsities also insinuated themselves. Hence arose schisms and heresies; which would never have been if charity had lived and ruled. Then a schism would not even have been called schism, nor a heresy heresy, but a doctrinal [belief] according to the opinion of him who held it; which they would have left to the conscience of every one,—if only it did not deny the principles, that is, the Lord, eternal life, and the Word; and if it was not against Divine order, that is contrary to the precepts of the Decalogue. (A. C. n. 1834.)

THE PRESENT STATE OF THIS CHRISTIAN CHURCH.

I have been told that good of the will, which was enjoyed by the men of the Most Ancient church, was entirely lost among the antediluvians; and that at this day, among the men of the Christian church, good of the understanding is beginning to perish, insomuch that but little of it remains,—for the reason that they believe nothing unless they comprehend it by the senses, and that at this day they not only reason from the senses concerning Divine arcana, but also by a philosophy unknown to the ancients. Through this means the light of the understanding is entirely darkened; and the darkness is become so great that it can scarcely be dispelled. (A. C. n. 2124.)

That within the church at this day faith is so rare that it can scarcely be said to exist at all, was made evident from many of the learned and many of the simple, whose spirits after death were examined as to what their faith had been in this world. It was found that every one of them supposed faith to be merely believing and persuading themselves that the truth is so; and that the more learned of them made it to consist entirely in believing, with trust or confidence, that they are saved by the Lord's passion and His intercession; and that hardly one among them knew that there is no faith if there is no charity or love. Nay, it was found that they did not know what charity to the neighbour is, nor the difference between thinking and willing. For the most part they turn their backs upon charity, saying that charity does nothing, but that faith alone is effective. When it was replied to them that charity and faith are one, as the will and the understanding are one, and that charity has its seat in the will, and faith in the understanding, and that to separate the one from the other is as it were to separate the will from the understanding, they did not comprehend. It was thus made evident to me that scarcely any faith exists at the present day. . . . Such then is the state of the church at this day; namely, that there is no faith in it because there is no charity; and where there is no charity there is no spiritual good, for that good exists from charity alone. It was declared from heaven that there is still good with some, but that it cannot be called spiritual, but natural good ; because essential Divine truths are in obscurity, and Divine truths introduce to charity, for they teach it, and regard it as their end and aim. There can therefore be no other charity than such as accords with the truths which form it. The Divine truths from which the doctrines of the churches are derived relate to faith alone; on which account they are called the doctrines of faith, and have no reference to life. But truths which regard faith alone, and not life, cannot make man spiritual; for so long as they are external to the life they are only natural, being merely known and thought of as common things. Hence it is that there is no spiritual good at the present day, but only natural good with some. (L. J. n. 37, 38.)

" *All these are the beginning of sorrows. Then shall they deliver you into tribulation, and shall kill you ; and ye shall be hated of all nations, for My name's sake. And then shall many be offended, and shall betray one another, and shall hate one another. And many false prophets shall rise, and shall seduce many. And because iniquity shall increase the charity of many shall wax cold. But he that shall remain steadfast unto the end, the same shall be saved. And this gospel of the kingdom shall be preached in all the inhabited world for a testimony unto all nations. And then shall the end be"* (Matt. xxiv. 8-14). By these words the second state of perversion of the church is described; which is, that good and truth would be despised, and also turned away from, and that thus faith in the Lord would expire according to the degree in which charity would cease. . . .

That such is the church does not appear to those who are in the church; namely, that they despise and are averse to all things which are of good and truth, and that they bear enmities against those things, and especially against the Lord Himself. For they frequent the temples, hear preaching, are in a kind of holy [state] while there, attend the Holy Supper, and sometimes converse among themselves in a becoming manner concerning these things. Thus do the bad equally with the good; they also live among themselves in civil charity or friendship. Hence it is that to the eyes of men no contempt appears, still less aversion, and less still enmity against the goods and truths of faith, and thus against the Lord. But these are external forms by which one seduces another; and the internal forms of the men of the church are quite unlike, even entirely contrary to the external forms. The internal forms are what are here described, and are of such a character. The real quality of these appears to the life in the heavens. For the angels do not attend to any other than internal things, that is to ends, or to intentions and volitions, and to thoughts from these. How unlike these are to the externals may be clearly seen from those who come from the Christian world into the other life; it is the internals alone according to which they think and speak in the other life, since the externals are left with the body. And there it is manifest that, although such appeared peaceable in the world, yet they entertained hatred to one another, and hatred towards all things of faith, especially towards the Lord. For when the Lord is only named before them in the other life, a sphere not only of contempt, but even of aversion and enmity against Him, manifestly goes forth from and surrounds them; even from those who in appearance talked piously of Him, and who also had preached. So when charity and faith are mentioned. Such are they in the internal form, which is there made manifest, that if external restraints had been removed while they lived in the world, that is, if they had not feared for life, and the penalties of the laws, and especially if they had not feared for reputation on account of the honours which they aspired to and sought to obtain, and the wealth which they desired and eagerly strove after, they would from intestine hatred have rushed one against another according to their impulses and thoughts; and without any conscience they would have seized the goods of others, and without conscience would also have cruelly murdered especially the inoffensive. Such are Christians at this day as to their interiors, except a few who are not known. From this it appears what the quality of the church is. (A. C. n. 3486-3489.)

"*For then shall be great tribulation, such as was not from the beginning of the world to this time, no, nor ever shall be; and except those days should be shortened, there should no flesh be saved*" (Matt. xxiv. 21, 22). This is said of the last time of the church, when the judgment takes place. That such is the state of the church at this day may be known from these considerations alone: That in the greatest part of the Christian world are those who have transferred to themselves the Divine power of the Lord, and would be worshipped as gods, and who invoke dead men,—and scarce any there invoke the Lord; and that the rest of the church make God three, and the Lord two, and place salvation, not in amendment of life, but in certain words devoutly uttered with the breath,—thus not in repentance, but in confidence that they are justified and sanctified, if only they fold their hands and look upwards, and utter some customary form of prayer. (A. R. n. 263.)

THE END OF THE FIRST CHRISTIAN CHURCH.

The greater part of mankind believe that when the last judgment comes all things in the visible world are to be destroyed, that the earth will be consumed by fire, the sun and the moon will be dissipated, and the stars will vanish away; and that afterwards a new heaven and a new earth will spring forth. This opinion they have taken from Prophetic revelations, wherein such things are mentioned. But the last judgment is nothing else than the end of the church with one nation, and its beginning with another; which end and which beginning take place when there is no longer any acknowledgment of the Lord, or, what is the same, when there is no faith. There is no acknowledgment or no faith when there is no charity; for faith cannot exist except with those who are in charity. That then is the end of the church and its transfer to others, clearly appears from all that the Lord Himself taught and foretold in the Evangelists concerning that last day, or the consummation of the age; namely, in Matt. xxiv., Mark xiii., and in Luke xxi. But as these teachings cannot be comprehended by any one without the key, which is their internal sense, it is permitted to unfold in order the things which are therein, beginning with these words in Matthew: "*The disciples came to Jesus, saying, Tell us when shall these things be, and what is the sign of Thy coming, and of the consummation of the age. And Jesus answering, said unto them, See that no one seduce you; for many shall come in My name, saying, I am Christ, and shall seduce many: but ye shall hear of wars and rumours of wars; see that ye be not disturbed; for all these things must needs be, but the end is not yet. For nation shall be stirred up against nation, and kingdom against kingdom; and there shall be famines, and pestilences, and earthquakes. But all these things are the beginning of sorrows*" (xxiv. 3-8). Those who adhere to the sense of the letter cannot know whether these, and the particulars which follow in this chapter, were spoken of the destruction of Jerusalem and the dispersion of the Jewish nation, or of the end of days, which is called the last judgment; but those who are in the internal sense see clearly that the end of the church is here treated of, which end is what here and elsewhere is called the coming of the Lord, and the consummation of the age. And as this is the end here meant, it may be known that all the above particulars signify things pertaining to the church; and what they signify is evident from the particulars, in the internal sense. As that "*many shall come in My name, saying, I am Christ, and shall seduce many.*" Here name does not signify a name, nor Christ, Christ; but name signifies that by means of which the Lord is worshipped, and Christ signifies the very truth. Thus the signification is that there would come those who would say, This is of faith, or, This is true, when yet it is neither of faith, nor true, but false. That they should *hear of wars and rumours of wars*, is, that there would be disputes and quarrels concerning truths, which are wars in the spiritual sense; that *nation should rise up against nation, and kingdom against kingdom*, signifies that evil would combat with evil, and the false with the false; and *there shall be famines and pestilences, and earthquakes in divers places*, is that there would no longer be any cognitions of good and of truth, and thus that the state of the church would be changed, which is [spiritually] an earthquake. (A. C. n. 3353.)

"*But immediately after the affliction of those days*" signifies the state of the Church as to the truth which is of faith, which state is treated of in what precedes; desolation of truth throughout the Word is called affliction. Hence it is evident that these words signify that when there is no longer any faith there will be no charity. For faith leads to charity, because it teaches what charity is; and charity receives its quality from the truths which are of faith, and the truths of faith receive their essence and their life from charity. "*The sun shall be darkened, and the moon shall not give her light,"* signifies love to the Lord, which is the sun, and charity towards the neighbour, which is the moon; to be darkened and not give light signifies that they would not appear, thus that they would vanish. The reason of this signification of the sun and moon is that in the other life the Lord appears as a sun to those in heaven who are in love to Him, who are called celestial, and as a moon to those who are in charity towards the neighbour, who are called spiritual. The sun and moon in the heavens, or the Lord, are never darkened, nor lose their light, but shine perpetually. Thus neither with the celestial is love to Him at any time obscured, nor charity towards the neighbour with the spiritual, in the heavens; nor on earth with those with whom those angels are, that is with those who are in love and in charity. But as to those who are in no love and charity, but in the love of self and of the world, and thence in hatreds and revenge,—they bring this darkness upon themselves. The case is the same as with the sun of the world; the sun shines perpetually, but when clouds interpose themselves it does not appear. "*And the stars shall fall from heaven,"* signifies that cognitions of good and truth shall be lost. Nothing else is signified in the Word by stars, wherever they are mentioned. "*And the powers of the heavens shall be shaken,"* signifies the foundations of the Church, which are said to be moved and shaken when these things perish; for the church on earth is the foundation of heaven, since the influx of good and truth through the heavens from the Lord ultimately terminates in the goods and truths of the man of the church. Thus when the man of the church is in such a perverted state as no longer to admit the influx of good and truth, the powers of the heavens are said to be shaken. On this account it is always provided by the Lord that somewhat of the church should remain; and that when an old church perishes a new church should be established. (*ib.* n. 4060.)

THE SECOND COMING OF THE LORD.

"*And then shall appear the sign of the Son of Man in heaven*" (Matt. xxiv. 30), signifies the appearing then of Divine Truth; a sign denotes an appearing; the Son of Man is the Lord as to Divine Truth. It is this appearing, or this sign, about which the disciples inquired when they said to the Lord, "*Tell us when shall these things come to pass, and what is the sign of Thy coming, and of the consummation of the age*" (ver. 3). For they knew from the Word that when the age was consummated the Lord would come, and they knew from the Lord that He would come again; and they understood by this that the Lord would come again into the world, not knowing as yet that as often as the church has been vastated, so often the Lord has come. Not that He has come in person, as when by nativity He assumed the Human and made this Divine, but by appearings,—either manifest, as when He appeared to Abraham in Mamre, to Moses in the bush, to the people of Israel on Mount Sinai, and to Joshua when he entered the land of Canaan; or not so manifest, as through the inspirations whereby the Word [was given], and afterwards through the Word. For the Lord is present in the Word; for all things of the Word are from Him and relate to Him, as is evident from what has been so frequently shown before. This is the appearing which is here signified by the sign of the Son of Man, and of which this verse treats. "*And then shall all the tribes of the earth mourn,*" signifies that all who are in the good of love and in the truth of faith shall be in grief. That mourning has this signification may be seen in Zechariah, chap. xii. verses 10-14; and tribes signify all things of good and truth, or of love and faith, consequently those who are in love and faith. They are called tribes of the earth, because they that are within the church are signified; the earth is the church. "*And they shall see the Son of Man coming in the clouds of the heavens, with power and great glory,*" signifies that then the Word shall be revealed as to its internal sense, in which the Lord is. The Son of Man is the Divine Truth which is therein. The clouds are the literal sense; power is predicated of the good, and glory of the truth that are therein. This is the coming of the Lord which is here meant; and not that according to the letter He will appear in the clouds. What now follows concerns the establishment of a New Church, which takes place when the old is vastated and rejected. "*He shall send forth His angels with a trumpet and a great voice,*" signifies election; not that it is effected by visible angels, still less by trumpets and by great voices, but by an influx of holy good and holy truth from the Lord through the angels. Therefore angels in the Word signify something appertaining to the Lord; here things which are from the Lord and concerning the Lord. By a trumpet and a great voice evangelization is signified, as also elsewhere in the Word. "*And they shall gather together the elect, from the four winds, from the end of the heavens even to the end of them,*" signifies the establishment of a New Church. The elect are they who are in the good of love and faith; the four winds, from which they shall be gathered together, are all states of good and truth; the end of the heavens even to the end of them are the internal and external things of the Church. These things then are what are signified by those words of the Lord. (A. C. n. 4060.)

THIS SECOND COMING OF THE LORD IS NOT A COMING IN PERSON, BUT IN THE WORD, WHICH IS FROM HIM, AND IS HIMSELF.

It is written in many places that the Lord will come in the clouds of heaven; but as no one has known what was meant by the clouds of heaven, men have believed that He would come in them in Person. That the clouds of heaven mean the Word in the sense of the letter, and that the glory and power in which He will also then come mean the spiritual sense of the Word, has hitherto been hidden; because no one hitherto has even conjectured that there is any spiritual sense in the Word, such as this in itself is. Now, since the Lord has opened to me the spiritual sense of the Word, and has granted me to be in company with angels and spirits in their world, as one of them, it is disclosed that by the clouds of heaven the Word in the natural sense is meant, and by power the Lord's might through the Word. That the clouds of heaven have this signification may be seen from these passages in the Word:—"*There is none like unto the God of Jeshurun, who rideth upon the heaven, and in His greatness upon the clouds*" (Deut. xxxiii. 26); "*Sing unto God, praise His name, extol Him who rideth upon the clouds*" (Ps. lxviii. 5); "*Jehovah rideth upon a swift cloud*" (Isa. xix. 1).

That the Lord is the Word is very certain from these words in John: "*In the beginning was the Word, and the Word was with God, and the Word was God, . . . and the Word was made flesh*"

(i. 1, 14). The Word here means Divine Truth; for Divine truth among Christians is from no other source than the Word. It is the fountain ·whence all churches bearing the name of Christ draw living waters in their fulness; although it is as in a cloud, in which its natural sense is, yet it is in glory and power, in which its spiritual and celestial sense is. It has been shown in the chapter on the Sacred Scripture, and in the chapter on the Decalogue or Catechism, that there are three senses in the Word, the natural, the spiritual, and the celestial, one within another. It is therefore clear that in John the Word means Divine Truth. . . . From all this it is plain that now also the Lord will appear in the Word. The reason why He will not appear in person is, that since His ascension into heaven He is in the glorified Human; and in this He cannot appear to any man unless He first open the eyes of his spirit; and these cannot be opened with any one who is in evils and thence in falsities; thus not with any of the goats which He sets at His left hand. Therefore when He manifested Himself to the disciples He first opened their eyes; for it is said, "*And their eyes were opened, and they knew Him; and He vanished out of their sight*" (Luke xxiv. 31). The same occurred with the women at the sepulchre after the resurrection; and therefore they then also saw angels sitting in the sepulchre and talking with them, whom no man can see with the material eye. Neither did the apostles see the Lord in the glorified Human before the Lord's resurrection with the eyes of the body, but in the spirit,—which appears after waking as if it were in sleep. This is evident from His transfiguration before Peter, James, and John, in that "*their eyes were heavy with sleep*" (Luke ix. 32). It is therefore vain to think the Lord will appear in person in the clouds of heaven; but He will appear in the Word which is from Him, thus which is Himself. (T. C. R. n. 776, 777.)

THIS SECOND COMING OF THE LORD IS EFFECTED BY MEANS OF A MAN, TO WHOM THE LORD HAS MANIFESTED HIMSELF IN PERSON, AND WHOM HE HAS FILLED WITH HIS SPIRIT, TO TEACH THE DOCTRINES OF THE NEW CHURCH FROM HIMSELF, THROUGH THE WORD.

Since the Lord cannot manifest Himself in Person, as shown just above, and yet has foretold that He would come and establish a New Church, which is the New Jerusalem, it follows that this will be effected by means of a man, who is able not only to receive the doctrines of that church into his understanding, but also to publish them by the press. I testify in truth, that the Lord manifested Himself to me His servant, and sent me to this office; and that afterwards He opened the sight of my spirit, and so intromitted me into the spiritual world, and has granted me to see the heavens and the hells, and also to converse with angels and spirits, and this now continually for many years; likewise that from the first day of that calling I have not received anything whatever relating to the doctrines of that church from any angel, but from the Lord alone, while I was reading the Word.

To the end that the Lord might continually be present, He has opened to me the spiritual sense of His Word, in which Divine Truth is in its light. And in this light He is continually present; for His presence in the Word is no otherwise than by the spiritual sense. By the light of this He passes through into the shade in which the sense of the letter is; comparatively as the light of the sun in the daytime does through an interposing cloud. (T. C. R. n. 779, 780.)

It has been given me to perceive distinctly what comes from the Lord, and what from the angels; what has come from the Lord has been written, and what from the angels has not been written. (A. E. n. 1183.)

The things which I have learned in representations, in visions, and from conversations with spirits, and with angels, are from the Lord alone.

Whenever there has been any representation, vision, or conversation, I was kept interiorly and most deeply in reflection upon it, as to what therefrom was useful and good, thus as to what I might learn (which reflection was not particularly observed by those who produced the representations and visions, and who conversed; nay, sometimes they were indignant when they perceived that I was reflecting). Thus have I been instructed; therefore by no spirit, nor by any angel, but by the Lord only, from whom is all truth and good. On the contrary, when they wished to instruct me on various subjects, there was scarcely anything but was false; for which reason I was prohibited from believing anything they said; nor was I permitted to infer any such thing whatever as was of their *proprium.* Moreover, when they wished to persuade me, I perceived an interior or inmost persuasion that it is so,—not as they wished; at which also they marvelled. The perception was manifest, but cannot easily be described to the apprehension of man. (S. D. n. 1647.)

The things related by me are not miracles, but are proofs that for certain ends I have been introduced by the Lord into the spiritual world.

In order that the true Christian religion might be unfolded, it was necessary that one should be introduced into the spiritual world, and receive from the mouth of the Lord genuine truths out of the Word.

In addition to the most evident proofs that the spiritual sense of the Word has been laid open by the Lord through me, who ever before [has had such experiences] since the Word was revealed in the Israelitish writings ? And this sense is the very Sanctuary of the Word. The Lord Himself is in this sense with His Divine ; and in the natural sense with His Human. Not even one jot of this could be opened but by the Lord Himself. This excels (*præstat*) all the revelations that have been made hitherto since the creation of the world.

The manifestation of the Lord and immission into the spiritual world excels all miracles. This has not been granted to any one in the same manner as to me since the creation of the world. The men of the golden age talked indeed with angels; but it was not granted them to be in any other than natural light; while to me it has been granted to be both in natural and in spiritual light at the same time. Thereby it has been granted me to see the wonders of heaven ; to be among the angels, as one of them; and at the same time to receive Divine Truths in the light, and so to perceive and teach them,—and therefore to be led of the Lord. (*Invitation to the New Church*, n. 29, 38, 44, 52.)

How the Lord's Advent becomes effective in the Individual Man.

The Lord's presence is perpetual with every man, the evil as well as the good ; for without His presence no man lives. But His advent is to those only who receive Him,—who are those that believe in Him, and do His Commandments. The effect of the Lord's perpetual presence is, that man is made rational, and that he can become spiritual. This is effected by the light proceeding from the Lord as a sun in the spiritual world, which man receives in his understanding; and that light is the truth by which he has rationality. But the Lord's advent is to him who conjoins heat with that light, that is, love with he truth ; for the heat proceeding from that same sun is love to God and towards the neighbour. The mere presence of the Lord, and enlightenment of the understanding thereby, may be compared to the presence of the light of the sun in the world ; unless it is conjoined with heat all things on earth become desolate. But the advent of the Lord may be compared to the advent of heat, which takes place in the springtime; and because heat then conjoins itself with the light, the earth is softened, seeds shoot forth and bear fruit. Such a parallelism exists between the spiritual things in which a man's spirit dwells, and the natural things in which his body lives. (T. C. R. n. 774.)

THE FIFTH OR NEW CHRISTIAN CHURCH.

IT was foretold in the Apocalypse, chap. xxi., xxii., that at the end of the former church a New Church would be established, in which this should be the primary doctrine: That God is One, both in person and in essence, and that the Lord is that God. This Church is what is there meant by the New Jerusalem; into which no one can enter but who acknowledges the Lord alone as God of heaven and earth. Wherefore this church is there called *the Lamb's Wife*. And this I am able to proclaim: That the whole heaven acknowledges the Lord alone, and that whoever does not acknowledge Him is not admitted into heaven; for heaven is heaven from the Lord. This acknowledgment, from love and faith, itself effects that those who are in heaven are in the Lord and the Lord in them; as He Himself teaches in John: "*At that day ye shall know that I am in My Father, and ye in Me, and I in you*" (xiv. 20); and in the same: "*Abide in Me, and I in you, . . . I am the vine, ye are the branches; he that abideth in Me and I in him the same bringeth forth much fruit; for without Me ye can do nothing. If a man abide not in Me he is cast forth*" (xv. 4-6; also xvii. 22, 23).

The reason why this was not seen before from the Word, is that if it had been seen it would not have been received; for the Last Judgment was not yet accomplished, and before that the power of hell prevailed over the power of heaven,—and man is in the midst between heaven and hell. If therefore this had been seen before, the devil, that is hell, would have plucked it from the hearts of men, and moreover would have profaned it. This condition of the power of hell was entirely broken by the Last Judgment, which has now been accomplished. Since that, that is, now, every man who will can be enlightened, and be wise. (D. P. n. 263.)

THIS NEW CHURCH IS SIGNIFIED BY THE NEW JERUSALEM.

That a New Church is meant by the New Jerusalem coming down from God out of heaven (Rev. xxi.), is because Jerusalem was the metropolis of the land of Canaan; and there were the temple and the altar, there the sacrifices were offered, and thus there the actual Divine worship was performed to which every male in the land was commanded to go up three times in the year; and because the Lord was in Jerusalem, and taught in its temple, and afterwards glorified His Human there. Hence it is that the church is signified by Jerusalem. That the church is meant by Jerusalem, is very evident from the prophecies in the Old Testament repecting the new church to be instituted by the Lord, in that it is there called Jerusalem. Only those passages shall be adduced from which every one endued with interior reason may see that the church is there meant by Jerusalem. Let these passages only be cited therefrom: "*Behold, I create a new heaven and a new earth ; the former shall not be remembered. . . . Behold I create Jerusalem a rejoicing, and her people a joy, and I will rejoice over Jerusalem, and joy over My people. . . . Then the wolf and the lamb shall feed together ; . . . they shall not do evil in all the mountain of My holiness*" (Isaiah lxv. 17-19, 25). "*For Zion's sake I will not hold my peace, and for Jerusalem's sake I will not rest, until the righteousness thereof go forth as brightness, and the salvation thereof as a lamp that burneth. Then the nations shall see thy righteousness, and all kings thy glory ; and thou shalt be called by a new name, which the mouth of Jehovah shall name. And thou shalt be a crown of glory . . . and a royal diadem in the hand of thy God. . . . Jehovah shall delight in thee, and thy land shall be married. . . . Behold, thy salvation cometh ; behold, His reward is with Him. . . . And they shall call them The holy People, The redeemed of Jehovah ; and thou shalt be called A city sought for, not forsaken*" (lxii. 1-4, 11, 12). "*Awake, awake, put on thy strength, O Zion ; put on the garments of thy beauty, O Jerusalem, the city of holiness ; for henceforth there shall no more come into thee the uncircumcised and the unclean. Shake thyself from the dust ; arise, sit down, O Jerusalem. . . . The people shall know my name in that day, for it is I that speak, behold, it is I. . . . Jehovah hath comforted His people, He hath redeemed Jerusalem*" (lii. 1, 2, 6, 9). "*Thus saith Jehovah, I am returned unto Zion, and will dwell in the midst of Jerusalem; wherefore Jerusalem shall be called the City of Truth, and the Mountain of Jehovah of Hosts, the Holy Mountain*" (Zech. viii. 3). "*Then shall ye know that I am Jehovah your God, dwelling in Zion the mountain of holiness ; and Jerusalem shall be Holiness. . . . And it shall come to pass in that day that the mountains shall drop down new wine, and the hills shall flow with milk, . . . and Jerusalem shall abide from generation to generation*" (Joel iii. 17, 20). "*In that day shall the branch of Jehovah be beautiful and glorious. . . . And it shall come to pass that he that is left in Zion, and he that re-*

maineth in Jerusalem shall be called holy, every one that is written among the living in Jerusalem " (Isaiah iv. 2, 3). *" At that time they shall call Jerusalem the Throne of Jehovah, and all nations shall be gathered into it, on account of the name of Jehovah at Jerusalem ; neither shall they walk any more after the stubbornness of their evil heart* " (Jer. iii. 17). *" Look upon Zion, the city of our festivities : Thine eyes shall see Jerusalem a quiet Habitation, a Tabernacle that shall not be taken down ; not one of the stakes thereof shall ever be removed, neither shall any of the cords thereof be broken* " (Isaiah xxxiii. 20). That by Jerusalem here the church is meant which was to be instituted by the Lord, and not the Jerusalem inhabited by the Jews, is manifest from every part of its description in the passages adduced ; as that Jehovah God would create a new heaven and a new earth, and also at the same time Jerusalem ; and that this Jerusalem would be a crown of glory and a royal diadem ; that it was to be called Holiness, and the City of Truth, the Throne of Jehovah, a Quiet Habitation, a Tabernacle that shall not be taken down ; that there the wolf and the lamb shall feed together ; and there it is said the mountains shall drop new wine, and the hills shall flow with milk, and that it shall abide from generation to generation ; and, besides many other things, it is also said of the people there that they should be holy, every one written among the living ; and that they should be called the Redeemed of Jehovah. Moreover, in all these passages the coming of the Lord is referred to ; especially His second coming, when Jerusalem will be such as is there described. For before she was not married, that is, made the bride and wife of the Lamb, as is said of the New Jerusalem in the Apocalypse. The former church, or that of the present day, is meant by Jerusalem in Daniel ; and its beginning is there described by these words : *" Know and perceive that from the going forth of the word for restoring and building Jerusalem, even to the Prince Messiah, shall be seven weeks ; after that in sixty and two weeks the street and the trench shall be restored and built, but in troublous times* " (ix. 25). And its end is there described by these words : *" At length upon the bird of abominations shall be desolation, and even to the consummation and decision it shall drop upon the devastation* " (ver. 27). These last are what are meant by the Lord's words in Matthew : *" When ye shall see the abomination of desolation, foretold by Daniel the prophet, standing in the holy place, let him that readeth observe well* " (xxiv. 25). That Jerusalem in the passages above quoted did not mean the Jerusalem inhabited by the Jews, may be seen from the passages in the Word where it is said of this that it was utterly lost, and that it was to be destroyed. (T. C. R. n. 782.)

THE NEW HEAVEN AND THE NEW EARTH.

"*And I saw a new heaven and a new earth*" (Rev. xxi. 1), signifies that a new heaven was formed by the Lord from among Christians, which at this day is called the Christian heaven; where they are who had worshipped the Lord and lived according to His commandments in the Word,—in whom therefore there is charity and faith. In this heaven are also all the infants of Christians. A natural heaven visible to the eyes, and a natural earth inhabited by men, are not meant by a new heaven and a new earth; but a spiritual heaven is meant, and the earth of that heaven, where angels dwell. That this heaven and the earth of this heaven are meant, every one may see and acknowledge if he can but withdraw himself somewhat from a merely natural and material conception when he reads the Word. It is plain that an angelic heaven is meant; for it is said in the verse immediately following, that he saw the holy city Jerusalem coming down from God out of heaven, prepared as a bride adorned for her husband; by which no Jerusalem descending is meant, but a church. And the church upon earth comes down from the Lord out of the angelic heaven, because the angels of heaven and men on earth in all things relating to the church form one. It may be seen from this how naturally and materially they have thought and think, who, from these words and those that follow in this verse, have fabricated the dogma of the destruction of the world, and of a new creation of all things. This new heaven is several times previously referred to in the Apocalypse, especially in chap. xiv. and xv. It is called the Christian heaven because it is distinct from the ancient heavens, which were composed of the men of the church before the Lord's coming. These ancient heavens are above the Christian heaven; for the heavens are like expanses one above the other. It is the same with each heaven; for each heaven by itself is distinguished into three heavens, an inmost or third, a middle or second, and a lowest or first heaven. So it is with this new heaven. I have seen those who are there and conversed with them. In this new Christian heaven are all, from the first formation of the Christian church, who have worshipped the Lord and lived according to His commandments in the Word, and who therefore were in charity and at the same time in faith from the Lord through the Word,— and thus who were not in a dead but a living faith. All the infants of Christians are likewise in that heaven, because they are educated by angels in those two essentials of the church; which are, an acknowledgment of the Lord as the God of heaven and earth, and a life according to the commandments of the decalogue. (A. R. n. 876.)

It is according to Divine order that a new heaven should be formed before a New Church on earth. For the church is internal and external, and the internal church forms one with the church in heaven, that is with heaven; and the internal must be formed before the external, and afterwards the external by the internal. That it is so is known among the clergy in the world. As this new heaven which constitutes the internal with man increases, the New Jerusalem, that is the New Church, comes down from that heaven. This cannot therefore come to pass in a moment, but takes place as the falsities of the former church are removed. For what is new cannot enter where falsities have previously been ingenerated unless these are eradicated; which will be effected among the clergy, and so among the laity. (T. C. R. n. 784.)

ALL THINGS MADE NEW.

"*And He that sat upon the throne said, Behold, I make all things new. And He said unto me, Write, for these words are true and faithful*" (ver. 5). This signifies the Lord saying these things, concerning the last judgment, to those who should come into the world of spirits, or should die, from the time when He was in the world until now; namely, that the former heaven with the former earth, and the former church, with each and all things in them, should perish, and that He would create a new heaven with a new earth, and a new church, which should be called the New Jerusalem; and that they may know this of a certainty, and keep it in remembrance, because the Lord Himself has testified and declared it. The things contained in this verse, and in the following as far as the 8th inclusive, were said to those in the Christian world who should come into the world of spirits,—which is immediately after death,—to the end that they might not suffer themselves to be seduced by the Babylonians[1] and dragonists. For, as was said above, all congregate after death in the world of spirits,—and they incline to association with one another, as in the natural world,—where they are in company with Babylonians and dragonists, who continually burn with the desire to lead astray; and who were also permitted to form heavens, as it were, for themselves, by imaginative and illusive arts,—by which, too, they were able to mislead. Lest this should be done these words were spoken by the Lord, that they might certainly know that these heavens with their earths would perish, and that the Lord would create a new heaven and a new earth; at which time those that did not suffer themselves to be led astray would be saved. But it should be known that these

[1] See note, p. 172.

things were said to those who lived from the Lord's time down to the last judgment, which was executed in the year of our Lord 1757,—because these could have been led astray. But this they cannot be hereafter there, because the Babylonians and dragonists have been separated and cast out. (A. R. n. 886.)

The Vision of the Holy City.

"*And he carried me away in the spirit to a great and high mountain, and showed me that great city, the holy Jerusalem, descending out of heaven from God*" (ver. 10). This signifies that John was translated into the third heaven, and that his sight was there opened, and the Lord's New Church was manifested before him, as to doctrine, in the form of. a city. "He carried me away in the spirit to a great and high mountain," signifies that John was translated into the third heaven, where they are who are in love to the Lord, and in the genuine doctrine of truth from Him. Great is also predicated of the good of love, and high of truths. Carried away into a mountain signifies taken up into the third heaven, because it is said "in the spirit," and he who is in the spirit as to his mind and its sight is in the spiritual world; and there the angels of the third heaven dwell upon mountains, the angels of the second heaven upon hills, and the angels of the lowest heaven in valleys among the hills and mountains. When, therefore, any one in the spirit is taken up into a mountain, it signifies that he is taken up into the third heaven. This elevation is effected in a moment, because it is done by a change of state in the mind. "He showed me," signifies that his sight was then opened, and manifestation. "That great city, the holy Jerusalem, descending out of heaven from God," signifies the Lord's New Church; for this reason it is called holy, and is said to descend out of heaven from God; it was seen in the form of a city, because a city signifies doctrine, and the church is a church by virtue of doctrine and life according to it. It was seen as a city also in order that it might be described as to its every quality; and it is described by its wall, its gates, its foundations, and various dimensions. The church is described in a similar manner in Ezekiel, where it is also said that the prophet was *led in the visions of God upon a very high mountain, and saw a city on the south, which the angel also measured as to its wall, and gates, and as to its breadth and height* (xl. 2, and following verses). The same is meant by these words in Zechariah: "*Then said I unto the angel, Whither goest thou? And he said unto me, To measure Jerusalem, to see what is the breadth thereof, and what is the length thereof*" (ii. 2). (A. R. n. 896.)

The City Four-square.

"*And the city lieth four-square*" (ver. 16). The reason why the city was seen four-square is that a quadrangle or square signifies justice, for a triangle signifies righteousness,—all these in the ultimate degree, which is the natural. A quadrangle or a square signifies justice because it has four sides and the four sides look to the four quarters, and to look equally to the four quarters is to look at all things from justice. Therefore three gates from each quarter opened into the city; and it is said in Isaiah, "*Open ye the gates, that the righteous nation, which keepeth truths, may enter in*" (xxvi. 2). The city lieth four-square, that the length and breadth thereof might be equal; and by the length is signified the good of that church, and by the breadth its truth; and when good and truth are equal there is justice. It is from this signification of a square, that in common speech a man is said to be square, who inclines neither to this side nor that from injustice. Because four-square signifies justice the altar of burnt-offering was four-square, by which worship from good and thence from celestial truth was signified (Exod. xxvii. 1); and the altar of incense, by which was signified worship from good and thence from spiritual truth, was also four-square (Exod. xxx. 1, 2; xxxix. 9). And the breastplate of judgment too, in which was the Urim and Thummim, was four-square doubled (Exod. xxviii. 15, 16); besides other things. (A. R. n. 905.)

The City pure Gold.

"*And the city was pure gold like unto pure glass*" (ver. 18) signifies that therefore the all of that church is the good of love, flowing in together with light out of heaven, from the Lord. By the city or Jerusalem the Lord's New Church is meant, as to every thing pertaining to it, viewed interiorly or within the wall; by gold the good of love from the Lord is signified; and like unto pure glass signifies pellucid, from Divine wisdom,—and since this appears in heaven as light, and flows from the Lord as the sun, by "like unto pure glass" is signified, flowing in together with light from heaven, from the Lord. . . . Since the good of love does not exist by itself or separate from the truths of wisdom, but that it may be the good of love must be formed, and it is formed by the truths of wisdom, therefore it is here said pure gold like unto pure glass. For the good of love without the truths of wisdom has no quality, because it has no form; and its form is according to its truths, flowing in, in their order and connection, together with the good of love, from the Lord; thus in man it is according to reception. It is said in man, but it is not meant that it is of the man, as his own, but of the Lord in him. From these considerations then, it is plain that by the city being pure gold like unto pure glass, it is signified that therefore the all of that church is the good of love, flowing in with light from heaven, from the Lord. (A. R. n. 912.)

THE TWELVE FOUNDATIONS.

" *The first foundation was jasper; the second, sapphire; the third, chalcedony; the fourth, emerald; the fifth, sardonyx; the sixth, sardius; the seventh, chrysolite; the eighth, beryl; the ninth, topaz; the tenth, chrysoprasus, the eleventh, jacinth; the twelfth, amethyst* " (ver. 19, 20). This signifies all things of that doctrine in their order from the literal sense of the Word, with those who immediately approach the Lord, and live according to the commandments of the decalogue by shunning evils as sins; for these and no others are in the doctrine of love to God, and of love towards the neighbour, which two are the fundamentals of religion. The twelve foundations of the wall signify all [truths] of doctrine of the New Jerusalem, from the literal sense of the Word. Precious stones in general signify all truths of doctrine from the Word translucent by the spiritual sense; here by each stone some truth in particular is signified thus translucent. There are in general two colours which prevail in the precious stones, red and white; the other colours, as green, yellow, blue, and many others, are composed of these by the mediation of black. By the colour red the good of love is signified and by the colour white the truth of wisdom. Red signifies the good of love because it derives its origin from the fire of the sun, and the fire of the sun of the spiritual world in its essence is the Lord's Divine love, thus the good of love; and white signifies the truth of wisdom because it derives its origin from the light which proceeds from the fire of that sun, and that proceeding light in its essence is Divine wisdom, thus the truth of wisdom; and black derives its origin from their shade or shadow, which is ignorance. But to explain separately what good and what truth is signified by each stone, would be too prolix. But yet that it may be known what good and what truth each stone in this order signifies, see the explanation given at chap. vii. ver. 5-8, where the twelve tribes of Israel are treated of; for the same is here signified by each stone as there by each tribe mentioned, since by the twelve tribes there described all the goods and truths of the church and its doctrine in their order are likewise signified. It is therefore said also in this chapter (ver. 14) *that in these twelve foundations were written the names of the twelve apostles of the Lamb;* and by the twelve apostles all things of doctrine concerning the Lord are signified, and concerning life according to His commandments.   The same also is signified by these twelve stones as by the twelve precious stones in the breast-plate of Aaron, which was called the Urim and Thummim,—of which in Exod. xxviii. 15-21, and which are separately explained in the *Arcana Cœlestia,*—with the difference, that upon those were the names of the twelve tribes of Israel, and upon these the names of the twelve apostles of the Lamb.   That the foundations are of precious stones is also said in Isaiah: " *O thou afflicted, . . . behold, I will lay thy stones with fair colours, and lay thy founda-tions with sapphires, . . . and thy gates of carbuncles, . . . and all thy children shall be taught of Jehovah* " (Isaiah liv. 11, 12). By the afflicted the church is meant that was to be established by the Lord among the Gentiles.   In the same: " *Therefore, thus saith the Lord Jehovah, Behold, I lay in Zion for a foundation, a stone, a tried stone, a precious corner stone, a sure foundation. . . . Judgment also will I lay to the line, and righteousness to the plummet* " (xxviii. 16, 17).   Since all truth of doctrine from the Word must be founded upon the acknowledgment of the Lord, therefore the Lord is called the Stone of Israel (Gen. xlix. 24); and the Corner Stone, which the builders rejected (Matt. xxi. 42); Mark xii. 10, 11; Luke xx. 17, 18).   That the corner stone is the foundation stone appears from Jerem. li. 26.   The Lord also in many places in the Word is called a rock; therefore by the rock He meant Himself when He said, " *Upon this rock will I build my church* " (Matt. xvi. 18, 19); and also when He said, " *Whosoever heareth my sayings and doeth them, is to be likened unto a prudent man, who buildeth a house and layeth the foundation upon a rock* " (Luke vi. 47, 48 ; Matt. vii. 24, 25).   By a rock the Lord as to the Divine truth of the Word is signified.   (A. R. n. 915.)

The Twelve Gates of Pearl.

" *And the twelve gates were twelve pearls ; every one of the gates was of one pearl* " (ver. 21), signifies that the acknowledgment and cognition [1] of the Lord conjoins into one all cognitions of truth and good which are from the Word, and introduces into the church.   By the twelve gates are signified, in a summary, the cognitions of truth and good by which man is introduced into the church ; by twelve pearls also cognitions of truth and good in a summary are signified.   Hence it is that the gates were pearls.   Every gate was of one pearl because all cognitions of

[1] See note, p. 284.

truth and good, which are signified by gates and by pearls, have reference to one cognition, which is their containant; which one cognition is cognition of the Lord. It is called one cognition, although there are several which constitute that one, because a cognition of the Lord is the universal of all things of doctrine, and hence of all things of the church. From this all matters of worship derive their life and soul; for the Lord is the all in all of heaven and the church, and therefore the all in all of worship. The reason why the acknowledgment and cognition of the Lord conjoins into one all cognitions of truth and good from the Word is, that there is a connection of all spiritual truths; and if you will believe it, their connection is like the connection of all the members, viscera, and organs of the body. Therefore, as the soul contains and holds all these in their order and connection, so that they are felt no otherwise than as one, so the Lord contains and holds together all spiritual truths in man. That the Lord is the very gate through which men must enter into the church and thence into heaven, He Himself teaches in John: "*I am the door; by Me if any man enter in, he shall be saved*" (x. 9); and that the acknowledgment and cognition of Him is the pearl of great price, is meant by these words of the Lord in Matthew: "*The kingdom of heaven is like unto a merchant-man seeking goodly pearls; who, when he had found one pearl of great price, went and sold all that he had, and bought it*" (xiii. 45, 46). The one pearl of great price is the acknowledgment and cognition of the Lord. (A. R. n. 916.)

The Temple of the City.

"*And I saw no temple therein; for the temple of it is the Lord God Almighty, and the Lamb*" (ver. 22). This signifies that in this church there will be no external separate from the internal, because the Lord Himself in His Divine Human, from whom is the all of the church, is alone approached, worshipped, and adored. I saw no temple therein, does not mean that in the New Church which is the New Jerusalem there will not be temples, but that in this church there will not be an external separate from the internal; the reason is that by a temple the church as to its worship is signified, and, in the highest sense, the Lord Himself as to His Divine Human, who is to be worshipped. And because the all of the church is from the Lord, therefore it is said, "For the Lord God Almighty and the Lamb is the Temple of it," by which the Lord in His Divine Human is signified; by the Lord God Almighty is meant the Lord from eternity, who is Jehovah Himself; and by the Lamb His Divine Human is signified. (A. R. n. 918.)

The Tree of Life in the Midst of the City.

" *In the midst of the street of it, and of the river on this side and on that, was the tree of life, which bare twelve manner of fruits* " (Rev. xxii. 2). This signifies that in the inmost of the truths of doctrine and thence of life in the New Church is the Lord in His Divine love, from whom flow all the goods that man does apparently as of himself. In the midst, signifies in the inmost and thence in all things around ; by the street the truth of the doctrine of the church is signified ; by a river is signified Divine truth in abundance. On either side, signifies on the right hand and on the left,—and the truth on the right hand is that which is in clearness, and on the left hand that which is in obscurity ; for in heaven the south, by which truth in its clearness is signified, is on the right hand, and the north, by which truth in obscurity is signified, is on the left. By the tree of life the Lord as to the Divine love is signified; by fruits are signified the goods of love and charity, which are called good works; by twelve all are signified, and it is predicated of the goods and truths of the church. From these particulars collated into one sense it follows that, " In the midst of the street and of the river, on this side and on that, was the tree of life bearing twelve manner of fruits," signifies that in the inmost of the truths of doctrine and of life in the New Church is the Lord in His Divine love, from whom flow all the goods that man does apparently as from himself. This is the case with those who approach the Lord immediately, and shun evils because they are sins, thus who will be in the Lord's New Church, which is the New Jerusalem. For they that do not approach the Lord immediately cannot be conjoined with Him; nor therefore with the Father ; and hence cannot be in the love which is from the Divine. For looking up to [Him] conjoins,—not intellectual looking alone, but intellectual looking from an affection of the will ; and there is no affection of the will unless a man keeps His commandments. Therefore the Lord says, " *He that hath My commandments, and keepeth them, he it is that loveth Me; and I will love him, and manifest Myself to him* " (John xiv. 21-24). It is said, in the inmost of the truths of doctrine and thence of life in the New Church, because in spiritual things all exist and all proceed from the inmost, as from fire and light in the centre to the circumferences ; or as from the sun, which in fact is the centre, heat and light proceed to all parts of the universe. It is thus the same in least things as in the greatest. Because the inmost of all truth is signified, therefore it is said, " in the midst of the street and of the river," and not on either side of the river, although this is meant. That all the goods of love and of charity exist and proceed from the Lord, because He is in the inmost, is plain from the Lord's own words in John: Jesus said, "*As the branch cannot bear fruit of itself, except it abide in the vine, no more can ye, except ye abide in Me. I am the Vine, ye are the branches; he that abideth in Me, and I in him, the same bringeth forth much fruit; for without Me ye can do nothing*" (xv. 4-6). (A. R. n. 933.)

THE LEAVES OF THE TREE FOR THE HEALING OF THE NATIONS.

"*And the leaves of the tree were for the healing of the nations*" (ver. 2), signifies rational truths therefrom, by which they who are in evils and thence in falsities are led to think sanely and to live becomingly. By the leaves of the tree rational truths are signified; by the nations they are signified who are in goods and thence in truths,—and, in the opposite sense, they who are in evils and thence in falsities. Here those who are in evils and thence in falsities are signified, because it is said "for the healing of them;" and those who are in evils and in falsities thence cannot be healed by the Word, for they do not read it, but if they are strong in judgment they can be healed by rational truths. A similar signification to that of this verse is contained in the following from Ezekiel: "*Behold waters went forth from under the threshold of the house . . . from which there was a river, upon whose bank on this side and on that were very many trees of meat, whose leaf doth not fall, neither shall be consumed; every month it springeth again; . . . and the fruit thereof is for meat, and the leaf thereof for medicine*" (xlvii. 1, 7, 12). Here also the New Church is referred to. Leaves signify rational truths, because by a tree man is signified, and therefore all things pertaining to a tree, as the branches, leaves, flowers, fruits, and seeds, signify corresponding things in man. By the branches are signified the sensual and natural truths in man; by the leaves, his rational truths; by the flowers, the earliest spiritual truths in the rational [mind]; by fruits, the goods of love and charity; and by seeds, the last and first [principles] of man. That leaves signify rational truths is very evident from those seen in the spiritual world; for there too trees appear, with leaves and fruits, and there are gardens and paradises of them. Among those who are in the goods of love and at the same time in the truths of wisdom, there appear luxuriant fruit trees, with beautiful leaves; and among those who are in truths of some wisdom, and speak from reason, but are not in the goods of love, trees full of leaves appear but without fruits; and among those who are neither in goods nor in truths of wisdom no trees appear unless denuded of their leaves, as in winter-time in the world. The man who is not rational is nothing else than such a tree. Rational truths are those which immediately receive spiritual truths. For the rational [faculty] of man is the first receptacle of spiritual truths; since in the rational of man there is, in some form, a perception of truth which the man himself does not see in thought, as he does the things which are under the rational, in the inferior thought that connects itself with external sight. Rational truths are likewise signified by leaves in Gen. iii. 7; viii. 11; Isa. xxxiv. 4; Jer. viii. 13; xvii. 8; Ezek. xlvii. 12; Dan. iv. 11, 12; Psa. i. 3; Lev. xxvi. 36; Matt. xxi. 19, 20; xxiv. 32; Mark xiii. 28. But the signification varies according to the kinds of trees; the leaves of the olive and the vine signify rational truths from celestial and spiritual light; the leaves of the fig tree, rational truths from natural light; and the leaves of the fir, the poplar, the oak, and the pine, rational truths from sensual light. The leaves of these last kinds excite terror in the spiritual world when they are shaken by a strong wind. These are what are meant in Levit. xxvi. 36; Job xiii. 25. But with the leaves of the former it is not so. (A. R. n. 936.)

Seeing the Face of the Lord.

"*And they shall see His face; and His name shall be in their foreheads*" (ver. 4). This signifies that they will turn themselves to the Lord, and that the Lord will turn Himself to them, because they will be conjoined by love. To see the face of God and of the Lamb, or of the Lord, does not mean to see His face, because no one can see His face, as He is in His Divine love and in His Divine wisdom, and live; for He is the sun of heaven and of the whole spiritual world. For, to see His face as He is in Himself would be as if one should enter into the sun; by the fire of which he would be consumed in a moment. Yet the Lord sometimes presents Himself to the sight out of His sun; but He then veils Himself, and thus presents Himself to their sight, —which is done by means of an angel. As He also did in the world, to Abraham, Hagar, Lot, Gideon, Joshua, and others; and therefore those angels were called both angels and Jehovah, for the presence of Jehovah was in them from afar. But here "they shall see His face," does not mean thus to see His face; but to see the truths which are from Him in the Word, and through them to have cognition of and acknowledge Him. For the Divine truths of the Word form the light in which the angels are, which proceeds from the Lord as a sun; and as they constitute the light, they are as mirrors in which the Lord's face is seen. That to see the Lord's face signifies to turn to Him will be shown below. The name of the Lord in their foreheads signifies that the Lord loves them and turns them to Himself. The name of the Lord signifies the Lord Himself, because it signifies every quality of Him whereby He is known, and according to which He is worshipped; and by the forehead love is signified; and written in the forehead signifies the Lord's love in them. From these considerations it may appear what is properly signified by these words. But the reason why it signifies that they will turn themselves to the Lord and the Lord will turn Himself to them is, that the Lord looks at all who are conjoined with Him by love in their forehead, and so turns them to Himself; wherefore the angels in heaven turn their faces only towards the Lord and the sun, and what is remarkable, this is done in every turning of their bodies. Hence it is in common speech that they have God always before their eyes. It is the same with the spirit of a man who lives in the world and by love is conjoined to the Lord. (A. R. n. 938.)

THE LIGHT OF THE CITY.

"*And there shall be no night there; and they need no lamp, neither light of the sun; for the Lord God giveth them light*" (ver. 5). This signifies that in the New Jerusalem there will be no falsity of faith, and that men there will be in cognitions concerning God not from natural light, which is from their own intelligence and from glory arising from pride, but will be in spiritual light from the Word from the Lord alone. "There shall be no night there," signifies the same as above, chap. xxi., where these words occur: "*And the gates of it shall not be shut at all by day, for there shall be no night there*" (ver. 25), by which is signified, that they are continually received into the New Jerusalem who are in truths from the good of love from the Lord, because there is no falsity of faith there. "They need no lamp, neither light of the sun, for the Lord God giveth them light," signifies the same as above, in chap. xxi., where are these words: "*And the city had no need of the sun, neither of the moon, to shine in it, for the glory of God did lighten it, and the Lamb is the lamp thereof*" (ver. 23), which signify that the men of that church will not be in the love of self and in their own intelligence, and hence only in natural light, but in spiritual light from the Divine truth of the Word from the Lord alone. But instead of the moon, which occurs there, the word lamp is used here, and instead of the sun there, it is here said the light of the sun; and by the moon as well as by a lamp, natural light from their own intelligence is signified, and by the light of the sun is signified the glory arising from pride. But it shall be briefly explained what is meant by natural light from the glory arising from pride. There is a natural light from the glory arising from pride, and also from glory that is not from pride. Light from the glory arising from pride is in those who are in the love of self, and thence in all manner of evils; which if for fear of loss of reputation they do not commit, and even condemn, as contrary to morality and against the public good, yet they do not regard them as sins. These are in natural light from the glory arising from pride; for love of self in the will becomes pride in the understanding, and this pride from that love can elevate the understanding even into the light of heaven. This [capability] is granted to man in order that he may be man, ånd that he may be capable of being re-formed. I have seen and heard many consummate devils who understood arcana of angelic wisdom when they heard and read them like the angels themselves; but the instant they returned to their love and their pride therefrom, they not only understood nothing of them, but even saw the contrary from the light of the confirmation of falsity within themselves. But natural light from glory not from pride is in those who are in the delight of uses from genuine love to the neighbour. The natural light of these is also rational light, within which interiorly there is spiritual light from the Lord. The glory in them is from the brightness of the light flowing in from heaven, where all things are splendid and harmonious; for in heaven all uses are re-splendent. The pleasantness in the ideas of thought in them from these is perceived as glory. It enters through the will and its goods, into the understanding and its truths, and in these becomes manifest. (A. R. n. 940.)

The New Jerusalem the Bride and Wife of the Lord.

It is said that John saw the holy city New Jerusalem coming down from God out of heaven, and here (Rev. xxi. 2) that he saw that city prepared as a bride for her husband; from which also it is evident that the church is meant by Jerusalem, and that he saw this, first as a city and afterwards as a virgin bride,—as a city representatively, and as a virgin bride spiritually. Thus that he saw it under a twofold idea, one within or above the other,—just as the angels do, who, when they see, hear, or read of a city in the Word, in the idea of their lower thought perceive a city, but in the idea of their higher thought perceive the church as to doctrine; and if they desire, and pray to the Lord, they see it as a virgin,—in beauty and apparel according to the quality of the church. Thus has it also been granted me to see the church. By "prepared" is signified, attired for her espousal; and the church is no otherwise made ready for espousal, and afterwards for conjunction or marriage, than by the Word; for this is the only medium of conjunction or marriage, because the Word is from the Lord and concerning the Lord, and thus the Lord; and therefore it is called also the covenant, and a covenant signifies spiritual conjunction. For this end indeed the Word was given. That the Lord is meant by "husband" is plain from verses 10 and 11 of this chapter, where Jerusalem is called "the bride, the Lamb's wife." From all this it may be seen, that by Jerusalem "prepared as a bride adorned for her husband" that church is signified, conjoined with the Lord by the Word. (A. R. n. 881.)

Memorabilia concerning the Tabernacle and Temple of the Holy City.

While I was engaged upon the explanation of the xxth chapter [of the Apocalypse], and was meditating upon the dragon, the beast, and the false prophet, one appeared to me, and asked, " What is the subject of your meditation ? " I said, " The false prophet." He then said, " I will lead you to a place where they are who are meant by the false prophet." He said they were the same that are meant in chap. xiii. by the " beast out of the earth, which had two horns like a lamb, and spake like a dragon." I followed him. And lo, I saw a multitude, in the midst of which were prelates, who taught that nothing but faith saves man, and that works are good, but not unto salvation; and yet that they are to be taught from the Word, in order that the laity, especially the simple, may be kept more strictly under the restraints of obedience to the magistracy, and forced, as if from religion thus interiorly, to exercise moral charity. And then one of them seeing me said, " Would you like to see our temple, in which there is an image representative of our faith ? " I went and saw it. And behold it was magnificent ! And in the midst of it there was an image of a woman clothed in a scarlet robe, holding in her right hand a gold coin, and in her left a string of large pearls. But both the temple and the image were produced by fantasies; for infernal spirits can represent magnificent things by fantasies, by closing the interiors of the mind and opening only its exteriors. But when I considered that they were illusions of this kind, I prayed to the Lord, and suddenly the interiors of my mind were opened, and then instead of a magnificent temple I saw a house full of chinks and crevices from

top to bottom, in which nothing was coherent; and instead of
the woman I saw hanging in that house a form, of which the
head was like a dragon's, the body like a leopard's, and the feet
like those of a bear,—thus like the beast described as rising out
of the sea in Rev. xiii.; and instead of a floor was a marsh, in
which there was a multitude of frogs; and I was told that beneath
the marsh there was a large hewn stone, under which the Word
lay, well hidden. Seeing this, I said to the juggler, "Is this your
temple?" And he said, "It is." But then suddenly his interior
sight also was opened, and he saw the same as I. Seeing which,
he cried out in a loud voice, "What is this, and whence is it?"
And I said, "It is from the light of heaven, which discovers the
quality of every form. And here is the quality of your faith
separate from spiritual charity." Then immediately an east wind
blew and carried away everything that was there, and also dried
up the marsh, and so laid bare the stone under which the Word
lay. And then there breathed a vernal warmth from heaven,
and lo! in the same place there appeared a tabernacle; as to
outward form, plain and simple. And the angels who were with
me said, "Behold the tabernacle of Abraham, as it was when the
three angels came to him and announced the future birth of
Isaac. It appears simple to the eye; but according to the influx
of light from heaven it is more and more magnificent." And it
was granted them to open the heaven in which the spiritual
angels dwell, who are in wisdom; and then by the inflowing light
from thence the tabernacle appeared as a temple, like that at
Jerusalem. And when I looked into it, I saw the foundation-
stone under which the Word was deposited set round about with
precious stones, from which as it were lightning flashed forth
upon the walls, on which there were forms of cherubim, and
beautifully variegated them with colours. I was wondering at
these things, when the angels said, "You shall see things still
more wonderful." And it was given them to open the third
heaven, in which the celestial angels dwell, who are in love;
and then by the inflowing light from thence that whole temple
vanished, and in its place the Lord alone was seen, standing upon
the foundation-stone, which was the Word, in the same form in
which He was seen by John (Rev. i.). But as a holiness then
filled the interiors of the minds of the angels, from which they
had a strong inclination to fall prostrate on their faces, the way
of the light from the third heaven was suddenly closed by the
Lord, and the way of light from the second heaven was opened,
by which the former appearance of the temple returned, and also
of the tabernacle, but within the temple. By these things it was
illustrated what is meant by the words in this chapter: "*Behold, the tabernacle of God is with men, and He will dwell with*

them" (ver. 3); and by these : "*And I saw no temple in the New Jerusalem; for the Lord God Omnipotent and the Lamb are the temple of it*" (ver. 22). (A. R. n. 926.)

The New Church in the Heavens signified by the Woman clothed with the Sun.

"*A woman clothed with the sun, and the moon under her feet*" (Rev. xii. 1), signifies the Lord's New Church in the heavens, which is the new heaven, and the Lord's New Church about to be on earth, which is the New Jerusalem. That by this woman the Lord's New Church is signified, appears from the particulars in this chapter understood in the spiritual sense. The church is signified by a woman in other parts of the Word also; and the church is signified because the church is called the bride and wife of the Lord. She appeared clothed with the sun because the church is in love to the Lord; for it acknowledges Him and does His commandments, and this is to love Him (John xiv. 21-24). The moon was seen under the feet of the woman because the church on earth is meant, which is not yet conjoined with the church in the heavens. The moon signifies intelligence in the natural man, and faith; and its appearing under the feet signifies that it is about to be on earth. Otherwise, by the feet that church itself is signified when it is conjoined. (A. R. n. 533.)

"*And upon her head a crown of twelve stars,*" signifies its wisdom and intelligence, from cognitions of Divine good and Divine truth from the Word. The crown upon her head signifies wisdom and intelligence; the stars signify cognitions of Divine good and Divine truth from the Word; and twelve signify all things of the church which relate to its good and truth. Thus the crown of twelve stars upon the woman's head signifies the wisdom and intelligence of the New Church, from cognitions of Divine good and Divine truth from the Word.

"*And she, being with child, cried, travailing in birth, and pained to be delivered*" (ver. 2), signifies the doctrine of the New Church about to come forth, and its difficult reception on account of the resistance of those who are meant by the dragon. To be with child signifies the doctrine about to come forth; because the child which was in the womb,—whose birth is spoken of in ver. 5,—signifies the doctrine of the New Church. For in the spiritual sense of the Word by being with child, travailing, and bringing forth, nothing is signified but the conception and bringing forth of things which are of spiritual life. "She cried, travailing in birth, and pained to be delivered," signifies difficult reception of that doctrine, because of resistance from those who are meant by the dragon. This is plain from what follows in this chapter; as that the dragon stood before the woman who was ready to be delivered, to devour her child; and afterwards pursued her into the wilderness. (*ib.* n. 534, 535.)

"*And behold a great red dragon*" (ver. 3), signifies those in the Reformed church who make God three, and the Lord two, and who separate charity from faith, and hold the latter,—and not together with the former,—to be saving. It is these who are meant, here and in what follows, by the dragon. For they are opposed to the two essentials of the New Church, which are : That God is one in essence and in person; in whom there is a trinity; and that the Lord is that God : And that charity and faith are one, as the essence and its form; and that none have charity and faith but those who live according to the commandments of the decalogue, which are commandments that evils are not to be done. And in so far as any one, by shunning evils as sins against God, does not do them, in so far he does the goods which are of charity, and believes the truths which are of faith. . . . By those who make God three, and the Lord two, they are meant who think of three persons as of three Gods, and separate the Lord's Human from His Divine. And who thinks otherwise, or can think otherwise, that prays, according to the formula of faith, "That God the Father, for the sake of the Son, will send the Holy Spirit ?" Does he not pray to God the Father as to one God, and for the sake of the Son as another, and concerning the Holy Spirit as a third ? It is plain that though one in his thought shall make the three persons one God, yet he divides them,—that is divides his conception,—when he thus prays, into three Gods. The same formula of faith also makes the Lord two; for the Lord's Human alone is then thought of, and not at the same time His Divine; since "for the sake of the Son" is for the sake of the Human which suffered on the cross. . . . Now, because these two essentials of doctrine in the Reformed churches are falsities, and falsities devastate the church,—for they take away its truths and goods,—therefore they were represented by a dragon. The reason is that by a dragon, in the Word, the devastation of the church is signified; as may appear from the following passages : "*I will make Jerusalem heaps, a habitation of dragons, and I will make the cities of Judah desolate*" (Jer. ix. 11). *Behold, . . . a great commotion out of the north country, to make the cities of Judah desolate, a habitation of dragons*" (Jer. x. 22). "*Hazor shall be a habitation of dragons, even a desolation for ever*" (Jer. xlix. 33). "*That it may be a habitation of dragons, a court for owls*" (Isa. xxxiv. 13). "*In the habitation of dragons where each lay*" (Isa. xxxv. 7). "*I will go stripped and naked, I will make a wailing like the dragons, and mourning as the owls*" (Mic. i. 8). "*I cried,*

I am a brother to dragons, and a companion to owls" (Job xxx. 28, 29). *" The wild beasts . . . shall cry in their desolate houses, and dragons in their pleasant palaces"* (Isa. xiii. 22). *" And Babylon shall become heaps, a habitation of dragons, an astonishment and a hissing"* (Jer. li. 37). *" Thou hast sore broken us in the place of dragons, and covered us with the shadow of death"* (Psa. xliv. 19). *" I have laid the mountains of Esau and his heritage waste for the dragons of the wilderness"* (Mal. i. 3). And other passages; as Isa. xliii. 20; Jer. xiv. 6; Psa. xci. 13, 14; Deut. xxxii. 33. That by the dragon here they are meant who are in faith alone, and reject the works of the law as not conducive to salvation, has sometimes been made manifest to me in the spiritual world by living experience. I have seen many thousands of them assembled in a crowd; and from a distance they appeared as a dragon with a long tail, that seemed covered with spines like a thorn, which signified falsities. Once also a still greater dragon was seen, which raising his back lifted up his tail towards heaven, with an effort to draw down the stars from thence. Thus it was manifested before my eyes that no others are meant by the dragon. (*ib.* n. 537.)

" Having seven heads," signifies insanity from the falsification and profanation of the truths of the Word. The head signifies wisdom and intelligence; and, in the opposite sense, insanity. And here by the seven heads, because they were of the dragon, insanity from the falsification and profanation of the truths of the Word is properly signified; for seven is predicated of things holy, and in the opposite sense of things profane. It therefore follows that upon his heads there appeared seven diadems, and by diadems the truths of the Word are signified,—here, falsified and profaned. (*ib.* n. 538.)

" And ten horns," signifies much power. A horn signifies power; and ten signifies much. It is said that the dragon has much power, because the salvation of man by faith alone, without the works of the law,—which faith is meant by the dragon,— captivates the minds of men, and then confirmations produce conviction. It captivates, because when a man hears that the damnation of the law is taken away, and that the Lord's merit is imputed to him through faith alone therein, he can indulge in the pleasures of mind and body without any fear of hell. Hence is the power which is signified by the dragon's ten horns. That such has been his power, is very plain from the reception of that faith throughout the whole reformed Christian world. (*ib.* n. 539.)

" And seven diadems upon his heads," signifies all the truths of the Word falsified and profaned. By diadems, or by precious stones, the truths of the Word are signified ; in particular, the truths of the literal sense of the Word,—but here, those truths falsified and

profaned ; for they were seen upon the seven heads of the dragon, which signify insanity from truths falsified and profaned. . . . The truths of the literal sense of the Word are signified by diadems or precious stones because, to the eyes of the angels, all things of the literal sense of the Word admit light from its spiritual sense through them, thus light from heaven, in which the spiritual truths of the Word are ; for a stone in the Word signifies truth in the ultimates, and therefore a precious stone is that truth pellucid. The reason why the truths of the Word falsified and profaned are also called diadems is, that they have a lustre of themselves, with whomsoever they are,—as diadems on earth, in whosesoever hand. It has sometimes been given me to see adulterous women adorned with diadems, when they first came from the earth into the world of spirits ; and also Jews selling diadems, which they had procured from heaven ; from which it was evident that evils and falsities with them do not change the light and lustre of the truths of the Word. Similar things are therefore signified by the ten diadems upon the horns of the beast that rose up out of the sea (Rev. xiii. 1); and by the precious stones on the woman sitting upon the scarlet coloured beast (xvii. 3-5). That the truths of the Word are what are signified by diadems plainly appears in the Apocalypse, in that many diadems were seen upon the head of Him who sat on the white horse, whose name was The Word of God (xix. 12, 13). (*ib.* n. 540.)

"*And his tail drew the third part of the stars of heaven, and did cast them to the earth*" (ver. 4). This signifies that by falsifications of the truths of the Word they have estranged all spiritual cognitions of good and truth from the church, and by applications to falsities have entirely destroyed them. By the tail, where the reference is to those who have confirmed heretical doctrines from the Word, the truths of the Word falsified are signified ; the stars signify spiritual cognitions of good and truth ; the third part signifies all ; to draw from heaven and cast them to the earth, signifies to estrange from the church and entirely destroy them. For when they are drawn from heaven they are also drawn from the church, because every truth of the Word is insinuated by the Lord into the man of the church through heaven; and truths are drawn away only by falsifications of them in the Word, since the truths of heaven and the church are there and therefrom. That all truths of the Word have been destroyed by those who are meant by the dragon, mentioned above, cannot be believed by any one in the world; and yet they have been so completely destroyed that not one doctrinal truth remains. This was put to the test among the learned of the clergy in the spiritual world, and was found to be so. The reasons I know, but will here mention only one of them:—They assert that whatever proceeds from man's will and judgment is not good; and that therefore the goods of charity or good works, because they are done by man, contribute nothing to salvation, but faith alone; when yet the one thing by virtue of which man is man, and by which he is conjoined with the Lord, is, that he can do good and believe truth as of himself, that is from his own will according to his own judgment. If this one thing were taken away, at the same time everything that is conjunctive of man with the Lord and of the Lord with man would also be taken away. For this is the ability of love to reciprocate; which the Lord gives to every one who is born a man, which He also preserves in him to the end of his life, and afterwards to eternity. If this were taken away from man every good and truth of the Word would also be taken away from him; insomuch that the Word would be nothing but a dead letter and an empty volume. For the Word teaches nothing else than the conjunction of man with the Lord through charity and faith,—both, from man as of himself. They who are meant by the dragon referred to above have sundered this only bond of conjunction, by asserting that the goods of charity or good works which proceed from man, and from his will and judgment, are only moral, civil, and political works, by which man has conjunction with the world, and none at all with God and with heaven; and when this bond is thus broken there is no doctrinal truth of the Word remaining. And if the truths of the Word are applied to confirm faith alone as saving without the works of the law, then they are all falsified. And if the falsification proceeds so far as to affirm that the Lord did not command good works in the Word for the sake of man's conjunction with Himself, but only for the sake of his conjunction with the world, then the truths of the Word are profaned; for thus the Word becomes no longer a holy but a profane book. (*ib.* n. 541.)

"*And the dragon stood before the woman who was ready to be delivered, to devour her child as soon as she should bring forth.*" This signifies that they who are meant by the dragon will be active to extinguish the doctrine of the New Church at its very birth. The woman signifies the New Church. To bring forth signifies to receive goods and truths of doctrine from the Word; the child which she would bring forth signifies the doctrine of the New Church. To devour signifies to extinguish, because the child signifies doctrine; and when in relation to the child it is said "to devour," in relation to the doctrine it is said "to extinguish." This is at its very birth; for it is said that the dragon stood before the woman, to devour her child as soon as she should bring forth. (*ib.* n. 542.)

"*And she brought forth a male child*" (ver. 5), signifies the doctrine of the New Church. By a son in the Word truth of doctrine is signified, and understanding and thought of truth and good therefrom; and by a daughter the good of doctrine is signified, and a will and thence affection for truth and good; and by a male child is signified truth conceived in the spiritual man and born in the natural. The reason is that in the Word generations and births signify spiritual generations and births, all which in general relate to good and truth; for nothing else is begotten and born of the Lord as a husband and the church as a wife. Now, as the woman who brought forth signifies the New Church, it is plain that the male child signifies the doctrine of that church. The doctrine which is here meant is THE DOCTRINE OF THE NEW JERUSALEM, published in London in 1758; and also THE DOCTRINE CONCERNING THE LORD, CONCERNING THE SACRED SCRIPTURE, AND CONCERNING LIFE, ACCORDING TO THE COMMANDMENTS OF THE DECALOGUE, published in Amsterdam. For by doctrine all the truths of doctrine are meant; because doctrine is the complex of them. When these doctrines were written the dragonists stood around me, and laboured together with all their fury to devour, that is, to extinguish them. This strange circumstance I am permitted to relate, because of a truth it thus occurred. The dragonists who stood around me were from every part of the reformed Christian world. (*ib.* n. 543.)

" *Who was to feed all nations with a rod of iron,*" signifies,— Which [doctrine] will convince all who are in dead worship from faith separated from charity, that are willing to be convinced, by truths from the literal sense of the Word, and at the same time by rational [considerations] from natural light. This is said concerning the doctrine of the New Church, because concerning the male child by which that doctrine is signified. To feed signifies to teach and instruct; here, to convince those who are willing to be convinced. Nations signify those who are in evils of life; here, those who are in dead worship, from faith separated from charity, for they are here treated of, and they are in evils of life. For while charity is separated there is no good of life; and where there is no good of life there is evil." (*ib.* n. 544.)

" *And her child was caught up unto God and His throne,*" signifies that the doctrine is protected by the Lord, and guarded by the angels of heaven, because it is for the New Church. (*ib.* n. 545.)

THE NEW CHURCH IS FIRST ESTABLISHED AMONG A FEW.

" *And the woman fled into the wilderness*" (ver. 6), signifies that the church which is the New Jerusalem is at first among a few. The New Church is signified by the woman; and the wilderness signifies where there are no longer any truths. That it is first among a few is signified, because it follows, " Where she hath a place prepared of God, that they should feed her there a thousand two hundred and sixty days;" by which its state at that time is signified,—that meanwhile it may be provided for among a larger number, until it increases to its appointed [state]. (A. R. n. 546.)

" *Where she hath a place prepared of God, that they should feed her there a thousand two hundred and sixty days,*" signifies the state of this church at that time, that meanwhile it may be provided for among a larger number, until it increases to its appointed [state]. By place state is signified; and to feed signifies to provide for its increase,—for thus the church is fed. Hence to have a place prepared of God that they may feed her, signifies the state of the church that meanwhile it may be provided for among a greater number. " A thousand two hundred and sixty days " signifies to the end and beginning; that is, to the end of the former church and the beginning of the new,— the same as " time, and times, and half a time " in ver. 14,—thus also to its appointed [state], that is until it comes forth, as was provided. It is of the Lord's Divine providence that the church should first exist among a few, and successively increase among a larger number; because the falsities of the former church must first be removed. For not before can truths be received; because truths which are received and implanted before falsities are removed do not remain, and are also refined away by the dragonists. The case was similar with the Christian church, in that it successively increased from a few to many. Another reason is that first a new heaven is to be formed, which shall act as one with the church on earth. We therefore read that John " *saw a new heaven, and the Holy Jerusalem coming down from God out of heaven* " (Rev. xxi. 1, 2). It is certain that a new church will arise, which is the New Jerusalem, for it is foretold in the Apocalypse (chap. xxi. xxii.); and it is also certain that the falsities of the former church must first be removed; for these are the subject of the Apocalypse as far as chapter xx. (*ib.* n. 547.)

There are several reasons why this New Church which is called the holy Jerusalem will first begin among a few, afterwards embrace a larger number, and finally be filled:—First, because its doctrine, which is the doctrine of love to the Lord and charity towards the neighbour, cannot be acknowledged and hence cannot be received, except by those who are interiorly affected by truths,—who are no others than those that can see them; and they only see them who have cultivated their intellectual faculty, and have not destroyed it'in themselves by the loves of self and the world. A second reason is, that the doctrine of that Church cannot be acknowledged, and hence cannot be received, except by those who have not confirmed themselves, in doctrine and at the same time in life, in faith alone. If confirmed only in doctrine it does not prevent; but if they have confirmed themselves at the same time in life it prevents; for then they neither know nor wish to know what love to God and charity towards the neighbour are. A third reason is, that the New Church on earth increases according to its increase in the world of spirits; for spirits from thence are with men, and are from those who were in the faith of their church while they lived in the world; and no others of them receive the doctrine but those that are in an affection for spiritual truth. They alone are conjoined with heaven, and conjoin heaven with man. Their number in the world of spirits now daily increases; and therefore, according to their increase, this church which is called the New Jerusalem increases on earth. These too were the reasons why the Christian church increased so slowly in the European world after the Lord left the earth, and did not come to its fulness (*ad plenum*) until after an age had elapsed. (A. E. n. 732.)

It is said that " *The woman fled into the wilderness, where she hath a place prepared of God;*" and afterwards that " *she received the wings of an eagle and flew to her own place,*"—which signifies that the church which is called the New Jerusalem will abide among those who are in the doctrine of faith separate [from charity] while it increases to a full [state] (*in plenum*), until it is provided for among a larger number. But in that church are the dragons, who separate faith from good works not in doctrine only but also in life; others however in the same church, who live the life of faith, which is charity, are not dragons although among them. . . . The church consisting of those who are not dragons is meant (ver. 16) by *the earth which helped the woman, and swallowed up the flood which the dragon cast out of his mouth.* . . . By these the New Church which is called the holy Jerusalem is helped, and also increases. (*ib.* n. 764.)

The Doctrine of the New Church is from Heaven, because from the Spiritual Sense of the Word.

The doctrine of the New Church is from heaven, because it is from the spiritual sense of the Word, and the spiritual sense of the Word is the same as the doctrine which is in heaven.[1] (H. D. n. 7.)

---

[1] This might seem at variance with the author's very explicit teaching elsewhere (see p. 117), that "The doctrine of the Church should be drawn from the

The doctrines of the church in very many instances recede from the literal sense of the Word. It should be known that the true doctrine of the church is what is called the internal sense; for in the internal sense are such truths as are with the angels in heaven. . . . They who teach and learn only the literal sense of the Word, without the regulating doctrine of the church, comprehend only those things that belong to the natural or external man; while those who teach and learn from true doctrine which is from the Word understand also the things that belong to the spiritual or internal man. The reason is that in the external or literal sense the Word is natural, and in the internal sense it is spiritual. (A. C. n. 9025; also 9424.)

All the Doctrines of the New Church are Essentials.

The essentials of the church, which conjoin themselves with faith in one God, are charity, good works, repentance, and a life according to the Divine laws; and as these, together with faith, affect and move the will and thought of man, they conjoin man to the Lord, and the Lord to man. . . .

All the dogmas or doctrinals of the New Church are essentials, in each of which is heaven and the church; and they look to this as their end, that man may be in the Lord, and the Lord in

literal sense of the Word, and confirmed by it." In reality however the two are in perfect harmony, and only different and very important phases of the same truth. In another place (S. S. n. 55) he teaches that, "In the literal sense the Word is as a man clothed, whose face and hands are naked; all things therein which relate to man's life, and so to his salvation, are naked, and the rest are clothed." The very doctrine of the Word is its internal sense (A. C. n. 9424, *et al.*), and those parts of the Word which are naked, or where the doctrine of the internal sense is uncovered in the letter, are the parts where genuine truth or true doctrine is taught in the letter. But this genuine truth can only be seen by those who are enlightened by the Lord; and when the church had sunk so low that all power to distinguish the true doctrine of the Word had been lost,—when "the sun was darkened, and the moon had ceased to give her light," the true doctrine could only be restored by a new revelation. It was then necessary that one should be enlightened in the spiritual sense itself of the Word, in order that in the light of that sense he might fully and certainly see which are the uncovered parts where the literal coincides with the spiritual sense, and genuine truth or the true doctrine of the church is taught. Thus it is true, both that the genuine doctrine of the church is from the spiritual sense of the Word, and that it must be drawn from the literal sense, and confirmed by it. But the doctrines lying uncovered in the letter of the Word are general truths (A. R. n. 378, *et al.*); and as the uncovered face is the index to the whole man, so these general truths involve all the particulars of doctrine contained in the internal sense itself. Now, it has pleased the Lord in this fulness of time, for the use of this future " crown of all the churches," not only to enlighten the mind of one raised up for the purpose, to see and teach the genuine doctrine thus contained in the letter of the Word, but also to reveal very many of the particulars of doctrine contained within these general truths; in other words, to reveal the spiritual sense which is the doctrine itself of the Word. (See also pp. 122, 123.)

man, according to His words in John xiv. 20; and xv. 4-6. (B. E. n. 96, 97.)

THIS CHURCH IS TO BE THE CROWN OF ALL THE CHURCHES, AND IS TO ENDURE FOR EVER.

This church is the crown of all the churches that have hitherto existed on the globe; because it will worship the one visible God, in whom is the invisible God as the soul is in the body. Thus and no otherwise can there be conjunction of God with man; because man is natural, and therefore thinks naturally, and conjunction must be in the thought, and so in the affection of his love; and this is effected when man thinks of God as a Man. Conjunction with an invisible God is like conjunction of the vision of the eye with the expanse of the universe, of which it sees no limit; and like sight in mid ocean, which falls into the air and into the sea and vanishes. But conjunction with a visible God is like seeing a man in the air or on the sea, spreading forth his hands and inviting to his arms. For all conjunction of God with man must also be a reciprocal conjunction of man with God; and there cannot be this latter reciprocation except with a visible God.

That this church is to succeed the churches which have existed since the beginning of the world; that it is to endure for ages of ages [*in sæcula sæculorum*]; and thus is to be the crown of all the churches that have existed before, was prophesied by Daniel:—First, when he told and explained to Nebuchadnezzar his dream concerning the four kingdoms,—by which are meant the four churches represented by the image seen by him,—saying, "*In their days the God of heaven shall cause to arise a kingdom, which for ages shall not be destroyed; . . . and it shall . . . consume all those kingdoms; and it shall stand for ages*" (Dan. ii. 44); and this was to be done by "*A stone which became a great rock, filling the whole earth*" (ver. 35). By a rock in the Word the Lord as to Divine truth is meant. And elsewhere the same prophet says, "*I saw in the visions of the night, and behold, with the clouds of heaven, as it were the Son of Man; . . . and there was given Him dominion and glory, and a kingdom; and all peoples, nations, and tongues shall worship Him. His dominion is the dominion of an age which will not pass away, and His kingdom one which shall not be destroyed*" (vii. 13, 14). And this he says after he saw the four great beasts coming up out of the sea (ver. 3), which also represented the four former churches. That these things were prophesied by Daniel concerning the present time, is evident from his words in chap. xii. 4; and from the Lord's words in Matt. xxiv. 15, 30. Similar things are said in the Apocalypse: " *The seventh angel sounded ; then there were great voices in heaven, saying, The kingdoms [of this world] are become [the kingdom] of our Lord and of His Christ, and He shall reign for ages of ages* " (xi. 15).

Moreover the other prophets have, in many places, predicted of this church what its character will be ; from which these few passages shall be adduced. In Zechariah: " *There shall be one day which shall be known to Jehovah, not day nor night, . . . for about the time of evening there shall be light. In that day living waters shall go forth out of Jerusalem, . . . and Jehovah shall be King over all the earth. In that day shall there be one Jehovah, and His name one* " (xiv. 7-9). In Joel: " *It shall come to pass in that day, that the mountains shall drop down new wine, and the hills shall flow with milk, . . . and Jerusalem shall remain to generation and generation* " (iii. 18, 20). In Jeremiah: " *At that time they shall call Jerusalem the throne of Jehovah ; and all the nations shall be gathered together, on account of the name of Jehovah, to Jerusalem ; neither shall they walk any more after the stubbornness of their evil heart* " (iii. 17; Rev. xxi. 24, 26). In Isaiah: " *Thine eyes shall see Jerusalem a quiet habitation, a tabernacle that shall not be taken down ; its stakes shall never be removed, and its cords shall not be broken* " (xxxiii. 20). In these passages by Jerusalem is meant the holy New Jerusalem described in Rev. xxi., which means the New Church. Again in Isaiah: " *There shall go forth a Rod out of the stem of Jesse, . ,. and righteousness shall be the girdle of His loins, and truth the girdle of His thighs. Wherefore the wolf shall dwell with the lamb, and the leopard shall lie down with the kid, and the calf and the young lion and the fatling together, and a little child shall lead them. And the cow and the bear shall feed, their young ones shall lie down together ; . . . and the sucking child shall play on the hole of the asp, and the weaned child shall put his hand over the den of the cockatrice. They shall not hurt nor destroy in all the mountain of My holiness ; for the earth shall be full of the knowledge of Jehovah. . . . In that day there shall be a Root out of Jesse, which standeth for an ensign of the people ; after it shall the Gentiles seek ; and His rest shall be glorious* " (xi. 1, 5-10). That such things have not yet come to pass in the churches, much less in the last, is well known. In Jeremiah: " *Behold the days come, . . . in which I will make a new covenant. . . . And this shall be the covenant: . . . I will put My law in their inward parts, and write it on their heart ; and I will be their God, and they shall be My people ; . . . they shall all know Me, from the least of, them even to the greatest of them* " (xxxi. 31-34; Rev. xxi. 3). That these things have not hitherto taken place in the churches is also known. The reason has been that they have not approached a visible God, whom all shall recognize ; and He is the Word or law which He will put in their inward parts and write upon their hearts. In Isaiah : " *For Jerusalem's sake I will not rest, until the righteousness thereof go forth as brightness, and the salvation thereof as a lamp that burneth. . . . And thou shalt be called by a new name, which the mouth of Jehovah shall name. And thou shalt be* A CROWN OF GLORY AND A ROYAL DIADEM *in the hand of thy God. . . . Jehovah shall delight in thee, and thy land* SHALL BE MARRIED. *Behold, thy Salvation cometh ; behold, His reward is with Him. . . . And they shall call them, The people of Holiness, The redeemed of Jehovah ; and thou shalt be called, A city sought out and not forsaken"* (lxii. 1-4, 11, 12). (T. C. R. n. 787-789.)

This new and true Christian Church, it is to be proved from the Word of both Testaments, will endure to eternity *(in æternum)*, and was foreseen from the foundation of the world. It is to be the crown of the four preceding churches, because of its true faith and true charity. (Cor. p. 70.)

FORMATION OF THE NEW HEAVEN.

" *And I saw, and, lo ! a Lamb stood upon Mount Zion, and with him an hundred forty and four thousand* " (Rev. xiv. 1). This signifies the Lord, now in the New Heaven, gathered from those in the Christian churches who have acknowledged the Lord alone as God of heaven and earth, and have been in truths of doctrine from the good of love from Him, by means of the Word. . . . The *one hundred forty and four thousand* were treated of in the seventh chapter ; but there [the circumstance] that they were *sealed upon their foreheads,* thus, that they were distinguished and separated from others. Here now [it is taught] that they were gathered together in one ; and that of them a heaven [was formed]. . . . This heaven is the New Heaven from which the Holy Jerusalem, that is the New Church on earth, will descend. (A. R. n. 612.)

THE NEW CHURCH FROM THIS NEW HEAVEN IS TO BE DISTINCT FROM THE FORMER CHURCH.

It should be known that when any church becomes no church, —that is when charity perishes,—and a new church is established by the Lord, seldom if ever does it take place among those with whom the old church existed, but among those with whom there was before no church, that is among Gentiles.[1]   It was so when the Most Ancient church perished; then a new church called Noah, or the Ancient church which existed after the flood, was established among Gentiles, that is among those with whom there was no church before.   In like manner when this church perished, the semblance of a church was established among the descendants of Abraham from Jacob; thus again among Gentiles, for Abram when he was called was a Gentile; the posterity of Jacob in Egypt became still more Gentile, insomuch that they were entirely ignorant of Jehovah, and therefore of all Divine worship.   After this semblance of a church was consummated, then the Primitive church was established among Gentiles, the Jews being rejected.   So will it be with this church, which is called Christian.   (A. C. n. 2986.)

The destruction of this [the first Christian] church is foretold by the Lord in the Evangelists, and through John in the Apocalypse; which destruction is what is called the last judgment. Not that then heaven and earth are to perish; but that a new church will be raised up in some part of the earth, this church still remaining in its external worship,—as the Jews in theirs; in whose worship it is well enough known there is nothing of charity and faith, thus nothing of the church.   (*ib.* n. 1850.)

When the church is fully devastated a New Church will be established, into which they who are of the former church will be invited.   (A. E. n. 948.)

"*And His wife hath made herself ready.*"   This signifies that they who will be of this New Church, which is the New Jerusalem, are to be gathered together, inaugurated, and instructed. That by *wife* the Lord's New Church is signified, which is the New Jerusalem, is clearly manifest from the following (twenty-first) chapter, where these words occur:—"*I saw the holy city New Jerusalem descending from God out of heaven, prepared as a bride adorned for her husband*" (ver. 2).   And in the same chapter: "*There came unto me an angel . . . saying, Come hither, I will show thee the bride, the Lamb's wife. . . . And he showed me that great city, the holy Jerusalem, descending out of heaven from God*" (ver. 9, 10).   By [the expression] "*His wife hath made herself ready,*" it is signified that they who will be of this New Church of the Lord are to be gathered together, inaugurated, and instructed. And because this is signified by "*hath made herself ready,*" it follows that that wife is to be "*arrayed in fine linen, clean and bright,*" by which inauguration by instruction is signified.   And therefore the subject of the white horse also follows, by which is signified the understanding of the Word [revealed] for them by the Lord.   (A. R. n. 813.)

[1] As to who are meant by *Gentiles* see p. 323.

By the New Jerusalem is meant a new church or congregation; the doctrines and articles of whose faith cannot shine in their true splendour, and give light to others, without the Divine aid; because they are only figuratively described in the Apocalypse, that is, according to correspondence. (*Letter to Oetinger, Swed. Doc.,* p. 208.)

The New Church at first External.

The New Church in its beginning will be external. (A. E. n. 403.)

Every church in its beginning becomes acquainted only with the general [principles] of doctrine; for it is then in its simplicity, or as it were in its childhood. In the course of time it adds particulars; which are partly confirmations of general principles, partly additions,—which yet are not repugnant to the general principle,—and also explanations, that open contradictions may be analyzed, and not clash with what common sense dictates. (A. C. n. 4720.)

The Necessity of Order, Internal and External.

Who does not see that there is no empire, kingdom, dukedom, republic, state, or household, that is not established by laws, which constitute the order and so the form of its government? In each of them the laws of justice are in the highest place, political laws in the second, and economical laws in the third. If compared with man, the laws of justice constitute the head; political laws the body; and economical laws the clothing,— wherefore these, like garments, may be changed.

But as regards the order in which the church is established by God, it is,—That God, and also the neighbour towards whom order is to be exercised, is in all and every thing of it. The laws of this order are as many as the truths in the Word. The laws which relate to God constitute its head; the laws that relate to the neighbour constitute its body; and ceremonial laws form its clothing. For unless these preserved the former in their order it would be as if the body were made bare, and exposed to the heat of summer and the cold of winter; or as if the roof and walls were removed from a temple, and the sanctuary, the altar, and the pulpit, daily stood thus openly exposed to various kinds of violence. (T. C. R. n. 55.)

BAPTISM.

BAPTISM was instituted for a sign that a man is of the church, and for a memorial that he must be regenerated; for the washing of Baptism is no other than spiritual washing, or regeneration.

All regeneration is effected by the Lord, by means of the truths of faith and a life according to them. Baptism therefore testifies that a man is of the church, and that he can be regenerated. For in the church the Lord is acknowledged, who alone regenerates; and there the Word is, wherein are the truths of faith by which regeneration is effected.

The Lord thus teaches in John:—" *Except a man be born of water and of the Spirit he cannot enter into the kingdom of God.*" In the spiritual sense *water* is the truth of faith from the Word; *the spirit* is life according to it; and to be born of them is to be regenerated by them.

Since every one who is regenerated also endures temptations, which are spiritual combats against evils and falsities, therefore these also are signified by the waters of baptism.

Because baptism is for a sign and a memorial of these things, a man may be baptized as an infant; and if not then, he may be as an adult.

Those who are baptized should therefore know that the Baptism itself confers neither faith nor salvation; but testifies that they may receive faith, and that they may be saved if they are regenerated.

From this it is evident what is meant by the Lord's words in Mark:—" *He that believeth and is baptized shall be saved; but he that believeth not shall be condemned*" (ch. xvi. 16). He that believeth is he who acknowledges the Lord and receives truths from Him through the Word; he that is baptized is he who is regenerated by means of them by the Lord. (H. D. n. 202-208.)

BAPTISM COMMANDED.

That baptism was commanded is very manifest from the baptism of John, in the Jordan, to which there went out all Judea and Jerusalem (Matt. iii. 5, 6; Mark i. 4, 5); and from the fact that the Lord our Saviour Himself was baptized by John (Matt. iii. 13-17). He moreover commanded the disciples that they should baptize all nations (Matt. xviii. 19). (T. C. R. n. 668.)

The reason why the Lord Himself was baptized by John was, not only that He might institute baptism for the future, and lead the way by His example, but also because He glorified His Humanity and made this Divine, as He regenerates man and makes him spiritual. (*ib.* n. 684.)

The First use of Baptism.

The first use of Baptism is introduction into the Christian church, and then, at the same time, insertion among Christians in the spiritual world. . . . Baptism was instituted in the place of circumcision; and as circumcision was a sign that the circumcised were of the Jewish church, so Baptism is a sign that the baptized are of the Christian church. But the sign effects nothing more than that they may be known; as the swaddling-clothes of different colour placed upon the infants of two mothers, that they may be distinguished, and not changed. . . . Not only infants are baptized, but also all foreign proselytes, young and old, who are converted to the Christian religion, and this before they have been instructed, merely upon a confession that they desire to embrace Christianity. This too did the Apostles, according to the Lord's command that they should " *make disciples of all nations, and baptize them* " (Matt. xviii. 19). . . But this is done on earth. In the heavens, on the other hand, the infants are introduced by Baptism into the Christian heaven; and angels are assigned them there by the Lord, who take care of them. As soon therefore as infants are baptized, angels are appointed over them, by whom they are kept in a state to receive faith in the Lord. But as they grow up, and come to act of their own right and of their own reason, the guardian-angels leave them, and they draw to themselves such spirits as make one with their life and faith; from which it is plain that Baptism is also insertion among Christians in the spiritual world. (T. C. R. n. 677.)

The reason why not only infants but in fact all are inserted by baptism among Christians in the spiritual world, is, that in that world peoples and nations are distinct, according to their religions. Christians are in the centre; Mahomedans around them; after them idolaters of various kinds; and at the sides the Jews.[1]

---

[1] The reader should not think of this as of an arrangement in space, but rather according to state. A little reflection will show an arrangement to some extent

Moreover, all of the same religion in heaven are arranged in societies, according to the affections of love to God and towards the neighbour; and in hell, in congregations, according to the affections opposed to these two loves, thus according to the lusts of evil. In the spiritual world,—by which we mean both heaven and hell,—all things are most distinctly organized, in the whole and in every part, or in general and in every particular. Upon the distinctive organization there the preservation of the whole universe depends; and there could not be this distinctiveness unless every one after he is born were known by some sign, [showing] to what religious body he belongs. For without the Christian sign, which is Baptism, some Mahomedan spirit or one of the idolaters might attach himself to Christian infants newly born, and also to children, and breathe into them an inclination for his religion, and so distract their minds and alienate them from Christianity; which would be to distort and destroy spiritual order. (T. C. R. 678.)

The Mahomedans, as all the Gentiles, who acknowledge one God, and love justice, and do good from a religious motive, have their heaven; but outside of the Christian heaven. (*ib.* n. 832.)

Infants and children born without the Christian church, [who depart this life in infancy or childhood] after reception of faith in the Lord, are designated for the heaven of their religion by other means than baptism; but they are not intermingled with those who are in the Christian heaven. (*ib.* n. 729.)

Every man as to his spirit, although he does not know it, is in society with spirits while he lives in the body. Through them a good man is in an angelic society, and an evil man in an infernal society. (H. H. n. 438.)

This first use of baptism is, that it is a sign in the spiritual world, that the baptized is a Christian,—where every one is inserted in the societies and congregations there, according to the quality of the Christianity within him or without him.[1] (T. C. R. n. 680.)

---

similar, although less perfect, in this world. Christians here are in the centre,—the centre of light and civilization ; others are grouped around them, and, in a common and important aspect, are considered nearer or more remote from Christendom according as they have more or less of the light and life which characterize it.

[1] What the author means by the Christianity without a man may be gathered from the following in the *Doctrine of the Sacred Scripture :*—" The church is in man ; the church which is without him is the church among the many who have the church in them." (S. S. n. 78.)

John's Baptism as an Illustration of the Effect of the Sign of Baptism in the Spiritual World, and thence upon the Baptized on Earth.

Baptism is holy, and a sacrament, because it is a sign and a memorial that the man can be regenerated by the Lord, by means of truths from the Word,—a sign for heaven, and a memorial for man; and that a man is introduced by it into the church,—as the children of Israel by passing over the Jordan were introduced into the land of Canaan, and as the inhabitants of Jerusalem were prepared by the Baptism of John for the reception of the Lord. For without that sign in heaven before the angels, the Jews could not have subsisted and lived at the coming of Jehovah, that is of the Lord, in the flesh. (A. R. n. 776.)

The Baptism of John prepared the heavens, that the Jewish people might subsist when God Himself should appear among them. (*Letter to Beyer, Swed. Doc.*, p. 170.)

John was the prophet who was sent to prepare the way of Jehovah God, who was to descend into the world and accomplish the work of redemption. He prepared that way by baptism, and then by announcing the coming of the Lord; and without that preparation all there would have been smitten with a curse, and would have perished. (T. C. R. n. 688.)

The reason why a way was prepared by John's Baptism was, that by that baptism they were introduced into the future church of the Lord, and in heaven were inserted among those who expected and desired the Messiah, and so were guarded by angels, that devils might not break forth from hell and destroy them. . . .

If the way had not been prepared for the descent of Jehovah into the world by means of Baptism, the effect of which in heaven was that the hells were closed, and the Jews were guarded from total destruction [they would have perished]. (*ib.* n. 689.)

After quotation and exposition of some illustrative and confirmatory passages from the Word, the author adds:—

These few examples illustrate with what a curse and destruction the Jews would have been smitten, if they had not been prepared by the Baptism of John to receive the Messiah, who was Jehovah God in the human form, and if He had not assumed the Human and so revealed Himself. And they were prepared by this, that in heaven they were enrolled and numbered among those who in heart expected and desired the Messiah; in consequence of which angels were then sent, and became their guardians. (*ib.* n. 691.)

The Second Use of Baptism.

The second use of Baptism is, that the Christian may know and acknowledge the Lord Jesus Christ, the Redeemer and Saviour, and follow Him. This second use of Baptism, which is that one may know the Lord the Redeemer and Saviour Jesus Christ, inseparably follows the first, which is introduction into the Christian church, and insertion among Christians in the spiritual world. And what is this first use without the second but a mere name? . . . To bear the name of a Christian, of one belonging to Christ, and not acknowledge Him, and follow Him, that is, live according to His commandments, is as empty as a shadow, as a smoke, and useless as a blackened picture. For the Lord says,—" *Why call ye me Lord, and do not the things which I say?*" (Luke vi. 46); " *Many will say unto Me in that day, Lord, Lord. . . . And then will I profess unto them, I never knew you*" (Matt. vii. 22, 23). (T. C. R. n. 681.)

The Third Use of Baptism.

The third use of Baptism, which is its final use, is that the man shall be regenerated. This is the very use for the sake of which Baptism was instituted, and is thus its final use; because a true Christian knows and acknowledges the Lord the Redeemer, Jesus Christ, who as He is the Redeemer is also the Regenerator; and because a Christian possesses the Word, in which the means of regeneration stand plainly described,—and the means therein are faith in the Lord and charity towards the neighbour. This is the same as what is said of the Lord, that,—" *He shall baptize with the Holy Spirit and with fire.*" The Holy Spirit means the Divine truth of faith; and fire, the Divine good of love or charity, both proceeding from the Lord; and by these two all regeneration is effected by the Lord. (T. C. R. n. 684.)

From what has been said before, and now, it may be seen that the three uses of Baptism cohere as one,—after the same manner as the first cause, the mediate, which is the efficient cause, and the ultimate cause, which is the effect; and the end itself for the sake of which the former exist. For the first use is that one may be named a Christian; the second, following from this, is that he may know and acknowledge the Lord the Redeemer, Regenerator, and Saviour; and the third is, that he may be regenerated by Him; and when this is done he is redeemed and saved. Since these three uses follow in order, and unite in the last, and hence in the conception of the angels cohere as one, therefore when Baptism is performed, read of in the Word, or mentioned, the angels who are present do not understand Baptism, but regeneration. Wherefore, by these words of the Lord, " *Whosoever believeth and is baptized shall be saved, but whosoever believeth not shall be condemned*" (Mark xvi. 16), it is understood by the angels in heaven, that he who acknowledges the Lord and is regenerated is saved. (*ib.* n. 685.)

As regards the Baptism of John, it represented the cleansing of the external man ; but the Baptism which is at this day among Christians represents the cleansing of the internal man, which is regeneration. We therefore read that John baptized with water, but that the Lord baptizes with the Holy Spirit and with fire ; and for this reason the Baptism of John is called the Baptism of repentance. . . . The Jews that were baptized were merely external men ; and the external man cannot become internal without faith in Christ. It may be seen in the Acts of the Apostles (ch. xix. 3-6) that those who were baptized with the Baptism of John became internal men when they received faith in Christ, and were then baptized in the name of Jesus. (*ib.* n. 690.)

BAPTISM ITSELF HAS NO SAVING EFFICACY.

He who believes that baptism contributes anything to the salvation of a man, unless he is at the same time in the truths of the church and in a life according to them, is greatly mistaken. For baptism is an external rite, which does nothing for salvation without its internal ; but when the external is conjoined with the internal it does. The internal of baptism is, that by means of truths from the Word and through a life according to them, evils and falsities are removed by the Lord, and man is thus regenerated,—as indeed the Lord teaches in Matthew xxiii. 26, 27. (A. E. n. 475.)

BAPTISM WITH THE HOLY SPIRIT.

It is said in John, that the Lord " baptized with the Holy Spirit," and in Luke, that He baptized " with the Holy Spirit and with fire." In the internal sense, to baptize signifies to regenerate ; to baptize with the Holy Spirit and with fire, is to regenerate by the good of love,—fire, is the good of love. . . . The Holy Spirit signifies, the Divine truth proceeding from the Lord ; fire, signifies the Divine good proceeding from Him ; and baptism signifies regeneration by the Lord, by means of Divine truths from the Word. (A. C. n. 9229 ; A. E. n. 475.)

THE HOLY SUPPER.

IN order that every one who repents should look to the Lord alone, the Holy Supper was instituted by Him, which to those who repent confirms the remission of sins. It confirms, because in that supper or communion every one is kept looking to the Lord only. (D. P. n. 122.)

Baptism is introduction into the church; but the Holy Supper is an introduction into heaven. These two Sacraments, Baptism and the Holy Supper, are as two gates to eternal life. By baptism, which is the first gate, every Christian man is intromitted and introduced into those things which the church teaches from the Word concerning another life; all which are means whereby a man may be prepared for and led to heaven. The second gate is the Holy Supper; through this every man who has suffered himself to be prepared and led by the Lord, is intromitted and introduced into heaven. (T. C. R. n. 721.)

The Holy Supper was instituted by the Lord that by means of it there may be a conjunction of the church with heaven, and so with the Lord; it is therefore the most holy thing of worship.

But how conjunction is effected by it, is not apprehended by those who do not know anything of the internal or spiritual sense of the Word; for they do not think beyond the external sense, which is the sense of the letter. From the internal or spiritual sense of the Word it is known what is signified by the body, and blood, and what by the bread and wine, also what is signified by eating.

In that sense, the body or flesh of the Lord is the good of love, as is the bread likewise; and the blood of the Lord is the good of faith, as also is the wine; and eating is appropriation, and conjunction. The angels who are attendant on man when he receives the Sacrament of the Supper understand these things no otherwise; for they perceive all things spiritually. Hence it is that with man the holiness of love and the holiness of faith then flow in from the Lord. From this is conjunction.

From these considerations it is evident that when a man takes the bread, which is the body, he is conjoined to the Lord by means of the good of love to Him from Him; and when he takes the wine, which is the blood, he is conjoined to the Lord by means of the good of faith in Him from Him. But it should be known that conjunction with the Lord by means of the Sacrament of the Supper is effected only with those who are in the good of love and faith in the Lord from the Lord. With these there is conjunction by means of the Holy Supper; with others there is presence, but not conjunction.

Moreover, the Holy Supper includes and comprehends all the Divine worship instituted in the Israelitish church; for the burnt-offerings and sacrifices, in which the worship of that church principally consisted, were called in one word bread; hence also the Holy Supper is its complement. (H. D. n. 210-214.)

They come to the Holy Supper worthily who are in faith in the Lord, and in charity towards the neighbour, thus who are regenerate. (T. C. R. n. 722.)

[Every one is regenerated by abstaining from the evils of sin. T. C. R. n. 510. The state of regeneration begins when a man determines to shun evil and do good. *ib.* n. 587.]

To those who come to it worthily the Holy Supper is as a signing and sealing that they are children of God; because the Lord is then present, and introduces those who are born of Him, that is who are regenerate, into heaven. The Holy Supper effects this because the Lord is then present even as to His Human; for it was shown above that in the Holy Supper the Lord is wholly present, and also the whole of His redemption; for He says of the bread " *This is My body*," and of the wine, " *This is My blood*." Consequently He then admits them into His body; and the church and heaven constitute His body. The Lord is indeed present whenever man is being regenerated, and by His Divine operation prepares him for heaven; but that He may actually enter, a man must actually present himself to the Lord. And because the Lord actually presents Himself to man, a man must actually receive Him,—and not as He hung upon the cross, but as He is, in His glorified Human in which He is present. The body of this is Divine Good, and the blood is Divine Truth. These are given to man, and by them man is regenerated, and is in the Lord and the Lord in him; for, as was shown above, the eating which takes place in the Holy Supper is spiritual eating. From all this, rightly apprehended, it is plain that the Holy Supper is as a signing and sealing that they who worthily approach it are children of God. (*ib.* n. 728.)

Conjunction with the Lord by means of the Holy Supper may be illustrated by the conjunction of the families descended from one father. From him descend brethren, and relations in succession by marriage and by blood; and they all derive something from the first stock. They do not, however, thus derive flesh and blood; but from flesh and blood they thus derive the soul and hence inclination to similar things, whereby they are conjoined. The very conjunction indeed commonly appears in their faces, and also in their manners; and they are therefore called one flesh (Gen. xxix. 14; xxxvii. 27; 2 Sam. v. 1; xix. 12, 13; *et al.*). It is similar in respect to conjunction with the Lord, who is the Father of all the faithful and blessed. Conjunction with Him is effected by love and faith, on account of which two they are called one flesh. Hence it is that He said:—"*He that eateth My flesh and drinketh My blood dwelleth in Me and I in him*" (John vi. 56). Who does not see that the bread and wine do not effect this, but the good of love which is meant by bread, and the truth of faith which is meant by wine, which are the Lord's own, and proceed and are communicated from Him alone? In truth all conjunction is effected by love; and love is not love without confidence. Those who believe that the bread is flesh and the wine blood, and are not able farther to elevate their thought, may remain in this belief; but ought not to think otherwise than that there is a something most holy [in the Sacrament], that is conjunctive with the Lord, which is attributed and appropriated to man as his although it continually remains the Lord's. (*ib.* n. 727.)

Divine Power in the Sacraments, by Correspondences.

That there is the greatest power in correspondences is shown by the fact that heaven and the world, or the spiritual and the natural, are together in them; and that for this reason the Word was written by pure correspondences; wherefore it is the conjunction of man with heaven, and so with the Lord. The Lord is thus in things first, and at the same time in things last. For the same reason the Sacraments were instituted by correspondences. (*Invitation to the New Church,* n. 59.)

THE PRIESTHOOD.

The church on earth comes down from the Lord out of the angelic heaven ; because the angels of heaven and men on earth in all things relating to the church make one. (A. R. n. 876. Also n. 486.)

A Priesthood and Ecclesiastical Governments in Heaven.

It should be known that there is a church in the heavens as well as on earth. For the Word is there; there are temples, and preachings in them; there are ministerial and priestly offices. For all the angels there have been men, and their going thither out the world was only a continuation of their life; therefore they too are perfected in love and wisdom, every one according to the degree of affection for truth and good which he brought with him from the world. (A. R. n. 533.)

The doctrine of the New Church is from heaven, because it is from the spiritual sense of the Word, and the spiritual sense of the Word is the same with the doctrine that is in heaven. For the church is in heaven as well as on earth. For the Word is there; there is doctrine from the Word; there are temples, and sermons delivered in them. For there are ecclesiastical and civil governments there. In a word, *there is no difference between the things which are in heaven and those that are on earth, except that in heaven all things are in a state of greater perfection;* because there all are spiritual, and spiritual things immensely exceed in perfection those that are natural. (H. D. n. 7.)

In the societies of heaven there are superior and inferior rulers (*præfecti*), all ordered and subordinated by the Lord, according to their wisdom and intelligence. The highest of them, who excels the others in wisdom, dwells in the midst, in a palace so magnificent that nothing in all the world can be compared with it. Its architectural qualities are so amazing that of a truth I can say they cannot even as to the hundredth part be described in natural language; for the art itself is there in its own skill. . . . The subordinate rulers have similar palaces, the splendour and magnificence of which are according to the degree of their wisdom; and they have wisdom according to their love of uses. Such things are not possessed by them only, but also by the inhabitants, all of whom love uses, and perform uses by various employments. (A. E. n. 1191.)

In heaven as on earth there are various administrations; for there are ecclesiastical affairs, civil affairs, and domestic affairs.

All things in the heavens are established according to Divine order, which is everywhere guarded by means of administrations by the angels; the wiser angels having charge of the things which belong to the general good or use, and the less wise of those that belong to particular goods or uses, and so on. They are subordinated just as in Divine order the uses are subordinated. Hence also dignity is attached to every employment according to the dignity of the use. And yet no angel arrogates dignity to himself, but ascribes it all to the use. And because the use is the good that he performs, and all good is from the Lord, he ascribes it all to the Lord.

Those are in ecclesiastical [administrations] in heaven who in the world loved the Word and earnestly sought after the truths therein, not for the sake of honour or gain, but for the use of life, both for themselves and others. According to their love and desire of use they are in illustration and in the light of wisdom there; into which they also come from the Word in the heavens,— which is not natural, as in the world, but spiritual. These perform the office of preachers; and according to Divine order there, those are in superior station who excel others in wisdom, from illustration. (H. H. n. 388, 389, 393.)

Divine worship in the heavens, as to externals, is not unlike Divine worship on earth; but as to internals it is different. Just as on earth, there are doctrines in the heavens; there are preachings; and there are temples. The doctrines agree as to essentials; but those that are held in the higher heavens are of more interior wisdom than those in the lower heavens. The preachings are according to the doctrines. And as there are houses and palaces, there are also temples in which the preaching is performed. . . . The preachings in the temples serve only as means of instruction in matters relating to life. . . . They are fraught with such wisdom that no preachings in the world can be compared with them; for in the heavens they are in interior light. The temples in the spiritual kingdom appear as of stone; and in the celestial kingdom, as of wood. For the reason that stone corresponds to truth, in which they are who are in the spiritual kingdom; and wood corresponds to good, in which they are who are in the celestial kingdom. In this kingdom the sacred edifices are not called temples, but houses of God. [Because "temple' signifies what is spiritual, and "house of God" what is celestial. A. C. n. 3720.] (H. H. n. 221-223.)

The preachers are all from the Lord's spiritual kingdom, and none from the celestial kingdom; because those who are of the spiritual kingdom are in truths from good, and all preaching is from truths. (*ib.* 225.)

As the celestial angels are still perfected in wisdom by hearing, therefore there are intermediate angels called celestial spiritual angels who preach and teach truths in their temples; which are called houses of God, and are of wood. (A. E. n. 831.)

There are angels intermediate between the spiritual and the celestial heaven, who are called spiritual celestial. Many of these are preachers in the highest heaven. (S. D. Pt. vii. Vol. 2. 2.)

The preachers in heaven are all appointed by the Lord, and thence are in the gift of preaching. No others but them are permitted to teach in the temples. They are called preachers, and not priests (*sacerdotes*), because the priesthood of heaven is the celestial kingdom; for the priesthood signifies the good of love to the Lord, in which they are who are in that kingdom.[1] (H. H. n. 226.)

The following was an occurrence in the intermediate state called the world of spirits:—I looked around, and saw two angels standing and conversing not far from me. One was clad in a woollen robe, resplendent with flaming purple, and under this a tunic of shining linen; the other in similar garments of scarlet, with a mitre, on the right side of which several rubies were set. I approached them, and with a salutation of peace reverently asked, "For what purpose are you here below?" They answered, " We have descended hither from heaven by the Lord's command, to talk with you about the blessed lot of those who from the love of uses desire to rule. We are worshippers of the Lord. I am the prince of a society. My companion is the highest priest there [*summus sacerdos*]. And the prince said that he was the servant of his society, because he served it by performing

---

[1] Although it is here said that the preachers in heaven are not *called* priests,— because the representative character of the priesthood is filled in heaven by "the celestial kingdom,"—yet it is evident that they are what are called priests on earth ; for, as will be observed in the extracts that follow, the author nearly everywhere else designates them priests, in describing their office, and in interpreting the language of angels to men. And it appears, moreover, that they are called priests on earth for the very reason on account of which they cannot properly be so called in heaven,—that is on account of the representative signification of *priest* (see below. p.435). In like manner, and for a similar reason, the author states that in the celestial kingdom "the sacred edifices are not *called* temples," and yet in the same paragraph he calls them temples; and more expressly in the passage just quoted above from A. E. n. 831. For a similar representative reason, we are informed, priests in heaven do not minister at marriage ceremonies, but at betrothals; and yet that on earth it is fitting that they minister at marriage ceremonies. (C. S. L. n. 21, cited below, p. 429).

uses. The other angel said that he was a minister of the church there, because in serving he administered sacred things for the uses of their souls; and that they were both in perpetual joys, from the eternal happiness that is in them from the Lord. They said that all things in that society are resplendent and magnificent,—resplendent with gold and precious stones, and magnificent with palaces and paradises. "The reason is that our love of ruling is not from self-love, but from the love of uses; and because the love of uses is from the Lord, all good uses in the heavens are resplendent and refulgent. And because in our society we are all in this love the atmosphere appears golden, from the light there, which it derives from the flame of the sun; and the sun's flame corresponds to that love." This being said, there appeared to me also a similar sphere around them; and there was perceived an aromatic fragrance from it; which also I remarked to them, and begged that they would add something more to what they had said about the love of uses. And they continued, saying,—" The dignities in which we are we indeed sought after; but for no other end than that we might be able more fully to perform uses, and more widely to extend them. We are also surrounded with honour; and we accept it, not for ourselves, but for the good of the society. For the brethren and associates who are of the people there scarcely know but that the honours of our dignities are in ourselves, and consequently that the uses we perform are from ourselves. But we feel otherwise; we feel that the honours of the dignities are without us, and that they are as the garments with which we are clothed; but that the uses we perform are from the love of them within us from the Lord. And this love receives its blessedness from communication by uses with others. And we know by experience, that so far as we perform uses from the love of them that love increases, and with the love the wisdom by which the communication is effected; and that so far as we retain the uses in ourselves, and do not communicate them, the blessedness perishes; and then use becomes as food hidden in the stomach, which does not by being dispersed nourish the body and its parts, but remains undigested, whence nausea arises. In a word, the whole heaven is nothing but a continant of use, from its first things to its last. What is use but active love to the neighbour? And what keeps the heavens together but this love?" Hearing this, I asked, "How can any one know whether he is performing uses from self-love, or from the love of uses? Every man, both good and bad, performs uses, and performs uses from some love. Suppose there be a society in the world composed of mere devils, and a society composed entirely of angels; I think the devils in their society, from the fire of self-love and the brightness of their own glory, would perform as many uses as the angels in theirs. Who then can know from what love and from what origin uses are?" To this the two angels responded, —"Devils perform uses for their own sakes, and for reputation, that they may be exalted to honours, or acquire wealth; but angels do not perform uses from such motives, but for the sake of the uses, from the love of them. Man cannot discern [the qualities of] these uses; but the Lord discerns them. Every one who believes in the Lord, and shuns evils as sins, performs his uses from the Lord; and every one who does not believe in the Lord, nor shun evils as sins, does uses from himself, and for his own sake. This is the distinction between uses performed by devils, and uses performed by angels." These things having been said, the two angels departed; and were seen, from a distance, carried like Elijah in a chariot of fire, and taken up into their heaven. (C. S. L. n. 266. Also T. C. R. n. 661.)

The author describes a marriage ceremony in heaven, at which ten strangers from the world of spirits were present, and narrates a conversation they had with a wise angel there; the latter part of which is as follows:—

They afterwards asked whether it is not appropriate that a priest be present and minister at these ceremonies? The wise man answered, "It is appropriate on earth, but not in the heavens; on account of the representation of the Lord Himself and the church [by the bridegroom and bride]. This is not known on earth. But even with us a priest ministers at betrothals, and hears, receives, confirms, and consecrates the consent. Consent is the essential of marriage; all the other things which follow are its formalities." . . . .

After this festive assembly all who had been invited to the wedding departed, and also those two men, with their angel. It was late in the evening, and they retired to rest. At dawn they heard a proclamation, TO-DAY IS THE SABBATH; and they arose, and asked the angel why it was. He answered, "It is for the worship of God, which recurs at stated times, and is proclaimed by the priests. It is performed in our temples, and continues about two hours. If you please, therefore, come with me and I will conduct you there." And they made ready and accompanied the angel, and entered. And lo, there was a large temple, suited to about three thousand, semi-circular, with steps or seats extended around in a continuous sweep, according to the form of the temple; the hinder seats more elevated than those in front. The pulpit in front of them was a little withdrawn from the centre. The door was behind the pulpit on the left. The ten strangers entered, with their angel conductor, and the angel assigned them places where they should sit, saying to them,

" Every one who enters into the temple knows his place; he knows it from something implanted within him, and cannot sit elsewhere. If he sit in any other place he hears nothing, and perceives nothing; and he also disturbs order, from which disturbance it results that the priest is not inspired."

When they were assembled the priest ascended the pulpit and preached a sermon full of the spirit of wisdom. The discourse was on the holiness of the Sacred Scripture, and on the conjunction of the Lord with both the spiritual world and the natural by means of it. In the state of illustration in which he then was he fully demonstrated that that Holy Book was dictated by the Lord Jehovah; and that therefore He is in it, even so that He is the wisdom therein; but that the wisdom which is Himself therein lies concealed under the sense of the letter, and is not opened except to those who are in truths of doctrine, and at the same time in goods of life, and so are in the Lord and He in them. To the discourse he added a votive prayer and descended. The hearers having departed, the angel requested the priest to speak a few words of peace with his ten companions; and he came to them, and they conversed about half an hour. He spoke of the Divine Trinity,—that it is in Jesus Christ, in whom all the fulness of the Divinity dwelleth bodily, according to the declaration of the Apostle Paul; and afterwards of the unity of charity and faith,—but he said, " the union of charity and truth," because faith is truth. After an expression of thanks they went home. (C. S. L. n. 21, 23, 24; also T. C. R. n. 748, 750, 751.)

At the beginning of the series of narrations of which the preceding is the last, the author says :—

" I foresee that many who read the things that follow will believe they are fictions of the imagination; but I declare in truth that they are not fictions, but were truly done and seen; and that I saw them, not in any state of the mind asleep, but in a state of full wakefulness. For it has pleased the Lord to manifest Himself to me, and to send me to teach the things which shall be of the New Church which is meant by the New Jerusalem in the Apocalypse. For this purpose He has opened the interiors of my mind and spirit; by which it has been granted me to be in the spiritual world with angels, and at the same time in the natural world with man; and this now [1768] for twenty-five years." (C. S. L. n. 1.)

And at the close of this narration he adds :—

" I again aver in truth that these things were done and said as they are related, in the society of heaven to which the angel conductor belonged." (*ib.* n. 26.)

A Priesthood and Ecclesiastical Governments Likewise on Earth.

There are two [classes of affairs] among men which must be in order, namely those that are of heaven, and those that are of the world. Those that belong to heaven are called ecclesiastical, and those that are of the world are called civil [affairs].

Order cannot be maintained in the world without rulers (*præfecti*), who shall observe all things that are done according to order, and that are contrary to order; and who shall reward those that live according to order, and punish those that live contrary to order. If this be not done the human race must perish. For the desire to rule over others, and to possess the goods of others, —whence come enmities, envyings, hatreds, revenges, deceits, cruelties, and many other evils,—is inborn in every one, from what is hereditary. Unless therefore men were kept in restraint, by laws, and by rewards suited to their loves for those that do good,—which are honours and gains,—and by punishments, against those loves, for those that do ill,—which are the loss of honours, of possessions, and of life,—the human race would perish.

There must therefore be those in authority who shall keep associations of man in order; who should be learned in the laws, men of wisdom, fearing God. Among the rulers also there must be order; lest any, from caprice or ignorance, should permit evils which are against order, and so destroy it. This is guarded against when there are men higher and lower in authority among whom there is subordination.

Rulers (*præfecti*) over those [affairs] among men which belong to heaven, or over ecclesiastical [affairs], are called priests, and their office is called the priesthood; and rulers over those [affairs] among men which are of the world, or over civil [affairs], are called magistrates, and their chief, where there is such a form of government, is the king.

As regards priests, they should teach men the way to heaven, and also lead them; they should teach them according to the doctrine of their church, from the Word, and should lead them to live according to it. Priests who teach truths, and lead by them to the good of life, and so to the Lord, are good shepherds of the sheep; and those who teach and do not lead to the good of life, and so to the Lord, are bad shepherds.

Priests ought not to claim for themselves any power over the souls of men, for they do not know in what state the interiors of a man are. Still less ought they to claim the power of opening and shutting heaven; for that power belongs to the Lord alone.

Priests should have dignity and honour on account of the holy tl.ings which they administer; but those that are wise render the honour to the Lord, from whom these holy things are, and not to themselves; and those who are not wise attribute the honour to themselves. These rob the Lord of it. They who attribute honour to themselves, on account of the holy things they administer, prefer honour and gain to the salvation of the souls which they ought to care for; but they who render the honour to the Lord, and not to themselves, prefer the salvation of souls before honour and gain. No honour of any function is in the person, but it is adjoined to him according to the dignity of the thing which he administers. And what is adjoined does not belong to the person himself; and is also separated from him with the function. Honour in the person is honour of wisdom and of the fear of the Lord.

As priests are the rulers for the administration of those things which belong to the Divine law, and to worship, so kings and magistrates are for the administration of those things which belong to the civil law, and to judgment. (H. D. n. 311-319; and A. C. n. 10,789-10,798; also A. R. n. 854.)

The common good consists of these [elements]:—That in the society or kingdom there be, 1, What is Divine among the people. 2, That there be justice among them. 3, That there be morality among them. 4, That there be industry, skill, and uprightness. 5, That there be the necessaries of life. 6, That there be the things necessary for resources. 7, That there be the things necessary for protection. 8, That there be a sufficiency of employments; for this is the source of the three preceding [kinds of] necessaries.

From these the common good results; and it does not come out of the very [society] itself, but from the individuals there, and through the goods of use which the individuals perform. Thus, even what is Divine exists there through ministers;[1] and

---

[1] Rightly interpreted,—that is, by the light of the author's own teaching elsewhere,—the doctrine that the Divine exists in human society through ministers, or men in the priestly office, is by no means opposed to the cardinal truth that the Divine Word is the actual source of Divine life and light in the world; nor to the concurrent truth which he so strongly inculcates, that it is the privilege and *duty* of every man to go for himself to the Word, with the lamp of genuine doctrine, and draw out freely for his daily spiritual nourishment. All his utterances bearing in any wise upon the subject of the priesthood and of external worship seem to converge to this, as the true explanation : That in the course of time "the Divine" would cease to exist among a people, private worship, and the private study of the Word would cease, and religion become extinguished, in the absence of stated public worship. But public worship would gradually cease to be maintained if there were not men whose special use and duty it is to lead in and administer the things belonging to it (H. D. 311-314). Therefore "the Divine" would cease to exist notwithstanding the Word and revelation from the Word, if there were not ministers; even as justice would cease to exist, however

justice, through magistrates and judges; through the Divine and the just morality exists; and the necessaries of life through employments and commerce; and so on. . . .

The goods of use which individuals perform, and from which the common good exists, are ministries, functions, offices, and various employments. By ministries are meant priestly offices, and the duties of them; by functions, various offices of a civil nature; by employments are meant labours, as those of artificers, which are many; by offices are meant various pursuits, businesses, and services. Of these four the commonwealth or society consists.

Those who belong to the ministries provide that there may be what is Divine; the various civil functionaries, that there may be justice, that there may be morality, and that there may be industry, skill, and uprightness; the various workmen, that there may be the necessaries of life; and merchants, that there may be the things necessary for employments; soldiers, that there may be protection; and these last especially, and also agriculturists, that there may be a sufficiency of resources.

Such is the form of heaven that every one there is in some ministry, office, employment, or work. Such also are all the heavenly societies, in order that no one may be useless. . . .

From heavenly society chiefly it has been given me to know not only that individuals arranged according to the varieties of affections form the common good, but also that every one derives his own good from the common good. In like manner on earth; for so earthly society corresponds to heavenly society. . . . There is [in heaven] what is Divine, there is justice, there is uprightness, there is wisdom, and there is skill; and the community inspires these into the individuals when [each] part, who is an angel, is in charity. (Ch. n. 65, 66, 69-72.)

By fruits and works in the Word it is meant that one should rightly, faithfully, sincerely, and justly perform the duty and

just and pure the laws if there were not judges to administer them. So when the author teaches elsewhere, in an exactly parallel passage (see p. 437), that the Holy Spirit, in descending from the Lord through heaven to men, "in the church passes chiefly through the clergy to the laity, . . . by preachings according to the reception of the doctrine of truth therefrom, and also by the Sacrament of the Holy Supper according to repentance before it," the language does not necessarily bear the extreme interpretation that there is but little influx of the Holy Spirit into men except *directly* through these ministrations; and his whole teaching on the operation of the Holy Spirit forbids this interpretation. But these ministrations are essential means by which "the Divine" continues to exist among a people; and in this way and in this sense it is that chiefly through these ministrations the Holy Spirit passes from the Lord through heaven to the men of the church. No one acquainted with his writings can presume that the author in these passages prescribes for the New Church the Romish dogma of priestly intercession. What he really teaches here is the true doctrine of which this dogma is a perversion. But the language of both passages is terse and synoptical; for such is the character of the works,—and needs to be studied in the light of the author's own teachings elsewhere.

work of his office. When he does this he consults the common or public good, thus that of the country, of society larger and smaller, and of the fellow citizen, the companion, and brother,—which are the neighbour in the extended and the limited sense. For then every one, whether he be priest, or ruler and officer, or merchant, or labourer, daily performs uses; the priest [*sacerdos*] by preaching, the ruler and officer by administration, the merchant by commerce, and the labourer by his work. For example, the judge who judges rightly, faithfully, sincerely, and justly, as often as he judges performs a use to the neighbour; the minister (*minister*) likewise, as often as he teaches (*docet*); and so the others. That such uses are meant by the goods of charity, and by works, is manifest from the Lord's government in the heavens; for in the heavens as in the world all are in some function or ministration, or in some office, or in some work. (D. W. in A. E. xi. 4.)

That there is to be a Priesthood in the New Church typically shown in a symbolic Temple.

One day there appeared to me a magnificent square temple, the roof of which was in the form of a crown, arched above and elevated round about. Its walls were continuous windows of crystals; its gate of pearly substance. Within, on the south side toward the west, was a pulpit; on which at the right hand lay the open Word, surrounded with a sphere of light, the brightness of which encircled and illuminated the whole pulpit. In the midst of the temple was a sanctuary, with a veil before it,—but now lifted,—wherein stood a cherub of gold, with a sword in hand, which waved rapidly to and fro. While I was beholding these things there flowed into my meditation [a perception of] what they severally signified, namely :—That the temple signified the New Church; the gate of pearly substance, entrance into it; the windows of crystals, the truths which enlighten it; the pulpit, the priesthood and preachings; the open Word thereon and illuminating the upper part of the pulpit, its internal sense revealed, which is spiritual; the sanctuary in the midst of the temple, the conjunction of that church with the angelic heaven; the cherub of gold within, the Word in its literal sense; the sword rapidly waving in his hand signified that this sense can be turned every way, if only it be made applicable to some truth; the lifting of the veil before the cherub signified that now the Word is laid open. Afterwards, when I came nearer, I saw within over the gate Now it is Permitted; which signified that now it is permitted to enter intellectually into the mysteries of faith. (T. C. R. n. 508.)

The Priestly Office Representative.

The priesthood is representative of the Lord as to the work of salvation. (A. C. n. 9989, 9809.)

The priesthood is one of the representatives that exist even at the present day. . . . All priests, whoever or whatever they are, by the priestly [office] itself represent the Lord. . . . The priestly [office] itself is holy, whatever the character of him who ministers. Hence it is that the Word which a wicked man reads is equally holy; also the Sacrament of Baptism, and the Holy Supper, and the like. From this also it is evident that no priest can arrogate to himself any of the holiness of his priesthood. In so far as he arrogates anything of this to himself, or attributes it to himself, he places the character of a spiritual thief, or the mark of spiritual theft upon him. And in so far too as he does evil, that is, acts contrary to justice and equity, and contrary to good and truth, the priest puts off the representation of the holy priesthood, and represents the opposite. (*ib.* n. 3670.)

Inauguration into the Priesthood by a Representative Rite.

Because a clergyman is to teach doctrine from the Word concerning the Lord, and concerning redemption and salvation by Him, he is to be inaugurated by the solemn promise [*sponsionem*] of the Holy Spirit, and by the representation of its translation; but it is received by the clergyman according to the faith of his life. (Canons, p. 29.)

Communication, translation, and also reception, are signified by the laying on of hands. (A. C. n. 10,023.)

The reason why the laying on of hands signifies communication and reception is that the hands signify power. (*ib.*)

The arms and hands, in the Word, signify power, and the right hand superior power, because the body determines its powers chiefly into the arms and hands. (D. L. W. n. 220; see also A. R. n. 55.)

The [faculties] themselves of man's understanding and will are in the head; and in the body are action and obedience according to them. To place the hand upon the head therefore [in ancient times] was representative that a blessing was communicated to the understanding and will, thus to the real man. The same ritual remains even to this day, and is in use in inaugurations; also in benedictions. (A. C. n. 6292.)

Because touching, and the laying on of hands, signifies the

communication and transfer of what is with one, to another, therefore the laying of hands on the heads of those who are inaugurated and blessed has been received in the churches from ancient times; as it was also commanded Moses that he should do to Joshua (Num. xvii. 18-23; Deut. xxxiv. 9). (A. E. n. 79.)

The reason why even communications of the mind are effected by the touch of the hands is that the hands are the ultimates of a man, and the first things of him are at the same time in the ultimate or last, whereby all things that are intermediate, both of the body and of the mind, are kept in unbroken connection. Hence it is that Jesus touched infants (Matt. xviii. 2-6; Mark x. 13-16); and that by a touch He healed the sick; and that those who touched Him were made whole. Hence also it is that inaugurations into the priesthood, at this day, are effected by the laying on of hands. (C. L. n. 396; see also A. C. n. 878.)

The Falsity nevertheless of the Dogma of Apostolic Succession.

The [apostolic] succession is an invention of the love of ruling from self-love; as also the translation of the Holy Spirit from man to man (*ab homine in hominem*). (A. R. n. 802.)

The holy [effluence] which is meant by the Holy Spirit is not transferred from man to man (*ab homine in hominem*), but from the Lord through man to man.[1] (Canons, p. 29.)

The Gifts and Offices of the Priesthood.

Priests are appointed for the administration of those things which are of the Divine Law, and of worship. (H. D. n. 319; also A. C. n. 10,799.)

The Holy Spirit is the Divine [effluence] that proceeds from the One, Infinite, Omnipotent, Omniscient, and Omnipresent God.

The Holy Spirit in its essence is that Very God; but in the subjects where it is received it is the Proceeding Divine.

The Divine [effluence] which is called the Holy Spirit, proceeding from God by His Humanity, passes through the angelic heaven, and through this into the world; thus through angels into men.

Thence [it passes] through man to man, and in the church

---

[1] From this, in connection with the preceding passage, it would appear that the dogma of Apostolic succession originated, as have most other falsities, by the perversion of a truth.

especially through the clergy to the laity;[1] what is holy is given continually, and recedes if the Lord be not approached.

The Proceeding Divine which is called the Holy Spirit, in its proper sense, is the Holy Word and the Divine Truth therein ; and its operation is instruction, reformation and regeneration, and thence vivification and salvation.

The Divine [effluence], which is meant, by the Holy Spirit, proceeds from the Lord through the clergy to the laity by preachings, according to reception of the doctrine of truth thence; and by the Holy Supper, according to repentance before it. (Coronis, pp. 26, 29.)

The Divine virtue and operation which are meant by the sending of the Holy Spirit, with the clergy in particular are illustration and instruction.

The operations of the Lord considered in the preceding section, —which are reformation, regeneration, renovation, vivification, sanctification, justification, purification, the remission of sins, and finally salvation,—flow in from the Lord with the clergy as well as the laity; and are received by those who are in the Lord and the Lord in them (John vi. 56; xiv. 20; xv. 4, 5). But the reasons why with the clergy in particular there is illustration, and instruction, are, that these pertain to their office, and inauguration into the ministry carries them with it. (T. C. R. n. 146.)

The good of the priesthood is to care for the salvation of souls, to teach the way to heaven, and to lead those who are taught. In the degree that a priest is in this good, from love and its desire he acquires the truths that he is to teach, and by which he is to lead. (Life, n. 39.)

Jesus said three times to Peter, " *Lovest thou Me ?* " and Peter three times replied that he loved Him. Jesus said three times, " *Feed My lambs, and My sheep* " (John xxi. 15-17). To feed lambs and sheep denotes the uses or goods of charity with those who preach the gospel, and love the Lord. (D. W. in A. E. xi. 3.)

Priests ought to teach the people, and to lead them by truths to the good of life; but yet they ought not to compel any one, since no one can be compelled to believe contrary to what from his heart he thinks to be true. He who believes differently from the priest, and makes no disturbance, should be left in peace ; but he who makes disturbance should be separated; for this, too, is of order, for the sake of which the priesthood is established. (H. D. n. 318.)

Good may be insinuated into another by any one in the country, but not truth except by those who are teaching ministers; if others insinuate truth heresies arise, and the church is disturbed and rent asunder. (A. C. n. 6822.)

[1] See note p. 432.

Among the externals of worship with priests is preaching, and also teaching privately; and with every one the instruction of children and servants in religious matters. (Ch. n. 101.)

Marriage ought to be consecrated by a priest. The reason is, that marriages in themselves considered are spiritual and therefore holy. For they descend from the heavenly marriage of good and truth, and things relating to marriage correspond to the Divine marriage of the Lord and the church; and hence they are from the Lord Himself, but according to the state of the church with the contracting parties. Now because the ecclesiastical order on earth administer those things which are of the priesthood with the Lord,—that is, those which are of His love, and so those also which pertain to blessing,—it is proper that marriages should be consecrated by His ministers; and then, because they are also the chief witnesses, that the consent to the covenant be heard, accepted, confirmed, and so, too, established by them. (C. L. n. 308; also *ib.* n. 21.)

CHARITY IN THE PRIEST.

If he looks to the Lord and shuns evils as sins, and sincerely, justly, and faithfully does the work of the ministry enjoined upon him, he does the good of use continually, and becomes charity in form. And he does the good of use, or the work of the ministry, sincerely, justly, and faithfully, when he is affected for the salvation of souls. And in proportion as he is thus affected truths affect him, because it is by means of them that he leads souls to heaven; and he leads souls by means of truths to heaven when he leads them to the Lord. His love then is to teach truths diligently from the Word; because when he teaches them from the Word he teaches them from the Lord. For the Lord not only is the Word, as He says in John (i. 1, 2, 14), but He is also "*the Way, the Truth, and the Life*" (John xiv. 6), and the *Door.* He therefore who enters the fold by the Lord as the door is a good shepherd; and he who does not enter the fold by the Lord as the door is a bad shepherd, who is called "*a thief and a robber*" (John x. 1-9). (Ch. n. 86.)

The priest who teaches truths from the Word, and leads by them to the good of life and so to heaven, practises charity in an eminent degree; because he exercises care for the souls of the men of his church. (T. C. R. n. 422.)

CHARITY TOWARDS THE PRIEST.

Since man was born for eternal life, and is introduced into it by the church, he ought to love the church as his neighbour in a higher degree. . . . It is not meant that the priesthood ought to be loved in a higher degree, and from it the church; but that the good and truth of the church ought to be loved, and the priesthood on account of them. The priesthood only serves; and according as it serves it ought to be honoured. (T. C. R. n. 415.)

It is one of the general uses of charity to make the contributions that are suitable and necessary for the ministry of the church. Which goods become uses of charity in so far as the church is loved as the neighbour in a higher degree. (D. W. in A. E. xi. 5.)

WHY PRIESTS ARE CALLED PASTORS.

To feed signifies, to instruct. The custom of calling those who teach, pastors, and those who are taught, the flock, is derived from the Word. The reason why they are so called [in the Word] has not hitherto been known, and shall therefore be explained:—In heaven, where all things that appear before the eyes are representative, they really represent under the natural appearance the spiritual things which the angels are thinking of and affected by; thus they present their thoughts and affections before their eyes in such forms as are in the world, or in like forms of natural things,—and this from the correspondence established by the Lord between spiritual things and natural. It is from this correspondence that flocks of sheep, lambs, and goats appear in heaven, feeding in green pastures and in gardens also,—which appearances spring from the thoughts of those who are in goods and truths of the church, and think from them intelligently and wisely. Hence it is, then, that the flock, pasture, feeding, and pastor (shepherd) are so often mentioned in the Word; for the Word in the letter is composed of such things as appear before the eyes in heaven, by which the spiritual things are signified that correspond to them. (A. E. n. 482.)

OF SOME, IN THE OTHER LIFE, WHO DISDAINED THE PRIESTLY OFFICE.

There were some who disdained the priestly office, saying that the priesthood is universal, that is, with all. Some of them read the Word diligently enough, but as they lived wickedly they drew therefrom abominable dogmas,—of which there are many These also were cast out of heaven, but behind; for the reason that they preached clandestinely, and were willing thus secretly to subvert the doctrine of the church. (S. D. n. 4904. See also pp. 427, 437.)

MARRIAGE.

IT is evident from the book of Creation, and at the same time from the Lord's words, that from creation there was given to man and woman an inclination and also a capability of conjunction, as into one. In the book of Creation, which is called Genesis, we read: "*Jehovah God builded the rib which he had taken from the man into a woman, and brought her to the man. And the man said, This now is bone of my bones, and flesh of my flesh. She shall be called Woman, because she was taken out of man. Therefore shall a man leave his father and his mother, and shall cleave unto his wife; and they shall be one flesh*" (ii. 22-24). The Lord also says the same in Matthew :—"*Have ye not read, that He which made them from the beginning made them male and female, and said, For this cause shall a man leave father and mother, and shall cleave to his wife; and they twain shall be one flesh? Wherefore they are no more twain, but one flesh*" (xix. 4-6). It is clear from these passages that the woman was created from the man (*vir*),[1] and that each has an inclination and capability of re-uniting themselves into one. That the re-union is into one man (*homo*) is also plain from the book of Creation, where both together are called man (*homo*) ; for we read :—*In the day that God created man* (homo), . . . *a male and a female created He them,* . . . *and called their name man* (homo)" (v. 1, 2). It is said, "He called their name Adam ; " but Adam and man in the Hebrew tongue are one word. They are both together called man too in chap. i. 27, and iii. 22, 23, 24, of the same book. One man is also signified by one flesh; as is evident from passages in the Word where all flesh is mentioned, meaning all mankind. (C. L. n. 156.)

THE NATURE AND ORIGIN OF MARRIAGE.

The origin of love truly conjugial is the love of the Lord towards the church. Hence in the Word the Lord is called the

---

[1] The author must not be understood to mean that this account is to be interpreted literally, and that the woman was created from the man after the manner of the literal sense. He distinctly states otherwise (A. C. n. 152). But that, as

Bridegroom, and Husband, and the church the bride, and wife. From this marriage the church is a church, in general and in particular. The church in particular is a man in whom the church exists. It is therefore evident, that the conjunction of the Lord with the man of the church is the very origin of love truly conjugial. But it shall be explained how that conjunction can be the origin. The conjunction of the Lord with the man of the church is the conjunction of good and truth. Good is from the Lord, and truth is with man; and from this comes the conjunction which is called the heavenly marriage. From this marriage love truly conjugial arises between a wedded pair who are in such conjunction with the Lord. From this it is plain, first, that love truly conjugial is from the Lord alone; and that it is with those who are in the conjunction of good and truth from the Lord. Because this conjunction is reciprocal, it is described by the Lord that " *they are in Him and He in them* " (John xiv. 20). This conjunction or this marriage was thus established from creation; the man was so created that he might be an understanding of truth, and the woman, that she might be an affection of good, that accordingly the man might be truth and the woman good. When the understanding of truth which is with the man makes one with the affection of good which is with the woman, there is a conjunction of the two minds into one. This conjunction is the spiritual marriage from which conjugial love descends; for when two minds are so conjoined that they become as one mind, there is love between them. This love, which is the love of spiritual marriage, when it descends into the body becomes the love of natural marriage. That this is so any one if he will may clearly perceive. A married pair who mutually and reciprocally love each other inwardly, in mind, also mutually and reciprocally love each other as to their bodies. It is known, that all love descends into the body from an affection of the mind; and that without this origin no love exists. (A. E. n. 983.)

When good united to truth flows down from the Lord into a lower sphere it forms a union of minds; when into a still lower, it forms a marriage. Actual conjugial love is therefore a union of minds from good united to truth from the Lord. (A. C. n. 2728.)

There cannot be wisdom in man except by the love of being wise. A man can by no means be wise if this love is taken away. Wisdom from this love is meant by the truth of good, or truth from good. But when a man has obtained wisdom and loves it in himself, or loves himself on account of it, he forms a

---

there recorded, the man was first created, and the woman from the man; but after a manner involved in that account,—as he says below (p. 459) of the formation of the woman into a wife after marriage,—" interiorly understood."

love which is the love of wisdom, and is meant by the good of truth, or good from that truth. With man there are therefore two loves, of which the one that is prior is the love of being wise; and the other, which comes after, is the love of wisdom. But this if it remains with a man is an evil love; and is called pride, or the love of his own intelligence. It was therefore provided from creation that this love should be taken out of the man, lest it destroy him, and be assigned to the woman; that it might become conjugial love, which makes him whole again. (C. L. n. 88.)

THE HOLINESS OF MARRIAGE.

How holy marriages are in themselves, that is from creation, may be seen from the fact that they are the seminaries of the human race, and as the angelic heaven is from the human race, are also the seminaries of heaven; that consequently by marriages not only the earths but also the heavens are filled with inhabitants. And as the human race and a heaven therefrom wherein the very Divine may dwell as in its own, and as it were in itself, is the end of the whole creation, and their procreation according to Divine order is established by marriages, it is manifest how holy they are in themselves, thus from creation, and how holy they ought therefore to be kept. The earth indeed may be filled with inhabitants by fornications and adulteries as well as by marriages; but not heaven. The reason is that hell is from adulteries, and heaven from marriages. . . . When the procreations of the human race are effected through marriages in which the holy love of good and truth from the Lord reigns, then it is done on earth as in the heavens, and the kingdom of the Lord on earth corresponds to the kingdom of the Lord in the heavens. For the heavens consist of societies arranged according to all varieties of affections, celestial and spiritual; from which arrangement arises the form of heaven, which pre-eminently surpasses all the forms in the universe. A similar form would exist on earth if the procreations there were effected by marriages in which love truly conjugial reigns; for then how many families soever should successively descend from one father, they would come forth so many images of the societies of heaven, in a similar variety. Families would then be as fruitful trees of various species, from which there should spring as many gardens, in each its own species of fruit, which gardens taken together should present the form of a heavenly paradise. But this is said comparatively, because trees signify men of the church, gardens intelligence, fruits the good of life, and a paradise heaven. It has been told me from heaven that with the most ancients, of whom the first church on this earth was constituted,—which was called also by ancient writers the golden age,—there was such a correspondence of the families on earth with the societies of heaven; for the reason that love to the Lord, mutual love, innocence, peace, wisdom, and chastity in marriages reigned. And it was also told me from heaven, that they were then interiorly horrified at adulteries, as at the abominable things of hell. (A. E. n. 988.)

The reason why the love of marriage is so holy and so heavenly is, that it begins from the Lord Himself in the inmosts of man, and descends according to order to the ultimates of the body, and so fills the whole man with heavenly love; and induces upon him a form of the Divine love, which is the form of heaven, and is an image of the Lord. (*ib.* n. 985.)

The Distinction of Sex is in the Spirit.

Since man lives a man after death, and man is male and female, and the masculine is one and the feminine another, and they are so different that the one cannot be changed into the other, it follows that after death the male lives a male, and the female lives a female, each a spiritual man (*homo*). It is said that the masculine cannot be changed into feminine, nor the feminine into masculine, and that therefore after death the male is male, and the female is female; but as it is unknown in what the masculine and in what the feminine essentially consist, this shall here be briefly stated :—The distinction consists essentially in the fact that in the male the inmost is love, and its vestment is wisdom,—or what is the same, it is love overveiled with wisdom; and that in the female the inmost is that wisdom of the male, and its vestment is the love therefrom. But this love is feminine love, and is given by the Lord to the wife through the wisdom of the husband ; and the former love is masculine love, and is the love of being wise, and is given by the Lord to the husband according to his reception of wisdom. It is from this that the male is the wisdom of love ; and that the female is the love of that wisdom. There is therefore, from creation, implanted in each a love of conjunction into one. That the feminine is from the masculine, or that the woman was taken out of the man, is certain from these words in Genesis : *Jehovah God . . . took out one of the ribs of the man and closed up the flesh instead thereof, and He builded the rib which He had taken out of the man into a woman, and now brought her unto the man. And the man said, This is bone of my bones, and flesh of my flesh, hence she shall be called Woman* (Isha), *because she was taken out of the man* (Ish) (ii. 21-

23). What is signified by the rib, and what by flesh, will be shown elsewhere.

It follows from this primitive formation that the male is born intellectual, and the female is born voluntary;[1] or what is the same, that the male is born into the affection of knowing, of understanding, and of being wise, and the female into the love of conjoining herself with that affection in the male. And since the interiors form the exteriors to their likeness, and the masculine form is a form of intellect, and the feminine form is a form of the love of that intellect, hence it is that the male has a different face, a different voice, and a different body from the female; that is to say, a harder face, a harsher voice, and a stronger body, and moreover a bearded chin; in general, a form less beautiful than the female. They differ also in bearing and in manners. In a word, nothing whatever is alike in them; and yet in the least things there is what is conjunctive. Nay, in the male the masculine is masculine in every even the least part of his body; and also in every idea of his thought, and in every particle of his affection. In like manner the feminine in the female. And as the one cannot therefore be changed into the other, it follows that the male is male, and the female is female after death. (C. L. n. 32, 33).

THE LOVE OF SEX, AND WITH THOSE WHO COME INTO HEAVEN CONJUGIAL LOVE, REMAINS AFTER DEATH.

Because the male is then a male, and the female a female, and the masculine in the male is masculine entirely and in his every part, and likewise the feminine in the female, and as in their single, yea in their very minutest parts there is what is conjunctive, therefore the love of sex remains with man (*homo*) after death. Now, because this that is conjunctive was implanted from creation, and therefore perpetually inheres, it follows that the one desires and breathes forth conjunction with the other. Love in itself regarded is nothing else than a desire and hence an urging to conjunction; and conjugial love, to conjunction into one. For the male and female man were so created that from two they may become as one man, or one flesh; and when they

---

[1] In the original the correlative terms here are *intellectualis* and *voluntaria*. As we have in English no adjective that is perfectly correlative to *intellectual*, the translator, in order to convey precisely the author's meaning without circumlocution, is constrained to use the word voluntary somewhat out of its usual sense. As here used it bears the same relation to the will that *intellectual* does to the understanding. Its sense would be suggested but hardly expressed by the word affectional, in its common acceptation: thus—"The male is born intellectual and the female affectional."

become one, then taken together they are man (*homo*) in his fulness; but without this conjunction they are two, and each is as it were a divided or half-man. Since then this that is conjunctive lies inmostly concealed in the least things of the male, and in the least things of the female, and there is in their least things the faculty and desire after conjunction into one, it follows that the mutual and reciprocal love of sex remains with men (*homines*) after death.

The love of sex and conjugial love are mentioned [distinctively] because the love of sex is different from conjugial love. The love of sex pertains to the natural man, and conjugial love to the spiritual man. The natural man loves and desires only external conjunctions, and the pleasures of the body from them; but the spiritual man loves and desires internal conjunction, and the satisfactions of the spirit therefrom, and these he perceives are given with one wife, with whom he can be perpetually conjoined more and more into one; and by so much the more as he is thus conjoined does he perceive his satisfactions ascending in a like degree, and perceive them to be enduring to eternity; but the natural man has no thought of this. Hence it is said, that conjugial love remains after death with those that come into heaven; who are those that become spiritual on earth. (C. L. n. 37, 38.)

The love of sex is love towards many and with many of the sex, but conjugial love is only towards one and with one of the sex, and love for many and with many is a natural love; for it is common with beasts and birds, and they are natural. But conjugial love is a spiritual love, and is proper and peculiar to men; because men were created and are therefore born to become spiritual. In so far then as a man becomes spiritual he puts off the love of sex, and puts on conjugial love. In the beginning of marriage the love of sex appears as if conjoined with conjugial love, but in the progress of marriage they are separated, and then with those who are spiritual the love of sex is put away, and conjugial love instilled; but with those who are natural it is otherwise. It is clear now from what has been said that the love of sex, because it is with many, and in itself natural, yea animal, is impure and unchaste; and because it is vague and unlimited it is incontinent. But conjugial love is entirely different. (*ib.* n. 48.)

MARRIAGES IN THE HEAVENS.

As heaven is from the human race, and the angels there are consequently of both sexes; and as it is of creation that the woman is for the man, and the man for the woman, thus that the one is the other's ; and as with both this love is innate ; it follows that there are marriages in the heavens as well as on earth. Yet the marriages in the heavens are very different from the marriages on earth.

In the heavens marriage is the conjunction of two in one mind. It shall first be explained what the nature of this conjunction is :—The mind consists of two parts, of which one is called the understanding, the other the will. When these two parts act as one they are called one mind. In heaven the husband acts the part which is called the understanding, and the wife the part which is called the will. When this conjunction, which is of the interiors, descends into the lower things that are of their body, it is perceived and felt as love. This love is conjugial love. It is plain from this that conjugial love derives its origin from the conjunction of two in one mind. This in heaven is called cohabitation ; and it is said that they are not two, but one. For this reason a married pair in heaven are not called two, but one angel.

That there is such conjunction of husband and wife even in the inmosts, which are of their minds, comes from creation itself. For the man is born to be intellectual, thus to think from the understanding, and the woman is born to be voluntary, and thus to think from the will ; and this is evident from the inclination or connate disposition of each, as also from their form. *From disposition,* in that the man acts from reason, and the woman from affection. *From form,* in that the man has a rougher and less beautiful face, a heavier voice, and harder body ; and the woman a milder and more beautiful face, a more tender voice, and softer body. There is a similar difference between the understanding and the will, or between thought and affection ; a similar difference also between truth and good, and between faith and love ; for truth and faith are of the understanding, and good and love are of the will.

Every one, both man and woman, has an understanding and will ; but yet in man the understanding predominates, and in woman the will predominates, and the character of the person is according to that which predominates. But in marriages in the heavens there is no predominance ; for the will of the wife is also that of the husband, and the understanding of the husband is that also of the wife, since the one loves to will and to think as the other, thus mutually and reciprocally. Hence their conjunction in one. This conjunction is an actual conjunction ; for the will of the wife enters into the understanding of the husband, and the understanding of the husband into the will of the wife, and this especially when they look each other in the face. For, as has often been stated above, there is a communication of thoughts and affections in the heavens, and especially of consort with consort, because they mutually love each other. From all this it may be seen what is the nature of the conjunction of minds which constitutes marriage and produces conjugial love in the heavens; namely, that it is that one wishes his own to be the other's, and so reciprocally.

I have been told by the angels, that in so far as a married pair are in such conjunction they are in conjugial love; and in so far they are at the same time in intelligence, wisdom, and happiness. For the reason that Divine good and Divine truth, from which is all intelligence, wisdom, and happiness, flow principally into conjugial love. Consequently, that conjugial love is the very plane of Divine influx, because it is at the same time the marriage of truth and good. (H. H. n. 366-370.)

It has been granted me also to see how they are united in marriage in the heavens. Everywhere in heaven those that are alike are consociated, and the unlike are dissociated. Hence each society of heaven consists of those that are of similar character; like are brought to like, not of themselves but of the Lord. In the same manner consort is drawn to consort, whose minds can be conjoined in one. They therefore inmostly love each other at first sight, see themselves to be consorts, and enter into marriage. Thus it is that all the marriages of heaven are from the Lord alone. They also celebrate a festival, which is attended by a numerous assemblage. The festivities are different in different societies. (H. H. n. 383.)

The Lord's Words concerning Marriage in the Heavenly World.

In the Evangelists we read these words:—"*Certain of the Sadducees, who say that there is no resurrection, asked Jesus, saying, Master, Moses wrote, . . . If any man's brother die, having a wife, and . . . without children, his brother shall take his wife and raise up seed unto his brother. Now there were seven brethren, one after the other of whom took a wife; but they died without children. At last the woman died also. Therefore, in the resurrection, whose wife of them is she? And Jesus, answering, said unto them, The sons of this age marry and are given in marriage, but they which shall be accounted worthy to attain another age, and the resurrection from the dead, shall neither marry nor be given in marriage; neither can they die any more; for they are like unto the angels, and are sons of God, being sons of the resurrection. But that the dead rise again, even Moses showed at the bush, when he calleth the Lord the God of Abraham, and the God of Isaac, and the God of Jacob. For He is not the God of the dead, but of the living; for all live unto Him."* (Luke xx. 27-38; Matt. xxii. 23-33; Mark xii. 18-27.) There are two things which the Lord taught by these words:—First, that man rises again after death; and secondly, that in heaven they are not given in marriage. That man rises again after death, He taught by the saying that *"God is not the God of the dead, but of the living,"* and that Abraham, Isaac, and Jacob are alive; and moreover in the parable of the rich man in hell and Lazarus in heaven (Luke xvi. 22-31). And that in heaven they are not given in marriage, He taught by the words: *"They which shall be accounted worthy to attain another age, neither marry nor are given in marriage."* From the words which immediately follow,—that they cannot die any more, because they are like the angels, and are sons of God, being sons of the resurrection,—it is very evident that no other marriage is here meant than spiritual marriage. By spiritual marriage conjunction with the Lord is meant, and this is effected on earth; and when it is effected on earth it is effected also in the heavens. The marriage therefore is not performed again in the heavens, and they are not given in marriage. This is also meant by the words: *"The sons of this age marry and are given in marriage, but they which are accounted worthy to attain another age neither marry nor are given in marriage."* They are also called by the Lord sons of the marriage (Matt. ix. 15; Mark ii. 19); and here angels, sons of God, and sons of the resurrection. That to marry is to be conjoined with the Lord, and that to enter into marriage is to be received in heaven by the Lord, is plain from the following passages:—*The kingdom of heaven is like unto a man, a king, which made a marriage for his son, and sent forth servants, and invited . . . to the wedding"* (Matt. xxii. 1-14). *" The kingdom of heaven is like unto ten virgins, which . . . went forth to meet the bridegroom; five of whom . . . that were ready went in to the marriage"* (Matt. xxv. 1, *seq.*). It is evident from verse 13,—where it is said, *" Watch ye, for ye know not the day nor the hour in which the Son of Man will come,"*—that the Lord here meant Himself. From the Revelation also:—*" The time of the marriage of the Lamb is come, and His wife hath made herself ready. . . . Blessed are they which are called to the marriage supper of the Lamb"* (xix, 7, 9). (C. L. n. 41.)

There are nuptials in the heavens, just as on earth; but there, only with those who are in the marriage of good and truth. Nor are others angels. Spiritual nuptials, therefore, which are those of the marriage of good and truth, are meant in the Word. These take place on earth, and not after death, thus not in the heavens. As it is said of the five foolish virgins who also were invited to the wedding, that they could not enter in, because they were not in the marriage of good and truth; for they had no oil, but only lamps. By oil good is meant, and by lamps, truth; and to be given in marriage is to enter into heaven where this marriage is. (*ib.* n. 44.)

No Procreation of Offspring in Heaven.

Marriages in the heavens differ from the marriages on earth in this, that marriages on earth, in addition to [their other uses], are for the procreation of offspring; but not in the heavens. In place of that procreation there is in the heavens a procreation of good and truth. The reason why there is this procreation in place of the former is, that marriage in the heavens is a marriage of good and truth, as was shown above; and in that marriage good and truth and their conjunction above all things are loved. These, therefore, are what are propagated from marriages in the heavens. Hence it is that in the Word by births and generations spiritual births and generations are signified, which are those of good and truth; by mother and father truth conjoined to good, which procreates; by sons and daughters, the truths and goods that are procreated; and by sons-in-law and daughters-in-law, the conjunctions of these; and so on. It is evident from this that marriages in the heavens are not like marriages on earth. The nuptials in the heavens are spiritual, —which ought not to be called nuptials, but conjunctions of minds from the marriage of good and truth; but they are nuptials on earth, because they are not only of the spirit but also of the flesh. And as in the heavens they are not nuptials, therefore the two consorts are there not called husband and wife; but the consort of another,—from the angelic idea of the conjunction of the two minds in one,—is called by a word which signifies, reciprocally, his [or her] mutual (*suum mutuum vicissim*). From these considerations it may be known how the Lord's words respecting marriages (nuptials) in Luke xx. 35, 36 are to be understood. (H. H. n. 382.)

The reason why marriages in the heavens are without prolification, and there is instead of this a spiritual prolification, which is that of love and wisdom, is that the third [degree] which is natural is wanting with those that are in the spiritual world, and this is the containant of things spiritual; and spiritual things without their containant do not abide, after the manner of those that are procreated in the natural world. And in themselves regarded spiritual things relate to love and wisdom;

these therefore are what are born of their marriages. It is said that these are born, because conjugial love perfects an angel; for it unites him with his consort, whereby he becomes more and more a man (*homo*). For, as was said above, a married pair in heaven are not two, but one angel. By conjugial unition, therefore, they fill themselves with the human,—which is the desire to be wise, and the love of that which pertains to wisdom. (C. L. n. 52.)

The conjunction of charity and faith is as the marriage of a husband and wife. All natural offspring are born of the husband as a father, and of the wife as a mother; so from charity as a father and from faith as a mother all spiritual offspring are born, which are cognitions of good and truth. (T. C. R. n. 377.)

A MARRIAGE CEREMONY IN HEAVEN.

Towards evening there came a swift-footed messenger clothed in linen to the ten strangers who accompanied the angel, and invited them to a wedding to be celebrated the next day; and the strangers greatly rejoiced that they were also to witness a marriage in heaven. After this they were conducted to one of the chief counsellors, and supped with him. And after supper they returned, and retired each to his own chamber, and slept until morning. When they awoke they heard the song of maidens and little girls from the houses around the public place. At this time the affection of conjugial love was sung. Deeply affected and moved by its sweetness, they perceived infused into their joys a blessed delightfulness, which exalted and renewed them. When the time was come the angel said, Make ready, and array yourselves in the garments of heaven which our prince has sent for you. They put them on, and lo! the garments shone as with a flaming light. And they asked the angel, Whence is this? He replied, Because you are going to a wedding. With us garments are then resplendent, and become wedding garments.

The angel afterwards conducted them to the house of the marriage, and a porter opened the doors. As soon as they were within the threshold they were received and saluted by an angel sent from the bridegroom, and were brought in and led to the seats appointed for them. Soon afterwards they were invited into an ante-room of the bridal chamber; where they observed, in the centre, a table whereon was placed a magnificent candlestick, with seven branches and sconces, of gold; and against the walls hung silver lamps, from which when lighted the atmosphere appeared as if golden. At the sides of the candlestick they saw two tables on which loaves were placed, in triple order; and in the four corners [of the room] there were tables on which were crystal cups. While they were observing these things, lo! a door was opened from a room next to the bridal chamber, and they saw six virgins coming out, and after them the bridegroom and bride holding each other by the hand, and leading each other to an elevated seat which was set over against the candlestick, whereon they seated themselves, the bridegroom on the left, and the bride at his right hand; and the six virgins stood at the side of the seat next to the bride. The bridegroom was clad in a radiant purple robe and tunic of shining linen, with an ephod, on which was a plate of gold set around with diamonds; and on the plate a young eagle was engraved,—the nuptial badge of this society. And the bride wore a scarlet mantle, and under it an embroidered dress, reaching from the neck to her feet, and below the breast a golden girdle, and on her head a coronet of gold, set with rubies. When they were thus seated the bridegroom turned to the bride and placed on her finger a gold ring, and drew forth bracelets and a necklace of pearls, and fastened the bracelets upon her wrists and the necklace about her neck, and said, Accept these pledges. And when she accepted them he kissed her, and said, Now thou art mine; and called her his wife. This being done the guests cried out, A blessing on you. This each one by himself said, and then altogether; one sent by the prince uttered the same for him. And at that moment the ante-room was filled with an aromatic vapour, which was the sign of a blessing from heaven. The attendants then took bread from the two tables near the candlestick, and cups, now filled with wine, from the tables in the corners, and gave to each of the guests his bread and his cup, and they ate and drank. After this the husband and his wife arose, the six virgins with the silver lamps in their hands, now lighted, following to the threshold; and the married pair entered the bridal chamber, and the door was shut. (C. L. n. 19, 20.)

A Conjugial Pair in Heaven.

One morning I was looking up into heaven, and saw over me expanse above expanse; and I saw that the first expanse which was near opened, and presently the second which was higher, and lastly the third which was the highest. And by illustration therefrom I perceived that upon the first expanse there were angels who compose the first or ultimate heaven; and upon the second expanse were angels who compose the second or middle heaven; and upon the third expanse were angels who compose the third or highest heaven. At first I wondered what and why this was; but presently a voice was heard from heaven, as of a trumpet, saying, We have perceived, and now see, that you are meditating on CONJUGIAL LOVE; and we know that as yet no one on earth knows whât love truly conjugial in its origin and in its essence is; and yet it is important that it should be known. It has pleased the Lord therefore to open the heavens to you, that illustrating light, and thence perception, may flow into the interiors of your mind. With us in the heavens, especially in the third heaven, our heavenly delights are chiefly from conjugial love. By permission given us we will therefore send down to you a married pair that you may see them. And lo! a chariot then appeared descending from the highest or third heaven, in which an angel was seen; but as it approached two were seen in it. At a distance the chariot glittered like a diamond before my eyes; and there were harnessed to it young horses, white as snow. And they that sat in the chariot held in their hands two turtle-doves. And they called to me, saying, Would you like us to come nearer? But take heed then that the effulgence which is from our heaven whence we have descended, and is flaming, does not penetrate too interiorly. By the influx of this the higher ideas of your understanding, which in themselves are heavenly, may indeed be illustrated; but in the world in which you are these are ineffable. Receive rationally therefore what you are about to hear, and so address it to the understanding. I answered, I will take heed; come nearer. And they came, and lo! it was a husband and his wife. And they said, We are a married pair. From the earliest age, which is called by you the golden age, we have lived happily in heaven; and perpetually in the same flower of youth in which you see us to-day. I looked at both attentively, for I perceived that they represented conjugial love in its life and in its adornment; in its life in their faces, and in its adornment in their apparel. For all the angels are affections of love in the human form; the governing affection itself shines forth from their faces; and their raiment is derived to them from the affection and in accordance with it. It is therefore said in heaven that his own affection clothes every one. The husband appeared of an age intermediate between manhood and youth. From his eyes shone forth a light, sparkling from the wisdom of love. His face was as if inwardly radiant from this light; and by irradiation therefrom the skin outwardly was as it were refulgent. His whole face was thence one resplendent comeliness. He was clothed in a long robe that reached to the ankles, and under the robe a vestment of blue, and this was girded about with a golden girdle, on which there were three precious stones,—two sapphires on the sides and in the middle a carbuncle ; his stockings were of shining linen interwoven with threads of silver, and his shoes were entirely of silk. This was the representative form of conjugial love with the husband. And with the wife it was this :—Her face I saw and did not see. I saw it as beauty itself, and did not see it because this was inexpressible to me. For there was a splendour of flaming light in her face,—such light as there is with the angels in the third heaven,— and it dimmed my sight, so that I was simply struck with amazement. Observing this, she spoke to me, saying, What do you see ? I answered, I see only conjugial love and a form of it ; but I see and do not see. At this she turned herself obliquely from her husband, and I could then regard her more attentively. Her eyes sparkled with the light of her heaven,—which, as was said, is flaming, and therefore is derived from the love of wisdom. For in that heaven wives love their husbands from wisdom and in their wisdom ; and husbands love their wives from that love and in that towards themselves ; and thus they are united. This was the origin of her beauty ; which was such that no painter could emulate and portray it in its form ; for there is no such lustre in his colour, nor any such beauty expressible in his art. Her hair was gracefully arranged in correspondence with her beauty, and flowers were inserted in it in the form of coronets. She wore a necklace of carbuncles, and pendent from this was a rosary of chrysolites ; and she had bracelets of pearl. She was clothed in a flowing robe of scarlet, and under this a waistcoat of purple, which was clasped in front with rubies. But what astonished me, the colours varied according to her aspect towards her husband ; and according to this they were also now more and now less brilliant,—more in a mutual aspect to each other and less in an oblique aspect. After I had observed these things they conversed with me again ; and when the husband was talking he spoke as if at the same time from his wife ; and when the wife was talking she spoke as if at the same time from her husband ; for such is the union of minds from which their speech flows. And then I also marked the tone of voice of conjugial love ; that inwardly it was simultaneous with and also a proceeding from the delights of a state of peace and innocence. At length they said, We are recalled ; we must depart. And then they appeared to be conveyed in a chariot again as before ; and were carried along a paved way among gardens of flowers, out of whose beds sprang olive trees and orange trees laden with fruit ; and when they were near their heaven virgins came to meet them, and received and conducted them in. (C. L. n. 42.)

The State of Married Partners after Death.

There are two states through which man passes after death, an external and an internal. He comes first into his external, and afterwards into his internal state. And while in the external, one married partner,—if both are dead,—meets and recognises the other, and if they have lived together in the world they consociate, and for some time live together. And while they are in this state one does not know the inclination of the other to him or her self, because this conceals itself in the internals. But afterwards when they come into their internal state the inclination manifests itself; and if it be concordant and sympathetic they continue their conjugial life, but if it be discordant and antipathetic they discontinue it. If a man has had several wives he joins himself to them in succession while in the external state; but when he enters the internal state, in which he perceives the inclinations of the love as they are, he then either chooses one or leaves them all. For in the spiritual world as well as in the natural, it is not permitted any Christian to take more than one wife, because this destroys and profanes religion. It is the same with a woman who has had several husbands. But they do not attach themselves to their husbands; they only present themselves, and the husbands attach them to themselves. It should be known that husbands rarely recognise their wives; but wives easily recognise their husbands. The reason is, that women have an interior perception of love, and men only an exterior. (C. L. n. 47.)

If they can live together they remain consorts; but if they cannot live together they separate,—sometimes the husband from the wife, sometimes the wife from the husband, and sometimes each from the other. Separations take place after death because the conjunctions that are formed on earth are seldom formed from any internal perception of love, but from an external perception which hides the internal. The external perception of love has its cause and origin from such things as pertain to the love of the world and of the body. Wealth and large possessions especially are [objects] of the love of the world; and dignities and honours are objects of the love of the body. And in addition to these there are also various seductive allurements; such as beauty, and a simulated elegance of manners, and sometimes also unchastity. And besides, marriages are contracted within the country, city, or village of birth or of abode, where no choice is given except as restricted and limited to the families that are known,—and within these limits to those of corresponding fortune. Hence it is that marriages entered into in the world for the most part are external, and not at the same time internal. And yet internal conjunction, which is a conjunction of souls, constitutes real marriage; and this conjunction is not perceivable until man puts off the external and puts on the internal, which he does after death. Hence now it is that separations then take place, and afterwards new conjunctions with those who are similar and congenial,—unless these had been provided on earth; which is done for those who from their early years have loved, desired, and asked of the Lord a legitimate and lovely union with one; and have spurned and, as an offence to their nostrils, detested wandering lusts. (*ib.* n. 49.)

TRUE MARRIAGE LOOKS TO WHAT IS ETERNAL.

They who are in love that is truly conjugial look to what is eternal, because there is eternity in that love. And its eternity is from the fact that love increases with the wife and wisdom with the husband to eternity; and in this increase or progression the married pair enter more and more interiorly into the blessed-nesses of heaven, which their wisdom and love of it together have in store within them. If therefore the idea of what is eternal were eradicated, or should by any event escape from their minds, it would be as if they were cast down from heaven. What the state of the married in heaven is when the idea of the eternal escapes from their minds and an idea of what is temporal enters in its place, came into open view with me from this experience:—By permission granted, there was once with me a married pair from heaven; and then, by a certain worthless wretch speaking artfully, the idea of the eternal in marriage was taken from them; which being taken away they began to lament, saying that they could no longer live, and that they felt a wretchedness which they had never felt before. This being perceived in heaven by their fellow angels, the worthless spirit was removed and cast down. When this was done the idea of what is eternal returned to them; whereat they rejoiced with joy of heart, and most tenderly embraced each other. In addition to this I have heard a married pair who cherished, now an idea of the eternal, and now an idea of the temporal, in respect to their marriage. The reason was that there was an internal dissimilitude between them. When they were in an idea of the eternal they rejoiced with each other, and when in an idea of the temporal, they said, " It is no longer marriage ; " and the wife said, " I am no more a wife, but a concubine ; " and the man, " I am no longer a husband, but a fornicator." Therefore, when their internal dissimilitude was made known to them, the man went away from the woman, and the woman from the man. But afterwards, as they were both in the idea of what is eternal in respect to marriage, they were united to partners who were in similitude with themselves. From these illustrations it may be clearly seen, that they who are in love that is truly conjugial look to what is eternal; and that if this vanishes from the inmosts of their thought they are disunited as to conjugial love, though not at the same time as to friendship; for this abides in the externals, but that in the internals. It is the same in marriages on earth. The married there, when they love each other tenderly, think of the eternal in respect to the marriage covenant, and not at all of its end by death; or if they think of this they grieve, yet are revived with hope from the thought of its continuing after their decease. (C. L. n. 216.)

Conjugial Love is perfected to Eternity.

As love that is truly conjugial endures to eternity, it follows that the wife becomes more and more a wife, and the husband more and more a husband. The actual reason is that in a marriage of truly conjugial love each becomes a more and more interior man (*homo*). For this love opens the interiors of their minds; and as these are opened man becomes more and more a man; and to become more a man in the case of the wife is to become more a wife, and with the husband it is to become more a husband. I have heard from the angels that the wife becomes more and more a wife as her husband becomes more and more a husband, and not *vice versa*; because it rarely if ever occurs that a chaste wife fails to love her husband, but the return of love by the husband fails; and that this fails for the reason that there is no elevation of wisdom, which alone receives the love of the wife. (C. L. n. 200.)

Those who are in love that is truly conjugial, after death when they become angels, return to their youth and early manhood. However worn out with age, husbands become young men; and wives, however worn out with age, become young women. Each consort returns to the flower and into the joys of the age in which conjugial love begins to exalt the life with new delights, and to inspire sportiveness, for the sake of prolification. Into this state,—first outwardly, and afterwards more and more interiorly to eternity,—does the man come who in the world had fled adulteries as sins, and was introduced by the Lord into conjugial love. As they are always growing more interiorly young, it follows that love which is truly conjugial continually increases and enters into its delights and satisfactions,—which were provided for it from the creation of the world, and which are the delights and satisfactions of the inmost heaven, arising from the love of the Lord towards heaven and the church, and therefore from the love of good and truth for each other; from which loves every joy in the heavens is derived. The reason why man thus grows young in heaven is because he then enters into the marriage of good and truth, and in good there is an inclination continually to love truth, and in truth there is a continual inclination to love good; and then the wife is good in form, and the man is truth in form. From this inclination man puts off all the austerity, dejection, and dryness of age, and puts on the liveliness, gladness, and freshness of youth,—whence the inclination lives and becomes joy. It has been told me from heaven that they have then a life of love which can only be described as a life of joy itself. (A. E. n. 1000.)

THEY WHO ARE IN LOVE TRULY CONJUGIAL FEEL AND SEE THEMSELVES TO BE A UNITED MAN.

I talked with the angels respecting conjugial love, or the love between two consorts who love each other. [They said] that it is the inmost of all loves, and is such that consort sees consort in his or her inner and outer mind (*animo et mente*[1]), so that each consort has the other within him or her. That is, that the image, yea, the similitude of the husband is in the mind of the wife, and the image and similitude of the wife is in the mind of the husband; so that the one sees the other in himself or herself, and in their inmosts they thus dwell together. This was represented by angelic conceptions, which cannot be expressed in words. (S. D. n. 4408.)

I have heard it testified by those who have lived for ages with their consorts in heaven, that they feel themselves to be thus united,—the husband that he is united with the wife, and the wife that she is united with the husband; and feel themselves to be each within the other, mutually and reciprocally, as also in

---

[1] There are in general four distinct terms which the author applies to the spiritual part of man, each with a different and very definite signification; viz. *spiritus, anima, mens,* and *animus*. *Spiritus* (the spirit) is the whole immortal part of man,—all that which lives as a man after death,—and includes the *anima, mens,* and *animus*. *Anima* (the soul), strictly, is the very inmost of man's spirit, the first receptacle of life from the Lord (C. L. n. 101, 315, *end*); and by derivation it inmostly pervades and is the life of the whole mind and body below it. *Mens* (the mind) is intermediate between the *anima* and the *animus*, and in itself comprises three discrete degrees, viz. the highest, middle, and lowest (C. L. n. 270). The *animus* is a still lower and outer mind, composed of "affections, and hence outward inclinations insinuated principally after birth, by education, association, and consequent habits of life." (*ib.* n. 246.) See Chapter on the Human Soul.

the flesh, although distinct. The reason of this phenomenon, rare on earth, is that the unition of their souls and minds is felt in the flesh; because the soul forms not only the inmosts of the head, but also the inmosts of the body; likewise the mind, which is intermediate between the soul and the body; this too although it appears to be in the head is yet actually in the whole body also. And they said that it is from this cause that the actions which the soul and mind intend flow instantly from the body; and that it is from this that they themselves, since the rejection of the body in the former world, are perfect men. Now as the soul and mind closely adjoin themselves to the flesh of the body, in order that they may operate and produce their effects, it follows that the unition of the soul and mind with the consort is felt, even in the body, as one flesh. (C. L. n. 178.)

MARRIAGES INDUCE UPON THE SOULS AND MINDS ANOTHER FORM.

It cannot be discerned in the natural world that marriages induce another form upon souls and minds, because there souls and minds are encompassed with a material body, and the mind rarely shines through this; and the men of this age also, more than the ancients, learn from infancy to put expressions on their faces by which they profoundly conceal the affections of the mind. This is the reason why the difference in the forms of minds before marriage and after marriage are not distinguished. That nevertheless the forms of souls and minds after marriage are different from what they were before it, manifestly appears from the same in the spiritual world. For then they are spirits and angels; who are nothing else than minds and souls in human form divested of their coverings, which were composed of the elements in waters and earths, and of exhalations therefrom diffused in the air,—which being cast off, the forms of the minds appear, as they had inwardly been in their bodies; and it is then clearly seen that with those who live in marriage and those who do not they are different. In general, with the married there is an inner beauty of the countenance; for the man takes from the wife the beautiful ruddiness of her love, and the wife from the man the brilliant lustre of his wisdom. For there the two consorts as to souls are united; and there appears besides a human fulness in each. This is in heaven; for there are no marriages elsewhere [in the spiritual world], but beneath the heavens are only nuptial bonds which are made and broken. (C. L. n. 192.)

The Woman is actually formed into a Wife according to the Description in the Book of Genesis.

It is said in this book that the woman was created out of the rib of the man, and that when she was brought to him the man said, " *This is bone of my bones, and flesh of my flesh ; and she shall be called woman* (isha), *because she was taken out of man*" (ish) (ii. 22-24). A rib of the breast in the Word, in the spiritual sense, signifies nothing else than natural truth. This is signified by the ribs which the bear carried between his teeth in Dan. vii. 5 ; for by bears they are signified who read the Word in the natural sense, and see the truths therein, without understanding. By the breast of a man that essential and peculiar thing is signified which is distinct from the breast of woman. This is wisdom ; for truth sustains wisdom, as a rib sustains the breast. These things are signified because it is the breast in which all things of man are as in their centre. It is therefore evident that the woman was created out of the man by the transfer of his own wisdom,—that is, out of natural truth ; and that the love of this was transferred from the man to the woman, that it might become conjugial love ; and that this was done in order that there may not be the love of himself in the man, but the love of the wife,—who, from the nature innate in herself, cannot but convert the love of himself in the man into his love for her. And I have heard that this is done from the wife's love itself, neither the man nor the wife being conscious of it. Hence it is that no one can ever really conjugially love his consort who from the love of himself is in the pride of his own intelligence. When this mystery of the creation of the woman from the man is understood, it can be seen that the woman is likewise as it were created or formed from the man in marriage ; and this is effected by the wife, or rather through the wife by the Lord, who has infused into women inclinations for becoming so. For the wife receives in herself the image of the man, by the fact that she appropriates to herself his affections ; and by the fact that she conjoins the internal will of the man with her own ; and also by the fact that she takes to herself the offspring of his soul. From all this it is plain that, according to the description in the book of Creation, interiorly understood, the woman is formed into a wife by means of such things as she takes from her husband, even from his breast, and inscribes upon herself. (C. L. n. 193.)

I was once in the midst of angels, and heard their conversation. The conversation was upon intelligence and wisdom :— That a man does not perceive but that both are in himself ; and thus that whatever he thinks from his understanding and intends

from his will is from himself. When yet not the least of it is
from the man, save the faculty of receiving the things which are
of the understanding and will, from God. And as every man from
birth inclines to love himself, lest man should perish on account
of the love of himself and the pride of his own intelligence, it
was provided from creation that this love of the man should be
transferred to the wife, and be implanted in her from nativity, so
that she may love the intelligence and wisdom of her husband,
and thus her husband. The wife therefore continually attracts
to herself her husband's pride in his own intelligence; and extinguishes it in him and vivifies it in herself, and so turns it into
conjugial love, and fills it with pleasantnesses beyond measure.
This was provided of the Lord, that the pride of his own intelligence might not so infatuate the man that he should believe that
his understanding and wisdom are of himself, and not from the
Lord; and thus be willing to eat of the tree of the knowledge of
good and evil, and therefore believe himself like God, and even
God,—as the serpent, which was the love of his own intelligence,
said and persuaded. Wherefore, after eating of it man was cast
out of paradise, and the way to the tree of life was guarded by a
cherub. Spiritually, paradise is intelligence; to eat of the tree of
life, spiritually, is to have understanding and wisdom from the
Lord; and to eat of the tree of the knowledge of good and evil,
spiritually, is to have understanding and wisdom from himself.
(*ib.* n. 353.)

Conjugial Love is Fundamental to all Loves, and the Treasury of all Joys and Delights.

That there is such conjugial love as is described in these
pages may indeed be acknowledged from the first state of that
love, when it insinuates and enters into the heart of a youth and
virgin; that is, with those who begin to love one only of the
sex, and to desire her to wife; and especially during the period
of betrothment, while it is lingering and progressing to the
nuptials; and at length at the nuptials, and during the first days
which follow them. Who does not then acknowledge and
consent to these things? That this is the fundamental love of
all loves? And that all joys and all delights from first to last
are gathered into it? And who does not know that after this
pleasant time these transports gradually decline and pass away,
till at length they are scarcely sensible of them? If then it be
said to them, as before, that this is the fundamental love of all
loves, and that all joys and delights are gathered into it, they do
not consent, nor acknowledge; and perhaps say these things are

nonsense, or mysteries that are incomprehensible. It is evident from this that the earliest love of marriage emulates love which is truly conjugial, and causes it visibly to appear in a certain image. This takes place because the love of sex, which is unchaste, is then cast away, and the love of one of the sex, which is a love truly conjugial and chaste, sits implanted in its place. Who does not then look on other women with indifference, and upon his only one with love? (C. L. n. 58.)

The reason why conjugial love viewed as to its essence is the fundamental love of all the loves of heaven and the church, is that its origin is from the marriage of good and truth, and from this marriage all the loves which constitute heaven and the church with man proceed. The good of this marriage constitutes love, and the truth of it constitutes wisdom; and when love draws near to wisdom or conjoins itself therewith, love becomes love, and when in its turn wisdom draws near to love, and conjoins itself therewith, wisdom becomes wisdom. Love that is truly conjugial is nothing else than the conjunction of love and wisdom. A married pair between whom or in whom together this love exists, are an image and form of it. And in the heavens, where the faces are genuine types of the affections of their love, all are similitudes of it; for it is in them in general, and in every part. Now since a married pair are this love in image and in form, it follows that every love that proceeds from a form of the love itself is a representation of it. If therefore conjugial love is heavenly and spiritual, the loves proceeding from it are also heavenly and spiritual. Conjugial love is therefore as the parent, and other loves are as its offspring. Hence it is that from the marriages of angels in the heavens spiritual offspring are generated, which are [generations] of love and wisdom, or of good and truth. (*ib.* n. 65.)

All delights whatsoever that are felt by man are of his love; through them the love manifests itself, yea, exists and lives. It is well known that delights are exalted in the degree that the love is exalted, and also as the incident affections touch the ruling love more nearly. Now, as conjugial love is the fundamental of all good loves, and as it is inscribed on the very least things of man, as was shown before, it follows that its delights exceed the delights of all loves, and also that it imparts delight to them according to its presence and at the same time its conjunction with them; for it expands the innermost things of the mind, and at the same time the innermost things of the body, as the delicious current of its fountain flows through and opens them. It is because of the superior excellence of its use above all others that all delights from first to last are gathered into this love. Its use is the propagation of the human race, and an angelic heaven therefrom; and because this use was the end of ends of the creation, it follows that all the states of blessedness, happiness, gladness, gratification, and pleasure, which could ever be conferred on man by the Lord the Creator, are gathered into this his love. That delights follow use, and are experienced by man according to the love of the use, is manifest from the delights of the five senses,—sight, hearing, smell, taste, and touch; each of these has its delights differing according to their specific uses. What then must be the delight of the sense of conjugial love, whose use is the complex of all other uses?

I know that few will acknowledge that all joys and all delights from first to last are gathered into conjugial love; because love that is truly conjugial, into which they are gathered, is at this day so rare that it is unknown what it is, and scarcely that it exists. For these joys and delights are in no other than genuine conjugial love ; and as this is so rare on earth it is impossible to describe its super-eminent felicities otherwise than from the mouth of angels, for they are in it. They have declared that its inmost delights, which are of the soul,—into which the conjugial [influence] of love and wisdom or good and truth from the Lord first flows,—are imperceptible and therefore ineffable, because they are delights at the same time of peace and innocence; but that in their descent they become more and more perceptible,—in the higher [regions] of the mind as states of blessedness, in the lower as states of happiness, in the breast as delights therefrom; and that from the breast they diffuse themselves into each and every part of the body, and finally unite in ultimates in the delight of delights. And the angels have related wonders respecting these delights, declaring also that the varieties of them in the souls of consorts, and from these in their minds, and from these in their breasts, are both infinite and eternal; and that they are exalted according to the wisdom in the husbands,—and this because they live to eternity in the flower of their age; and because to them nothing is more blessed than to grow wiser and wiser. (*ib.* n. 68, 69.)

Wisdom and Intelligence are in Proportion to Conjugial Love.

The amount and the quality of intelligence and wisdom that a man has is according to the amount and quality of conjugial love with him. The reason is that conjugial love descends from the love of good and truth, as an effect from its cause, or as the natural from its spiritual; and all intelligence and wisdom are from the marriage of good and truth, even with the angels of the three heavens. For intelligence and wisdom are nothing else than the reception of light and heat from the Lord as a sun; that is, the reception of Divine truth conjoined with Divine good, and Divine good conjoined with Divine truth; thus it is the marriage of good and truth from the Lord. It was clearly apparent that this is so from the angels in the heavens. Separated from their consorts they are in intelligence it is true, but not in wisdom; but when they are with their consorts they are in wisdom also. And what surprised me, they are in a state of wisdom just in proportion as they turn their faces towards their consorts; for the conjunction of truth and good in the spiritual world is effected by the look, and the wife there is good, and the husband is truth; therefore as truth turns itself to good, so it is vivified. By intelligence and wisdom is not meant ingenuity in reasoning about truths and goods, but the faculty of seeing and understanding truths and goods; a faculty which man has from the Lord. (A. E. n. 998.)

The reason why the capability of being wise increases with those who are in love that is truly conjugial, is that this love with the married is from wisdom and according to it; and also because the sense of this love is the touch, and this sense is common to all the senses, and is also full of delights. It therefore opens the interiors of the mind as it opens the interiors of the senses, and with them the organic forms of the whole body. It follows from this that they who are in that love, love nothing more than to be wise; for a man is wise in proportion as the interiors of his mind are opened. (C. L. n. 211.)

The Qualifications for receiving Conjugial Love.

None can be in love which is truly conjugial but those who receive it from the Lord; who are those that directly come to Him, and from Him live the life of the church. The reason is, that viewed from its origin and its correspondence that love is heavenly, spiritual, holy, pure, and clean, beyond every love that exists among the angels of heaven and among the men of the church; and these its attributes cannot be given except to those who are conjoined to the Lord, and are consociated by Him with the angels of heaven. For these shun extra-conjugial loves, which are conjunctions of one with others than his or her own consort, as injuries to the soul, and as they would the lakes of hell; and in so far as consorts shun such conjunctions, even as to the lusts of the will and intentions from them, in so far this love is purified in them, and gradually becomes spiritual,—first while they live on earth, and afterwards in heaven. No love can ever become pure with man; nor with the angels. Nor therefore can this love. But as the Lord primarily regards the intention, which is of the will, in the degree that a man is in this intention, and perseveres in it, he is introduced into and gradually progresses in its purity and holiness. (C. L. n. 71.)

They that love the truths of the church and do its goods come into this love, and can abide in it, because [they and] no others are received by the Lord; for they are in conjunction with Him, and on this account can be kept by Him in this love. There are two things which constitute the church and therefore heaven in man; namely, truth of faith, and good of life. Truth of faith constitutes the presence of the Lord, and good of life according to truths of faith effects conjunction with Him; and thus these produce heaven and the church. Truth of faith constitutes the presence of the Lord because it is [of the nature] of light. Spiritual light is nothing else. Good of life effects conjunction because it is [of the nature] of heat. Spiritual heat is nothing else; for it is love, and good of life is of love. And it is known that all light, even of winter, produces presence, and that heat united with light effects conjunction; for fruit and flower gardens appear in all light, but do not blossom and bear fruit except when heat conjoins itself with the light. From these considerations the conclusion is obvious, that they who only know the truths of the church cannot be gifted with love that is truly conjugial, but they that know them and do its goods. (*ib.* n. 72.)

Love that is truly conjugial in its first essence is love to the Lord. Hence it is that no one can be in truly conjugial love, and in its states of pleasantness, delight, blessedness, and joy, but who acknowledges the Lord alone, that is the Three in Him. They who go to the Father as a person by Himself, or to the Holy Spirit as a person by Itself, and not to them in the Lord, have not conjugial love. The genuine conjugial principle is given especially in the third heaven; because the angels there are in love to the Lord, acknowledge Him to be the only God, and do His commandments. To do His commandments, with them, is to love Him. The commandments of the Lord, to them, are the truths in which they receive Him. There is a conjunction of the Lord with them, and of them with the Lord; for they are in the Lord because in good, and the Lord is in them because in truths. This is the heavenly marriage from which love that is truly conjugial descends. (A. E. n. 995.)

OBSTACLES TO CONJUGIAL LOVE.

From what has been said respecting the origin of conjugial love it may be concluded who are in that love, and who are not: That they are in conjugial love who from Divine truths are in Divine good; and that conjugial love is the more genuine in proportion as the truths which are conjoined to good are more genuine. And as all the good which is conjoined to truths is from the Lord, it follows that no one can be in love that is truly conjugial unless he acknowledge the Lord, and His Divinity; for without that acknowledgment the Lord cannot flow in, and be conjoined to the truths that are with man.

It is evident from these considerations that they who are in falsities are not in conjugial love, and not at all they that are in falsities from evil. Besides, with those that are in evil and thence in falsities, the interiors, which are of the mind, are closed; there cannot therefore be any origin of conjugial love therein. (H. H. n. 376, 377.)

Nor can there be love that is truly conjugial between one husband and several wives; for this destroys its spiritual origin, which is, that of two there is formed one mind. It therefore destroys the interior conjunction, which is of good and truth; which is that from which comes the very essence of that love. Marriage with more than one wife is as an understanding divided between several wills; and as a man attached not to one but to several churches, for thus his faith is distracted so that it becomes no faith. The angels declare that to marry more wives than one is entirely contrary to Divine order. And that they know this from several causes; and in addition to others, from the fact that as soon as they have a thought of marriage with more than one they are alienated from internal blessedness and heavenly happiness, and that then they become as if intoxicated, because good in them is disjoined from its truth. And as the interiors, which are of their mind, come into such a state from the mere thought with any intention, they perceive clearly that marriage with more than one wife closes the internal, and causes the love of lasciviousness to enter,—a love which leads away from heaven,—in place of conjugial love. They say further that man scarcely comprehends this, because there are few who are in genuine conjugial love, and they that are not in it know nothing at all of the interior delight that is in that love, but only know of the delight of lasciviousness; a delight which after a brief cohabitation is turned into what is undelightful. But the delight of love that is truly conjugial not only endures to old age in the world, but also becomes the delight of heaven after death; and is then filled with interior delight, which is perfected to eternity.

The love of domination of one over the other entirely banishes conjugial love and its heavenly delight; for, as was said above, conjugial love and its delight consists in the fact that the will of the one is that of the other, and this mutually and reciprocally. This the love of dominion destroys in marriage; for he who domineers wishes that his will alone should be in the other, and none of the other's reciprocally in himself There is therefore nothing mutual, and accordingly no communication of any love and its delight with the other, and no reciprocal return; yet this communication, and the consequent conjunction, is the very interior delight that is called blessedness in marriage. This blessedness the love of domination utterly extinguishes, and with it all that is heavenly and spiritual in that love, even to such a degree that it is unknown that there is [anything heavenly and spiritual in it]. (*ib.* n. **379, 380.**)

Difference of Religion incompatible with Conjugial Love.

Neither is there love that is truly conjugial between two who are of different religion; since the truth of the one does not accord with the good of the other, and two dissimilar and discordant principles cannot make of two one mind. The origin of their love takes nothing therefore from the spiritual. If they cohabit and agree, it is only from natural causes. For this reason marriages in the heavens are formed with those that are within the same society, because they are in similar good and truth; and not with those that are out of the society. (C. L. n. 378.)

They that are born within the church, and from infancy have imbibed the principles of truth of the church, ought not to unite in marriage with those who are out of the church and so have imbibed such principles as are not of the church. The reason is that there is no conjunction between them in the spiritual world; for in that world every one is consociated according to good and the truth therefrom. And as there is no conjunction between such in the spiritual world, there ought to be no conjunction on earth; for in themselves regarded marriages are conjunctions of the inner and outer minds (*animorum et mentium*), the spiritual life of which is from goods and truths of faith and charity. For this reason marriages on earth between those who are of different religion are ever regarded in heaven as heinous; and more so between those who are of the church and those that are out of the church. This too was a reason why the Jewish and Israelitish nation was prohibited from contracting marriages with the Gentiles (Deut. vii 3, 4); and that it was utterly heinous to commit fornication with them (Numb. xxv. 1-9). This is the more evident from the origin of conjugial love, which is from the marriage of good and truth. When conjugial love descends from this it is heaven itself with man. This [heaven] is destroyed when a married pair are dissimilar in heart from a dissimilar faith. Now it is on this account that a maid-servant of the daughters of Israel, that is of those who are of the church, might not be sold to a strange people, that is to those who are out of the church; for they would afterwards betroth her, that is be conjoined to her, and so profane those things which pertain to the church. It is therefore said (Ex. xxi. 8) that this is to act perfidiously. (A. C. n. 8998.)

Conjugial Pairs are born for each other.

For those who desire love that is truly conjugial the Lord provides similitudes; and if they are not granted on earth He provides them in the heavens. And how they are provided in the heavens I have heard thus described by the angels:— That the Divine Providence of the Lord respecting marriages, and in marriages, is most particular and most universal; for the reason that all the enjoyments of heaven stream forth from the enjoyments of conjugial love, as sweet waters by the streamlet of a fountain. And it is therefore provided that conjugial pairs be born, and that they be educated for their marriage, both the boy and the girl being unconscious of it, continually under the auspices of the Lord. And after the required time they some-where meet, as if by chance, and see each other,—she then a maiden and he a youth, fit for marriage; and then at once, as by a certain instinct, they recognise that they are mates, and from a kind of inward dictate, as it were, think within themselves, the young man "She is mine," and the maiden, "He is mine." And when for some time this has been settled in the minds of both, they deliberately speak to each other, and betroth themselves. It is said, as if by chance, instinct, and dictate; but the meaning is, by the Divine Providence, because when it is unknown this so appears. In reality the Lord opens the internal similitudes, that they may see themselves. (C. L. n. 229.)

That conjugial pairs are born, and, both being unconscious of it, are educated for marriage, the angels confirmed by the conjugial similitude visible in both their faces; as well as by the eternal union of their inner and outer minds (*animorum et mentium*), which could not be, as it is in heaven, unless forseen and provided by the Lord. (*ib.* n. 316.)

Marriages that are interiorly conjunctive can with difficulty be entered into on earth, because there the choice of internal similitudes cannot be provided of the Lord just as in the heavens. For it is restricted in many ways; as, to equals in rank and station, within the country, city, and village of their abode. And accordingly for the most part external [attractions], and so not internal [qualities] there bind them together. These do not come forth until after an interval of marriage, and are only known when they force themselves into the externals. (*ib.* n. 320.)

True Conjugial Love is scarcely known at this Day.

Love which is truly conjugial is at this day so rare that it is unknown what the nature of it is, and almost that it exists; because the state of pleasurable gratifications before marriage is changed after it into a state of indifference, from insensibility to them. The reasons of this change of state are more than can here be adduced, but will be referred to hereafter, when the causes of coldness, separation, and divorce are to be laid open in their order; from which it will be seen, that with most persons at this day that image of conjugial love which exists in the first state after marriage is so completely destroyed, and with it the cognition of it, that it is not known what conjugial love is, and scarcely that there is such a love. It is known that every man when he is born is merely corporeal; and that from corporeal he becomes more and more interiorly natural, and thus rational, and finally spiritual. That he is thus progressive is because the corporeal is as the ground in which the natural, rational, and spiritual in their order are implanted. Thus man becomes more and more a man. Almost the same takes place when he enters into marriage. Man then becomes a completer man, because he is conjoined with a consort with whom he acts as one man. But this takes place in the first state in a certain image, referred to above. Then likewise he begins from the corporeal, and advances into the natural,—but in respect to conjugial life and thence conjunction into one. They who then love corporeal-natural things, and only love rational things from them, cannot be conjoined with a consort as into one, except as to these externals; and when the externals fail coldness enters into the internals, which dissipates the delights of that love, as from the mind so from the body, and afterwards as from the body so from the mind; and this until no reminiscence is left of the first state of their marriage, and consequently no cognition of it. Now, as this takes place with the most at this day, it is plain that it is not known what truly conjugial love is, and scarcely that there is such love. It is otherwise with those who are spiritual. With them the first state is the initiation to perpetual happinesses; which are progressive in proportion as the spiritual-rational of the mind, and from this the natural-sensual of the body, of the one and the other conjoin and unite themselves. But these instances are rare. (C. L. n. 59.)

Semblances of Conjugial Love.

There is a certain resemblance of conjugial love with some; but yet there is not conjugial love if they are not in the love of good and of truth. It is a love that appears like conjugial love, but is from causes relating to the love of the world, or of self; such as, that they may be served at home; that they may live in security ; that they may live in ease; that they may be ministered to in sickness and in old age; for the sake of the care of children whom they love. With some it is constrained, by fear, —in respect to the married partner, to reputation, to adversities. With some it is the love of lasciviousness that induces it. This in the first period appears like conjugial love; for then they emulate something of innocence, sport like little children, and perceive a joy as a something of heavenly origin. But in process of time they are not united more and closer like those who are in conjugial love, but separated. Conjugial love also differs in married partners; with one there may be more or less, with the other little or none. And since it differs, to one it may be heaven, to the other hell. Affection and reception determine this. (A. C. n. 2742.)

There are marriages in which conjugial love does not appear, and yet exists; and there are marriages in which conjugial love appears, and yet does not exist. The reasons are many on either hand,—knowable in part, from what has been said above concerning love that is truly conjugial, and the causes of coldnesses and separations; and concerning the causes of apparent love and friendship in marriages. But appearances in the externals determine nothing as respects the ascription. The one only thing that determines is the conjugial [principle], which has its seat in one's will, and is protected in whatsoever state of marriage a man may be. This conjugial principle is as the balance in which that love is weighed; for the conjugial [union] of one man with one wife is the jewel of human life, and the repository of the Christian religion. And because it is so, that love can exist in one consort, and at the same time not in the other. And that love may lie more deeply hidden than that the man (*homo*) himself shall observe any thing of it; and may also be manifested in the course of life. The reason is that that love accompanies religion in its steps; and religion, because it is the marriage of the Lord and the church, is the rudiment (*initiamentum*) and inoculation of that love. Conjugial love is therefore ascribed to every one after death according to his spiritual rational life; and for him to whom that love is ascribed marriage is provided after death in heaven, of whatsoever quality his marriage may have been in the world. From these considerations, now, there results this conclusion:—That it is not to be concluded respecting anyone from the appearances of marriage, nor even from the appearances of fornication, that he has or has not conjugial love. Wherefore *Judge not, that ye be not condemned* (Matt. vii. 1). .C. L. n. 531.)

SECOND MARRIAGES.

[Whether] to marry again after the death of a consort depends on the preceding conjugial love. Love that is truly conjugial is as a scale of the balance in which the inclinations to repeated marriages are weighed. In so far as the preceding conjugial love approaches that love, inclination to another marriage recedes; and in so far as the preceding love recedes from conjugial love the inclination to another marriage is wont to approach. The reason is obvious:—Because conjugial love is in a like degree a conjunction of minds, which remains in the bodily life of the one after the death of the other; and this holds the inclination as a balance, with two scales, and causes a preponderance according to the appropriation of true love. But as at this day no approach is made to this love, except for a few paces, the scale of preponderance of inclination at the utmost raises itself to an equipoise; and from this wavers,—and inclines to the other side, that is to marriage. The contrary is the case with those whose preceding love, in the former marriage, receded from love that is truly conjugial. The reason is, that recession from this is in like degree a disjunction of minds; which also remains in the bodily life of the one after the death of the other; and this enters into the will disjoined from the other, and causes an inclination to a new conjunction,—in favour of which the thought excited by the inclination of the will induces the hope of a more united, and so more delightful cohabitation. (C. L. n. 318.)

With those who had not a truly conjugial love there is no obstacle or hindrance to their marrying again. There is no spiritual or internal bond, but only a natural or external bond, between those who have not had a truly conjugial love; and if an internal bond does not hold the external together in its order and tenor this does not endure,—save as a bundle with the fastening removed, which, according as it is tossed, or driven by the wind, flows apart. The reason is that the natural derives its origin from the spiritual, and in its existence is nothing else than an assemblage from things spiritual, combined. If then the natural be separated from its spiritual, which produced and as it were begat it, it is no longer inwardly held together, but only outwardly, by the spiritual that encompasses and binds it in common, and does not bring it together and keep it together in particular. Hence it is that the natural separated from the spiritual in two consorts produces no conjunction of minds, and so none of wills, but only a conjunction of some external affections which are connected with the senses of the body. The reason why with such there is no obstacle or hindrance to their marrying again is, that they have not had the essentials of marriage, nor therefore are there any such essentials in them after separation by death. They are for this reason then in full liberty to bind their sensual affections, if a widower with any woman, and if a widow with any man they please, in case there is no legal impediment. Nor do they themselves think of marriages otherwise than naturally, and as of advantage on account of various outward needs and benefits, —which at death can be restored again by another person in place of the former . . . It is allowable for these to marry again and again, for the reason above mentioned; because conjunctions that are only natural are dissolved and flow asunder of themselves after death. For external affections at death follow the body, and are entombed with it,—those remaining which are connected with the internals. (*ib.* n. 320.)

Those who have lived together in love which is truly conjugial do not desire another marriage, unless for reasons apart from conjugial love . . . Two such are not separated by the death of one, since the spirit of the departed continually dwells with the spirit of the one not yet deceased; and this even until the death of the other, when they meet again and are re-united, and love each other more tenderly than before, because in the spiritual world. From these facts there follows this undeniable consequence; that those who have lived in love that is truly conjugial do not desire another marriage, and if afterwards they contract something like marriage it is for reasons apart from conjugial love. And these reasons are all external; as, if there are little children in the household, and there must be provision for the care of them; if the house is large and provided with servants of both sexes; if the management of affairs out of doors withdraws the mind from the concerns of the household; if mutual aids and offices are necessities ; and other such reasons. (*ib.* n. 321.)

THE NATURE OF THE INTELLIGENCE OF WOMEN AND OF MEN.

The intelligence of women, in itself, is modest, refined, pacific, yielding, gentle, tender ; and the intelligence of men, in itself, is grave, harsh, unyielding, bold, and fond of license. That such is the nature of women and of men is very plain from the body, the countenance, the tone of voice, the speech, the bearing, and manners of each :—From the body, in that men are hard and women soft in skin and flesh. From the countenance, in that the faces of men are harder, more resolute, rougher, tawnier, and also bearded, and therefore less beautiful ; and the features of women are softer, more flexible, more delicate, whiter, and therefore more beautiful. From the tone of voice, in that the tone of men is deep, and of women soft. From the speech, in that with men it is fond of licence, and bold ; and with women modest, and pacific. From the bearing, in that with men it is stronger, and firmer ; and with women weaker, and feebler. From the manners, in that with men they are more unrestrained, and with women more elegant. How much from very birth the genius of men differs from the genius of women, has been made very clear to me from boys and girls seen in their assemblages. I have at different times, through a window, observed them on the street in a great city, where more than twenty gathered in a day. The boys, according to their innate disposition, played by making an uproar, shouting, fighting, beating, and throwing stones at each other ; but the girls sat peacefully at the doors of their houses, some playing with little children, some dressing their dolls, some sewing, on bits of linen, some kissing each other. And what I wondered at, they yet looked with delighted eyes at the boys, who were so different. I could plainly see from these manifestations that man is born an understanding, and woman a love ; and also what the nature of the understanding, and what the nature of love is, in their beginnings ; and so what the understanding of the man in its progress would be, without conjunction with feminine and after that with conjugial love. (C. L. n. 218.)

The wife cannot enter into the proper duties of the man ; nor the man, on the other hand, into the proper duties of the wife ; because they differ, as wisdom and its love, or thought and its affection, or understanding and its will. In the proper duties of men the understanding, thought, and wisdom act the chief part ; but in the proper duties of wives the will, affection, and

love act the chief part. And from these the wife performs her
duties, and from those the man performs his. Their duties are
therefore in their nature different,—but yet conjunctive, in a
successive series. It is believed by many that women can perform the duties of men, if only they are initiated into them, in
the same manner as boys, from their earliest age; and they can
come into the exercise, but not into the judgment of them, on
which the right performance of duties inwardly depends. For
this reason those women who are initiated into the duties of
men are bound in matters of judgment to consult with men;
and then, if they are free to choose, they elect that which is
favourable to their love. By some it is also imagined that
women are equally capable of elevating the sight of their understanding, into the sphere of light in which men may be, and
of viewing things in the same [intellectual] altitude; an
opinion to which they have been led by the writings of certain
learned authoresses. But these being examined in their presence
in the spiritual world were found to be products not of judgment and wisdom, but of genius and eloquence; and what comes
of these two, from elegance and beauty in the style of composition, appears as if it were sublime and erudite,—but only to
those who call cleverness wisdom. The reason why men, on
the other hand, cannot enter into the proper duties of women,
and rightly perform them, is that they are not in their affections,
which are entirely distinct from the affections of men. As the
affections and perceptions of the male sex are by creation and
hence by nature thus distinguished, therefore among the statutes
given to the children of Israel there was also this:—"*A woman
shall not put on the garment of a man, neither shall a man put on
a woman's garment; for this is an abomination.*" (Deut. xxii. 5).
The reason of this was, that in the spiritual world all are
clothed according to their affections, and the two affections, of
woman and of man, cannot be united except [reciprocally]
between two, and never in one person. (*ib.* n. 175.)

The Wife should be under the Guidance of the Husband.

Since every law and every precept springs from what is
celestial and spiritual, as from its beginning, it follows that
this law also, which is a law of marriage, does:—That the wife,
because she acts from desire, which is of the *proprium*, and
not so much from reason as the man, is subject to the prudence of the man. (A. C. n. 266.)

The Beauty of the Angels originates from Conjugial Love.

That is beautiful which in the sight of the eye is true and good. (D. P. n. 312.)

All beauty is from good in which there is innocence. Good itself produces beauty when it flows from the internal man into the external. All human beauty is from this origin. This may be seen too, from the fact that no one is affected merely by the face of another, but by the affection which beams from the face; and that those who are in good are affected by the affection of good that is in them; and in the degree that there is innocence in the good. Thus it is the spiritual in the natural that affects [as beauty], and not the natural without the spiritual. They that are in good are affected in a similar manner by little children, who appear beautiful to them in proportion as the innocence of charity is in their face, action, and speech. (A. C. n. 3880.)

Spiritual beauty is an affection of interior truth, because truth is the form of good. It is good itself, which is from the Divine in heaven, from which the angels have life; but the form of their life is by the truths which are from that good. Yet the truth of faith does not produce beauty, but the affection itself that is in the truths of faith, which affection is from good. Beauty from the truth of faith only is like the beauty of a painted or sculptured face; but beauty from an affection of truth which is from good, is like the beauty of a living face animated with heavenly love. For such as is the quality of the love, or such as is the quality of the affection beaming from the face, such is the beauty. Hence it is that the angels appear of ineffable beauty. The good of love beams from their faces by the truth of faith; which not only appear to the sight, but are perceived also by the spheres that proceed from them. (*ib.* n. 5199.)

The marriage union of good and truth is the origin of conjugial love. (C. L. n. 60.)

The angels derive all their beauty from conjugial love; so that each angel is beautiful according to that love in him. For all the angels are forms of their affections; for the reason, that in heaven no one is permitted to feign with the countenance things which are not of his affection. Their face is therefore the type of their mind. And consequently when they are possessed of conjugial love, of love to the Lord, of mutual love, of the love of good and the love of truth, of the love of wisdom, these loves in them give form to their faces, and present themselves as the fires of life in their eyes; to which moreover innocence adds itself, and peace, which complete their beauty. Such forms are forms of the inmost angelic heaven, and are truly human forms. (A. E. n. 1001).

Genuine conjugial love is an image of heaven; and when it is represented in the other life, this is done by the most beautiful things that eyes can ever see or mind conceive. It is represented by a maiden of inexpressible beauty, encompassed with a white cloud; so beautiful that it may be said she is beauty itself in essence and in form. It is declared that in the other life all beauty is from conjugial love. The affections and thoughts of it are represented by brilliant auras, sparkling as if with particles of ruby and carbuncle;[1] and this with delights that affect the inmosts of the mind. But as soon as anything unchaste intervenes they are dissipated. (A. C. n. 2735.)

A form of beauty appeared to me, very slightly presented [to view], veiled as it were with a kind of cloud lest I should look upon it; and at the same time a perception was given me that it was the beauty of conjugial love. It was such,—it was given me, from an affection, to perceive,—that scarcely anything can be said of it but that it was beauty itself. For it is conjugial love thus *formed*, so that it is conjugial love itself, which constitutes beauty, affecting to the inmosts. All beauty is from this source. (S. D. n. 4175.)

A Likeness of Marriage in all Created Things.

This conjugial sphere fills the universe, pervading it from first to last; which is evident from the consideration that there

---

[1] The original of this descriptive clause is,—"*per auras adamantinas ex quasi rubinis et pyropis scintillantes.*" The adjective *adamantinus*, here and elsewhere in the author's writings, has commonly been rendered by "adamantine," a word which has an established meaning in our language,—referring merely to the *hardness* of the diamond,—quite different from that intended by the author, as explained by him, with an excuse for its inadequacy, in A. C. n. 1526. He there speaks of the "living sparkle of diamond light" ("*rutilatio viva lucis adamantinæ*"), and adds, "I cannot otherwise describe the light, for it was as a diamond sparkling in its minutest particles." But in the extract above he evidently uses the word *adamantinas* with reference exclusively to the sparkling brilliancy of the diamond, apart from its colour. To translate it with "diamond," or "diamond like," would therefore be at the least incongruous. The reading of the sentence above given is believed to express the author's meaning, as interpreted by the light of the explanation just referred to, more exactly than a strictly literal or verbal rendering. But the reader will bear in mind that the author is endeavouring to convey some faint suggestion of what is in its nature indescribable,—being spiritual,—by a comparison confessedly inadequate. If the reader would carry this obviously just consideration continually in mind, as applicable generally to the author's descriptions of scenes and occurrences in the heavenly world, it would undoubtedly help to prevent a certain materiality of conception with regard to them, and possibly some substantial misapprehension.

are marriages in the heavens, the most perfect in the third or highest heaven; and that on earth, besides the marriages among men, it is in all the subjects of the animal kingdom, even down to the worms; and, also, in all the subjects of the vegetable kingdom, from the olives and palms down to the smallest grasses. This sphere is more universal than the sphere of heat and light that proceeds from the sun of our world; of which reason may be convinced, from the fact that it is even operative in the absence of the sun's heat, as in the winter, and in the absence of its light, as in the night, especially among men. The reason why it is thus operative is that it is from the sun of the angelic heaven, and there is a constant equilization of the heat and light therefrom, that is, a conjunction of good and truth; for heaven is in perpetual spring. The changes of good and truth, or of the heat and light of that sun, are not such variations of it as those that take place on earth by the changes of the heat and light from the sun there, but arise from the subjects that receive them. (C. L. n. 222.)

ORIGIN OF THE LOVE OF INFANTS.

The love of infants is originally from conjugial love. It is known that mothers have a more and fathers a less tender love of infants. It is evident from the lovely and winning affection of little girls for infants, and for the images of them which they carry, dress, kiss, and press to their very heart, that the love of infants is inscribed upon the conjugial love into which women are born. With boys there is no such affection. It appears as if mothers had the love of infants from the nourishment of them in the womb from their own blood, and hence from the appropriation of their own life to them, and so from a sympathetic union But yet this is not the origin of that love; for if without the mother's knowledge, after birth, another infant be substituted for the genuine one, she will love this with just as much tenderness as if it were her own. Besides, infants are sometimes loved by their nurses more than by their mothers. It follows from all this, that that love is from no other source than the conjugial love implanted in every woman; to which is adjoined the love of conceiving, from the delight of which the wife is prepared for reception. This is the beginning of that love, which after the birth passes fully over, with its delight, to the offspring. (C. L. n. 393.)

A sphere of innocence flows into infants, and through them into parents and affects them. That infants are innocent is known, but it has not been known that their innocence flows into them from the Lord. It flows in from the Lord because He is innocence itself; and nothing can flow in, for nothing exists, except from its beginning, which is its very self. . . The innocence of the Lord flows into the angels of the third heaven, where all are in the innocence of wisdom, and passes through the lower heavens,—but only through the innocences of the angels there,—and so immediately and mediately into infants. They are scarcely otherwise than as if sculptured forms, but yet capable of receiving life from the Lord through the heavens. But if parents did not also receive that influx into their own souls and the inmosts of their minds, they would be affected to no purpose by the innocence of infants. There must be in another a something adequate and homogeneous, through which communication may be effected, and which will produce reception, affection, and hence conjunction. Otherwise it would be like soft seed falling upon flint, or as a lamb thrown to a wolf. Hence it is then that innocence flowing into the souls of parents conjoins itself with the innocence of infants. Experience teaches that this conjunction is effected through the medium of the bodily senses,—but especially, with parents, through the sense of touch; as, for instance, that the sight is inmostly delighted by looking at them, the ear by their speech, the smell by the odour of them. That the communication and therefore the conjunction of innocences is effected especially through the medium of the touch, is clearly perceived from the pleasure of carrying them in the arms; from embracing and kissing them,—particularly with mothers, who are delighted with laying the mouth and face of infants upon their breasts, and at the same time with the touch there of the palms of their hands; in general it is perceived from their sucking of the breasts, and in yielding them milk; and also from stroking their naked body, and from the unwearied labour of washing and swathing them upon their knees. It has several times been pointed out above that the communications of love and its delights between married partners are effected by the sense of touch. The reason why even communications of the mind are effected by this sense is, that the hands are the ultimates of a man, and his first [principles] are at the same time in the ultimates; by this means all things of the body and all things of the mind that are intermediate are also held in unbroken connection. Hence it is that Jesus touched infants (Matt. xix. 13-15; Mark x. 13-16); and that by the touch he healed the sick; and that they who touched him were healed. Hence also it is that at this day inaugurations into the priesthood are effected by the laying on of hands. From all this it is plain that the innocence of parents and the innocence of infants meet each other through the touch, especially of the hands, and so conjoin themselves, as it were by kisses. (*ib.* n. 395, 396.)

It is the inmost heaven through which the Lord insinuates true conjugial love. Its beginning or origin is from the inmost heaven ; and then [it passes] through the medium of the lower heavens. From thence also is parental love. For the celestials of the inmost heaven love infants much more than parents,—even than mothers ; yea they are present with infants, and have care of them.[1] It was told me, indeed, that they are present and are watchful over them, that they may be nourished, in the maternal womb. They therefore preside over the womb during gestation. (S. D. n. 1201.)

DIFFERENT QUALITY OF THE LOVE OF INFANTS AND CHILDREN WITH THE SPIRITUAL AND THE NATURAL.

To appearance the love of infants with married partners who are spiritual is the same as with those that are natural ; but in fact it is more interior and hence more tender, because that love springs from innocence, and from the nearer and so more present perception of it in them. For the spiritual are spiritual in so far as they partake of innocence. And in truth spiritual fathers and mothers, after that they have tasted the sweetness of innocence in their infants, love their children altogether differently from fathers and mothers who are natural. The spiritual love their children from their spiritual intelligence and moral life. They therefore love them from the fear of God and from actual piety, or piety of life ; and at the same time from an affection for and devotion to uses beneficial to society, thus from the virtues and good morals in them. From the love of these, principally, they provide for and supply their wants. If therefore they do not see such virtues in them they withdraw their favour from them, and do nothing for them except from duty. The love of infants is indeed from innocence with fathers and mothers also, who are natural ; but this received by them is wrapped about their own love, and they therefore love infants from the one and at the same time from the other,—kissing, embracing, carrying them, pressing them to their bosoms, and caressing them beyond all measure,— and regard them as one heart and one mind with themselves. And then after their state of infancy, up to and beyond early manhood, when innocence is no longer operative, they do not love them from any fear of God and actual piety, or piety of life ; nor from any rational and moral intelligence in them ; and they pay little regard,—scarcely any at all indeed,—to their internal affections, and hence to their virtues and good morals, but only to the outward things towards which they are inclined. To these they attach, affix, and fasten their love. Hence they also shut

[1] Matt. xviii. 10.

their eyes to their faults, excusing and favouring them. The reason is that with them the love of their offspring is also the love of themselves, and this cleaves to the subject outwardly, and does not enter into it, as neither does it into themselves.

The quality of the love of infants, and of the love of children, with the spiritual and the natural is manifestly perceived from them after death. For most fathers when they come into the other life remember their children who have gone before them ; and they become present to and mutually acknowledge each other. Spiritual fathers only see them, ask after their condition, and rejoice if it is well, and grieve if it is ill with them. And after some converse, instruction, and admonition respecting the heavenly moral life they separate from them ; but before separating they teach them that they ought no longer to be remembered as fathers, because the Lord is the only Father to all in heaven,— according to His words in Matt. xxiii. 9,—and that they never think of them as their children. But natural fathers, as soon as they observe that they are living, after death, and recall to mind their children who have gone before them, and in accordance with their longing desire become present also to them, are instantly conjoined, and cleave to them as a bundle of rods bound together ; and the father is then delighted continually by the sight of them, and by converse with them. If the father is told that some of these his sons are satans, and that they have inflicted injuries upon the good, he none the less keeps them in a group around him, or in a company before him. If he himself sees that they do harm and commit evils, yet he pays no regard at all to these things, nor does he dissociate any from himself. Therefore in order that such a mischievous company may not continue, they are of necessity sent away together into hell; and there before his children the father is placed under guard, and the children are separated and each is removed to the place of his life. (C. L. n. 405, 406.)

The Recession of Infantile Innocence, and hence of Parental Love.

In the degree that innocence recedes in infants, affection and conjunction are also loosened, and this successively, even to separation. It is known that the love of infants, or parental love, recedes from parents according to the recession of innocence from them ; and that with man it recedes to the point of separation of children from home, and with beasts and birds even to the rejection of them from their presence and forgetfulness that they are of their stock. From this also, as from an established fact, it may be seen that innocence flowing in on both sides produces the love called parental love. (C. L. n. 398.)

DIVINE PROVIDENCE.

DIVINE Providence is the government of the Lord's Divine Love and Divine Wisdom. (D. P. n. 1.)

All that the Lord does is Providence; which, because as it is from the Divine, has within it what is eternal and infinite,—eternal because it looks to no limit from which, nor any limit to which it extends; infinite because it looks at once in every least particular to the universal, and in the universal to every least particular. This is called Providence. And there is such in each and all that the Lord does. His doing cannot be expressed by any other word than Providence. (A. C. n. 5264.)

THE LORD'S DIVINE PROVIDENCE HAS FOR ITS END A HEAVEN FROM THE HUMAN RACE.

Since heaven is from the human race, and is an abiding with the Lord to eternity, it follows that this was the Lord's end in the creation; and, as it was the end of creation it is the end of His Divine Providence. The Lord did not create the universe for His own sake, but for the sake of those with whom He will dwell in heaven; for spiritual love is of such a nature that it wills to give its own to another, and in so far as it can do this it is in its being, in its peace, and in its blessedness. This nature spiritual love derives from the Lord's Divine Love, which is such infinitely. Hence it follows that the Divine Love, and therefore the Divine Providence, has for its end a heaven; which shall consist of men become and who are becoming angels, to whom He can impart all the varieties of blessedness and happiness which are of love and wisdom, and impart them from Himself in them. (D. P. n. 27.)

DIVINE FORESIGHT WITH THE DIVINE PROVIDENCE.

As regards Foresight and Providence in general: Relatively to man it is Foresight, relatively to the Lord it is Providence The Lord foresaw from eternity what the human race would be, and what each individual of the human race would be; and that evil would continually increase, until at length man of himself would rush headlong into hell. On this account the Lord not only provided means by which man might be turned from hell and led to heaven, but also by Providence He continually turns and leads him. The Lord foresaw, too, that no good could ever take root in man except in his freedom; for whatever does not take root in freedom, at the first approach of evil and temptation is dissipated. This the Lord foresaw, and also that of himself or of his freedom man would thus incline towards the deepest hell; and therefore the Lord provides, that if a man should not suffer himself to be led in freedom to heaven he might still be turned to a milder hell; and that if on the other hand he should suffer himself to be led in freedom to good he may be led to heaven. From this it is plain what Foresight and what Providence are, and that what is foreseen is thus provided for. It is therefore evident how greatly a man errs who believes that the Lord will not have foreseen, and does not see the least particulars relating to man, and that He does not in the least particulars foresee and lead; when yet the truth is that the Foresight and Providence of the Lord is in the very minutest of all the particulars relating to a man,— even in things so exceedingly minute that it is impossible by any power of thought to comprehend one out of myriads of myriads of them. For every least moment of a man's life has a series of consequences following one after another to eternity. For every moment is as a new beginning of sequences; and so each and all the moments of his life, both as regards his understanding and his will. And as the Lord foresaw from eternity what he would be, even what he would be to eternity, it is evident that Providence is present in the very least particulars, which He governs and bends, as was said, in order that the man may be such,—and this by a continual moderation of his freedom. (A. C. n. 3854.)

DIVINE PROVIDENCE IS UNIVERSAL AND PARTICULAR.

The Divine Providence is universal, but universal from the fact that it is in the very least things, and that not even a hair falls from the head, that is, that there is nothing so minute, but it is foreseen and accordingly provided for. (A. C. n. 2694.)

It is Jehovah from whom order proceeds. It may therefore be said that Jehovah is order itself; for He from Himself governs order, not as is believed in the universal only, but also in the very least particulars. For it is from the least particulars that the universal exists, and to speak of a universal, and separate the particulars from it, would be like talking of a whole in which there are no parts; thus like talking of something in which there is nothing. It is therefore most false, and a mere creature of

the reason, as it is called, to say that the Lord's Providence is
universal and not at the same time over the minutest particulars;
for to provide and govern in the universal, and not at the same
time in the least particulars, is not to provide and rule at all.
This is philosophically true; and yet it is remarkable that philosophers themselves, even the more distinguished, conceive and
think otherwise. (A. C. n. 1919.)

If by Providence in the universal any one understands the
conservation of the whole according to an order of universal
nature enstamped upon it at its first creation, he does not consider that nothing can subsist unless it perpetually springs into
being; for, as is known in the learned world, subsistence is a
perpetual coming into existence, thus conservation is perpetual
creation; consequently Providence is continually in the least
particulars. (*ib.* n. 6482.)

In all that it does the Divine Providence looks to what is Infinite and Eternal from itself, especially in the Salvation of the Human Race.

That the Divine Providence, in all that it does, looks to what
is infinite and eternal from itself, is certain from the fact that
everything created from the First, who is Infinite and Eternal,
proceeds to ultimates, and from ultimates to the First from which
it sprung; as was shown in the treatise on the Divine Love and
Divine Wisdom, in the Part where it treats of the creation of the
universe. And as the First from which it originates is inmostly
in all progression, it follows that the Divine Proceeding or Divine
Providence, in all that it does, has regard to some image of the
infinite and eternal. This it has regard to in all things, but in
some it is evident to the perception and in some not so. It presents
that image to clearness of perception in the variety of all things,
and in the fructification and multiplication of all things. An
image of the infinite and eternal appears in the variety of all
things, in the fact that there is no one thing which is the same as
another, and that there cannot be to eternity. This is manifest to
the eye in the faces of men, from the first creation; likewise from
their outer minds [*animi*], of which their faces are the types;
and also from their affections, perceptions, and thoughts, for of
these their outer minds consist.[1]   Hence it is, that in the universal
heaven there are not two angels or two spirits the same, nay, and
cannot be to eternity. It is the same with every object of sight
in both worlds, the natural as well as the spiritual. From these
examples it is evident that variety is infinite and eternal. The
image of the infinite and eternal in the fructification and multi-

[1] See note, p. 457.

plication of all things, is evident in the power implanted in seeds in the vegetable kingdom; and in prolification in the animal kingdom,—especially in the race of fishes, which if they fructified and multiplied according to their ability within an age would fill the space of the whole world, nay, of the universe. Whence it is plain, that in that power there lies hidden an endeavour to propagate itself to infinity; and as fructifications and multiplications have not failed since the beginning of creation, and will not fail to eternity, it follows that in that ability there is also an endeavour to propagate itself to eternity.

It is the same with men in respect to their affections, which are of love; and their perceptions, which are of wisdom. The variety of both these is infinite and eternal, so also are their fructifications and multiplications, which are spiritual. No man has delight in an affection and perception so like another's that they are the same, nor can this be to eternity; and affections can also be fructified and perceptions multiplied without end. That knowledges can never be exhausted is known. This capability of fructification and multiplication without end, or to infinity and eternity, with men is in natural things, with spiritual angels in spiritual things, and with celestial angels in celestial things. Such are not only affections, perceptions, and knowledges in general, but also every even the least thing of them in particular. They are such because they spring from the Infinite and Eternal in itself, by the infinite and eternal from itself. But as the finite possesses nothing of that which is Divine in itself, therefore there is no such thing, not even the least, in man or angel as his own; for man and angel are finite, and only receptacles, in themselves dead. Their living principle is from the proceeding Divine conjoined to them by contiguity, which appears to them as their own. That this is so will be seen in what follows.

The Divine Providence looks to what is infinite and eternal from itself in the salvation of the human race, especially because the end of the Divine Providence is a heaven from the human race; and this being the end, it follows that what the Divine Providence especially regards is the reformation and regeneration of man, and thus his salvation, for heaven consists of the saved or regenerated. Since to regenerate man is to unite good and truth or love and wisdom in him, as they are united in the Divine which proceeds from the Lord, therefore the Divine Providence regards this especially in the salvation of the human race. The image of the infinite and eternal in man no otherwise exists than in the marriage of good and truth.

It has not as yet been known that in all its progress with man the Divine Providence looks to his eternal state. It can indeed look to nothing else; for the Divine is Infinite and Eternal, and the Infinite and Eternal or Divine is not in time, and therefore to Him all things future are present. And as such is the nature of the Divine it follows that the eternal is in each and every thing that it does. (D. P. n. 56-59.)

Since the universal heaven in the Lord's sight is as one man, therefore heaven is distinguished into as many general societies as there are organs, viscera· and members in man ; and every general society into as many less general or particular societies as there are larger parts of each viscus and organ. (*ib.* n. 65.)

Now since by creation man is a heaven in the least form, and therefore an image of the Lord, and since heaven consists of as many affections as there are angels, and each affection in its form is a man, it follows that the continual [purpose] of the Divine Providence is, that man may become a heaven in form, and thereby an image of the Lord ; and as this is effected through an affection for good and truth, that he may become that affection. This therefore is the continual [purpose] of the Divine Providence. But its inmost [purpose] is, that he may be here or there in heaven, or here or there in the Divine heavenly Man, for thus he is in the Lord.   And this comes to pass with those whom the Lord can lead to heaven ; and as the Lord foresees this, he also provides continually that man may become such ; for thus every one who suffers himself to be led to heaven is prepared for his place in heaven.

It was said above that heaven is distinguished into as many societies as there are organs, viscera and members in man. Among these no one part can be in any other place than its own. Since therefore angels are such parts in the Divine heavenly Man, and no angels are created but who have been men in the world, it follows that a man who suffers himself to be led to heaven is continually prepared by the Lord for his place ; which is done by such an affection for good and truth as corresponds.   To this place also every angelic man after his departure from the world is assigned.   This is the inmost of the Divine Providence respecting heaven.

But the man who does not suffer himself to be led and assigned to heaven, is prepared for his place in hell.   For of himself man continually tends to the lowest depth of hell, but is continually withdrawn by the Lord.   And he who cannot be withdrawn is prepared for a certain place there, to which also he is assigned immediately after his departure from the world ; and this place there is opposite to a certain place in heaven,—for hell is in the opposite over against heaven.   Wherefore as a man angel is allotted his place in heaven according to his affection for good and truth, so a man devil is allotted his place in hell according to his affection for evil and falsity ; for two opposites set in like position over against each other are held in connection. This is the inmost of the Divine Providence concerning hell. (*ib.* n. 67-69.)

What other end can the Divine Providence have than the reformation of the human race and its salvation ? And no one can be reformed of himself by his own prudence, but of the Lord by His Divine Providence. It follows from this that unless the Lord leads man every minute, nay, every least moment, man would depart from the way of reformation and perish. Every change and variation of state of the human mind changes and varies something in the series of things present, and hence of the things consequent. Why not progressively to eternity ? It is as an arrow shot from a bow; which, if in its aim it swerve in a very slight degree from the mark, at the distance of a thousand paces and more it would deviate immensely. So would it be if every least moment the Lord did not direct the states of human minds. This the Lord does, according to the laws of His Divine Providence; according to which also it is that it appears to man as if he led himself. But the Lord foresees how he leads himself, and continually accommodates [His Providence]. (*ib.* n. 202.)

That the Providence of the Lord is infinite, and looks to what is eternal, is evident from the formation of the embryo in the womb. Lineaments of things to come are there continually projected, so that one thing is always a plane for another, and this without any error, until the embryo is formed. And also afterwards when it is born, one thing is prepared in succession to another and for another, that the perfect man may come forth, and finally such a man as can receive heaven. If the least particulars are thus provided during man's conception, birth, and growth, why not in respect to his spiritual life ? (A. C. n. 6491.)

THE LAW OF DIVINE PROVIDENCE RESPECTING MAN'S FREEDOM AND REASON.

It is a law of the Divine Providence that man should act from freedom according to reason. It is known that man has freedom to think and will as he pleases, but not freedom to say whatever he thinks, nor to do whatever he wills. The freedom therefore that is here meant is spiritual, and not natural freedom, except when they form one; for to think and will is spiritual, and to speak and act is natural. They are in fact clearly distinguished in man; for a man can think what he does not speak, and will what he does not do,—from which it is plain that the spiritual and natural in man are distinct. A man cannot therefore pass from one to the other except by determination. This determination may be compared to a door, which must first be unfastened and opened. But this door stands open, as it were, with those who from reason think and will in accordance with the civil laws of the kingdom and the moral laws of society; for they speak what they think, and do as they will. On the other hand, with those who think and will contrary to those laws the door remains as it were closed. He who attends to his volitions and consequent acts will observe that such a determination intervenes, and sometimes frequently in a single conversation, and in a single action. These things are premised that it may be known that by acting from freedom according to reason is meant thinking and willing freely, and then doing freely what is according to reason.

But as there are few who know that this can be a law of the Divine Providence,—from the fact especially that man thus has freedom to think evil and falsity also, and yet the Divine Providence continually leads man to think and will good and truth,—therefore, that this may be perceived, the development of the subject must advance clearly; which shall be in the following order :[1]—

I. *Man has reason and free-will, or rationality and liberty; and these two faculties are from the Lord in man.* . . . As many doubts may arise respecting both of these faculties when one reflects upon them, I will, at this threshold of the subject, only advance something concerning the freedom in man of acting according to reason. But first it should be known that all freedom is of love, insomuch that love and freedom are one; and as love is the life of man freedom also is of his life. For all the delight that man has is of his love; there is no delight from any other source. And to act from the delight of his love is to act from freedom; for delight leads a man, as a river that which is carried by it along its course. Now, as there are many loves, some concordant and some discordant, it follows that there are likewise many varieties of freedom. But in general there are three kinds, natural, rational, and spiritual freedom. *Natural freedom* every man possesses hereditarily. From this a man loves nothing but himself and the world; his first life is nothing else. And as all evils spring from these two loves, and evils therefore become [a part] of the love, it follows that his natural freedom is [freedom] to think and will evils; and when he has confirmed them in himself he does them from freedom according to his reason. So to act is from his faculty which is called liberty; and

---

[1] The reader will understand that what follow are only extracts from the author's argument, and not the complete argument.

to confirm them is from his faculty which is called rationality.
. . . . *Rational freedom* is from the love of reputation, for the
sake of honour, or for the sake of gain. It is the delight
of this love to appear outwardly as a moral man; and because
he loves this reputation he does not defraud, he does not commit
adultery, he does not revenge, he does not blaspheme; and as
he abstains from these of his own reason, from freedom according to his reason also he acts sincerely, justly, chastely,
amicably. Nay, from reason he can speak well for these virtues.
But if his rationality is only natural and not at the same time
spiritual, this freedom is only external and not internal freedom;
for he nevertheless does not inwardly love these goods, but only
outwardly, for the sake of reputation, as was said. The goods
that he does are therefore not good in themselves. He can even
say that they ought to be done for the public good; but this he
does not say from a love of the public good, but from the love
of his own honour or gain. His freedom therefore derives
nothing from a love of the public good; nor does his reason, for
this assents to his love. This rational freedom therefore is
interior natural freedom. This freedom also, by the Divine
Providence of the Lord, is left remaining to every one.
Spiritual freedom is from the love of eternal life. No one
comes into this love and its delights but who regards evils as
sins, and for that reason, does not purpose them, and who at
the same time looks to the Lord. As soon as a man does that
he is in this freedom; for no one has power not to purpose evils,
because they are sins, and therefore not to do them, but from an
interior or higher freedom, which is from his interior or higher
love. This freedom at first does not appear as freedom; but yet
it is, and afterwards so appears; and then he acts from very
freedom according to very reason in thinking, willing, speaking,
and doing good and truth. As natural freedom decreases
and becomes subject, this freedom increases; and it conjoins itself
with rational freedom and purifies it. Any one can come into
this freedom if only he will reflect that life is eternal; and that
the delight and happiness of life in time and for time is but as
a fleeting shadow, to the delight and happiness of life in eternity
and to eternity. And this a man can think if he will, because
he has rationality and liberty; and because the Lord, from whom
these two faculties are, continually gives him the ability to do
so. (D. P. n. 71-73.)

II. *Whatever a man does from Freedom, whether an act of
reason or not of reason, if only it be according to his reason,
appears to him as his own.* . . . . Every one with rationality
unobscured can see or comprehend that man cannot be in any
affection of knowing, nor in any affection of understanding,

without the appearance that is his; for all delight and pleasure, thus every thing of the will, is from an affection which is of love. Who can desire to know and desire to understand any thing, unless he has some pleasure of affection [in it]? And who can have that pleasure of affection, unless that with which he is affected appears as his own? If nothing were his own, but all were another's, that is, if any one from his affections should pour any thing into the mind of another who had no affection for knowing and understanding it as if of himself, would he receive it? Nay, could he receive it? Would he not be like what is called a brute or stock? It is therefore very evident that although all things that man perceives and hence thinks and knows, and according to perception wills and does, flow in, yet it is of the Lord's Divine Providence that it should appear as man's own; for, as was said, otherwise man would receive nothing, and therefore could not be gifted with any intelligence and wisdom. It is known that good and truth are all, not man's but the Lord's, and yet that it appears to man as if they were his; and because all good and truth so appears, all things of the church and heaven also, and therefore all things of love and wisdom, as well as of charity and faith, so appear; and yet nothing of them is man's own. No one can receive these from the Lord, unless it appears to him that he perceives them as of himself. From these considerations the truth of this matter is evident; that whatever man does from freedom, whether it is of reason or not of reason, if only it is according to his reason, appears to him as his own. (*ib.* n. 74, 76.)

III. *Whatever a man does from freedom according to his thought is appropriated to him and remains.* . . . . It is said that what a man does from freedom according to his thought also remains, because nothing whatever that a man has appropriated to himself can be eradicated; for it has become [a part] of his love and at the same time of his reason, or of his will, and at the same time of his understanding,—and therefore of his life. It can be set aside indeed, but not expelled; and when it is set aside it is transferred as from the centre to the circumference, and there abides. This is meant by saying that it remains. As for example, if in boyhood and youth a man has appropriated to himself a certain evil by doing it from the delight of the love of it,—as, if he has indulged in fraud, in blasphemy, in revenge, in fornication,—then as he had done these things from freedom according to thought, he has even made them his own; but if afterwards he repents, shuns them, and looks upon them as sins which must be held in aversion, and thus from freedom according to reason abstains from them, the goods are then appropriated to him to which those evils are the opposites. These goods then

form the centre, and remove the evils towards the circumferences,—farther and farther according to his aversion and
abhorrence of them. But yet they cannot be so cast out that it
can be said they are extirpated; nevertheless, by that removal
they may appear as if extirpated. This comes to pass through
the fact that he is withheld by the Lord from evils and kept
in goods. This takes place with respect to all hereditary evil,
and likewise with respect to all man's actual evil. This too I
have seen proved by the experience of some in heaven; who
because they were kept by the Lord in good supposed themselves
to be without evils. But that they might not believe the good
in which they were was their own, they were let down from
heaven and let into their evils, until they acknowledged that of
themselves they were in evils, but in goods from the Lord.
After this acknowledgment they were restored to heaven. Let
it therefore be understood, that these goods are no otherwise
appropriated to man than that they are constantly the Lord's in
him; and that in so far as a man acknowledges this, in so far the
Lord grants that the good appears to man as his; that is, that
to the man he appears to love his neighbour or have charity as
of himself, to believe or have faith as of himself, to do good
and understand truth, and so to be wise as of himself. From
which one who is enlightened can see the nature of and how
strong is the appearance in which the Lord wills that man
should be. And this the Lord wills for the sake of his salvation; for no one can be saved without this appearance. (*ib.*
n. 78, 79.)

IV. *By means of these two faculties man is reformed and
regenerated by the Lord, and cannot be reformed and regenerated
without them* . . . The reason why man is regenerated by means
of the two faculties called rationality and liberty, and why he
cannot be reformed and regenerated without them is, that by
rationality he can understand and know what is evil and what
is good, and consequently what is false and what is true; and
by liberty he can will what he understands and knows. (*ib.* n.
82, 85.)

V. *Man can be reformed and regenerated by means of these
two faculties in so far as he can be led by them to acknowledge
that all the truth and good that he thinks and does is from the
Lord, and not from himself* . . . From rationality man has ability
to understand, and from liberty he has ability to will, both as of
himself; but he cannot be able freely to will what is good, and
hence to do it according to reason, unless he is regenerated.
An evil man can only freely will evil, and do it according to his
thought,—which by confirmations he makes to appear as of
reason. For evil equally with good can be confirmed; but evil

is confirmed by fallacies and appearances, which when confirmed became falsities; and when evil is confirmed it appears as if of reason.

Every one who has any thought from interior understanding can see that the power to will and the power to understand is not from man, but from Him who has Power itself, that is, to whom Power in its essence belongs. Only consider from whence power comes. Is it not from Him who has it in its very potency? That is, who has it in Himself, and so from Himself? Power therefore is in itself Divine. To every power there must be an abundant supply which must be imparted, and thus a determination by an interior or higher self. The eye cannot see of itself; nor the ear hear of itself; neither can the mouth speak of itself; or the hand act of itself; there must be a supply [of power], and a consequent determination from the mind. Nor can the mind think and purpose this or that of itself, unless there be something interior or higher which determines the mind to it. It is the same with the power to understand, and the power to will. These powers cannot be conferred by any other than Him who in Himself is able to will and able to understand. From which it is plain that these two faculties which are called rationality and liberty are from the Lord, and not from man. And as they are from the Lord, it follows that man wills nothing whatever from himself, neither understands from himself, but only as if from himself. That it is so any one can confirm within him, who knows and believes that the will of all good and the understanding of all truth is from the Lord and not from man. That *a man can receive nothing of himself, and do nothing of himself,* the Word teaches in John iii. 27, xv. 5. (*ib.* n. 87, 88.)

It is said that a man can be reformed and regenerated in so far as, by means of these two faculties, he can be led to acknowledge that all the good and all the truth that he thinks and does is from the Lord, and not from himself. The reason why a man cannot acknowledge this except through these two faculties is that these are from the Lord, and are the Lord's in man, as is clear from what has been said above. It follows therefore that a man cannot do this from himself, but from the Lord. But yet he can do it as of himself; this [power] the Lord gives to every one. Grant that he believes it to be from himself; yet when he is wise he will acknowledge that it is not from himself. Otherwise, the truth that he thinks and the good that he does are not true and good in themselves, for the man and not the Lord is in them; and good in which man is, if it be done for the sake of salvation, is good done for merit; but good in which the Lord is is not for merit. (*ib.* n. 87, 89, 90.)

VI. *The conjunction of the Lord with man, and the reciprocal conjunction of man with the Lord, is effected through these two faculties.* . . . . Every one can see, from reason alone, that there is no conjunction of minds unless it be reciprocal, and that reciprocation conjoins. If one loves another and is not loved in return, then as the one advances the other recedes; but if he is loved in return, as the one advances the other advances also, and a conjunction takes place. Love desires to be also loved; this is implanted in it; and in so far as it is loved in return it is in itself and in its own delight. From these considerations it is plain that if only the Lord loved man, and were not loved by man in return, the Lord would approach and man would withdraw; thus the Lord would continually will to come to man and enter in to him, and man would turn back and go away. It is so with those who are in hell; but with those who are in heaven there is mutual conjunction. Since the Lord wills conjunction with man for the sake of his salvation, He also provides that with man there shall be reciprocation. Reciprocation with man is, that the good which he purposes and does from freedom, and the truth which from that purpose he thinks and speaks according to reason, appear as from him; and that that good in his will and that truth in his understanding appear as his. They actually do appear to man as if from himself and as his,—entirely as if they were his; there is no difference. Observe whether any one, by any sense, perceives otherwise. The only difference is that man ought to acknowledge that he does not do good and think truth from himself, but from the Lord; and therefore that the good which he does and the truth which he thinks are not his. Thus to think, from some love of the will, because it is the truth, effects conjunction; for so man looks to the Lord, and the Lord looks to man. (*ib.* n. 92.)

VII. *The Lord keeps these two faculties in man inviolate, and as sacred, in every proceeding of His Divine Providence.* The reasons are that without these two faculties man would not have understanding and will, and thus would not be man; and that he could not be conjoined with the Lord without these two faculties, and so could not be reformed and regenerated; and also, that without these two faculties man would not have immortality and eternal life. (*ib.* n. 96.)

VIII. *It is therefore of the Divine Providence that man should act from freedom according to reason.* To act from freedom according to reason, and to act from liberty and rationality, are the same; as also to act from the will and understanding. But it is one thing to act from freedom according to reason or from liberty and rationality, and another to act from true freedom according to true reason, or from true liberty and true rationality.

For the man who does evil from the love of evil, and confirms it in himself, acts indeed from freedom according to reason; but yet his freedom in itself is not freedom, or is not true freedom, but infernal freedom, which in itself is servitude ; and his reason in itself is not reason, but is either spurious or false reason, or merely apparent through confirmations. And yet both are of the Divine Providence. For if the freedom to will evil, and to make it [appear] as of reason by confirmations, were taken away from the natural man, his liberty and rationality would perish, and at the same time his will and understanding, and he could not be led away from evils and be reformed; thus he could not be conjoined to the Lord and live to eternity. Therefore does the Lord so guard freedom in man, as a man guards the apple of his eye. But still by means of his freedom the Lord continually leads man away from evils; and in so far as He can lead him by his freedom, in so far through freedom He implants goods. Thus He successively introduces heavenly freedom in the place of infernal freedom. (*ib.* n. 97.)

The Law of the Divine Providence respecting the Removal of Sins in the internal and external Man.

It is a law of the Divine Providence that man, as of himself, should remove evils, as sins, in the external man ; and that thus and not otherwise the Lord can remove the evils in the internal man, and then at the same time in the external. (D. P. n. 100.)

The internal cannot be purified from the concupiscences of evil so long as the evils in the external man are not removed, because they obstruct. . . . The external of ɾa man's thought, in itself, is of the same character as the internal of his thought ; and they cohere, as things of which one is not only within the other, but one also is from the other. One cannot therefore be separated [from a man] unless at the same time the other. It is so with everything external which is from an internal, and with everything posterior which is from a prior, and with every effect which is from a cause. Now since with the evil concupiscences together with subtleties constitute the internal of thought, and the delights of concupiscences together with their machinations constitute the external of thought with them, and these are conjoined with those in one, it follows that the internal cannot be purified from concupiscences, so long as the evils in the external man are not removed. It should be known that it is a man's internal will which is in concupiscences, and his internal understanding which is in subtleties ; and that it is his external will which is in the delights of concupiscences, and his external understanding which is in machinations from subtleties. Any one can see that concupiscences and their delights form one; and that subtleties and their machinations form one; and that these four are in a series, and together make as it were one bundle. From which again it is plain that the internal which consists of concupiscences cannot be cast out, except by the removal of the external which consists of evils. Concupiscences through their delights produce evils; but when evils are considered allowable, which comes to pass by consent of the will and the understanding, then the delights and the evils make one. It is well known that consent is an act. This also is what the Lord says :—*If any man looketh on the woman of another to lust after her, he hath committed adultery with her already in his heart*" (Matt. v. 28). It is the same with the other evils. (D. P. n. 111.)

When a man as of himself removes evils, then the Lord purifies the man from the concupiscences of evil. The reason is, that the Lord cannot purify him before. For evils are in the external man, and the concupiscences of evil in the internal; and they are connected as roots with the trunk. Unless the evils are removed therefore there is no opening, for they obstruct and close the door; which cannot be opened by the Lord except by means of the man, as has been shown just above. When as of himself a man thus opens the door, then at the same time the Lord extirpates the concupiscences. A further reason is that the Lord acts in the inmost of man, and from the inmost in the sequences, down to the ultimates; and in the ultimates man is together [with the Lord]. So long therefore as the ultimates are kept closed by the man himself there cannot be any purification; but only a work can be wrought by the Lord in the interiors, of such a nature as is that of the Lord in hell,—of which the man who is in concupiscences and at the same time in evils is a form; which work is only an arrangement that one thing may not destroy another, and that good and truth may not be violated. That the Lord continually urges and entreats man to open the door to Him, is plain from the Lord's words in the Apocalypse :—"*Behold, I stand at the door and knock: if any man hear My voice, and open the door, I will come in to him, and will sup with him, and he with Me*" (iii. 20.)

Man knows nothing at all of the interior state of his mind, or of his internal man; yet infinite things take place there, not one of which comes to his knowledge. For the internal of man's thought, or his internal man, is his spirit itself; and there are things as infinite or as innumerable therein as in man's body; nay, even more innumerable; for man's spirit in its form is a man, and all the things pertaining to it correspond to all things of man in his body. Now as a man knows nothing, by any sensation, of how his mind or soul operates in all things of his body, together and separately, so neither does a man know how the Lord operates in all things of his mind or soul, that is, in all things of his spirit. The operation is continual; man has no part in it; and yet the Lord cannot purify a man from any concupiscence of evil in his spirit or internal man, so long as the man keeps the external closed. It is by evils that man keeps his external closed; each of which appears to him as one, although there are infinite things in each. When a man removes this as one, then the Lord removes the infinite things within it. This is what is meant by the Lord then purifying man from the concupiscences of evil in the internal man, and from the evils themselves in the external. (*ib.* n. 119, 120.)

The Lord acts from inmosts and from ultimates simultaneously; because thus and not otherwise each and all things are held in connection. For the intermediates are in successive dependance, from the inmosts to the ultimates; and in the ultimates they are together, for in the ultimates is the simultaneous [order] of all things, from the first. . . . . The Lord cannot act at the same time from inmosts and from ultimates except together with man; for man is with the Lord in the ultimates. As man therefore acts in the ultimates, which are under his control because subject to his free will, so the Lord acts from his inmosts and in the things following, down to the ultimates. The things that are in man's inmost parts, and in those that follow from the inmosts to the ultimates, are entirely unknown to a man; and man is therefore altogether ignorant of how and what the Lord there operates. But as they are connected as one with the ultimates, it is on this account unnecessary for man to know more than that he should shun evils as sins, and look to the Lord. Thus and not otherwise his life's love, which by birth is infernal, can be removed by the Lord, and the love of a heavenly life be implanted in its place. (*ib.* n. 125.)

THE LAW OF THE DIVINE PROVIDENCE RESPECTING COMPULSION IN MATTERS OF FAITH AND OF RELIGION.

It is a law of the Divine Providence that a man should not be compelled to think and to will, and so to believe and love, the things which pertain to religion, by external means; but that a man should bring and sometimes compel himself to it. This law of the Divine Providence follows from the two preceding. . . . . Every one knows that no man can be compelled to think what he will not think, and to will what he thinks not to will; nor therefore to believe what he does not believe, and by no means what he will not believe; and especially can he not be compelled to love what he does not love, and by no means what he will not love. For the spirit or mind of a man is in full liberty to think, will, believe, and love. . . . . A man may be compelled to say that he thinks and wills this and that, and that he believes and loves this and that; but if they are not and do not become objects of affection and thence of his reason he yet does not think, will, believe, and love them. A man may even be compelled to speak in favour of religion, and to act according to it; but he cannot be compelled to think in favour of it from any faith, and to desire it from any love. In kingdoms where justice and judgment are protected every one is in fact compelled not to speak against religion, and not to act against it; but yet no one can be compelled to think and will in favour of it. For it is within the liberty of every one to think with hell, and to will in favour of hell, as well as also to think and will in favour of heaven; but reason teaches what is the nature of the one and of the other course, and what lot awaits the one and the other; and from reason the will has its option and election. It may appear from these considerations that the external cannot compel the internal; but yet this is sometimes done. But that it is injurious will be shown in the following order:—

I. *No one is reformed by miracles and signs, because they compel.* . . . . It cannot be denied that miracles induce a faith and strongly persuade that that is true which he who performs the miracles teaches and says; and that this at first so occupies the external of a man's thought that it as it were binds and fascinates him. But a man is thereby deprived of his two faculties called rationality and liberty, so that he cannot act from freedom according to reason; and then the Lord cannot flow in through the internal into the external of his thought, but can only leave the man to confirm by his rationality that which by miracle was made a matter of his faith. Man's state of thought is such, that from the internal of thought he sees a subject in the external of thought as in a kind of mirror; for as was said above, a man can see his thought,—which can only be from an interior thought. And when he sees the subject as in a mirror, he can turn it over, this way and that way, and shape it until it appears to himself beautiful. This subject if it is a truth may be compared to a virgin or youth, living and beautiful. But if a man cannot turn a subject this way and that way, and shape it, but only believe it from a persuasion induced by miracle, if then it is a truth it may be compared to a virgin or youth sculptured out of stone or wood, in which there is no life. And it may also be compared to an object that is perpetually before the sight, which only is seen, and puts out of sight all that is on either side and that is behind it. And it may be compared to a sound continually in the ear, that takes away the perception of harmony from many sounds. Such blindness and deafness are induced upon the human mind by miracles. It is the same with every thing confirmed, which is not looked at from some rationality before it is confirmed.

It is evident from these considerations that a faith induced by miracles is not faith, but persuasion; for there is nothing rational in it, still less is there anything spiritual. It is in fact only the external without the internal. It is the same with all that a man does from that persuasive faith; whether he acknowledges God, or worships Him, at home or in temples, or does good. When only a miracle induces a man to acknowledgment, worship, and piety, he acts from the natural man and not from the spiritual. For a miracle introduces faith by an external way, and not through the internal way; thus from the world, and not from heaven; and the Lord does not enter into man by any other than the internal way, which is by means of the Word, through doctrine and preachings from it. And because miracles close this way, therefore at this day no miracles are wrought. That such is the nature of miracles is very evident from the miracles wrought before the Jewish and Israelitish people. Although they saw so many miracles in the land of Egypt and afterwards at the Red Sea, and others in the desert, and especially upon Mount Sinai when the law was promulgated, yet within a month, while Moses was tarrying upon that mountain, they made themselves a golden calf, and acknowledged it as Jehovah who led them forth out of the land of Egypt (Ex. xxxii. 4-6). And it is evident again from the miracles performed afterwards in the land of Canaan; and yet they as often departed from the worship commanded them. It is equally evident from the miracles which the Lord wrought before them; and yet they crucified Him. The reason why miracles were wrought among them was, that they were merely external men, and were led into the land of Canaan only that they might represent a church and its internals by the externals of worship,—and a bad man can represent equally with a good man. For the externals are rituals, all of which among them signified things spiritual and celestial . . . And because they could not be led by the internals of worship to represent these things, they were led, nay, driven and compelled to it, by miracles. That they could not be led by the internals of worship was because they did not acknowledge the Lord,—although the whole Word, which was with them, treats of Him alone; and he who does not acknowledge the Lord cannot receive any internal of worship. But after the Lord manifested Himself, and was received and acknowledged in the churches as the eternal God, miracles ceased. (D. P. n. 129-132.)

II. *No one is reformed by visions and by conversations with the departed, because they compel.* . . . That no one is reformed by conversations with the departed is evident from the Lord's words concerning the rich man in hell, and concerning Lazarus in Abraham's bosom. For the rich man said, *" I pray thee, father Abraham, that thou wouldest send Lazarus to my father's house for I have five brethren, that he may testify unto them, lest they also come into this place of torment. Abraham saith unto him, They have Moses and the prophets ; let them hear them. And he said, Nay, father Abraham, but if one went unto them from the dead they would repent. And he said unto him, If they hear not Moses and the prophets, neither will they be persuaded though one rose from the dead "* (Luke xvi. 27-31). Speaking with the dead would produce the same effect as miracles, of which just above ; namely, that a man would be persuaded and driven to worship for a short time ; but because this deprives a man of rationality, and at the same time shuts in his evils, as was said above, this fascination or internal bond is loosed, and the pent-up evils break forth with blasphemy and profanation. But this takes place only when spirits lead into some dogma of religion ; which is never done by any good spirit, still less by any angel of heaven.

And yet conversation with spirits occurs,—but rarely with the angels of heaven,—and has occurred for many ages back. But when it takes place they speak with a man in his mother tongue ; yet only a few words. But those who speak by permission of the Lord never say any thing that takes away the freedom of reason ; nor do they teach. For the Lord alone teaches man ; but mediately through the Word, .in illustration. (*ib.* n. 134, 135.)

III. *No one is reformed by threats and punishments, because they compel.* . . . To compel man to Divine worship by threats and punishments is injurious. . . . Forced worship shuts evils in ; which then lie hidden like fires in wood beneath the ashes, that continually foment and spread until they burst forth into a flame. But worship that is not forced, but spontaneous, does not shut evils in ; and they are therefore like fires that at once burn out and are dissipated. . . . The internal of thought cannot be coerced by any fear ; but it can be constrained by love and by the fear of losing it. The fear of God, in the genuine sense, is nothing else. To be constrained by love, and by the fear of losing it, is to compel one's-self. It will be shown below that to compel one's-self is not against liberty and rationality.

Forced worship is corporeal, inanimate, unintelligible, and sad ; corporeal, because it is of the body and not of the mind ; inanimate, because the life is not in it ; unintelligible, because the understanding is not in it ; and sad because the delight of heaven is not in it. But worship that is not forced, when it is genuine, is spiritual, living, luminous, and joyful; spiritual, because there is a spirit from the Lord in it; living, because there is life from the Lord in it; luminous, because there is wisdom from the Lord in it; and joyful, because there is heaven from the Lord in it. (*ib.* n. 136, 137.)

IV. *No one is reformed in states that are not of rationality and liberty.* . . . There are many states that are not states of rationality, and of liberty. But in general they may be referred to the following: to states of fear, of misfortune, of mental disorder, of bodily disease, of ignorance, and of blindness of the understanding. But something shall be said of each state in particular.

The reason why no one is reformed in a *State of Fear,* is that fear takes away freedom and reason, or liberty and rationality. For love opens the interiors of the mind; but fear closes them. And when they are closed a man thinks little, and only of those subjects which then present themselves to his outer mind [*animus*] or to his senses. Of such effect are all the fears that invade the outer mind. It was shown above that man has an internal of thought and an external of thought. Fear can never invade the internal of his thought; this is always in freedom, because in his life's love. But it can invade the external of thought, and when it invades this, the internal of thought is closed; which being closed, the man can no longer act from freedom according to his reason, and therefore cannot be reformed. The fear which invades the external of thought and closes the internal is chiefly the fear of loss of honour or of gain. But the fear of civil punishments and of outward ecclesiastical punishments does not close it, because these laws only prescribe punishments for those who speak and act contrary to the civil [interests] of the kingdom and the spiritual [interests] of the church; and not for those who think contrary to them. The fear of infernal punishments does indeed invade the external of thought, yet only for a few moments, or hours, or days; but it is soon remitted to the freedom it derives from the internal of thought, which is properly of his spirit and life's love, and is called the thought of the heart. On the other hand, the fear of loss of honour and of gain invades the external of a man's thought, and when it invades it closes the internal of thought from above against influx from heaven, and renders it impossible that the man can be reformed. The reason is that the life's love of every man by birth is the love of self and the world; and the love of self makes one with the love of honour, while the love of the world makes one with the love of gain. When therefore a man is in honour or in possession of wealth, from fear of the loss of them he confirms in himself the means which serve him for honour and gain, which are civil as well as ecclesiastical, both being of authority [*utraque imperii*]. So does he who is not yet in honour or in possession of wealth, if he aspires to them ; but from fear of the loss of reputation on account of them. It is said that this fear invades the external of thought, and closes the internal from above against influx from heaven. This is said to be closed when it absolutely makes one with the external; for then it is not in itself, but in the external. But as the loves of self and of the world are infernal loves, and are the fountain heads of all evils, it is plain what the character of the internal of thought is, in itself, with those in whom these loves are the life's loves, or in whom they govern ; namely, that it is full of the concupiscences of evils of every kind. They do not know this who from fear of loss of dignity and opulence are strongly persuaded of the religion in which they are ; especially if in a religion which involves that they are worshipped as deities, and at the same time as Plutos in hell. These can burn as if with zeal for the salvation of souls, and yet from infernal fire. As this fear especially takes away rationality itself and liberty itself, which from their origin are heavenly, it is manifest that it so stands in the way that a man cannot be reformed.

The reason why no one is reformed in a *State of Misfortune*, if then only he thinks of God and implores His aid, is that it is a state of constraint; and therefore when he comes into a state of freedom he returns into the former condition, in which he had thought little if anything about God. It is different with those who feared God before, in a state of freedom. By fearing God is meant fearing to offend Him,—and to offend Him is to sin ; and this is not of fear, but of love. Who that loves one does not fear to do him wrong ? and fear it the more the more he loves ? Without this fear love is vapid and superficial,—of the thought only, and not of the will. By states of misfortune are meant states of desperation from perils,—as in battles, duels, shipwrecks, falls, fires, imminent or unexpected loss of wealth, also loss of office and hence of honour, and other such things. In these states alone to think of God is not from God, but from self. For the mind is then imprisoned as it were in the body ; thus is not in liberty, nor therefore in rationality, without which there is no reformation.

The reason why no one is reformed in a *Disordered State of the lower Mind* [*animus*] is that disorder of the lower mind takes away rationality, and therefore the freedom of acting according to reason ; for then the higher mind [*mens*] is disordered and unsound, and not a disordered but a sound mind is rational. Such disorders are states of melancholy, spurious and false consciences fantasies of various kinds, griefs of mind [*animus*] on account of misfortunes and anxieties, and anguish of mind [*mens*] from a vitiated condition of the body; things which are sometimes regarded as temptations, but are not so. For genuine temptations have for their objects things that are spiritual, and in these temptations the mind is sensible; but those troubled states have natural things for their objects, and in those states the mind is unsound.

No one is reformed in a *State of bodily Disease,* because the reason is then not in a free state; for the state of the mind depends on the condition of the body. When the body is ill the mind also is ill; if from nothing else, yet on account of its withdrawal from the world; for a mind withdrawn from the world thinks indeed of God, but not from God, because it has not freedom of reason. Man has freedom of reason from the fact that he is intermediate between heaven and the world, and that he can think both from heaven and from the world; equally from heaven concerning the world, and from the world about heaven. When therefore a man is in sickness and thinks of death, and of the state of his soul after death, he is then not in the world, but is withdrawn into the spirit; in which state alone no one can be reformed. But if he was reformed before his sickness he may be confirmed by it. It is the same with those who renounce the world and all business therein, and give themselves up solely to thoughts about God, heaven and salvation; but of this subject more in another place. If therefore they were not reformed before their sickness, after it, in case they die, they become such as they were before. It is vain then to suppose that any can repent or receive any faith in sickness; for there is nothing of action in that repentance, and nothing of charity in that faith. In both therefore it is all of the mouth, and nothing of the heart.

The reason why no one is reformed in a *State of Ignorance,* is that all reformation is effected by means of truths and a life according to them. They therefore who do not know truths cannot be reformed. But if they desire truths from an affection for them, they are reformed in the spiritual world after death.

Nor can any one be reformed in a *State of Blindness of the Understanding.* These also do not know truths, nor therefore life; for the understanding must teach truths, and the will do them; and when the will does what the understanding teaches, then its life comes into accordance with truths. But when the understanding is blinded the will too is closed, and does from freedom according to its reason nothing but the evil confirmed in the understanding, which is falsity. Besides the want of knowledge, a religion that teaches a blind faith also blinds the understanding. So also does the teaching of falsity; for as truths open the understanding, so falsities close it. They close it above, but open it below; and the understanding open only below cannot see truths, but can only confirm whatever it wishes, especially falsity. The understanding is blinded also by the lusts of evil. So long as the will is in them it actuates the understanding to confirm them; and in so far as the lusts of evil are confirmed the will cannot be in the affections of good, and from them see truths, and so be reformed. (*ib.* n. 138-144.)

V. *It is not contrary to rationality and liberty to compel one's self.* . . . Since the internal and external of the mind are so distinct as has been shown above, the internal can even fight with the external, and by conflict force it to agreement. Conflicts arise when a man thinks evils to be sins, and for that reason determines to abstain from them; for when he abstains the door is opened, and then the concupiscences of evil which occupy the internal of thought are cast out by the Lord, and affections of good are implanted in their place. This is in the internal of thought. But as the delights of the concupiscences of evil, which occupy the external of thought, cannot at the same time be cast out, a conflict therefore arises between the internal and the external of thought; the internal determines to cast out these delights,—because they are delights of evil and are not consonant with the affections of good in which the internal now is,—and to introduce delights of good, which are consonant, in place of the delights of evil. Delights of good are what are called goods of charity. The conflict springs from this contrariety, which, if it becomes severe is called temptation. Now, as a man is man by virtue of the internal of his thought,— for this is man's very spirit,—it is evident that when a man compels the external of his thought to agreement, or to receive the delights of his affections, which are goods of charity, he compels himself. It is plain that this is not contrary to rationality and liberty, but in accordance with them; for rationality produces the conflict, and liberty carries it on. Moreover, genuine liberty together with genuine rationality resides in the internal man, and from this in the external. When therefore the internal conquers,—which takes place as soon as the internal has reduced the external to consent and obedience,—then genuine liberty and genuine rationality is given to man by the Lord; for then the man is taken by the Lord out of infernal freedom, which in itself is servitude, and is brought into heavenly freedom, which in itself is genuine freedom, and he has consociation with the angels. That they who are in sins are servants, and that the Lord makes free those who through the Word receive truth from Him, He teaches in John viii. 31-36. (*ib.* n. 145.)

All who voluntarily serve for the sake of freedom compel themselves. And when they compel themselves they act from freedom according to reason; but from an interior freedom, from

which exterior freedom is looked upon as servitude.   (*ib.* n
148.)

The Divine Providence unseen and unfelt, but to be known and acknowledged.

*It is a law of the Divine Providence that man should not per-
ceive and feel anything of the operation of Divine Providence, but
yet that he should know and acknowledge it.* The natural man, who
does not believe in the Divine Providence, thinks within himself,
How can there be a Divine Providence, when the evil are
raised to honours and acquire wealth rather than the good ? and
when many such things succeed with those who do not believe in
the Divine Providence better than with those that do believe ?
Nay, that the faithless and impious can inflict injuries, losses,
and misfortunes, and sometimes death, upon the faithful and
devout, and this with craft and malice ? And so he thinks, Do
I not see, from very experience, as in the clear light of day, that
wily machinations, if only a man by ingenious shrewdness can
make them appear as if reliable and just, prevail over fidelity
and justice ? What remains but necessities, consequences, and
chance, in which there appears nothing of Divine Providence ?
Are not necessities of nature ? Are not consequences conditions
flowing from natural or civil order ? And are not matters
of chance from causes that are unknown, or from no cause ?
Such things does the natural man think within himself, who
ascribes nothing to God but all things to nature ; for he who
attributes nothing to God does not attribute anything to the
Divine Providence either ; for God and the Divine Providence
make one. But the spiritual man says or thinks otherwise
within himself. Although he does not in thought perceive,
nor by the sight of the eye discern the Divine Providence in
its progression, yet he knows and acknowledges it. Now since
the above-mentioned appearances and delusions therefrom have
blinded the understanding, and it can receive no sight unless
the delusions and the falsities are dispelled which have induced
the blindness and the thick darkness, and this can only be
done by truths, in which there is power to dispel falsities,
therefore these truths are to be set forth.

If man perceived and felt the operation of Divine Providence he would not act from freedom according to reason, nor
would any thing appear to him as from himself. So if man
foreknew events. . . . If man perceived and felt the operation
of the Divine Providence he would yet be led by it ; for the
Lord leads all by His Divine Providence, and man only apparently

leads himself, as has been shown above. If therefore he had a living perception and sensation that he is led he would not be conscious of life, and would then be moved to utterance and action scarcely otherwise than as a graven image. If he were still conscious of life, then he would be led but as one bound with handcuffs and fetters, or as a beast under the yoke before a cart. Who does not see that man would then have no freedom? And if he had no freedom neither would he have any reason; for every one thinks from freedom and in freedom, and whatever he does not think from freedom and in freedom does not appear to him to be from himself, but from another. Nay, if you weigh the matter interiorly you will perceive that he would neither have thought, nor still less reason, and would therefore not be man. (D. P. n. 175, 176.)

It is also in order that he may act from freedom according to reason that it is not given man to know future events. For it is known that whatever a man loves, he desires its effect; and to this, by reason, he directs himself. Then, that there is nothing that a man revolves in his reason, which is not from the love that through thought it may come into effect. If therefore the effect or event were known by Divine prediction the reason would acquiesce, and with the reason the love; for love with reason terminates in the effect, and then from this begins anew. The very delight of reason is, that from love it sees the effect in thought; not in the effect but before it, or not in the present but in the future. Hence it is that man has what is called *hope;* which increases and diminishes in the reason as he sees or expects the event. This delight is completed in the event; but after that it is obliterated, together with the thought of it. So would it be with an event foreknown. Because the foreknowledge of future events takes away the very human, which is to act from freedom according to reason, therefore it is given no one to know the future; but it is permitted any one from reason to form conclusions respecting future events; reason, with all its attributes, is then in its proper life. It is on this account that man does not know his lot after death; or know any event before he is in it. For if he knew he would no longer from his interior self consider how to act and live that he might attain it; but would only from his outer self think that he is to attain it,—and this state closes the interiors of his mind wherein the two faculties of his life, which are liberty and rationality, chiefly reside. The desire to foreknow the future is innate with very many, but this desire originates from the love of evil. It is therefore taken away from those who believe in the Divine Providence, and trust is given to them, in that the Lord disposes their lot. And therefore they do not desire to foreknow it, lest in some way they should intrude themselves upon the Divine Providence. This the Lord teaches by the several admonitions in Luke xii. 14-48. (*ib.* n. 178, 179.)

The Lord therefore who provides all things and foresees all things, conceals the operations of His Providence, so that man scarcely knows whether there ever is any Providence; and it is permitted him to attribute the things that are accomplished to prudence, and those that happen to fortune; nay, to ascribe many things to nature, rather than that by visible and palpable signs of Providence and of the Divine Presence he should untimely cast himself into sanctities in which he does not abide. The Lord permits such things also by the other laws of His Providence; certainly, by these; that man should have freedom; and that what he does he should do according to reason, thus entirely as of himself. For it is better that a man should ascribe the operations of the Divine Providence to prudence and fortune, than that he should acknowledge them and yet live as a devil. (A. E. n. 1159.)

The Divine Providence seen from behind, and not in the Face.

It is given man to see the Divine Providence from behind, but not in the face; and in a spiritual state, but not in his natural state. To see the Divine Providence from behind and not in the face, is to see it after and not before; and to see it from a spiritual but not from a natural state, is to see it from heaven and not from the world. All who receive influx from heaven, and acknowledge the Divine Providence,—and especially those who by reformation have become spiritual,—when they see events in a certain wonderful series, they see and confess it as it were from an interior acknowledgment. They do not wish to see it in the face, that is before it comes to pass; for they fear lest their will should enter into any thing of its order and tenor. It is otherwise with those who do not admit any influx from heaven, but only from the world; especially with those who by confirmation of appearances in themselves have become natural. They see nothing of the Divine Providence from behind or after it, but wish to see it in the face, or before it comes to pass; and as the Divine Providence operates through means, and the means are produced through man or through the world, therefore, whether they see it in the face or from behind, they attribute it either to man or to nature, and so confirm themselves in the denial of it. The reason why they thus attribute it is that their understanding is closed from above, and open only from beneath, —thus is closed towards heaven and open towards the world; and the Divine Providence is not seen from the world, but from heaven. I have sometimes thought within me, whether they would acknowledge the Divine Providence if their understanding were opened above, and they saw as in clear daylight that nature in itself is dead and human intelligence in itself is nothing, but that it is from influx that both appear to be. And I perceived that those who have confirmed themselves in favour of nature and of human prudence, would not acknowledge; because natural light flowing in from below would instantly extinguish the spiritual light flowing in from above. (D. P. 187.)

THE DIVINE PROVIDENCE AND HUMAN PRUDENCE.

Man's own Prudence is nothing, and only appears to be, and moreover ought so to appear; but the Divine Providence from the very least particulars is universal. It is entirely contrary to the appearance that man's own prudence is nothing, and it is therefore contrary to the belief of many. And because it is so, no one who, according to the appearance, is in the belief that human prudence accomplishes everything, can be convinced, unless by means of profounder investigation, which must be deduced from the causes; and the causes discover whence it is.

The affections of a man's life's love are known to the Lord alone. Man knows his thoughts, and therefore his intentions, because he sees them in himself; and as all his prudence is from them he sees this also in himself. If then his life's love is the love of self he comes into the pride of his own intelligence, and ascribes prudence to himself; and he gathers arguments in favour of it, and so recedes from acknowledgment of the Divine Providence. The same he does if the love of the world is his life's love; but yet this does not recede in a like degree. It is plain from these considerations that these two loves ascribe all to man and his prudence; and if they are examined interiorly nothing to God and His Providence. When therefore perchance they hear that the truth is that human prudence is nothing, but that it is the Divine Providence alone which governs all things, if they are thorough atheists they laugh at it; but if they retain something of religion in the memory, and it is said to them that all wisdom is from God, they assent indeed at the first hearing, but yet interiorly in their spirit they deny it.

There is no thought of man but from some affection of his life's love; and the thought is nothing else than the form of the affection. Therefore since a man sees his thought, and cannot see the affection,—for this he feels,—it follows that from sight, which is in the appearance, and not from the affection, which does not come into the sight but into sensation, he sets it down that his own prudence accomplishes everything. For the affection manifests itself only by a certain delight of thought and pleasure of reasoning upon the subject; and then this pleasure and delight make one with the thought, in those who from the love of self or from the love of the world believe in their own prudence. And thought flows in its delight, as a ship in the current of a river,—to which the master does not direct his attention, but only to the sails, which he spreads.

A man can indeed reflect upon the delight of his external affection, when this acts as one with the delight of some bodily sense; but yet he does not reflect upon the fact that this delight is from the delight of his affection within the thought. . . . The delights govern the thoughts, and the thoughts are nothing without them. But it is believed that they are thoughts only, when yet the thoughts are nothing but the affections composed into forms by the life's love, that they may appear in the light; for all affection is in heat, and thought is in light. The affections of external thought manifest themselves it is true in the sensation of the body, yet rarely in the thought of the mind. But the affections of internal thought, from which the external spring, never manifest themselves to a man. Of these a man knows no more than one sleeping in a carriage does of the road; and is no more sensible of them than of the circumrotation of the earth. Now as a man knows nothing of the things that are being done in the interiors of his mind, which are so infinite that they cannot be limited by numbers; and yet the few external things that come to the sight of thought are produced from those that are interior, and the interior are governed by the Lord alone through His Divine Providence, and these few external things by Him together with man; how can any one say that his own prudence accomplishes everything? If you should see but one idea of thought laid open you would see more wonderful things than tongue can tell. (D. P. n. 191, 197-199.)

No one knows how the Lord leads and teaches a man in his internals; just as one does not know how his soul operates that the eye may see, the ear hear, the tongue and the mouth speak, the heart impel the blood, the lungs respire, the stomach digest, the liver and the pancreas distribute, the kidneys secrete, and innumerable other things. These operations do not come to a man's perception and consciousness. So with those that are wrought by the Lord in the interior substances and forms of the mind, which are infinitely more. The Lord's operations in these do not appear to a man; but the effects appear, which themselves are many, and some causes of the effects. These are the externals, in which the man is, together with the Lord. And as the externals make one with the internals,—for they are connected in a series,—for this reason he can only be disposed by the Lord in the internals iu accordance with what is disposed in the externals by means of the man. (*ib.* n. 174.)

It has been fully shown in the preceding pages that if it did not appear to man as if he lived from himself, even so that he does think and will, speak and act just as if from himself, he would not be man. It follows from this that if man did not, as by his own prudence, dispose all things that pertain to his activity and life, he could not be led and disposed by the Divine Providence. For he would be as one who stands with hands down, mouth open, eyes shut, and holding his breath, in expectation of influx. He would divest himself of the human, which he has from a perception and sense that he lives, thinks, wills, speaks, and acts, as of himself; and then at the same time he would divest himself of his two faculties by which he is distinguished from animals, which are liberty and rationality. . . . If therefore you would be led of the Divine Providence use prudence, as a servant and minister who faithfully dispenses the goods of his master. This prudence is the pound that was given the servants to trade with, of which they were to render an account (Luke xix. 13-25 ; Matt. xxv. 14-31). The prudence itself appears to man as his own; and is believed to be his own so long as man keeps inclosed within him the most malignant enemy of God and of the Divine Providence,—which is the love of self. This dwells in the interiors of every man from birth. If you do not take cognizance of it (for it does not wish to be recognized) it dwells securely, and keeps the door, lest it should be opened by man and it should thus be cast out by the Lord. Man opens the door by shunning evils as sins, as of himself, with the acknowledgment that it is of the Lord. This is the prudence with which the Divine Providence acts as one. (*ib.* n. 210.)

The Divine Providence respecting temporal Things.

It is of the Divine Providence that man puts off natural and temporal things by Death, and puts on things spiritual and eternal. Natural and temporal things are the extremes and ultimates into which man enters,—which takes place when he is born,—to the end that afterwards he may be introduced into things interior and higher. For the extremes and ultimates are containants ; and these are in the natural world. . . . But as the extremes and ultimates of nature cannot receive things spiritual and eternal, for which the human mind is formed, as they are in themselves, and yet man is born that he may become spiritual and live to eternity, therefore man puts them off, and retains only the interior natural [substances] which harmonize and unite with the spiritual and celestial and serve them as containants. This is done by the rejection of the temporal and natural ultimates; which is the death of the body.

The Lord by His Divine Providence conjoins Himself to natural things by means of spiritual, and to temporal things by means of eternal, according to uses. Natural and temporal things are not only those that are peculiar to nature, but also those that are peculiar to man in the natural world. Both of these man puts off by death, and puts on the spiritual and eternal things corresponding to them. He puts them on according to uses. The natural things that are peculiar to nature relate in general to time and space; and in particular to the things which are seen on the earth. Man leaves these by death, and in place of them receives spiritual things which as to outward form or appearance are similar to them, but not so as to internal form and very essence. The temporal things which are peculiar to men in the natural world relate in general to dignities and possessions; and in particular to the necessities of every man, which are food, clothing, and habitation. These also are put off and left behind by death, and such things are put on and received as are similar to them in outward form or appearance, but not as to internal form and as to essence. They all have their internal form and essence from the uses of temporal things in the world. The uses are the goods which are called goods of charity. From these considerations it may be seen that the Lord by His Divine Providence conjoins spiritual and eternal things to natural and temporal according to uses. . . . Dignities, and honors, and wealth, and influence, are each in outward form natural and temporal; but in inward form they are spiritual and eternal. Dignities with their honors are natural and temporal when a man looks to himself personally in them, and not to the commonwealth and uses; for then a man cannot but think within himself, interiorly, that the commonwealth exists for him, and not he for the commonwealth. He is as a king who thinks that the kingdom and all the people in it exist for him, and not he for his kingdom and people. But the same dignities with their honours are spiritual and eternal when a man looks upon himself personally as existing for the sake of the commonwealth and uses, and not these for him. If a man does this, then he is in the truth and in the essence of his dignity and his honour; but if the former he is in the correspondence and appearance,—

which if he confirm within him he is in fallacies, and no otherwise in conjunction with the Lord than as those who are in falsities and thence in evils; for fallacies are the falsities with which evils conjoin themselves. Such have indeed performed uses and good works, but from themselves and not from the Lord; thus they have put themselves in place of the Lord. It is the same with wealth and influence, which also are natural and temporal, as well as spiritual and eternal. Wealth and influence are natural and temporal with those who look only to them and to themselves in them, and in these two find all their pleasure and delight; but the same are spiritual and eternal with those who look to good uses in them, and in these find interior pleasure and delight. With them even outward pleasure and delight becomes spiritual, and the temporal becomes eternal. (D. P. n. 220.)

Whoever duly considers may know that eminence and opulence in the world are not actual Divine blessings,—although man from his pleasure in them calls them so; for they are transient, and also seduce many and turn them away from heaven. But life in heaven and happiness there are actual blessings, which are from the Divine. These things the Lord teaches in Luke:— "*Provide yourselves . . . a treasure in the heavens that faileth not, where no thief approacheth, neither moth corrupteth. For where your treasure is, there will your heart be also*" (xii. 33, 34). (A. C. n. 10,776.)

They who place all prosperity in worldly and corporeal things, that is in honours and riches, and believe that these only are Divine blessings, in their hearts reject and deny the Divine Providence in particulars, when they see many of the evil abound in such things, and not so much the good; not considering that Divine blessing consists in being happy to eternity, and that such things as are momentary,—which the things of this world are, comparatively,—the Lord looks upon but as means to eternal things. On this account the Lord also provides for the good, who receive His mercy, such things in time as conduce to the happiness of their eternal life,—riches and honours to those whom they do not injure, and not riches and honours to those to whom they are hurtful. Yet to these He gives, in time, in place of honours and riches, more to rejoice in a few things, and to be more content, than the rich and honoured. (*ib.* n. 8717.)

THE DIVINE PROVIDENCE RESPECTING THE RECEPTION OF TRUTH AND GOOD.

The Lord does not admit a man interiorly into the truths of wisdom, and at the same time into the goods of love, except in the degree that the man can be kept in them to the end of life. . . . That this mystery of the Divine Providence may be explained, so that the rational man can see it in its light, it shall be unfolded in this order. I. There cannot be evil and at the same time good in man, in his interiors, nor therefore the falsity of evil and at the same time the truth of good. II. Good and the truth of good cannot be introduced by the Lord into the interiors of a man, except in so far as the evil therein and the falsity of evil are removed. III. If good with its truth were introduced therein before or more than evil with its falsity is removed, a man would depart from good and go back to his evil. IV. While man is in evil many truths may be introduced into his understanding, and these be stored up in the memory, and yet not be profaned. V. But the Lord by His Divine Providence takes the greatest care that it may not be received from thence by the will, before and more than in the degree in which the man as of himself puts away evil in the external man. VI. If it were done before, and more, then the will would adulterate the good and the understanding would falsify the truth, by mingling them with evils and with falsities. VII. Therefore the Lord does not admit a man interiorly into the truths of wisdom and into the goods of love, except in the degree that the man can be kept in them to the end of life.

I. That in the interiors of man there cannot at the same time be evil with its falsity and good with its truth, may be seen by the rational man without explanation. For evil is opposite to good, and good is opposite to evil; and two opposites cannot be together. There is also inherent in all evil a hatred against good, and there is inherent in all good a love of protecting itself against evil, and of putting it away from itself. Whence it follows that the one cannot exist in company with the other; and if they were together, there would arise first a conflict and battle, and then destruction. This indeed the Lord teaches in these words :—" *Every kingdom divided against itself is brought to desolation ; and every city or house divided against itself shall not stand.* . . . *He that is not with Me is against Me ; and he that gathereth not with Me scattereth abroad* " (Matt. xii. 25-30) ; and in another place; " *No man can at once serve two masters ; for he will either hate the one, or love the other* " (Matt. vi. 24). Two opposites cannot exist together in one substance and form without its being distracted and destroyed. If one should advance and draw near the other they would certainly separate ; like two enemies, one of whom would retire within his encampment, or within his fortifications, and the other remain without. This is the case with the evils and goods in a hypocrite. He is in both ; but the evil is within, and the good is without,—and so the two are separate and not commingled.

II. That good and the truth of good cannot be introduced by the Lord into the interiors of a man except in so far as the evil therein and the falsity of evil are removed, is the very consequence of the foregoing. For since evil and good cannot exist together, good cannot be introduced until the evil is removed. It is said, into the interiors of a man; by which are meant the internals of his thought. These are the interiors referred to,—in which either the Lord must be, or the devil. After reformation the Lord is there ; but before it the devil is there. In so far then as a man suffers himself to be reformed the devil is cast out; but in so far as he does not suffer himself to be reformed the devil remains. Who is not able to see that the Lord cannot enter so long as the devil is there ? And he is there so long as man keeps the door closed,—in which man is, together with the Lord.[1] That the Lord enters when by means of man this door is opened the Lord teaches in the Apocalypse :—" *Behold, I stand at the door and knock : if any man hear My voice, and open the door, I will come in to him, and will sup with him, and he with Me*" (iii. 20.)

III. If good with its truth were introduced before or more than evil with its falsity is removed, man would depart from good, and go back to his evil. The reason is that evil would be in power, and that which is in power conquers,—if not then yet afterwards. So long as evil is still in power good cannot be introduced into the inmost chambers, but only into the outer courts,—since, as was said, evil and good cannot dwell together ; and that which is only in the outer courts is removed by its enemy which occupies the inner apartments. Hence occurs the departure from good and the return to evil, which is the worst kind of profanation. Besides, the very delight of man's life is to love himself and the world above all things. This delight cannot be removed in a moment, but successively. Yet in the degree that this delight remains in a man evil is in power there ; and this evil can only be removed by the love of self becoming a love of uses, or by the love of rule coming to be exercised not for the sake of self, but for the sake of uses. . . . Since therefore the state of man's life must be inverted, so that what is above may be below, and this inversion cannot be affected in a moment,—for the veriest delight of life, which is from the love of self and the consequent love of rule, cannot be diminished and turned into the love of uses otherwise than successively,—therefore good cannot be introduced by the Lord before and more than in the

---

[1] The reader is referred to pp. 493, 494, 501, where the author explains that this door which man must open, and wherein he acts "together with the Lord," is the ultimate or external man ; which is the region of man's consciousness, and therefore within the scope and control, under the Lord, of his free-will and reason.

degree that evil is removed; and if it were done before, and more, man would depart from good and return to his evil.

IV. While man is in evil many truths may be introduced into his understanding, and these stored up in the memory, and yet not be profaned. The reason is that the understanding does not flow into the will, but the will into the understanding. And as it does not flow into the will, many truths may be received by the understanding, and these be laid up in the memory, and yet not be mingled with the evil of the will, and so holy things not be profaned. And it is also incumbent upon every one to learn truths from the Word or from preachings, to lay them up in the memory, and to meditate upon them; for, from the truths which are in the memory and which come thence into thought the understanding must teach the will, that is, must teach the man, what he should do. This therefore is the principal means of reformation. While truths are only in the understanding, and hence in the memory, they are not within the man, but without him. Man's memory may be compared to the ruminatory stomach of certain animals, into which they introduce their food; which so long as it is there is not within their body, but without it; but as they take it from thence and eat it, it becomes of their life, and the body is nourished. But in man's memory there is not material food but spiritual, which is meant by truths; and in themselves they are cognitions. In proportion as a man takes these out from thence, by meditating, ruminating as it were upon them, his spiritual mind is nourished. It is a love of the will which desires and as it were hungers, and causes them to be drawn out and nourished. If that love is evil it desires and as it were hungers for what is impure; but if good it desires and as it were hungers for what is pure; and those things which do not agree with it, it separates, removes, and expels,—which is done in various ways.

V. The Lord by His Divine Providence takes the greatest care that it may not be received from thence by the will, before and more than in the degree that the man as of himself puts away evil in the external man. For what is received by the will enters into the man, and is appropriated by him, and becomes of his life; and in his very life, which man has from the will, evil and good cannot dwell together; for thus he would perish. Yet these can both be in the understanding,—which are there called falsities of evil or truths of good; but not together, else a man could not distinguish evil from good and know good from evil; but they are distinguished and separated there, as a house into the interior and exterior. When an evil man thinks and speaks of goods he thinks and speaks outwardly; and when of evils, inwardly. When he speaks of goods therefore his speech comes as from the wall; and may be compared to fruit outwardly beautiful which is worm-eaten and rotten within, and also to the shell of a dragon's egg.

VI. If it were done before, and more, then the will would adulterate the good and the understanding falsify the truth, by mingling them with evils and the falsities therefrom. When the will is in evil, it adulterates the good in the understanding; and good adulterated in the understanding is evil in the will, for it confirms that evil is good and good evil. Evil does this to all good, because it is the opposite to itself. Evil also falsifies truth, because the truth of good is opposite to the falsity of evil; this also the will does in the understanding, and not the understanding of itself. Adulterations of good are described in the Word by adulteries, and falsifications of truth by fornications. These adulterations and falsifications are effected by reasonings from the natural man, who is in evil; and are also effected by confirmations from the appearances in the literal sense of the Word. The love of self, which is the head of all evils, surpasses other loves in its capacity for adulterating goods and falsifying truths; and it does this by the abuse of the rationality, which every man has from the Lord, the evil as well as the good. Nay, it can by confirmations make evil appear precisely as if it were good, and falsity as if it were truth.

VII. Therefore the Lord does not admit a man interiorly into the truths of wisdom and into the goods of love, except in the degree that the man can be kept in them to the end of life. The Lord does this that man may not fall into the most grievous kind of profanation of what is holy. On account of this danger the Lord even permits evils of life, and many things that are heretical pertaining worship. (D. P. n. 232, 233.)

Permissions of the Divine Providence.

There are no laws of permission by themselves, or separate from the laws of the Divine Providence, but they are the same. It is therefore said that God permits; by which is meant not that He wills, but that on account of the end, which is salvation, He cannot avert. Whatever is done for the sake of the end, which is salvation, is according to the laws of the Divine Providence. For, as was said before, the Divine Providence continually moves in a contrary direction and in opposition to the will of man, perpetually stretching forward to the end. Therefore, in every moment of its operation, or in every step of its progress, whenever it observes man to wander from the end, according to its laws it directs, bends, and disposes him, by leading him away from evil, and leading to good. That this cannot be done without the permission of evil, will be seen in what follows. Moreover, nothing can be permitted without a cause; and there is no cause elsewhere than in some law of the Divine Providence, which law teaches why it is permitted. (D. P. n. 234.)

Every worshipper of self and worshipper of nature, when he sees so many impious in the world, and their so many impieties, and at the same time the gloryings of some of them, and yet no punishment of them therefor by God, confirms himself against the Divine Providence. And he confirms himself the more against the Divine Providence when he sees that machinations, craft, and deceit succeed even against the pious, just and sincere; and that injustice triumphs over justice in judicial investigations, and in business. Especially does he confirm himself when he sees the impious raised to honours, and become great, and leading men, and abound too in riches, and live in luxury and magnificence; and sees the worshippers of God, on the contrary, in contempt and poverty. He also confirms himself against the Divine Providence when he considers that wars are permitted; and then the violent death of so many men, and the plundering of so many cities, nations, and families; and also that victory stands on the side of prudence, and sometimes not on that of justice; and that it makes no difference whether the commander be upright or not upright; besides other such things, all which are permissions in accordance with the laws of the Divine Providence.

The natural man likewise confirms himself against the Divine Providence when he beholds the religions of the different nations. As for instance, that there are those who are ignorant of God; that there are those who worship the sun and moon; and those who worship idols, graven images, and even monsters; and those also who worship dead men. Above all, when he observes that the Mahometan religion is received by so many empires and kingdoms, while the Christian religion prevails only in the smallest quarter of the habitable globe, which is called Europe; and that there it is divided; that there are those there who claim for themselves Divine power, and would be worshipped as gods; and who invoke dead men; and that there are those who place salvation in certain words that they think and say; and that there are few who live according to their religion. . . . . The denier of the Divine Providence concludes from these facts that religion is nothing in itself; but yet that it is necessary because it serves as a restraint. . . . . All these things are mentioned to the end that it may be shown that each and all things that take place in the world, the evil as well as the good, are of the Divine Providence. (D. P. n. 237, 238, 240.)

PERMISSIONS OF PROVIDENCE WITH RESPECT TO WORLDLY POSSESSIONS
AND HONOURS.

The worshipper of self and the worshipper of nature believes
dignities and possessions to be the highest and only happiness
that can be given, thus happiness itself. And if from being
initiated into worship in infancy he thinks anything about God,
he calls them Divine blessings; and so long as from these he
does not aspire to anything higher he thinks there is a God, and
worships Him. But there is concealed in his worship what he
himself is then ignorant of,—[the hope] that he may be elevated
by God to still higher dignities, and to yet more ample possessions. And if he comes into them his worship becomes more and
more external until it glides away, and at length he thinks slight-
ingly of God, and denies Him. He does the same if he is cast
down from the dignity and opulence on which he has set his heart.
What then are dignities and possessions but stumbling-blocks, to
the evil? But they are not so to the good; because they do not set
their heart upon them, but upon the uses or goods for the
accomplishment of which dignities and possessions serve as
means. No one therefore can confirm himself against the Divine
Providence by the fact that the impious are advanced to dignities
and honours, and become great, and leading men, but who is a
worshipper of himself and a worshipper of nature. Besides,
what is greater or less dignity? and greater or less opulence?
Is it other, in itself, than a something imaginary? Is the one
more fortunate and happy than the other? Is not dignity with
a great man, nay, with a king or emperor, after a year's time,
regarded but as a common thing, which no longer exalts the
heart with its joy, and which may even become worthless to him?
Are they by reason of their dignities in a greater degree of
happiness than those who are in less dignity? nay, who are in
the least, as husbandmen, and even their servants? These may
be in a greater degree of happiness, when it is well with them
and they are content with their lot. What is more restless at
heart, what more frequently irritated, what more violently rages,
than the love of self? This is the case as often as it is not honoured according to the pride of its heart; and as often as anything
does not prosper with it according to its will and pleasure. What
then is dignity but an idea, if it be not for some object or use?
Can there be such an idea in any thought but thought about self
and the world?—in its very self, even the thought that the world
is everything and eternity nothing? Now something shall be said
about the Divine Providence, as to why it permits that men impious in heart are elevated to dignities and acquire wealth. The

impious or evil equally with the pious or good can perform uses;
nay, from a more ardent fire; for they have regard to themselves
in uses, and regard honours as uses. In the degree therefore that
the love of self rises the lust of performing uses for the sake of
their own glory is enkindled. There is no such fire with the pious
or good, unless it is fomented beneath by honour. The Lord therefore governs the impious in heart who are in dignities through
the celebrity of their name, and excites them to perform uses to
the state or their native country, to the society or city in which
they live, and also to their fellow-citizens or neighbours among
whom they dwell. This is the Lord's government, which is
called the Divine Providence, with such. For the kingdom
of the Lord is a kingdom of uses; and when there are but
few who perform uses for the sake of uses He causes worshippers of self to be exalted to the more conspicuous offices,
in which every one is excited by his love to do good. . . . .
Light your candle and seek how many there are in the kingdoms at this day, who aspire to dignities, that are not lovers
of themselves and the world. Will you find fifty among a
thousand who are lovers of God? And among these there are
but few who aspire to dignities. Since then they are so few in
number who are lovers of God, and so many who are lovers of
themselves and of the world, and since these from their own
fires perform more uses than the lovers of God from theirs, how
can any one confirm himself [against the Divine Providence] by
the fact that the evil are in eminence and opulence more than
the good? (D. P. n. 250.)

PERMISSION OF PROVIDENCE WITH RESPECT TO WARS.

It is not from the Divine Providence that wars exist; for they
are connected with murders, plunderings, acts of violence,
cruelties, and other enormous evils, which are diametrically
opposed to Christian charity. And yet they cannot but be
permitted, because the life's love of men, since the most ancient
who are meant by Adam and his wife, has become such that it
desires to rule over others, and at length over all, and desires
to possess the wealth of the world, and finally all wealth. These
two loves cannot be kept in bonds, since it is in accordance with
the Divine Providence that every one should be permitted to
act from freedom according to reason ; and since without permissions man cannot be led by the Lord from evil, thus cannot
be reformed and saved. For if evils were not permitted to break
out man would not see them, therefore would not acknowledge
them, and so could not be led to resist them. Hence it is

that evils cannot be repressed by any Providence; for thus they would remain shut in, and, like the disease called cancer, and gangrene, would spread and consume all that is vital in man. For man is by birth as a little hell, between which and heaven there is a perpetual disagreement. No man can be extricated from his hell by the Lord unless he sees that he is in it, and unless he wishes to be extricated; and this cannot come to pass without permissions,—the causes of which are laws of the Divine Providence. It is for this reason that there are wars, greater and less; the less between possessors of estates and their neighbours, and the greater between the monarchs of kingdoms and their neighbours. Greater and less makes no difference, save that the less are kept within bounds by the laws of the nation, and the greater by the law of nations; and that the less as well as the greater wish to transgress their laws, but the less cannot and the greater can,—but yet not beyond what is possible. There are many causes, which lie hidden in the treasury of Divine wisdom, why the greater wars,—because they are connected with murders, plunderings, acts of violence, and deeds of cruelty,—are not repressed by the Lord in the kings and the generals, neither in their inception nor in their progress, but at the end, when the power of one or the other has become so weak and that it is in imminent danger of destruction. Some of these have been revealed to me; among which is this:—That all wars, howsoever political they are, are representative in heaven of states of the church; and that they are correspondences. Such were all the wars described in the Word; and such also are all wars at this day. The wars described in the Word are those that the children of Israel waged with different nations; as for instance with the Amorites, the Ammonites, the Moabites, the Philistines, the Syrians, the Egyptians, the Chaldeans, and the Assyrians. And when the children of Israel, who represented the church, departed from the commandments and statutes, and fell into the evils which were signified by those nations, (for every nation with which the children of Israel waged war signified some kind of evil,) then they were punished by that nation. Thus when they profaned the holy things of the church by foul idolatries, they were punished by the Assyrians and Chaldeans; because by Assyria and Chaldea the profanation of what is holy is signified. Similar things are represented by wars wherever they are, the present day; for all things that occur in the natural world correspond in the spiritual world to spiritual things, and all spiritual things concern the church. It is not known in this world what kingdoms in Christendom represent the Moabites and Ammonites, what the Syrians and Philistines, the Chaldeans and Assyrians, and the other nations with whom the children of Israel waged war; yet there are those that represent them. But it also cannot be seen at all in this world what the character of the church is on earth, and what the evils are into which it is falling, and on account of which it is punished by wars; for in this world only the externals are visible, which do not constitute the church. But it is seen in the spiritual world, where the internals appear, in which the church itself consists. And there they are all connected according to their various states. The conflicts of these in the spiritual world correspond to wars; which are on both sides governed by the Lord correspondentially according to the course of His Divine Providence. The spiritual man acknowledges that wars in the world are governed by the Lord's Divine Providence; but not the natural man,— save that when a festival is proclaimed on account of a victory, he can then upon his knees give thanks to God that He has given him the victory; and also in a few words before he goes to battle. But when he returns into himself he ascribes the victory either to the prudence of the general, or to some device or occurrence in the midst of the battle which they had thought nothing of, yet from which came the victory. It has been shown[1] that the Divine Providence,—which is called fortune,—is in the very least particulars even of trivial things. If you acknowledge the Divine Providence in these you must certainly acknowledge it in the affairs of war. The successes and events of war, resulting favourably, are indeed said by the common voice to be by the fortune of war; and this is the Divine Providence,—especially in the plans and deliberations of the general, —although he should then and afterwards ascribe them all to his own prudence. But this he can do if he will, for he is in the full liberty to think in favour of the Divine Providence or against it; nay, in favour of God and against Him. But let him know that no jot of his plan and deliberation is from himself. It all flows in either from heaven or from hell,—from hell by permission, from heaven by Providence. (D. P. n. 251.)

PERMISSION OF PROVIDENCE WITH RESPECT TO THE RELIGIONS OF THE VARIOUS NATIONS.

They who deduce arguments against the Divine Providence from these permissions do not know the mysteries of heaven, which are innumerable,—scarcely one of which does man become acquainted with. Among them is this; that man is not taught immediately from heaven, but mediately. And as it is done

[1] See p. 536.

mediately, and the gospel could not come through missionaries to all that dwell on the whole globe, but yet by various ways a religion could be communicated even to the nations that dwell in the corners of the world, therefore by the Divine Providence this has been done. For no man has a religion from himself, but through another, who either himself or by communication from others knew from the Word that there is a God, that there is a heaven and a hell, that there is a life after death, and that God must be worshipped in order that a man may become blessed. Religion was transplanted throughout the whole globe from the ancient Word,[1] and afterwards from the Israelitish Word. Unless there had been a Word no one could have known of God, of heaven and hell, of the life after death, and still less, of the Lord. When once religion is implanted [in a nation] that nation is led by the Lord according to the precepts and tenets of their religion. And the Lord provides that in every religion there shall be precepts such as are in the decalogue; as, that God is to be worshipped; His name is not to be profaned; a solemn day is to be kept; parents are to be honoured; that one must not kill; nor commit adultery; nor steal; nor bear false witness. A nation which esteems these precepts Divine, and lives according to them from religion, is saved. Very many nations remote from Christendom do in fact regard these laws not as civil, but as Divine, and hold them sacred. Among the mysteries of heaven is this also :—That the angelic heaven before the Lord is as one man, whose soul and life is the Lord; and that this Divine man is in every form a man ; not only as to the external members and organs, but also as to the internal members and organs, which are more numerous ; and even as to the integuments, membranes, cartilages, and bones. Yet none of these in that man are material, but they are spiritual. Now it is provided by the Lord that even they to whom the gospel could not come, but only a religion, might also have a place in that Divine man, that is in heaven,—by constituting those parts which are called integuments, membranes, cartilages, and bones,—and that they like the others might be in heavenly joy. For it matters not whether they are in such joy as is felt by the angels of the highest heaven; or in such as is felt by the angels of the lowest heaven; for every one who comes into heaven comes into the greatest joy of his heart. A greater joy he could not endure, for he would be suffocated in it. It is as with a farmer and a king. A farmer may be in the greatest joy when he goes clad in new clothing of coarse wool, and sits down to a table upon which there is set pork, a piece of beef, cheese, beer, and a rough wine. He would be oppressed at heart if like a king he were clothed

[1] See p. 134.

in purple and silk and gold and silver, and a table were set
before him on which there were delicacies and costly luxuries of
various kinds, with the choicest wine.   From which it is plain
that for the last as well as the first there is heavenly happiness,
—for each in his degree.   So it is also with those who are out
of the Christian world, if only they shun evils as sins against
God, because they are contrary to religion.   There are a few who
are totally ignorant of God   But these also, if they have lived
a moral life, are instructed by the angels after death, and receive
a spiritual principle into their moral life.   So with those who
worship the sun and moon, and believe God to be there.   They
know no otherwise; therefore this is not imputed to them as
sin.   For the Lord says:—" *If ye were blind,*" that is if ye did
not know, " *ye should have no sin* " (John ix. 41).   And there are
many even in the Christian world who worship idols and graven
images.   This in truth is idolatrous, but not with all ; for there
are those to whom graven images serve as a means of awakening
thought concerning God.   For it is owing to influx from heaven
that he who acknowledges God desires to see Him ; and as these
cannot like interior spiritual men lift the mind above sensual
things, therefore they arouse it by a graven image or picture.
They who do this and do not worship the image itself as God,
if also from religion they live the precepts of the Decalogue, are
saved.   From these considerations it is clear that, as God wills
the salvation of all, He has also provided that every one, if he
lives well, may have some place in heaven.   (D. P. n. 254.)

PERMISSION OF PROVIDENCE WITH RESPECT TO THE MAHOMETAN
RELIGION.

The fact that this religion is received by more kingdoms than
the Christian religion may be a stumbling-block to those who
think of the Divine Providence, and at the same time believe
that no one can be saved but who is born a Christian, thus
where the Word is and by means of it the Lord is known.   But
to those who believe that all things are of the Divine Providence
the Mahometan religion is not a stumbling-block.   They inquire,
and they also find, wherein it is [of the Divine Providence].   It
is in this :—That the Mahometan religion acknowledges the
Lord as the Son of God, as the wisest of men, and as the greatest
prophet, who came into the world that he might teach men.
The greater part of them make Him greater than Mahomet.
That it may be fully known that that religion was raised up by
the Lord's Divine Providence to destroy the idolatries of many
nations, it shall be explained in a certain order.   First, therefore,

concerning the origin of idolatries. Before that religion the worship of idols was common throughout the whole earth. The reason was, that the churches before the Lord's advent were all representative churches. Such was the Israelitish church. The tent there, the garments of Aaron, the sacrifices, all things of the temple at Jerusalem, and also the statutes, were representative. And among the ancients there was a knowledge of correspondences, which is also the knowledge of representations,—the very knowledge of the wise,—especially cultivated in Egypt; whence their hieroglyphics. From this knowledge they understood what animals of every kind signified; and trees of every kind; and also mountains, hills, rivers, fountains; and the sun, moon, and stars. And as their worship was all representative, consisting of pure correspondences, therefore they had worship upon mountains and hills, and also in groves and gardens. And therefore they consecrated fountains, and in their adoration of God turned their faces to the rising sun; and moreover made sculptured horses, oxen, calves, lambs, and even birds, fishes and serpents. And these they placed in their houses and elsewhere, in an order according to that of the spiritual things of the church to which they corresponded, or which they represented. They placed similar representative things in their temples also, that they might call to remembrance the holy things which they signified. After a time, when the knowledge of correspondences was blotted out of remembrance, their posterity began to worship the sculptured images, as in themselves holy; not knowing that their ancient progenitors saw nothing holy in them, but only that according to correspondences they represented and therefore signified holy things. Hence arose the idolatries that filled the whole world,— Asia with the neighbouring islands, and Africa and Europe. That all these idolatries might be extirpated, it was brought to pass, by the Divine Providence of the Lord, that a new religion should arise, accommodated to the genius of the orientals, in which there should be something from both Testaments of the Word, and which should teach that the Lord came into the world, and that he was the greatest prophet, the wisest of all men, and the Son of God. This was accomplished through Mahomet, from whom that religion is called the Mahometan religion. This religion was raised up of the Divine Providence of the Lord, and was, as was said, accommodated to the genius of the orientals, to the end that it should destroy the idolatries of so many nations, and give some knowledge of the Lord before they should come into the spiritual world. This religion would not have been received by so many kingdoms, and could not have extirpated the idolatries, unless it had been made conformable to and on a level with the ideas of the thoughts and of the life of them all. The reason why it did not acknowledge the Lord as God of heaven and earth, was that the orientals acknowledged God the Creator of the universe, and could not comprehend that He came into the world and assumed the Human. So neither do Christians comprehend it; who therefore in their thought separate His Divinity from His Humanity, and place the Divinity beside the Father in heaven, and His Humanity,—they know not where. It may be seen from these statements that the Mahometan religion arose in fact out of the Lord's Divine Providence; and that all of that religion who acknowledge the Lord as the Son of God, and at the same time live according to the commandments of the Decalogue, which they also possess, by shunning evils as sins, come into the heaven which is called the Mahometan heaven. This heaven also is divided into three heavens, a highest, a middle, and a lowest. In the highest heaven are those who acknowledge the Lord as one with the Father, and thus as Himself the only God; in the second heaven are those who renounce polygamy and live with one wife; and in the last heaven are those who are being initiated. (D. P. n. 255.)

PERMISSION OF PROVIDENCE WITH RESPECT TO THE LIMITED PREVALENCE OF THE CHRISTIAN RELIGION.

The reason why the Christian religion exists only in the smaller portion of the habitable globe called Europe [1] is, that it was not adapted to the genius of the Orientals, like the Mahometan religion,—which, as was said above, is mixed; and a religion that is not adapted is not received. For example, a religion which decrees that it is unlawful to have more than one wife, is not received but rejected by those who for ages back have been polygamists. So also with respect to some other things ordained by the Christian religion. Nor does it matter whether a less or greater part of the world receive it, if only there are peoples with whom the Word exists; for from thence

[1] Though the knowledge of the Christian religion has been much more widely extended during the more than a century that has elapsed since this was written, yet the disparity, to a vast extent, and especially the principle involved in this permissive dispensation of Providence, remains. There does not appear to be anything, however, in the fact or in the principle, discouraging to the hope, inspired by the marvellous universal circulation of the Divine Word in this age, that the "*living waters*" that "*go forth out of Jerusalem*" (Zech. xiv. 8), will be gradually received, as the nations become prepared to receive, and the true Christian religion more and more extended, until "*all shall know the Lord, from the least unto the greatest*" (Jer. xxxi. 34). The author's writings elsewhere, in fact, give support to this belief; and these very permissions of the Divine Providence look undoubtedly, by accommodation, to this ultimate end.

there is light to those who are out of the Church and have not the Word.[1] And it is marvellous that where the Word is devoutly read and the Lord is worshipped from the Word, there the Lord is, together with heaven. This is because the Lord is the Word, and the Word is the Divine Truth which makes heaven. The Lord therefore says;—" *Where two or three are gathered together in My name, there am I in the midst of them*" (Matt. xviii. 20). This may be done with the Word by Europeans in many parts of the habitable globe; because they have commerce over the whole earth, and everywhere the Word is read or taught by them. This appears like an invention; but yet it is true. (D. P. n. 256.)

PERMISSION OF PROVIDENCE WITH RESPECT TO THE DIVISIONS AND CORRUPTIONS OF THE CHRISTIAN RELIGION.

The natural man may think within him that if the Divine Providence were universal, in the very least things, and had for its end the salvation of all, it would have caused that there should be one true religion throughout the world, and that it should not be divided, still less rent with heresies. But exercise your reason, and if you are able think more profoundly. Can a man be saved if he is not first reformed? For he is born into the love of self and of the world; and, as these loves have not within them anything of love to God, nor anything of love towards the neighbour except for the sake of self, he is also born into evils, of every kind. What is there of love or mercy in these loves? Does he make anything of defrauding another? Of blaspheming him? Of hating him, even to the death? Of committing adultery with his wife? Of venting his rage upon him, when in a state of revenge?—Seeing that in his lower mind (*animus*) he bears the desire to be highest of all, and to possess the goods of all; thus seeing that he looks upon others as trivial and of small account in comparison with himself. That such a man may be saved, must he not first be led away from his evils, and thus reformed? It has been shown above, upon many considerations, that this cannot be done except according to many laws; which are the laws of the Divine Providence. These laws are for the most part unknown, and yet they are of the Divine wisdom, and at the same time of the Divine love; against them the Lord cannot act, for to act against them would be to destroy man, and not to save him. Scan briefly the laws which have been adduced, and you will see. Since therefore it is also in accordance with these laws that there

[1] See page 130.

is no immediate influx from heaven, but a mediate influx through the Word, doctrines, and preaching; and since the Word, in order that it should be Divine, could not be written otherwise than by pure correspondences;[1] it follows that dissensions and heresies are inevitable,[2] and that the permission of them is also in accordance with the laws of the Divine Providence. And are the more when the Church itself had taken for its essentials such things as relate to the understanding, thus to doctrine, and not such as relate to the will, and thus to life, and when those that relate to life are not essentials of the church. Man is then, from his understanding, in mere darkness, and wanders about as one blind, who everywhere runs against things and tumbles into pitfalls. For the will must see in the understanding, and not the understanding in the will. Or what is the same, the life and its love must lead the understanding to think, speak, and act, and not the reverse; if the reverse then the understanding, from an evil, nay, a diabolical love, might seize upon whatever impressed it through the senses and enjoin upon the will to do it. From these considerations it may be seen whence come dissensions and heresies. But it is provided that every one, in whatever heresies he may be as to his understanding, may yet be reformed and saved,—if only he shuns evils as sins, and does not confirm the heretical falsities in himself. For by shunning evils as sins the will is reformed, and through the will the understanding; which then first from darkness comes into the light. There are three essentials of the church;—the acknowledgment of the Lord's Divinity; the acknowledgment of the holiness of the Word; and the life which is called charity. According to the life which is charity every man has faith; from the Word, he has a knowledge of what his life must be; and reformation and salvation are from the Lord. If these three had remained as the essentials of the church intellectual differences would not have divided, but only varied it; as the light gives various colours in beautiful objects; and as the various gems add beauty to the crown of a king. (D. P. n. 259.)

The Permission of Evils.

If man had not full liberty he not only could not be saved, but would even utterly perish. Hear now the reason:—Every man by birth is in evils, of many kinds. These evils are in his will; and what is in his will is loved; for what a man inwardly wills he loves, and what he loves he wills. And the love of the will flows into the understanding, and there causes its delight to

---

[1] See p. 98.   [2] See p. 121.

be felt. From thence it comes into the thoughts, and also into the intentions. If therefore a man were not permitted to think according to the love of his will, which is from inheritance in him, that love would remain shut in, and would never come to the man's sight; and the love of evil not apparent is as an enemy in ambush, as purulent matter in an ulcer, as poison in the blood, and corruption in the breast, which if kept confined lead to dissolution. But on the other hand when a man is permitted to meditate the evils of his life's love, even to intention, they may be healed by spiritual means, as diseases are by natural means.

The Lord might heal the understanding in every man, and thus cause him not to meditate evils but goods. This He might do by various fears, by miracles, by converse with the departed, and by visions and dreams. But to heal the understanding only, is merely to heal man outwardly; for the understanding with its thought is the external of man's life, and the internal of his life is the will with its affection. The healing of the understanding only would therefore be like a palliative cure, whereby the interior malignity, shut in and prevented from coming out, would consume first the neighbouring and afterwards the remoter parts, until the whole were mortified. It is the will itself that is to be healed,—not by influx of the understanding into it, for that does not take place, but by instruction and exhortation by the understanding. If only the understanding were healed man would become as a dead body embalmed, or covered over with fragrant spices and with roses; which soon would so absorb the fetid odor of the body, that they could not be applied to the nostrils of any one. So would it be with heavenly truths in the understanding if the evil love of the will were obstructed. (D. P. n. 281, 282.)

THE DIVINE PROVIDENCE IS EQUALLY WITH THE EVIL AND THE GOOD.

The Divine Providence, not only with the good but also with the evil, is universal, in the very least particulars, and yet is not in their evils. It was shown above that the Divine Providence is in the very least particulars of a man's thoughts and affections; by which is meant that a man can think and will nothing from himself, but all that he thinks and wills and therefore says and does, is from influx,—if it is good, from influx out of heaven, and if evil, from influx out of hell; or what is the same, that the good is from influx from the Lord, and the evil from the man's *proprium*. But I know that this can with difficulty be comprehended, because a distinction is made between that which flows in from heaven, or from the Lord, and that which flows in from hell, or from man's *proprium,* and yet it is said that the Divine Providence is in the very least particulars of a man's thoughts and affections,—even so far that a man cannot think and will from himself; and as it is also said that he can do this from hell, and again, from his *proprium,* it appears as if it were contradictory; but yet it is not. That it is not so will be seen in what follows. (D. P. n. 287.)

That everything that man thinks and wills and therefore that he says and does flows in from the one only fountain of life, and yet that that only fountain, which is the Lord, is not the cause of man's thinking evil and falsity, may be illustrated by these facts in the natural world:—From its sun proceed heat and light; and these two flow into all subjects and objects that appear before the eyes,—not into good subjects and beautiful objects only, but also into evil subjects and unsightly objects,— and produce varieties in them. For they flow not only into trees that bear good fruits, but into trees also that bear evil fruits; nay, even into the fruits themselves, and give them sustenance. In like manner they flow into good seed, and into tares; and into shrubs that are of good use, or wholesome, and into shrubs that are of evil use, or poisonous. And yet it is the same heat, and the same light,—in which there is no cause of evil; but this is in the recipient subjects and objects. The heat that hatches eggs wherein lurk the owl, the screech-owl, the asp, acts in the same way as when it hatches eggs in which the dove, the beautiful bird, and the swan are concealed. Place eggs of each kind under a hen, and·by her heat, which in itself is harmless, they will be hatched. But what has the heat therefore in common with these evil and noxious things? So heat in marshy, stercoraceous, putrid and cadaverous substances, operates just as when it flows into things vinous and fragrant, and into living plants and animals. Who does not see that the cause is not in the heat, but in the recipient subject? The same light also presents pleasing colours in one object, and disagreeable colours in another; nay, is lustrous and effulgent in dazzling white objects, and covers itself with shade and with darkness in things verging to black. It is the same in the spiritual world. There are heat and light there also from its sun, which is the Lord; which flow from it into their subjects and objects. The subjects and objects there are angels and spirits; in particular, their voluntary and intellectual faculties. The heat there is the proceeding Divine love, and the light is the proceeding Divine wisdom. The cause is not in them of their being differently received by one and by another; for the Lord says, that "*He maketh His sun to rise on the evil and on the good, and sendeth rain on the just and on the unjust* " (Matt. v. 45). In the highest spiritual sense the Divine Love is meant by the sun, and by rain the Divine Wisdom. (*ib.* n. 292.)

The Particular Leading of the Good and the Evil by the Divine Providence.

There are men in the world who are angels, and there are men who are devils. Heaven is from the men-angels, and hell is from the men-devils. With a man-angel all the degrees of his life are open, even up to the Lord; but with a man-devil only the ultimate degree is open, and the higher degrees are closed. A man-angel is led of the Lord both from within and from without; but a man-devil is led of himself from within, and of the Lord from without. A man-angel is led of the Lord according to order,— from within from order, from without towards order; but a man-devil is led of the Lord towards order from without, but of himself from within against order. A man-angel is continually withdrawn by the Lord from evil and led to good; and a man-devil is also continually withdrawn by the Lord from evil,— but from a more to a less grievous evil; for he cannot be led to good. A man-angel is continually led by the Lord away from hell, and led more and more interiorly into heaven ; and a man-devil is also continually led by the Lord away from hell,—but from a more grievous to a milder hell, for he cannot be led to heaven. A man-angel being led of the Lord is led by the civil law, by the moral law, and by spiritual law, on account of the Divine in them; a man-devil is led by the same laws,—but for the sake of his own in them. A man-angel from the Lord loves the goods of the church, which are also the goods of heaven, because they are goods ; likewise its truths, because they are truths ; and from himself he loves the goods of the body and of the world, because they are of use, and because they are for enjoyment ; likewise truths which appertain to the sciences ; yet he loves them from himself apparently, but actually from the Lord. And a man-devil also from himself loves the goods of the body and of the world because they are of use, and because they are for enjoyment ; likewise truths appertaining to the sciences; but he loves them apparently from himself, and actually from hell. A man-angel is in freedom and in the delight of his heart while he is doing good from good, and likewise when he is not doing evil; but a man-devil is in freedom and in the delight of his heart when he is doing good from evil, and likewise when he is doing evil. A man-angel and a man-devil may appear alike as to externals, but they are entirely unlike as to internals. They are therefore manifestly unlike when the externals are laid aside by death; the one is carried up into heaven, and the other is borne down into hell. (A. E. n. 1145.)

The Lord flows into the interiors of man's mind, and through these into its exteriors; and into the affection of his will, and through this into the thought of his understanding; and not contrariwise. To flow into the interiors of man's mind and through these into the exteriors, is to form a root and from the root to produce,—the root being in the interiors and production in the exteriors; and to flow into the affection of the will and through this into the thought of the understanding, is first to inspire a soul, and through this to form the things following. For the affection of the will is as the soul through which the thoughts of the understanding are formed. This, too, is influx from the internal into the external, which there is. Man knows nothing at all of what flows into the interiors of his mind, nor of what flows into the affection of his thought. . . . But how the Lord flows in, and man is thus led, can only be known from the spiritual world. As to his spirit, and therefore as to his affections and the thoughts from them he is in that world; for both these are of his spirit. It is this which thinks from his affection, not the body. The affections of a man, whence his thoughts proceed, have an extension into societies there, in every direction; into more or fewer societies, according to the strength and character of the affection. As to his spirit man is within these societies, is bound to them as with extended cords which circumscribe the space wherein he walks. And then as he proceeds from one affection into another, so he proceeds from one society into another; and the society in which he is, and his place in it, is the centre from which the affection and its thought runs out to the other societies, as to the circumferences,—which are thus in unbroken connection with the affection of the centre from which he then thinks and speaks. This sphere, which is the sphere of his affections and the thoughts from them, a man procures for himself in the world,—in hell if he is an evil man, if he is a good man in heaven. Man does not know that it is so, for he is unaware that such things exist. Through these societies man—that is his mind—walks, free though bound, and the Lord leads him; nor does he take a step in which and by which He does not lead. And He continually gives man to know no otherwise than that he goes in full liberty, of himself;[1] and he is permitted to persuade

---

[1] This alone, or apart from the light of the author's teaching elsewhere, might seem to imply that man's freedom is not actual; but it is necessary to bear in mind the important distinction he makes between acting freely "from himself" (*ex se*), which man does not, and acting freely "*as if* from himself" (*sicut ex se*), which he does. The freedom is actual; but that the action is from himself is only apparent, inasmuch as man has no life and source of anything in himself.

himself of this, because it is according to a law of the Divine Providence that man should be carried whithersoever his affection wills. If his affection be evil he is carried about through infernal sôcieties; and if he does not look to the Lord he is brought more inwardly and profoundly into them; and yet the Lord leads him as by the hand, permitting, and withdrawing, so far as he is willing from freedom to follow. But if he looks to the Lord he is led out of these societies, in succession, according to the order and connection in which they are,—which order and which connection is known to none but the Lord only; and thus he is brought by continual steps out of hell upwards towards heaven, and into heaven. This the Lord does while man is ignorant of it, for if a man knew he would disturb the continuity of that progress by conducting himself. · (*ib.* n. 1173, 1174.)

It shall now be explained what affection is; and then why man is led of the Lord by affections and not by thoughts. . . . *What is affection?* By affection the same is meant as by love: but love is as the fountain, and affections are as the streams from it. Thus they are also continuations of it. Love as the fountain is in man's will; the affections which are its streams flow by continuity into the understanding, and these by means of the light from truths produce thoughts,—just as the influences of heat in a garden cause germinations by means of the rays of light. In fact love in its origin is the heat of heaven, truths in their origin are rays of the light of heaven, and thoughts are germinations from their marriage union. . . . It shall now be explained, *Why man is led of the Lord by affections and not by thought.* If a man is led of the Lord by affections he can be led according to all the laws of His Divine Providence, but not if led by thoughts. Affections do not manifest themselves to a man;.but thoughts are manifested. Then, affections produce thoughts; but thoughts do not produce affections. It appears as if they produce them; but it is a fallacy. And as affections produce thoughts they likewise produce all things of the man, for they are his life. This in fact is known in the world. If you hold a man by his affection you hold him fast, and may lead him whither you will; and then one reason has the weight of a thousand. But if you do not hold a man by his affection reasons are of no avail; for the affection not agreeing either perverts, or rejects, or extinguishes them. So would it be if the Lord were to lead man by thoughts immediately, and not by affections.

And besides, when a man is led of the Lord by his affections it appears to him as if he thought freely from himself, and as if he freely spake and also acted from himself. This now is the reason why the Lord does not teach man immediately, but mediately through the Word, by doctrines and preachings from the Word, and by conversations and social intercourse; for through these means man thinks freely as if from himself. (A. E. n. 1175.)

THE DIVINE PROVIDENCE IN WITHDRAWING MAN FROM EVIL.

What the Divine Providence is with the good can be more easily comprehended than what it is with the evil. And as this is now treated of it shall be explained in the following order:—

FIRST: *In every evil there are things innumerable.* Every evil appears to man as one simple thing. So hatred and revenge, so theft and fraud, so adultery and whoredom, so pride and arrogance, and the other evils appear; and it is not known that in each evil there are innumerable things. They are more than the fibres and vessels in a man's body. For an evil man is a hell in the least form, and hell consists of myriads of myriads; and every one there is as a man in form, although monstrous and all the fibres and all the vessels in him are inverted. The spirit himself is an evil, appearing to himself as one; but the concupiscences of that evil are as innumerable as the things that are in him. For every man is his evil or his good, from the head to the sole of the foot. Since then an evil man is so constituted, it is plain that one evil is composed of things various and innumerable, which distinctly are evils, and are called the concupiscences of evil. It follows from this that all these in the order in which they are, must be restored and converted by the Lord, in order that man may be reformed; and that this can only be done by the Lord's Divine Providence successively, from a man's earliest age to his last . . . And it cannot be effected otherwise than, comparatively, as in the grafting of trees, the roots of which with some of the trunk remain; but yet the ingrafted branch converts the sap extracted through the old root into sap forming good fruit. The branch to be ingrafted cannot be taken from elsewhere than from the Lord, who is the Tree of Life; which indeed is according to the Lord's words in John xv. 1-7.

SECONDLY: *An evil man, from himself, continually brings himself more deeply into his evils.* It is said from himself, because all evil is from man; for he turns the good which is from the Lord into evil, as was said above. The real cause of an evil man leading himself more deeply into evil is, that as he wills and does evil he brings himself more and more interiorly, and also more and more deeply into infernal societies. Hence the delight of evil also increases, and this so takes possession of his thoughts that at length he feels nothing more delightful. And whoever has brought himself more interiorly and more deeply into infernal societies, becomes as it were bound about with cords. But so long as he lives in the world he does not feel the cords. They are as of soft wool or tender threads of silk, which he likes because they titillate; yet after death those cords from soft become hard, and from titillating become galling. That the delight of evil receives increase is known from thefts, robberies, plunderings, revenge, tyrannies, the love of gain, and other evils. Does not a man feel an elation of delight in them according to their success and unrestrained exercise ? . . . If the evils are in thought only and not in the will a man is not yet connected with evil in an infernal society; but when they are also in the will he then enters it. If then he also considers that this evil is contrary to the precepts of the Decalogue, and regards these as Divine, he commits it from purpose, and thereby lets himself down deeply [into the infernal society], from which he cannot be drawn out save by actual repentance.

THIRDLY : *The Divine Providence with the evil is a continual permission of evil, to the end that there may be a continual withdrawal from it.* The reason why the Divine Providence with evil men is a continual permission is that nothing but evil can come forth from their life. For a man, whether he is in good or in evil, cannot be in both at the same time, nor alternately unless he is lukewarm; and evil of life is not introduced into the will and through it into the thought by the Lord, but by man; and this is called permission. Now as every thing that an evil man wills and thinks is of permission, it is asked, What then is the Divine Providence therein, which is said to be in the very least things with every man, the evil as well as the good? But it consists in this; that it continually permits for the sake of the end, and that it permits such things as are for the end, and no others; and that the evils which proceed from permission it continually observes, separates, purifies, and those that are not concordant [with the end] it removes, and through unknown ways discharges. These things are done chiefly in man's interior will, and from this in his interior thought. The Divine Providence is continual also in this; that it is watchful that the things removed and discharged be not received again by the will, since all things that are received by the will are appropriated to man; but those that are received by the thought, and not by the will, are separated and banished. This is the continual Providence of the Lord with the evil; which, as was said, is a continual permission, to the end that there may be a perpetual withdrawal. Of these things man knows scarcely anything, because he does not perceive them. The primary reason why he does not perceive them is, that they are evils of the concupiscences of his life's love, and these evils are not felt as evils, but as delights, to which no one pays attention. Who attends to the delights of his love ? His thought floats in them, as a skiff that is borne upon the current of a river ; and is perceived as a fragrant atmosphere, which is inhaled with a full breath. He is only able to perceive something of them in his external thought ; yet he does not attend to them there unless he well knows that they are evils. But more respecting these things in what now follows.

FOURTHLY: *The withdrawal from evil is effected by the Lord in a thousand, and moreover in most mysterious ways.* Of these a few only have been disclosed to me, and indeed none but the most general ; which are, that the delights of the concupiscences,—of which a man knows nothing,—are emitted in troops and bundles into the interior thoughts, which are those of man's spirit, and thence into his exterior thoughts in which they appear,—under a certain sense of enjoyment, pleasant or passionate,—and are there mingled with his natural and sensual delights. These are the means of separation and purification, and also the ways of withdrawal and discharge. The means are chiefly the delights of meditation, thought, and reflection, with a view to certain ends which are uses ; and the ends which are uses are as many as are the particulars and least particulars of any one's business and employment ; and then they are also as many as are the delights of reflection to the end that he may appear as a civil, and a moral, and also as a spiritual man,—besides the undelightful things which interpose. These, because they are the delights of his love in the external man, are means for the separation, purification, excretion and withdrawal of the delights of the concupiscences of evil in the internal man. Take for example an unjust judge, who looks to gain or to friendships as the ends or the uses of his function. Inwardly he is continually in these ends ; but so that outwardly he may act as lawyer and a just man. He is continually in the delight of meditation, thought, reflection, and intention, as to how he may bend, turn, adapt and adjust the right, so that it shall appear conformable to the law, and analogous to justice ; nor is he conscious that his internal delight consists in cunning, fraud, deceit, clandestine theft, and many other evils ; and that that delight, composed of so many delights of the concupiscences of evil, governs in each and all the particulars of his external thought, in which are the delights of the appearance that he is just and sincere. The internal delights are let down into these external delights, and commingled like food in the stomach, and are there separated, purified, and conducted away,—but yet no others than the more baneful delights of the concupiscences of evil. For in a wicked man there is no other separation, purification, and removal, than of the more grievous evils from the less grievous. But in a good man there is a separation, purification, and removal, not only of the more grievous but of the less grievous. And this is done by the delights of affections for good and truth, and justice and sincerity, into which he comes in so far as he regards evils as sins and therefore shuns and holds them in aversion; and the more if he fights against them. These are the means by which the Lord purifies all who are saved. He also purifies them by external means, which are [the delights] of fame, of honour, and sometimes of gain. But into these the delights of affections for truth and good are introduced by the Lord, by which they are so directed and adapted that they become delights of the love of the neighbour. . . . . That the withdrawal from evils is effected by the Lord in innumerable and most mysterious ways, cannot better be seen, and thus placed beyond doubt, than from the secret operations of the soul in the body. Those of which man has cognizance are; that he looks at the food he is about to eat, perceives its odor, hungers for it, tastes it, grinds it with his teeth, rolls it with his tongue into the œsophagus, and so into the stomach. While, on the other hand, the secret operations of the soul, of which a man knows nothing, because he has no sensation of them, are; that the stomach rolls about the food received, opens and separates it by solvents, that is digests it, and offers suitable parts to the little mouths opening there and to the vessels, which imbibe them; and that it sends away some into the blood, some into the lymphatic vessels, some into the lacteal vessels of the mesentery, and some it sends down into the intestines; then that the chyle, drawn from its receptacle in the mesentery through the thoracic duct, is carried into the *vena cava,* and so into the heart, and from the heart into the lungs, and from them through the left ventricle of the heart into the aorta, and from this through its branches into the viscera of the whole body, and also into the kidneys,—in each of which there then takes place a separation and purification of the blood, and a withdrawal of heterogeneous substances. To say nothing of how the heart sends its blood, defecated in the lungs, into the brain, which is done through the arteries called the carotids; and how the brain returns the vivified blood into the *vena cava,*—just above where the thoracic duct brings in the chyle,—and so back again into the heart. These with innumerable others are the secret operations of the soul in the body. Man has no sensation of them, and he who is not versed in the science of anatomy knows nothing of them. And yet similar things take place in the interiors of a man's mind; for nothing can be effected in the body but from the mind. For the mind of man is his spirit, and his spirit is equally a man, with the only difference that the things that are done in the body are done naturally, and the things done in the mind are done spiritually; there is in every way a similarity. From these considerations it is plain that the Divine Providence operates with every man in innumerable and moreover in most secret ways; and that its continual end is to purify him, because its end is to save him; and that nothing more is incumbent upon man than to remove the evils in the external man. The rest the Lord provides if he is implored. (D. P. n. 296.)

Every Man may be reformed, and there is no Predestination.

Sound reason dictates that all are predestined to heaven, and no one to hell. . . . . The end of creation is a heaven from the human race. . . . . Every man is created that he may live to eternity in a state of happiness; thus every man is created that he may come into heaven. Divine Love cannot but will this, and Divine Wisdom cannot but provide for it. . . . . It is therefore of the Divine Providence that every man can be saved; and that they are saved who acknowledge God and live uprightly. . . . . To live uprightly is to shun evils because they are contrary to religion and therefore against God. . . . . Man is himself at fault if he is not saved. . . . . Any other predestination than to heaven is contrary to the Divine Love, which is infinite; . . . and it is contrary to the Divine Wisdom, which also is infinite. . . . . The means by which the Divine Providence works out its end, which is the salvation of man, are Divine truths whereby he has wisdom, and Divine goods whereby he has love; for he who purposes an end purposes also the means. (D. P. n. 322-331.)

The Operations of Providence for Man's Salvation are continual and progressive.

The operation of the Divine Providence to save man begins at his birth and continues to the end of his life, and afterwards to eternity. . . . . All things that are exterior to man and subserve a use to him are secondary ends of creation; which ends in the aggregate have relation to all things that exist in the three kingdoms, the animal, the vegetable, and the mineral. Since all things in these kingdoms constantly proceed according to the laws of Divine order established in their first creation, how then is it possible for the primary end, which is the salvation of the human race, not to proceed constantly according to the laws of its order, which are laws of the Divine Providence? Look only at a fruit tree. Is it not first born as a tender germ from a diminutive seed? And does it not afterwards, successively, grow to a trunk, and spread forth branches, and they are covered with leaves, and then put forth blossoms, and bear fruit, and in it form new seeds, by which it provides for its perpetuation? It is the same with every shrub, and with every herb of the field. Do not all things, even the least particulars, in them constantly and wonderfully proceed from end to end according to the laws of their order? Why not likewise the primary end, which is a heaven from the human race? Can there be anything in its progression that does not most constantly proceed according to the laws of the Divine Providence? Since there is a correspondence of the life of man with the growth of a tree, let there be a parallelism or comparison drawn between them:—The infancy of man is comparatively as the tender germ of the tree springing forth from a seed out of the earth; the childhood and youth of man are like that germ growing to a trunk, with branchlets; the natural truths with which every man is first imbued are as the leaves with which the branches are covered,—leaves have no other signification in the Word; man's initiations into the marriage of good and truth, or the spiritual marriage, are as the blossoms that the tree produces in the time of spring; spiritual truths are the leaflets of those blossoms; the earliest [effects] of the spiritual marriage are as the inchoate forms of the fruit; spiritual goods, which are goods of charity, are as the fruit,— they also are signified by fruits in the Word; the procreations of wisdom from love are as the seeds,—by which procreations man becomes as a garden and a paradise. Man is indeed described by a tree in the Word, and his wisdom from love by a garden; nothing else is signified by the Garden of Eden. It is true that man is an evil tree from the seed; but there is vouchsafed a grafting or inoculation with branchlets taken from the Tree of Life, whereby the sap drawn out of the old root is turned into sap forming good fruit. This comparison is made that it may be seen, that since there is a so constant progression of the Divine Providence in the vegetation and regeneration of trees, it must certainly be constant in the reformation and regeneration of men, who are of far more value than the trees,—according to these words of the Lord:—"*Are not five sparrows sold for two farthings, and not one of them is forgotten before God? But even the very hairs of your head are all numbered. Fear not therefore; ye are of more value than many sparrows. . . . . And which of you with taking thought can add to his stature one cubit? If ye then be not able to do that which is least, why take ye thought for the rest? Consider the lilies, how they grow. . . . . If then God so clothe the grass, which is to-day in the field, and to-morrow is cast into the oven, how much more [will he clothe] you, O ye of little faith.*" (Luke xii. 6, 7, 25-28.)   (D. P. n. 332.)

REASON WHY THE DIVINE PROVIDENCE OPERATES INVISIBLY AND INCOMPREHENSIBLY.

The Divine Providence operates invisibly and incomprehensibly in order that a man may be able to ascribe it, freely, either to Providence or to chance.   For, if Providence should act visibly and comprehensibly, there would be danger that from the visible and comprehensible a man might believe a thing to be of Providence, and afterwards come into the opposite belief. Truth and falsity would thus be conjoined in the interior man, and the truth would be profaned,—which carries damnation with it.   Such a man is therefore rather kept in unbelief, than that he should once be in the faith and then recede from it. This is what is meant in Isaiah:—"*Say unto this people, Hearing, hear ye but understand not; and seeing, see ye, and perceive not; make the heart of this people fat, and make their ears heavy, and shut their eyes; lest peradventure they see with their eyes, and hear with their ears, and their heart understand, and they be converted and healed*" (vi. 9, 10; John xii. 40).   And hence it is that at this day no miracles are wrought; for these, like all visible and comprehensible things, would constrain men to believe; and whatever constrains takes away the freedom; whereas, all reformation and regeneration of a man is effected in his freedom.   Whatever is not implanted in freedom does not remain.   It is implanted in freedom when the man is in an affection for good and truth. . . . . That at this day a man ought to believe what he does not see is established by the Lord's words to Thomas, in John:—"*Thomas, because thou hast seen me thou hast believed; blessed are they that do not see, and yet believe*" (xx. 29).   (A. C. n. 5508.)

FATE.

While I was conversing with the angels respecting the Lord's Divine Providence there were also spirits present, who had im pressed upon themselves that there was something of fate or absolute necessity in it. They supposed the Lord to act from that necessity because he cannot but proceed according to the veriest essentials, therefore according to those [principles] which are of the most perfect order. But it was shown them that man has freedom ; and that if he has freedom it is not of necessity. This was illustrated by reference to houses that are to be built; in that the bricks, the lime, the sand, the stones serving for pedestals and pillars, the joists and beams, and many such materials, are brought together, not in the order in which the house is to be constructed, but at pleasure ;—and that the Lord only knows what kind of a house can be built of them. All things are most essential which are from the Lord ; but they do not follow in order from necessity, but in accommodation to man's freedom. (A. C. n. 6487.)

FORTUNE AND CHANCE.

Who does not speak of fortune ? And who since he speaks of it, and since he knows something of it from experience, does not acknowledge it ? Yet who knows what it is ? That it is something cannot be denied, for it is real and is ordained ; and nothing can really be and be ordained without a cause. But the cause of this something, or fortune, is unknown. And lest it should be denied, from mere ignorance of the cause, take dice or playing cards, and play; or consult players. Who of them denies fortune ? For they play with it, and it with them, wonderfully: Who can strive against it, if it be obstinate ? Does it not then laugh at prudence and wisdom ? Is it not, while you shake the dice and shuffle the cards, as if it knew and disposed the movements and turnings of the joints of the hand, to favour one more than another for some cause ? Can there be a cause from elsewhere than the Divine Providence in ultimates, where by means of certainties and uncertainties it deals wonderfully with human prudence, and at the same time conceals itself ? It is known that the heathen anciently acknowledged Fortune, and built a temple to it, as did also the Italians at Rome. Respecting this Fortune,—which as was said is the Divine Providence in ultimates,—it has been given me to know many things that I am not permitted to make public, from which it was evident to me, that it is no illusion of the mind, nor freak of nature ; nor any thing without a cause, for this is nothing ; but that it is ocular evidence that the Divine Providence is in the very least particulars of the thoughts and actions of men. Since there is a Divine Providence in the very least particulars of things so trivial and unimportant, why not in the very least particulars of things not trivial and unimportant, such as the affairs of peace and war in the world, and matters pertaining to salvation and life in heaven ? (D. P. n. 212.)

ACCIDENTS.

I have often conversed with spirits respecting fortune ; which in the world appears as a fortuitous event, because they know not whence it is,—and because they know not whence it is some deny that it is. When such a thing befell me as appeared an accident, it was said by the angels, that it occurred because there were such spirits present : and that when the accident is evil the sphere of such spirits prevailed. In truth the evil spirits by their arts contrived to produce a sphere from which unfortunate cirumstances arose which plainly appeared as by chance. And it was further said that all things, nay, the least of all, even to the least particulars of the least, are directed by the Lord's Providence,—even as to the very steps ; but when such a sphere as is contrary to it prevails misfortunes occur. And it was confirmed by them that there is no chance ; and that apparent accident or fortune is Providence in the ultimate of order, in which all things are relatively inconstant. (A. C. n. 6493.)

All evils, even those that occur by accident, come from hell. Of this the infernal genii are ignorant ; they nevertheless burst forth from them. For the inmost and interior heaven, as *media* or mediations, dispose and minister the things which are foreseen and provided by God the Messiah because they are salutary to the human race. These, with men who trust in themselves and indulge in the loves of self and the world, are immediately changed into evils,—also into accidents. Thus there is not even the least evil that befalls man which does not break forth from hell. (S. D. n. 224.)

DIVINE PROVIDENCE IN RESPECT TO THE TIME OF MAN'S DEATH.

The life of every man, both how long and how he will live, is foreseen by the Lord ; and therefore from the earliest infancy he is directed towards life in eternity. So that the Lord's Providence begins with the earliest infancy. There are reasons why some die in childhood, some in youth, some in adult age, and some in old age. The first regards a man's use to men in the world. The second has regard to the use [arising out of the fact that] while he is in the world he is with angels and spirits ; for he **is** with spirits as to his interiors, and so long as he is in the world there is that there in which all things close. The third regards use to himself in the world ; either that he may be regenerated, or that he may be let into his evils, so that they may not lie dormant and afterwards break forth,—which would be to his eternal ruin. So also the fourth reason has regard to his use in the other life, and to eternity, after death. For every one who goes to heaven has his place in the Greatest Man,—or who goes to hell, in the opposite ; wherever men are wanting to preserve an equilibrium thither they are brought by the Lord's Providence. Thus is the Lord's kingdom cared for, the welfare of which is universal Providence. (S. D. n. 5002, 5003. See also A. C. n. 6807.)

CARE FOR THE MORROW.

The manna was given to the Israelites every morning, and worms were bred in the residue ; by which is signified that the Lord daily provides necessaries, and that therefore men ought not to be anxious about acquiring them of themselves. This is also meant by the *daily bread* in the Lord's Prayer ; and like-wise by the Lord's words in Matthew :—" *Take no thought for your life, what ye shall eat, or what ye shall drink ; nor yet for your body, what ye shall put on.* . . *Why take ye thought for raiment ? Consider the lilies of the field, how they grow ; they toil not, neither do they spin.* . . . *Therefore, take no thought, saying, What shall we eat ? or, What shall we drink ? or, Wherewithal shall we be clothed ? For after all these things do the Gentiles seek. For your heavenly Father knoweth that ye have need of all these things. But seek ye first the kingdom of God, and His righteous-ness; and all these things shall be added unto you. Take therefore no thought for the morrow ; for the morrow shall take thought for the things of itself* " (vi. 25-34). For the subject treated of in this verse (Ex. xvi. 20) and the following, in the internal sense, is care for the morrow ; and it teaches that this care it not only prohibited but also condemned. That it is prohibited is signified by the injunction that they should not leave a residue of the manna until the morning ; and that it is condemned is signified by the fact that worms were bred in the residue, and that it be-came putrid. One who looks at the subject no farther than according to the sense of the letter may believe that all care for the morrow is to be cast off, and thus that necessaries are to be daily expected from heaven ; but he who looks at the subject more deeply than from the letter, that is to say from the internal sense, is able to understand what is meant by care for the morrow. It does not mean the care of procuring for one's self food and raiment, nor even provision for the time to come ; for it is not contrary to order to exercise forethought for one's self and one's own. But they have care for the morrow who are not content with their lot ; who do not trust in the Divine [Being], but in themselves ; and who only look to worldly and terrestrial things, and not to heavenly. There universally prevails with them a solicitude about things to come, a longing to possess all things, and to rule over all, which is inflamed and increased with their aggrandizement, and finally beyond all measure. They grieve if they do not obtain the objects of their desire, and are in anguish when they suffer the loss of them. Nor is there any consolation for them ; for they are then angry against the Divine, reject it together with all faith, and curse themselves. Such are they with whom there is care for the morrow. It is entirely different with those who trust in the Divine [Being]. Although they have a care for the morrow yet they have it not ; for they do not think of the morrow with solicitude, still less with anxiety. They are of tranquil mind whether they obtain the objects of their desire or not ; nor do they grieve at their loss. They are content with their lot. If they become opulent they do not set their heart upon opulence; if exalted to honours, they do not regard themselves more worthy than others. If they become poor they are not made sad ; if in humble condition they are not dejected. They know that to them who trust in the Divine [Being] all things advance to a happy state in eternity; and that whatever circumstances befall them in time they are yet conducive to that end. It should be known that the Divine Providence is universal, that is, in the very least particulars of all things ; and that they who are in the stream of Providence are continually borne along to happinesses, however the means may appear; and that they are in the stream of Providence who put their trust in the Divine [Being] and ascribe all things to Him ; and that they who trust in themselves only, and attribute all things to themselves, are not in the stream of Providence. They are indeed in opposition to it ; for they derogate from the Divine Providence, and ascribe it to themselves. It should be known also, that in so far as any one is in the stream of Providence he is in a state of peace ; and in so far as one is in a state of peace from the good of faith, or trust, he is within the Divine Providence. (A. C. n. 8478.)

THE HUMAN SOUL.

THE soul as to its every quality is unknown, especially in the learned world. This is evident from the fact that some believe it to be an ethereal principle, some a sort of flame or fire, some merely the thinking principle, some the vital principle in general, some the natural active principle. And what still further attests their ignorance of the nature of the soul, they assign it to various places in the body ; some place it in the heart, some in the brain and in the fibres there, some in the *corpora striata*, others in the ventricles, and others in the *exigua glandula;* some in every part. But then what they conceive of is a vital principle that is common to every living thing. From all which it is plain that nothing is known about the soul. This is the reason why all that has been offered respecting the soul is conjectural. And because they could thus form no idea of the soul, very many could but believe that it is nothing else than a vital something which when the body dies is dissipated. Hence it is then that the learned have less belief than the simple in a life after death ; and as they do not believe in it, neither can they believe in the things relating to that life, which are the celestial and spiritual things of faith and love. This is evident also from the Lord's words in Matthew : " *Thou hast hid these things from the wise and prudent, and hast revealed them unto babes* " (xi. 25) ; and again :— " *Seeing they see not, and hearing they hear not, neither do they understand* " (xiii. 13). For the simple have no such thoughts about the soul, but believe that they shall live after death ; in which simple faith is concealed,—although they are not aware of it,—a belief that they shall live there as men, shall see the angels, converse with them, and enjoy happines. (A. C. n. 6053.)

WHAT THE SOUL IS.

In the universal sense a soul is that from which another thing exists and lives. Thus the soul of the body is its spirit, for from this the body lives; and the soul of the spirit is its still more interior life, from which it discerns and understands. (A. C. n. 2930.)

There are three parts of which every man consists, and which follow in order within him; the soul (*anima*), the mind (*mens*), and the body. His inmost is the soul, his intermediate is the mind, and his ultimate is the body. All that flows from the Lord into man flows into his inmost, which is his soul, and descends thence into his intermediate, which is the mind, and through this into his ultimate, which is the body. (C. L. n. 101.)

The soul is the inmost and highest part of man; and into this influx from God takes place, and descends thence into the parts that are below it, and vivifies them according to reception. The truths which are to be truths of faith do indeed flow in through the hearing, and so are implanted in the mind (*mens*), thus below the soul; but by these truths a man is only set in order for the reception of the influx from God through the soul; and such as the order is such is the reception, and such the transformation of natural faith into spiritual faith. (T. C. R. n. 8.) See also pp. 24, 57.

As regards the soul, of which it is said it shall live after death, it is nothing else than the man himself who lives in the body; that is, the interior man, who through the body acts in the world, and who confers life upon the body. This man when he is loosed from the body is called a spirit,[1] and then appears completely in the human form; yet he can in nowise be seen by the eyes of the body. But he can be by the eyes of the spirit, and to the eyes of the spirit he appears as a man in the world; has senses, touch, smell, hearing, sight, far more exquisite than in the world; has appetites, pleasures, desires, affections, loves, such as he had in the world, but in a surpassing degree; thinks also as in the world, but more perfectly; converses with others; in a word, is there as in the world, insomuch that if he does not reflect upon the fact that he is in the other life he does not know but that he is in the world,—as I have sometimes heard

---

[1] The soul is here considered, in its wider and more general sense, as including its derivations. Specifically and strictly the soul is the inmost, and is the very man; but comprehensively, as here represented, it is the whole spirit of man, or all that lives after death. All of this that is below the soul is derived from and is as it were an extension of the soul. Thus the author says in another place:—"The soul is a human form, from which not the least can be taken away, and to which not the least can be added; and it is the inmost form of all the forms of the whole body; and the forms that are without receive both essence and form from the inmost. . . . In a word, the soul is the very man, because it is the inmost man; and therefore its form is fully and perfectly the human form. Yet it is not life, but is the proximate receptacle of life from God, and so is the habitation of God." (C. L. n. 315.) See also p. 457, *note.*

from spirits. For the life after death is a continuation of the life in the world. This then is the soul of man, which lives after death. But lest the idea should fail to be apprehended (*cadat in ignotum quid*) through using the term soul,—in consequence of the conjectural or hypothetical [preconceptions] concerning it,—it is better to say the spirit of man, or, if you prefer, the interior man. For he there appears entirely as a man, with all the members and organs in which man appears, and is in truth the man himself that was in the body. That this is so is indeed evident from the angels seen, of which we read in the Word, who all appeared in the human form; for all the angels in heaven have the human form because the Lord is in that form, who so often appeared as a man, after his resurrection. (A. C. n. 6054.)

It should be known that man's spirit in the body is in the whole and in every part of it; and that it is the purer substance of it,—as well in its organs of motion as of sense, and every where else; and that his body is the material substance every where annexed to it, adapted to the world in which he then is. This is what is meant by saying that man is a spirit, and the body serves him for uses in the world; and that the spirit is the internal of man, and the body his external. (*ib.* n. 4659.)

Origin of the Soul.

By no wise man is it doubted that the soul is from the father. It is in fact manifestly to be seen from the minds (*animi*), and also from the faces which are the types of the minds, in descendants which proceed in regular line from the fathers of families; for as in an image the father returns, if not in his sons yet in his grandsons and great-grandsons. And this comes from the cause, that the soul constitutes the inmost of man; and though this may be covered over in the next offspring yet it comes forth and reveals itself in the descendants afterwards. That the soul is from the father, and its clothing from the mother, may be illustrated by analogies in the vegetable kingdom. Here the earth or ground is the common mother; It receives into itself as in a womb and clothes the seeds; nay, it as it were conceives, bears, brings forth, and nurtures, as a mother her offspring from the father. (C. L. n. 206.)

Discrete and Continuous Degrees.

He who does not know the method of Divine order in respect to degrees cannot comprehend in what manner the heavens are distinct, nor indeed the nature of the internal and the external man. Most men in the world have no other idea of things interior and exterior, or higher or lower, than as of what is continuous, or connected by continuity from purer to grosser; but things interior and exterior in respect to each other are not continuous but discrete. Degrees are of two kinds; there are continuous degrees, and degrees that are not continuous. Continuous degrees are as the degrees of diminution of light, from the flame to darkness; or as the degrees of diminution of sight, from the things that are in the light to those that are in the shade; or as the degrees of purity of the atmosphere from lowest to highest. Distances determine these degrees. But degrees that are not continuous but discrete are distinguished as prior and posterior, as cause and effect, and as that which produces and that which is produced. Whoever investigates will see that in all, even the least things in the universal world, whatever they are, there are such degrees of production and composition; namely, that from one thing proceeds another, and from that a third, and so on. He who does not acquire a perception of these degrees can by no means have a knowledge of the distinctions of the heavens, and the distinctions of the interior and exterior faculties of man; nor of the distinction between the spiritual world and the natural world; nor of the distinction between the spirit of man and his body: and therefore cannot understand what and whence correspondences and representations are, nor what is the nature of influx. Sensual men do not comprehend these distinctions; for they make increase and decrease even according to these degrees continuous. They are therefore unable to conceive of the spiritual except as a purer natural. (H. H. n. 38.)

The knowledge of degrees is as it were the key to open the causes of things, and give entrance into them. Without this knowledge scarcely any thing of cause can be known; for, the objects and subjects of both worlds appear, without this knowledge, of one significance (*univoca*),—as if there were nothing in them except of such a nature as that which is seen with the eye; when yet this, relatively to the things that lie concealed within, is as one to thousands, nay to myriads. Unless degrees are understood the interior things which lie concealed can by no means be discovered, for exterior things advance to interior, and these to inmost, by degrees,—not by continuous but by discrete degrees . . . They are called discrete degrees, because the prior exists by itself, the posterior by itself, and the ultimate by itself, and yet taken together they form one. The atmospheres, which are called ether and air, from highest to lowest, or from the sun to the earth, are discrete in such degrees; and are as simples, the congregates of these simples, and the congregates of these again, which taken together are called a composite.

All things, even the least that exist in the spiritual world and in the natural world, coexist from discrete degrees and at the same time from continuous degrees, or from degrees of height and degrees of breadth. That dimension which consists of discrete degrees is called height, and that which consists of continuous degrees is called breadth. Their situation relative to the sight of the eye does not change their denomination.

That it may be still better comprehended what discrete degrees are and the nature of them, and what the difference is between them and continuous degrees, take for example the angelic heavens:—There are three heavens, and these are distinguished by degrees of height; one heaven is therefore below another; nor do they communicate with each other except by influx, which proceeds from the Lord through the heavens in their order to the lowest, and not contrariwise. But each heaven in itself is distinguished not by degrees of height but by degrees of breadth; they who dwell in the midst or in the centre are in the light of wisdom, and they who dwell towards the circumferences even to the boundaries are in the shade of wisdom. Thus wisdom decreases to ignorance just as light decreases to shade, which is by continuity. It is the same with men. The interiors which are of their minds are distinguished into as many degrees as the angelic heavens, and one of these degrees is above another. The interiors of men which are of their minds are therefore distinguished by discrete degrees, or degrees of height. Hence it is that a man may be in the lowest degree, then in the higher, and even in the highest, according to the degree of his wisdom; and that when he is only in the lowest degree, the higher degree is closed, and that this is opened as he receives wisdom from the Lord. There are also in man, as in heaven, continuous degrees or degrees of latitude. That a man is similar to the heavens is because, as to the interiors of his mind in so far as he is in love and in wisdom from the Lord, he is heaven in its least form. (D. L. W. n. 184-186.)

All things that exist in the world of which threefold dimension is predicated, or which are called compound, consist in degrees of height or discrete degrees. But this shall be illustrated by examples:—It is known by ocular experience that each muscle in the human body consists of very minute fibres, and that these composed in little bundles form the larger fibres called moving fibres, and that from the bundles of these arises the composite, which is called a muscle. It is the same with the nerves; of the very small fibres in them the larger are composed, which appear as filaments; of an assemblage of these is the nerve composed. So is it with the other combinations, fasciculations, and assemblages of which the organs and viscera consist; for they are compositions of fibres and vessels variously fashioned through similar degrees. It is the same too with each and every thing in the vegetable kingdom, and with each and every thing in the mineral kingdom. In wood there is a combination of filaments in threefold order; in metals and in stones also there is an accumulation of parts in threefold order. It is plain from these illustrations what is the nature of discrete degrees; namely, that one is from another, and by means of the second a third, which is called composite; and that each degree is discrete from the other.

From these examples a conclusion may be formed respecting those things which are not visible to the eyes, for the case is the same with them; as for example, with the organic substances which are the receptacles and abodes of the thoughts and affections in the brain; with the atmospheres; with heat and light; and with love and wisdom. For the atmospheres are receptacles of heat and light, as heat and light are receptacles of love and wisdom. Since therefore there are degrees of atmospheres, there are also similar degrees of heat and light, and of love and wisdom; for the method of these is not different from that of the former. (*ib.* n. 190, 191.)

The first degree is all in all in the subsequent degrees. The reason of this is that the degrees of every subject and of every thing are homogeneous; and they are homogeneous because produced from the first degree. For the formation of them is such that the first, by confasciculations or conglobations, in a word by assemblages, produces the second, and by this the third; and distinguishes each from the other, by a covering thrown around it. It is therefore plain that the first degree is the principal, and is solely regnant in the subsequent degrees; consequently that the first degree is all in all in the subsequent degrees. (*ib.* n. 194, 195.)

Successive and Simultaneous Order of Discrete Degrees.

There is a successive order, and a simultaneous order. The successive order of these degrees is from the highest to the lowest, or from summit to base. The angelic heavens are in this order; the third heaven is the highest in order, the second is the middle, and the first is the lowest; such is their relative situation. The states of love and wisdom with the angels there is in similar successive order; so also the states of heat and light, and of the spiritual atmospheres. In similar order are all the perfections of forms and powers there. When degrees of height or discrete degrees are in successive order, they may be compared to a column divided into three degrees, through which there is an ascent and descent; in the highest abode of which are things most perfect and most beautiful, in the middle things less perfect and beautiful, and in the lowest things still less perfect and beautiful. But the simultaneous order which consists of similar degrees presents another appearance. In this order the highest things of successive order, —which as was said are the most perfect and most beautiful,— are in the inmost, the lower things are in the middle, and the lowest in the circumference. They are as in a solid consisting of these three degrees; in the middle or centre of which are the most subtile parts, around this are the less subtile parts, and in the extremes which form the circumference are the parts composed of these, and therefore the grosser. It is like the column mentioned just above subsiding into a plane, the highest part of which forms the inmost, the middle part forms the intermediate, and the lowest forms the extreme. (*ib.* n. 205.)

THREE DISCRETE DEGREES OF THE MIND.

These three degrees of height are from birth in every man; and may be successively opened; and as they are opened the man is in the Lord and the Lord in him. It has hitherto been unknown that there are three degrees of height in every man; for the reason that the degrees have been unrecognized, and so long as these degrees lay hidden none but continuous degrees could be known; and when these only are known, it may be supposed that love and wisdom in a man increase only by continuity. But it should be known that there are three degrees of height or discrete degrees in every man from his birth, one degree above or within another; and that each degree of height or discrete degree has also degrees of breadth, or continuous degrees, according to which it increases by continuity. For there are both kinds of degrees in the greatest and the least of all things.

These three degrees are named natural, spiritual, and celestial. When a man is born he comes first into the natural degree; and this increases within him by continuity, according to his knowledge and the understanding acquired thereby, to the highest point of understanding called the rational. But yet the second degree which is called spiritual is not thereby opened. This is opened by the love of uses from things intellectual, that is by a spiritual love of uses, which is love towards the neighbour. This degree likewise may increase by degrees of continuity to its highest; and it increases by cognitions of truth and good, or by spiritual truths. Yet even by these the third or celestial degree is not opened; but this is opened by a celestial love of use, which is love to the Lord; and love to the Lord is nothing else than committing to life the precepts of the Word; the sum of which is to flee from evils because they are infernal and diabolical, and to do good works because they are heavenly and Divine. In this manner these three degrees are successively opened in man.

A man knows nothing of the opening of these degrees within him, so long as he lives in the world; because he is then in the natural which is the ultimate degree, and from this thinks, wills, speaks, and acts; and the spiritual degree, which is interior, does not communicate with the natural degree by continuity but by correspondence, and communication by correspondence is not felt. But when a man puts off the natural degree, which he does when he dies, he comes into the degree that was opened within him in the world; into the spiritual degree he in whom the spiritual degree has been opened; into the celestial degree he in whom the celestial degree has been opened. (D. L. W. n. 236-238.)

A knowledge of these degrees is at this day of the greatest utility; since many because they do not know them abide and stick fast in the lowest degree, wherein their bodily senses are; and on account of their ignorance, which is intellectual darkness, cannot be elevated into the spiritual light which is above them. Hence they are as it were spontaneously seized with naturalism, as soon as they undertake to search into and investigate any matter relating to the human soul and mind, and its rationality; and especially if anything relating to heaven and the life after death. (Influx, n. 16.)

In each Degree there is a Will and Understanding.

Since there are three degrees of love and wisdom and therefore of use in man, it follows that there are three degrees of the will and of the understanding, and therefore of conclusion and so of determination to use, in him. For the will is the receptacle of love, and the understanding is the receptacle of wisdom, and the conclusion from them is use. From which it is plain that in every man there is a natural, a spiritual, and a celestial understanding,—potentially from birth, and actually when they are opened. In a word, the mind (*mens*) of man, which consists of will and understanding, from creation and therefore from birth is of three degrees; so that man has a natural mind, a spiritual mind, and a celestial mind; and he can thereby be elevated to and possess angelic wisdom while he lives in the world. But yet he cannot enter into it until after death; and then, if he becomes an angel, he talks of things that to the natural man are ineffable and incomprehensible. (D. L. W. n. 239.)

A YET INTERIOR REGION OF THE UNDERSTANDING, ABOVE THE CELESTIAL, IN THE INMOST MAN.

There are three degrees of things intellectual in man; his lowest [degree] is the knowing [faculty]; the intermediate is the rational;[1] the highest is the intellectual. These are so distinct that they are never confounded. But that man is not cognizant of this, is because he places life in the sensual and knowing [faculty]; and while he cleaves to this [notion] he cannot even be aware that the rational is distinct from the knowing, still less then that it is so from the intellectual. When yet the truth is that the Lord flows into man through the intellectual into his rational, and through the rational into the knowing [faculty] of memory. Thence comes the life of the senses,—of the sight, and of the hearing. This is the true influx; and this is the true intercourse of the soul with the body. Without an influx of the Lord's life into things intellectual in man,—or rather into things of the will, and through these into things intellectual,—and through things intellectual into things rational, and through things rational into his matters of knowledge, which are of the memory, life cannot be imparted to man. And although a man is in falsities and in evils, yet there is an influx of the Lord's life through things of the will into things intellectual,—but the things that flow in are received by the rational according to its form; and this enables man to reason, to reflect, and to understand what is true and good. (A. C. n. 657.)

There are in man things intellectual, rational, and of knowledge; his inmost things are the intellectual, his interior are the rational, and his exterior are matters of knowledge. These are called his spiritual things, which are in such order. (*ib.* n. 1443.)

In every man intellectual truth, which is internal and in his

---

[1] In the aspect of the understanding here presented, its spiritual and celestial degrees appear to be taken together,—as in the following section,—as constituting the rational mind, of which they are respectively the exterior and the interior.

inmost, is not man's but the Lord's in man. From this the Lord flows into the rational, where truth first appears as if it were man's own; and through the rational into the knowing [faculty]. From which it is clear that a man can never think as of himself from intellectual truth; but from rational and known truth; because these appear as his own. (*ib.* n. 1904.)

The Lord, while He lived in the world, thought from intellectual truth; which, because it is above the rational, could perceive and see what was the nature of the rational. . . . The interior can perceive what exists in the exterior, or what is the same, the higher can see what is in the lower; but not *vice versa.* . . . Perception is an interior [intellection] *in* the rational. . . . What it is to think from intellectual truth cannot be explained to the apprehension; and this the less because no one has thought from that affection and from that truth except the Lord. Who thinks from that is above the angelic heaven; for the angels of the third heaven do not think from intellectual truth, but from interior rational truth. (*ib.* n. 1904, 1914). See also pp. 24, 57, 542.

In man there is no pure intellectual truth, that is truth Divine;[1] but the truths of faith which are in man are appearances of truth, to which fallacies which are of the senses adjoin themselves. (*ib.* n. 2053.)

The Rational and the Natural Mind.

By the natural and the rational the man himself is meant, in so far as he is formed to receive the celestial and the spiritual; but by the rational his internal is meant, and by the natural his external. (A. C. n. 5150.)

By the natural, here and elsewhere, the natural mind is meant. For there are two minds in man; the rational mind and the natural mind. (*ib.* n. 5301.)

It must be stated in a few words what the rational is:—The intellectual [part] of the internal man is called the rational; on the other hand, the intellectual [part] of the external man is called the natural. Thus the rational is internal, and the natural is external; and they are most distinct from each other. But a man is not truly rational unless he is what is called a celestial man, who has a perception of good, and from good a perception of truth; while he who has not this perception, but only a cognition that it is truth, because he is so instructed, and from this a conscience, is not truly a rational man, but an

---

[1] See pp. 566, 567.

interior natural man. Such are they who are of the Lord's spiritual church. They differ from each other as the light of the moon differs from the light of the sun; and therefore the Lord actually appears as a moon to the spiritual, and as a sun to the celestial. Many in the world think a man is rational who can reason ingeniously on many subjects, and can so connect his reasonings that his conclusion appears as the truth. But this [ability] falls to the lot even of the worst men, who can skilfully reason and show that evils are goods and that falsities are truths, and also the contrary. But whoever reflects must see that this is depraved phantasy, and not rational. The rational is [the faculty] to see and perceive from within that a good is good, and from this that a truth is truth; for the sight and perception of these is from heaven. (*ib.* n. 6240.)

The interior rational constitutes the first degree in man; in this are the celestial angels, or in this is the inmost or third heaven. The exterior rational forms another degree, in which are the spiritual angels, or in which is the intermediate or second heaven. The interior natural forms a third degree, in which are good spirits, or the ultimate or first heaven. The exterior natural forms a fourth degree, in which man is. (*ib.* n. 5145.)

Evils and Falsities reside in the Natural degree of the Mind.

All evils, and the falsities from them, both hereditary and acquired, reside in the natural mind. The reason is that that mind in its form or image is a world; while the spiritual mind in its form or image is a heaven, and evil cannot be a guest in heaven. This mind therefore is not opened from birth, but is only in the capability of being opened. The natural mind also takes its form in part from the substances of the natural world; but the spiritual mind, only from the substances of the spiritual world,—which are preserved by the Lord in their integrity, that man may be capable of becoming a man. He is born an animal; but becomes a man. The natural mind, with all things pertaining to it, revolves in spiral motions from right to left; but the spiritual mind, in spiral motions from left to right. These minds are thus in a contrary movement relatively to each other; an indication that evil resides in the natural mind, and that of itself it acts against the spiritual mind. And the spiral motion from right to left is downwards, thus towards hell; but the spiral movement from left to right goes upwards, thus towards heaven. (D. L. W. n. 270.)

The Action and Reaction of the Natural and Spiritual Mind.

If the spiritual mind is closed the natural mind continually acts against the things which are of the spiritual mind, and is afraid lest any thing should flow in from thence, because it would disturb its own states. All that flows in through the spiritual mind is from heaven, for the spiritual mind in its form is a heaven ; and all that flows into the natural mind is from the world, for the natural mind is a world in form. From which it follows, that when the spiritual mind is closed the natural mind reacts against all things of heaven, and does not admit them,—except in so far as they serve it as means for acquiring and possessing the things of the world. And when those things even which belong to heaven serve the natural mind as means to its ends, then those means, though they appear heavenly, become natural; for the end qualifies them. They in truth become as matters of knowledge belonging to the natural man, in which internally there is nothing of life. But as heavenly things cannot be so conjoined to natural that they act as one, they separate, and things heavenly with merely natural men take their place without, round about the natural things that are within. Hence it is that a merely natural man can talk of heavenly things, and preach them, and even simulate them in his actions, although within he thinks against them. This he does when alone, and that when he is in company. (D. L. W. n. 261.)

But when the spiritual mind is opened the state of the natural mind is entirely different. Then the natural mind is disposed to obedience to the spiritual mind, and is subordinated. The spiritual mind acts upon the natural mind from above or from within, and removes the things therein which react, and adapts to itself those that act in the same manner with itself. It thereby gradually takes away the predominant reaction. (*ib.* n. 263.)

The Closing of the Spiritual Degree of the Mind.

With those who as to life are in evils the spiritual degree is closed, and more completely with those who from evils are in falsities. It is the same as with the fibril of a nerve, which from the least touch of any heterogeneous body contracts itself. So every motive fibre of a muscle, nay, the whole muscle itself, and even the whole body contracts from the touch of any thing hard or cold. Thus do also the substances or forms of the spiritual degree in man shrink from evils and the falsities from them, because they are heterogeneous. For the spiritual degree since it is in the form of heaven admits nothing but goods, and truths which are from good. These are homogeneous to it; but evils and the falsities which are from evil are heterogeneous to it. This degree is contracted and by contraction is closed, especially, with those who in the world are in the love of rule from the love of self, because this love is the opposite of love to the Lord. It is closed also, but not so entirely, with those who from the love of the world have a mad desire to possess the goods of others. The reason why these loves close the spiritual degree is that they are the origins of evils. The contraction or shutting of this degree is like the retortion of a spiral in the opposite direction; for which reason that degree, after it is closed, turns back the light of heaven. Hence instead of the light of heaven there is darkness there, so that truth which is in the light of heaven becomes nauseous. With these not only is the spiritual degree itself closed, but also the higher region of the natural, which is called the rational,—until the lowest region of the natural degree only, which is called the sensual, stands open; for this is nearest to the world and to the outward senses of the body, from which the man afterwards thinks, speaks, and reasons. (D. L. W. n. 254.)

A Man is perfected in the other Life according to the Degree opened in the World.

Every angel is perfected in wisdom to eternity; but each one according to the degree of affection for good and truth in which he was when he departed from the world. It is this degree which is perfected to eternity; what is beyond this degree is without the angel, and not within him; and that which is without him cannot be perfected within him. (D. P. n. 334.)

The Will and Understanding are Organic Forms.

Since the will and understanding are receptacles of love and wisdom, therefore they are two organic forms, or forms organized from the purest substances; they must be such that they may be receptacles. It is no objection that their organization is not visible to the eye; it is interior to its vision, even when increased by microscopes. Even very small insects are interior to the sight, yet there are within them organs of sense and motion;

for they feel, and walk, and fly. That they have also brains, hearts, pulmonary tubes, viscera, has been discovered from their anatomy by acute observers, by means of the microscope. Since the little insects themselves are not manifest to the sight, and still less the minute viscera of which they are constituted, and it is not denied that even to least particulars within them they are organized, how then can it be said that the two receptacles of love and wisdom, which are called the will and the understanding, are not organic forms? How can love and wisdom, which are life from the Lord, act upon what is not a subject, or upon something which does not substantially exist? How else can thought endure? and how can any one speak from thought that is not enduring? Is not the brain, where the thought comes forth, full, and every thing therein organized? The organic forms themselves appear there, even to the naked eye; and manifestly in the cortical substance, the receptacles of the will and understanding in their beginning,—where, as it were, minute glandules are observed. Do not, I pray, think of these things from the notion of a vacuum. A vacuum is nothing; and in nothing nothing takes place, and from nothing nothing comes. (D. L. W. n. 373.)

THE UNDERSTANDING CAN BE ELEVATED ABOVE THE WILL.

Wisdom and Love proceed from the Lord as a Sun and flow into heaven, universally and particularly,—from which source the angels have wisdom and love; and also, universally and particularly, into this world,—whence men have wisdom and love. But these two proceed in union from the Lord; and in union they likewise flow into the souls of angels, and of men. But they are not received in union into their minds; light is first received there, which forms the understanding, and love, which forms the will, is received gradually. This too is of Providence; because every man is to be created anew, that is, reformed, and this is effected by means of the understanding; for he must from infancy imbibe cognitions of truth and good, which shall teach him to live well, that is, rightly to purpose and to act. Thus the will is formed by means of the understanding. For this end there is given to man the capability of elevating his understanding almost into the light in which the angels of heaven are; that he may see what he ought to purpose and therefore do, in order that he may be prosperous for a time in the world, and after death be blessed to eternity. He becomes prosperous and blessed if he acquires wisdom, and keeps his will under obedience to it; but unprosperous and unhappy if he allows his understanding to be under obedience to his will. The reason is that from birth the will inclines to evils, even to enormous evils; if therefore it were not curbed by the understanding, man would rush into acts of heinous wickedness, nay, from his inmost bestial nature he would for the sake of himself ruin and destroy every one who does not favour and yield to him. Besides, if the understanding could not be separately perfected, and the will by means of it, a man would not be man, but a beast. For without this separation, and without the ascent of the understanding above the will, he would be unable to think, and from thought to speak, but could only utter his affection by sound. Nor would he be able to act from reason, but only from instinct; still less would he be able to acquire a knowledge of the things that are of God, and a knowledge of God by means of them, and thus to be conjoined with him and live to eternity. For man thinks and wills as if from himself, and this " as if from himself " is the reciprocal of conjunction; for there can be no conjunction without a reciprocal,—just as there is no conjunction of an active with a passive without a reactive. God alone acts, and man suffers himself to be actuated; and reacts to all appearance as from himself, though interiorly from God. (Influx, n. 14.)

THE WILL RATHER THAN THE UNDERSTANDING CONSTITUTES THE MAN.

As the quality of the love is such is the wisdom, and therefore such is the man; for such as the love and the wisdom are such are the will and the understanding; because the will is the receptacle of love, and the understanding is the receptacle of wisdom, as has been shown above,—which two make the man and his character. Love is manifold; even so manifold that its varieties are indefinite,—as is evident from the human race on earth and in the heavens. There is not one man or one angel so like another that there is no distinction. Love is what distinguishes; for every man is his own love. It is supposed that wisdom distinguishes. But wisdom is from love; it is its form; for love is the *esse* of life, and wisdom is the *existere* of life from that *esse*. It is believed in the world that the understanding constitutes the man; but this is because the understanding can be elevated as was shown above into the light of heaven, and man may thus appear wise. But so much of the understanding as transcends the love, that is, as is not of the love, though it appears to be of the man, and therefore that the man is such, yet this is only an appearance. For so much of his understanding as transcends, is in fact from the love of knowing and being wise, but not at the same time from the love of applying to his life what he knows and understands. It therefore either passes away in the world, in the course of time, or abides outside the subjects of the memory, upon its boundaries, as a something deciduous. It is therefore separated after death, and nothing more remains than accords with the proper love of the spirit. (D. L. W. n. 368.)

THOUGHTS AND AFFECTIONS ARE VARIATIONS OF STATE AND FORM OF
THE ORGANIC SUBSTANCES OF THE MIND.

There was a philosopher who died some years ago,—among the more celebrated and sound,—with whom I conversed respecting the degrees of life in man; saying, that man consists of mere forms for receiving life; and that one form is interior to another, yet that one exists and subsists from another; also that when a lower or exterior form is dissolved, the higher or interior form still lives. It was further said that all operations of the mind are variations of its form, which variations are in such perfection in its purer substances that they cannot be described; that the ideas of thought are nothing else; and that these variations proceed according to the changes of state of the affections. How exceedingly perfect variations these are in the purer forms may be inferred from the lungs, which variously ply themselves, and change their forms, to each particular utterance of speech, to every note of song, to the particular motions of the body, and also to the particular states of thought and affection. What must not be the case then with more interior things, which are in the most perfect state, in comparison with so large an organ? The philosopher confirmed this, and declared that such things had been known to him when he lived in the world; and that the world should apply philosophy to such uses, and not give their attention to naked forms of words, and disputes about them, and so labour in the dust. (A. C. n. 6326.)

Affections, which are of the will, are mere changes of state of the purely organic substances of the mind; and thoughts, which are of the understanding, are mere changes and variations of their form; and the memory is the permanent state of these changes and variations. Who does not assent when it is said that there are no affections and thoughts except in substances and their forms, which are subjects? And as they exist in the brains, which are full of substances and forms, they are called purely organic forms. There is no one who thinks rationally but must smile at the fancies of some, that affections and thoughts are not in substantial subjects, but that they are exhalations modified by heat and light,—like images appearing in the air and ether; when yet there can no more be thought apart from a substantial form, than sight apart from its form, which is the eye, hearing from its form, which is the ear, and taste from its form, which is the tongue. Examine the brain and you will see innumerable substances, and likewise fibres, and that there is nothing there which is not organized. What need is there of other than this ocular confirmation? But it is asked, What is affection then, and what is thought? This may be inferred from all and each of the things that are in the body. There are many viscera there, each fixed in its place, and they perform their functions by changes and variations of state and form. That they are in the performance of their functions is known; the stomach in its function; the intestines in theirs; the kidneys in theirs; the liver, pancreas, and spleen in theirs; and the heart and lungs in theirs. And all these operations are set in motion only from within; and to be moved from within is to be moved by changes and variations of state and form. It is therefore evident that the operations of the purely organic substances of the mind are nothing else; with the difference, that the operations of the .organic substances of the body are natural, while those of the mind spiritual; and that by correspondences these and those make one. What is the nature of the changes and variations of state and form of the organic substances of the mind, which are affections and thoughts, cannot be shown to the eye; but yet they may be seen as in a mirror from the changes and variations of state of the lungs in speaking and singing. There is in fact a correspondence; for the tone in speaking and singing, and also the articulations of sound, which are the words of speech and the modulations of song, are made by the lungs; but the tone corresponds to an affection, and the speech to thought. They are in truth produced from them,— and this is done by changes and variations of the state and form of the organic substances in the lungs; and from the lungs, through the trachea or *arteria aspera*, in the larynx and glottis; and then in the tongue; and finally in the lips. The first changes and variations of the state and form of sound are made in the lungs; the second in the trachea and larynx; the third in the glottis, by the manifold openings of its orifice; the fourth in the tongue, by its manifold applications to the palate and teeth; the fifth in the lips, by their manifold forms. From these things it is evident that mere changes and variations of state of organic forms, continued successively, produce the sounds and the articulations of them which are speech and song. Now as sound and speech are produced from no other source than from affections and thoughts of the mind,—for they come from these, and never without them,—it is plain that affections of the will are changes and variations of state of the purely organic substances of the mind; and that thoughts of the understanding are changes and variations of the form of those substances,—in like manner as in the lungs. Since affections and thoughts are mere changes of state of the forms of the mind, it follows that the memory is no other than their permanent state; for all changes and variations of state in organic substances are such, that being once habitual they are permanent. Thus the lungs are accustomed to produce various sounds in the trachea, and to vary them in the glottis, to articulate them with the tongue, and modify them by the mouth; and when these organic [changes] are once accustomed they are in the organs and can be reproduced. These changes and variations are infinitely more perfect in the organic substances of the mind than in those of the body. (D. P. n. 279.)

IDEAS OF THOUGHT.

The thought of man is distinguished into ideas; and one idea follows another as one word follows another in speech. But the ideas of thought succeed each other with such rapidity that the thought appears to a man while in the body as if it were continuous, and therefore as if there were no distinction [of the thought into ideas]. But in the other life it becomes manifest that thought is distinguished into ideas; for then speech is effected by ideas. . . . . There are things innumerable in a single idea of thought; and still more innumerable in a thought composed of ideas. (A. C. n. 6599.)

How much more perfect are the ideas of thought than the words of speech may appear from the fact that a man can think more in a moment than he could utter or describe in an hour. The language after death is distinguished into ideas, and consists of ideas; which among spirits are in the place of words and of sounds. For among spirits sound corresponds to thought,—which in itself is tacit speech, yet audible to spirits. From this it is evident what is the nature of the language of spirits; that in fact it is as much more perfect than human language as thought is than a language of words. (S. D. Minus, n. 4617.) See also pp. 578, 579, 604.

THE APPEARANCE OF UNDERSTANDING IN BRUTES—DIFFERENCE BETWEEN THEM AND MAN.

They who judge only from the appearance to the bodily senses conclude that beasts in like manner as men have will and understanding; and therefore that the only distinction is that man is able to speak, and thus to tell what he thinks and what he desires, while beasts can only make them known by a sound. Nevertheless beasts have not will and understanding, but merely a semblance of each; what the learned call an analogue. That man is a man is because his understanding can be elevated above the desires of his will,—even so that from above he can cognize, and observe them, and also moderate them; but a beast is a beast because its desires drive it to do whatever it does. A man is therefore a man by the fact that his will is under obedience to his understanding; but a beast is a beast by the fact that its understanding is under obedience to its will. From these considerations this conclusion follows; that the understanding of man, because it receives inflowing light from heaven, and apprehends and apperceives this as its own, and from this light thinks analytically precisely as if from itself, with all variety, is a living and therefore a true understanding; and that his will because it receives the inflowing love of heaven, and from this acts as from itself, is a living and therefore a true will; and that with beasts it is the reverse. For this reason they who think from the desires of the will are likened to beasts, and in the spiritual world they also appear as beasts at a distance; and they act like beasts, with the only difference that they can act otherwise if they will. But they who restrain the desires of their will by the understanding, in the spiritual world appear as men, and are angels of heaven. In a word, with beasts the will and the understanding always cohere; and as the will in itself is blind,—for it is [the receptacle] of heat and not of light,—it makes the understanding blind also. Hence a beast does not know and understand what it does, and yet it acts; for it acts by virtue of influx from the spiritual world, and such action is instinct. It is believed that a beast thinks from the understanding about what it does. But not in the least; it is impelled to action only by a natural love that is in it from creation, recruited by its bodily senses. Man thinks and speaks solely because his understanding is separable from his will, and capable of being elevated even into the light of heaven; for the understanding thinks, and thought speaks. That beasts act according to the laws of order inscribed upon their nature, and some as if morally and rationally, and differently from many men, is because their understanding is in blind obedience to the desires of their will; and therefore they could not, like men, pervert them by depraved reasonings. It is to be observed that by the will and understanding of beasts, in what has been said, their semblance and analogue is meant. The analogues are thus called from the appearance. The life of a beast may be compared with a night-walker, who, the under-

standing being asleep, walks and acts from the will; and with a
blind man, who walks the streets led by a dog. . . . It is evident
from these considerations how mistaken they are who believe
that beasts enjoy rationality, and are only to be distinguished
from men by their outward form, and by the fact that they cannot
utter the rational things which they lay up within. From which
fallacies many conclude also that if man lives after death beasts
will live also; and on the other hand, that if beasts do not live
after death neither will man; and many other dreams, arising
from ignorance respecting the will and understanding, and also
respecting the degrees by which the mind of man, as by a ladder,
mounts up to heaven. (Influx, n. 15.)

How the Spirit dwells within the Body.

It has been said above that man is a spirit, and that the
body serves him for the performance of uses in the world; and
elsewhere, in different places, that the spirit is the internal of
man and the body his external. They that do not comprehend
how it is with respect to the spirit of man and his body, may
therefore assert that the spirit dwells thus within the body, and
the body, as it were, incloses and invests it. But it should be
known, that the spirit of man within the body is in the whole
and in every part, and is the purer substance of it, in its organs
of motion and of sense, and everywhere else, and that the body
is material annexed to it everywhere adapted to the world in
which he then is. This is what is meant by saying that man
is a spirit, and the body serves him for the performance of uses
in the world, and that the spirit is man's internal and the body
his external. It is clear, therefore, that man is in active and
sensitive life likewise after death; and also in the human
form, as in the world, but in a more perfect human form.
(A. C n. 4659.)

INFLUX,

AND INTERCOURSE BETWEEN THE SOUL AND THE BODY.

FORMER HYPOTHESES CONCERNING THE INTERCOURSE BETWEEN THE SOUL AND THE BODY.

RESPECTING the intercourse between the soul and the body, or the operation of the one upon the other, and of one with the other, there are three opinions and teachings, which are hypotheses; the first is called physical influx, the second spiritual influx, and the third pre-established harmony. The first, which is called *Physical Influx,* is from appearances to the senses, and the fallacies arising out of them; because it appears as if the objects of sight which affect the eyes flow into thought, and produce it; in like manner, as if speech, which affects the ears, flows into the mind and there produces ideas. And so with the smell, the taste, and the touch. As the organs of these senses first receive the impressions flowing to them from the world, and according to the affections of them the mind appears to think and also to will, therefore ancient philosophers and schoolmen supposed influx to be derived from them into the soul, and so adopted the hypothesis of physical or natural influx. The second hypothesis, which is called *Spiritual Influx* (by some occasional influx), is from order and its laws. Since the soul is a spiritual substance, and is therefore purer, prior, and interior; while the body is material, and therefore grosser, posterior, and exterior; and it is according to order that the purer should flow into the grosser, the prior into the posterior, and the interior into the exterior, thus the spiritual into the material, and not the contrary; consequently it is according to order that the thinking mind should flow into the sight, according to the state induced by objects upon the eyes,—which state that mind also disposes at its pleasure. In like manner the perceptive mind into the hearing, according to the state induced on the ears by speech. The third hypothesis, which is called *Pre-established Harmony,* is from appearances and fallacies of reason, seeing that the mind in its very operation acts together and simultaneously with the body. But then every operation is first successive, and afterwards simultaneous. The successive operation is influx ; and the simultaneous operation is harmony.   As when the mind thinks, and afterwards speaks ; or when it wills, and afterwards acts.   It is therefore a fallacy of reason to establish the simultaneous and exclude the successive. Beyond these three opinions there cannot be a fourth respecting the intercourse between the soul and the body, since either the soul must operate upon the body, or the body upon the soul, or both continually together.

Since spiritual influx, as was said, is according to order and its laws, this hypothesis therefore is acknowledged and received by the wise in the learned world in preference to the other two. Because all that is according to order is truth, and truth manifests itself by its inherent light,—even in the shade of reason, where hypotheses are.   But there are three things which involve this hypothesis in shade,—ignorance as to what the soul is; ignorance as to what is spiritual; and ignorance as to the nature of influx. These three must therefore be explained before reason will see the truth itself.   For hypothetical truth is not truth itself, but a conjecture respecting the truth.   (Influx, n. 1, 2.)

The spiritual influx hitherto treated of by men of refined talent is from the soul into the body ; and not any influx into the soul, and through this into the body ; although it is known that all the good of love and all the truth of faith flows in from God.   They flow in first into the soul ; and through the soul into the rational mind ; and through this into the things that constitute the body.   If otherwise any one investigates the subject of spiritual influx, it is if one should stop up the vein of a fountain and yet seek perennial waters there ; or should deduce the origin of a tree from the root, and not from the seed ; or throw light upon derivations without the first principle.   (*ib.* n. 8.)

There is one only Life, which flows into and vivifies all Forms.

I have been taught by very much experience that there is but one only life, which is that of the Lord ; which flows in and makes man to live, nay, makes both the good and the evil to live.   To this life forms which are substances correspond ; which by continual Divine influx are vivified in such wise that to themselves they appear to live from themselves.   (A. C. n. 3484.)

By various degrees of influx into the heavens the Lord disposes, regulates, tempers; and moderates all things there and in the hells, and, through the heavens and the hells all things in the world.   (A. R. n. 346.)

Man is not life, but an organ recipient of life from God ; and love together with wisdom is life; furthermore, God is love itself and wisdom itself, and thus life itself. Hence it follows that in so far as a man loves wisdom, or in so far as wisdom in the bosom of love is in him, he is an image of God, that is a receptacle of life from God; and on the contrary in so far as he is in an opposite love, and thence in insanity, he does not receive life from God, but from hell, which life is called death. Love itself and wisdom itself are not life, but are the *esse* of life; and the delights of love and the pleasures of wisdom, which are affections, constitute life,—for by these the *esse* of life exists. The influx of life from God carries with it those delights and pleasures; just as does the influx of light and heat, in the spring-time, into human minds, and also into birds and beasts of every kind, nay, into vegetables, which then germinate and become prolific. For the delights of love and pleasures of wisdom expand the mind (*animus*), and adapt it to reception, just as joy and gladness expand the face and adapt it to the influx of the exhilarations of the soul. (Influx, n. 13.)

With regard to the influx from the spiritual world into man, the fact in general is this; a man can neither think nor will any thing actually from himself, but everything flows in,—good and truth from the Lord through heaven, thus through the angels who are with man; evil and falsity from hell, and so through the evil spirits that are with man,—and this into man's thought and will. (A. C. n. 5846.)

INFLUX FROM THE LORD IS BOTH IMMEDIATE AND MEDIATE THROUGH THE HEAVENS.

Life flows into man from God through the soul; and through this into his mind, that is into his affections and thoughts; and from these into the senses, speech, and actions of the body; because these are in the successive order of life. For the mind is subordinate to the soul, and the body is subordinate to the mind. And the mind has two lives, one of the will and another of the understanding. The life of its will is the good of love, the derivations of which are called affections; and the life of its understanding is the truth of wisdom, the derivations of which are called thoughts; through both of these the mind lives. And the senses, speech, and actions are the life of the body; that these are by the soul through the mind, follows from the order in which they are; and according to this they manifest themselves to a wise man without investigation. The human soul, because it is a higher spiritual substance, receives influx immediately from God; and the human mind, because it is a lower spiritual substance, receives influx from God mediately, through the spiritual world; while the body, because it is of the substances of nature, which are called material, receives influx from God mediately through the natural world. (Influx, n. 7.)

It has been given me, by revelation, to know how the case is with regard to the influx of each life from the Lord ; that is to say, the life of thought and the life of the will. Namely, that the Lord flows in in a twofold manner, that is mediately through heaven, and immediately from Himself; and that from Himself He flows in both into the rational things of man which are his interiors, and into the natural, which are his exteriors. (A. C. n. 6472.)

The very celestial and the very spiritual, which flow from the Divine of the Lord into heaven, dwell principally in the interior rational ; [1] for there the forms are more perfect, and adapted to reception. But yet the celestial and spiritual from the Lord's Divine flow also into the exterior rational, and even into the natural,—both mediately and immediately ; mediately through the interior rational, and immediately from the Lord's Divine itself. What flows in immediately disposes ; and what flows in mediately is disposed. So is it in the exterior rational ; and so it is in the natural. (*ib.* n. 5150.)

The natural is not regenerated until it is conjoined to the rational. This conjunction is effected by means of immediate and mediate influx of the rational into the good and truth of the natural ; that is to say, immediately by the good of the rational into the good of the natural, and through this into the truth of the natural ; mediately through the truth of the rational into the truth of the natural, and thence into the good of the natural. . . . The rational mind,—that is the interior will part and intellectual part in man,—ought to represent itself in his natural mind, as this mind represents itself in the face and its expression ; insomuch that just as the face is the expression of the natural mind, so the natural mind ought to be the expression of the rational mind. When there is this conjunction, as in those who are regenerated, then whatever a man wills and thinks interiorly, in his rational mind, presents itself to view in his natural mind, and this presents itself visibly in the face. Such a countenance have the angels, and such a countenance had the Most Ancients who were celestial men. (*ib.* n. 3573.)

As regards every good that constitutes heavenly life, and so eternal life, with man and with angel, the case is this : The inmost of good is the Lord Himself, even the good of love which is immediately from Him. The good which next succeeds is the good of mutual love ; after that the good of charity towards the neighbour ; lastly the good of faith. This is the successive order of goods from the inmost. It may be seen from this how it is with regard

[1] See p. 551.

to immediate and mediate influx. In general, in the degree that a good succeeding in order, or an exterior good, has interior good within it, in that degree it is a good, for in that degree it is nearer to the Lord Himself, who, as was said, is the inmost good. But the successive disposition and ordination of interior goods in the exterior, varies in each and every subject according to reception; and reception varies according to the spiritual and moral life of each one in the world. For the life in the world remains with every one to eternity. The influx of the Lord is immediate also with every one, because without immediate influx the mediate is of no effect. Immediate influx is received according to the order in which the man or angel is; thus according to Divine truth which is from the Divine, for this is order. It is order itself therefore with man that he should live in the good which is from the Lord; that is that he should live from the Lord. This influx is continual, and is connected with each and all things of man's will, and as far as possible it directs them to order; for man's own will continually leads away. It is as with things voluntary and involuntary in man. His voluntary [activities] continually lead away from order; but the involuntary continually restore to order. Hence it is that the motion of the heart, which is involuntary, is entirely exempt from man's will; in like manner the action of the cerebellum; and that the motion of the heart and the powers of the cerebellum govern the voluntary [activities], that these may not rush beyond bounds, and extinguish the life of the body before its time. For this reason the active principles from each, that is to say, from the involuntary and from the voluntary things in the whole body, proceed in conjunction. These things are mentioned to illustrate in some measure the idea of immediate and mediate influx of the celestial things of love and the spiritual things of faith from the Lord. (*ib.* n. 9683.)

The Divine truth which proceeds immediately from the Lord is above all understanding of angels. But that which proceeds mediately is adapted to the angels in the heavens, and also to men; for it passes through heaven, and from thence puts on angelic quality, and human quality. But into this truth the Lord also flows immediately; and thus He leads angels and men both mediately and immediately. For each and all things are from the First Being; and order is so established that the First Being is present in derivatives both mediately and immediately, thus equally in the ultimate of order and in the first of order. For Divine truth itself is the one only substantial; derivatives are nothing else than successive forms thence resulting. It is therefore evident that the Divine also flows into each and all things immediately; for by Divine truth all things were created. For Divine truth is the one only essential, and therefore that from which all things are. The Divine truth is what is called the Word in John; " *In the beginning was the Word, and the Word was with God, and God was the Word; . . . all things were made by Him; and without Him was not any thing made that was made.*" (i. 1, 2.). (*ib.* n. 7004.)

GENERAL AND PARTICULAR INFLUX.

There is a general influx from the Lord, through the spiritual world into the subjects of the natural world, and there is a particular influx. The general influx is into those things which are in order; the particular influx into those things which are not in order. Animals of every kind are in the order of their nature; therefore into them there is a general influx. That they are in the order of their nature is evident from the fact that they are born into all things proper to them, and have no need to be introduced into them by any instruction. But men are not in order, nor in any law of order. Into them therefore there is a particular influx; that is, there are angels and spirits with them through whom there is influx; and unless these were with men they would rush into every abomination, and plunge themselves in a moment into the profoundest hell. Through these spirits and angels man is under the protection and guidance of the Lord. The order of man into which he was created would be, that he should love his neighbour as himself, nay, more than himself; and thus the angels do. But man loves only himself and the world, and hates his neighbour,—except in so far as he is favourable to his command and possession of the world. Therefore, because man's life is entirely contrary to heavenly order, he is governed by the Lord through separate spirits and angels. (A. C. n. 5850.)

THE INFLUX INTO AND THROUGH THE HEAVENS IS IN SUCCESSIVE ORDER, FROM THE FIRST TO THE ULTIMATES OF NATURE.

The truth which proceeds immediately from the Lord, inasmuch as it is from the infinite Divine Being Himself, can in nowise be received by any living substance which is finite; thus not by any angels. Therefore the Lord had created things successive, through which as mediums the Divine truth proceeding immediately might be communicated. But the first [medium] in succession from this is more full of the Divine than that as yet it can be received by any living substance which is finite; thus by any angel. The Lord therefore created a further successive [medium] through which the Divine truth immediately proceeding might in some measure be receptible. This successive [medium] is the truth Divine which is in heaven. The first two are above the heavens ; and are as it were radiant belts of flame that encompass the sun, which is the Lord. Such is the successive order even to the heaven nearest to the Lord, which is the third heaven, where they are who are innocent and wise. From this it is continued successively even to the ultimate heaven ; and from the ultimate heaven to the sensual and corporeal degree of man, which last receives the influx. It is certain from these facts that there are continual successions, from the First, that is from the Lord, to the last things that are in man, nay, to the last things that are in nature. The last things in man, as also in nature, are relatively inert, and therefore cold, and are relatively general, and therefore obscure. Hence also it is manifest that by these successions there is a continual connection of all things with the First Being. In accordance with these successions influx takes place ; for the Divine truth which proceeds immediately from Divine good flows in successively ; and on the way, or about each new successive [medium], it becomes more general, and therefore grosser and more obscure ; and becomes less active, thus more inert and colder. From these considerations it is clear what is the Divine order of things successive, and therefore of influxes. But it should be well understood that the truth Divine which flows into the third heaven, nearest the Lord, also at the same time, without successive formation, flows down even into the ultimates of order ; and there too, from the First, immediately governs and provides each and all things. The successive things are thereby preserved in their order and connection. That this is so may indeed in some measure be seen from a maxim not unknown to the learned in the world, that there is one only substance which is substance, and the rest are formations therefrom ; and that this one only substance governs in the formations just as in their origin, not only as form, but also not as form. If this were not so, the thing formed could in nowise subsist and act. But these things are said for the intelligent. (A. C. n. 7270.)

THE INFLUX INTO MAN IS ALSO IN SUCCESSIVE ORDER, ACCORDING TO THE DISCRETE DEGREES OF THE MIND.

There are three things in man which concur and unite,—the natural, the spiritual, and the celestial. His natural receives no life except from the spiritual, nor his spiritual except from the celestial, nor his celestial except from the Lord alone, who is life itself. But that an idea of this may be more fully comprehended; the natural is a receptacle that receives, or vessel into which is poured, the spiritual; and the spiritual is a receptacle that receives, or vessel into which is poured, the celestial; thus through the celestial life is received from the Lord. Such is the order of influx. (A. C. n. 880.)

Order is that the celestial shall flow into the spiritual and adapt it to itself; that thus the spiritual shall flow into the rational, and adapt it to itself; and so the rational into the knowing and adapt it to itself. But, though there is a similar order while man is being instructed in his earliest childhood, yet it appears otherwise, viz., that he progresses from things known to things rational, from these to things spiritual, and so at length to things celestial. That it so appears is because the way must thus be opened to things celestial, which are the inmost. All instruction is but an opening of the way; and as the way is opened, or what is the same, as the vessels are opened, there flow in, as was said, in order, from the celestial-spiritual, things rational; within them are things celestial-spiritual, and within these, things celestial. These are continually going forth, and also preparing for themselves and forming the vessels which are opened. Which may indeed appear from the consideration, that the knowing and the rational faculties in themselves are dead; and though they appear to live, they have this appearance from the interior life that flows in. This may be manifest to any one from thought, and the faculty of judging. In these lie concealed all the secrets of art and of analytical science, which are so numerous that they can never as to one in myriads be explored; not only in adult men, but even in children, all their thought, and all their speech thence is most full of them,—although the man, even the most learned, is unaware of it; which could never be if the celestial and spiritual things that are within were not proceeding, flowing in, and producing all these things. (*ib.* n. 1495.)

THE INFLUX IS INTO THE WILL AND UNDERSTANDING,[1] AND THROUGH THESE INTO THE BODY.

It is known that all things, universally, relate to good and truth, and that there is no single entity in which there is not the relative to these two. Hence it is that there are two receptacles of life in man; one that is called the will, which is the receptacle of good, another that is called the understanding, which is the receptacle of truth. And as good is of love

[1] See pp. 548, 549.

and truth is of wisdom, the will is the receptacle of love and the understanding is the receptacle of wisdom. That good is of love is because what a man loves he wills, and when he performs it he calls it a good ; and that truth is of wisdom is because all wisdom is from truths,—nay, the good that a wise man meditates is truth, and this when he wills and does it becomes a good. He who does not rightly distinguish between these two receptacles of life, the will and the understanding, and does not form for himself a clear notion of them, will seek in vain to obtain a knowledge of spiritual influx. For there is an influx into the will, and there is an influx into the understanding ; into the will of man there is an influx of the good of love, and into his understanding there is an influx of the truth of wisdom,— each immediately from Jehovah God, through the sun in the midst of which He is, and mediately through the angelic heaven. These two receptacles, the will and the understanding, are as distinct as heat and light ; for as was said above, the will receives the heat of heaven, which in its essence is love, and the understanding receives the light of heaven, which in its essence is wisdom. There is an influx from the human mind into the speech, and into the actions. Influx into the speech is from the will through the understanding ; and influx into the actions is from the understanding through the will. They who only take cognizance of the influx into the understanding, and not at the same time of that into the will, and who reason and form conclusions from it, are as those that are blind of one eye, who only see the objects that are on one side and not at the same time those that are on the other. (Influx, n. 7.)

The soul flows into the human mind, and through this into the body ; and carries with it the life that it continually receives from the Lord, and thus mediately transfers it to the body, where by the closest union it makes the body as it were to live. From this, and from a thousand attestations of experience, it is plain that the spiritual united to the material,— as it were a living power to a dead power,—enables man to speak rationally and act morally. It appears as if the tongue and lips speak from some life in themselves ; and that the arms and hands act in like manner. But it is the thought, which in itself is spiritual, that speaks ; and the will, which likewise is spiritual, that acts ; and both through their organs, which in themselves are material, because taken from the natural world. That it so appears in the light of day, if only attention be given to this consideration:—Take away the thought from speech ; does not the mouth instantly become mute ? And take the will from action ; do not the hands instantly cease ? (*ib.* n. 12.)

INFLUX ILLUSTRATED BY THE SIGHT OF THE EYE.

"*Thou God seest me*" (Gen. xvi. 13). Looking from a higher [region] into a lower, or what is the same, from an interior into an exterior, is called influx; for it is effected by influx. It is as the interior sight in man. Unless this flowed continually into his external sight, or that of the eye, it could never take in and distinguish any object; for it is the interior sight which, by means of the eye, takes in the things that the eye sees; and not the eye, although it appears so. From these principles it may be seen, too, how much the man is in the fallacies of the senses who believes that the eye sees; when yet it is the sight of his spirit, which is the interior sight, that sees by means of the eye. Spirits who were with me have seen through my eyes the objects that are in the world, as well as I; and some of them who were still in the fallacies of the senses supposed that they saw through their own eyes. But it was shown them that it was not so; for when my eyes were shut they saw nothing in this atmospheric world. The case is similar with man. It is his spirit that sees, not the eye; but it is through the eye. The same may also appear from dreams, in which a man sometimes sees as in the light of day. But further: it is the same with this interior sight, or that of the spirit. This does not see of itself, but from a still more interior sight, or that of its rational mind; nay, neither does this see of itself, but there is a sight yet more interior, which is that of the internal man,—of which in n. 1940.[1] But even this does not see of itself; but it is the Lord through the internal man who alone sees, because He alone lives; and He grants to man that he may see, even so that it appears as if he saw from himself. Thus it is with influx. (A. C. n. 1954.)

IN TRUE ORDER SPIRITUAL INFLUX WOULD GUIDE MAN INTO ALL INTELLIGENCE AND WISDOM.

It is plain, not only from the things that exist in the heavens, but even from those that exist in inferior nature, that in the good of love which flows in from the Lord through the angels there is all truth which truth would manifest itself, of itself, if man had lived in love to the Lord and in love towards the

---

[1] By "the internal man" in this instance,—as is explained in the paragraph, n. 1940, to which the author refers,—he means "that which is his inmost, and by which he is distinguished from brute animals, which have no such inmost; and is, as it were, the gate or entrance of the Lord into man, that is of the Lord's celestial and spiritual [influences]." See also pp. 24, 57.

neighbour. Some of those that exist in inferior nature, as they are visible to the eyes, may be adduced in illustration. Brute animals are impelled to action no otherwise than by the loves, and the affections of them, into which they were created, and afterwards are born; for every animal is carried whither its affection and love draws. And because it is so they are also in all the knowledges that in any wise pertain to that love. For from a love emulative of conjugial love they know how to copulate,—beasts in one way, and birds in another; birds know how to build their nests, how to lay their eggs, and to sit on them, how to hatch their young, and how to nourish them,—and this without any instruction, merely from a love emulative of conjugial love, and from love towards their offspring; which loves have all these knowledges connected with them. In like manner they know with what kinds of food to feed themselves, and how to obtain it. And what is more, bees know how to gather food from flowers of various kinds ; and also to collect the wax of which they make their cells, wherein they first deposit their offspring, and then lay up food; they also know how to provide for themselves against the winter; not to mention very many other things. All these knowledges are included in their loves, and dwell therein, from their first origin. They are born into these knowledges, because they are in the order of their nature, into which they were created; and then they are moved to action by the general[1] influx from the spiritual world. If man were in the order into which he was created, that is in love towards the neighbour, and in love to the Lord,—for these loves are proper to man,—he above all animals would be born, not only into knowledges, but also into all spiritual truths and celestial goods, and thus into all wisdom and intelligence. For he is capable of thinking about the Lord, and of being conjoined to Him by love; and so of being elevated to what is Divine and eternal, which brute animals are incapable of. Thus man would then be governed by no other than the general influx from the Lord through the spiritual world. But because he is not born into order but in a state of opposition to his order, therefore he is born into ignorance of all things; and because this is so it is provided that he may afterwards be re-born, and thus come into so much of intelligence and wisdom as from freedom he receives of good, and by good of truth. (A. C. n. 6323.)

The Influx into the World of Nature.

There is a continual influx from the spiritual world into the natural. He who does not know that there is a spiritual world,

[1] See p. 566.

and that it is distinct from the natural world,—as the prior and the posterior, or as the cause and the thing caused,—can know nothing of this influx. This is the reason why those who have written on the origin of vegetables and animals could not but deduce it from nature; or if from God, have inferred that from the beginning God indued nature with the power of producing such things,—thus not knowing that nature is indued with no power. For nature in itself is dead, and no more contributes to the production of these things than the instrument to the work of the artist, which must perpetually be moved that it may act. It is the spiritual principle, which derives its origin from the sun wherein the Lord is and proceeds to the ultimates of nature, that produces the forms of vegetables and animals, and exhibits the wonders that there are in both ; and it clothes them with material substances from the earth that these forms may be fixed and enduring. As it is now known that there is a spiritual world ; and that the spiritual is from the sun wherein the Lord is, and which is from the Lord; and that it moves nature to action, as the living actuates the dead ; also that in that world there are things similar to those in the natural world; it can be seen that vegetables and animals must have existed from no other source than from the Lord through that world, and that through it they perpetually exist; and thus that there is a continual influx from the spiritual world into the natural. (D. L. W. n. 340.)

I heard two Presidents of the English Royal Society, Sir Hans Sloane and Martin Folkes, conversing together in the spiritual world on the existence of seeds and eggs, and the productions from them on earth. The former ascribed them to nature; and maintained that from creation nature is indued with force and power to produce such things, by means of the sun's heat. The other said that this power is continually from God the Creator in nature. To settle the dispute a beautiful bird appeared to Sir Hans Sloane; and he was requested to examine it, to see whether in any least respect it differed from a similar bird on earth. He held it in his hand, examined it, and said that there was no difference. Yet he knew that it was but an affection of some angel represented out of him as a bird, and that it would vanish or cease with its affection; which indeed it did. Sir Hans Sloane was convinced by this experience that nature contributes nothing at all to the production of vegetables and animals, but that only which flows in from the spiritual world into the natural. He said, if that bird in its minutest parts were filled with corresponding material substances from the earth, and so fixed, it would be a durable bird, like the birds on earth ; and that it is the same with those things that are from hell. He said further, that if he had known what he now knew of the spiritual world, he would have ascribed no more to nature than that it served the spiritual, which is from God, in fixing the things that continually flow into nature. (*ib.* n. 344.)

ORIGIN OF NOXIOUS ANIMALS, PLANTS, AND MINERALS.

Evil uses were not created by the Lord, but all originated with hell. All goods that exist in act are called uses; and all evils that exist in act are also called uses,—but these are called evil uses, and the former good uses. Now as all goods come from the Lord, and all evils from hell, it follows that none other than good uses were created by the Lord, and that evil uses originated from hell. By the uses treated of in this section, in particular, all things are meant that appear on the earth, such as animals of all kinds and vegetables of all kinds; those of each that perform a use to man are from the Lord, and those that do injury to man are from hell. By uses from the Lord all things are likewise meant that perfect man's rational mind and cause him to receive what is spiritual from the Lord; and by evil uses all things are meant that destroy the rational, and render man unable to become spiritual. The things that do injury to man are called uses because they are used by the evil in doing evil; and because they serve to absorb malignities, and thus also as remedies. In each sense it is called use, just as we speak of love as a good love or an evil love; and that which is done by itself love calls use. (D. L. W. n. 336.)

By evil uses on the earth all noxious things are meant both in the animal and the vegetable kingdom, and also the noxious things in the mineral kingdom. It would be vain to enumerate all the noxious things in these kingdoms; for it would be but to bring together names, and to gather the names without an indication of the injury that each kind produces would not promote the use which this work has for its end. It is sufficient for our knowledge to mention here a few of them. Such in the animal kingdom are poisonous serpents, scorpions, crocodiles, dragons, horned owls, screech owls, mice, locusts, frogs, spiders; also flies, drones, roaches, lice, mites,—in a word, those that consume grasses, leaves, fruits, seeds, food and drink, and do injury to beasts and men. In the vegetable kingdom they are all mischievous, poisonous, and malignant herbs, and similar leguminous plants and shrubs. In the mineral kingdom all poisonous earthy substances. From these few examples it may be seen what is meant by evil uses on earth; for evil uses are all things that are contrary to good uses.

Before it can be seen that the evil uses which exist on the earth are not from the Lord, but are all from hell, something respecting heaven and hell must be premised. Unless this is known evil uses, as well as good, may be attributed to the Lord; and they may be believed to exist together from creation, or be attributed to nature, and their origin to the sun of nature. A man cannot be delivered from these two errors, unless he knows that nothing whatever exists in the natural world which does not derive its cause and therefore its origin from the spiritual world; and that the good is from the Lord, and the evil from the devil, that is from hell. By the spiritual world both heaven and hell are meant. All those things that are good uses appear in heaven; and all those that are evil uses, enumerated just above, appear in hell. There are wild beasts there of every kind, such as serpents, scorpions, dragons, crocodiles, tigers, wolves, foxes, swine, horned owls, night owls, screech owls, bats, rats, mice, frogs, locusts, spiders, and noxious insects of many kinds; there also appear hemlock, and aconite, and every kind of poison, both in herbs as in earthy substances; in a word, all things that are hurtful and deadly to men. Such things appear in the hells to the life, precisely like those upon and in the earth. It is said that they appear there; but yet they are not there as on earth, for they are mere correspondences of the lusts that stream forth from evil loves, and which present themselves in such forms before others. Since there are such things in the hells they therefore gush forth also with abominable stenches, cadaverous, stercoraceous, urinous, putrid, with which the diabolical spirits there are delighted; just as certain animals are with things that have an offensive odor. From these facts it may be concluded that the similar things in the natural world did not derive their origin from the Lord, and were not created from the beginning, and that they did not originate from nature by her sun, but that they are from hell. That they are not from nature by her sun is very manifest, from the fact that the spiritual flows into the natural, and not the contrary. And that they are not from the Lord is evident from the fact that hell is not from Him, and therefore nothing in hell that corresponds to their evils. (*ib.* n. 338, 339.)

Influx from hell produces the things that are evil uses, in places where there are such things as correspond. The things that correspond to evil uses, that is to mischievous plants and noxious animals, are cadaverous, putrid, excrementitious, and stercoraceous, rancid and urinous matters. In places therefore where there are these, such plants and little animals spring forth as are mentioned above; and in the torrid zone the larger animals of similar character, such as serpents, basilisks, crocodiles, scorpions, mice, and others. Every one knows that marshes, stagnant pools, dung, and rotten soil are filled with such things; also that noxious insects like clouds fill the atmosphere; and noxious worms like armies, the earth, and consume the herbage even to the roots. I once observed in my garden, that for the space of an ell almost all the dust was turned into very small insects; for being stirred with a stick they rose up like a cloud. That cadaverous and putrid substances agree with these noxious and useless little animals, and that they are homogeneous, is evident from experience alone. This may also be plainly seen from the cause; which is that there are similar stenches and effluvia in the hells, where such little animals also appear.

Now, the question is whether such things spring from eggs carried thither, either through the air, or by rains, or by water-courses, or whether they spring from the damps and stenches themselves in such places. That such noxious animalcules and insects as are mentioned above are hatched from eggs carried there, or hidden everywhere in the earth even from the creation, is opposed to all evidence; since worms spring forth in little seeds, in nuts, in wood, in stones, nay, from leaves; also lice and grubs which are accordant with them upon plants and in them. Then of flying insects, there are those which appear in the summer in houses, in the fields, and in the woods,—likewise arising from no oviform matter in such abundance; those that devour meadows and lawns, and in some hot countries fill and infest the air; besides those animalcules that invisibly swim and fly in filthy waters, sour wines, and pestilential air. These facts are favourable to those who say that also the odors, effluvia, and exhalations emitted from the plants, soils, and stagnant waters themselves, give origin to such things. That after-wards, when they have come forth, they are propagated by eggs or spawn, does not take away the fact of their immediate origin; since every animal along with its minute viscera receives also organs of generation and the means of propagation. The fact, not known before, that there are similar things also in the hells, is in agreement with these phenomena.

That the hells mentioned above not only have communication but also a conjunction with such things on earth, may be con-cluded from the fact that the hells are not remote from men, but are about them, nay, within those who are wicked; thus they are contiguous to the earth. For as to his affections and lusts and the thoughts therefrom, and as to his actions from the former and the latter, which are good or evil uses, man is in the midst either of the angels of heaven or of the spirits of hell; and as such things as are on earth are also in the heavens and the hells, it follows that the influx therefrom, when the conditions (*temperies*) are favourable, immediately produces such things. For all things that appear in the spiritual world, both in heaven and in hell, are the correspondences [respectively] of affections and lusts, for they spring forth there in accordance with them. When therefore affections and lusts, which in themselves are spiritual, meet with homogeneous or corresponding things on earth, there is present the spiritual that gives a soul, and the material that furnishes a body ; there is also inherent in every thing spiritual, an endeavour to clothe itself with a body. That the hells are about men, and therefore contiguous to the earth, is because the spiritual world is not in space, but is where there is a corresponding affection.   (*ib.* n. 341-343.)

How the Soul acts into and by means of the Body.

The mind of man is his spirit, and the spirit is the man ; for the mind means, all things of man's will and understanding ; and these in principles are in the brains, and in derivatives in the body. With respect to their forms they are all things of the man. Because it is so, the mind, that is the will and understanding, actuates the body and all things belonging to it, at will. Does not the body do whatever the mind thinks and determines ? The mind incites the ear to hear, and directs the eye to see ; the mind moves the tongue and lips to speak ; impels the hands and fingers to do whatever it pleases ; and the feet to walk whither it wills. Is the body anything but obedience to its mind ? Can it be such, unless the mind is in its derivatives in the body ? Is it consonant with reason to think that the body acts in obedience, because the mind so wills ?[1] They would thus be two, one above and the other beneath ; and one would command and the other obey. As this is not consistent with reason, it follows that a man's life in principles is in the brains, and in derivatives in the body, as was said above , also that such as the life is in the principles, such is it in the whole and in every part ; and that by these principles the life is from every part in the whole, and from the whole in every part. All things of the mind refer to the will and understanding ; and the will and understanding are receptacles of love and wisdom from the Lord ; and these two constitute man's life.   (D. L. W. n. 387.)

[1] The distinction the author here makes, if at first sight a little obscure, is yet very important. It is true that " the body is nothing but obedience to its mind ; ' and yet *the body does not act* in obedience. It is the mind, the living organic force, that acts in and by the body.

THE ETERNAL WORLD.

ALL ANGELS AND SPIRITS WERE ONCE MEN.

IT is entirely unknown in the Christian world that heaven and hell are from the human race; for it is believed that the angels were created from the beginning, and that this was the origin of heaven; and that the devil or satan was an angel of light, but because he became rebellious, was cast down with his crew, and that this was the origin of hell. Angels wonder exceedingly that there should be such a belief in the Christian world; and still more that they should know nothing at all about heaven, when yet that is the primary of doctrine in the church. And because such ignorance prevails, they rejoiced in heart that it had pleased the Lord now to reveal to mankind many things respecting heaven, and also respecting hell; and thereby as far as possible to dispel the darkness, which is daily increasing because the church has come to its end. They therefore wish me to assert from their mouths, that there is not a single angel in the universal heaven who was created such from the beginning; nor any devil in hell who was created an angel of light and cast down; but that all, both in heaven and in hell, are from the human race; in heaven those who in the world lived in heavenly love and faith, in hell those who lived in infernal love and faith; and that hell in its whole complex is what is called the devil and satan; the hell which is at the back, where they are who are called evil genii, is the devil; and the hell in front, where they are who are called evil spirits, is satan. (H. H. n. 311.)

THE IMMENSITY OF THE SPIRITUAL WORLD.

From the immense multitude of men who have passed into the spiritual world since the first creation, and are there assembled; and from the continual increase that will be added to them from the human race hereafter, and this without end; it is obvious that that world is such and so vast that the natural world cannot be compared with it. How immense is the multitude of men already there it has sometimes, when my eyes have been opened, been granted me to see. There were so many,—and this only in a single place in one region,—that they could scarcely be numbered; there were some myriads. What must not the numbers be in all the rest ? For all are connected into societies there; and the societies are very numerous, and each society in its own place forms three heavens; and there are three hells under them. There are therefore some there who are in elevated regions, some who are in intermediate regions, and some who are below these ; and there are some who are in the lowest parts, or in the hells. And they who are in the higher regions dwell together as men dwell in cities in which there are hundreds of thousands assembled. It is plain therefore that the natural world, the abode of men on earth, cannot be compared with that world, as regards the multitude of the human race. So that when a man passes from the natural world into the spiritual it is as from a village into a mighty city. (L. J. n. 27.)

In so large a kingdom, where all the souls of men from the beginning of creation flock together,—nearly a million coming weekly from this earth,—and each has his peculiar genius and nature different from every other, and where there is a communication of all the ideas of every one, and yet each and all things must be brought into order, and that continually. it cannot be but that there exist indefinite things which have never entered into the idea of man. But as scarcely any one has conceived other than a very obscure idea of heaven or hell, the things here related must appear strange and wonderful ; especially from the fact that men believe spirits have no power of sensation ; when yet they have a more exquisite sense than men. (A. C. n. 969.)

Outward Aspect of the Spiritual World.

In outward appearance the spiritual world is quite similar to the natural world. Countries, with mountains, hills, valleys, plains, fields, lakes, rivers, fountains, appear there, as in the natural world; thus all things of the mineral kingdom are there. And paradises, gardens, groves, and woods appear, in which there are trees and shrubs of every kind, with fruits and seeds; and plants, flowers, herbs and grasses; all things therefore of the vegetable kingdom. Animals, birds, and fishes of every kind appear also ; and thus all things that belong to the animal kingdom. Man is there an angel and spirit. This is premised, that it may be known that the universe of the spiritual world is entirely similar to the universe of the natural world,—with the only difference that there things are not fixed and stationary, as in the natural world, because nothing there is natural, but all is spiritual.

It can be manifestly seen that the universe of that world reflects the image of man,—from the fact that the things above mentioned all spring forth and appear to the life about an angel, and about the angelic societies, just as if produced or created from them; and they remain about them, and do not pass away. That they are as if produced or created from them, is evident from the fact that when an angel goes away, or a society passes to another place, they no longer appear; and that when other angels come in their place, then the face of all things about them changes,—the paradises change, as to their trees and fruits; the gardens change, as to their flowers and seeds; the fields, as to their herbs and grasses; and the species of animals and birds are changed. The reason why such things appear, and are so changed, is, that they all spring forth in accordance with the affections and hence the thoughts of the angels; for they are correspondences, and as things that correspond make one with that to which they correspond, they are therefore a representative image of it. When viewed as to their forms the very image does not appear, but it is seen when they are regarded as to their uses. (D. L. W. n. 321, 322.)

THE BOOK OF LIFE.

It has scarcely been known to any one hitherto that every man has two memories, one exterior, the other interior; and that the exterior memory is proper to his body; and the interior to his spirit.

So long as he lives in the body, a man can scarcely know that he has an interior memory, because the interior memory then acts almost as one with his exterior memory. For the ideas of thought,[1] which belong to the interior memory, flow into the things that are in the exterior memory, as into their vessels, and they are there conjoined. It is the same as when angels and spirits speak with man; their ideas, by which they converse with each other, then flow into and so conjoin themselves with the words of a man's language, that they do not know but that they themselves are speaking in the man's vernacular; when yet the ideas only are theirs, and the words into which they flow are the man's,—about which I have often conversed with spirits.

These two memories are entirely distinct from each other. To the exterior memory, which is proper to man while he lives in the world, pertain all the words of languages, and objects of outward sense; as also the knowledges that belong to the world. To the interior memory pertain the ideas of speech

[1] See p. 558.

of spirits, which are of the interior sight; and all things
rational, from the ideas of which springs thought itself. A
man has no cognizance that these are distinct from each other,
both because he does not reflect upon the subject, and because
he is in things corporeal, and cannot so easily withdraw his
mind from them.

Hence it is that, while they live in the body men cannot
speak with each other except by languages divided into articulate sounds, that is into words, and cannot understand each
other, unless they are acquainted with these languages. The
reason is that it takes place from the exterior memory. But
spirits converse with each other by a universal language distinguished into ideas, such as those of thought itself, and thus
can converse with every spirit, of whatsoever language and
nation he had been in the world; the reason is that it takes
place from the interior memory. Every man, immediately
after death, comes into this universal language, because he
comes into this interior memory, which is proper to his spirit.

The interior memory vastly excels the exterior; it is as
myriads to one, or as a thing that is luminous to one that is
dark. For myriads of ideas of the interior memory flow into
one of the exterior memory, and there form a certain indistinct
general [impression]. All the faculties of spirits, and especially
of angels, are therefore in a more perfect state, their sensations
as well as their thoughts and perceptions. How great is the
superiority of the inner memory to the outer, may be seen
from examples :—When a man calls another to remembrance,
friend or enemy, whose character he has known from the
intercourse of many years, what he then thinks of him is
presented as an indistinct [outline]; and this because he
thinks from his exterior memory. But when the same man
becomes a spirit and remembers him, then what he thinks of
him is presented as to all the ideas that he ever conceived
respecting him; and this because he thinks from his interior
memory. It is the same with regard to every thing; a thing
itself of which he knows many particulars presents itself in
the exterior memory as a certain general [conception], but in
the interior memory it is presented as to all the least particulars
respecting it of which he had ever formed an idea; and this in
a wonderful form.

Whatever things a man hears and sees, and is affected by,
these as respects ideas and ends are insinuated into his interior
memory,—the man not being aware of it,—and there they remain; so that nothing whatever perishes, although the same
things in the exterior memory are obliterated. Such therefore
is the interior memory that the particulars, nay, the very least

particulars, of what a man has at any time thought, said and done, or even that as a faint impression has appeared to him, from earliest infancy to latest old age, are with the utmost minuteness inscribed upon it. Man has the memory of all these things within him when he comes into the other life, and is successively brought into the recollection of them all. This is his BOOK OF LIFE, which is opened in the other life, and according to which he is judged. Man can scarcely believe this; but yet it is most true. All his ends, which to him were obscure, and all that he had thought as well as all that he had said and done from them, to the minutest point, are in that book, that is, in his interior memory; and whenever the Lord permits, they are laid open before the angels, as in the clear light of day. This has sometimes been shown me, and has been attested by so much experience that there remains not the least doubt of it. . . . A man leaves nothing at all behind him at death save only his bones and flesh, which of themselves were not animate while he lived in the world, but were animated by the life of his spirit, which was his purer substance annexed to the corporeal.

But with respect to his exterior memory the case is this: he has with him each and all things pertaining to it; but he is not then permitted to use this, but only the interior memory. There are many reasons. The first is that, as was said, from the interior memory in the other life a man is able to speak and converse with all throughout the universe. A second reason is, that this is the memory proper to the spirit, and is adequate to his state in which he then is. For outward things, that is to say matters of outward knowledge, things worldly and corporeal, are adapted to man and correspond to his state while he is in the world and the body; while interior things, that is things rational, spiritual, and celestial, are adapted and correspond to the spirit. (A. C. n. 2469-2476.)

THE ETERNITY OF HEAVEN AND HELL.

The life of man cannot be changed after death. He then remains such as he had been in the world. For the whole spirit of a man is such as his love is; and infernal love cannot be changed into heavenly love, because they are opposite. This is meant by the words of Abraham to the rich man in hell: *" Between us and you there is a great gulf; so that they which would pass from hence to you cannot; neither can they pass from thence to us"* (Luke xvi. 26). It is plain from this that they who enter into hell remain there to eternity; and that they who enter into heaven remain there to eternity. (H. D. n. 239.)

After death a man puts off all that does not agree with his love; nay, he successively puts on the face, the tone of voice, the speech, the bearing, and the manner of his life's love. (C. L. n. 36.)

That after death a man remains to eternity such as he is as to his will or reigning love, has been confirmed by abundant experience. It has been given me to speak with some who lived two thousand years ago, whose lives are described in history and therefore known. They were found to be still like themselves, and precisely such as they were described,—such, as to the love from which and according to which their life was. There were others who lived seventeen centuries ago, who were also known from history; and there were others who lived four centuries ago, and some three, and so on, with whom also it was granted me to converse; and it was found that a similar affection still reigned with them,—with no other difference than that the delights of their love were turned into such things as were correspondent. It was said by the angels that the life of the reigning love is never changed with any one to eternity, since every one is his own love; to change that love in a spirit would therefore be to deprive him of his life, or annihilate him. They also stated the reason, which is, that after death a man can no longer be reformed, by instruction, as in the world; because the ultimate plane which consists of natural cognitions and affections is then quiescent, and as it is not spiritual cannot be opened; that the interiors which are of the internal or external mind rest upon that plane, as a house upon its foundation; and that it is on this account that a man remains to eternity such as the life of his love had been in the world. (H. H. n. 480.)

They who are being elevated into heaven, and afterwards when they have been elevated, are perfected to eternity. But they who are being cast into hell,[1] and afterwards when they have been cast in, suffer more grievous evils continually, and this until they dare not do evil to any one; and they afterwards remain in hell to eternity. They cannot be delivered therefrom,

---

[1] The evil are spoken of as being *cast* into hell only according to the appearance. The author abundantly teaches that in reality the Lord casts no one into hell, but constantly withholds from hell; but that the evil of themselves plunge into hell, by following the bent of their evil loves (see p. 527). The apparent casting into hell is really a gradual process,—that of voluntarily choosing and living an evil life. The necessary restraint of evil by punishments, whether in this world or the other, is essentially mercy. (See also p. 597.)

because it cannot be given them to will good to any one; but only, from fear of punishment, not to do evil to any one,—the lust always remaining.   (A. C. n. 7541.)

WHY THE WICKED CANNOT BE SAVED AFTER DEATH.

The life of any one can by no means be changed after death; an evil life can in no wise be converted into a good life, or an infernal into an angelic life; because every spirit, from head to foot, is of the character of his love, and therefore of his life; and to convert this life into its opposite would be to destroy the spirit utterly.   The angels declare that it would be easier to change a night owl into a dove, or a horned owl into a bird of paradise, than an infernal spirit into an angel of heaven. From these considerations it is evident that no one can be received into heaven by immediate mercy.   (H. H. n. 527.)

The affection of a man's love is his life.   If a man's affection is that of self and the world, then his whole life is nothing else; nor can he strive against it, for this would be to strive against his very life.   Principles of truth effect nothing; if the affection of these loves has dominion it draws truth over to its own side, and thus falsifies it, and if it does not entirely favour rejects it. Hence it is that principles of the truth of faith have not the least efficacy with a man unless the Lord insinuates an affectior of spiritual love, that is of love towards the neighbour; and in so far as a man receives this affection he receives also the truths of faith.   The affection of this love is what constitutes the new will.   It is manifest from these considerations that a man never sets his heart to any truth if the will resists.   It is on this account that the infernals cannot receive the truths of faith, and therefore cannot be amended,—because they are in the affection or lust of evil.   (A. C. n. 7342.)

MEANING OF THE SAYING, AS THE TREE FALLETH SO IT LIES.

So long as a man lives [in the world] he is in the ultimate of order and has a corporeal memory, which increases, and in which the things that belong to his interior memory must be enrooted. Hence the more there are in them and between them of things concordant and correspondent with good and truth, the more he has of life from the Lord, and the more he can be perfected in the other life.   But the exterior or corporeal memory is that in which the interiors are rooted.   After death, indeed, man has all his exterior or corporeal memory, or each and all things belonging to it; but this can no longer increase, and when it does not, new concordance and correspondence cannot be formed; and hence all things of his interior memory are there, and are terminated, in his exterior memory, although he cannot now use this. From this it may appear why it is that, "*As the tree falleth so it lies.*" [1] Not that he who is in good cannot be perfected; he is perfected immensely, even to angelic wisdom,—but conformably to the concordance and correspondence that there was between his internals and externals while he lived in the world. After the life of the body no one receives external, but interior and internal things.

With respect to the dogma that where the tree falleth it remains, it is not to be understood as it has been explained, but thus:—It is the concordance of the internal or spiritual man with the external or natural which remains as it falls. Man has both with him in the other life; the internal or spiritual is terminated in his external or natural as in its ultimate. The internal or spiritual man is perfected in the other life; yet only so far as it can have concordance in the external or natural. But this, that is the external or natural, cannot be perfected in the other life, but remains of the same character that it has acquired in the life of the body; and it is perfected in this life by the removal of the love of self and of the world, and so by the reception of the good which is of charity and the truth which is of faith from the Lord. Hence is the concordance, or the non-concordance, which is the tree with its root, that after death remains where it falls. (S. D. Minus, n. 4645, 4646.)

Scriptural Explanation of the final State.

" *He that is unjust let him become unjust still; and he that is filthy let him become filthy still; and he that is just let him become just still; and he that is holy let him become holy still* " (Rev. xxii. 11). This signifies in particular the state of every one after death and before his judgment, and in general before the last judgment; that from those who are in evils goods will be taken away, and from those who are in falsities truths will be taken away; and on the other hand that from those who are in goods evils will be taken away, and from those who are in truths falsities will be taken away. By the unjust he who is in evils is signified, and by the just he who is in goods; by the filthy or unclean he is signified who is in falsities, and by the holy he is signified who is in truths. From this it follows that he that is unjust let him become unjust still, signifies that he who is in

[1] Eccles. xi. 3.

evils will be still more in evils ; and that he who is filthy let him become filthy still, signifies that he who is in falsities will be still more in falsities ; and on the other hand that he that is just let him become just still, signifies that he who is in goods will be still more in goods ; and that he that is holy let him become holy still, signifies that he who is in truths will be still more in truths. And the reason why it is signified that from those who are in evils goods will be taken away, and from those who are in falsities truths will be taken away ; and that on the other hand from those who are in goods evils will be taken away, and from those who are in truths falsities will be taken away, is that in so far as goods are taken away from one who is in evils he is so much the more in evils, and in so far as truths are taken away from one who is in falsities, so much the more is he in falsities ; and on the other hand in so far as evils are taken away from one who is in goods so much the more is he in goods, and in so far as falsities are taken away from one who is in truths so much the more is he in truths. Either this or the other takes place with every one after death ; for thus the evil are prepared for hell and the good for heaven. For an evil man cannot carry goods and truths with him to hell ; neither can a good man carry evils and falsities with him to heaven ; for heaven and hell would thus be confounded. But it should be well understood that those who are interiorly evil, and interiorly good are meant. For they who are interiorly evil may be outwardly good ; for they can act and speak like the good, as hypocrites do. And they who are interiorly good may sometimes be outwardly evil ; for outwardly they may do evils, and speak falsities ; but yet they repent, and desire to be instructed in truths. This is the same as the Lord says, " *Whosoever hath, to him shall be given, that he may have more abundance ; but whosoever hath not from him shall be taken away even that he hath* " (Matt. xiii. 12). (A. R. n. 948.)

The Universals of Hell and of Heaven.

The universal [principles] of hell are three ; but they are diametrically opposite to the universal [principles] of heaven. The universals of hell are these three loves ; the love of ruling, from the love of self ; the love of possessing the goods of others, from the love of the world ; and scortatory love. The universals of heaven opposite to them are these three loves ; the love of ruling, from the love of use ; the love of possessing the goods of the world, from the love of performing uses by means of them ; and love truly conjugial. (T. C. R. n. 661.)

THE INTERMEDIATE STATE OR
WORLD OF SPIRITS.

THE world of spirits is not heaven, nor is it hell; but it is a place or state intermediate between the two. For thither man first goes after death; and then after the required time, according to his life in the world, he is either elevated into heaven, or cast into hell.

The world of spirits is a place intermediate between heaven and hell, and is also the intermediate state of man after death. That it is an intermediate place, has been made manifest to me by the fact that the hells are beneath and the heavens above; and that it is an intermediate state, by the fact that so long as he is there a man is not yet in heaven, nor in hell. The state of heaven in man is the conjunction of good and truth within him; and the state of hell is the conjunction of evil and falsity within him. When good is conjoined to truth in a man-spirit [1] he then enters into heaven; for as was said, that conjunction is heaven within him. And when evil is conjoined with falsity in a man-spirit he enters into hell; for that conjunction is hell within him. This conjunction is effected in the world of spirits, because man is then in an intermediate state. It is the same whether you say the conjunction of the understanding and the will, or the conjunction of truth and good. (H. H. n. 421, 422.)

Almost every man at this day is in such a state that he knows truths, and from knowledge and also from understanding thinks of them; and he either does much of them, or little of them, or nothing of them, or acts contrary to them from the love of evil and thence a belief in what is false. In order therefore that he may be a subject either of heaven or hell, he is first after death brought into the world of spirits; and there a conjunction of good and truth is effected in those who are to be elevated into heaven; and a conjunction of evil and falsity in those who are to be cast into hell. For it is not permitted any one, in heaven or in hell, to have a divided mind, that is, to understand one thing and will another; but what he wills he must also understand, and what he

---

[1] Man-spirit (*homo spiritus*) is an expression used occasionally by the author to designate the spirit of man newly entered into the spiritual world, while he is yet in externals, and in a state similar to that in which he was in the world.

understands he must also will. In heaven therefore, he who wills good must understand truth ; and in hell he who wills evil must understand falsity. For this reason with the good falsities are removed in the world of spirits, and truths suitable and conformable to their good are given ; and with the evil truths are there removed and falses are given suitable and conformable to their evil. It is plain from these facts what the world of spirits is.

There is a vast number in the world of spirits, because the first meeting of all is there ; and all are there examined and prepared. There is no fixed term of duration for their sojourn there ; some only enter that world, and are presently either taken up into heaven, or cast down into hell ; some remain there only for weeks ; some for years, but not more than thirty. The differences in the duration of their sojourn arise from the correspondence or want of correspondence of the interiors and exteriors in man. But it shall be told in what follows, how a man is brought from one state into another in that world and prepared.

As soon as men come into the world of spirits after their decease they are perfectly distinguished by the Lord ; the evil are immediately bound to the infernal society in which as to their ruling love they were in the world; and the good are immediately bound to the heavenly society in which they were in the world, as to love, charity, and faith. But although they are thus distinguished, yet those who have been friends and acquaintances in the life of the body all meet and converse with each other in that world, when they desire,—especially wives and husbands, and also brothers and sisters. I have seen a father converse with six sons and recognize them ; and have seen many others with their relatives and friends ; but as they were of different mind (*animus*) owing to their life in the world, after a short time they were separated. But those who pass into heaven, and who pass into hell, from the world of spirits, afterwards neither see nor know each other more, unless they are of similar character from a similar love. That they see each other in the world of spirits, and not in heaven and hell, is because those who are in the world of spirits are brought into states similar to those which they experienced in the life of the body, [passing] from one into another ; but afterwards all are brought into a permanent state, similar to the state of their ruling love, in which one knows another only from the similitude of love ; for similitude conjoins, and dissimilitude separates. (H. H. n. 425-427.)

The Resurrection and Last Judgment of everyone is immediately after Death.

I have conversed with some a few days after their decease ; and as they were then recently come, they were in a degree of light there which to them differed little from the light of the world. And because the light so appeared to them they doubted whether the light came to them from any different source. They were therefore taken up into the first confine of heaven, where the light was brighter; and from there speaking with me, they said that they had never seen such light. And this took place when already the sun was set . . . Some of them believed no otherwise than that men after death would be as phantoms ; in which opinion they confirmed themselves by the apparitions of which they had heard. But they drew no other conclusion therefrom than that the ghost was some gross vital principle that is first exhaled from the life of the body, but falls back again into the dead body, and is thus extinguished. And some believed that they should first rise again at the time of the last judgment, when the world would perish; and that they should then rise with the body, which though fallen into dust would then be collected together ; and thus that they were to rise again with flesh and bone. And since for many ages mankind have looked in vain for that last judgment or destruction of the world, they have lapsed into the error that they shall never rise again ; thinking nothing then of what they have learned from the Word, and from which too they have sometimes therefore said that when a man dies his soul is in the hand of God, among the happy or the unhappy according to the life that he had acquired to himself; nor of what the Lord said concerning the rich man and Lazarus. But they were instructed that the last judgment of every one is when he dies ; and that he then appears to himself endowed with a body as in the world ; and to enjoy every sense as in the world,—but purer and more exquisite, because things corporeal do not hinder, and the things that pertain to the light of the world do not overshadow those that are of the light of heaven ; thus that they are in a body purified as it were ; and that he could never carry about a body of flesh and bone there such as he had in the world, for this would be to be encompassed with earthly dust. With some I conversed on this subject on the same day that their bodies were entombed,—who through my eyes saw their own corpse, the bier, and the burial. And they said that they reject that body; that it had served them for their uses in the world in which they had been ; but that now they live in a body that serves them for uses in the world in which they now are. They also desired that I would tell this to their relatives who were in mourning. But it was given me to reply that if I should tell them they would mock at it, because they believe that to be nothing which they themselves cannot see with their own eyes; and so they would reckon it among the visions which are illusions. (A. C. n. 4527.)

THE DREAD OF DEATH AN INDICATION OF THE QUALITY OF A MAN'S LIFE.

Whatever a man loves he fears to lose; and therefore in sickness, when death is impending, it may especially be known what things a man has loved, or what were his ends in life. As for example, if he has striven for honours, and has placed his delight in them, he then greatly fears to die; and also upon the bed of death talks about such things as had been the source of his delight. As he does not abstain from such matters, so he is even devoted to himself. So also with the man who has his delight in possessions, in gains, and other worldly things; then in thought he clings to the same, and disposes of them at the point of death, by will and similar means. But he who is not solicitous about these things lightly regards them, and thinks only of eternal salvation; and all other things he esteems of very trifling value, as not worthy to be mentioned, even though it were the whole world.

But yet for the sake of one's children to be unwilling to die is natural, both in the good and the evil. For the evil also love their children, but for the ends that prevail in themselves, that is to say, that they may be eminent in honours, and so on.

The evil too, at the point of death, can lightly regard worldly things, and their own [possessions], and think only of eternal things; but this is done in despair of life, that is when he no longer sees any hope of life. Then too he can talk piously, and despise worldly things; but rarely those who are led by the love of self.

But they who are reckless of death, from the love of self, that they may be famous after the life of the body, and who at the same time are regardless of worldly things, have a different motive; that they wish to be kept in remembrance as heroes, for it is thus that they desire to die. (S. D. n. 1235-1238.)

THE PROCESS OF DYING, RESURRECTION, ETC.

When the body is no longer capable of performing its functions in the natural world,—corresponding to the thoughts and affections of its spirit, which it has from the spiritual world,—then a man is said to die. This takes place when the respiratory motions of the lungs and the systolic motions of the heart cease. But yet the man does not die, but is only separated from the corporeal part which was of use to him in the world; for the man himself lives. It is said that the man himself lives, because a man is not man by virtue of the body, but by virtue of the spirit; for it is the spirit in man which thinks, and thought together with affection makes the man. From this it is plain that when a man dies he only passes from one world into the other. Hence it is that in the Word, in its internal sense, death signifies resurrection and the continuation of life.

The inmost communication of the spirit [with the body] is with the respiration and with the motion of the heart; its thought communicates with the respiration, and its affection, which is of love, with the heart. When therefore these two motions in the body cease there is immediately a separation. These two motions, the respiratory motion of the lungs and the systolic motion of the heart, are the very bonds which being broken the spirit is left to itself; and the body, being then without the life of its spirit, becomes cold and putrifies. That the inmost communication of man's spirit is with the respiration and with the heart, is because all the vital motions thereon depend, not only in general, but also in every part.

The spirit of a man remains in the body for a short time after the separation; but no longer than till the total cessation of the motion of the heart, which takes place sooner or later according to the nature of the disease of which a man dies. For with some the motion of the heart continues a long time, and with some not long. As soon as this motion ceases the man is resuscitated; but this is done by the Lord alone. By resuscitation is meant the withdrawal of man's spirit from the body, and its introduction into the spiritual world; which is commonly called the resurrection. The reason why man's spirit is not separated from the body until the motion of the heart has ceased is, that the heart corresponds to affection, which is of love, which is the very life of man; for the vital heat of every one is from love.[1] So long therefore as this motion[2] continues, there is a correspondence, and the life of the spirit therefore in the body.

It has not only been told me how the resuscitation is effected, but has also been shown me by living experience. I

[1] See p. 25.
[2] The word in the original here is *conjunctio ;* but as suggested by Mr. Noble, in his translation of the work from which this extract is taken, it seems evident from the context that this has been written or printed, by mistake, for the very different word *motus.*

was subjected to this very experience in order that I might fully understand how it is effected.

I was brought into a state of insensibility as to the bodily senses, thus almost into the state of the dying; the interior life with the faculty of thought, however, remaining entire, so that I could perceive and retain in the memory the things which came to pass, and which take place with those who are resuscitated from the dead. I perceived that the respiration of the body was almost taken away, the interior respiration which is of the spirit remaining, connected with a slight and tacit respiration of the body. Then there was given, in the first place, a communication as to the pulsation of the heart with the celestial kingdom, since that kingdom corresponds to the heart in man. Angels from that kingdom were also seen,—some at a distance, and two were sitting near my head. All affection proper to myself was thereby taken away, but yet thought and perception remained. I was in this state for some hours. The spirits who were about me then withdrew, supposing that I was dead. An aromatic odor was also perceived, as of an embalmed body; for when celestial angels are present what is cadaverous is perceived as aromatic,—which when spirits perceive they cannot approach. Thus, too, evil spirits are kept away from the spirit of man when he is first introduced into eternal life. The angels who were sitting at my head were silent, communicating only their thoughts with mine; and when these are received the angels know that the spirit of the man is in the state in which it can be withdrawn from the body. The communication of their thoughts was effected by looking into my face; for thus communications of thoughts are effected in heaven. As thought and perception remained with me, in order that I might know and remember how resuscitation is effected, I perceived that these angels first examined what my thought was,—whether it was like that of those who die, which is usually about eternal life; and that they wished to keep my mind in that thought. I was afterwards told that a man's spirit is held in its last thought when the body is expiring, until he returns to the thoughts which come from his general or ruling affection in the world. It was given me, especially, to perceive and also to feel that there was an attraction, and as it were a pulling of the interiors of my mind, thus of my spirit, out of the body; and it was said that this is of the Lord, and that thereby the resurrection is effected.

Since the celestial angels are with the resuscitated they do not leave him, because they love every one. But if the spirit is such that he can no longer remain in the company of celestial angels he longs to depart from them; and when this is the case there come angels of the Lord's spiritual kingdom, through whom the enjoyment of light is given him; for before he saw nothing, but only thought. It was also shown me how this is effected. These angels appeared as it were to roll off the tunic of the left eye towards the septum of the nose, that the eye might be opened and be enabled to see. The spirit perceives no otherwise than that it is effected in this manner; but it is an appearance. When the tunic appears to have been rolled off a certain brightness is visible, but obscure; as when a man looks through the eyelashes on first awakening. This obscure brightness appeared to me of an azure colour, but it was told me afterwards that this takes place with variety. After this something is felt to be gently rolled from off the face; which being done spiritual thought is induced. This rolling from off the face is also an appearance; for it is represented thereby that from natural thought he comes into spiritual thought. The angels are extremely careful lest any idea should come from the resuscitated that does not savour of love. They then tell him that he is a spirit. After the enjoyment of light has been given, the spiritual angels perform for the new spirit all the kindly services that he can ever desire in that state; and instruct him respecting the things that are in the other life,—yet only so far as he can comprehend them. But if he is not such as to be willing to be instructed, then the resuscitated spirit desires to separate from the companionship of these angels. But still the angels do not leave him; he in fact dissociates himself from them. For the angels love every one, and desire nothing more than to perform kindly services, to give them instruction, and take them into heaven; in this consists their highest delight. When a spirit thus dissociates himself he is received by good spirits, and all kindly services are also rendered him while he is in company with them. But if his life in the world had been such that he cannot abide in the company of the good, then he also desires to withdraw from them; and thus he continues to do until he associates himself with such as are in entire agreement with his life in the world, with whom he finds his own life. And then, which is remarkable, he pursues a life similar to that which he led in the world. (H. H. n. 445-450.)

THREE SUCCESSIVE STATES OF MAN IN THE WORLD OF SPIRITS.

There are three states through which man passes after death, before he comes either into heaven or into hell; the first state is that of his exteriors; the second state is that of his interiors; and the third is his state of preparation. These states man passes through in the world of spirits. But there are some who do not pass through these states, but are either taken up into heaven or cast into hell immediately after death.[1] They who are immediately taken up into heaven are those that have been regenerated, and thus prepared for heaven, in the world. Those who have been so regenerated and prepared that they have need only to reject natural impurities with the body, are immediately carried by the angels into heaven. I have seen them taken up soon after the hour of death. But they who interiorly have been wicked and outwardly as to appearance good, thus who have filled their malignity with deceit, and have used goodness as a means of deceiving, are immediately cast into hell. I have seen some such cast into hell directly after death. . . . But both these are few in comparison with those who are kept in the world of spirits, and there, according to Divine order, are prepared for heaven or for hell. (H. H. n. 491.)

The First State of Man after Death.

The first state of man after death is similar to his state in the world, because then in like manner he is in externals. He also has a similar face, similar speech, and a similar external mind (*animus*), and therefore a similar moral and civil life. Hence it is that he then knows no otherwise than that he is still in the world, unless he adverts to the things he meets with, and to what was said to him by the angels when he was raised up, that he is now a spirit. Thus one life is continued into the other, and death is only the transit.

Because the spirit of a man soon after his life in the world is such, he is therefore then recognized by his friends, and by those whom he had known in the world; for spirits have this perception, not from his face and speech only, but also from the sphere of his life as they approach. When any one thinks of another in the other life he also brings his face before him in thought, and at the same time many things that pertain to his life; and when he does this the other becomes present, as if he were sent for and called. This in the spiritual world arises from the fact that there thoughts are communicated; and that there are no spaces there, such as exist in the natural world. Hence it is that all, when they first come into the other life, are recognized by their friends, their relatives, and those with whom in any way they are acquainted; and that they converse together, and afterwards associate, according to their friendship in the world. I have frequently heard that those who have come from the world have rejoiced at seeing their friends again, and that their friends in

[1] See pp. 582, 597.

turn have rejoiced that they had come to them. It is a common occurrence that consort meets consort, and they mutually congratulate each other. They remain together too, but for a longer or shorter time according to the delight of their life together in the world. But yet if love truly conjugial,—which is a conjunction of minds, from heavenly love,—has not joined them together, after remaining together some time they are separated. And if the minds of consorts have been in disagreement, and they inwardly loathed each other, they burst forth into open enmity, and sometimes fight; but yet they are not separated until they enter the second state,—of which in what presently follows.

As the life of spirits recently arrived is not unlike their life in the natural world, and as they know nothing about the state of their life after death, and nothing about heaven and hell, except what they have learned from the literal sense of the Word, and from preaching thence; therefore, after they have wondered that they are in a body, and in the possession of every sense that they had in the world, and that they see similar objects, they come into the desire, to know what heaven is, and what hell is, and where they are. They are therefore instructed by their friends respecting the state of eternal life; and are also led about to various places, and into various companies; and some into cities, and also into gardens and paradises; generally to magnificent scenes, since such things delight the externals in which they are. They are then brought by turns into their thoughts, which they had entertained in the life of the body, about the state of their souls after death, and about heaven, and about hell; and this until they feel indignant that they have been entirely ignorant, and that the church is ignorant, of such things. Almost everyone desires to know whether he will go to heaven; very many believe that they shall go to heaven, because they led a moral and civil life in the world; not considering that the evil and the good lead a similar life in externals, alike doing good to others, and alike frequenting places of public worship, hearing sermons and praying; not knowing at all that external acts and the externals of worship effect nothing, but the internals from which the externals proceed. Scarcely one out of some thousands knows what the internals [of life and worship] are, and that in them man has heaven and the church; and less do they understand that external acts are of the same quality as the intentions and thoughts and the love and faith in these from which the actions spring. And when they are instructed, they do not comprehend that thinking and willing effect anything, but only speaking and acting. There are very many such at this day who come from the Christian world into the other life.

Yet they are examined by good spirits, as to their quality, and this in various ways; for in this first state the evil as well as the good utter truths and do good deeds,—for the reason mentioned above, that they alike lived a moral life, in outward form, since they lived under governments and subject to laws, and since thereby they acquired a reputation for justice and sincerity, and secured favour, and so were exalted to honours and acquired wealth. But evil spirits are distinguished from the good especially by the fact that the evil attend eagerly to what is said about external things, and little to what is said about internal things, which are the truths and goods of the church and of heaven. These indeed they hear, but not with attention and joy. They are also distinguished by the fact that they frequently turn themselves towards certain quarters, and when left to themselves walk in the ways that lead in those directions. From their turning to such quarters and walking in such ways it becomes known what is the nature of the love that leads them.

The spirits who arrive from the world are in truth all attached to some society in heaven, or to some society in hell. But this is only as to their interiors, and the interiors of no one are manifested so long as they are in exteriors; for external things cover and conceal the internal, especially with those who are in interior evil. But afterwards, when they come into the second state, they manifestly appear; for then their interiors are opened, and the exteriors are laid asleep.

This first state of man after death continues with some for days, with some for months, and with some for a year; but rarely with anyone beyond a year; with a difference in each case according to the agreement or disagreement of the interiors with the exteriors. For the exteriors and interiors with every one must act in unity, and correspond. It is not allowable in the spiritual world for any one to think and will in one way, and speak and act in another. There every one must be the image of his own affection or his own love; and therefore such as he is in his interiors, he must be in his exteriors. For this reason the exteriors of a spirit are first uncovered and reduced to order, that they may serve as a plane corresponding to the interiors. (H. H. n. 493, 498.)

The Second State of Man after Death.

After the first state is passed through,—which is the state of the exteriors, treated of in the foregoing article,—the man-spirit is let into the state of his interiors, or into the state of his interior will and the thought therefrom, in which he had been in the world, when being left to himself he thought freely and without restraint. Into this state he glides unconsciously, much as when, in the world, he withdraws the thought that is nearest to the speech, or from which the speech proceeds, towards his interior thought, and abides in that. Therefore when the man-spirit is in this state he is in his very self and in his very life; for to think freely from his own affection is the very life of man, and is himself. (H. H. n. 502.)

All men without exception are let into this state after death, because it is the proper state of their spirit. The former state is such as the man was as to his spirit when in company, which is not his proper state. (*ib.* n. 504.)

When a spirit is in the state of his interiors it manifestly appears what the character of the man was, in himself, when in the world; for he then acts from his own. He who was interiorly in good in the world then acts rationally and wisely, more wisely indeed than in the world; because he is released from connection with the body, and therefore with terrestrial things, which caused obscurity and interposed as it were a cloud. But he who was in evil in the world then acts foolishly and insanely, in truth more insanely than in the world; because he is in freedom, and under no restraints. For while he lived in the world he was sane in externals, because he thereby presented the appearance of a rational man. When therefore his externals are taken away from him, his insanities are revealed. A bad man who in externals puts on the appearance of a good man, may be compared to a vessel outwardly polished and elegant, and covered with a lid, within which is concealed every kind of filth; according to the Lord's saying:—"*Ye are like unto whited sepulchres, which appear beautiful outwardly, but within are full of the bones of the dead, and of all uncleanliness*" (Matt. xxiii. 27). (*ib.* n. 505.)

When spirits are in this second state they appear precisely as they were, in themselves, in the world; and whatever they have done and said in secret is also divulged. For then, as external considerations do not restrain them, they say such things and also endeavour to do such things openly; nor do they fear, as in the world, for their reputation. They are also then brought into the many states of their own evils; that they may appear to angels and good spirits as they are. Thus things hidden are laid open, and secret things are revealed, according to the Lord's words:—"*There is nothing covered that shall not be uncovered, neither hid, that shall not be known. Whatsoever ye have spoken in darkness shall be heard in the light; and that which ye have spoken in the ear in closets shall be proclaimed upon the house tops*" (Luke xii. 2, 3). And in another place:—"*I say unto you, that every idle word that men shall have spoken, they shall give account thereof in the day of judgment*" (Matt. xii. 36). (*ib.* n. 507.)

Because evil spirits when they are in this second state rush into evils of every kind, they are frequently and grievously punished. The punishments in the world of spirits are manifold; nor is there any respect of person, whether in the world a man were king or servant. Every evil carries its punishment with it; they are conjoined. Whoever therefore is in evil is also in the punishment of evil. But yet no one there suffers punishment on account of the evils that he had done in the world; but for the evils that he then does. It however amounts to the same, and is the same, whether it be said that men suffer punishment on account of their evils in the world, or that they suffer punishment on account of the evils that they do in the other life; since every one after death returns into his own life, and thus into similar evils. For the character of a man is such as it had been in the life of his body. They are punished because in this state the fear of punishment is the only means of subduing evils. Exhortation is no longer of any avail, nor instruction, nor fear of the law, and of public opinion and reputation; since the spirit now acts from his nature, which can neither be restrained nor broken except by punishments. But good spirits are never punished, although they have done evils in the world; for their evils do not return. And it is also given me to know that their evils were of a different kind or nature; for they were not of purpose against the truth, and from no other evil heart than what they received by inheritance from their parents,—into which, when they were in externals separate from internals, they were carried by a blind delight. (*ib.* n. 509.)

While an evil spirit is in the state of his interiors, he is turned by degrees towards his own society, and at length before this state is ended, directly to it; and when the state is ended the evil spirit of his own accord casts himself into the hell where they are who are like him. The act itself appears to the sight as one falling backwards, with the head down and feet uppermost. The reason why it so appears is that he is in inverted order; for he has loved infernal things and rejected heavenly things. Some evil spirits in this second state by turns enter the hells, and come out again; but they do not then appear to fall backwards, as when they are fully vastated. The society itself in which they had been, as to their spirit, while in the world, is also shown them when they are in the state of their exteriors; that they may know thereby that they have been in hell even in the life of the body,—but yet not in a similar state with those that are in hell itself, but in a state similar to those that are in the world of spirits ; of whose state in comparison with that of those that are in hell more will be said in what follows. (*ib.* n. 510.)

The separation of evil spirits from good spirits is effected in this second state. For in the first state they are together; since while a spirit is in his exteriors he is as he had been in the world; thus, just as there, the evil is with the good, and the good with the evil. When he is brought into his interiors, and left to his own nature or will, it is otherwise. The separation of the good from the evil is effected in various ways; generally by leading them about to those societies with which they had had communication by good thoughts and affections in their first state ; and so to those that they had induced, by external appearances, to believe that they were not evil. They are usually led about through a wide circuit, and are every where shown to good spirits as they are in themselves. At the sight of them good spirits turn away ; and as they turn away, the evil spirits also who are carried about are turned away from them, with their face to the quarter where their infernal society is, into which they are about to enter. As to other methods of separation, which are many, I say nothing. (*ib.* n. 511.)

The Third State of Man after Death.

The third state of man or of his spirit after death is a state of instruction. This state is for those who go to heaven, and become angels ; but not for those that pass into hell, since these cannot be instructed. Therefore the second state of these is also their third, which ends in this ; that they are turned entirely to their own love, and so to the infernal society which is in similar love. When this comes to pass they think and will from that love ; and as the love is infernal they will nothing but what is evil, and think nothing but what is false. These are their delights, because they are of their love. And hence they reject every thing good and true, which they had before adopted because they served their love as means. But the good are brought from the second state into a third, which is the state of their preparation for heaven, by instruction. For no one can be prepared for heaven except by cognitions of good and truth, and therefore by instruction ; since no one can know what spiritual good and truth are, and what the evil and the falsity are which are opposite to them, unless he be instructed.

The instruction is given by the angels of many societies ; especially by those which are in the northern and southern quarters, for these angelic societies are in intelligence and wisdom from cognitions of good and truth. The places of instruction are towards the north, and are various ; being arranged and distinguished according to the genera and species of heavenly goods, so that each and everyone may be instructed there according to his genius and faculty of reception. These places extend to a great distance there, all around. The good spirits who are to be instructed are guided to them by the Lord, after they have passed through their second state in the world of spirits. But yet not all ; for they who have been instructed in the world were there also prepared by the Lord for heaven, and are taken into heaven by another way ; some immediately after death ; some after a brief sojourn with good spirits,—where the grosser things of their thoughts and affections, which they derived from honours and riches in the world, are removed, and they are thus purified. Some are first vastated ; which is effected in places beneath the soles of the feet which are called the lower earth,[1] where some suffer severely. These are they who have confirmed themselves in falsities, and yet have led good lives ; for confirmed falsities inhere with great tenacity, and until they are dispersed truths cannot be seen, and therefore cannot be received. (H. H. n. 512, 513.)

But all are not instructed in a similar manner, nor by similar societies of heaven. They who from infancy have been educated in heaven are instructed by angels of the interior heavens,—since they have not imbibed falsities from falsities of religion, nor defiled their spiritual life by grossness from honors and riches in the world. Those who have died in adult age are for the most part instructed by angels of the ultimate heaven, because these angels are more suited to them than the angels of the interior heavens ; for they are in interior wisdom, which is not as yet received. But Mahomedans are instructed by angels who had before been in the same religion, and were converted to Christianity.[2] The [gentile] nations also are instructed by their angels.

All instruction there is from doctrine derived from the Word ; and not from the Word without doctrine. Christians are instructed from heavenly doctrine, which is in perfect agreement with the internal sense of the Word. All others, as the Mahomedans, and [gentile] nations, are instructed from doctrines suited to their apprehension ; which differ from heavenly doctrines only in this, that spiritual life is taught through

---

[1] See note, p. 601.
[2] That is, as the author sets forth in another section (H. H. n. 514), Mahomedans who, having lived a good life on earth, had been instructed in the Christian religion and so prepared for heaven, in the world of spirits.

moral life, in agreement with the good dogmas of their religion, from which they derived their life in the world.

Instruction in the heavens differs from instruction on earth in this respect; that the knowledges are not committed to memory, but to the life. For the memory of spirits is in their life; inasmuch as they receive and imbibe all things that are in agreement with their life, and do not receive, still less imbibe, the things that are not in agreement; for spirits are affections, and are therefore in a human form similar to their affections. Because they are so, an affection for truth for the sake of the uses of life is continually inspired; for the Lord provides that every one may love the uses suited to his genius,—which love is also exalted by the hope of becoming an angel. And as all the uses of heaven have reference to the common use, which is for the Lord's kingdom,—which then is their country; and as all special and particular uses are excellent in proportion as they more nearly and more fully regard this common use; therefore all the special and particular uses, which·are innumerable, are good and heavenly. With every one therefore an affection for truth is conjoined with an affection for use, insomuch that they act as one. Truth is thereby implanted in use, so that the truths which they learn are truths of use. Thus are angelic spirits instructed, and prepared for heaven. An affection for the truth suitable to the use is insinuated by various means, most of which are unknown in the world; chiefly by representatives of uses, which in the spiritual world are exhibited in a thousand ways, and with such delights and charms that they penetrate the spirit, from the interiors which are of his mind to the exteriors which are of his body, and thus affect the whole. Hence the spirit becomes as it were his own use. When therefore he enters his own society, into which he is initiated by instruction, he is in his own life while in his own use. From these considerations it may be seen that knowledges, which are external truths, do not enable any one to enter heaven, but the life itself, which is a life of use, inspired by knowledges. (*ib.* n. 515-517.)

After spirits by means of instruction have been prepared for heaven, in the places mentioned above,—which is effected in a short time, for the reason that they are in spiritual ideas, which embrace many things together,—they are then arrayed in angelic garments, which for the most part are white, as if of fine linen; and in this state are brought to a way that leads upwards to heaven, and are confided to the angel guards there; and afterwards they are received by other angels, and introduced into societies, and into many gratifications there. Every one is afterwards led by the Lord to his own society; which also is done by various ways, sometimes in a mysterious manner. The ways by which they are led no angel knows, but the Lord only. When they come to their own society their interiors are opened; and as these are conformable to the interiors of the angels who are in that society, therefore they are immediately acknowledged, and are received with joy. (*ib.* n. 519.)

VASTATION.

There are many who during their abode in the world, through simplicity and ignorance, have imbibed falsities as to faith; and have formed a certain kind of conscience, according to the principles of their faith; but have not, like others, lived in hatred, revenge, and adulteries. These in the other life, so long as they are in falsity, cannot be introduced into heavenly societies, lest they should contaminate them; and therefore they are kept for a certain time in the lower earth,[1] that they may there put off their false principles. The periods for which they remain there are longer or shorter according to the nature of the falsity, the life thence contracted, and the principles which they have confirmed in themselves. Some suffer severely there, others not severely. These states are what are called vastations; and are frequently mentioned in the Word. When the time of vastation is over they are taken up into heaven, and being novitiates, are instructed in truths of faith by the angels by whom they are received.

There are some who freely desire to be vastated, and thus to put off the false principles which they had brought with them from the world; but one can never put away false principles in the other life except in the course of time, and by means provided of the Lord. While they remain in the lower earth they are kept by the Lord in the hope of deliverance, and in consideration of the end; which is that thus they may be amended and prepared for the reception of heavenly happiness. (A. C. n. 1106, 1107.)

INDISCRIMINATE EARTHLY FRIENDSHIPS HURTFUL AFTER DEATH.

A friendship of love contracted with a man, regardless of his spiritual character, is detrimental after death. By a friendship of love interior friendship is meant; which is of such a nature that not his external man only but also his internal is loved,—and this without scrutiny as to his internal or spiritual

[1] See Eph. v. 9; Ezek. xxxi. 16; Rev. vi. 9, etc.

character, that is, as to the affections of his mind, whether they are affections of love towards the neighbour and love to God, and thus are associable with angels of heaven, or of a love opposed to the neighbour and a love opposed to God, and therefore associable with devils. Such friendship is contracted, by many, from various causes and for various ends. This is distinct from that external friendship which is for the person only, and is for the sake of various bodily and sensual delights, and for various mutual intercourse. This friendship may be formed with any one, —even with the clown that jests at a prince's table. This is called simply friendship, and the former the friendship of love; because friendship is a natural conjunction, and friendship of love is a spiritual conjunction.

That a friendship of love is detrimental after death, may appear from the state of heaven, from the state of hell, and from the state relatively of man's spirit . . . Those who have contracted friendships of love with one another in the world cannot like others be separated according to order, and assigned to the society corresponding to their life; for inwardly, as to the spirit, they are bound together, and cannot be severed, because they are as branch ingrafted in branch. If therefore one as to his interiors is in heaven, and the other as to his interiors is in hell, they cleave scarcely otherwise than as a sheep tied to a wolf, or as a goose to a fox, or a dove to a hawk; and he whose interiors are in hell breathes his infernal influences into him whose interiors are in heaven. For among the things well known in heaven is also this, that evils may be inspired into the good, but not goods into the evil; for the reason that every one is in evils by birth. Hence in the good who are thus connected with the evil the interiors are closed, and both are thrust down into hell, where the good spirit suffers severely; but at length after an interval of time he is delivered, and then first is prepared for heaven.

It is entirely different with those who love the good in another, that is, who love the justice, judgment, sincerity, and benevolence from charity; especially who love faith and love to the Lord. These, since they love the things that are within a man apart from those that are without him, if they do not observe the same in his person after death immediately withdraw from the friendship, and are associated by the Lord with those who are in similar good. It may be said that no one can search into the interiors of the mind of those with whom he is in fellowship and correspondence. But this is not necessary; only let him beware of a friendship of love with every one; external friendship, for the sake of various uses, is not hurtful. (T. C. R. n. 446-449.)

THE CHARACTER OF EVERY ONE IS PERCEIVED IN THE OTHER LIFE FROM THE SPHERE THAT ENCOMPASSES HIM.

That the truths or falsities which are from his loves encompass a man and also flow forth from him, may appear from the consideration that all things in the world, both animate and inanimate, pour forth a sphere from themselves, which sometimes is perceptible to the senses at a distance; as animals in the woods, which dogs exquisitely smell out and pursue from step to step by the scent; and plants in gardens and in woods, which emit a fragrant sphere in every direction likewise the ground and its various minerals. But these are natural exhalations. The case is similar in the spiritual world; from every spirit and angel there flows forth a sphere of his love, and thence a sphere of his truth or falsity, and this in every direction. Hence it is that all spirits, as respects their character, may be known from the spiritual sphere alone that goes out from them; and that in accordance with these spheres they have conjunction with societies which are in similar love, and thence in a similar truth or falsity. They who are in the love of good and thence of truth, are with societies of heaven, and they who are in the love of evil and thence of falsity, are with societies of hell. I am able to affirm that neither a spirit nor a man has even a single thought that does not communicate by that sphere with some society. As yet man does not know that this is so; but it has been made evident to me by a thousand experiences in the spiritual world. Therefore when spirits are examined as to their character it is traced out whither their thoughts extend; and from this it is known with what societies they are conjoined, and thus what their character is; and that the evil are conjoined with societies of hell, and the good with societies of heaven. (A. E. n. 889.)

The character of another is known in the other life at his first approach, even though he does not speak. From which it may be seen that the interiors of man are in a certain unconscious activity; and that from this the character of a spirit is perceived. That this is so has been made evident from the fact that the sphere of this activity not only extends itself to a distance, but sometimes, when the Lord permits, is also made sensibly manifest in various ways.

I have also been informed how these spheres are acquired which become so sensible in the other life. That it may be clearly explained, take for example one who has conceived a high opinion of himself, and of his own excellence, in comparison with others. He acquires at length such a habit, and as it

were nature, that wherever he goes, and whenever he sees and
converses with others, he fixes his attention on himself. This at
first he does perceptibly ; but afterwards not perceptibly, so that
he is not aware of it. But still this regard for himself prevails,
as in every particular of his affection and thought, so in every
particular of his bearing and of his speech. This men are able
to see in others. Such is that which produces a sphere in the
other life ; which is perceived, but not oftener than the Lord
permits. So is it with other affections. There are therefore as
many spheres as there are affections and combinations of
affections, which are innumerable. The sphere is as it were a
man's image extended without him, and indeed an image of all
that pertains to him. But what is presented to the sight or
perception in the world of spirits is only a something general.
Yet the nature of it as to its particulars is discerned in heaven.
But its nature as to the least particulars no one knows but the
Lord only. (A. C. n. 1504, 1505.)

Conversation and Language of Spirits.

Spirits converse with each other in the other life, just as men
do on earth ; and they that are good, with all familiarity of
friendship and love,—of which I have frequently been a witness ;
and this they do in their own language, by which they express
more in a minute than man can do in an hour. For their speech
is the universal of all languages, by means of ideas, the primitives
of words. They converse on subjects so acutely and clearly,
through so many series of well-connected and persuasive reasons,
that if a man perceived he would be astonished. They join
persuasion with affection, and so give life to their reasoning. At
the same time they also enliven it sometimes by representations
to the sight, and thus to the life. For example, if the conversation
be about shame, whether it can exist without reverence. This
cannot be discussed among men except by much reasoning, with
arguments and examples ; and will yet remain in doubt. But
with spirits it is done in a moment, by states of the affection of
shame and of reverence, varied in regular order ; and thus by
perceptible agreements and disagreements,—and perceptible at
the same time in the representatives connected with the conversation,—from which they instantly perceive the conclusion,
flowing of itself from the discords thus brought into harmony.
So in all other matters. Souls come into this faculty immediately
after death ; and then good spirits like nothing better than to
instruct the novitiate and ignorant. Spirits are themselves not
aware that they talk with each other in language so surpassing,

and are furnished with so excellent a gift, unless it is granted them by the Lord to reflect upon it; for the language is natural to them, and then inherent. It is with them as with a man; when his mind is intent on the sense of the subject, not upon the words and language, he sometimes does not know without reflection what language he is using.

This then is the language of spirits. But the language of angelic spirits is yet more universal and more perfect; and the language of angels is more universal and more perfect still. For there are three heavens; the first is the abode of good spirits; the second of angelic spirits; and the third of angels. Perfections therefore ascend in a relation like that of things exterior to things interior; to make it known by comparison, almost as hearing is to the sight, and as sight is to the thought. For what the hearing would derive from speech in an hour, could be presented to the sight in a moment; for example, a prospect of plains, palaces, and cities. And what the eye can see in many hours can be comprehended in a moment by the thought. Such is the ratio of the speech of spirits to that of angelic spirits; and of the speech of angelic spirits to that of angels. For angelic spirits distinctly comprehend more in one idea of speech and of thought, than spirits by a thousand; and so with the angels in respect to angelic spirits. How then must it be with the Lord, from whom is all the life of affection, of thought, and of language, and who alone is speech, and is the Word! (A. C. n. 1641, 1642.)

THE CASE OF THOSE WHO HAVE ONLY NATURAL HEREDITARY GOOD.

There are some who enjoy natural good hereditarily; from which they have a delight in doing good to others, but are not imbued with principles from the Word or the doctrine of the Church, or from their religion, from which they do good. They cannot therefore be gifted with any conscience; for conscience does not come of natural or hereditary good, but from doctrine of truth and good, and a life according to it. When such come into the other life they wonder that they are not received into heaven; saying, that they have led a good life. But they are told that a good life from what is natural or hereditary is not a good life; but only a life from those things which are of the doctrine of good and truth, and thence of the life. By these they have principles respecting truth and good impressed on them, and receive conscience; which is the plane into which heaven flows. That they may know that this is the case they are sent into various societies; and they then suffer themselves to be led astray into evils of every kind, merely by reasonings and persuasion thereby that evils are goods, and goods are evils. And wherever they are they are thus persuaded, and are driven as chaff before the wind. For they are without principles, and without a plane in which the angels may operate and withdraw them from evils. (A. C. n. 6208.)

The Case of those who in the World were Idiots.

Those who in the world were idiots are also foolish and idiotic on their arrival in the other world; but having been divested of their externals, and their internals opened,—which takes place with them all,—they acquire an understanding in accordance with their former quality and life ; since the actual follies and madness dwell in the external natural man, and not in the internal spiritual man.—*Letter to Dr. Beyer.*

The Delights of every one are Changed into the Corresponding Delights after Death.

All the delights that a man has are of his ruling love; for he feels nothing as delightful but what he loves. That therefore is most delightful which he loves above all things. Whether you say the ruling love, or that which is loved above all things, it is the same. These delights are various. In general they are as many as there are ruling loves, consequently as many as there are men, spirits, and angels; for the ruling love of one is not in every respect like that of another. Hence it is that no one has a face exactly like that of another ; for the face of every one is an image of his mind (*animus*), and in the spiritual world it is an image of every one's ruling love. In particular, the delights of each one also are of infinite variety ; nor is there a single delight of any onethat is in all respects similar to or the same as another ; whether those delights that succeed one after another, or those that come together, one with another, there is not one that is the same as another. But yet these delights, with each one in particular, have reference to the one love which is his ruling love; for they compose it, and thus make one with it. In like manner all delights in general have reference to one universally ruling love ; in heaven to love to the Lord, and in hell to the love of self. (H. H. n. 486.)

Those who have loved Divine truths, and the Word, from an interior affection, or from an affection for truth itself, in the other life dwell in light, in elevated places which appear as mountains, and are there continually in the light of heaven.

They do not know what darkness is, like that of night in the world. And they also live in a vernal temperature. There are presented to their view as it were fields with standing corn, and also vineyards. In their houses every thing is refulgent, as if from precious stones; the view through their windows is as through pure crystals. These are the delights of their sight. But the same things are interiorly delightful, from their correspondence with Divine celestial things; for the truths from the Word which they have loved correspond to standing corn, to vineyards, to precious stones, to windows, and crystals. Those who have applied the doctrinals of the church which are from the Word immediately to life, are in the inmost heaven, and more than all others are in the delight of wisdom. In every object they behold things Divine. They indeed see the objects, but the corresponding Divine things flow immediately into their minds, and fill them with a blessedness with which all their sensations are affected. To their eyes therefore all things as it were laugh, sport, and live. They who have loved the sciences, and have cultivated their rational mind by means of them, and thereby have acquired intelligence, and at the same time have acknowledged the Divine, their pleasure and rational delight in the sciences is turned in the other life into a spiritual delight, which is a delight in cognitions of good and of truth. They dwell in gardens where there appear beds of flowers, and grass plots beautifully arranged, with rows of trees round about, and porticoes and walks. The trees and flowers are varied every day. In general, the view of the whole gives delight to their minds; and in particular, the varieties continually renew this delight. And as these correspond to things Divine, and they have a knowledge of correspondences, they are always being replenished with new knowledges, and their spiritual-rational mind is perfected by them. They have these delights because gardens, beds of flowers, grass plots, and trees, correspond to sciences, to knowledges, and to intelligence from them. Those who have ascribed all things to the Divine, and have regarded nature relatively as dead, and only subservient to things spiritual, and have confirmed themselves in this, are in heavenly light; and all things that appear before their eyes derive from that light the property of being transparent; and in that transparency they behold innumerable variegations of the light, which their internal sight as it were immediately imbibes. From these they perceive interior delights. The objects that appear in their houses are as it were of diamond, in which there are similar variegations. I was told that the walls of their houses are as if of crystal, thus also transparent; and there appear in them as it were flowing forms representative of heavenly things, and with perpetual variety. And this is because such transparency corresponds to an understanding enlightened by the Lord, free from the shades arising from the faith and love of natural things. Such, and infinite others, are the things of which it is said, by those who have been in heaven, that they have beheld what eye hath never seen, and,—from a perception of things Divine communicated to them from these things,—that they have heard what ear hath never heard. They that have not acted clandestinely, but have been willing that all that they thought so far as civil life permitted should be known,—because from the Divine they have thought nothing but what was sincere and just,—in heaven their faces are radiant with light; and from that light all their affections and thoughts appear in the countenance, as in a form. And as regards their speech and actions, they are as it were the likenesses of their affections. Hence they are loved more than others. When they speak, the face becomes somewhat obscured; but when they have done speaking, the same things that they have spoken appear together in the face, fully in view. All things that exist around them too, because they correspond to their interiors, have such an appearance that it is perceived clearly by others what they represent and signify. Spirits whose delight it has been to act clandestinely shun them from afar, and appear to themselves to creep from them like serpents. Those who have regarded adulteries as abominable, and have lived in the chaste love of marriage, are beyond all others in the order and form of heaven; and therefore are in all beauty, and continually in the flower of youth. The delights of the love are ineffable, and increase to eternity. For into that love all the delights and joys of heaven flow; because that love descends from the conjunction of the Lord with heaven and the church, and in general from the conjunction of good and truth,—which conjunction is heaven itself in general, and is heaven in particular with each individual angel. Their external delights are such as no human language can describe. But these are only a few of the things that have been told me respecting the correspondences of delights among those who are in heavenly love. (*ib.* n. 489.)

UNCONSCIOUS ASSOCIATION OF ANGELS AND SPIRITS WITH MAN.

With every man there are good spirits and evil spirits; by good spirits man has conjunction with heaven, and by evil spirits with hell. These spirits are in the world of spirits, which is intermediate between heaven and hell. When these come to a man they enter into all his memory, and thence into all his thought; evil spirits into those things of the memory and thought that are evil, and good spirits into those things of the memory and thought that are good. Spirits do not know at all that they are with man, but believe when they are with him that all things that are of the man's memory and thought are their own; neither do they see the man, because the objects in our solar world do not fall within their vision. The Lord takes exceeding care that spirits may not know that they are with man; for if they knew they would speak with him, and then evil spirits would destroy him. For evil spirits, because they are conjoined with hell, desire nothing more than to destroy man; not only as to the soul, that is as to faith and love, but also as to the body. It is otherwise when they do not speak with man. Then they do not know that what they think and also what they say among themselves is from him,—for even among themselves they speak from man,—but believe that what they think and say is their own, and every one esteems and loves his own. Thus spirits are constrained to love and esteem man, although they are not aware of it. That there is such a conjunction of spirits with man has been made so known to me by the continual experience of many years, that there is nothing better known.

The reason why spirits who communicate with hell are also adjoined to man, is that man is born into evils of every kind, and therefore his first life is only from them. If then spirits of similar character to himself were not adjoined to a man he could not live, and could by no means be withdrawn from his evils and be reformed. He is therefore kept in his own life by evil spirits, and is withheld from it by good spirits. By means of the two also he is in equilibrium; and because he is in equilibrium he is in his freedom. (H. H. n. 292, 293.)

The spirits adjoined to man are such as he himself is as to affection or as to love. But the good spirits are adjoined to him by the Lord, while the evil spirits are invited by the man himself. The spirits with man, however, are changed according to the changes of his affections. Hence some spirits are with him in infancy; others in childhood; others in youth and manhood; and others in old age. In infancy spirits are present who are in innocence, thus who communicate with the heaven of innocence, which is the inmost or third heaven; in childhood spirits are present who are in the affection of knowing, thus who communicate with the ultimate or first heaven; in youth and manhood spirits are present who are in the affection of truth and good, and thence in intelligence, thus who communicate with the second or middle heaven; and in old age spirits are present who are in wisdom and innocence, thus who communicate with the inmost or third heaven. But this adjunction is effected by the

Lord with those who can be reformed and regenerated. It is different with those who cannot be reformed and regenerated. To them also good spirits are adjoined, that they may be withheld by them as much as possible from evil; but their immediate conjunction is with evil spirits who communicate with hell,—from whence they have spirits of such character as the men are themselves. If they are lovers of themselves, or lovers of gain, or lovers of revenge, or lovers of adultery, similar spirits are present, and as it were dwell in their evil affections. And in so far as the man cannot be kept from evil by good spirits, these evil spirits inflame him; and in so far as the affection reigns they cleave to him, and do not go away. Thus is a bad man conjoined to hell, and a good man conjoined to heaven. (*ib.* n. 295.)

So long as man remains unregenerate he is governed altogether differently from what he is when regenerated. While he is unregenerate evil spirits are with him, and so rule over him that the angels, although they are present, can scarcely do anything more than give him such a direction that he may not plunge into the very depths of evil, and incline him to a sort of good; to good indeed through his own peculiar desires; and to truth through the good, and the fallacies of the senses. He then, through the spirits that are with him, has communication with the world of spirits; but not so much with heaven, because the evil spirits rule, and the angels only turn him away. But when he is regenerated the angels rule, and inspire him with all good and truth, and with a horror and fear of what is evil and false. The angels indeed lead man, but they only serve; for it is the Lord alone who governs man, by means of angels and spirit. (A. C. n. 50.)

Only angels from the Lord know that they are with man; for they are adjoined to his soul or spirit, and not to his body. For the things which from the thoughts are determined into speech, and from the will into acts in the body, in a state of order flow into act by common influx, according to correspondences with the Greatest Man. The spirits that are with man have therefore nothing in common with these things; thus they do not speak with man's tongue, for this would be obsession; nor do they see through his eyes what is in the world; nor hear through his ears what is passing there. It is different with me; for the Lord has opened my interiors, that I may be able to see the things that are in the other life. Spirits therefore have known that I was a man in the body; and the faculty was given them of seeing through my eyes what is in the world, and of hearing those speak who were in company with me.

If evil spirits perceived that they were with man, and that they were spirits separate from him, and if they could flow into the things pertaining to his body, they would attempt in a thousand ways to destroy him; for they hate man with a deadly hatred. And because they have known that I was a man in the body, therefore they have been in a continual effort to destroy me; not only as to the body, but especially as to the soul. For to destroy man, or any spirit, is the very delight of life of all those who are in hell; but I have been continually protected by the Lord. From this it may appear how dangerous it is for a man to be in living association with spirits, unless he is in the good of faith. (*ib.* n. 5862, 5863.)

WHY THERE ARE TWO SPIRITS AND TWO ANGELS WITH EVERY MAN.

The reason why there are two is, that there are two kinds of spirits in hell, and two kinds of angels in heaven; to which the two faculties in man, the will and the understanding, correspond. The first kind are simply called spirits; and they act upon the things of the understanding. The other kind are called genii; and these act upon the things of the will. They are also most distinct from each other. For those that are simply called spirits pour in falsities; for they reason against the truth, and are in the delight of their life when they can make truth appear as falsity and falsity as truth. But those that are called genii pour in evils, and act upon a man's affections and concupiscences; and they scent in a moment what a man desires. If this be good they turn it most dexterously into evil, and are in the delight of their life when they can make good appear as evil and evil as good. . . . Those that are called genii have nothing whatever in common with those that are called spirits. The genii care nothing for what a man thinks, but only for what he loves; the spirits care nothing for what a man loves, but for what he thinks. The genii take delight in being silent; the spirits, in speaking. They are are also separated entirely from each other. The genii are at a great depth in the hells behind, and they are almost invisible to the spirits, and when they look in that direction appear as shades that flit about; but the spirits are in the hells at the sides and in front. Hence it is then that there are two spirits from hell.

There are two angels with every man because the angels also are of two kinds; one that act upon the things of man's will, another that act upon the things of his understanding. Those that act upon the things of man's will act upon his loves and ends, consequently upon his goods; and those that act upon the things of his understanding act upon his faith and principles, consequently upon his truths. They are also most distinct from each other. Those who act upon the things of man's will are called celestial angels; and those who act upon the things of his understanding, spiritual angels. To the celestial the genii are opposed ; to the spiritual, the spirits. These things it has been given me to know by much experience; for I am continually in company and conversation with both. (A. C. n. 5977, 5978.)

It has been given me to learn by experience the kind of wickedness with those who are called genii. Genii do not operate upon and flow into the thoughts, but into the affections. These they perceive and scent, as dogs the wild beasts in a forest. Where they perceive good affections in another they turn them in a moment into evil, leading and bending them through his delights in a wonderful manner; and this so clandestinely, and with such malignant art, that he knows nothing of it, —dexterously taking care least any thing should enter his thought, since thus they would be discovered. They have their seat in man beneath the occiput. In the world they were men who deceitfully captivated the minds of others, leading and persuading them by their affections or their lusts. But they are kept away by the Lord from every man of whom there is any hope of reformation ; for they are of such a character that they are able not only to destroy the conscience, but also to excite in man his hereditary evils, which otherwise lie concealed. Therefore, lest man should be led into them, it is provided of the Lord that these hells should be entirely closed; and when any man who is such a genius comes, after death, into the other life, he is immediately cast into their hell. When viewed as to their deceit and subtlety they appear as vipers. (H. H. n. 579.)

Such Spirits and Angels are subject Spirits of some heavenly or Infernal Society.

The spirits and genii with man are nothing else than subjects, through whom he has communication with hell ; and the celestial and spiritual angels are subjects, through whom he has communication with the heavens. (A. C. n. 5983.)

A subject is one in whom are concentrated the thoughts and speech of many ; and thus the many are presented as one. And because the subject thinks and says nothing at all from himself, but from the others, and the thoughts and speech of the others are made to appear to the life in his thought and speech, therefore those that flow in imagine that the subject is as nothing, and scarcely animate,—merely receptive of their thoughts and speech. But the subject on the other hand imagines that he thinks and speaks not from others, but from himself. Thus do fallacies play with both. It has often been given me to tell a subject that he thinks and says nothing from himself, but from others; and also that those others imagine a subject to be unable to think and say any thing from himself, and that therefore he appears to them as one in whom of himself there is nothing of life. He that was the subject was exceedingly indignant on hearing this. But that he might be convinced of its truth, it was given him to speak with the spirits who were flowing in; who then said they confessed that the subject thinks and says nothing at all from himself; and that he thus appears to them as a something scarcely animate. On one occasion it came to pass that he who declared a subject to be nothing himself became a subject, and then the others said of him that he was nothing; whereat he was very angry. But yet he was instructed by the experience as to how it is. (*ib.* n. 5985.)

The Angels Associated with Man, or Guardian Angels.

It is the office of the angels by whom the Lord leads and also protects man to inspire charity and faith; and to observe man's delights, to what direction they turn, and as far as they can consistently with man's freedom to moderate and bend them towards good. They are not suffered to act violently, and so to break man's lusts and principles, but gently. It is also their office to control the evil spirits who are from hell, which is effected by methods innumerable; of which these only may be mentioned:— When the evil spirits infuse evils and falsities, the angels insinuate truths and goods; which, if not received, they are yet tempered by them. The infernal spirits continually attack, and the angels defend; such is the order. The angels especially regulate the affections; for these constitute the life of man, and also his freedom. The angels also observe if any hells are opened that were not opened before, from which there is an influx into man; which takes place when man enters himself into any new evil. These hells, so far as man suffers them, the angels close; and if any spirits attempt to emerge from them the angels drive them back. They also dissipate strange and new influx from which there are evil effects. The angels especially call forth the goods and truths that are in man, and oppose them to the evils and falsities which the evil spirits excite. Man is therefore in the midst, and [of himself] apperceives neither the evil nor the good; and because he is in the midst he is in freedom to turn himself either to the one or to the other. By such means do the angels from the Lord lead and protect man,—and this every moment and moment of a moment; for if only for one moment the angels should intermit, man would be plunged into evil from which he could never afterwards be extricated. These things the angels do from love, which they receive from the Lord; for they perceive nothing more delightful and more happy than to remove evils from man, and lead him to heaven. That they have joy in these things may be seen from Luke xv. 7. That the Lord has such care for man, and this continually, from the first beginning to the end of his life, and afterwards to eternity, scarcely any man believes. (A. C. n. 5992.)

It is provided of the Lord that spirits flow into the things of man's thought and will; but the angels into his ends, and thus through his ends into the things which follow from the ends. The angels also flow in, through good spirits, into those things in man which are goods of life and truths of faith; by which as much as possible they withdraw him from evils and falsities. The influx is silent, imperceptible to man, yet all the while secretly working and producing effects. The angels especially avert evil and insinuate good ends. But in so far as they cannot effect this they withdraw, and flow in more distantly and without being present; and then the evil spirits draw nearer. For the angels cannot be present in evil ends, that is in the loves of self and of the world; but yet they are present from a distance. The Lord could, through the angels, lead man into good ends with omnipotent power; but this would be to deprive him of life, for his life is a life of loves entirely contrary to such ends. It is therefore an inviolable Divine law that man shall be in freedom, and that good and truth or charity and faith shall be implanted in his state of freedom, by no means in a state of compulsion; for what is received in a state of compulsion does not remain, but is dissipated. For to force a man is not to insinuate anything into his will. It is in truth the will of another from which he would act; and therefore when he returns to his own will, that is to his freedom, it is extirpated. For this reason the Lord governs man through his freedom, and as far as possible withholds him from the freedom of thinking and willing evil; for if he were not withheld by the Lord man would cast himself continually into the deepest hell. It was said that, through the angels, the Lord could lead man into good ends with omnipotent power; for the evil spirits, if even these were myriads around a man, could be driven away in a moment, and that by a single angel. But man would then come into such torment and into such a hell as he could by no means endure; indeed he would be miserably deprived of life. For man's life is from lusts and fantasies contrary to good and truth; and if this life were not sustained by evil spirits and so amended, or at least guided, he would not survive for a moment. Nothing else in fact possesses him but the love of self and of gain, and the love of reputation for the sake of them; thus whatever possesses him is contrary to order. Unless therefore he were to be reduced to order moderately, and by degrees through the guidance of his freedom, he would instantly expire. (*ib.* n. 5854.)

Only good Spirits and Angels are with Infants.

Spirits clothe themselves with all things of man's memory, at their first approach. . . . . Evil spirits cannot come near to infants, because they have as yet nothing in the memory that they can put on. Good spirits and angels are therefore with them. (A. C. n. 5857.)

The Lord's Providential Guardianship of Man from Evil Spirits in Sleep.

Evil spirits vehemently desire and burn to infest and assault man while he sleeps; but then especially he is watched over by the Lord; for love never sleeps. The spirits who thus infest are miserably punished. I have heard their punishments oftener than can be told. . . . . They that chiefly beset man during the night, and endeavour then to pour themselves into his interior thoughts and affections, are sirens, who are interior magicians. But they are continually kept away by angels from the Lord, and are at length deterred by the most grievous punishments. They have even talked with others in the night just as if from me, as it were my speech; so like it that it could not be distinguished from mine, pouring forth filthy things, and persuading to falsities. I was once in a most sweet sleep, in which I had no sensation but of delightful rest. When I awoke certain good spirits began to chide me for having infested them, so atrociously, as they said, that they supposed themselves to be in hell; casting blame upon me. To whom I replied that I knew nothing whatever about the matter, but that I had slept most quietly, so that it was quite impossible I could have been troublesome to them. Being amazed at this they perceived at length that it had been done by the magical arts of sirens. The like was shown to me also afterwards, that I might know the nature of the siren crew. They are chiefly those of the female sex who in the life of the body sought, by interior wiles, to allure male companions to themselves, insinuating themselves by external [enticements], captivating their minds by whatever means, entering into the affections and delights of every one; but with an evil intent, especially to get command over them. . . . . It was given me to perceive their interiors, how filthy they are,—defiled with adulteries and hatreds. It was also given me to perceive how powerful their sphere is. (A. C. n. 1983.)

I was awaked one night from sleep, and heard spirits about me, who wished to ensnare me in my sleep; and presently dozing, I had a sorrowful dream. But I awoke, and suddenly there were present chastising spirits,—which surprised me ; and they miserably punished the spirits who were ensnaring me in my sleep. They clothed them as it were with bodies, which were visible, and bodily senses, and in this condition tortured them, by violent collisions of the parts forward and backward, attended with pains induced by resistance. The chastisers had a mind to kill them if they could; hence their very great violence. Those that were punished were for the most part sirens. The punishment continued for a long time, and extended to several troops around me ; and what astonished me, all who were ensnaring me were discovered, although they endeavoured to conceal themselves. Being sirens they tried by many arts to elude punishment, but they could not. Now, they sought to withdraw themselves secretly into an interior nature ; now, to persuade that they were others ; now, to divert the punishment to others by translations of ideas ; now they pretended that they were infants whom they were punishing; now good spirits ; now angels ; besides many other artifices ; but ever in vain. I wondered that they were so grievously punished ; but perceived that such a crime is enormous, from the necessity that man should sleep in safety ; that if he did not, the human race would perish. Hence, the so great punishment is of necessity. I also perceived that the same takes place about other men, whom they insidiously endeavour to assail in sleep, although a man is not aware of it. For, one to whom it has not been granted to speak with spirits, and by internal sense to be with them, can hear no such thing, still less see it; and yet similar things are constantly arising about others. The Lord most especially watches over man while he sleeps. (*ib.* n. 959.)

THE DANGER OF CONSCIOUS INTERCOURSE WITH SPIRITS.

It is believed by many that man may be taught of the Lord by spirits speaking with him; but they who believe and desire this do not know that it is connected with danger to their souls. So long as, man lives in the world, he is as to his spirit in the midst of spirits, and yet the spirits do not know that they are with man; nor does a man know that he is with spirits. The reason is that they are conjoined immediately as to affections of the will, and mediately as to the thoughts of the understanding. For man thinks naturally, and spirits think spiritually; and natural and spiritual thought do not make one otherwise than by correspondences,—and unity by correspondences causes that one knows nothing of the other. But as soon as spirits begin to speak with a man they come out of their spiritual state into the natural state of the man; and then they know that they are with the man, and conjoin themselves with the thoughts of his affection, and from these speak with him. They cannot enter into any thing else; for a similar affection and consequent thought conjoins all, and a dissimilar separates. It is owing to this that the spirit speaking is in the same principles as the man, be they truths or be they falsities; and also that he excites them, and by his affection conjoined to the man's affection strongly confirms them. It is therefore evident that no other than similar spirits speak with a man, or manifestly operate upon a man; for manifest operation coincides with speech. It comes from this that no other than enthusiastic spirits speak with enthusiasts; and that no other than Quaker spirits operate upon Quakers; and Moravian spirits upon Moravians. It would be the same with Arians, with Socinians, and with other heretics. The spirits that speak with a man are all none others than men who have lived in the world, and were then of such a character. It has been given me to know that it is so by much experience. And what is ridiculous, when a man believes that the Holy Spirit speaks with him, or operates upon him, the spirit also believes himself to be the Holy Spirit; this is common with enthusiastic spirits. From these considerations it is evident to what danger a man is exposed who speaks with spirits, or manifestly feels their operation. Man is ignorant of the quality of his own affection, whether it be good or evil, and with what other beings it is conjoined; and if he has a conceit of his own intelligence the spirits favour every thought that comes from it. So it is if any one, inflamed with a sort of fire, has a leaning to certain principles; which is the case with those who are not in truths from a genuine affection. When a spirit favours a man's thoughts or principles, from a similar affection, the one leads the other as the blind the blind, until both fall into the pit. Such were the Pythonic [diviners] of old; [1] and also the magicians in Egypt and in Babylon, who on account of their converse with

---

[1] That is, those who were believed to be inspired by Apollo, the Pythian god.

spirits, and on account of the operation of them upon themselves, manifestly felt, were called wise. But the worship of God was thereby converted into the worship of demons, and the church perished. For this reason such communications were forbidden to the children of Israel under penalty of death. (A. E. n. 1182.)

It is rarely permitted to speak with spirits at the present day, because it is perilous. For the spirits then know that they are with a man; which otherwise they do not know; and evil spirits are of such a character that they hold man in deadly hatred, and desire nothing more than to destroy him as to soul and body. This also comes to pass with those who have much indulged in fantasies,—so far that they have put away from themselves the enjoyments suitable to the natural man. Some indeed who lead a solitary life, occasionally hear spirits speaking with them, and without danger. But the spirits present with them are removed by the Lord at intervals, lest they should know that they are with the man; for most spirits do not know that there is another world than that in which they are. They therefore also do not know that there are men elsewhere; and for this reason it is not permitted man to speak, in turn, with them; for if he spoke with them they would know. They who think much on religious subjects, and are so intent upon them as inwardly to see them as it were within themselves, also begin to hear spirits speaking with them; for matters of religion whatever they are, when of himself a man dwells upon them, and does not vary them with the different affairs that are uses in the world, pass more within and there abide, and occupy the whole spirit of the man, and enter the spiritual world, and act upon the spirits who are there. But such persons are visionaries and enthusiasts; and whatever spirit they hear they believe to be the Holy Spirit, when yet they are enthusiastic spirits. Such spirits see falsities as truths; and because they see them they persuade themselves that they are truths, and likewise persuade those into whom they flow. (H. H. n. 249.)

When spirits begin to speak with a man he ought to be beware that he believes nothing whatever from them; for they say almost any thing. Things are fabricated by them, and they lie. For instance if they were permitted to describe what heaven is, and how things are in the heavens, they would tell so many lies, and indeed with solemn affirmation, that a man would be astonished. Therefore when spirits are speaking, I have not been permitted to have faith in the things which they related. For they have a passion for inventing; and whenever any subject of conversation is presented they think they know it, and give their opinions upon it, one after another, one in one way and another in another, quite as if they knew; and if a man then listens and believes they press on, and deceive, and seduce in divers ways. For example, if they were permitted to tell of things to come, of things unknown, in the universal heaven, of any thing whatever that a man desires, while speaking from themselves they would not tell the truth, but all things falsely. Let men beware therefore how they believe them. For this reason the state of speaking with spirits on this earth is most perilous, unless one is in true faith. They induce so strong a persuasion that it is the Lord Himself who speaks, and who commands, that a man cannot but believe and obey. (S. D. n. 1622.)

Spirits can be introduced who represent another person; and the spirit, as also any one who has been acquainted with the spirit, cannot know but that he is the same. It has been shown me many times that the spirits speaking with me did not know but that they were the men of whom I was thinking; neither did other spirits know to the contrary. Thus yesterday, and to-day, one known to me in life [was personated]. The personation was so like him in all respects, so far as known to me, that nothing could be more like. Let those who speak with spirits beware therefore lest they be deceived when they say that they are those whom they have known and that have died.

For there are genera and species of spirits of similar faculty; and when like things are called up in the memory of man, and so are represented to them, they think that they are the same persons. Then all those things that represent them are called forth from the memory; as well as the words, the speech, the tone of voice, the bearing, and many other things. Moreover, they are induced so to think when other spirits inspire them; for then they are in the fantasy of these, and think that they are the same.—Aug. 19, 1748. (S. D. n. 2860, 2861.)

When Angels or Spirits speak with Man they speak in his own Language, from his Memory.

When angels converse with a man they do not speak in their own language, but in the language of the man; and in other languages also that the man knows, but not in language unknown to him. The reason why it is so, is that when angels speak with a man they turn themselves to him, and conjoin themselves with him; and the conjunction of an angel with a man brings each into similar thought. And as man's thought is connected with his memory, and his speech flows from thence, therefore each is in the same language. Besides, when an angel or spirit comes to a man, and by turning to him is conjoined with him, he enters into all his memory, so completely that he is scarcely aware that he does not know of himself what the man knows, and therefore the languages also that he knows. I have conversed with the angels on this subject; and said that perhaps they supposed that they spoke with me in my mother tongue, because it is so perceived, when yet it was not they who spoke, but I; and that this is evident, from the fact that angels cannot utter one word of human language. (H. H. n. 246.)

The speech of an angel or a spirit with man is heard as sonorously as the speech of man with man; yet it is not heard by others who stand near, but only by himself. The reason is, that the speech of an angel or spirit flows first into man's thought, and by an internal way into his organ of hearing, and thus moves this from within; but the speech of man with man flows first into the air, and into his organ of hearing by an external way, and moves it from without. It is therefore evident that the speech of an angel or of a spirit with a man is heard within the man; and since it equally moves the organs of hearing, that it is also equally sonorous. That the speech of an angel or spirit flows down from within even into the ear, was manifest to me from the fact that it flows also into the tongue, and causes it slightly to vibrate, but not with any such motion as when the sound of speech is articulated by it into words, by the man himself. (H. H. n. 248.)

That the speech of spirits with man is in his mother tongue is among the wonders that exist in the other life. This they speak as readily and skilfully as if they had been born in the same country, and had been brought up in the same language; and this, whether they are from Europe, or from Asia, or from any other part of the globe. It is the same with those who lived thousands of years before the language existed. Nay, the spirits do not know but that the language in which they are speaking with man is their own proper and native tongue. So it is with the other languages that the man is acquainted with. But beyond these they cannot pronounce a syllable of another language, unless it be immediately given them by the Lord. Infants speak in like manner also, who departed this life before they had learned any language. And the reason is that the language which is familiar to spirits is not a language of words, but the language of ideas of thought,—a language which is the universal of all languages; and when spirits are with man the ideas of their thought glide into the words which are with the man,—and this so correspondently, and fitly, that the spirits do not know but that the very words are their own, and that they are speaking in their own language, while yet they are speaking in the language of the man. I have sometimes conversed with spirits on these subjects. All souls, as soon as they enter into the other life, are gifted with the faculty of being able to understand the speech of all that dwell upon the whole earth, just as if it had been born in them; because they perceive whatever man thinks. Besides other faculties, which are still more excellent. Hence it is that after the death of the body souls are able to talk and have intercourse with all, of whatever country and language.

The words with which they speak,—that is, which they excite or call forth out of man's memory, and imagine to be their own,—are well chosen and clear, full of meaning, distinctly pronounced, and applicable to the subject. And what is surprising, they know how to choose expressions better and more readily than the man himself; nay, as has been shown me, they are acquainted with the various meanings of words, which they instantly apply, without any premeditation; for the reason, as has been said, that the ideas of their language cannot but flow into those words that are suitable. It is almost as when a man is speaking, and thinks nothing about his words, but dwells only upon the sense of the words; then his thought falls rapidly and spontaneously into words, according to the sense of them. It is the internal sense that brings forth the words. In such internal sense, but yet more subtle and more excellent, consists the speech of spirits; by this man, however unaware of it, communicates with spirits. (A. C. n. 1637, 1638.)

As soon as angels and spirits turn themselves away from a man they are in their own angelic or spiritual language, and know nothing whatever of the language of the man. The same has occurred with me. When I have been in company with the angels and in a similar state with them, I have then spoken with them also in their language, and knew nothing whatever of my own,—of which I had no recollection; but as soon as I was not in company with them I was in my own language.

It is not permitted any angel or spirit to speak with a man from his own memory, but from that of the man; for angels and spirits have memory as well as men. If a spirit were to speak with a man from his own memory, the man would not know but that the things he would then think were his, when yet they would belong to the spirit. It is as the recollection of a thing which yet the man never heard or saw. It has been given me to know that this is so from experience. Hence the opinion among some of the ancients, that after some thousands of years they would return into their former life, and into all its acts, and that they actually had so returned. They were led to this conclusion by the fact that there sometimes occurred to them, as it were, a recollection of things which yet they never saw or heard. This came to pass from the fact that spirits flowed from their own memory into the ideas of their thought. (H. H. n. 255, 256.)

MAN IS NOT ENLIGHTENED BY INTERCOURSE WITH SPIRITS, BUT FROM THE WORD.

There is a belief that man might be more enlightened and become more wise if he had immediate revelation, by converse with spirits and with angels; but the reverse is the case. Enlightenment through the Word is effected by an interior way; while enlightenment by immediate revelation is effected by an exterior way. The interior way is through the will into the understanding; the exterior way is through the hearing into the understanding. A man is enlightened by the Lord through the Word in proportion as his will is in good; but a man may be instructed and as it were enlightened by hearing though his will is in evil. And what enters into the understanding in a man whose will is in evil is not within the man, but without him; it is only in his memory, and not in his life. And what is without a man and not in his life is gradually separated, if not before, yet after death; for the will which is in evil, either casts it out, or suffocates it, or falsifies and profanes it. For the will constitutes the life of man; and it continually acts upon the understanding, and regards that as extraneous which is in the understanding from the memory. On the other hand the understanding does not act on the will, but only teaches how the will should act. If therefore a man knew from heaven all that the angels ever know, or if he knew all that is contained in the Word, and that is contained in all the doctrines of the Church, and besides, what the fathers have written and councils have declared, and his will is yet in evil, after death he would be regarded as one who knows nothing, because he does not will what he knows. And as evil hates truth the man himself then casts out truths, and in place of them adopts such falsities as are in agreement with the evil of his will. Moreover, there is not granted to any spirit nor to any angel leave to instruct any man on this earth in Divine truths; but the Lord Himself teaches every one, by means of the Word, and He teaches in proportion as a man receives good from the Lord in his will; and thus he receives in proportion as he shuns evils as sins. Every man, moreover, as to his affections and as to his thoughts from them, is in a society of spirits, in which society his mind is as it were one with them. Spirits speaking with a man therefore speak from his affections, and according to them. A man cannot converse with other spirits unless the society in which he is be first removed, which cannot be done except by a reformation of his will. For every man is in a society with spirits who are of the same religion with himself. The spirits who speak with him, therefore, confirm whatever the man has made a part of his religion; thus enthusiastic spirits confirm in a man all that pertains to his enthusiasm; Quaker spirits all things of Quakerism; Moravian spirits all things of Moravianism; and so on. Hence result confirmations of falsities which can never be extirpated. It is plain from these facts, that the mediate revelation which is effected by means of the Word is superior to an immediate revelation, which is effected by means of spirits. As regards myself, it was not permitted me to take any thing whatever from the mouth of any spirit, nor from the mouth of any angel, but from the mouth of the Lord alone.[1] (S. S. *Post,* n. 13.)

The Lord does not teach man truths immediately, either from Himself or by the angels; but teaches mediately by the Word, through preaching, reading, conversation, and intercourse with others, and so by meditations in private upon what is taught. A man is then enlightened according to his affection for truth on account of use. Otherwise man would not act as of himself. (A. E. n. 1173.)

Visions and Dreams.

It is known to few how visions take place, or what visions are genuine; and as I have been now for some years almost continually with those who are in the other life, and have there seen amazing things, so I have been instructed by actual experience respecting visions and dreams; concerning which I am permitted to relate the following particulars.

By genuine visions are meant visions or sights of the objects that really exist in the other life; which are nothing else than realities, that can be seen with the eyes of the spirit though not with the eyes of the body; and which appear to man when his interior sight is opened by the Lord,—that is, the sight which his spirit possesses, into which, he also comes when being separated from the body he passes into the other life. For man is a spirit clothed with a body. Such were the visions of the prophets. When this sight is opened, the things that actually exist among the spirits are seen in daylight clearer than the noonday light of the world; not representatives only but also spirits themselves, together with a perception as to who they are, and what they are, where they are, whence they come, whither they go, of what affection, of what persuasion, nay, of what faith they are; all confirmed by living converse, precisely as of men, and this without any deception.

The visions that appear to the eyes of good spirits are repre-

[1] See also p. 383.

sentatives of the things that exist in heaven; for what appears before the eyes of the angels in heaven when it descends into the world of spirits is changed into representatives, by which and in which what they signify can be clearly seen. Such representations are perpetual among good spirits; with a beauty and delightfulness scarcely utterable. (A. C. n. 1966, 1970, 1971.)

Real visions, which are visions of such things as actually appear in the spiritual world, corresponding exactly with the thoughts and affections of the angels, are therefore real correspondences. Such were the visions of the prophets who prophesied truths; and such also were the visions that were seen by John, which are described throughout the Apocalypse. But visions that are not real are such as appear similar to real visions in the external form, but are not so in the internal. They are produced by spirits, through fantasies. Such were the visions of the prophets who prophesied vain things, or lies. All these visions, because they were not real, were fallacies; and therefore signify fallacies. . . . There are also appearances in the spiritual world that are not correspondences; which are produced by spirits, chiefly by evil spirits, through fantasies. For through these means those spirits can present to view palaces and houses, full of decorations, and splendid garments, and can induce upon themselves beautiful faces, and other like appearances; but as soon as the fantasy is at an end all these things too vanish, because they are external appearances in which there is no internal. (A. E. n. 575.)

As regards dreams, it is known that the Lord revealed the secrets of heaven to the prophets not only by visions, but also by dreams; that the dreams were equally representative and significative with the visions, and that they were for the most part of one kind; and that to others also as well as the prophets things to come were made known by dreams; as by the dream of Joseph, and the dreams of those who were with him in prison, and those also of Pharaoh, of Nebuchadnezzar, and others. From which it is evident that dreams of this kind, equally with visions, flow in from heaven; with the difference, that dreams are experienced when the corporeal man is asleep, and visions when he is not asleep. How prophetic dreams, and such dreams as are in the Word flow in, nay, descend from heaven, has been shown me to the life; respecting which I may state from experience these particulars :—

There are three kinds of dreams. The first kind come from the Lord, mediately through heaven; such were the prophetic dreams of which we read in the Word. The second kind come through angelic spirits,—especially those who are at the front, above, towards the right, where there are paradisiacal scenes.

From thence the men of the Most Ancient Church had their dreams, which were instructive. The third kind come through the spirits who are near man while he sleeps; which also are significative. But fantastic dreams have another origin. (A. C. n. 1975, 1976.)

WHAT IS MEANT BY BEING IN THE SPIRIT.

Since by the spirit of man his mind is meant, therefore by being "*in the spirit*," which is sometimes spoken of in the Word, is meant a state of the mind separate from the body; and because in this state the prophets saw such things as exist in the spiritual world, it is called "the vision of God." Their state was then like that of the spirits and angels themselves in that world. In this state the spirit of man,—like his mind as respects the sight,—can be transported from place to place, the body remaining in its position. This is the state in which I have been now for twenty-six years; with the difference, that I have been in the spirit and at the same time in the body, and only sometimes out of the body. That Ezekiel, Zechariah, Daniel, and John when he wrote the Revelation, were in this state, is evident from the following passages:—Ezekiel xi. 1, 24; iii. 12, 14; viii. 3, *seq.*; i. 10; xl.—xlviii.; Zech. i. 8, *seq.*; i. 18; ii. 1-5; iii. 1 *seq.*; iv. i. *seq.*; v. 1-6; vi. 1, *seq.*; Daniel vii. 1, *seq.*; viii. 1, *seq.*; ix. 21; Rev. i. 10; xvii. 3; xxi. 10; ix. 17. (T. C. R. n. 157.)

WHAT IT IS TO BE TAKEN OUT OF THE BODY, AND TO BE CARRIED BY THE SPIRIT INTO ANOTHER PLACE.

There are two kinds of visions out of the common course, into which I was introduced only that I might know the nature of them, and what is meant by that which we read of in the Word, that some were "*taken out of the body*," and some were "*carried by the Spirit into another place*."

As regards the first, namely, being taken out of the body, the case is this: The man is brought into a certain state which is intermediate between sleep and wakefulness. While he is in this state he cannot know but that he is quite awake; all the senses are as much awake as in the completest state of bodily vigilance, the sight as well as the hearing, and what is remarkable, the touch, which is then more exquisite than it can ever be in bodily wakefulness. In this state spirits and angels have been seen exactly to the life, and also heard, and what is amazing, touched; and almost nothing of the body then intervenes. This

is the state described as being "taken out of the body," and of which it is said of those who are in it that, "whether in the body or out of the body, they cannot tell."[1]   Into this state I have been introduced only three or four times; merely that I might know the nature of it, and that spirits and angels enjoy every sense,—even the touch, more powerful and more exquisite than the touch of the body.

With respect to the other, the being carried by the Spirit into another place, what this is and how it is was also shown me by living experience; but only twice or three times.   I may merely relate an experience:—Walking through the streets of a city and through the country, and in conversation at the same time with spirits, I was not aware but that I was equally awake and in the enjoyment of my sight as at other times, walking thus without error; and all the while I was in a vision, seeing groves, rivers, palaces, houses, men, and many other objects.   But after I had been walking thus for some hours, suddenly I was in bodily vision, and observed that I was in a different place. Greatly amazed at this, I apperceived that I had been in such a state as they were in of whom it is said, that they were "carried by the spirit to another place."[2]   For while the state lasts there is no reflection respecting the way, and this although it were many miles; nor upon the time, though it were many hours or days; neither is there any sense of fatigue.   Then, the man is led also through ways of which he himself is ignorant, until he comes to the place intended.   This was done that I might know also that a man can be led of the Lord without his knowing whence or whither.

But these two kind of visions are uncommon, and were shown me only to the end that I might know the nature of them.   But all those things which by the Lord's Divine mercy you may see related in the First Part of this work, prefixed and annexed to each chapter, are ordinary sights; they are not visions, but things seen in utmost wakefulness of the body, and this now for many years.   (A. C. n. 1882, 1885.)

The Difference between a State of Vision and direct Revelation from the Lord.

What John saw [in the Revelation] he did not see with the eyes of the body, but with the eyes of the spirit; as may appear from the passages where he says that he was in the spirit, and in vision; ch. i. 10; ix. 17; xvii. 3; xxi. 10,—thus in every

---

[1] 2 Cor. xii. 3.
[2] 1 Kings xviii. 12; 2 Kings ii. 16; Ez. iii. 12, 14; Acts viii. 39.

place where he says he saw. No one can enter into that state, and be kept in it, but by angels who are in near conjunction with the man, and who inspire their spiritual state into the interiors of his mind; for thus the man is elevated into the light of heaven; and in this light he sees the things that are in heaven, and not the things that are in the world. In a similar state at times were Ezekiel, Zechariah, Daniel, and the other prophets; but not when they spake the Word. Then they were not in the spirit but in the body, and heard the words that they wrote from Jehovah Himself, that is from the Lord. These two states of the prophets should be carefully distinguished. The prophets themselves indeed carefully distinguish them; for they say everywhere, when they wrote the Word from Jehovah, that Jehovah spake with them, and to them, and very often, Jehovah said, and saith Jehovah; but when they were in the other state, they say that they were in the spirit, or in vision,—as may appear from many passages. (A. R. n. 945.)

EXTENSION OF MAN'S THOUGHT INTO THE SPIRITUAL WORLD.

It has been plainly shown me that the thought of man, and also of spirits, and likewise of angels, diffuses itself around into many societies in the spiritual world; but the thought of one in a different manner from that of another. That I might know this for a certainty it was given me to discourse with some societies to which my thought penetrated; and thereby it was given me to know what flowed into the thought, from what society it flowed, also where it was, and of what quality, so that I could not be mistaken. According to the extension of the thoughts and affections into societies is the faculty of understanding and perceiving, with man, spirit, and angel. He who is in the good of charity and of faith has extension into societies of heaven,—ample according to the degree in which he is in them, and in which he is in genuine good; for these are concordant with heaven, and therefore spontaneously and widely flow in thither. There are constantly some societies into which affection for truth, and others into which affection for good penetrates. Affection for truth penetrates to societies of spiritual angels, and affection for good to societies of celestial angels. But on the other hand, the thought and affection of those who are in evil and falsity have extension into infernal societies; and this also according to the degree of evil and falsity in them. It is said that the thought and affection of man, spirit, and angel, diffuse themselves around into societies, and that hence come understanding and perception. But it should be known that this is said according to the appearance; for there is not an influx of thoughts and affections into societies, but from societies,—and this through the angels and spirits that are with man. For all influx is from the interior; thus with the good it is from heaven,—that is, through heaven from the Lord; and with the evil it is from hell. (A. C. n. 6600.)

How Spirits can be enabled to see into this World.

Spirits with their sight, that is with the sight of the spirit cannot see anything whatever in the world,—still less can the angels; for the light of the world, or of the sun, is as thick darkness to them. So man with his sight, that is with the sight of the body, can see nothing whatever in the other life; for to him the light of heaven, or the heavenly light of the Lord, is as thick darkness. And yet when it pleases the Lord, spirits and angels can see the objects that are in the world through the eyes of a man; but this the Lord vouchsafes with none but to whom He gives to speak with spirits and angels, and to be in company with them. It has been given them to see through my eyes the things that are in this world, and as distinctly as I; and also to hear men talking with me. It has happened several times that some, through me, have seen their friends which they had in the life of the body, as actually present as before, and were astonished. They have also seen their partners and children; and desired that I would tell them they were present and saw them, and that I would inform them of their state in the other life. But it was forbidden me to tell them, and to reveal that they were thus seen; for the reason indeed that they would have declared me insane, or would have thought these things to be mental hallucinations. For I knew that although with their mouth they might say, yet in heart they would not believe that there are spirits, and that the dead are raised again. When first my interior sight was opened, and through my eyes they saw the world and the things that are in the world, the spirits and angels were so astonished that they declared it to be the miracle of miracles, and were affected with a new joy, that thus communication was given of earth with heaven, and of heaven with earth. And this delight lasted for months; but afterwards the thing became familiar. Now they do not wonder. I have been informed that the spirits and angels with other men see nothing at all that is in the world, but only perceive the thoughts and affections of those with whom they are. From these facts it must appear that man was so created that while he is living among men on earth he might also at the same time live among angels in heaven, and *vice versa ;* so that heaven and earth might be associated together and act as one, and men might know what is in heaven, and the angels what is in the world. And when men depart, they would thus pass from the Lord's kingdom on earth into the Lord's kingdom in the heavens not as into another, but as into the same in which they have been while they were living in the body. But because man has become so corporeal he has closed heaven against himself. (A. C. n. 1880.)

How long Men remain in the World of Spirits.

Some abide in the world of spirits only a month, or a year, and some from ten even to thirty years. Those who were permitted to make, as it were, heavens for themselves, remained there for some centuries. But at this day they do not remain beyond twenty years. (A. R. n. 866.)

Purgatory a Fiction.

As to purgatory, I am able to assert that it is purely a Babylonish fiction, for the sake of gain ; and that there is no such thing, and cannot be. Every man, after death, enters first into the world of spirits,—which is intermediate between heaven and hell,—and is there prepared either for heaven or for hell, each according to his life in the world. And no one is tormented in that world ; but the wicked first come into torment when, after preparation, they go into hell. In that world there are innumerable societies, and enjoyments in them, similar to those on earth,—for the reason that those who are there are conjoined with men on earth, who also are intermediate between heaven and hell. Their externals are there gradually put off, and their internals thus discovered ; and this until the reigning love, which is the life's love, and inmost and dominant over the externals, is revealed,—which being revealed, the man appears as he is ; and according to the quality of that love he is sent from the world of spirits to his own place ; if good, into heaven, if evil, into hell. That it is so has been given me certainly to know; for it has been granted me by the Lord to be with those who are in that world, and to see all things, and so from very experience to relate what I have seen, and this now for twenty years. I can therefore assert that purgatory is a fiction; which may be called diabolical, because for the sake of gain, and for the sake of power over souls, even of the deceased, after death. (A. R. n. 784.)

HEAVEN.

Heaven is Divided into Two Kingdoms.

Since there are infinite varieties in heaven, and no one society is exactly similar to another, nor indeed one angel to another, therefore heaven is distinguished generally, specifically, and particularly; generally into two kingdoms, specifically into three heavens, and particularly into innumerable societies. (H. H. n. 20.)

There are angels who more and who less interiorly receive the Divine proceeding from the Lord. Those who more interiorly receive are called celestial angels; and those who receive less interiorly are called spiritual angels. Heaven is therefore distinguished into two kingdoms; of which one is called the Celestial Kingdom, the other the Spiritual Kingdom. (*ib.* n. 21.)

The love in which they are who are in the celestial kingdom is called celestial love; and the love in which they are who are in the spiritual kingdom is called spiritual love. Celestial love is love to the Lord; and spiritual love is charity towards the neighbor. And as all good is of love,—for what any one loves is good to him,—therefore the good also of one kingdom is called celestial, and the good of the other spiritual. It is evident from this in what these two kingdoms are distinguished; namely, that they are distinguished as the good of love to the Lord, and the good of charity towards the neighbor. And because the former good is more interior good, and the former love is more interior love, therefore the celestial angels are more interior and are called higher angels. (*ib.* n. 23.)

The angels in the Lord's celestial kingdom in .wisdom and glory greatly excel the angels who are in the spiritual kingdom, because they receive the Divine of the Lord more interiorly; for they are in love to Him, and are therefore nearer and more closely conjoined to Him. These angels are such because they have received and do receive Divine truths immediately into the life, and not as the spiritual into previous memory and thought. They therefore have them inscribed on their hearts, and perceive them and as it were see them in themselves; nor do they ever reason about them, whether it be so or not so. They are such as are described in Jeremiah: "*I will put my law in their mind, and write it in their heart. . . . They shall teach no more every man his friend and every man his brother, saying, Know ye Jehovah; they shall know me, from the least of them unto the greatest of them*" (xxxi. 33, 34). And they are called in Isaiah the "*Taught of Jehovah*" (liv. 13). That they who are taught of Jehovah are they who are taught of the Lord, the Lord Himself teaches in John vi. 45, 46. (*ib.* n. 25.)

Because there is such a distinction between the angels of the celestial kingdom and the angels of the spiritual kingdom, they are not together, nor have they intercourse with each other. There is only a communication by intermediate angelic societies, which are called celestial-spiritual; through these the celestial kingdom flows into the spiritual. Hence it is that although heaven is divided into two kingdoms, yet it makes one. The Lord always provides such intermediate angels, through whom there is communication and conjunction. (*ib.* n. 27.)

There are three Heavens.

There are three heavens, and they are most distinct from each other; the inmost or third, the intermediate or second, and the ultimate or first. They follow and are related to each other as the highest part of man, which is called the head, his middle part, which is called the body, and his lowest which is called the feet; and as the highest, middle, and lowest parts of a house. In such order also is the Divine which proceeds and descends from the Lord. Hence, from a necessity of order, heaven is threefold.

The interiors of man, which are of his higher mind (*mens*) and lower mind (*animus*), are also in similar order; he has an inmost, an intermediate, and an ultimate. For all things of Divine order were brought together in man when he was created, so that he was made Divine order in form, and therefore heaven in its least image. As to his interiors therefore man also communicates with the heavens; and he likewise comes among the angels after death,—among the angels of the inmost heaven, or of the intermediate, or the ultimate heaven, according to his reception of Divine good and truth from the Lord while he lived in the world.

The Divine which flows in from the Lord and is received in the inmost or third heaven is called celestial, and the angels there are therefore called celestial angels. The Divine which flows in from the Lord and is received in the second or middle heaven is called spiritual, and therefore the angels who are there are called spiritual angels. And the Divine which flows in from the Lord and is received in the ultimate or first heaven is called natural. But as the natural of that heaven is not as the natural of the world, but has the spiritual and the celestial within it, that heaven is called spiritual and celestial-natural; and hence the angels who are there are called spiritual and celestial-natural. Those are called spiritual-natural who receive influx from the intermediate or second heaven, which is the spiritual heaven; and those are called celestial-natural who receive influx from the third or inmost heaven, which is the celestial heaven. The spiritual-natural and the celestial-natural angels are distinct from each other; but yet they constitute one heaven, because they are in the same degree. (H. H. n. 29-31.)

Because there is such a distinction, an angel of one heaven cannot enter among the angels of another heaven; nor can any one ascend from a lower heaven, or any one descend from a higher heaven. When the Lord elevates any from a lower heaven into a higher, that they may see the glory there, which is often done, they are first prepared, and encompassed by intermediate angels through whom there is communication. From these facts it is plain that the three heavens are most distinct from each other. (*ib.* n. 35.)

But although the heavens are so distinct that the angels of one heaven cannot associate with the angels of another heaven, yet the Lord conjoins all the heavens by immediate and mediate influx; by immediate influx from Himself into all the heavens, and by mediate influx from one heaven into another. And thus He effects that the three heavens are one, and that all, from the first to the last, are in connection; even so that nothing is unconnected. Whatever is not connected by intermediates with the first does not subsist, but is dissipated and becomes nothing. (*ib.* n. 37.)

The Heavens were not three before the Lord's Advent.

Before the Lord's advent heaven was not distinguished into three heavens,—that is into an inmost or third, an intermediate or second, and an ultimate or first heaven,—as after the Lord's advent, but was one. As yet the spiritual heaven was not. The region where the spiritual heaven was about to be was occupied by those who were in falsity and evil, but who could be kept in some truth and good by external means,—especially by ideas of eminence and dignity; in like manner as is the case in the world, where they who are in evil and falsity are yet obliged as it were to think and speak truths, and as it were to will and do goods, by external means, such as honours and gains. The reason why that region of heaven was then occupied by such was that the good were wanting, and they who were of the spiritual church were not yet prepared; and yet it must everywhere be filled with spirits, in order that there might be a continuity from the Lord even to man, for if there had not been a continuity man would have perished. There are at this day also some regions of heaven occupied by such;[1] but they who are there are withheld by a strong force from doing evil. . . . These regions are thus occupied when the evil are increased in the world, and the good are diminished. For then evil spirits draw near to man, and good spirits recede from him; and in proportion as they recede the regions nearest to man are occupied by the evil. When this comes to pass generally the inhabitants of these regions are changed. This takes place when the church is near its end; for then evil and falsity prevail. But at about the end of the church they are cast down, and the regions occupied are given to the good who in the meantime have been prepared for heaven.[2] This is meant by these words in the Apocalypse: " *There was war in heaven; Michael and his angels fought against the dragon; and the dragon fought and his angels, but prevailed not; neither was their place found any more in heaven* " (xii. 7, 8). (A. C. n. 8054.)

In each Heaven there are Innumerable Societies.

The angels of each heaven are not assembled together in one place, but distinguished into societies greater and smaller, according to the differences of the good of love and faith in which they are. Those that are in similar good form one society. Goods in the heavens are infinite in variety; and each angel is such as his own good. The angelic societies in the heavens are also distant from each other according as their goods differ generally and specifically. For in the spiritual world distances are from no other origin than from a difference of state of the interiors. Therefore in the heavens they are from a difference in the states of love; they that differ much are widely distant, and they that differ little are but little distant. Similarity brings them together.

In one society all are in like manner distinct from each other; those who are more perfect, that is who excel in good, and therefore in love, wisdom and intelligence, are in the midst; those

[1] It is important to understand that when the work was published from which this extract is taken, the Last Judgment (see p. 704) had not yet taken place.
[2] See p. 156.

who less excel are round about them, at a distance increasing by degrees as they diminish in perfection. It is as light decreasing from a centre to the circumferences. Those who are in the midst are in fact in the greatest light; and those who dwell towards the circumferences, in less and less.

Like, as it were of themselves, are brought to like; for with their like they are as with their own, and at home; but with others they are as with strangers, and abroad. When they are with their like they are also in their freedom, and therefore in every delight of life.

From this it is plain that good consociates all in the heavens, and that they are distinguished according to its quality. And yet it is not the angels that thus consociate themselves, but the Lord, from whom is good. He leads them, conjoins them, distinguishes them, and keeps them in freedom so far as they are in good; and thus preserves every one in the life of his love, of his faith, of his intelligence and wisdom, and thereby in happiness.

All who are in similar good also know each other,—although they have never seen each other before,—just as men in the world know their kindred, their relations, and their friends. The reason is that in the other life there are no kindreds, relationships and friendships but such as are spiritual, thus which are of love and faith. This it has sometimes been given me to see, when I have been in the spirit and thus withdrawn from the body, and so in company with angels. Some of them have then appeared as if known to me from infancy; and others as if entirely unknown. Those who appeared as if I had known them from infancy, were such as were in a state similar to the state of my spirit; and those who were not known were in a dissimilar state. (H. H. n. 41-46.)

The larger societies consist of myriads of angels, the less of some thousands, and the least of some hundreds. There are also angels who dwell apart, as it were house by house, and family by family. Although they live thus dispersed, yet they are arranged in a similar manner as those who dwell in societies; that is, the wiser of them are in the midst, and the more simple upon the boundaries. These are more nearly under the Divine auspices of the Lord, and are the best of the angels. (*ib.* n. 50.)

The Universal Heaven is in the Form of a Man.

That heaven in its whole complex resembles a man, is an arcanum not yet known in the world; but in the heavens it is very well known. To know this, and the specific and particular things concerning it, is a chief part of the intelligence of the angels there. On this indeed many other things depend, which without it as their general principle would not enter distinctly and clearly into the ideas of their mind. Because they know that all the heavens together with their societies resemble a man, they also call heaven THE GREATEST, and THE DIVINE MAN; Divine, from the fact that the Divine of the Lord makes heaven. (H. H. n. 59.)

The angels do not indeed see heaven in its whole complex in such a form, for the whole heaven does not fall into the view of any angel. But they sometimes see remote societies, which consist of many thousands of angels, as one in such a form; and from a society, as from a part, they form a conclusion as to the whole, which is heaven. For in the most perfect form things general are as the parts, and the parts as the general; the only distinction is as between similar things greater and less. Hence they say that the whole heaven is in such a form in the sight of the Lord; because the Divine, from the inmost and supreme, sees all things.

Because heaven is such it is therefore also governed by the Lord as a man, and hence as one; for it is known that although a man consists of an innumerable variety of things, both in the whole and in part,—in the whole, of members, organs, and viscera, in part, of series of fibres, nerves, and blood-vessels,—thus of members within members and parts within parts, yet when a man acts he nevertheless acts as one. Such also is heaven under the auspices and guidance of the Lord.

That so many various things in a man act as one is because there is nothing there that does not some thing for the common weal, or that does not perform a use. The whole performs use to its parts, and the parts perform use to the whole; for the whole is from the parts, and the parts constitute the whole. They therefore provide for each other, have respect to each other, and are conjoined in such form that each and all things have reference to the whole and its good. Hence it is that they act as one. Such are the consociations in the heavens; they are there conjoined in similar form according to uses. Any therefore who do not perform a use to the whole are cast out of heaven, because they are heterogeneous.

Because the whole heaven resembles a man, and also is a Divine spiritual man in the greatest form, even as to figure, therefore heaven as a man is distinguished into members and parts; and they are also named in like manner. The angels also know in what member one society is, and in what another; and they say, that this society is in the member or in some province of the head, this in the member or in some province of the breast, that in the member or in some province of the loins, and so on. In general, the highest or third heaven forms the head as far as the neck; the intermediate or second heaven forms the breast down to the loins and knees; the ultimate or first heaven forms the feet down to the soles, and also the arms to the fingers; for the arms and hands are ultimates of a man, although at the sides. From this again it is evident why there are three heavens. (*ib.* n. 62-65.)

Because heaven in the whole and in part resembles a man, from the Divine Human of the Lord, the angels say that they are in the Lord, and some that they are in His body; by which they mean that they are in the good of His love. As indeed the Lord Himself teaches, saying :—" *Abide in Me, and I in you. As the branch cannot bear fruit of itself, except it abide in the vine, no more can ye, except ye abide in Me ;* . . . *for without Me ye can do nothing.* . . . *Continue ye in My love. If ye keep My commandments, ye shall abide in My love* " (John xv. 4-10). (*ib.* n. 81.)

The Correspondence of Heaven with all Things of Man.

In general the celestial kingdom corresponds to the heart, and to all things of the heart in the whole body; and the spiritual kingdom to the lungs, and to all things of them in the whole body. The heart and the lungs constitute two kingdoms also in man; the heart governs therein by the arteries and veins, and the lungs by the nervous and moving fibres,—both, in every force and action. In every man there are two kingdoms also in his spiritual world, which is called his spiritual man; one is the kingdom of the will, and the other of the understanding. The will governs by affections for good, and the understanding by affections for truth. These kingdoms also correspond to the kingdoms of the heart and lungs in the body. So in the heavens. The celestial kingdom is the will principle of heaven, and therein the good of love reigns; and the spiritual kingdom is the intellectual principle of heaven, and therein truth reigns. These are what correspond to the functions of the heart and of the lungs in man. It is from this correspondence that in the Word the heart signifies the will, and also the good of love; and the breath of the lungs signifies the understanding, and the truth of faith. Hence also it is that the affections are ascribed to the heart, although they are not there nor thence.

The correspondence of the two kingdoms of heaven with the heart and lungs is the general correspondence of heaven with man. But there is a less general correspondence with his particular members, organs, and viscera; what the nature of this is shall also be explained. They who are in the head in the Greatest Man, which is heaven, excel all others in every good; for they are in love, peace, innocence, wisdom, intelligence, and thence in joy and happiness. These flow into the head and into the things in man which belong to the head and correspond to them. Those who are in the breast in the Greatest Man, which is heaven, are the good of charity and faith; and these also flow into the breast of man, and correspond to it. And those who are in the loins and in the organs dedicated to generation there, in the Greatest Man or heaven, are in conjugial love. Those who are in the feet are in the ultimate good of heaven, which good is called natural-spiritual. Those who are in the arms and hands are in the power of truth from good. Those who are in the eyes are in understanding. Those who are in the ears are in hearing and obedience. Those who are in the nostrils are in perception. Those who are in the mouth and tongue are in discourse from understanding and perception. Those who are in the kidneys, are in truth that is searching, separating, and corrective. Those who are in the liver, pancreas, and spleen, are in the various purification of good and truth. So in a different manner with the other organs. These flow into the like parts in man, and correspond to them. The influx of heaven is into the functions and uses of the members; and the uses, because they are from the spiritual world, give themselves form by means of such things as are in the natural world, and thus present themselves in effect. Hence is the correspondence.

It is from this that similar things are signified by these same members, organs, and viscera, in the Word; for all things therein have a signification according to their correspondences. By the head is therefore signified intelligence and wisdom; by the breast, charity; by the loins, conjugial love; by the arms and hands, the power of truth; by the feet, the natural; by the eyes, the understanding; by the nostrils, perception; by the ears, obedience; by the kidneys, examination of truth; and so on. Hence also it is that it is usual for a man to say of one who is intelligent and wise, that he has a head; of one who is in charity, that he is a bosom friend; of one who excels in perception, that he has a quick scent; of one who is intelligent, that he has a keen sight; of one who is in power, that he has long arms ; of one who purposes from love, that he does it from the heart. These and many other things that are in human speech, are from correspondence; for such forms of speech, although man is ignorant of it, are from the spiritual world. (H. H. n. 95-97.)

But although all things of man as regards his body correspond to all things of heaven, yet man is not an image of heaven as to his external form, but as to his internal form ; for the interiors of man receive heaven, and his exteriors receive the world. So far therefore as his interiors receive heaven, a man as to them is a heaven in the least form, after the image of the greatest. But in so far as his interiors do not receive he is not a heaven and an image of the greatest ; and yet his exteriors which receive the world may be in form according to the order of the world, and hence in various beauty. For external beauty, which is of the body, derives its cause from parents, and from formation in the womb, and is afterwards preserved by a common influx from the world. Hence it is that the form of the natural man differs exceedingly from the form of his spiritual man. It has sometimes been shown me what the spirit of a man was in form ; and it was seen that in some who were of beautiful and lovely countenance the spirit was deformed, black, and monstrous,—so that you would call it an image of hell, not of heaven. And in some who were not beautiful, the spirit was comely, beautiful and angelic. After death the spirit of a man actually appears such as it had been in the body while he lived in the world. (*ib.* n. 99.)

CORRESPONDENCE OF HEAVEN WITH ALL THINGS ON EARTH.

Nothing ever comes into existence and subsists without correspondence with the Greatest Man, that is with heaven, or, what is the same with the spiritual world ; for the reason that it would have no connection with anything prior to itself, nor consequently with the First, that is with the Lord. Anything unconnected and thus independent cannot even for one moment subsist ; for that a thing subsists is from its connection with and dependence upon that from which is every thing of existence, since subsistence is perpetual existence. Hence it is that not only each and all things in man correspond, but also each and all things in the universe. The sun itself corresponds, and also the moon ; for in heaven the Lord is the sun, and likewise the moon. The sun's flame and heat, and also light, correspond ; for it is the Lord's love towards the whole human race to which the flame and heat, and Divine truth to which light corresponds. The very stars correspond ; it is to the societies of heaven and their habitations that they correspond ; not that they are there, but that they are in such order. Whatever appears beneath the sun corresponds ; as each and all the subjects of the animal kingdom, and also each and all the subjects of the vegetable kingdom ; which, individually and collectively, would sink and fall in ruins in a moment, if there were not an influx into them from the spiritual world. This also it has been given me to know by much experience ; for it was shown me with what in the spiritual world many things that are in the animal kingdom, and still more that are in the vegetable kingdom, correspond ; and also that they can in nowise subsist without influx. For if the prior be taken away, the posterior necessarily falls ; so if the prior be separated from the posterior. (A. C. n. 5377.)

It shall be briefly stated how the conjunction of heaven with the world by correspondences is effected. The kingdom of the Lord is a kingdom of ends, which are uses; or what is the same, a kingdom of uses, which are ends. Therefore the universe was so created and formed by the Divine that uses may everywhere be clothed with such things as present them in act or in effect, —in heaven first, and then in the world ; thus, by degrees and in succession down to the ultimates of nature. It is therefore plain that the correspondence of natural things with spiritual or of the world with heaven is through uses, and that uses conjoin them; and that the forms with which uses are clothed are correspondences, and are conjunctions, in so far as they are forms of the uses. In the nature of the world, in its threefold kingdom, all things that exist therein according to order are forms of uses, or effects formed from use for use. From this cause the things that are therein are correspondences. (H. H. n. 112.)

The Sun and Moon in Heaven.

The sun of the world does not appear in heaven, nor any thing which is from that sun, because all this is natural; for with that sun nature begins, and whatever is produced by means of it is called natural. But the spiritual [world], in which heaven is, is above nature, and altogether distinct from the natural; nor do they communicate with each other except by correspondences.

But although the sun of the world does not appear in heaven, nor any thing from that sun, yet there is a sun in heaven, and there is light, and heat. The sun of heaven is the Lord; the light there is the Divine truth, and the heat there is the Divine good, which proceed from the Lord as a sun. All things that exist and appear in the heavens are from this origin. The reason why the Lord appears in heaven as a sun is, that He is Divine Love, from which all things spiritual exist; and also, by means of the sun of the world, all natural things. It is this love which shines as a sun.

The Lord appears as a sun, not in heaven, but high above the heavens; nor yet overhead or in the zenith, but before the faces of the angels, at a middle altitude. He appears, at a very great distance, in two places; in one before the right eye, in the other before the left eye. Before the right eye He appears exactly like a sun, of similar fire as it were, and of similar magnitude to the sun of the world. But before the left eye he does not appear as a sun but as a moon, of similar but more brilliant whiteness, and of similar magnitude to the moon of our earth; but this appears encompassed with several smaller moons as it were, each of which is similarly white and brilliant. The reason why the Lord appears in two places, with such a difference, is that He appears to every one according to the quality of his reception of Him; and therefore in one way to those who receive Him in the good of love, and in another to those who receive Him in the good of faith. To those who receive Him in the good of love He appears as a sun, fiery and flaming according to reception. They are in His celestial kingdom. But to those who receive Him in the good of faith He appears as a moon, white and brilliant according to reception. These are in His spiritual kingdom. The cause of this is, that the good of love corresponds to fire, and therefore fire in the spiritual sense is love; and the good of faith corresponds to light, and light also in the spiritual sense is faith. The reason why He appears before the eyes is, that the interiors, which are of the mind, see through the eyes; through the right eye from the good of love, and through the left eye from the good of faith. For with an angel, and also with a man, all things that are on the right side correspond to good from which is truth; and those on the left, to truth which is from good. The good of faith in its essence is truth from good.

Hence it is that the Lord as to love is compared to the sun, and as to faith to the moon, in the Word; and also that love from the Lord to the Lord is signified by the sun, and faith from the Lord in the Lord is signified by the moon. As in the following passages: " *The light of the moon shall be as the light of the sun, and the light of the sun shall be sevenfold, as the light of seven days* " (Isaiah xxx. 26). " *When I shall extinguish thee I will cover the heavens, and make the stars thereof dark: I will cover the sun with a cloud, and the moon shall not make her light to shine. All the bright lights in the heavens I will make dark over thee, and will set darkness upon thy land* " (Ezek. xxxii. 7, 8.) " *I will darken the sun in its going forth, and the moon shall not cause her light to shine* " (Isaiah xiii. 10). " *The sun and the moon shall be darkened, and the stars shall withdraw their shining. . . . The sun shall be turned into darkness, and the moon into blood* " (Joel ii. 2, 10, 31; ch. iii. 15). " *The sun became black as sackcloth of hair, and the moon became as blood, and the stars fell to the earth* " (Apoc. vi. 12, 13). " *Immediately after the tribulation of those days shall the sun be darkened, and the moon*

shall not give her light, and the stars shall fall from heaven"
(Matt. xxiv. 29) ; and in other places. By the sun in these passages love is signified, by the moon faith, and by stars cognitions
of good and truth. These are said to be darkened, to lose
their light, and to fall from heaven, when they no longer exist.
That the Lord appears in heaven as a sun, is evident also from
His actual transfiguration before Peter, James, and John, where it
is said that " *His face did shine as the sun*" (Matt. xvii. 2). The
Lord was thus seen by those disciples when they were withdrawn from the body, and were in the light of heaven. Hence
it was that the ancients, with whom the church was representative, turned their faces to the sun in the east when they were in
Divine worship. From them the custom is derived of placing
temples with their aspect towards the east. (H. H. n. 116-119.)

But when the Lord appears in heaven, which frequently
occurs, He does not appear encompassed with the sun, but in an
angelic form, distinguished from the angels by the Divine shining through and from His face. In truth He is not there in
person, for in person the Lord is constantly surrounded with
the sun; but He is in the presence [of the angels] by aspect.
It is indeed common in heaven for them to appear as if present
in the place to which the view [*aspectus*] is earnestly directed, or
where it is terminated; although it may be very far from the
place where they actually are. This presence is called presence
to the internal sight, of which hereafter. The Lord has also
been seen by me out of the sun, in an angelic form, a little
beneath the sun on high; and also near, in a similar form, with
a resplendent countenance ; once also as a flaming splendour
in the midst of the angels. (*ib.* n. 121.)

Let every one take care that he does not think the sun of
the spiritual world to be God Himself. God Himself is a Man.
The first proceeding from His love and wisdom is a fiery
spiritual [emanation] which appears to the angels as a sun.
Therefore when the Lord manifests Himself to the angels in
person He manifests Himself as Man ; and this sometimes in the
sun, sometimes out of the sun. (D. L. W. n. 97.)

The Heat and Light of Heaven.

The heat of heaven like the light of heaven is everywhere
various ; different in the celestial kingdom from what it is in the
spiritual kingdom, and also different in every society of each.
It not only differs in degree but also in quality. It is more
intense and pure in the Lord's celestial kingdom, because the
angels there receive more of the Divine good ; it is less intense

and pure in the Lord's spiritual kingdom, because the angels there receive more of Divine truth. It differs in each society also, according to reception. . . . That love is heat from a spiritual origin is manifest from the increase of warmth according to love; for a man is inflamed and heated according to its degree and quality, and its ardor is manifested when it is assaulted. From this too it has become customary to speak of being inflamed, of growing warm, of burning, boiling, and being on fire, both when speaking of the affections which are of the love of good, and of the concupiscences which are of the love of evil.

The reason why the love proceeding from the Lord as a sun is felt in heaven as heat is, that from the Divine good which comes from the Lord the interiors of the angels are in love; whence the exteriors, which therefore grow warm, are in heat. It is from this cause that in heaven heat and love mutually so correspond to each other that every one there is in heat such as his love, agreeably to what was said just above.

Angels like men have an understanding and will. The light of heaven constitutes the life of their understanding,—because the light of heaven is Divine truth, and thence Divine wisdom; and the heat of heaven constitutes the life of their will,—because the heat of heaven is Divine good, and thence Divine love. The veriest life of the angels is from heat; and not from light, except in so far as there is heat within it. That life is from heat is manifest; for this being removed life perishes. It is the same with faith without love, or with truth without good; for truth, which is called the truth of faith, is light, and good which is of love, is heat. These things more plainly appear from the heat and light of the world, to which the heat and light of heaven correspond. From the heat of the world conjoined to the light all things that exist on the earth are vivified and flourish; they are conjoined in the seasons of spring and summer. But by the light separate from the heat nothing is vivified and flourishes, but all things become inactive and dead; they are not conjoined in the season of winter,—then heat is absent though the light continues. On account of this correspondence heaven is called paradise; since truth there is conjoined to good, or faith to love; just as the light is to heat in the season of spring on earth. (H. H. n. 134-136.)

Such is the light in heaven that it exceeds the very noon-day light of this solar world, to a degree surpassing belief. But the angels receive no light from the world; because they are above or within the sphere of this light. But they receive light from the Lord, who is their sun. The light, even the noonday light, of this world, is as thick darkness to the angels. When it is given them to see this light it is as if they beheld mere darkness; which it has been given me to know by experience. It may be seen from this what a difference there is between the light of heaven and the light of the world. (A. C. n. 1521.)

THE FOUR QUARTERS IN HEAVEN.

In heaven as in the world there are four quarters, the east, the south, the west, and the north,—in both, determined by their sun; in heaven by the sun of heaven, which is the Lord; in the world by the sun of the world. But yet there are great differences. The first is, that in the world it is called south where the sun is at its greatest altitude above the earth; north, where it is at the opposite point below the earth; east where the sun rises at the equinoxes; and west where it then sets. Thus, in the world all the quarters are determined from the south. But in heaven it is called the east where the Lord appears as a sun; the west is opposite; on the right in heaven is the south; and on the left there is the north; and this in every turning of their face and body. Thus, in heaven all the quarters are determined from the east. The reason why it is called east [*oriens*] where the Lord appears as a sun, is that all the origin of life is from Him as a sun;[1] and also that in proportion as heat and light, or love and intelligence, are received from Him by the angels the Lord is said to arise with them. Hence also it is that the Lord is called the East, in the Word.

Another difference is that to the angels the east is always before the face, the west is behind them, the south on their right, and the north on their left. But as this can with difficulty be comprehended in the world,—for the reason that man turns his face to every quarter, it shall therefore be explained:—The whole heaven turns itself to the Lord as to its common centre; hence all the angels turn themselves thither. It is well known that on earth also there is a tendency of every thing to a common centre; but in heaven the direction differs from the direction in the world,—in that in heaven the anterior parts are turned to its common centre, but in the world the lower parts. This tendency in the world is what is called the centripetal force, and also gravitation. The interiors of the angels are in fact actually

---

[1] It is scarcely possible to find complete expression for the sense of this passage in our language. To understand its full significance, and the doctrinal truth it involves respecting the Lord, it is necessary to know that the Latin word for east, *oriens*, is the present participle of the verb *orior*, "to rise," and literally signifies "the (sun) rising;" and that from the same verb was formed the Latin word for origin, *origo*, meaning literally the rising, *i.e.* coming forth, of things.

turned forwards ; and as the interiors present themselves in the face, the face is therefore what determines the quarters.

But it is still more difficult to comprehend, in the world, that with the angels the east is before the face at every turning of their face and body; for the reason that to man every quarter comes before the face, according as he turns himself. This therefore shall also be explained :—The angels, in like manner with men, turn and direct their faces and their bodies whithersoever they will ; and yet they always have the east before their eyes. But the turnings of the angels are not as the turnings of men; they are in fact from a different origin. They indeed appear alike ; but yet they are not alike. The ruling love is the origin; all determinations are from this, with angels and with spirits. For, as was said just above, their interiors are actually turned to their common centre ; thus, in heaven, to the Lord as a sun. As their love is therefore continually before their interiors, and the face exists from the interiors,—for it is the external form of them,—it results that the love which predominates is always before the face. And consequently in the heavens the Lord as a sun is continually before the face ; for it is He from whom they receive love. And as the Lord Himself is in His own love with the angels, therefore it is the Lord who causes them to look to Him which way soever they turn.

That there is such a turning to the Lord is among the wonders of heaven ; for many may be together there in the same place, and one turn the face and body in one way, and another in another, and yet all see the Lord before them, and each have the south on his right hand, the north on his left, and the west behind his back. It is also among the wonders of heaven that although the whole aspect of the angels is towards the east, yet they have an aspect also towards the three other quarters ; but their aspect towards these is from their interior sight, which is that of the thought. Among the wonders is this too, that in heaven one is never permitted to stand behind another and look at the back of his head, and if this is done the influx of good and truth which comes from the Lord is disturbed. (H. H. n. 141-144.)

All that is here said of the angels and of their turning to the Lord as a sun, is also to be understood of man, as to his spirit ; for as to his mind man is a spirit, and if he is in love and wisdom he is an angel. After death therefore, when he puts off his externals which he had derived from the natural world, he actually becomes a spirit or an angel. And as the angels constantly turn their faces eastward towards the sun, and thus towards the Lord, it is said also of the man who is in love and wisdom from the Lord, that he sees God, that he looks to God, and that he has

God before his eyes; by which is meant, that he lives as an angel. Such things are said in the world both because they actually exist in heaven, and because they actually exist in man's spirit. Who does not in prayer look before him up to God, to whatever quarter his face is turned?

The reason why the angels constantly turn their faces towards the Lord as a sun is, that they are in the Lord and the Lord in them; and the Lord interiorly leads their affections and thoughts, and constantly turns them to Himself. For this reason they cannot otherwise than look towards the east, where the Lord as a sun appears. It is plain from this that the angels do not turn themselves to the Lord, but that the Lord turns them to himself. For when the angels think interiorly of the Lord, they do not think of Him otherwise than within themselves. Interior thought does not itself cause distance; but the exterior thought does this, which acts as one with the sight of the eyes. The reason is that the exterior and not the interior thought is in space; and where as in the spiritual world it is not in space, it is yet in the appearance of space. (D. L. W. n. 129, 130.)

All in the heavens have distinct abodes according to the quarters. Towards the east and the west dwell those who are in the good of love; towards the east those who are in a clear perception of it, towards the west those who are in an obscure perception of it. Towards the south and the north dwell those who are in wisdom from that good; towards the south those who are in the clear light of wisdom, towards the north those who are in an obscure light of wisdom.

In like manner do the angels dwell among themselves in each society of heaven; towards the east dwell those who are in a greater degree of love and charity, towards the west those who are in a less degree; towards the south those who are in a greater light of wisdom and intelligence, towards the north those who are in a less.

Hence it is that the quarters in the heavens signify such things as pertain to those who dwell there; for the east signifies love and its good in clear perception; the west, the same in obscure perception; the south, wisdom and intelligence in clear light; and the north the same in obscure light. And because such things are signified by these quarters, therefore similar things are signified by them in the internal or spiritual sense of the Word; for the internal or spiritual sense of the Word is entirely in accordance with the things that exist in heaven. (H. H. n. 148-150.)

Changes of State in Heaven.

The angels are not constantly in the same state as to love, nor therefore in the same state as to wisdom; for all their wisdom is from love, and according to love. They are sometimes in a state of intense love, and sometimes in a state of love not intense. It decreases by degrees from its greatest to its least. When they are in their greatest degree of love they are in the light and heat of their life, or in their clearness and delight; but when they are in their least degree they are in shade and cold, or in their obscurity and undelight. From the last state they return again to the first; and so on. These changes follow one after the other, but with a diversity. The states succeed each other as the variations of the state of light and shade, of heat and cold; or as the morning, midday, evening, and night, every day in the world, with perpetual variety throughout the year. They also correspond; the morning to the state of their love in clearness, the midday to the state of their wisdom in clearness, the evening to the state of their wisdom in obscurity, and the night to a state of no love and wisdom. But it should be known that there is no correspondence of night with states of life of those who are in heaven; but there is a correspondence of the twilight that comes before the morning. The correspondence of night is with those who are in hell. (H. H. n. 155.)

I have been informed from heaven why there are changes of state there. The angels have told me that there are several reasons. The first is, that the delight of life and of heaven, which they derive from the love and wisdom that proceed from the Lord, would by degrees lose its value if they were in it continually; as is the case with those who are in conditions of delight and pleasantness without variety. Another reason is, that they as well as men have a *proprium*, and that this consists in loving themselves; and that all who are in heaven are withheld from their *proprium*, and in so far as they are withheld from it by the Lord are in love and wisdom; but in so far as they are not withheld they are in the love of self; and as every one loves his *proprium*, and is attracted by it, they have changes of state, or successive alternations. A third reason is, that they are thus perfected, since they are thus accustomed to be kept in the love of the Lord, and to be withheld from the love of self; and also that by alternations of delight and undelight the perception and sensation of good becomes more exquisite. They added, that the Lord does not produce their changes of state, for the Lord as a sun is always flowing in with heat and light, that is with love and wisdom; but that they themselves are the cause, for that they love their *proprium*, which is continually drawing them away. This was illustrated by comparison with the sun of the world; in that the cause of the changes of state of heat and cold, and of light and shade, every year and every day, is not in the sun, for it stands still, but the cause is in the earth. (*ib.* n. 158.)

TIME IN HEAVEN.

The angels do not know what time is,—although all things successively advance with them just as in the world, even so completely that there is no difference,—because in heaven there are not years and days, but changes of state; and where there are years and days, there are times, and where there are changes of state, there are states. The reason why there are times in the world is, that there to appearance the sun advances successively from one degree to another, and makes the times that are called seasons of the year; and also apparently revolves around the earth, and causes the periods that are called times of the day,— and each by stated alternations. It is otherwise with the sun of heaven. This does not by successive progressions and circumvolutions cause years and days, but to appearance changes of state; and these not by stated alternations, as was shown in the preceding article. Hence it is that the angels can have no conception of time, but of state in its stead.

Since the angels have no idea derived from time, like men in the world, they have therefore no idea concerning time, nor concerning the things that relate to time. The things proper to time, such as the year, month, week, day, hour, to-day, to-morrow, yesterday,—they do not even know what they are. When the angels hear of them from man (for angels are always adjoined to man by the Lord), instead of these they perceive states, and such things as pertain to state; thus the natural idea of man with the angels is turned into a spiritual idea. Hence it is that times signify states in the Word, and that the things proper to time, such as are mentioned above, signify the spiritual things corresponding to them.

It is the same with all things that exist from time; as with the four seasons of the year, called spring, summer, autumn and winter; the four times of the day, called morning, noon, evening, and night; and with the four ages of man, called infancy, youth, manhood, and old age; and with all other things that either exist from time, or follow in succession according to time. In thinking of these a man thinks from time, and an angel from state. Therefore whatever is from time in these things with man, is changed into an idea respecting state with an angel; spring and morning are changed into an idea of the state of love and wisdom, as they are in the first state with the angels; summer and noon are changed into an idea of love and wisdom as they are in the second state; autumn and evening as they are in the third state; night and winter into an idea of such a state as exists in hell. Hence it is that similar things are signified by these times in the Word. It may be seen from this how the natural things that are in the thought of man become spiritual with the angels who are with man. (H. H. n. 163-166.)

Space and Distance in Heaven.

Although all things in heaven appear in place, and in space, just as in the world, yet the angels have no notion or idea of place and space. As this cannot but seem a paradox, I wish to present the subject in a clear light; for it is of great moment.

All progressions in the spiritual world are made by changes of the state of the interiors; so that the progressions are nothing else than changes of state. Thus too have I been brought by the Lord into the heavens, and also to earths in the universe; and this, as to the spirit, while the body remained in the same place. Thus do all the angels move forward. To them therefore there are no distances; and if there are not distances neither are there spaces, but instead of them states, and their changes.

As progressions are thus made, it is evident that approaches are similitudes as to the state of the interiors, and that withdrawals are dissimilitudes. Hence it is that they are near to each other who are in a similar state, and they at a distance who are in a dissimilar state; and that spaces in heaven are nothing but the external states corresponding to internal. It is from no other cause that the heavens are distinct from each other; and the societies also of each heaven; and every one in a society. Hence likewise it is that the hells are completely separated from the heavens; because they are in a contrary state.

It is also from this cause that in the spiritual world one is presented in person to another if only he intensely desires his presence; for thus he sees him in thought, and puts himself in his state; and conversely, that one is removed from another in proportion as he is averse to him. And as all aversion is from contrariety of affections and disagreement of thoughts, it therefore comes to pass that several who are in one place there appear so long as they agree, but disappear as soon as they disagree.

When also any one goes from one place to another, whether in his own city, or in courts, or in gardens, or to others out of his own society, he arrives sooner when he desires, and later when he does not desire; the very way, although it is the same, is

lengthened and shortened according to the desire. This I have
often seen and wondered at. From these facts again it is evident
that distances, and therefore spaces, with the angels, are exactly
in accordance with the states of their interiors ; and because it is
so, that the notion and idea of space cannot enter into their
thought, although there are spaces with them equally as in the
world. (H. H. 191-195.)

Representatives and Appearances in Heaven.

The things that spring forth in the heavens are not produced in
the same manner as those that spring forth on earth. In the
heavens all things come forth from the Lord, according to correspondence with the interiors of the angels. For the angels have
both interiors and exteriors ; the things that are in their interiors
all have relation to love and faith, thus to the will and the understanding,—for the will and understanding are their receptacles ;
and the exteriors correspond to the interiors. This may be
illustrated by what was said above concerning the heat and
light of heaven. It is the same with all other things that appear
to the senses of the angels. (H. H. n. 173.)

Because all things that correspond to the interiors also represent
them, they are called *representatives*. And because they are
varied according to the state of the interiors with the angels, they
are called *appearances ;* and yet the things which appear before
the eyes of angels in the heavens, and are perceived by their
senses, appear and are perceived as much to the life as
the things that are on the earth do to man,—nay, much more
clearly, distinctly, and perceptibly. The appearances from this
origin in the heavens because they really exist, are called *real*
appearances. There are also appearances that are not real, which
are those things that do indeed appear but do not correspond to
the interiors. But of these hereafter.

In illustration of the nature of the things that appear to the
angels according to correspondences, I will here adduce a single
example :—To those who are in intelligence gardens and paradises
appear, full of trees and flowers of every kind. The trees
therein are set in most beautiful order, joined together by inter-
lacing branches, forming fretted avenues and walks among them
round about, all of such beauty that they cannot be described.
They who are in intelligence walk also there, and gather flowers,
and weave garlands, with which they adorn little children.
There are species of trees and flowers there too, which are never
seen and cannot exist in the world. There are also fruits on the
trees, according to the good of love in which the intelligent are.

They see such things because a garden and paradise, and fruit trees and flowers, correspond to intelligence and wisdom. That such things exist in the heavens is known indeed on earth, but only to those who are in good, and who have not extinguished the light of heaven within them, by natural light and its fallacies; for they think and say, when speaking of heaven, that such things exist there " as ear hath not heard, nor eye seen." (*ib.* n. 175, 176.)

Besides these paradisiacal scenes there are also cities presented to view, with magnificent palaces, contiguous to each other, of splendid colours, exceeding all architectural art. Nor is this surprising. Similar things were seen also by the prophets when their interior sight was opened ; and so manifestly, indeed, that nothing could be more manifest in the world. For example, the New Jerusalem seen by John, which is described by him in these words :—" *He carried me away in the spirit to a great and high mountain, and shewed me that great city the Holy Jerusalem,* . . . *having a wall great and high, having twelve gates.* . . . *The building of the wall was of jasper ; and the city was pure gold, like unto golden glass. The foundations of the wall were garnished with all manner of precious stones. The first foundation was jasper ; the second, sapphire ; the third, chalcedony ; the fourth, emerald ; the fifth, sardonyx ; the sixth, sardius ; the seventh, chrysolite ; the eighth, beryl ; the ninth, topaz ; the tenth, chrysoprasus ; the eleventh, jacinth ; the twelfth, amethyst* " (Rev. xxi. 10, 12, 18, 19, 20).

Besides cities and palaces it has been given me also to look at their decorations; such as those of the steps and gates,—and these were moving as if with life, and varying as with ever new beauty and symmetry. And I was informed that there can thus be successive variations perpetually, even though it were to eternity, with constantly new harmony; the very succession also forming a harmony. And it was said that these were some of the least of their wonders. (A. C. n. 1626, 1627.)

Representatives of things spiritual and celestial sometimes appear in a long series, continued for an hour or two, in such order one after another as is wonderful. There are societies among whom these take place, and it was granted me to be with them for several months ; but the representations are such that if I were to recount and describe only one in its order it would fill several pages. They are extremely delightful, inasmuch as something new and unexpected is continually following, until that which is represented is fully completed ; and when all the representatives are completed, it is permitted to contemplate them in one view, and at the same time it is given to perceive what each particular thing signifies. Good spirits are thus also introduced into spiritual and celestial ideas. (A. C. n. 3214.)

THE GARMENTS OF ANGELS.

Like other things, the garments with which angels are clothed correspond; and because they correspond they also really exist. Their garments correspond to their intelligence; and therefore all in the heavens appear clothed according to their intelligence; and as one excels another in intelligence, one therefore has more excellent garments than another. The most intelligent have shining garments as of flame, some resplendent as of light; the less intelligent have garments of shining white, and of white without lustre; and those still less intelligent have garments of diverse colors. But the angels of the inmost heaven are naked. (H. H. n. 178.)

The reason why they go naked is, that nakedness in the spiritual sense is innocence, and that garments signify truths investing good; and the investing truths are in the memory and thence in the thought; but with them truths are in the life and thus concealed, and only manifest themselves to the perception,—while others talk of them, and their ministers preach them from the Word.[1] Yet they are perfected by the discourse of those who are in the understanding of truth, by preachings, and also by books. They also write; but not as the other angels, by letters; but by curves and inflections, which involve mysteries that transcend the understanding of the angels in the lower heavens. (A. E. n. 828.)

Because the angels are clothed with garments in heaven, therefore they have appeared clothed with garments also when seen in the world. As for example those who were seen by the prophets, and those who were seen at the Lord's sepulchre, *whose countenance was like lightning, and whose raiment white and shining* (Matt. xxviii. 3; Mark xvi. 5; Luke xxiv. 4; John xx. 12, 13); and those seen by John in heaven *whose raiment was of fine linen and white* (Apoc. iv. 4; chap. xix. 11, 13). And because intelligence is from Divine truth, the Lord's garments when He was transfigured, were *shining and white as the light* (Matt. xvii. 2; Mark ix. 3; Luke ix. 29). Light is Divine truth proceeding from the Lord. Hence it is that in the Word garments signify truths, and intelligence from them; as in the Apocalypse:—" *Those which have not polluted their garments, shall walk with Me in white, for they are worthy. He that overcometh shall be clothed in white ‧ raiment* " (iii. 4, 5); " *Blessed is he that watcheth, and keepeth his garments* " (xvi. 15); and elsewhere.

That the garments of the angels not only appear as garments,

[1] See p. 427.

but really are garments, is evident from the fact that they not only see but also feel them; and that they have many garments; and that they put them off and put them on; and those that are not in use they keep, and when in use resume them. That they are clothed with various garments I have seen a thousand times. I inquired whence they had their garments, and they said it was from the Lord; that they are given to them, and that they are sometimes clothed unconsciously to themselves. They said also that their garments are changed according to the changes of their state; and that in the first and second state they are shining and of dazzling white, in the third and fourth states a little more dull; and this too from correspondence, because they have changes of state in respect to intelligence and wisdom.

Since every one in the spiritual world has garments according to his intelligence, thus according to the truths from which he has intelligence, therefore those who are in the hells, being without truths, though they appear clothed yet they are in ragged, squalid and filthy garments,—each one according to his insanity; and they can wear no others. It is given them by the Lord to be clothed, that they may not appear naked. (*ib.* n. 180, 182.)

THE HABITATIONS AND MANSIONS OF THE ANGELS.

Since there are societies in heaven and the angels live as men, they also have habitations, and these also are various according to every one's state of life; magnificent for those who are in a higher state of dignity, and less magnificent for those who are in a lower. I have sometimes talked with the angels about the habitations in heaven, and said that scarcely any one at this day would believe that they have habitations and mansions; some because they do not see them; some because they do not know that angels are men; some because they believe that the angelic heaven is the heaven that is seen with their eyes round about them,—and because this appears empty, and they suppose that angels are ethereal forms, they conclude that they live in the ether. Moreover, they do not comprehend that there are such things in the spiritual world as are in the natural world, because they know nothing of what is spiritual.

But it is better to adduce the evidences of experience. As often as I have talked with the angels face to face, I have been with them in their habitations. They are precisely like the habitations on earth called houses, except that they are more beautiful; there are rooms, closets, and bed-chambers in them in great number; and there are courts; and round about them are gardens, shrubberies, and fields. Where they are associated together the habitations are contiguous, one close to another, disposed in the form of a city, with streets, passages, and public squares, quite after the manner of cities on our earth. It has been given me to pass through them, and look about me on every side, and some times to enter the houses. This has been done in full wakefulness, while my interior sight was opened.

I have seen palaces in heaven which were so magnificent that they cannot be described. Above they glistened as if they were of pure gold; and below as if of precious stones. Some palaces were more splendid than others. It was the same within; the apartments were ornamented with such decorations as neither language nor science can adequately describe. On the side looking to the south there were paradises, wherein all things were equally resplendent. In some places the leaves were as of silver, and the fruits as of gold, and the flowers in their beds presented by their colors the appearance of rainbows. On the boundaries again palaces were seen, in which the view terminated. Such is the architecture of heaven that you would declare the art is there in its own skill; and no wonder, for this art itself is from heaven. The angels said that such things, and innumerable others which are still more perfect, are presented before their eyes by the Lord; but yet that they delight their minds more than their eyes, because they see the correspondences in every least thing, and through correspondences things Divine.

Respecting correspondences, I have been informed too that not only their palaces and houses, but also each and all things that are within and without them correspond to things interior that are within them from the Lord; that the house itself in general corresponds to their good, and the several things that are within the houses to the various particulars of which their good consists; and the things outside of the houses correspond to the truths which are from their good, and likewise to perceptions and knowledges; and that because they correspond to the goods and truths within them from the Lord, they correspond to their love, and therefore to their wisdom and intelligence,—for love is of good, wisdom is of good and at the same time of truth, and intelligence is of truth from good; and that such are the things which the angels perceive when they look at these objects, and that for this reason they delight and affect their minds more than their eyes. (H. H. n. 183, 186.)

Governments in Heaven.

Since heaven is distinguished into societies, and the larger societies consist of some hundreds of thousands of angels, and though all within a society are in similar good, yet they are not in similar wisdom, it of necessity follows that there are governments also in heaven. For order must be observed, and all things pertaining to order must be watched over. But the governments in the heavens are various; of one kind in the societies that constitute the Lord's celestial kingdom, and of another kind in the societies that consitute the Lord's spiritual kingdom. They also differ according to the ministries performed by each society. Yet there is no government in the heavens but the government of mutual love; and government of mutual love is heavenly government.

The government in the Lord's celestial kingdom is called *Justice*, because all who are there are in the good of love to the Lord from the Lord, and what is from that good is called just. The government there is of the Lord alone; He leads them and teaches them in the affairs of life. The truths which are called the truths of judgment are inscribed upon their hearts. Every one knows, perceives, and sees them; matters of judgment therefore never come into dispute there, but matters of justice, which are of life. The less wise interrogate the more wise upon these subjects, and they the Lord, and receive answers. Their heaven, or their inmost joy, is to live justly from the Lord.

The government in the Lord's spiritual kingdom is called *Judgment;* because there they are in spiritual good, which is the good of charity towards the neighbor, and this good is the essence of truth,—and truth is of judgment, and good is of justice. They also are led by the Lord, but mediately; they therefore have governors, few or more, according to the need of the society in which they are: they have laws too, according to which they live together. The governors administer all things according to the laws. As they are wise, they understand them; and in doubtful cases they are enlightened by the Lord. (H. H. n. 213-215.)

There are various forms of government in the Lord's spiritual kingdom, differing in different societies; the variety is according to the ministries which the societies perform. Their ministries are in accordance with the functions of all the parts in man to which they correspond; and that these functions are various is well known; for the heart has one function, the lungs another, the liver another, the pancreas and spleen another, and each organ of sense also another. As the administrations of these functions in the body are various, so the administrations of the societies in the Greatest Man, which is heaven, are various; for there are societies that correspond to them. But all the forms of government agree in this; that they regard the public good as the end, and in that the good of every individual.

From these statements it may appear what is the character of the governors; namely, that they are those who excel others in love and wisdom, thus who from love will do good to all, and from wisdom know how to provide that it shall be done. They who are of such a character do not rule and command, but minister and serve; for to do good to others from the love of good is to serve, and to cause it to be done is to minister. Nor do they make themselves greater than others, but less; for they have the good of society and of their neighbor in the first place, but their own in the last place, and what is in the first place is the greater, and what is in the last is the less. And yet they have honor and glory. They dwell in the midst of the society, more exalted than others, and also in magnificent palaces; and they accept this glory and honor, yet not for themselves, but for the sake of obedience; for all there know that they have this honor and glory from the Lord, and that for this reason they ought to be obeyed. These are the things that are meant by the Lord's words to his disciples: *" Whosoever would be great among you, let him be your minister ; and whosoever would be chief among you let him be your servant; even as the Son of man came not to be ministered unto but to minister "* (Matt. xx. 27, 28). *" He that is the greatest among you, let him be as the younger, and he that is leader, as he that doth minister "* (Luke xxii. 26).

There is also a similar government, in the least form, in every household. There is a master, and there are servants ; the master loves the servants, and the servants love the master; so that they serve each other, from love. The master teaches them how they ought to live, and tells what is to be done; the servants obey, and perform their duties. To perform use is the delight of life with all. It is therefore evident that the kingdom of the Lord is a kingdom of uses. *(ib.* n. 217-219.)

Divine Worship in Heaven.

Divine worship in the heavens as to its externals is not unlike Divine worship on earth, but as to internals it is different. Just as on earth, there are doctrines in the heavens; there are preachings ; and there are temples. The doctrines agree as to essentials; but are of more interior wisdom in the higher than in the lower heavens. The preachings are according to the doctrines. And as there are houses and palaces, so also there are temples, in which the preaching is performed. The reason why there are such things in the heavens also is, that the angels are being continually perfected in wisdom and in love. For they, like men, have an understanding and a will; and the understanding is of such a nature that it can be perfected continually, and likewise the will; the understanding by truths, which are matters of intelligence, and the will by goods, which are of love.

But Divine worship itself in the heavens does not consist in frequenting temples, and in listening to preaching, but in a life of love, charity, and faith, according to the doctrines. The preachings in the temples serve only as means of instruction in matters relating to life.

That I might know what their meetings are in the temples, it has been given me several times to go in and hear the preaching. The preacher stands in a pulpit on the east. Those who more than others are in the light of wisdom sit before his face; at the right and left of them sit those who are in less light. They sit in the form of a circle, so that all are in view of the preacher; no one is at the sides on either hand, so as to be out of his sight. At the door, which is on the east side of the temple, and at the left of the pulpit, stand those who are being initiated. No one is permitted to stand behind the pulpit; if any one is there the preacher is confused. It is the same if any one in the congregation dissent; it therefore becomes him to turn away his face. The preachings are fraught with such wisdom that no preachings in the world can be compared with them; for in the heavens they are in interior light. The temples in the spiritual kingdom appear as if of stone; and in the celestial kingdom as if of wood; for the reason that stone corresponds to truth, in which they are who are in the spiritual kingdom, and wood corresponds to good, in which they are who are in the celestial kingdom. In this kingdom the sacred edifices are not called temples, but houses of God. In the celestial kingdom the sacred edifices are without magnificence; but in the spiritual kingdom they are more or less magnificent. (H. H. n. 221-223.)

The preachers are all from the Lord's spiritual kingdom, and none from the celestial kingdom. They are from the spiritual kingdom, because there they are in truths from good, and all preaching is from truths; that no preacher is from the celestial kingdom, is because there they are in the good of love, and from this good they see and perceive truths but do not talk about them. Notwithstanding that the angels who are in the celestial kingdom perceive and see truths, yet there are preachings there, because by preaching they are enlightened in the truths that they know, and are perfected by many that they did not know before. And they acknowledge and thus perceive them as soon as they hear them. The truths which they perceive they also love, and by living according to them they make them a part of their life; to live according to truths, they say, is to love the Lord.

The preachers are all appointed by the Lord, and thence are in the gift of preaching. None but these are permitted to teach in the temples. They are called preachers, and not priests, because the priesthood of heaven is the celestial kingdom; for the priesthood signifies the good of love to the Lord, in which they are who are in that kingdom. But the royalty of heaven is the spiritual kingdom; for royalty signifies truth from good, in which they are who are in that kingdom.

The doctrines according to which they preach all regard life as the end, and none of them faith without life. The doctrine of the inmost heaven is more full of wisdom than the doctrine of the intermediate heaven; and this is more full of intelligence than the doctrine of the ultimate heaven. For the doctrines are adapted to the perception of the angels in each heaven. The essential of all the doctrines is acknowledgment of the Lord's Divine Humanity. (*ib.* n. 225-227.)

The Power of Angels.

They who know nothing of the spiritual world, and of its influx into the natural world, cannot comprehend that the angels have power. They think angels cannot have power because they are spiritual, and so pure and attenuate that they cannot even be seen with the eyes. But they who look more interiorly into the causes of things, think differently. They know that all the power that man has is from his understanding and will; for without them he cannot move a particle of his body. The understanding and will are his spiritual man. This actuates the body and its members at its pleasure; for what it thinks the mouth and tongue speak, and what it wills the body does. It also gives its powers at pleasure. The will and understanding of man are governed by the Lord, through angels and spirits; and the will and understanding being thus governed, so also are all things of the body, for they are from them; and if you will believe it, a man cannot even move a step without the influx of heaven. That it is so has been shown me by much experience. It has been given the angels to move my steps, my actions, my tongue, and speech, as they pleased, and this by influx into my will and thought; and I found by experience that of myself I could do nothing. They said afterwards, that even man is so governed; and that he may know this from the doctrine of the church and from the Word; for he prays that God will send His angels, that they may lead him, direct his steps, teach him, and inspire what he should think and what he should say; and more to this effect; and yet when by himself he thinks without doctrine he says and believes otherwise. These things are mentioned that it may be known what power the angels have over man.

And in the spiritual world the power of the angels is so great, that if I were to proclaim respecting it all that I have seen, it would exceed belief. If anything resists there, which ought to be removed because it is contrary to Divine order, they cast it down and overturn it by a mere effort of the will and a look. I have thus seen mountains which were occupied by the evil cast down and overthrown, and sometimes shaken from one end to the other, as they are in an earthquake. Rocks I have also seen cleft asunder in the midst down to the deep, and the evil who were upon them swallowed up. And I have seen hundreds of thousands of evil spirits dispersed and cast into hell by them. Numbers avail nothing against them, nor arts, nor cunning and confederacies; for they see them all, and disperse them in a moment. Such power have they in the spiritual world. That the angels have similar power in the natural world also, when it is granted, is evident from the Word. For example, in that they gave whole armies to destruction; that an angel wrought a pestilence, of which seventy thousand men died. Of this angel we read:—" *The angel stretched out his hand against Jerusalem, to destroy it; but Jehovah repenting the evil, said to the angel that destroyed the people, It is enough, stay now thy hand.* . . . *And David . . . saw the angel that smote the people*" (2 Sam. xxiv. 15-17); and elsewhere. Because they have such power they are called powers. As in David:—" *Bless Jehovah, ye His angels, most powerful in strength*" (Ps. ciii. 20).

But it should be known that the angels have no power at all from themselves, but that all the power they possess is from the Lord; and that they are powers in so far as they acknowledge this. Whoever among them believes that he has power from himself instantly becomes so weak that he cannot resist even one evil spirit; which is a reason why the angels attribute nothing at all of merit to themselves, and are averse to all praise and glory for anything done, and ascribe it to the Lord.

It is the Divine truth proceeding from the Lord to which all power pertains in the heavens. . . . So far therefore as an angel is truth from the Divine, and good from the Divine, he is a power, because so far the Lord is in him. And as no one is in precisely similar, or in the same good and truth as another (for in heaven as in the world, there is perpetual variety), therefore one angel is not in similar power to another. They are in the greatest power who constitute the arms of the Greatest Man or heaven; because they who are there are in truths more than others, and into their truths good flows from the universal heaven. Moreover the power of the whole man transfers itself into the arms, and through these the whole body exercises its powers. Hence it is, that power is signified by the arms and the hands in the Word. (H. H. n. 228-231.)

THE SPEECH OF ANGELS.

Angels converse with each other just as men do in the world; and also on various subjects, such as domestic affairs, matters relating to their civil condition, the affairs of moral life, and the affairs of spiritual life. Nor is there any difference except that they converse more intelligently than men, because from more interior thought. It has been granted me often to be in company with them, and to talk with them as friend with friend,—and sometimes as a stranger with a stranger; and being then in a similar state with them, I knew not but that I was conversing with men on earth.

Angelic speech like human speech is distinguished into words. In like manner it is also uttered with a sound, and is heard as sound. For they equally with men have a mouth, a tongue, and ears; and they have also an atmosphere, in which the sound of their speech is articulated; but it is a spiritual atmosphere, accommodated to the angels, who are spiritual. The angels also breathe in their atmosphere, and pronounce their words by means of the breath, as men do in theirs.

In the universal heaven they have all one language; and they all understand each other, from whatever society they are, whether near or distant. The language there is not learned, but is inherent with every one; for it flows from their very affection and thought. The sound of speech corresponds to their affection; and the articulations of sound, which are words, correspond to the ideas of thought, which are from affection; and as the language corresponds to these it also is spiritual, for it is affection sounding and thought speaking. Whoever directs his attention to the subject may know that every thought is from an affection, which is of love; and that the ideas of thought are the various forms into which the general affection is distributed. For there is no thought or idea without an affection; from thence is their soul and life. Hence it is that the angels know the character of another from his speech alone; from the sound they know what his affection is, and from the articulations of the sound, or words, what his mind is. The wiser angels, from a single series of words know the character of the ruling affection, for to this they principally attend. That every one has various affections, is known; one affection when he is in a state of joy, another in grief, another when in clemency and mercy, another in sincerity and truth, another in love and charity; another when in zeal or in anger, another when in simulation and deceit, another when in quest of honour and glory, and so·on. But the ruling affection or love is in them all; wherefore the wiser angels, because they perceive this, know all the state of another from his speech. It has been given me to know that it is so by much experience. I have heard angels laying open the life of another merely from listening to his speech. They also told me that they know all things of another's life from a few ideas of his thought; because from thence they know his ruling love, in which they are all contained in their order; and that man's book of life is nothing else.

Angelic language has nothing in common with human languages, save with some words that sound from a certain affection; and then not with the words themselves, but with the sound. . . . I have been told that the first language of men on our earth was in agreement with that of the angels, because they received it from heaven; and that the Hebrew language agrees with it in some particulars. Since the speech of angels corresponds to their affection, which is an affection of love, and the love of heaven is love to the Lord and love towards the neighbour, it is evident how elegant and delightful must be their discourse. It indeed affects not the ears only, but also the interiors of the mind of those who hear. There was a certain hard-hearted spirit, with whom an angel conversed. He was at length so affected by his speech that he shed tears, saying that he could not help it, for it was love speaking, and that he had never wept before. (H. H. n. 234-238.)

The same kind of speech that is in the spiritual world is inherent in every man, but in his interior intellectual part. But as with man this does not fall into words analogous to affection, as with the angels, man is not aware that he is in it. Yet it is from this that when a man comes into the other life he speaks the same language as the spirits and angels there, and knows how thus to speak without instruction. (*ib.* n. 243.)

The speech of the celestial angels is distinct from that of the spiritual angels, and is still more ineffable and inexpressible. The things into which their thoughts are insinuated are the celestial things and goods of ends; and they are therefore in the enjoyment of happiness itself. And what is remarkable, their speech is far more copious; for they are in the very fountains and origins of the life of thought and speech. (A. C. n. 1647.)

The angels in the Lord's celestial kingdom speak in a similar manner as the angels in the Lord's spiritual kingdom; but the celestial angels speak from more interior thought than the spiritual angels. And as the celestial angels are in the good of love to the Lord they speak from wisdom; but the spiritual angels being in the good of charity to the neighbour, which in its essence is truth, speak from intelligence; for wisdom is from good, and intelligence is from truth. Hence the speech of the celestial angels is like a gentle stream, soft, and as it were continuous; but the speech of the spiritual angels is a little vibratory and discrete. (H. H. n. 241. See also p. 604.)

WRITINGS IN HEAVEN.

As the angels have a language, and their language is a language of words, therefore they have writings also, and express the sentiments of their minds by writings as well as by speech. Sometimes papers have been sent me covered with writings, precisely like papers written by hand, and also like printed papers in the world. I could read them too in the same manner; but I was not permitted to take from them more than an idea or two; the reason was that it is not according to Divine order to be instructed by writings from heaven, but by the Word, because by this alone is there communication and conjunction of heaven with the world, and so of the Lord with man. Papers written in heaven also appeared to the prophets; as may be seen in Ezekiel:—" *When I looked, behold a hand put forth by a spirit unto me, and a roll of a book was therein, which he unfolded in my sight; it was written on the front and on the back*" (ii. 9, 10). And in John: "*I saw at the right hand of Him who sat on the throne, a book written within and on the back, sealed with seven seals*" (Apoc. v. 1). (H. H. n. 258.)

A little paper was also once sent to me from heaven, on which a few words only were written, in Hebrew letters; and it was said that every letter involved arcana of wisdom, and that they were contained in the inflections and curvatures of the letters, and thence also in the sounds. By this it was made clear to me what is signified by the words of the Lord: " *Verily I say unto you, Till heaven and earth pass away, one iota or one little horn* [*i.e.* of a letter] *shall not pass from the law*" (Matt. v. 18). It is known indeed in the Church that as to every tittle of it the Word is Divine; but where in every tittle the Divine is concealed is not known as yet. It shall therefore be declared :—The writing in the inmost heaven consists of various inflected and circumflected forms ; and the inflexions and circumflexions are according to the form of heaven. By these the angels express the arcana of their wisdom, and many things too which they cannot utter by words. And what is wonderful, the angels know this writing without acquired skill, and without a master ; like their speech itself[1] it is inherent in them. This writing therefore is heavenly writing. It is inherent, because all extension of thoughts and affections, and therefore all communication of the intelligence and wisdom of the angels, proceed according to the form of heaven. It comes from this that their writing flows into that form. I have been told that the most ancient people on this earth also had such writing, before letters were invented ; and that it was translated into the letters of the Hebrew language, which letters in ancient times were all inflected, and none of them were terminated, as some of them are at this day, as lines. Hence it is that in the Word there are things Divine, and arcana of heaven, even in the points, apexes, and little horns of its letters.

This writing which is done with characters of a heavenly form is in use in the inmost heaven, where they excel all others in wisdom. Affections are expressed by means of them, from which thoughts flow and follow in order according to the subject treated of. Hence these writings involve arcana which cannot be exhausted by thought. These writings also it has been granted me to see. But in the lower heavens there are not such writings. The writings in these heavens are similar to writings in the world ; in similar letters, but yet not intelligible to man, because they are in angelic language, and angelic language is such that it has nothing in common with human languages ; for by the vowels they express affections, by the consonants ideas of thought from affections, and by the words formed of them their sense of the subject. This writing also involves more in a few words than a man can write down in several pages. These writings too have been seen by me. They have the Word thus written in the lower heavens; and by heavenly forms in the inmost heaven.

It is worthy of remark that the writings in the heavens flow naturally from their thoughts themselves ; with so little exertion that it is as if thought cast itself forth. Nor does the hand hesitate in the choice of any word ; for the words that they write as well as those which they speak correspond to the ideas of their thought, and all correspondence is natural and spontaneous. There are also writings without the aid of the hand,

[1] See p. 659.

in the heavens; from the mere correspondence of the thoughts; but these are not permanent. (*ib.* n. 260-262.)

The Knowledge of the Angels.

With regard merely to the knowledge of the angels of the interior heaven, their knowledge of the structures and forms of the body alone may serve as an example. For while any one, no matter which, of the viscera of the body is under consideration, they are able to know not only its whole structure and operation, but every experimental knowledge whatever, that anatomy can discover in the least parts, as to whether it be true or genuine. And they know in an instant whether what is said of each of the viscera be correct; nay, very many more interior things, which none of the human race can ever know, as has sometimes been proved to me. They also know to what they correspond in spiritual things. So great is their knowledge,—although they had never investigated such subjects in the life of the body,— that if men were aware of it they would be astounded. It flows as it were spontaneously from the fact that, through an intelligence bestowed by the Lord, they know how everything is in the Greatest Man, in general, and in its parts; so that it seems as it were innate with them. But they could never possess such knowledge were it not that the whole heaven represents the entire man with his several parts, and that the Lord, thus Life itself, is the life of that man, and that the universal heaven is organic. Thus they are in the principles of things; and from principles, or things interior and inmost, they can know those that are below or without. (S. D. n. 1625.)

The Wisdom of the Angels.

The nature of the wisdom of the angels of heaven can with difficulty be comprehended; because it so far transcends human wisdom that they cannot be compared, and that which is transcendent appears as if it were nothing. Some of the things also by which it must be described are unknown; and until these become known they are as shadows in the understanding, and so actually conceal the subject as it is in itself. But yet they are such things as can be known, and can be comprehended when they are known, if only the mind is delighted with them. For delight carries light with it, because it is from love; and upon those who love such things as are of Divine and heavenly wisdom light shines from heaven, and they receive illustration.

The nature of the wisdom of angels may be inferred from the fact that they are in the light of heaven, and the light of heaven in its essence is Divine truth or Divine wisdom ; and this light enlightens at the same time their internal sight, which is that of the mind, and their external sight, which is that of the eyes. The angels are also in heavenly heat, which in its essence is Divine good, or Divine love, from which they have the affection and desire to be wise. To such a degree are the angels in wisdom that they may be called wisdoms, as may be concluded from the fact that all their thoughts and affections flow in accordance with the heavenly form, which is the form of Divine wisdom; and that their interiors which receive wisdom are fashioned to that form. That the angels have supereminent wisdom, may also appear from the fact that their speech is the speech of wisdom ; for it flows immediately and spontaneously from the thought, and this from their affection, so that their speech is thought and affection in external form. Hence there is nothing that withdraws them from the Divine influx, and nothing external intrudes from other thoughts, as with man in his speech. To such wisdom of the angels this also conspires, that all things which they see with their eyes and perceive by the senses agree with their wisdom, since they are correspondences ; and the objects are therefore forms representative of such things as are of wisdom. Moreover the thoughts of the angels are not, like human thoughts, bounded and contracted by ideas derived from space and time ; for spaces and times are proper to nature, and things that belong to nature draw the mind away from spiritual things, and deprive the intellectual sight of extension. Nor are the thoughts of angels drawn down to earthly and material things; nor interrupted by any cares about the necessaries of life. Thus they are not withdrawn by these things from the delights of wisdom, as the thoughts of men are in the world. For all things come to them without recompense from the Lord ; they are clothed without recompense, they are nourished without recompense, they have habitations without recompense. And moreover they are gifted with delights and pleasures according to their reception of wisdom from the Lord. These things are mentioned, that it may be known whence the angels have so great wisdom. (H. H. n. 265, 266.)

How great is the wisdom of the angels may appear from the fact that in the heavens there is a communication of all things ; the intelligence and wisdom of one is communicated to another; heaven is a communion of all goods. The reason is, that heavenly love is of such a nature that it desires that what is its own may be another's. No one in heaven therefore perceives his own good in himself as good, unless it be also in another ; and hence is the happiness of heaven. The angels derive this quality from the Lord, whose Divine love is of such a nature.

Their wisdom is to human wisdom as a myriad to one; comparatively, as the moving forces of the whole body, which are innumerable, to an action from them,—which to human sense appears as one ; or as the thousand minutiæ of an object seen with a perfect microscope to the one indistinct thing that appears to the naked eye. I will also illustrate the subject by example :—An angel from his wisdom described regeneration, and brought forth mysteries concerning it, in their order, up to hundreds, and filled each mystery with ideas in which there were yet more inferior mysteries. And this he did from the beginning to the end ; for he explained how the spiritual man is conceived anew, is carried as it were in the womb, is born, grows up, and is successively perfected. He said, that he could increase the number of mysteries to thousands; and that those which he explained only related to the regeneration of the external man, and that there were innumerably more relating to the regeneration of the internal. From these and other similar things that have been heard from the angels it was made manifest to me how great is their wisdom; and how great relatively is the ignorance of man, who scarcely knows what regeneration is, and knows no movement of the progress while he is being regenerated.

The wisdom of the angels of the third or inmost heaven is incomprehensible even to those who are in the ultimate heaven. The reason is, that the interiors of the angels of the third heaven are opened to the third degree, and the interiors of the angels of the first heaven only to the first degree ; and all wisdom increases towards the interiors, and according to the opening of them. . . . Divine truths appear as inscribed upon these angels, or as if inherent and innate. As soon therefore as they hear genuine Divine truths they immediately acknowledge and perceive them, and afterwards inwardly see them as it were within themselves. Such being the character of the angels of that heaven, they never reason about Divine truths ; still less do they dispute about any truth, as to whether it is so or not so. Nor do they know what it is to believe, or have faith ; for they say, Why have faith ? For I perceive and see that it is so. They illustrate the matter by comparisons ; such as, that it would be as when one with a companion sees a house and the various things within and around it, and should say to his companion that he ought to believe that they exist, and that they are such as he sees them ; or as if one should see a garden, and trees and fruits therein, and should say to his companion that he ought to have faith that it is a garden, and that there are trees and fruits, when yet he sees them plainly with his eyes. Hence it is that these angels never mention faith, and have no idea of it; nor therefore do they reason about Divine truths, still less dispute about any truth, as to whether it be so or not so. But the angels of the first or ultimate heaven have not Divine truths inscribed thus on their interiors, because with them only the first degree of life is open. They therefore reason about truths; and those who reason scarcely see anything beyond a phase of the matter about which they reason; or go beyond the subject, except merely to confirm it by certain considerations; and when they have confirmed it they 'say that it must be a matter of faith, and ought to be believed. I have conversed with angels on these subjects; who said that the difference between the wisdom of the angels of the third heaven, and the wisdom of the angels of the first heaven, is as between what is clear and what is obscure. Yet the angels of the inmost heaven are continually being perfected in wisdom; but in a different manner from the angels of the ultimate heaven. The angels of the inmost heaven do not lay up Divine truths in the memory, thus they do not make them a matter of knowledge, but as soon as they hear they perceive them, and apply them to life. Hence it is that Divine truths remain with them, as if inscribed on them; for what is applied to the life thus internally abides. But it is different with the angels of the ultimate heaven. These first lay up Divine truths in the memory, and store them in the form of knowledge; and from thence bring them forth and perfect their understanding by them, and without interior perception whether they are truths, will them, and commit them to life; hence they are relatively in obscurity. It is worthy of mention that the angels of the third heaven are perfected in wisdom by hearing, but not by sight. The truths that they hear from preaching do not enter into their memory, but immediately into their perception and will, and become a part of their life; but the things which these angels see with their eyes enter into their memory, and they reason and talk about them. It is therefore evident that the way of hearing is to them the way of wisdom. This too is from correspondence; for the ear corresponds to obedience, and obedience is a matter of life; but the eye corresponds to intelligence, and intelligence relates to doctrine.

To the reasons already given why the angels are capable of receiving so great wisdom, this is to be added, which in heaven indeed is the primary reason; that they are without self-love. For in so far as any one is without that love, he is capable of becoming wise in things Divine. It is that love which closes the interiors against the Lord and heaven, and opens the exteriors and turns them to self. Therefore all those with whom that love rules, however they may be in light as to the things of the world, are in thick darkness as to the things that pertain to heaven. But on the other hand the angels, because they are without that love, are in the light of wisdom; for the heavenly loves in which they are,—which are love to the Lord and love towards the neighbour,—open the interiors, because these loves are from the Lord, and the Lord Himself is in them. (*ib.* n. 268-272.)

The Innocence of Angels.

The innocence of infancy, or of little children, is not genuine innocence; for it is innocence only in external form, and not in the internal. Yet it may be learned from this what innocence is ; for it shines forth from their faces, from some of their gestures, and from their earliest speech, and affects those about them. The reason is that they have no internal thought, for they do not yet know what is good and evil, and true and false, —from which thought proceeds. Hence they have no prudence from the *proprium*, no purpose and deliberation, and therefore no intention of evil. They have no *proprium* acquired from the love of self and of the world; they do not attribute anything to themselves; all that they receive they ascribe to their parents. Content with the few and the little things that are given them, they rejoice in them ; they have no solicitude about food and raiment, and none about the future; they do not look to the world, and covet many things therefrom. They love their parents, their nurse, and their infant companions, with whom they innocently play; they suffer themselves to be led; they hearken, and obey. And because they are in this state they receive all things into the life. Hence although they know not whence, they acquire becoming manners ; hence they acquire speech ; and hence the rudiment of memory, and of thought, for the receiving and implanting of which their state of innocence serves as a medium. But this innocence as was said above is external, because only of the body, not of the mind. Their mind in fact is not yet formed ; for the mind is the understanding and will, and thought and affection therefrom. It has been told me from heaven that infants especially are under the auspices of the Lord, and that their influx is from the inmost heaven, where there is a state of innocence ; that the influx passes through their interiors, and that in passing through it affects them only with innocence ; and that hence innocence shows itself in the face, and in some of their gestures, and becomes apparent ; and that it is this by which parents are inmostly affected, and which causes the love that is called storge.

Genuine innocence is the innocence of wisdom, because this is internal; for it is of the mind itself, thus of the will itself, and thence of the understanding; and when there is innocence in these there is also wisdom, for wisdom pertains to them. Hence it is said in heaven that innocence dwells in wisdom, and that an angel has as much of wisdom as he has of innocence. That it is so they confirm by the fact that those who are in a state of innocence attribute nothing of good to themselves, but render and ascribe all they receive to the Lord; that they desire to be led of Him, and not by themselves; that they love everything that is good, and are delighted with everything that is true,—because they know and perceive that to love good, that is to will and do it, is to love the Lord, and to love truth is to love their neighbour; that they live contented with their own, whether it be little or much, because they know that they receive as much as is profitable for them,—little, they for whom little is profitable, and much, they for whom much is profitable; and they do not know what is profitable for them, but the Lord only, to whom all things that He provides are eternal. And therefore they are not solicitous about the future; they call solicitude for the future care for the morrow, which they say is grief on account of the loss or non-reception of such things as are not necessary to the uses of life. Among their associates they never act from an evil end, but from goodness, justice, and sincerity; acting from an evil end they call craft, which they shun as the venom of a serpent, since it is altogether contrary to innocence. (H. H. n. 277, 278.)

I have conversed much with the angels respecting innocence, and have been informed that innocence is the *esse* of all good, and that therefore good is so far good as innocence is within it; consequently that wisdom is so far wisdom as it is derived from innocence; and so with love, charity, and faith; and that hence it is that no one can enter heaven unless he has innocence; and that this is what is meant by the Lord when He says:—" *Suffer little children to come unto Me, and forbid them not; for of such is the kingdom of the heavens. Verily I say unto you, Whosoever shall not receive the kingdom of the heavens as a little child, he shall not enter therein* " (Mark x. 14, 15; Luke xviii. 16, 17; Matt. xix. 14). By little children here, as elsewhere also in the Word, are meant those who are innocent. A state of innocence is also described by the Lord in Matt. vi. 25-34, but by pure correspondences. The reason why good is good in proportion as there is innocence in it is, that all good is from the Lord, and innocence consists in a desire to be led of the Lord. I have also been informed that truth cannot be conjoined to good, and good to truth, except by means of innocence; and hence it is that an angel is not an angel of heaven unless innocence be in him; for heaven is not within any one until truth is conjoined to good in him. Therefore the conjunction of truth and good is called the heavenly marriage; and the heavenly marriage is heaven. (*ib.* n. 281.)

The Peace of Heaven.

The inmost things of heaven are two, namely, innocence and peace; they are said to be inmost because they proceed immediately from the Lord. It is from innocence that all the good of heaven proceeds, and from peace all the delight of good. (H. H. n. 285.)

In the first place the origin of peace shall be mentioned. Divine peace is in the Lord, arising from the union of the very Divine and the Divine Human in Him. The Divine of peace in heaven is from the Lord, arising from His conjunction with the angels of heaven; and in particular, from the conjunction of good and truth in every angel. These are the origins of peace. From which it may be seen that in the heavens peace is the Divine inmostly affecting every good there with blessedness; thus, that it is that from which comes all the joy of heaven; and that in its essence it is the Divine joy of the Lord's Divine love, from his conjunction with heaven and with every one there. This joy, perceived by the Lord in the angels, and by angels from the Lord, is peace. From this, by derivation, the angels have all that is blessed, delightful and happy, or what is called heavenly joy. (*ib.* n. 286.)

The peace of heaven, because it is the Divine inmostly affecting with blessedness the good itself which is with the angels, does not come to their manifest perception, except by a delight of heart when they are in the good of their life, and by a pleasantness when they hear truth which agrees with their good, and by a cheerfulness of mind when they perceive the conjunction of them; yet it flows thence into all the acts and thoughts of their life, and presents itself therein as joy, even in the outward form. . . . . That innocence and peace dwell together, like good and its delight, may be seen in infants, who because they are in innocence are also in peace; and because they are in peace all things with them are therefore full of sport. (*ib.* n. 288.)

I have also conversed with angels respecting peace; and said that in the world it is called peace when wars and hostilities cease between kingdoms, and when enmities and discords cease among men; and that internal peace is believed to be a rest of mind on the removal of cares, and especially tranquillity and delight from success in business. But the angels responded, that rest of mind and tranquillity and delight from the removal of cares, and from success in business, appear as of peace; but that they are not of the nature of peace, except with those who are in heavenly good; since there is no peace except in that good. For peace flows from the Lord into their inmost, and from their inmost descends and flows down into their lower degrees, and produces rest of mind [*mens*], tranquillity of the lower mind [*animus*], and thence joy. (*ib.* n. 290.)

Concerning the state of peace which there is in heaven, it may be said to be such as no words can describe. Nor can it enter into the thought and perception of man, so long as he is in the world, by any idea derived from the world. It is then beyond every sense. Tranquillity of the lower mind (*animus*), content and gladness derived from successes, are relatively nothing; for these affect the externals only, while peace affects the inmosts of all,—the first substances and principles of substances in man; and thence it derives and pours itself forth into what is substantiated and originated from those principles, and affects them and the sources of ideas with pleasantness, and so the ends of man's life with satisfaction and happiness. And thus it makes the mind of man a heaven. (A. C. n. 8455.)

Peace in heaven is as the spring or as the day-dawn on earth, which affect not by sensible varieties, but by a universal pleasantness, which flows into the least things that are perceived, and imbues not only the perception itself, but also the single objects with pleasantness. . . . Because peace is of such a nature, that is to say, is the inmost of every happiness and blessedness, and therefore is a thing universal, reigning in all particulars, therefore the ancients used, as a common formula, to say, when they meant, may it be well, Peace be to you; and to inquire, when they would know if it was well with them, whether they were at peace. (*ib.* n. 5662.)

The State in Heaven of the Nations and Peoples out of the Church.

It is a common opinion that those who are born out of the Church, who are called Heathen, and Gentiles, cannot be saved; for the reason that they have not the Word, and therefore are ignorant of the Lord, without whom there is no salvation. But that they also are saved, may be known from this single consideration; that the mercy of the Lord is universal, that is, it extends to every individual; that they, equally with those that are within the Church, who are comparatively few, are born men; and that it is not by their fault that they are ignorant of the Lord. Every one who thinks from any enlightened reason may see that no man is born for hell; for the Lord is Love itself, and His love is a desire to save all men. And He therefore provides that there may be a religion with all, and through it an acknowledgment of the Divine, and interior life. For, to live according to a religion is to live interiorly, for then a man looks to the Divine; and in so far as he looks to this he does not look to the world, but removes himself from the world, and therefore from the life of the world, which is an exterior life.

They who understand what it is that constitutes heaven in man, may know that Gentiles equally with Christians are saved; for heaven is within a man,[1] and they who have heaven within them come into heaven after death. It is heaven in man to acknowledge the Divine [Being], and to be led by the Divine. The first and chief thing in every religion is the acknowledgment of a Divine [Being]. A religion that does not acknowledge a Divine [Being] is no religion. And the precepts of every religion have regard to worship, thus, to how the Divine [Being] is to be worshipped so that it may be acceptable to Him. And when this is settled in a man's mind, that is to say, in so far as he wills it, or in so far as he loves it, he is led by the Lord. It is known that gentiles live a moral life as well as Christians, and many of them live a better life than Christians. A moral life is lived either from regard to the Divine [Being], or out of regard to men in the world. A moral life that is lived out of regard to the Divine [Being] is a spiritual life. Both appear alike in outward form; but in the internal they are entirely different. One saves a man; the other does not save. For he who lives a moral life from regard to the Divine [Being] is led by the Divine; but he who lives a moral life out of regard to men in the world is led by self. . . . . The man whose moral life is spiritual has heaven within him; but he whose moral life is only natural has not heaven within him. . . . From these considerations it may be seen who receive heaven within themselves, and who do not. But heaven is not the same in one as in another; it differs in each according to his affection for good and hence for truth. They who are in an affection for good out of regard to the Divine [Being] love Divine truth; for good and truth mutually love each other, and desire to be conjoined. For this reason gentiles, although they are

[1] Luke xvii. 21.

not in genuine truths in the world, yet receive them in the other life, according to their love. (H. H. n. 318, 319.)

I have been instructed by many experiences that gentiles who have led a moral life, and have been obedient, and lived in mutual charity, and have received a sort of conscience according to their religious belief, are accepted in the other life, and with anxious care are there instructed by the angels in goods and truths of faith. While they are being instructed they are modest, intelligent, and wise in their deportment, and easily receive truths and become imbued with them; for they have formed to themselves no principles contrary to the truths of faith, which must be dissipated, still less scandals against the Lord, as many Christians have done who have led an evil life. Such gentiles, moreover, have no hatred towards others; nor do they avenge injuries; nor devise machinations and frauds. Nay, they wish well to Christians; while they, on the other hand, despise them, and as far as they can do violence to them. But they are delivered and protected by the Lord from their unmercifulness. The case with Christians and gentiles in the other life, in fact, is this; that Christians who have acknowledged the truths of faith, and at the same time have led a good life, are received before gentiles,—but there are few such at this day; on the other hand, gentiles who have lived in obedience and in mutual charity are received before Christians who have not led so good a life. (A. C. n. 2590.)

It is a Divine truth that without the Lord there is no salvation. But this is to be understood thus; that there is no salvation except from the Lord. There are many earths in the universe, and all full of inhabitants; scarcely any therein know that the Lord assumed the Human on our earth; and yet, because they adore the Divine [Being] under a human form, they are accepted and led of the Lord. (H. H. n. 321.)

There are gentiles who while they lived in the world knew, from intercourse with them, and from common report, that Christians lead an evil life; for example, live in adultery, in hatred, in quarrels, in drunkenness, and the like,—which they abhorred, because such things are contrary to their religion. These are more fearful than others about receiving the truths of faith. But they are instructed by the angels that the Christian doctrine, and the Faith itself, teaches an entirely different life; but that Christians live less according to their doctrine than gentiles. When they apprehend this they receive the truths of faith, and adore the Lord; but more slowly than others. (*ib.* n. 325.)

INFANTS IN HEAVEN.

It is the belief of some that only infants who are born within the church go to heaven, and not those that are born out of the church; because, they say, infants within the church are baptized, and are initiated by baptism into the faith of the church. But they are not aware that no one receives either heaven or faith by baptism. For baptism is only for a sign and a memorial that the man ought to be regenerated, and that he who is born within the church can be regenerated; because the Word is there, wherein the Divine truths are through which regeneration is effected, and there the Lord is known, by whom regeneration is accomplished. Let them know therefore that every infant, wherever born, within the church or without the church, of pious parents or of impious, is received by the Lord when he dies, and is educated in heaven; and according to Divine order is taught and imbued with affections for good, and through them with cognitions of truth. And afterwards, as he is perfected in intelligence and wisdom, he is introduced into heaven and becomes an angel. Every one who thinks from reason may know that no one is born for hell, but all for heaven; and that man himself is in fault if he goes to hell; and that infants as yet can be in no fault.

Infants who die are infants still in the other life. They have the same infantile mind, the same innocence in ignorance, and the same tenderness in all respects. They are only in states rudimentary to those of angels; for infants are not angels, but become angels. For every one that passes out of the world is yet in the same state of his life; an infant is in the state of infancy, a child in the state of childhood, a youth, a man, an old man, in the state of youth, of manhood, and of an old age. But afterwards the state of each is changed. But the state of infants excels the state of all others in the fact that they are in innocence, and that evil from actual life is not yet rooted in them. And such is the nature of innocence that all things of heaven may be implanted in it; for innocence is the receptacle of the truth of faith and of the good of love.

The state of infants in the other life is far better than that of infants in the world; for they are not clothed with an earthly body, but with a body like that of the angels. The earthly body in itself is gross. It receives its first sensations and first motions not from the inner or spiritual world, but from the outer or natural world. In the world therefore infants must learn to walk, to move their limbs, and to talk; nay, their senses, as the sight, and hearing, must be opened by use. It is different with infants in the other life. Being spirits they act immediately according to their interiors. They walk, and also talk, without practice; but their speech is at first from general affections, not yet so well distinguished into ideas of thoughts. In a short time however they are initiated into these also, because their exteriors are homogeneous with their interiors.

As soon as infants are resuscitated,—which takes place immediately after their decease,—they are taken up into heaven, and are confided to angels of the female sex who in the life of the body tenderly loved infants, and at the same time loved God. As in the world they loved all infants with almost maternal tenderness, they receive them as their own; and the infants, from an innate disposition, love them too as their own mothers. Each one has as many infants in her charge as, from a spiritual maternal affection, she desires. . . . All infants are under the immediate auspices of the Lord; the heaven of innocence, which is the third heaven, also flows into them. (H. H. n. 329, 332.)

It shall also be stated briefly how infants are educated in heaven. From their instructress they learn to talk. Their earliest speech is merely the sound of affection, which by degrees becomes more distinctive, as ideas of thought enter; for ideas of thought from affection constitute all angelic speech. Into their affections, which all proceed from innocence, such things as appear before their eyes and are delightful are first insinuated; which being of a spiritual origin, the things of heaven at the same time flow into them, whereby their interiors are opened; and thus they are daily perfected. When this first age is past they are transferred to another heaven, where they are instructed by masters; and so on.

Infants are instructed chiefly by representatives, adapted to their capacity; which are so beautiful, and at the same time so full of wisdom from within, as to exceed all belief. By degrees an intelligence is thus insinuated into them which derives its soul from good.

It was also shown me how tender their understanding is. When I was praying the Lord's prayer, and they then flowed in from their intellectual faculty into the ideas of my thought, it was perceived that their influx was so tender and soft, that it was almost of affection alone; and then it was observed at the same time that their intellectual faculty was opened even from the Lord, for what emanated from them was as if it flowed through them. The Lord does in reality flow into the ideas of infants chiefly from the inmosts, for nothing closes their ideas, as with adults; no principles of falsity hinder the understanding of truth, and no life of evil prevents the reception of good, and thus the attainment of wisdom. It is evident from these considerations that infants do not come into the angelic state immediately after death, but are gradually led into it, b y cognitions of good and truth, and this in accordance with all heavenly order. For the least things of their natural character are known to the Lord ; and therefore they are led to receive the truths of good and the goods of truth, according to all and each particular of the movements of their inclination.

It was also shown me how all things are insinuated into them by delights and pleasures suited to their genius. It was indeed given me to see little children most beautifully clothed, with garlands of flowers resplendent with the most delightful and heavenly colours about their breasts and likewise around their tender arms. Once it was given me also to see children with their instructresses and accompanied by virgins, in a paradisiacal garden, beautifully adorned not so much with trees as with espaliers as if of laurel, and so forming porticoes with paths leading towards interior recesses. The little children themselves were clothed then in a similar manner ; and when they entered, the flowers above the entrance shone forth most joyfully. It may be seen from this what delights they have, and also that by means of things pleasant and delightful they are led into the goods of innocence and charity ; which goods are continually insinuated into them by the Lord, through such delights and pleasures. (*ib.* n. 334, 336.)

It was shown me, by a mode of communication familiar in the other life, what the ideas of infants are when they behold any object. Their conceptions were as if each and all things were alive ; there is life therefore in every idea of their thought. And I perceived that little children on earth have nearly the same ideas, while they are engaged in their little pastimes ; for as yet they have no reflection, like adults, as to what is inanimate.

Infants are of a genius either celestial or spiritual ; those who are of a celestial genius are quite distinct from those of a spiritual genius. The former think, speak, and act very gently, so that there appears scarcely anything but what flows from the good of love to the Lord and love towards other children ; and the latter not so gently, but in all things with them a certain tremulous fluttering, as it were (*quoddam quasi alatum vibratile*), is manifest. It also appears from their displeasure, and from other indications. (*ib.* 338, 339.)

The innocence of infants is not genuine innocence, because it is as yet without wisdom. Genuine innocence is wisdom, for in so far as any one is wise he loves to be led by the Lord ; or what is the same, in so far as any one is led by the Lord he is wise. Infants therefore are led on from the external innocence which is called the innocence of infancy, in which they first are, to internal innocence, which is the innocence of wisdom. This innocence is the end of all their instruction and progress. When therefore they attain to the innocence of wisdom, then the innocence of infancy, which in the meantime had served them as a plane, is conjoined to them.

I have conversed with the angels respecting infants, as to whether they are free from evils, because they have no actual evil like adults. But I was told that they are equally in evil, nay, that they too are nothing but evil; but that like all the angels they are withheld from evil and kept in good by the Lord, so that it appears to them as if of themselves they were in good. Therefore lest infants, after they become adults in heaven, should be in the false opinion respecting themselves that the good in them is from them, and not from the Lord, they are sometimes let back into their evils which they have hereditarily received, and are left in them until they know, acknowledge, and believe that the case is so. No one ever suffers punishment in the other life on account of hereditary evil; because it is not his own, and therefore it is not by his fault that he is such. But he suffers for the actual evil that is his own, and therefore in so far as he has appropriated hereditary evil to himself by actual life. Infants therefore are let back into the state of their hereditary evil when they become adults, not that they may suffer punishment for it, but that they may know that of themselves they are nothing but evil; and that by the Lord's mercy they are taken out of the hell that is in them into heaven; and that they are in heaven not on account of any merit of their own, but through the Lord; and that they may not therefore boast to others of the good that is in them,—for this is as contrary to the good of mutual love as it is contrary to the truth of faith. (*ib.* n. 341, 342.)

It shall also be stated what the difference is between those who die in infancy and those who die in adult age. Those who die in adult age have and carry with them a plane acquired from the terrestrial and material world. This plane is their memory, and its corporeal natural affection. This remains fixed, and is then quiescent; but it still serves their thought after death as the ultimate plane, for the thought flows into it. Hence it follows that such as is the character of that plane, and such as is the manner of correspondence of the rational with the things that are therein, such is the man after death. But infants who die in infancy and are educated in heaven have not such a plane, but a spiritual natural plane; for they derive nothing from the material world and the earthly body. They therefore cannot be in so gross affections and consequent thoughts; for they derive all things from heaven.

Infants moreover do not know that they were born in the world, and so believe that they were born in heaven. They therefore know of no other birth than spiritual birth, which is effected by cognitions of good and truth, and by intelligence and wisdom, by virtue of which man is man. And as these are from the Lord, they believe and love to believe that they are [children] of the Lord Himself. But yet the state of men who grow up on earth may become just as perfect as the state of infants who grow up in heaven, if they put away corporeal and earthly loves, which are the loves of self and of the world, and receive spiritual loves in their place. (*ib.* n. 345.)

THE RICH AND POOR IN HEAVEN.

From much converse and life with the angels, it has been given me to know for a certainty that the rich as easily enter heaven as the poor; that a man is not excluded from heaven because he has great abundance, and is not received into heaven because he is in indigence. Both rich and poor are there, and many rich are in greater glory and happiness than the poor.

It may be observed at the outset that, so far as it is granted him, a man may acquire riches and accumulate wealth, if only it is not done with craft and dishonesty; that he may have delicate food and drink, if he does not place his life in them; that he may dwell in magnificence according to his condition; may associate with others, as others do; frequent places of amusement, and talk about the affairs of the world; and that he has no need to assume a devout aspect, to be of sad and mournful countenance, to bow down his head—but may be glad and cheerful,— nor to give his goods to the poor, except so far as affection leads him. In a word, he may live in outward form precisely as a man of the world, and these things do not hinder his going to heaven, if only he thinks within himself as it behoves him about God, and acts sincerely and justly to his neighbour. (H. H. 357, 358.)

It is a life of charity towards the neighbour, which consists in doing what is just and right in all one's dealings, and in every occupation, that leads to heaven; and not a life of piety without this. Consequently, the exercises of charity, and the increase of the life of charity by their means, can take place in proportion as a man is in the duties of some occupation; and in proportion as he withdraws from these they cannot take place. Of this I will speak now from experience:—Many of those who in the world were engaged in business and in mercantile pursuits, and also who became enriched by them, are in heaven; but fewer of those who have been in stations of honour, and became rich by their offices. The reason is, that the latter, by the gains and honours bestowed on them on account of their dispensation of justice and right, and of emoluments and honours, were induced to love themselves and the world, and thereby to withdraw their thoughts and affections from heaven, and turn them to themselves; and in so far as a man loves himself and the world, and regards himself and the world 'in everything, in so far he alienates himself from the Divine, and removes himself from heaven. (*ib.* n. 360.)

The poor do not go to heaven on account of their poverty, but on account of their life. Every one's life follows him, whether he be rich or poor. There is no peculiar mercy for the one more than for the other. Besides, poverty seduces and withdraws man from heaven equally with wealth. There are very many among the poor who are not content with their lot, who are covetous of many things, and believe riches to be blessings. They are angry, therefore, and think ill of the Divine Providence when they do not receive them. They also envy others their goods; and moreover equally defraud others when they have opportunity, and equally live also in sordid pleasures. But it is otherwise with the poor who are content with their lot, who are careful and diligent in their calling, and love labour better than idleness, and act sincerely and faithfully, and at the same time live a Christian life.

It is believed that the poor easily enter heaven, and the rich with difficulty, because the Word has not been understood where the rich and poor are mentioned. By the rich therein, in the spiritual sense, they are meant who abound in cognitions of good and of truth; thus those who are within the church where the Word is. And by the poor they are meant who are wanting in these cognitions, and yet desire them; thus those that are without the church, where the Word is not. By the rich man who was clothed in purple and fine linen and was cast into hell, the Jewish nation is meant, which is called rich because it had the Word, and therefore abounded in cognitions of good and truth; cognitions of good are also signified by garments of purple, and cognitions of truth by garments of fine linen. And by the poor man who lay at his gate and desired to be filled with the crumbs that fell from the rich man's table, and was carried by the angels into heaven, the gentiles are meant, who had not cognitions of good and truth, and yet desired them (Luke xvi. 19, 31). The Jewish nation also is meant by the rich who were called to a great supper, and excused themselves; and the gentiles who are out of the church are meant by the poor brought in in their place (Luke xiv. 16-24). It shall also be explained who are meant by the rich man, of whom the Lord says, "*It is easier for a camel to go through the eye of a needle, than for a rich man to enter into the kingdom of God*" (Matt. xix. 24). By the rich man here the rich in both senses are meant, the natural as well as the spiritual. In the natural sense the rich are those who abound in riches and set their heart upon them; and in the spiritual sense they are those who abound in cognitions and knowledges (for these are spiritual riches), and desire by means of them to introduce themselves into the things that pertain to heaven and the church by their own intelligence. And because this is contrary to Divine order, it is said that it is easier for a camel to pass through the eye of a needle; for in this sense, by a camel is signified the cognitive or knowing [faculty] in general; and by the eye of a needle, spiritual truth. (*ib.* n. 364, 365.)

ETERNAL REST.

Eternal rest is not idleness, since from idleness comes languor, torpor, dullness and stupefaction of mind, and therefore of the whole body; and these are death and not life, and still less eternal life, in which the angels of heaven are. Eternal rest is therefore a rest which dispels these, and causes a man to live; and this is no other than such rest as elevates the mind. It is therefore some study and work by which the mind is excited, vivified, and delighted; and this effect is produced according to the use from which, in which, and for which it works. Hence it is that the universal heaven is regarded by the Lord as the containant of use; and every angel is an angel according to his use. The delight of use carries him along as a favourable current a ship, and causes him to be in eternal peace, and in the rest of peace. Eternal rest from labours is thus to be understood. (C. L. n. 207.)

THE OCCUPATIONS OF ANGELS.

The employments in the heavens cannot be enumerated; nor can they be described specifically, but only something in general can be said of them; for they are innumerable, and also vary according to the offices of the societies. Each society performs a peculiar office; for, as the societies are distinguished according to goods, so are they according to uses, since with all in the heavens goods are goods in act, which are uses. Each one there performs a use; for the kingdom of the Lord is a kingdom of uses.

There are various administrations in the heavens, just as on earth; for there are ecclesiastical affairs, civil affairs, and domestic affairs. . . . It is evident from this that there are many occupations and administrations in each heavenly society. All things in the heavens are established according to Divine order, which is everywhere preserved by means of administrations by the angels; by the wiser angels those things that relate to the general good or use; by the less wise, those that relate to the particular uses, and so on. They are subordinated just as in Divine order the uses are subordinated. Hence also dignity is attached to every employment, according to the dignity of the use. And yet no angel arrogates the dignity to himself, but ascribes it all to the use; and as the use is the good that he performs, and all good is from the Lord, he therefore ascribes it all to the Lord. For this reason one who thinks of honour for himself and hence for a use, and not for the use and hence for himself, can perform no office in heaven; for he looks back, away from the Lord, regarding himself in the first place, and use in the second. (H. H. n. 387-389.)

There are societies whose occupations consist in the care of infants; there are other societies whose occupations are to instruct and educate them as they grow up; there are others who in like manner instruct and educate boys and girls who have acquired a good disposition from their education in the world, and who come thence into heaven. There are others who teach the simple good from the Christian world, and lead them into the way to heaven; others, who in like manner teach and lead the various gentile nations; others, who defend novitiate spirits,—which are those who have recently come from the world,—from infestations by evil spirits. There are some also who are present with those that are in the lower earth; and some too who are present to those that are in the hells, and restrain them from tormenting each other beyond prescribed limits; and there are some who are present to those who are being raised from the dead. In general, angels of every society are sent to men; that they may guard them, and withdraw them from evil affections, and thereby from evil thoughts, and, in so far as from freedom they receive them, inspire them with good affections; whereby they also rule the deeds or works of men, as far as it is possible removing evil intentions. While they are with men the angels dwell, as it were, in their affections; and are near a man in so far as he is in good from truths, and more remote in proportion as his life is distant from good. But all these occupations of the angels are functions performed by the Lord through the angels; for the angels perform them not for themselves but from the Lord. Hence it is that by angels in the Word, in its internal sense, angels are not meant, but some [attribute] of the Lord; and hence it is that in the Word angels are called gods.

These employments of the angels are their general occupations, but every one has his particular charge; for every general use is composed of innumerable uses, which are called mediate, administering, and subservient uses. Each and all are co-ordinated and subordinated according to Divine order; and taken together they constitute and perfect the general use, which is the general good.

In ecclesiastical affairs in heaven are those who in the world loved the Word, and with ardent desire sought after the truths therein, not for the sake of honour or gain, but for the use of life, both for themselves and others. According to their love and desire for use there they are in illustration, and in the light of wisdom ; into which they come from the Word in the heavens, which is not natural, as in the world, but spiritual. These perform the office of preachers ; and according to Divine order there, those are in higher station who from illustration excel others in wisdom. In civil [offices] are those who in the world loved their country and its general good in preference to their own, and did what was just and right from a love of what is just and right. They are in the ability to administer offices in heaven in proportion as from an earnest desire of love they have searched into and have thus become intelligent in the laws of justice ; which they also administer in that place or degree which accords with their intelligence ; which is then also in equal degree with their love of use, for the common good. . . . The offices, administrations, and employments on earth are few in comparison with the heavens ; and all, how many soever they are, are in the delight of their occupation and labour, from a love of the use, and no one from the love of self or of gain. (H. H. n. 391-393.)

THE EMINENCE AND OPULENCE OF ANGELS.

The eminence and opulence of angels of heaven shall also be described. In the societies of heaven there are superior and inferior rulers, all ordered and subordinated by the Lord, according to their wisdom and intelligence. The highest of them, who excels the others in wisdom, dwells in the midst, in a palace so magnificent that nothing in all the world can be compared with it. Its architectural qualities are so amazing that of a truth I can declare, that they cannot as to the hundredth part be described in natural language ; for the art itself is there in its own skill. Within the palace there are chambers and bedchambers, in which all the furniture and ornaments are resplendent with gold and various precious stones, in forms such as no master in the world, by painting or by sculpture, can portray; and, what is wonderful, every, even to the very least particular thing of them, is for use. Every one who enters sees for what use they are; he in truth perceives it, as it were, from a transpiration of the uses through their forms. But any wise man who enters does not long keep his eye fixed upon their forms; but directs his mind to their uses; for these delight his wisdom. Round about the palace there are colonnades, paradisiacal gardens, and little palaces; and every single thing is a heavenly pleasantness itself, in a form of its own beauty. In addition to these magnificent objects there are attendants, each clad in shining garments; and many things besides. The subordinate rulers have similar palaces, the magnificence and splendour of which are according to the degree of their wisdom; and they have wisdom according to the degrees of their love of uses. Not only do the rulers possess such things, but the inhabitants also; all of whom love uses, and perform them by various occupations. But there are few things that can be described. Those that cannot be described are innumerable; which because they are of a spiritual origin do not fall into the conceptions of the natural man, nor therefore into the words of his language,—save only as to these [general principles]; that wisdom builds for itself a habitation, and conforms to herself; and that all that lies hidden in the inmost of any science or of any art there, convenes and gives effect. These things now are written that it may be known that all things in the heavens also have reference to eminence and opulence; but that eminence there is of wisdom, and opulence there is of knowledge; and that such are the things to which man is led of the Lord by His Divine Providence. (A. E. n. 1191.)

HEAVENLY JOY AND HAPPINESS.

All the delights of heaven are connected with and are in uses; because uses are goods of the love and charity in which the angels are. Every one therefore has delights according to the nature of his uses; and also in degree proportioned to his affection for use. (H. H. n. 402.)

That I might know what heaven is, and heavenly joy, and the nature of them, it has been granted me by the Lord, often and for a long time, to perceive the delights of heavenly joys. I can therefore, because from living experience, know them, but can never describe them. Yet something shall be stated merely to give an idea of them.

Heavenly joy is an affection of delights and joys innumerable, which together present a certain general [emotion]; in which gene-

ral [emotion], or in which general affection, are the harmonies
of innumerable affections,—which do not come distinctly to
perception, but obscurely, because the perception is most general.
Yet it was given me to perceive that there are [joys] innumerable
within it, in such order as can never be described. These
innumerable [joys] are such as flow from the order of heaven.
There is such an order in the single and least particulars of an
affection; which are presented and perceived, according to the
capacity of him who is the subject, only as a most general unit.
In a word, there are infinite things in most orderly form in every
general thing; and there is nothing that does not live, and
affect,—and all indeed from the inmosts; for from the inmosts
heavenly joys proceed. I perceived also that the joy and
delight came as from the heart, diffusing themselves most
gently through all the inmost fibres, and thence into the
congregated fibres, with such an inmost sense of enjoyment
that every fibre is as it were nothing but joy and delight; and
everything perceptive and sensitive therefrom is in like manner
alive with happiness. The joy of bodily pleasures is to these
joys as a gross and pungent fog to a pure and most gentle
aura. It was observed, that when I desired to impart all my
delight to another, a more interior and fuller delight than before
continually flowed in in its place, and the more I desired this,
the more it flowed in; and it was perceived that this was from
the Lord. (*ib.* n. 413.)

Such is the angelic state that each communicates his own
blessedness and happiness to another. For there is a most
exquisite communication and perception of all affections and
thoughts in the other life, whereby each communicates his delight
to all, and all to each; so that each one is as it were a centre of
all. This is the heavenly form. The more they are, therefore,
who constitute the Lord's kingdom the greater is their happiness;
for it increases in the ratio of their number. Hence it is that
the happiness of heaven is ineffable. There is such communication of all with each and each with all when one loves another
better than himself. But if any one wishes better to himself
than to another, then the love of self prevails; and this communicates nothing from itself to another save the idea of self,
which is most foul, and when it is perceived is instantly separated
and rejected. (A. C. n. 549.)

The Aged return to the Spring-time of Life in Heaven.

They who dwell in heaven are continually advancing to the
spring-time of life; and to a spring more and more delightful

and happy the more thousands of years they live; and this to eternity, with increase according to the progress and degrees of love, charity, and faith. Those of the female sex who have died old and infirm with age, and have lived in faith in the Lord, in charity towards the neighbour, and in happy conjugial love with a husband, after a succession of years, come more and more into the flower of youth and adolescence, and into a beauty which surpasses every conception of beauty ever perceptible by the sight. It is goodness and charity which form and present an image of themselves; and they cause the delight and beauty of charity to shine forth from every least feature of the countenance, so that they are very forms of charity. Some have seen them, and were astonished. Such is the form of charity,—which is seen to the life in heaven,—that charity itself is what portrays and is portrayed; and this in such wise that the whole angel, especially the face, is charity, as it were,—which is both manifestly seen, and is perceived. This form when seen is ineffable beauty, affecting the very inmost life of the mind with charity. In a word, to grow old in heaven is to grow young. They who have lived in love to the Lord and in charity towards the neighbour become such forms, or such beauties, in the other life. (H. H. n. 414.)

The Immensity of Heaven.

That the heaven of the Lord is immense may appear from many things that have been said and shown in the preceding sections; especially from the fact that heaven is from the human race; and not from those only that are born within the church, but also from those that are born out of the church; from all therefore since the first beginning of this earth who have lived in good. How great the multitude of men is, in all this terrestrial globe, any one may judge who knows anything of the parts, regions and kingdoms of this earth. Whoever goes into the calculation will find that many thousands of men depart thence every day, and therefore some myriads or millions within a year; and this has been so from the earliest times, since which some thousands of years have elapsed. All these after their decease have passed into the other world, which is called the spiritual world, and are passing in continually. But how many of them have become and do become angels of heaven cannot be told. It has been told me that in ancient times very many became angels, because then men thought more interiorly and more spiritually, and thence were in heavenly affection; but not so many in the following ages, because in process of time man became exterior, and began to think more naturally, and thence to be in earthly affection. It is evident, in the first place, from these considerations, that the heaven from the inhabitants of this earth alone is great.

That the heaven of the Lord is immense may appear from this single fact ; that all infants, whether they are born within the church or without it, are adopted by the Lord and become angels, —the number of whom amounts to a fourth or fifth part of the whole human race on the earth. . . . It may be concluded therefore how great a multitude of angels of heaven from the first creation to the present time have come from these alone.

How immense the heaven of the Lord is may further appear from the fact that all the planets visible to the eye in our solar system are earths ; and that there are innumerable earths in the universe beyond this, and all full of inhabitants ; of which in a little special work on those earths. (H. H. n. 415, 417.) See chapter below on " The Earths in the Universe."

It was given me also to see the extent of the inhabited heaven, and of that too which is not inhabited ; and I saw that the extent of the uninhabited heaven was so great that it could not be filled to eternity, even if there were many myriads of earths, and in each earth as great a multitude of men as in ours. (*ib.* n. 419.)

HEAVEN IS NEVER FILLED, BUT MORE PERFECT BY INCREASE.

It is worthy of mention that the more there are in a society of heaven, and the more they act as one, the more perfect is its human form ; for variety disposed in heavenly form gives perfection, and where there are many there is variety. Every society of heaven, moreover, increases in number from day to day, and as it increases it becomes the more perfect ; and not the society only is thus perfected, but heaven in general also, for the societies constitute heaven. Since heaven is perfected by its increasing multitude, it is evident how greatly they mistake who believe that heaven may be closed by becoming full ; when in fact the opposite is true, that heaven will never be closed, and that its greater and greater fullness perfects it ; and therefore the angels desire nothing more earnestly than that new angel guests may come to them.

Every society, when it appears together as one, is in the human form ; for the whole heaven has that form, and in the most perfect form,—which the form of heaven is,—there is a likeness of the parts to the whole, and of the less to the greatest. The less, and the parts of heaven, are the societies of which it consists, which are heavens in lesser form. (H. H. n. 71. 72.)

HELL.

THE ORIGIN OF EVIL AND OF HELL.

IT is plain from the first chapter of Genesis,—where it is said (v. 10, 12, 18, 21, 25), "*God saw that it was good*," and finally (v. 31), "*God saw everything that He had made, and behold it was very good*,"—and also from the primeval state of man, in Paradise, that everything that God created was good. And it is plain from the second state of Adam, or that after the fall,—in that he was cast out of Paradise,—that evil arose from man. From these facts it is clear that if man had not been gifted with free will in spiritual things, God Himself, and not man, would have been the cause of evil, and thus that God must have created both good and evil. It is impious to think that He also created evil. That God did not, because He endued man with free agency in spiritual things, create evil, and that He never inspires any evil into man, is because He is good itself; and in this God is omnipresent, and continually urges and entreats that He may be received. And if He is not received yet He does not withdraw; for if He should withdraw man would instantly die, nay, would lapse into nonentity; for man's life and the subsistence of all things of which he consists, is from God. The cause of the fact that God did not create evil, but that man introduced it is, that man turns into evil the good which continually flows in from God, by turning himself away from God and turning to himself; and when this is done the delight of good remains, and this then becomes the delight of evil. For without a remaining delight, apparently similar, man could not live; since delight constitutes the life of his love. (T. C. R. n. 490.)

The love of self and the love of the world constitute hell; but it shall be shown what is the origin of those loves :—Man was created to love himself and the world, to love his neighbour and heaven, and also to love the Lord. Hence it is that after man is born he first loves himself and the world, and then in proportion as he grows wise he loves his neighbour and heaven, and as he becomes more wise he loves the Lord. When this is the case then he is in Divine order, and is led of the Lord actually, and of himself apparently. But in so far as he is not wise he abides in the first degree, which is to love himself and the world,—and if he loves his neighbour, heaven, and the Lord, it is for the sake of himself before the world. And if he is altogether unwise then he loves himself alone, and the world, and likewise the neighbour, for the sake of himself; and, as to heaven and the Lord, he either makes light of, or denies, or hates them,—if not in words, yet in his heart. These are the origins of the love of self and the love of the world; and as these loves are hell, it is evident whence hell is. (A. E. n. 1144.)

The author gives the following further explanation of the origin of evil, in a conversation with certain angels from the heaven of innocence, who, having been removed from the world in infancy, were ignorant of and doubted the existence of evil. Being asked by them to explain, how a love could exist which not only was not from creation, but is contrary to creation, he says :—

I rejoiced in heart that it was given me to speak with angels of such innocence, ... and I opened my mouth and said :—" Do you not know that there is good and evil, and that good, and not evil, is from creation ? And yet evil in itself regarded is not nothing, although it is nothing of good. Good is from creation, and there is good also in the greatest and least degree ; and when the least becomes none, on the other side evil arises. There is therefore no relation nor progression of good to evil, but a relation and progression of good to more and less good, and of evil to more and less evil ; for in each and all respects they are opposites. And since good and evil are opposites there is an intermediate, and an equilibrium there, in which evil acts against good ; but as it does not prevail it abides in effort. Every man is nurtured in this equilibrium ; which, as it is between good and evil, or what is the same, between heaven and hell, is a spiritual equilibrium, which brings liberty to those who are in it. From this equilibrium the Lord draws all to Himself ; and the man who from freedom follows is led out of evil into good, and so into heaven." . . . . The two angels asked, " How could evil arise when nothing but good had existed from creation ? That anything may exist it must have an origin. Good cannot be the origin of evil ; for evil is nothing of good. It is in fact privative and destructive of good. And yet it exists, and is felt. It is not nothing, but is something. Say, then, whence arises this something after nothing ?" To this I responded :—" This mystery cannot be explained, unless it be known that there is none good but the Lord only ; and that there is no good, which is good in itself, except from God. He therefore who looks to God, and desires to be led of God, is in good; but he who turns himself away from God, and wishes to be led of himself, is not in good. For the good that he does is either for the sake of himself, or on account of the world; thus it is either for the sake of reward, or it is simulated, or even hypocritical. From which it is plain that man himself is the origin of evil; that this origin was not introduced into man from creation, but that he introduced it into himself, by turning from God to himself. This origin of evil was not in Adam and his wife; but when the serpent said, "*In the day that ye eat of the tree of knowledge of good and evil ye shall be as God,*" and they then turned away from God, and turned them to themselves as to a god, they made in themselves the origin of evil. To eat of that tree signified to believe that one knows and does good from himself, and not from God." But the two angels then asked, " How could man turn away from God and turn to himself, when yet man can will, think, and therefore do nothing except from God?" But I answered, that man was so created that what he wills, thinks, and does, appears to him as in himself, and so from himself. Without this appearance man would not be man; for he could not receive, retain, and as it were appropriate to himself, anything of good and truth, or of love and wisdom. Whence it follows, that without this, as it were living appearance, man would have no conjunction with God, and therefore no eternal life. But if on account of this appearance he induces upon himself a belief that he wills, thinks, and therefore does good, from himself, and not from the Lord, —although in every appearance it is as from himself,—he turns good into evil within him, and so causes within himself the origin of evil. This was the sin of Adam. (C. L. n. 444.)

The Lord Governs the Hells.

It shall be briefly stated how the hells are governed by the Lord. The hells in general are governed by a general influx of Divine good and Divine truth from the heavens, whereby the general effort issuing forth from the hells is checked and restrained; and likewise by a special afflux from each heaven, and from each society of heaven. The hells in particular are governed by angels, to whom it is given to look into the hells, and restrain the insanities and disturbances there; sometimes also angels are sent thither, and being present moderate them. And in general all who are in the hells are governed by their fears; some by fears implanted and yet in them from the world; but as these fears are not sufficient, and also by degrees lose their force,

they are governed by fears of punishment. By these principally
they are deterred from doing evils. The punishments in hell are
manifold, more gentle and more severe, according to the evils.
For the most part the more malignant, who excel in cunning and
artifice, and are able to keep the rest in submission and servitude
by punishments and the terror of punishments, are set over
others. These rulers do not dare to pass beyond the limits
prescribed to them. It should be known that the fear of punishment is the only means of restraining the violence and fury of
those who are in the hells. There is no other means.

It has hitherto been believed in the world that there is some
one devil who presides over the hells; and that he was created
an angel of light, but afterwards became rebellious, and was cast
down with his crew into hell. This belief has prevailed because
in the Word mention is made of the Devil and Satan, and also
of Lucifer, and the Word has been understood in these passages
according to the sense of the letter. When yet by the Devil
and Satan hell is there meant; by the Devil the hell which is
behind, and where the worst dwell, who are called evil genii,[1]
and by Satan the hell which is in front, where they are not so
malignant, and are called evil spirits; by Lucifer they are meant
who are of Babel or Babylon,[1]—who are those that extend their
dominion even into heaven. That there is no one Devil to
whom the hells are subject is evident indeed from the fact that
all who are in the hells, as all who are in the heavens, are from
the human race; and that, from the beginning of creation to the
present time, there are myriads of myriads there, and every one
of them is a devil of such character as he had acquired in the
world, by opposition to the Divine. (H. H. n. 543, 544.)

THE LORD CASTS NO ONE INTO HELL, BUT THE SPIRIT CASTS
HIMSELF THEREIN.

An opinion has prevailed with some that God turns away His
face from man, rejects him from Himself, and casts him into hell;
and that He is angry with him on account of his evil; and by
some it is still further supposed that God punishes man and
brings evil upon him. They confirm themselves in this opinion
from the literal sense of the Word, where such things are declared,
—not being aware that the spiritual sense of the Word,[2] which
explains the sense of the letter, is entirely different; and that
therefore the genuine doctrine of the church, which is from the
spiritual sense of the Word,[3] teaches otherwise; namely, that
God never turns away his face from man and rejects him from
Himself, that He casts no one into hell, and is angry with no one.

[1] See p. 611.   [2] See pp. 141, 172, *note.*   [3] See p. 409, *note.*

This in fact any one whose mind is in a state of illustration when he reads the Word perceives, from this consideration alone, that God is Good itself, Love itself, and Mercy itself; and that Good itself cannot do evil to any one, and Love itself and Mercy itself cannot reject man from them,—because it is contrary to the very essence of mercy and love, thus contrary to the Divine itself. (H. H. n. 545.)

Evil in man is hell in him; for whether we speak of evil or of hell, it is the same. Now since man is in the cause of his own evil, he therefore, and not the Lord, brings himself into hell; for so far is the Lord from bringing man into hell that He delivers him from hell, in the degree that a man does not will and love to be in his evil. All man's will and love remains with him after death; he who in the world wills and loves an evil, wills and loves the same evil in the other life; and then he no longer suffers himself to be withdrawn from it. Hence it is that a man who is in evil is bound to hell, and even, as to his spirit, is actually there; and after death he desires nothing more than to be where his evil is. A man therefore casts himself into hell after death, and not the Lord. (H. H. n. 547.)

The wicked thrust themselves into hell not instantaneously, but successively. This fact originates in a universal law of the order established by the Lord; that the Lord never casts any one into hell, but that evil itself, or an evil man thrusts himself into hell; and this he does successively, until his evil is consummated, and there no longer appears anything of good. So long as anything of good remains he is lifted out of hell; and when there is nothing left but evil he is plunged by himself into hell. The one must first be separated from the other, for they are opposed to each other; and to hang in suspense between the one and the other is not permitted. (A. C. n. 1857.)

ALL IN THE HELLS ARE IN EVILS AND FALSITIES.

All who are in the hells are in evils and thence in falsities; and no one there is in evils and at the same time in truths. Very many of the evil in the world are acquainted with spiritual truths, which are truths of the church; for they have learned them in childhood, and then from preaching and from reading the Word, and afterwards have discoursed from them. Some have even induced others to believe that they were Christians in heart, because they knew how to discourse from truths with simulated affection, and also to act sincerely as if from spiritual faith. But such of them as have thought within themselves contrary to these truths, and have abstained from doing the evils agreeable to their thoughts only on account of the civil laws, and for the sake of reputation, honours, and gain, are all evil in heart, and are in truths and goods only as to the body, and not as to the spirit. When therefore the externals are taken away from them in the other life, and the internals which were of their spirit are revealed, they are entirely in evils and falsities, and not in any truths and goods ; and it is then evident that truths and goods resided only in their memory, no otherwise than as things known; and that they brought them forth from thence in discourse, and made a pretence of good as if from spiritual love and faith. When such men are let into their internals, and so into their evils, they can no longer speak truths, but only falsities, since they then speak from evils ; for to speak truths from evils is impossible, since the spirit is then nothing but his own evil, and falsity proceeds from evil. (H. H. n. 551.)

INFERNAL SPIRITS ARE THE FORMS OF THEIR OWN EVILS.

Viewed in any light of heaven all the spirits in the hells appear in the form of their evil. Every one indeed is the image of his evil ; for the interiors and exteriors with every one act as one, and the interiors visibly present themselves in the exteriors, which are the face, the body, the speech, and actions. Thus their character is recognized as soon as they are seen. In general, they are forms of contempt of others ; of menace against those who do not pay them respect; they are forms of hatred of various kinds ; they are forms also of various kinds of revenge. Fierceness and cruelty from their interiors transpire through them ; but when others commend, venerate, and worship them, their faces are contracted, and have an appearance of gladness from delight. It is impossible in a few words to describe all these forms such as they appear, for no one is like another. Only between those who are in similar evil and are therefore in a similar infernal society is there a general likeness, from which, as from a plane of derivation, the faces of the individuals therein appear to have a certain resemblance. Their faces in general are horrible, and void of life like corpses ; those of some are black, of some fiery, like torches, of some hideous with pimples, warts, and ulcers ; with many no face appears, but in its place a something hairy or bony, and with some only the teeth appear. Their bodies also are monstrous ; and their speech is as the speech of anger, or of hatred, or of revenge; for every one speaks from his falsity, and the tone of his voice is from his evil. In a word, they are all images of their own hell. In what form hell itself is, in general, it has not been given me to see. I have only been told that as the universal heaven in one complex is as one man, so the universal hell in one complex is as one devil, and may also be presented in the image of one devil. But it has often been given me to see in what form the hells or infernal societies in particular are; for at their apertures, which are called the gates of hell, there usually appears a monster, which in general represents the form of those that are within. The fierce passions of those that dwell there are at the same time represented by abominable and frightful [appearances], which I forbear to name. It should be understood however that such is the appearance of infernal spirits in the light of heaven; but among themselves they appear as men. It is of the Lord's mercy, that their hideousness may not appear among themselves as it appears before the angels. But the appearance is a fallacy; for as soon as any ray of light from heaven is let in their human forms are turned into monstrous forms, such as they are in themselves, as described above. For in the light of heaven everything appears as it is in itself. Hence it is that they shun the light (*lux*)[1] of heaven, and cast themselves down into their own light (*lumen*); a light which is like the light from glowing coals, and in some places like that from burning sulphur. But even this light is turned into thick darkness, when any particle of light from heaven flows in there. Hence it is that the hells are said to be in thick darkness, and in darkness; and that thick darkness and darkness [in the Word] signify falsities from evil, such as are in hell.

From the contemplation of those monstrous forms of spirits in the hells,—which, as was said, are all forms of contempt of others, and of menace against those that do not pay them honour and respect, and forms of hatred and revenge against those that do not favour them,—it was evident that in general they were all forms of the love of self and the love of the world; and that the evils of which they are the specific forms derive their origin from those two loves. (H. H. n. 553, 554.)

The Nature of Self-Love.

I wondered at first why it is that the love of self and the love of the world are so diabolical, and that they who are in those loves are such monsters to look upon; since in the world little thought is given to self-love, but only to that puffed-up state of mind [*animus*] outwardly manifest which is called pride, and which alone is believed to be self-love, because it appears to the

[1] See *note*, p. 152

sight. Moreover self-love, when it does not so inflate itself, is believed in the world to be the fire of life, by which a man is incited to seek employment, and to perform uses, in which unless a man saw honour and glory his mind would grow torpid. Who, it is said, has done any worthy, useful, and distinguished action, but for the sake of being celebrated and honoured by others, or in the minds of others? And whence is this but from the ardour of love for glory and honour, consequently for self? It is therefore unknown in the world that self-love in itself regarded is the love that rules in hell, and which produces hell in man.

The love of self consists in a man's wishing well to himself alone, and to no others except for the sake of himself,—not even to the church, his country, or any human society; as also in doing good to them for the sake of his own reputation, honour, and glory; which unless he sees in the uses he performs to others, he says in his heart, What does it concern me? What does it concern me? Why should I do this? Of what advantage is it to me? And so he lets it pass. Whence it is evident that one who is in the love of self neither loves the church, nor his country, nor society, nor any use, but himself alone. His delight is only the delight of the love of self; and as the delight that comes from his love constitutes the life of a man, his life is a life of self; and a life of self is a life from a man's *proprium*, and the *proprium* of man, in itself regarded, is nothing but evil. He who loves himself loves also his own; who in particular are his children and grandchildren; and in general, all who make one with him, whom he calls his own. To love these is also to love himself; for he looks upon them in himself, as it were, and himself in them. Among those whom he calls his are also all who praise, honour, and reverence him. (H. H. n. 555, 556.)

Such indeed is the nature of the love of self, that in so far as the reins are given to it, that is, in so far as external restraints are removed,—which are the fear of the law and its penalties, and of the loss of reputation, of honour, of gain, of employment, and of life,—in so far it rushes on, until at length it not only desires to rule over the whole terrestrial globe, but also over the whole heaven, and over the Divine [Being] Himself. It has no limit or bound. This propensity lurks within every one who is in self-love, although it is not evident before the world, where the above-mentioned restrains keep it back. That this is so no one can fail to see in potentates and kings, with whom there are no such curbs and restraints; who, so far as they succeed in their purposes, rush on and subjugate provinces and kingdoms, and aspire after unlimited power and glory. That it is so is still more manifest from the Babylon of this day, which has extended its dominion to heaven, and transferred to itself all the Divine power of the Lord, and lusts continually for more.   (*ib.* n. 559.)

THE FIRE OF HELL AND THE GNASHING OF TEETH.

Infernal fire or love comes from the same origin as heavenly fire or love, namely, from the sun of heaven or the Lord ; but it is made infernal by those who receive it.   For all influx from the spiritual world varies according to reception, or according to the forms into which it flows ; not differently from the heat and light from the sun of the world.   The heat flowing thence into plantations and gardens produces vegetation, and also brings forth grateful and delicious odours ; and the same heat flowing into excrementitious and cadaverous substances produces putrefaction, and draws forth noisome and disgusting stenches.   So the light from the same sun produces in one subject beautiful and charming colours, in another those that are ugly and disagreeable.   It is the same with the heat and light from the sun of heaven, which is love.   When the heat or love thence flows into goods,—as in good men and spirits, and in angels,—it renders their goods fruit-. ful ; but when it flows into the wicked it produces a contrary effect, for their evils either suffocate or pervert it.   So with the light of heaven ; when it flows into the truths of good it gives intelligence and wisdom ; but when it flows in into the falsities of evil, it is there turned into insanities and fantasies of various kinds.   Thus everywhere the effect is according to reception.

Infernal fire being the love of self and of the world is therefore every lust which comes of those loves; since lust is the love in its continuity, for what the man loves he continually lusts after.   And it is likewise delight ; for what the man loves or lusts after, when he obtains it he perceives to be delightful, nor is delight of heart communicated to the man from any other source.   Infernal fire, therefore, is the lust and delight which stream forth from these two loves as their origins.   (H. H. n. 569, 570.)

Since by infernal fire is meant every lust to do evil which flows from the love of self, therefore by the same fire is also meant such torment as there is in the hells.   For the lust from that love is a lust to injure others who do not honour, venerate, and worship them ; and in proportion to the anger thence conceived, and the hatred and vindictiveness from anger, is the lust of venting their rage upon them.   And when there is such a lust in every one, in a society where they are coerced by no external restraints,— which are fear of the law, and of the loss of reputation, of honour, of gain, and of life,—there every one, out of his own evil, rushes upon another, and in so far as he is able subjugates and subjects the rest to his dominion; and with delight raves against those that do not submit. This delight is closely connected with the delight of tyrannous rule, insomuch that they exist in a similar degree; for the delight of inflicting injury is inherent in enmity, envy, hatred, and vindictiveness, which, as was said above, are the evils of that love. All the hells are such societies. Every one there bears hatred against others therefore in his heart; and as far as he is able, from hatred breaks forth into cruelties. These cruelties and the torments from them are also meant by infernal fire; for they are the effects of lusts. (*ib.* n. 573.)

The gnashing of teeth is the continual disputing and combating of falsities, and consequently of those who are in falsities, with each other, joined also with contempt of others, with enmity, derision, mockery, and blaspheming; which evils likewise burst forth into violent assaults of various kinds; for every one fights for his own falsity and calls it truth. These disputings and combatings are heard without those hells as the gnashings of teeth; and are actually turned into gnashings of teeth, when truths from heaven flow in there. In these hells are all those who have acknowledged nature and denied the Divine [Being]; those who have confirmed themselves in such acknowledgment and denial are in profounder hells. These, because they can receive nothing of light from heaven, and can therefore inwardly see nothing within themselves, are for the most part sensual-corporeal spirits, or such as believe nothing but what they see with their eyes and touch with their hands. Hence all the fallacies of the senses to them are truths; and it is from these that they dispute. It is from this cause that their disputes are heard as the gnashings of teeth; for in the spiritual world all falsities are grating, and teeth correspond to the ultimate things in nature, and also to the ultimate things in man, which are sensual-corporeal things. That there is gnashing of teeth in the hells may be seen in Matt. viii. 12; xiii. 42, 50; xxii. 13; xxiv. 51. (*ib.* n. 575.)

THE PROFOUND WICKEDNESS AND NEFARIOUS ARTS OF INFERNAL SPIRITS.

In the same degree that there is wisdom and intelligence among the angels, there is also wickedness and cunning among infernal spirits. . . . In the life of the body the evil in the spirit of a man was under the restraints which are imposed upon every man by the law, by his love of gain, of honour, and the fear of losing them; and therefore the evil of the spirit could not then break forth and manifest itself, as it was in itself. Besides, the evil in the spirit of a man then also lay wrapped up and veiled in the outward probity, sincerity, justice, and affection for truth and good, which such a man manifested and feigned for the sake of the world. The evil lay so concealed and in such obscurity under these semblances, that he scarcely knew himself that his spirit contained so much wickedness and craft, and that therefore in himself he was such a devil as he becomes after death, when his spirit comes into itself and into his own nature. Such wickedness then manifests itself as exceeds all belief. There are thousands of evils which then burst forth from evil itself; among which are even such as no words of any language can express. It has been given me to know and also to apperceive their nature by much experience; for it has been granted me by the Lord to be in the spiritual world as to the spirit, and at the same time in the natural world as to the body. This I can testify, that their wickedness is so great that it is scarcely possible to describe even a thousandth part of it; and also that if the Lord did not protect man he could never be rescued from hell.

The worst of all are those who have been in evils from self-love, and who at the same time, in their interior selves, have acted from deceit; for deceit enters more deeply than any other evil into the thoughts and intentions, and infects them with poison, and so destroys all the spiritual life of a man. Most of these are in the hells behind, and are called genii; and their delight there is to make themselves invisible and flit about others like phantoms, secretly infusing evils into them, which they spread around like the charms of the viper. These are more direfully tormented than others. And those who were not deceitful, and not so eaten up with malignant cunning, and yet were in evils from self-love, are also in the hells behind, but not in so deep hells. But those who have been in evils from the love of the world are in the hells in front, and are called spirits. They are not in such evils, that is not in such hatreds and vindictiveness, as those who are in evils from the love of self; consequently they have not such profound wickedness and cunning. Their hells are therefore more mild. (H. H. n. 577, 578.)

The nature of the wickedness of infernal spirits is evident from their nefarious arts, which are so many that to enumerate them would fill a volume, and to describe them, many volumes. These arts are almost all unknown in the world. One kind relates to the abuse of correspondences; another, to abuses of the ultimates of Divine order; a third, to the communication and influx of thoughts and affections, by conversions, by searching looks, and by other spirits distant from themselves, and by emissaries from themselves; a fourth relate to operations by means of fantasies; a fifth, to a certain casting themselves out beyond themselves, and consequent presence elsewhere than where they are in the body : a sixth, to pretences, persuasions, and lies. Into these arts the spirit of a wicked man comes of itself, when released from the body; for they are inherent in the nature of its evil, in which it then is. By these arts they torment each other in the hells. But as all of these arts, except those that are effected by pretences, persuasions, and lies, are unknown in the world, I will not here describe them specifically, both because they would not be comprehended, and because they are abominable. (*ib.* n. 580.)

The Torments and Punishments of Hell.

Infestation by evils and falsities is signified by having no rest (Rev. xiv. 11); because those that are in hell are continually withheld from their loves, and as often as they break forth into them they are punished; for their loves are the various forms of hatred, vindictiveness, enmity, and lusts to do evil,—which to them are so delightful that they may be called the very delights of their life. To be withheld from them therefore is to be tormented. For every one is in the joy of his heart when he is in his ruling love; and so, on the other hand, he is in anguish of heart when he is withheld from it. This is the common torment of hell; out of which innumerable others arise. (A. E. n. 890.)

Infernal torments are not, as some suppose, the stings of conscience; for they who are in hell have no conscience, and therefore cannot be so tormented. For such as had conscience are. among the blessed. (A. C. n. 965.)

As love to the Lord and towards the neighbour, together with the joy and happiness therefrom, constitute heaven; so hatred against the Lord and the neighbour, together with the punishment and torment therefrom, constitute hell. (*ib.* n. 693.)

The torment does not arise from grief on account of the evil they have done, but from the fact that they cannot do evil; for this is the delight of their life. For when they do evil to others in hell they are punished and tormented by those to whom they do it. They do evil to each other especially from the lust of dominion, and of subjugating others for the sake of it; which is done,—if they do not suffer themselves to be subjugated to another,—by a thousand modes of punishment and torment. But the dominion which they continually aim at there, is in a perpetual state of vicissitude; and thus they who had punished and tormented others are in their turn punished and tormented by others; and this until at length such ardour abates, from fear of punishment. (*ib.* n. 8232.)

The hells have such form and order induced upon them by the Lord that all are held in restraint, and bound by the lusts and fantasies in which their veriest life consists; and as this life is [spiritual] death, it becomes changed into torments, which are so dreadful that they cannot be described. For the veriest delight of their life consists in their ability to punish, torture, and torment each other ; which they do by means of artifices altogether unknown in the world, whereby they excite exquisitely painful sensations, just as if they were in the body, and dire and horrible fantasies, as well as extreme alarm and terror; and by many such means. The diabolical crew perceive so great pleasure in this that were it possible for them infinitely to increase and extend these pangs and torments, yet they would not be satisfied, but would burn with the desire to eternity. The Lord, however, frustrates their efforts, and mitigates the torment they inflict.

Such is the equilibrium of all and every thing in the other life that wickedness punishes itself, so that in evil is the punishment of evil, and falsity returns upon him who is in falsity. Every one therefore brings the punishment and torment upon himself, and then rushes among the diabolical crew which inflict such punishment. (*ib.* n. 695, 696.)

The wicked are not punished in the other life until their evils have reached their utmost ; and this in general, and in particular. For such is the equilibrium in the other life that evil punishes itself, or that the wicked run into the punishment of their evil ; but only when their evil has attained its utmost. Every evil has its limit, though it is different with each individual. This limit they are not permitted to pass ; and when a wicked spirit does pass it he plunges himself into punishment. (*ib.* n. 1857.)

The Use and Effect of Punishments in Hell.

The Lord never casts any one into hell, but would lead all out of hell ; still less does He occasion torment. But as an evil spirit himself rushes into it, the Lord turns all his punishment and torment to good, and to some use. There can never be any punishment but with the Lord there is an end to use in it, for the Lord's kingdom is a kingdom of ends and uses. But the uses which infernal spirits are able to perform are of the basest kind. When they are in these uses they are not so much in torment. But as soon as the use ceases they are remitted into hell. (A. C. n. 696.)

The reason why torments are permitted in the hells by the Lord is, that evils cannot be restrained and subdued otherwise. The fear of punishment is the only means of checking and subduing them, and thus of keeping the infernal crew in restraint. There is no other means. For without the fear of punishment and torment evil would burst forth into madness, and the whole would be scattered, as a kingdom on earth where there is no law and no punishment. (H. H. n. 581.)

While man lives in the world he is continually kept in such a state that he can be reformed, if only of free choice he desists from evils. . . . . But the state of the wicked in the other life is such that as to his interiors he can no longer be amended,[1] but only as to his exteriors, that is to say, by fear of punishment; which when he has frequently suffered he at length abstains,— not of free choice, but by compulsion, his lust to do evil remaining; which lust is held in check, as was said, by fears, which compel, and are the means of an external amendment. (A. C. n. 6977.)

Appearance, Situation, and Plurality of the Hells.

The hells do not appear, because they are closed, but only the entrances, which are called gates,—when they are opened to let in other similar spirits. All the gates to the hells open from the world of spirits, and none from heaven.

The hells are everywhere, both under mountains, hills, and rocks, and under plains and valleys. The apertures or gates to the hells that are under the mountains, hills, and rocks, appear to the sight as holes and clefts of rocks; some stretching wide and large, some strait and narrow, some rugged. They all when looked into appear dark and gloomy, but the infernal spirits that are within them are in a light of similar quality to that from a fire of coals. Their eyes are accommodated to the reception of that light; and this by reason of the fact that while they lived in the world they were in thick darkness as to Divine truths, in consequence of denying them, and in light as it were in respect to falsities, through affirming them,—whereby the sight of their eyes was thus formed. Hence also it is that the light of heaven is thick darkness to them; and therefore when they come out of their dens they see nothing.

The apertures or gates to the hells that are beneath the plains and valleys appear in different forms to the sight; some, like those that are beneath the mountains, hills, and rocks; some as dens and caverns; some as great chasms and gulfs; some as bogs; and some as stagnant lakes of water. All are entirely covered, nor are they opened except when evil spirits from the world of spirits are cast into them; and when they are opened

[1] See p. 582.

there is an exhalation from them, either like that of fire and smoke, such as appears in the air from a conflagration, or like a flame without smoke, or like soot such as comes from a chimney on fire, or like a mist and dense cloud. I have heard that the infernal spirits do not see these things, and are not sensible of them, because when they are in them they are as it were in their own atmosphere, and thus in the delight of their life; and this for the reason that these things correspond to the evils and falsities in which they are; namely, fire to hatred and revenge; smoke and soot to the falsities therefrom; flame to the evils of the love of self; and mist and dense cloud to the falsities from them.

It has also been granted me to look into the hells, and see what is the character of them within. For when it is the Lord's good pleasure a spirit or angel who is above may penetrate by sight into the depths beneath, and explore their character, notwithstanding the coverings. Thus too has it been permitted me to look into them. Some hells appeared to the sight as holes and caves in rocks extending inwards, and thence also obliquely or perpendicularly into an abyss. Some hells appeared to the sight like dens and caverns, such as are inhabited by the wild beast in a forest; some like vaulted caverns and subterraneous passages, such as there are in mines, with caves in the direction of lower parts. Most of the hells are threefold. The higher appear within in thick darkness, because inhabited by those who are in falsities of evil; and the lower appear fiery, because inhabited by those who are in evils themselves. For thick darkness corresponds to the falsities of evil, and fire to the evils themselves; for they who have acted from evil interiorly are in deeper hells; and they who have done the same exteriorly, that is from falsities of evil, are in those that are less deep. In some hells there is an appearance as of the ruins of houses and cities after a fire, in which ruins the infernal spirits dwell, and conceal themselves. In the milder hells there is an appearance as of rude cottages, in some cases contiguous in the form of a city, with lanes and streets. Within the houses are infernal spirits, where there are continual quarrels, enmities, fightings, and violence; in the streets and lanes are robberies and plunderings. In some of the hells there are nothing but brothels, which are disgusting to the sight, full of every kind of filth and excrement. There are also dark forests, in which infernal spirits roam like wild beasts, and where likewise there are subterraneous caves into which they flee who are pursued by others. There are deserts too, where all is barren and sandy, and where in some places there are rugged rocks in which there are caverns, and in some places huts. Such as have suffered the extremity [of punishment] are cast out of the hells into these desert places; especially those who in the world had been more cunning than others in plotting and devising deceptions and intrigues. Their last condition is such a life. (H. H. n. 583-586.)

The hells are innumerable, near to and remote from one another according to the differences of evils, general, specific and particular. There are likewise hells beneath hells. There are communications of some [with others] by passages, and there are communications of more [with others] by exhalations, and this exactly according to the affinities of one genius and one species of evil with others. How great is the number of the hells it has been given me to know from the fact that there are hells under every mountain, hill, and rock, and also under every plain and valley [in the spiritual world], and that they extend themselves in length, breadth, and depth beneath them. In a word, the whole heaven, and the whole world of spirits, are as it were excavated beneath, and under them there is a continuous hell. (*ib.* n. 588.)

Equilibrium between Heaven and Hell.

Hell in like manner with heaven is distinguished into societies, and also into as many societies as heaven; for every society in heaven has a society opposite to it in hell, and this for the sake of equilibrium. But the societies in hell are distinct according to evils and the falsities from them, because the societies in heaven are distinct according to goods and the truths therefrom. That to every good there is an opposite evil, and to every truth an opposite falsity, may be known from the fact that there is nothing without a relation to its opposite; and that from the opposite its quality is cognized, and in what degree it is; and that hence comes all perception and sensation. The Lord continually provides that every society of heaven has its opposite in a society of hell, and that there is an equilibrium between them. (H. H. n. 541.)

The equilibrium between the heavens and the hells is diminished and increases according to the number of those who enter heaven and who enter hell, which amounts to many thousands daily. But no angel can know and perceive this, and regulate and equalize the balance, but the Lord alone. For the Divine proceeding from the Lord is omnipresent, and everywhere observes which way there is any preponderance; whereas an angel only sees what is near himself, and has not even a perception within him of what is doing in his own society.

How all things are ordered in the heavens and in the hells, that all and each of those who are there may be in their equilibrium, may in some measure appear from what has been said and shown respecting the heavens and the hells; namely, that all the societies of heaven are distinct in the most perfect order, according to goods and their genera and species; and all the societies of hell, according to evils and the genera and species of them; and that beneath every society of heaven there is a society of hell corresponding by opposition, from which opposite correspondence equilibrium results. It is therefore continually provided of the Lord that no infernal society beneath a heavenly society shall prevail; and as soon as it begins to prevail it is restrained by various means, and reduced to a just ratio for equilibrium. (*ib.* n. 593, 594.)

FREEDOM OF THE INFERNALS.

I have listened to evil spirits who inwardly were devils, and who in the world rejected the truths of heaven and the church; when the affection for knowing, in which every man is from childhood, was excited in them, by the glory that like the brightness of a fire surrounds every love, they could perceive arcana of angelic wisdom equally as well as good spirits, who inwardly were angels. Nay, the diabolical spirits declared that they could indeed will and act according to them, but that they will not. When told that they might will them if only they would shun evils as sins, they said they could do that also, but that they will not. Whence it was evident that the wicked equally with the good have the faculty which is called liberty. Let any one consult himself, and he will observe that it is so. (D. L. W. n. 266.)

EVIL SPIRITS ARE RESTRAINED FROM PLUNGING INTO GREATER DEPTHS OF EVIL THAN THEY HAD REACHED IN THE WORLD.

After death a man who is in evil is no longer capable of being reformed; and, lest he should have communication with some society of heaven, all truth and good is taken away from him,[1] and he therefore remains in evil and falsity; which evil and falsity increase there according to the faculty of receiving them which he has acquired to himself in the world. But yet he is not permitted to go beyond the limits acquired. (A. C. n. 6977.)

[1] See Vastation, p. 601.

It was perceived that the moment a spirit rushes or endeavours to rush beyond those things which he has by actuality acquired to himself in life, that is to say, into greater evils, he instantly incurs punishment, that he may not acquire more evil to himself by actuality in the other life. (S. D. n. 4055.)

If evil spirits do any evil in the world of spirits beyond what they have been imbued with by their life in the world, punishers are instantly at hand, and chastise them just according to the degree that they overstep [this limit]; for it is a law in the other life, that no one must become worse than he had been in the world. Those that are punished are entirely ignorant whence these chastisers know that the evil is beyond what they have been imbued with. But they are informed that such is the order in the other life that evil itself has the punishment within it, so that the evil of a deed is entirely conjoined with the evil of the punishment; that is, that its punishment is in the evil itself; and therefore that it is according to order that recompensers be instantly at hand. Thus it is when evil spirits do evil in the world of spirits. But in his own hell one chastises another, according to the evil with which they were actually imbued in the world; for this evil they carry with them into the other life. (A. C. n. 6559.)

The Deadly Sphere of Hell.

It has been given me sometimes to perceive the sphere of falsity from evil flowing from hell. It was like a perpetual effort to destroy all good and truth, combined with anger, and as it were fury, because it could not. The effort was especially to destroy and annihilate the Divinity of the Lord; and this, because all good and truth are from Him. But a sphere from heaven was perceived, of truth from good, by which the fury of the effort ascending from hell was restrained. Hence there was an equilibrium. This sphere from heaven was perceived to be from the Lord alone, although it appeared to be from the angels in heaven. That it was perceived to be from the Lord alone, and not from the angels, was because every angel in heaven acknowledges that nothing of good and truth is from himself, but that all is from the Lord.

In the spiritual world all power is of truth from good, and there is no power at all in falsity from evil; because the Divine itself in heaven is Divine good and Divine truth, and all power is from the Divine. . . . Hence it is that in heaven is all power, and in hell none. (H. H. n. 538, 539.)

THE LAST JUDGMENT.

BY the last judgment the last time of a church is meant; and also, the last time of life with every one. As regards its being the last time of a church :—There was a final judgment of the Most Ancient church, or that before the flood, when their posterity perished, whose destruction is described by the flood. There was a final judgment of the Ancient church, which was after the flood, when almost all who were of that church became idolaters, and were dispersed. There was a final judgment of the representative church which succeeded, among the posterity of Jacob, when the ten tribes were led away into captivity, and dispersed among the nations; and subsequently the Jews, after the advent of the Lord, were driven out of the land of Canaan, and scattered over the whole earth. The last judgment of this church which is called the Christian church is what is meant, by John in the Apocalypse, by the new heaven and the new earth. (A. C. 2118.)

Every one, whether evil or good, is judged immediately after death,—when he enters the spiritual world, in which he is to live to eternity. For a man is then immediately designated either for heaven or for hell; he who is designated for heaven is allied to some heavenly society, into which he will afterwards enter; and he who is designated for hell is allied to some infernal society, into which he will afterwards enter. But a period of time intervenes, before they enter there, in order, especially, that they may be prepared; the good, that the evils may be wiped away, which adhere to them from the body in the world; and the evil, that the good may be taken away which outwardly adheres to them from education and religion; according to the Lord's words in Matthew :—" *Whosoever hath, to him shall be given, that he may have more abundantly; but whosoever hath not, from him shall be taken away even that which he hath*"—(xiii. 12; xxv. 29). This delay is effected in order that the affections, which are of many kinds, may be set in order and subjected to the reigning love, so that the man-spirit shall be entirely his own love. But yet, many of them, both of the evil and of the good, are reserved till the last judgment ; but, of the evil, only those who from habit in the world could live an outwardly moral life ; and of the good, those who from want of knowledge and from religion have been imbued with falsities. But the rest, after a suitable time, are separated from them, the good being taken up into heaven, and the evil cast into hell, and this before the last judgment. (A. E. n. 413.)

THE LAST JUDGMENT DOES NOT INVOLVE THE DESTRUCTION OF THE WORLD.

They who are unacquainted with the spiritual sense of the Word, have understood no otherwise than that at the day of the last judgment all things that appear before the eyes in the world will be destroyed ; for it is said that then heaven and earth will perish, and that God will create a new heaven and a new earth. They have also confirmed themselves in this opinion, by the fact that it is said that all are then to rise from their graves, and that then the good are to be separated from the evil, and so on. But it is thus said in the literal sense of the Word, because the literal sense of the Word is natural, and in the ultimate of Divine order, where each and all things contain a spiritual sense within them. For which reason he who only comprehends the Word according to the sense of the letter may be carried away into various opinions ; as has actually been the case in the Christian world, where so many heresies hence arise, and every one of them confirmed from the Word. But as no one has known hitherto that there is a spiritual sense in each and all things of the Word, nor even what a spiritual sense is, they are therefore to be excused who have embraced this opinion respecting the last judgment. But they may even now know, that neither the visible heaven nor the habitable earth will perish, but that both will remain ; and that by a new heaven and a new earth a new church is meant, both in the heavens and on earth. It is said a new church in the heavens, because the church is there equally as on earth. For the Word is equally there, and there are preachings, and similar Divine worship as on earth ; but with the difference that there all things are in a more perfect state, because there they are not in the natural world but the spiritual. Hence all there are spiritual men, and not natural, as they were in the world.

The passages in the Word where it speaks of the destruction of heaven and earth are the following :—" *Lift up your eyes to heaven, and look upon the earth beneath ; the heavens shall vanish away like smoke, and the earth shall wax old like a garment* " (Isa li. 6). "*Behold, I will create new heavens and a new earth ; neither shall former things be remembered*" (Isa. lxv. 17). "*I will make new heavens and a new earth*" (Isa. lxvi. 22). "*The stars of heaven fell unto the earth,* . . . . *and the heaven departed as a scroll when it is rolled together*" (Rev. vi. 13, 14). "*I saw a great throne, and One sitting thereon, from whose face the earth and the heaven fled away, and the place of them was not found*" (Rev. xx. 11). "*I saw a new heaven and a new earth, for the first heaven and the first earth were passed away*" (Rev. xxi. 1.) By the new heaven in these passages the heaven visible to our eyes is not meant, but the very heaven where the human race was assembled. For a heaven was collected from all the human race, from the beginning of the Christian church ; but they who were there were not angels, but spirits,[1] of various religions. This heaven is meant by the first heaven which was to perish. . . . . . Every one indeed, who thinks from a somewhat enlightened reason, may perceive, that it is not the starry heaven, the so immense firmament of creation, that is meant, but heaven in the spiritual sense, where angels and spirits are.

Hitherto it has been unknown that by "a new earth" a new church on earth is meant ; because by earth, in the Word, every one has understood the earth, when yet it means the church. In the natural sense the earth is the earth, but in the spiritual sense it is the church. The reason is that they who are in the spiritual sense,—that is who are spiritual, as the angels are,—when the earth is mentioned in the Word, do not understand the earth itself, but the people who are there, and their Divine worship. It is from this that the earth signifies the church. I will adduce one or two passages from the Word, from which it may in some measure be perceived that the earth signifies the church. "*The flood-gates from on high are opened, and the foundations of the earth do shake ; by breaking the earth is broken ; by quaking the earth doth quake ;* . . . *by reeling the earth doth reel like a drunkard ; it swayeth to and fro like a cottage ; and heavy upon it is the transgression thereof*" (Isa. xxiv. 18-20). "*I will make a man to be more rare than fine gold ;* . . . . . *therefore I will shake the heaven, and the earth shall be removed out of her place,* . . . . . *in the day of the fierceness of the anger of Jehovah*" (Isa. xiii. 12, 13). "*The land did quake before Him, the heavens trembled, the sun and the moon were darkened, and the stars withdrew their shining*" (Joel ii. 10). "*The earth shook and trembled, the foundations also of the mountains moved and were shaken*" (Psalm xviii. 7, 8). And many other places.

Moreover in the spiritual sense of the Word, to create signi-

---

[1] By spirits the author invariably means those who are yet in the intermediate state, called the world of spirits. See below, p. 711.

fies to form, to establish, and to regenerate; so that to create a new heaven and a new earth signifies to establish a new church in heaven and on earth. This is plain from the following passages :—" *The people which shall be created shall praise Jah* " (Psalm cii. 18). " *Thou sendeth forth Thy spirit, they are created ; and Thou renewest the faces of the earth* " (Psalm civ. 30). " *Thus said Jehovah, thy Creator, O Jacob, thy Former, O Israel, ... for I have redeemed thee ; and I have called thee by thy name ; thou art Mine. . . . . . Every one that is called by My name, even for My glory I have created, I have formed him, yea, and I have made him* " (Isa. xliii. 1, 7); and elsewhere. Hence it is that the new creation of man is his reformation; since he is made new, that is, from natural is made spiritual. And hence it is that a new creature is a reformed man. (L. J. 1-4.)

THE EARTH AND THE HUMAN RACE WILL ABIDE FOR EVER.

They who have adopted the belief concerning the last judgment, that all things that are in the heavens and on the earth will then be destroyed, and that a new heaven and a new earth will arise in the place of them, believe,—because it follows from the connection of things,—that generations and procreations of the human race are thenceforth to cease. For they think that all things will then have been accomplished, and that man will be in a different state from that before. But as the destruction of the world is not meant by the day of the last judgment,—as was shown in the preceding article,—it follows too that the human race will continue, and that procreations will not cease.

That procreations of the human race will continue to eternity, is evident from many considerations, the chief of which are these :—

I. That the human race is the basis on which heaven is founded.

II. That the human race is the seminary of heaven.

III. That the extent of heaven, which is for angels, is so immense that it cannot be filled to eternity.

IV. That they of whom heaven as yet consists are comparatively few.

V. That the perfection of heaven increases according to its plurality.

VI. And that every Divine work looks to Infinity and Eternity.

The human race is the basis on which heaven is founded because man was last created, and that which is last created is the basis of all that precedes. Creation began from the highest or inmost, because from the Divine, and went forth to the ultimates or extremes, and then first subsisted. The ultimate of the creation is the natural world, and in it the terraqueous globe with all things thereon. When these were completed then man was created, and into him were gathered all things of Divine order, from the first to the last. In his inmost parts were gathered the things which are in the first [degrees] of that order, and in his ultimates those which are in the last; so that man was made Divine order in form. Hence it is that all things in man and with man are both from heaven and from the world; from heaven those which are of his mind, and from the world those which are of his body. For the things which are of heaven flow in into his thoughts and affections, and dispose them according to reception by his spirit; and those which are of the world flow in into his sensations and pleasures, and dispose them according to reception in his body, yet fitly according to the agreement [therewith] of the thoughts and affections of his spirit.

From this it appears that the connection between the angelic heaven and the human race is such that the one subsists from the other, and that without the human race the angelic heaven would be as a house without a foundation, for heaven terminates in it and rests upon it. The case is the same as with a man himself in particular; his spiritual things, which are of his thought and will, flow in into his natural things, which are of his sensations and actions, and there terminate and subsist. If man did not delight also in these, or were without these boundaries and ultimates, his spiritual things which pertain to the thoughts and affections of his spirit would flow away, as things interminate, or that have no bottom. In a similar manner it occurs that when a man passes from the natural world into the spiritual,—which takes place when he dies,—since he is then a spirit, he no longer subsists upon his own basis, but upon the common basis, which is the human race. He who does not know the mysteries of heaven, may believe that angels subsist without men, and men without angels; but I can asseverate from all experience of heaven, and from all discourse with angels, that no angel or spirit subsists without man, and no man without spirit and angel, and that there is a mutual and reciprocal conjunction. From this it can first be seen that the human race and the angelic heaven make one, and subsist mutually and in turn from each other, and thus that the one cannot be removed from the other. (L. J. 6-9.)

It is the angelic heaven for which all things in the universe were created; for the angelic heaven is the end for which the human race was created, and the human race is the end for which the visible heaven and the earths therein exist. Therefore that

Divine work, the angelic heaven, looks primarily to what is infinite and eternal, and accordingly, to its multiplication without end, for the very Divine dwells therein. From this also it is evident that the human race will never cease; for if it were to cease the Divine work would be limited by a certain number, and thus its regard to infinity would disappear. (*ib.* n. 13.)

When the Last Judgment takes place.

A judgment is said to take place when evil has been brought to its height, or as it is expressed in the Word when it is consummated, or when iniquity is consummated. The case is this. All evil has its limits, as far as which it is permitted to go; but when it is carried beyond these limits the transgressor runs into the punishment of evil, and this in particular, and in general. The punishment of evil is what is then called a judgment. (A. C. n. 1311.)

The last judgment takes place when there is an end of the church; and the end of the church is when there is no faith, because there is no charity. There are many reasons why a last judgment takes place when it is the end of the church. The chief reason is, that then the equilibrium between heaven and hell, and with it man's essential liberty, begins to perish; and when man's liberty perishes he can no longer be saved, for he cannot then be led in freedom to heaven, but without freedom is borne down to hell. For no man can be reformed without free will, and all man's free will is from the equilibrium between heaven and hell.

That the equilibrium between heaven and hell begin to perish at the end of the church, may appear from the fact that heaven and hell are from mankind; and that when many go to hell and few to heaven, evil on the one hand increases over good on the other. For in proportion as hell increases evil increases; and all evil is derived to man from hell, and all good from heaven. Now, since evil increases over good at the end of the church, all are then judged by the Lord; the evil are separated from the good, all things are reduced to order, and a new heaven is established, with a new church on earth; and thus the equilibrium is restored. It is this, then, which is called the last judgment. (L. J. n. 33, 34.)

The last judgment of every one in particular is immediately after his death; for he then passes into the other life, in which, when he comes into the life that he had in the body, he is judged either to death or to life. (A. C. n. 1850.)

The Last Judgment must be in the Spiritual World.

The last judgment must be where all are together, and therefore in the spiritual world, and not upon earth. . . . Moreover, no one is judged from the natural man, nor therefore so long as he lives in the natural world, for man is then in a natural body; but he is judged in the spiritual man, and therefore when he comes into the spiritual world, for man is then in a spiritual body. . . . In the spiritual body man actually appears as he is, with respect to love and faith; for every one in the spiritual world is the likeness of his love, not only as to the face and body, but even as to speech and actions. Hence it is that the true qualities of all are known, and their instantaneous separation is effected whenever the Lord pleases. (L. J. n. 28, 30.)

I will here add a certain heavenly arcanum, which indeed has been mentioned in the work on HEAVEN AND HELL, but has not yet been described. Every one after death is bound to some society, even when first he comes into the spiritual world; but in his first state the spirit is ignorant of it, for he is then in externals and not yet in internals. When he is in this state he goes hither and thither, wherever the desires of his outer mind (*animus*) impel him; but still, actually, he is where his love is, that is in a society composed of those who are in similar love. While the spirit is in such a state, he then appears in many other places, in all of them also present as it were with the body; but this is only an appearance. As soon therefore as he is brought by the Lord into his ruling love, he instantly vanishes from the eyes of the others, and is among his own in the society to which he was bound. This peculiarity exists in the spiritual world, and is a wonder to those who are ignorant of its cause. Hence now it is that as soon as spirits are congregated together and separated they are also judged, and every one is presently in his own place, the good in heaven and in a society there among their own, and the wicked in hell in a society there among their own. From these facts also it is evident that the last judgment can take place nowhere but in the spiritual world; both because every one there is in the likeness of his own life, and because he is with those who are in similar life, and therefore every one is with his own. But in the natural world it is not so; the good and the evil can dwell together there; one does not know the quality of another, nor are they separated from each other according to the life's love. Indeed, no one in the natural body can be either in heaven or in hell. Therefore, in order that a man may go to one or the other of them he must put off the natural body, and be judged after he has put it off, in the spiritual body. Hence it is, as was said above that the spiritual man is judged, and not the natural. (*ib.* n. 32.)

The Last Judgment of the First Christian Church has been Accomplished.

It has been granted me to see with my own eyes that the last judgment has now been accomplished; that the evil have been cast into the hells, and the good elevated into heaven ; and thus that all things have been reduced to order, and the spiritual equilibrium between good and evil, or between heaven and hell, has thereby been restored. It was granted me to see from beginning to end how the last judgment was accomplished; and also how the Babylon[1] was destroyed (Rev. xviii.); how those who are understood by the dragon were cast into the abyss; and how the new heaven was formed; and a new church was instituted in the heavens, which is meant by the New Jerusalem. It was granted me to see all these things with my own eyes, in order that I might be able to testify to them. This last judgment was commenced in the beginning of the year 1757, and was fully accomplished at the end of that year.

But it should be known that the last judgment was effected upon those who had lived from the Lord's time to this day, and not upon those who had lived before ; for a last judgment had twice before taken place on this earth. Of these two judgments, the one is described in the Word by the flood, the other was effected by the Lord Himself when He was in the world ; which also is meant by the Lord's words, " *Now is the judgment of this world, now is the prince of this world cast out* " (John xii. 31); and in another place, " *These things I have spoken unto you, that in Me ye may have peace;* . . . *be of good cheer, I have overcome the world* " (xvi. 33); and by these words also in Isaiah, " *Who is this that cometh from Edom,* . . . . *travelling in the multitude of His strength,* . . . . *mighty to save?* . . . *I have trodden the winepress alone,* . . . *therefore I have trodden them in Mine anger; wherefore their victory is sprinkled upon My garments,* . . . . *for the day of vengeance is in Mine heart, and the year of My redeemed is come.* . . . *So He became a Saviour* " (Isa. lxiii. 1-8). And elsewhere in many places. (L. J. 45, 46.)

The Former Heaven and its Abolition.

It is said in the Apocalypse :—" *I saw a great throne, and One sitting upon it, from whose face the heaven and the earth fled*

[1] See *note*, p. 172.

away ; and their place was not found " (xx. 11). And afterwards :—" *I saw a new heaven and a new earth ; the first heaven
and the first earth had passed away* " (xxi. 1).

Before showing what is meant by the first heaven and the
first earth, it should be known that by the first heaven is not
meant the heaven which was formed of those who became
angels from the first creation of the world to that time; for
that heaven is abiding, and endures to eternity.   For all who
enter heaven are under the Lord's protection ; and he who has
once been received by the Lord can never be plucked away from
Him.   By the first heaven a heaven is meant which was made
up of others than those who have become angels ; and for the
most part of those who could not become angels. . . . It is
this heaven of which it is said that it " passed away."   It was
called a heaven because they who were in it formed societies on
high, upon rocks and mountains, and were in delights similar to
natural delights ; but yet they were in none that were spiritual.
For very many who pass from the earth into the spiritual world
believe themselves to be in heaven when they are on high, and
in heavenly joy when they are in such delights as they experienced in the world.   Hence it is that it was called a heaven,
but " *the first heaven which passed away.*"

It should be known, further, that this heaven which is called
the first did not consist of any who had lived before the Lord's
advent into the world ; but that all who composed it lived after
His advent.   For, as was shown above, a last judgment takes
place at the end of every church, a former heaven being then
abolished, and a new heaven created or formed.   (L. J. n. 65-67.)

The first heaven was composed of all those upon whom the
last judgment was effected.   For it was not effected upon those
in hell ; nor upon those in heaven ; nor upon those in the world
of spirits ; nor upon any who were yet living in this world ;
but only upon those who had made to themselves the likeness
of a heaven, of whom the greater part were upon mountains and
rocks.   These indeed are they whom the Lord meant by the
goats, which He placed on the left, in Matt. xxv. 32, 33, and
following verses.   It is therefore evident that the first heaven
arose not merely from Christians, but also from Mahometans
and Gentiles, who all had formed to themselves such heavens in
their own places.   What manner of men they were shall be
stated in few words.   They were those who in the world had
lived in a holy external, and in no holy internal ; who were
just and sincere on account of the civil and moral laws, but not
on account of the Divine laws ; who therefore were external or
natural, and not internal or spiritual men ; who were also in the
doctrinals of the church, and were able to teach them, but

whose lives were not accordant with them; and who filled various offices, and performed uses, but not for the sake of uses. These and all throughout the whole world who were like them, who lived after the Lord's coming, constituted the first heaven. This heaven therefore was such as the world is, and such as the church is on earth among those who do good not because it is good, but because they fear the laws, and the loss of reputation, honour, and gain. They that do good from no other origin fear not God, but men, and have no conscience. In the first heaven of the Reformed there was a large proportion of spirits who believed that man is saved by faith alone, who did not live the life of faith, which is charity, and who loved much to be seen of men. In all these spirits, so long as they were associated together, the interiors were closed, that they might not appear. But when the last judgment was at hand they were opened, and then it was found that inwardly they were possessed with falsities and evils of every kind; and that they were in opposition to the Divine, and were actually in hell. For after death every one is immediately bound to his like, the good to their like in heaven, and the evil to their like in hell; but they do not go to them until the interiors are unveiled. In the meantime they can live together in society with those who resemble them in externals. But it should be known that all who inwardly were good, and therefore spiritual, were separated from them and elevated into heaven; and that all who outwardly as well as inwardly were evil were also separated from them, and cast into hell; and this from the time immediately after the Lord's advent down to the last time, when the judgment took place; and that they only who were of the character above described were left to form among themselves the societies of which the first heaven consisted.

There were many reasons why such societies or such heavens were tolerated. The chief reason was, that by outward sanctity, and by outward sincerity and justice, they were connected with the simple good who were in the ultimate heaven, and who were still in the world of spirits and not yet introduced into heaven. For in the spiritual world there is a communication and thereby a conjunction of all with their like; and the simple good in the ultimate heaven and in the world of spirits look chiefly at the externals, but yet are not inwardly evil. If therefore these spirits had been forcibly removed from them before the appointed time, heaven would have suffered in its ultimates; and yet it is upon the ultimate that the higher heaven rests, as it were upon its basis. That for this reason these spirits were tolerated until the last time, the Lord teaches in these words:—
" The servants of the householder came and said unto him, Didst thou not sow good seed in thy field? whence then hath it the tares?

*And they said, Wilt thou then that we go and gather them up ?
But he said, Nay ; lest while ye gather up the tares, ye root up
also the wheat with them.　Let both therefore grow together until
the harvest ; and in the time of harvest I will say to the reapers,
Gather ye together first the tares, and bind them in bundles to
burn them ; but gather the wheat into my barn. . . . He that
sowed the good seed is the Son of Man ; the field is the world ;
the good seed are the sons of the kingdom, the tares are the sons
of evil, the harvest is the consummation of the age. . . . As
therefore the tares are gathered together and burned in the fire,
so shall it be in the consummation of this age "* (Matt. xiii. 27-30,
37, 40).　(L. J. n. 69, 70.)

Of those meant by the Sheep, the Saints that slept, and the Souls under the Altar.

Of the salvation of the sheep.　After the last judgment was
accomplished there was such joy in heaven, and such light also
in the world of spirits, as there had not been before.　What joy
there was in heaven after the dragon was cast down is described
in the Apocalypse (ch. xii. 10-12) ; and the light in the world
of spirits was because those infernal societies had been interposed
like clouds which darken the earth.　A similar light then arose
also upon men in the world, giving them new enlightenment.
I then saw angelic spirits, in great numbers, rising from below, [*ex inferis,*] and elevated into heaven.　They were the sheep
reserved and guarded there by the Lord for ages back, lest they
should come into the malignant sphere flowing from dragonists, and their charity be suffocated.　These are they who are
meant in the Word by them that "*came forth out of the
graves,*"[1] and by "*the souls of them that were slain*"[2] for the
testimony of Jesus who were watching ; and by them that
have part in "*the first resurrection.*"[3]　(C. L. J. n. 30, 31.)
They who lived according to the Lord's precepts in the Word
and acknowledged His Divinity, thus a life of charity from the
Lord, ... were reserved by the Lord below the heavens, and
protected from the infestation of the hells, until the last judgment ; which being accomplished, they were raised up out of
their places, and elevated into heaven.　The reason why they
were not raised before was, that before the judgment the hells
prevailed, and there was a preponderance on their part ; but
after that the heavens prevailed, and then there was a preponderance on their part.　By the last judgment all things
were reduced to order, both in the hells and in the heavens.　If

---

[1] Matt. xxvii. 52, 53.　　[2] Rev. vi. 9 ; xx. 4.　　[3] Rev. xx. 5, 6.

therefore they had been elevated before, they would not have been able to resist the power with which the hells prevailed over the heavens. That they were elevated it was given me to see ; for I saw whole phalanxes rising up, and elevated from the lower earth where they were reserved by the Lord, and translated into heavenly societies. This took place after the last judgment, treated of in a little work on that subject. The same took place after the former judgment, which was accomplished by the Lord when He was in the world ; of which also in the same work. This arcanum is what is meant by the resurrection of those who before that lived a life of charity. The same is also meant by these words in John : " *Now is the judgment of this world ; now shall the prince of this world be cast out : I, if I be lifted up from the earth, will draw all men unto Me* " (xii. 31-32) ; and was represented by the declaration that :—" *Many of the saints which slept were raised up, and came out of the graves after the Lord's resurrection, and went into the holy city, and appeared unto many* " (Matt. xxvii. 52-53). (A. E. 899.)

" *I saw under the altar the souls of them that were slain for the Word of God, and for the testimony which they held* " (Rev. vi. 9). This signifies those who were hated, abused, and rejected by the wicked, on account of their life according to the truths of the Word and their acknowledgment of the Lord's Divine Humanity, who were guarded by the Lord that they might not be led astray. " Under the altar " signified the lower earth, where they were guarded by the Lord ; the altar signifies the worship of the Lord from the good of love. By " the souls of them that were slain " the martyrs are not here signified, but those that are hated, abused, and rejected by the wicked in the world of spirits, and who might be led astray by dragonists and heretics. " For the Word of God, and for the testimony which they held," signifies for living according to the truths of the Word, and acknowledging the Lord's Divine Humanity. Testimony in heaven is not given to others than those who acknowledge the Lord's Divine Humanity ; for it is the Lord who testifies, and gives the angels to testify : " *For the testimony of Jesus is the spirit of prophecy* " (Apoc. xix. 10). Since they were under the altar it is plain that they were guarded by the Lord ; for they who led in any sort a life of charity were all guarded by the Lord, that they might not be injured by the wicked ; and after the last judgment, when the wicked were removed, they were released from captivity and elevated into heaven. I frequently saw them after the last judgment liberated from the lower earth and translated into heaven. (A. R. n. 325.)

The State of the World and the Church after and in consequence of the Last Judgment.

Before the last judgment was effected much of the communication between heaven and the world, and therefore between the Lord and the church, was intercepted. All enlightenment comes to man from the Lord through heaven, and enters by an internal way. So long as there were congregations of such spirits between heaven and the world, or between the Lord and the church, man could not be enlightened. It was as when a sunbeam is cut off by a black interposing cloud, or as when the sun is eclipsed and its light arrested by the interjacent moon. If therefore anything had then been revealed by the Lord, it either would not have been understood, or if understood, yet it would not have been received, or if received, it would afterwards have been stifled. Now, since all these interposing congregations were dissipated by the last judgment, it is plain that the communication between heaven and the world, or between the Lord and the church, has been restored.

Hence it is that after and not before the last judgment revelations were made for the New Church. For now that communication has been restored by the last judgment, man can be enlightened and reformed ; that is, he can understand the Divine Truth of the Word, can receive it when understood, and retain it when received, for the interposing obstacles are removed. Therefore John said, after the former heaven and the former earth had passed away, that he " *saw a new heaven and a new earth ; and then, the holy city Jerusalem descending from God out of heaven, prepared as a bride adorned for her husband ; . . . . and heard Him that sat upon the throne say, Behold, I make all things new* " (Rev. xxi. 1, 2, 5). (C. L. J. n. 11, 12.)

The state of the world hereafter will be precisely similar to what it has been hitherto ; for this great change which has been effected in the spiritual world does not induce any change in the natural world as to the outward form. So that hereafter there will be affairs of states, there will be peace, treaties, and wars, and other things that belong to societies of men, in general and in particular, just as before. The Lord's saying, that " *in the last times there will be wars, and that nation will then rise against nation, and kingdom against kingdom, and that there will be famines, pestilences, and earthquakes in divers places*" (Matt. xxiv. 6, 7), does not signify such things in the natural world, but corresponding things in the spiritual world. For the Word in its prophecies does not treat of kingdoms or of nations on earth, consequently not of their wars ; nor of famines, pestilences, and earthquakes in nature, but of such things as correspond to them in the spiritual world. What these things are is explained in the ARCANA CŒLESTIA. But as regards the state of the church, it is this which will be dissimilar hereafter; it will indeed be similar as to the outward, but dissimilar as to the internal form. To outward appearance there will be divided churches as before; their doctrines will be taught as before; and likewise the religions among the gentiles. But the man of the church will hereafter be in a more free state of thinking on matters of faith, that is on the spiritual things that relate to heaven, because spiritual liberty has been restored. For all things in the heavens and in the hells are now reduced into order, and all thought on Divine things and against Divine things flows in from thence,—from the heavens all that is in harmony with Divine things, and from the hells all that is in opposition to them. But man does not observe this change of state in himself, because he does not reflect upon it, and because he knows nothing of spiritual liberty, or of influx; nevertheless it is perceived in heaven, and also by man himself after his death. Because spiritual liberty has been restored to man the spiritual sense of the Word is now unveiled, and thereby interior Divine truths are revealed, for in his former state man would not have understood them, or he who would have understood them would have profaned them.

I have had various converse with the angels respecting the state of the church hereafter. They said that they know not things to come; for that the knowledge of things to come belongs to the Lord alone; but that they know that the slavery and captivity in which the man of the church was until this time has been removed; and that now, from the fact that his liberty is restored, he can better perceive interior truths, if he desires to perceive them, and thus become more internal, if he wills to become so; but yet that they have slender hope of the men of the Christian church, but much of some nation distant from the Christian world, and therefore removed from infesters (*infestores*), a nation which is such that it can receive spiritual light, and become a celestial-spiritual man. And they said that interior Divine truths are at this day revealed to that nation, and are also received in spiritual faith, that is in life and heart: and that they worship the Lord. (L. J. n. 73, 74.)

THE EARTHS IN THE UNIVERSE.

IT is well known in the other life that there are many earths, and men upon them, and spirits and angels from them. For, to every one there who desires it from a love of truth, and hence of use, it is granted to converse with the spirits of other earths, and thereby to be assured of a plurality of worlds, and to be informed that the human race is not from one earth only, but from innumerable earths. I have at different times conversed with spirits of our earth on this subject; and it was said that any intelligent person may know, from numerous facts with which he is acquainted, that there are many earths, inhabited by men. For it may be concluded from reason that so large masses as the planets, some of which exceed this earth in magnitude, are not empty bodies, and created only to whirl and travel round the sun, and shine with their scanty light for one earth; but that they must have a nobler use than that. He who believes, as every one ought to believe, that the Divine [Being] created the universe for no other end than that the human race might exist, and thence heaven,—since the human race is the seminary of heaven,—cannot but believe that wherever there is any earth there must also be men. That the planets which are visible to our eyes,—because within the limits of this solar system,—are earths, may be manifestly perceived from the fact that they are bodies of earthy matter, for they reflect the sun's light; and when seen through a telescope appear, not as stars glowing with a flame, but as earths variegated with dark spots. From the fact also that they, in like manner with our earth, revolve around the sun and travel through the path of the zodiac, and thereby cause years, and the seasons of the year, spring, summer, autumn, and winter; likewise that like our earth they revolve upon their own axis, and thereby form days, and times of the day, morning, midday, evening, and night; and moreover that some of them have moons, called satellites, which revolve around their globes in fixed periods, as the moon around ours; and that the planet Saturn, because it is very far distant from the sun, has also a great luminous belt, which gives that earth much though reflected light. Who that knows these facts, and thinks from reason, can ever say that these are empty bodies ? Moreover, when with spirits, I have said that it might be believed by man that there are more earths than one in the universe from the fact that the starry heaven is so immense, and the stars therein of various magnitudes so innumerable; each of which in its place or in its system is a sun, and similar to our sun. Whoever duly considers the subject, must conclude that this so immense whole cannot but be the means to an end, which is the ultimate end of creation ; and this end is a heavenly kingdom, in which the Divine may dwell with angels and men. The visible universe, or the heaven lighted with so innumerable stars, which are so many suns, is in fact only a means that earths may spring forth, and men upon them, from whom there may be a heavenly kingdom. A rational man cannot but think that so immense means to so great an end were not produced for the human race and hence a heaven of one earth. What would this be for the Divine [Being], who is infinite, to whom thousands, nay, myriads of earths, and all filled with inhabitants, would be little, and indeed scarcely anything ? (H. H. n. 417.)

PERMISSION TO DISCOURSE WITH THE INHABITANTS OF OTHER EARTHS.

Since by the Divine mercy of the Lord the interiors, which are of my spirit, are open to me, and thereby it has been granted me to converse not only with the spirits and angels who are near our earth, but also with those that are near other earths ; and as I had a desire to know whether there are other earths, and what they are, and what is the character of their inhabitants ; there-fore it has been granted me of the Lord to converse and be in company with spirits and angels from other earths ; with some for a day, with some for a week, and with some for months ; and to be informed by them respecting the earths from which and near which they were ; and respecting the lives, customs, and worship of the inhabitants of them ; and various other matters there worthy to be mentioned. And as it has been granted me in this manner to know these things, I am permitted to describe them, from things heard and seen. (E. U. n. 1.)

THE POSSIBILITY OF SUCH CONVERSE, AND HOW EFFECTED.

What I have seen was not beheld with my bodily eyes, but with the eyes of my spirit ; for a spirit can see things that are on earth when the Lord grants it.

As I know that many will doubt whether it is ever possible, that a man should be able with the eyes of his spirit to see anything on an earth so distant, I may state how it is effected. Distance in the other life is not like distance on earth. In the other life distances are precisely according to the states of the interiors of every one. They that are in a similar state are together in one society and in one place. All presence there is from similarity of state, and all distance is from its dissimilarity. Hence it was that I could be near an earth when I was led by the Lord into a state similar to that of the spirits and of the inhabitants there, and that being present I then conversed with them. . . . As regards the fact that a spirit, or what is the same a man as to his spirit, can seen things that are on earth, I will explain how it is. Neither spirits nor angels, by their own sight, can see anything that is in the world ; for to them the light of the world, or of the sun, is as thick darkness ; just as a man with his bodily sight can see nothing that is in the other life, because to that sight the light of heaven is as thick darkness. And yet, when it pleases the Lord, spirits and angels can see things in the world, through the eyes of a man. But this is only granted by the Lord with those whom He permits to converse with spirits and angels, and to be in company with them. It has been permitted them to see through my eyes things that are in the world, as plainly as I, and to hear men conversing with me. Sometimes it has occurred that through me some have seen their friends that they had known in the world, and they were amazed. (E. U n. 134, 135.)

The Planet Mercury.

Some spirits came to me, and it was declared from heaven that they were from the earth nearest to the sun, and which on our earth is known by the name of the planet Mercury. As soon as they came they searched out of my memory what I knew. Spirits can do this most adroitly ; for when they come to a man they see in his memory the particular things it contains. During their search after various things, and among others, after the cities and places where I had been, I observed that they had no inclination to know anything of temples, palaces, houses, or streets, but only of the things I knew which were done in those places ; also whatever related to the government there, and to the genius and manners of the inhabitants, and things of this nature. For such things are connected with places in man's memory ; so that when the places are called to remembrance, these things are also brought to view at the same time. I was surprised at this peculiarity, and therefore asked them why they disregarded the magnificence of the places, and only attended to the things and circumstances connected with them? They answered, that they had no delight in looking at things material, corporeal, and terrestrial, but only at things real. It was proved by this experience that the spirits of that earth have relation in the Greatest Man to the memory of things, apart from what is material and terrestrial.

It was told me that such is the life of the inhabitants of that earth; that is to say, that they have no concern about things terrestrial and material, but only about the statutes, laws, and forms of government of the nations there; and also about the things of heaven, which are innumerable. I was further informed that many of the men of that earth converse with spirits, and that thereby they have knowledges of spiritual things, and of the states of life after death. And hence also is their contempt of things corporeal and terrestrial; for they who know of a certainty and believe that they shall live after death are concerned about heavenly things, because they are eternal and happy, and not about worldly things, except so far as the necessities of life require. (E. U. n. 11, 12.)

The spirits of Mercury above all other spirits possess a knowledge both of the things in this solar system, and in the earths in the starry heaven; and what they have once acquired they retain, and also recall to mind as often as similar things occur. (*ib.* n. 14.)

They are averse to verbal discourse, because it is material. When therefore I conversed with them without intermediate spirits I could only do it by a kind of active thought. Their memory being of things, not of images purely material, brings its objects nearer to the thought; for thought, which is above the imagination, requires for its objects things abstracted from what is material. But although it is so, yet the spirits of Mercury are little distinguished by the faculty of judgment; having no delight in matters of judgment, and deducing conclusions from knowledges. Bare knowledges, in fact, are the things which give them pleasure. (*ib.* n. 17.)

The spirits of Mercury differ entirely from the spirits of our earth; for the spirits of our earth do not care so much about immaterial things, but about worldly, corporeal, and terrestrial things, which are material. On this account the spirits of Mercury cannot abide with the spirits of our earth, and therefore wherever they meet them they fly away; for the spiritual spheres exhaled from each are entirely contrary the one to the other. The spirits of Mercury are accustomed to say that they have no wish to look at the husk, but at the things, stripped of the husk, that is, the interiors. (*ib.* n. 20.)

The spirits of Mercury who were with me while I was writing, and explaining the Word as to its internal sense, and who perceived what I wrote, said that the things which I wrote were exceedingly gross (*admodum crassa*), and that almost all the expressions appeared as material. But it was given me to reply, that to the men of our earth what was written appeared subtle and elevated, many things of which they do not apprehend. (*ib.* n. 27.)

I asked whether they had the art of printing among them? But they said they had not, yet they knew that we had printed papers on our earth. They had no inclination to say more; but I perceived that they thought knowledges with us were upon our paper, and not so much in our understandings, thus derisively insinuating, that our papers knew more than we ourselves. But they were informed how the case really is. (*ib.* n. 28.)

I was desirous to know what kind of face and person the inhabitants have upon the earth Mercury, whether they were like the men on our earth. There was then presented before my eyes a woman precisely like the women on that earth. She was of beautiful countenance, but it was smaller than that of a woman of our earth; her body also was more slender, but her height was equal. On her head she wore a linen cap, artlessly but yet gracefully put on. A man also appeared, who likewise was more slender in body than the men of our earth. He was clad in raiment of dark-blue, fitting closely to his body, without folds or skirts. I was told that such is the form of body, and the costume of the men of that earth. Afterwards there was presented to view a species of their oxen and cows; which indeed did not differ much from those on our earth, only that they were smaller, and approached in some degree to a species of stag and hind.

They were asked about the sun of the solar system; how it appears from their earth? They affirmed that it appears large, —larger there than when seen from other earths. They said that they knew this from the ideas of other spirits respecting the sun. They stated further that they enjoy a medium temperature, neither too hot nor too cold. It was given me then to tell them that it was so provided of the Lord, in regard to them, that they should not be exposed to excessive heat from the fact that they are nearer than others to the sun; since the heat does not arise from nearness to the sun, but from the altitude and density of the atmosphere,—as appears from the cold on high mountains even in hot climates; and also that heat is varied according to the direct or oblique incidence of the sun's rays, as is plain from the seasons of winter and summer in every region. (*ib.* n. 44, 45.)

The Planet Venus.

In the planet Venus there are two kinds of men, of opposite character; the first mild and humane, the second savage and almost brutal. Those who are mild and humane appear on the farther side of the earth , and those that are savage and almost brutal appear on the side looking this way. But it should be understood that they thus appear according to the states of their life; for in the spiritual world the state of life determines every appearance of space and of distance.

Some of those who appear on the farther side of the planet, and are mild and humane, came to me and were visibly presented above my head, and conversed with me on various subjects. Among other things they said that when they were in the world they acknowledged our Lord, and acknowledged Him the more now, as their only God. They affirmed that they had seen Him on their earth, and also represented how they had seen Him.

But I did not converse with those spirits who appear from the side looking this way, and who are savage and almost brutal. I was informed by the angels, however, respecting their character, and whence they have so brutal a nature; that in fact they are exceedingly delighted with rapine, and more especially with feeding upon their spoils. Their delight when they think of eating of their spoils was communicated to me, and was perceived to be extreme. . . . I was also informed that these inhabitants are for the most part giants, and that the men of our earth only reach to their navel : and moreover that they are stupid, not inquiring about heaven or eternal life, but that they care only for those things that relate to their land and their cattle. (E. U. n. 106-108.)

The Moon of our Earth.

Certain spirits appeared above my head, and from thence voices were heard like thunder ; for their voices roared like the thunderings from the clouds after lightning. I at first conjectured that it was owing to a great multitude of spirits, who had the art of uttering voices with such a noise. The more simple spirits who were with me derided them, at which I was greatly surprised. But the cause of their derision was presently discovered; which was that the spirits who thundered were not many, but few, and also as small as children , and that before this they had terrified them by such noises, and yet were unable to do them the least harm. In order that I might know their character some of them descended from on high where they were thundering; and what surprised me, one carried another on his back, and thus two of them approached me. Their faces appeared not unhandsome, but longer than the faces of other spirits. In stature they were like children of seven years, but more robust; thus they were diminutive men. It was told me by the angels, that they were from the Moon. He who was carried by the other came to me, applying himself to my left side under the elbow, and thence spoke to me, saying, that whenever they cry out with the voice, they thus thunder ; and that they thereby terrify spirits who would do them injury, and some take to flight ; and that thus they go in security wherever they will. That I might certainly know that this kind of sound was theirs, he retired from me to some others, but not entirely out of sight, and thundered in like manner. And they showed, moreover, that their voice thus thundered by being emitted from the abdomen, after the manner of an eructation. It was perceived that this arose from the fact that the inhabitants of the Moon do not speak from the lungs, like the inhabitants of other earths, but from the abdomen, and so from a quantity of air gathered there; for the reason that the Moon is not surrounded by a similar atmosphere to that of other earths.

That even upon the Moon there are inhabitants is well known to spirits and angels ; and in like manner, that there are inhabitants upon the moons or satellites which revolve about Jupiter and Saturn. Those who have not seen and conversed with spirits coming from those moons, yet entertain no doubt that there are men inhabiting them ; for they equally with the planets are earths, and wherever there is an earth there are men ; for man is the end for which an earth is created, and nothing is made by the Great Creator without an end. (E. U. n. 111, 122.)

The Planet Mars.

The spirits of Mars are the best of all the spirits that come from the earths of this solar system ; being for the most part celestial men, not unlike those who were of the Most Ancient church on this earth. (E. U. n. 85.)

It was given to know that the speech of the inhabitants of Mars was different from that of the inhabitants of our earth, in that it was not sonorous, but almost tacit, insinuating itself into the interior hearing and sight by a shorter way ; and that for this reason it was more perfect, fuller of ideas, thus approaching nearer to the speech of spirits and angels. With them the very affection of the speech is also represented in the face, and its thought in the eyes ; for among them the thought and speech, and the affection and countenance, act in unity. They account it wicked to think one thing and speak another, and to wish one thing while the face expresses another. Hypocrisy is entirely unknown to them; and also fraudulent pretence and deceit. The same kind of speech prevailed among the earliest inhabitants of our earth. (*ib.* n. 87.)

The angelic spirits spoke to me of the life of the inhabitants on their earth; informing me, that they are not under governments, but are in distinct societies, larger and smaller, and are associated together there with such as are of congenial mind; that they know whether they are so instantly by the face and speech; and that they are rarely deceived. They are then instantly friends. They said further that their consociations are delightful; and that they converse with each other about what passes in their societies, and especially about what passes in heaven, for many of them have open communication with the angels of heaven. Such of them in their societies as begin to think perversely and thereby to purpose evil they dissociate from, and leave them to themselves alone; in consequence of which they lead an extremely miserable life out of society, among the rocks or elsewhere, being no longer regarded by the rest. Some societies endeavour to compel such to repentance by various means, but if this is in vain, they dissociate themselves from them. Thus they take care lest the lust of dominion and the lust of gain should creep in, that is, lest any from the lust of dominion should subject any society, and afterwards many others to themselves; and lest any, from the lust of gain, should deprive others of their possessions. Every one there lives content with his own goods, and with his own share of honour; that of being reputed upright, and a lover of his neighbour. This delightful and tranquil state of mind would perish unless those who think and purpose evil were cast out, and a prudent but severe check given to the first encroachments of self-love and the love of the world.

In regard to the Divine worship of the inhabitants of that earth, they informed me that they acknowledge and adore our Lord, saying, that He is the only God, and that He governs both heaven and the universe; that every good is from Him; and that He leads and directs them; also that He often appears among them on earth. It was given me then to tell them that Christians on our earth know also that the Lord governs heaven and earth,—according to His own words in Matthew:—"*All power is given unto Me in heaven and on earth*" (xxviii. 18); but that they do not believe it like those of the earth Mars. (*ib.* n. 90, 91.)

An inhabitant of that earth was presented to me. He was not actually an inhabitant, but like one. His face was like the faces of the inhabitants of our earth; but the lower part of the face was black,—not from a beard, for he had none, but from a blackness in place of a beard. This blackness extended under the ears on both sides; the upper part of the face was tawny, like the faces of the inhabitants of our earth who are not perfectly white. They said that on that earth they subsist on the fruits of trees,—especially on a kind of round fruit which springs out of their ground; and also on pulse; that they are clothed with garments wrought from the fibres of the bark of certain trees, which have such consistence that they can be woven, and also be joined together by a kind of gum which they have among them. They told me also that they know there how to make fluid fires, whereby they have light during the evening and night. (*ib.* n. 93.)

THE PLANET JUPITER.

It was granted me to enjoy longer social intercourse with the spirits and angels of the planet Jupiter than with the spirits and angels from the other planets. I can therefore say more regarding their state of life, and that of the inhabitants of that planet. It was clear to me from many circumstances that those spirits were from that planet, and it was also declared from heaven.

The earth or planet Jupiter itself does not actually appear to spirits and angels, for no material earth is visible to the inhabitants of the spiritual world, but only the spirits and angels who are from it. . . . The spirits of every earth are near their own earth, because they are from the inhabitants of it (for every man becomes a spirit after death), and are therefore of similar genius, and can be with the inhabitants, and be of service to them.

They informed me that the multitude of men in the region of the earth where they dwelt when they were in the world was as great as the earth could support; and that it was fertile, and everything was abundant; that the inhabitants desired nothing beyond the necessaries of life; and accounted what was not necessary as not useful; and that hence was the multitude of inhabitants so great. They said their greatest care was the education of their children; and that they loved them most tenderly.

They stated further that the inhabitants are distinguished into nations, families, and houses; that they all dwell separately, with their own kindred, and that their intercourse is therefore among their relatives. No one covets another's goods;

and it never enters their minds to desire the possessions of another, much less to obtain them fraudulently, and less still to extort them by violence. This they consider a crime contrary to human nature, and regard it with horror. When I would have told them that on this earth there are wars, depredations, and murders, they turned away and were unwilling to hear.

By long intercourse with the spirits of the earth Jupiter, it was evident to me that they were of more excellent character than the spirits of many other earths. Their quiet approach when they came to me, their abode with me, and their influx at the time, were inexpressibly gentle and sweet. In the other life the quality of every spirit manifests itself by an influx which is the communication of his affection; goodness of disposition manifests itself by gentleness and sweetness; by gentleness, in that it is afraid to do harm, and by sweetness, in that it loves to do good. I could clearly distinguish a difference between the gentleness and sweetness of the influx from the spirits of Jupiter, and that from the good spirits of our earth. (E. U. n. 46-50.)

It was also shown me what kind of a face the inhabitants of the earth Jupiter have. Not that the inhabitants themselves appeared to me, but spirits appeared with faces similar to what they had when they were on their earth. But before this was shown, one of their angels appeared behind a bright cloud, who gave permission. And then two faces appeared; they were like the faces of the men of our earth, fair and beautiful. Sincerity and modesty beamed forth from them. . . . . They maintain that the face is not body, since they see, hear, speak, and manifest their thoughts by it, and since the mind thus shines through it. They therefore have an idea of the face as the mind in form. . . . . For this reason the inhabitants of that earth frequently wash and cleanse the face, and also carefully protect it from the sun's heat. They have a covering for the head, made from the inner or outer bark of a tree, of a bluish colour, with which they shade the face. Respecting the faces of the men of our earth, which they saw through my eyes, they said that they were not beautiful; and that the beauty they possess is in the outer skin, and does not consist in the fibres from within. They were surprised that the faces of some were disfigured with warts and pimples, or otherwise deformed. They said that such faces never appear among them. Yet there were some faces that pleased them; namely, such as were cheerful and smiling, and which were a little prominent about the lips.

The reason why they were pleased with the faces that were prominent about the lips was, because their speaking is effected chiefly by the face, and especially by the part of it about the lips; and also because they never use deceit, that is, never speak otherwise than they think; the face therefore is not restrained, but sends forth [its expression] freely. It is otherwise with those who from childhood have learned to dissemble. Their faces are thereby contracted from within, lest anything of the thought should show itself; nor is it outwardly uttered, but is held in readiness either to express or withhold, as shrewdness dictates. The truth of this is evident from an examination of the fibres of the lips, and round about them; for there are manifold series of fibres there, complex, and interwoven, which were not created merely to perform their part in chewing, and speaking by words, but also to express the ideas of the mind.

It was also shown me how thoughts are expressed by the face. Affections, which are of love, are manifested by the looks and their changes; and thoughts, by variations in them as to the interior forms therein. They cannot be further described. The inhabitants of the earth Jupiter have also a language of spoken words, but it is not so loud as with us. One kind of speech aids the other; and life is insinuated into vocal speech by the language of the countenance. I have been informed by the angels, that the first language of all on every earth was expressed by the face, and this from two origins there, the lips and the eyes. The reason why the first language was of this kind was, that the face was formed to portray man's thoughts and volitions. The face is therefore called the likeness and index of the mind. Another reason is, that in the most ancient or earliest times sincerity prevailed, and man had no thought, nor wished to have any, but that he was willing should shine forth from his face. And the affections of the mind, and the thoughts from them, could thus be presented to the life, and fully; they thus actually appeared visibly to the eye, as very many things together in a form. This language, therefore, was as much superior to a language of words as the sight is to the hearing, that is, as the sight of a country is to a verbal description of it. They added that such discourse was in agreement with that of the angels, with whom men in those times had communication; and that when the face speaks, or the mind by the face, angelic speech is with man in its ultimate natural form, but not so when the mouth speaks by words. Every one may comprehend also that with the most ancient people there could not be a language of words, inasmuch as the expressions of vocal language are not poured in, immediately, but must be invented, and applied to things; which could only come to pass in the course of time. So long as man continued sincere and upright such language also remained; but as soon as the mind began to think one thing and speak another,—which it did when man began to love himself, and not his neighbour,—then vocal language began to increase, the face being either silent or deceitful. The internal form of the face was thereby changed, contracted itself, hardened, and began to become almost void of life; while the external form, inflamed with the fire of self-love, appeared to the eyes of men as if it were alive. For this want of life which is under the external does not appear to the eyes of men; but it does to the eyes of the angels, since they see interior things. Such are the faces of those who think one thing and speak another; for simulation, hypocrisy, cunning, and deceit, which at this day are called prudence, induce such faces.

I was further informed by the spirits who were from that earth of various things relating to the inhabitants there, such as their manner of walking, their food, and their habitations. As regards their manner of walking, they do not walk erect like the inhabitants of this and many other earths, nor do they creep, after the manner of animals, but they assist themselves with their hands as they advance, and by turns half raise themselves on their feet; and also at every third step of their progress turn the face to one side and behind them, and at the same time bend the body a little,—which is done hastily; for it is thought unseemly among them to be looked at by others except in the face. As they thus walk they always keep the face elevated, as with us,—that thus they may look to the heavens also as well as to the earth. They do not hold the face down, so as to look at the earth; this they called accursed. The meanest among them do this; who if they do not become accustomed to elevate the face are driven out of their society. When they sit they appear like men of our earth, erect as to the upper part of the body, but they usually sit with the feet crossed. They are very solicitous, not only when they walk but also when they sit, not to be looked at behind, but in the face. They are indeed willing to have their faces seen, because therein the mind appears; for with them the face is never at variance with the mind, and cannot be. Those present with them, therefore, openly know what disposition they are in towards them, which they do not conceal,—especially whether apparent friendship is real, or whether it is constrained. These things were shown me by their spirits, and confirmed by their angels. Hence their spirits also are seen to walk, not as others, erect, but almost as swimmers advance, aiding themselves with their hands, and by turns looking around.

Those who live in their warm zones go naked, with a covering, however, about the loins; nor are they ashamed of their nakedness, for their minds are chaste, loving none but their consorts, and abhorring adultery. They were greatly astonished that spirits of our earth derided and thought lasciviously when they heard that they walked in this way, and were naked, and did not at all regard their heavenly life, but only such things. They said it was a sign that things corporeal and terrestrial were of more concern to them than heavenly things, and that indecencies occupied their minds. Those spirits of our earth were told that nakedness is no shame nor scandal to those who live in chastity and in a state of innocence, but only to those who live in lasciviousness and lewdness. (*ib.* n. 52, 56.)

They take delight in making long meals, not so much for the pleasure of eating, as for the pleasure of conversation at the time. When they sit at meat, they do not sit on chairs or benches, nor on turfy banks, nor on the grass, but upon the leaves of a certain tree. They were not willing to tell of what tree the leaves were; but when I had guessed at several, and at last named it, they affirmed that they were leaves of the fig-tree. They said, moreover, that they did not dress their food to please the taste, but chiefly with a view to what is wholesome. They affirmed that wholesome food is savoury to them. A conversation took place among the spirits on this subject, and it was urged that this would be well for man; for thus he would have at heart, that a sound mind must be in a sound body. It is otherwise with those with whom the taste governs; the body thereby becomes diseased, at the least is inwardly enfeebled, and consequently the mind also; for this acts according to the interior state of the bodily parts receiving it,—just as the sight and hearing depend on the state of the eye and ear. Hence the insanity of placing all the delight of life in luxury and pleasure. From this also come dulness in matters of thought and judgment, and acuteness in such as relate to the body and the world. From this comes man's likeness to a brute animal; with which such men not incongruously compare themselves.

Their dwellings were also shown me. They are low, constructed of wood, and within are lined with bark, of a pale blue colour; and the walls and ceiling were pricked as it were with little stars, in imitation of the heavens. For they are fond of thus picturing the visible heaven with its stars upon the interiors of their houses, because they believe the stars to be the abodes of the angels. They have also tents, which are rounded above, and extended in length, dotted likewise within with little stars on a blue ground. They retire into these in the middle of the day, lest their faces should suffer from the heat of the sun. They bestow great care upon the construction and cleanliness of these their tents. In these they also take their meals.

When the spirits of Jupiter saw the horses of this earth the horses appeared to me smaller than usual, although they were rather robust and large. This was from the idea of those spirits of the horses there. They said there were horses among them also, but much larger ; but that they were wild, or in the woods, and that when they are seen they terrify the inhabitants, although they are harmless. They added, that the fear of horses is innate or natural to them. (*ib.* n. 59, 60.)

The inhabitants of the earth Jupiter make wisdom to consist in thinking well and justly on all occurrences in life. This wisdom they imbibe from their parents from childhood, and it is transmitted in succession to their posterity ; and from the love of it, because it was with their forefathers, it increases. Of knowledges such as are cultivated in our earth they know nothing, nor wish to know. They call them shades, and compare them to clouds that intercept the sun. This idea of knowledges they have conceived from some spirits from our earth who commended themselves to them as wise on account of their knowledge. The spirits from our earth who thus boasted were such as made wisdom to consist in such things as belong merely to the memory ; as in the languages, especially Hebrew, Greek, and Latin ; in things memorable in the world of literature ; in criticism ; in bare experimental discoveries ; and in terms, especially philosophical ; and things of this kind. They do not use them as means to wisdom, but make wisdom to consist in these things themselves. (*ib.* n. 62.)

As regards their Divine worship, its chief characteristic is that they acknowledge our Lord as Supreme, who governs heaven and earth, whom they call the one only Lord. And as they acknowledge and worship Him during their life in the body, they seek and find Him after death. He is the same with our Lord. They were asked whether they know that the only Lord is a Man ? They replied, that they all know that He is a Man, for in their world He has been seen by many as a Man ; and that He instructs them concerning the truth, preserves them, and gives eternal life to those who from good worship Him. They said further that it is revealed to them from Him how they should live, and how believe ; and that what is revealed is handed down from parents to children ; and from this, doctrine is spread abroad to all families, and so to the whole nation which is descended from one father. They added that it appears to them as if they had the doctrine written upon their minds. This they conclude from the fact that they instantly perceive and acknowledge as of themselves, whether it be true or not that is said by others respecting the life of heaven in man. They do not know that their only Lord was born a Man on our earth ; they said that it does not concern them to know it, but only that He is a Man, and governs the universe. When I told them that on our earth

He is named Jesus Christ, and that Christ signifies Anointed or King, and Jesus, Saviour, they said, they do not worship Him as a King, because a king savours of what is worldly, but that they worship Him as the Saviour. (*ib.* n. 65.)

They said that they have no holy days, but that every morning at sunrise, and every evening at sunset, they perform holy worship to the one only Lord in their tents; and that after their manner they also sing psalms. (*ib.* n. 69.)

I afterwards talked with the angels about some of the remarkable things on our earth, especially about the art of printing, about the Word, and the various doctrinals of the Church from the Word; and I told them that the Word and the doctrinals of the Church are widely published, and thus learned. They wondered exceedingly that such things could be made public by writing and by printing. (*ib.* n. 81.)

They do not fear death there, except for the reason that they must leave their conjugial partner, their children, or parents; for they know that they shall live after death, and that they do not quit life, for they go to heaven. They therefore do not call death dying, but being heaven-made. Those on that earth who have lived in truly conjugial love, and have taken such care of their children as behoves parents, do not die of disease, but tranquilly as in sleep, and so pass over from the world into heaven. The age of men there for the most part is thirty years, according to the years of our earth. It is of the Lord's Providence that they die within a space of time so brief, that the multitude of men there may not increase beyond the number which that earth can support. And because when they have fulfilled those years, they do not suffer themselves to be led by spirits and angels, like those who have not fulfilled them, therefore spirits and angels rarely approach them after that period of life. They also mature more rapidly than on our earth. Even in the first flower of youth they marry; and then their delights are to love their consort and to take care of their children. Other delights indeed they call delights, but relatively external. (*ib.* n. 84.)

The Planet Saturn.

It was given me to speak with spirits from the planet Saturn, and thereby to become acquainted with their character in comparison with others. They are upright, and they are modest, and as they esteem themselves small, they therefore also appear small in the other life.

In worship they are extremely humble; for in this they esteem themselves as nothing. They worship our Lord and acknowledge Him as the one only God. The Lord also sometimes appears to them, under an Angelic Form, and thus as a Man, and the Divine then beams forth from His face and affects the mind. The inhabitants also speak with spirits, when they come of age, by whom they are instructed concerning the Lord, and how they ought to worship, and how to live. When any attempt is made to seduce the spirits who come from the earth Saturn, and to withdraw them from faith in the Lord, or from humiliation towards Him, and from uprightness of life, they say they wish to die. (*ib.* n. 98.)

They said that there are some also on their earth who call the nocturnal light, which is great, the Lord; but that they are separated from the rest, and are not tolerated by them. This nocturnal light comes from the great belt which encircles that earth at a distance, and from the moons which are called the satellites of Saturn.

I was further informed by the spirits of that earth respecting the associations of the inhabitants, and other matters. They said that they live apart in families, each particular family by itself; that is a husband and wife, with their children; and that these children, when they marry, are separated from the house of their parents, and have no further care about it. The spirits from that earth therefore appear two and two. They have little solicitude about food and raiment. They subsist on fruits and pulse which their earth produces; and are slightly clothed, being girt about with a coarse covering or coat, which keeps out the cold. Moreover, all on that earth know that they shall live after death; and therefore they make nothing of their bodies, only so far as is needful to life, which they say is to remain and serve the Lord. For this reason also they do not bury the bodies of the dead, but cast them forth, and cover them with branches of trees from the wood.

Being asked about the great ring which appears from our earth to rise above the horizon of that planet, and vary its situations, they said, it does not appear to them as a ring, but only as a something white as snow in the heavens, in various directions. (*ib.* n. 103, 104.)

EARTHS OF OTHER SOLAR SYSTEMS.

He who does not know the mysteries of heaven cannot believe that man is capable of seeing earths so remote, and of giving any account of them from sensible experience. But he should know, that the spaces and distances and consequent progressions which exist in the natural world, in their origin and first cause are changes of state of interior things, and that with angels and spirits they appear according to such changes , and that therefore angels and spirits by such changes can be apparently translated from one place to another, and from one earth to another,—even to earths at the farthest limits of the universe. So can a man also, as to his spirit, his body remaining in its place. This has occurred with me; since, by the Lord's Divine Mercy, it has been given me to be in company with spirits as a spirit, and at the same time with men as a man. . . . . . The truth which I am now about to state respecting earths in the starry heaven is from actual experimental evidence. From which it will also appear in what manner as to my spirit I was translated thither, my body remaining in its place. (E. U. n. 125, 126.)

At a time when I was wide awake I was led by angels from the Lord, as to the spirit, to a certain earth in the universe, accompanied by some spirits from this globe. Our progress was to the right, and continued for two hours. Near the boundary of our solar system appeared first a whitish but dense cloud, and after it a fiery smoke ascending from a great chasm. It was a vast gulf separating our solar system on that side from some other systems of the starry heaven. The fiery smoke appeared at a considerable distance. I was carried through the midst of it, and there then appeared a great number of men in the chasm or gulf beneath, who were spirits (for spirits all appear in the human form, and are actually men). And I heard them talking together; but whence or what they were it was not given me to know. One of them, however, told me they were guards, to prevent spirits passing from this world to any other in the universe without permission. That this was so was indeed confirmed; for some spirits who were in the company, who had no permission to pass, when they came to this great gulf began to cry out vehemently that they were lost; for they were as persons struggling in the agonies of death. They therefore stopped on that side of the gulf; nor could they be carried further; for the fiery smoke exhaling from the gulf overpowered and thus tormented them.

After I was conveyed through this great chasm, I arrived at length at a place where I stopped; and then there appeared to me spirits from above, with whom it was given to converse. From their speech, and their peculiar manner of apprehending and explaining things, I clearly perceived that they were from another earth; for they differed entirely from the spirits of our solar system. They perceived also from my discourse that I came from afar.

After conversing for some time on various subjects, I asked what God they worshipped ? They said that they worshipped a certain Angel, who appears to them as a Divine man, for He is refulgent with light; and that He instructs them, and gives them to perceive what they ought to do. They said further that they know the Most High God is in the Sun of the angelic heaven, and that He appears to His angel, and not to them; and that He is too great for them to dare to adore Him. The angel whom they worshipped was an angelic society, to which it was granted by the Lord to preside over them, and teach them the way of what is just and right. (*ib.* n. 128-130.)

Being questioned concerning the sun of their system, which enlightens their earth, they said it has a flaming appearance; and when I represented the size of the sun of our earth, they said theirs was less. For their sun to our eyes is a star, and I was told by the angels that it is one of the lesser stars. They said that the starry heaven is also seen from their earth; and that to the westward a star larger than the rest appears to them, which was declared from heaven to be our sun.

After this my sight was opened, so that I could in some degree look upon their earth; and there appeared many green fields, and forests with trees in foliage, and also fleecy sheep. Afterwards I saw some of the inhabitants, who were of the meaner class, clothed nearly like peasantry in Europe. I saw also a man with his wife. She appeared of beautiful form, and graceful mien; so likewise did the man. But I remarked that he had a stately carriage, and a deportment which had a semblance of haughtiness; but the woman's deportment was humble. I was informed by the angels that such is the manner on that earth; yet that the men who have such a bearing are beloved, because they nevertheless are good. I was also informed that they are not permitted to have more than one wife; for it is contrary to the laws. The woman whom I saw had before her breast a wide garment, behind which she could conceal herself, which was so made that she could insert her arms, and clothe herself in it, and so walk away. As to the lower part it could be gathered up, and when gathered up and applied to the body it looked like a stomacher, such as are worn by the women of our earth. But the same also served the man for a covering; he was seen to take it from the woman, put it on his back, and loosen the lower part, which then flowed down to his feet like a toga; and thus clothed he walked away.

What I saw on that earth was not seen with the eyes of my body, but with the eyes of my spirit; for a spirit can see the things which are on any earth, when it is granted by the Lord. (*ib.* n. 133, 134.)

Of a Second Earth beyond our Solar System.

I was afterwards led of the Lord to an earth in the universe which was farther distant from our earth than the first, just spoken of. That it was farther distant was plain from the fact that I was two days in being led thither, as to my spirit. This earth was towards the left, whereas the former was towards the right. Since remoteness in the spiritual world does not arise from distance of place, but from difference of state, as was said above, therefore from the length of my progress thither I could infer that the state of the interiors among them, which is the state of the affections and thence thoughts, differed as much from the state of the interiors among the spirits of our earth. Being conveyed thither, as to the spirit, by changes of state of the interiors, it was given me to observe the successive changes themselves, before I arrived there. This was done while I was wide awake.

When I arrived there the earth was not seen by me, but only the spirits who were from that earth. Those spirits were at a considerable height above my head, whence they beheld me as I approached. From where they stood they observed that I was not from their earth, but from some other at a great distance. They therefore accosted me with questions on various subjects, to which it was given me to reply. Among other things I told them to what earth I belonged, and what kind of an earth it is; and then I told them about the other earths in our solar system; and at the same time also of the spirits of the earth or planet Mercury, that they wander about to many earths to procure for themselves knowledges on various matters. On hearing this they said that they had also seen those spirits among them. (E. U. n. 138, 139.)

Being asked about the God they worship, they replied that they worshipped a God visible and invisible, God visible in the Human Form, and God invisible not in any form; and it was discoverable from their conversation, and also from the ideas of their thought, as communicated to me, that the visible God was our Lord Himself; and they also called Him Lord. (*ib.* n. 141.)

The spirits who were seen on high were asked, whether they live under the rule of princes or kings on their earth? To which they replied, that they do not know what rule is; and that they live under themselves, distinguished into nations, families, and houses. They were asked whether they are thus in a state of security? They said that they are secure, since one family never envies another in any respect, or desires to deprive another of its just rights. They were indignant that such questions should be asked as suggested hostility, or any protection against robbers. What, said they, have we need of but food and raiment, and thus to live content and quiet under ourselves ?

They were further asked about their earth and its produce. They said that they have green fields, flower gardens, forests filled with fruit-trees, and also lakes abounding with fish ; that they have birds of a blue colour with golden wings, and animals, larger and smaller. Among the smaller they mentioned one kind, which has the back elevated like camels on our earth. They do not however eat the flesh of animals, but only the flesh of fishes ; and besides this the fruits of trees and pulse of the earth. They said, moreover, that they do not live in houses that are built, but in groves, among the leafy branches of which they make themselves a covering from the rain and from the heat of the sun.

Being asked about their sun, which appears from our earth as a star, they said that it has a fiery appearance, and is not larger to the sight than a man's head. I was told by the angels that the star which is their sun is among the lesser stars, not far distant from the equator.

Some spirits [of them] were seen who were like what they had been during their abode on their earth as men. They had faces not unlike those of the men of our earth, except that their eyes, and also their nose, was small. This appearing to me somewhat of deformity, they said that with them small eyes and a small nose were accounted marks of beauty. A female was seen, clad in a gown ornamented with roses of various colours. I asked whence they are supplied with materials for clothing on their earth ? They answered, that they gather from certain plants a substance which they spin into thread ; and that they then immediately lay the threads in double and triple rows, and moistened them with a glutinous liquid which gives them consistency. They afterwards colour the cloth thus prepared with the juices of plants. It was also shown me how they make the thread. They sit reclining backwards upon a seat, and wind it by the help of their toes, and when wound draw it towards them, and twist it with the hand.

They also told me that on that earth a husband has only one wife ; and they bear children to the number of ten to fifteen. (*ib.* n. 143-147)

Note.—For an account of other earths beyond our solar system the reader is referred to the author's little work, " The Earths of the Universe."

MISCELLANEOUS EXTRACTS.

CONTINUAL REFLECTION, AND CONTINUAL PRESENCE OF THE LORD.

IT was perceived how it is with regard to continual reflection, that it is not innate with man, but a man is accustomed to it by habit from infancy, so that at length it becomes as it were natural. Thus it is with reflection upon the things one meets with in walking, upon the motions of his body and limbs, upon his steps, —into all which he is led by habit. For if he had not previously learned it he would not even know how to walk upon his feet; and of such things there are a great many with man that are at once acquired and yet naturalized. So it is also with his speech, whether vernacular or foreign; the sense falls into words while the man does not think of it, from custom, although it is the result of previous training. It is the same with those who practise upon musical instruments. All things of the external body are thus habituated, the muscles being wonderfully taught; and even the sight and hearing. When one speaks, the sight is present; and the hearing, in a different manner. Especially when one speaks with a person of dignified rank, there is a sentiment of respect in every single particular of his behaviour, which is in like manner acquired. It is the same also with the man who is regenerated. It was perceived that in matters of conscience, conscientiousness is present in every particular of the man's thought and action, though he is not aware of it; with the pious man, piety is in everything; with the obedient, obedience; with the charitable, charity; with the conjugial, conjugial love. In all these cases the ruling principle is perpetually present, in the minutest particulars, though the man is not conscious of it. So is the presence of the Lord with the celestial angels; which, although they do not know it, is yet the Lord's. When therefore it is said that the Lord is continually to be thought of, this is what is meant by it; not that man is to hold his thoughts perpetually and sensibly on that one theme. This may be done in the beginning, until such continuity [of reflection] is acquired. (S. D. n. 4226.)

CONSCIENCE.

The real spiritual life of man resides in a true conscience; for therein is his faith conjoined with his charity. To act from conscience therefore, with those who are possessed of it, is to act from their own spiritual life, and to act contrary to conscience, with them is to act contrary to their own spiritual life. Hence it is that they are in the tranquillity of peace, and in internal blessedness, when they act according to conscience, and in intranquillity and pain when they act contrary to it. This pain is what is called remorse of conscience.

Man has a conscience of what is good, and a conscience of what is just. The conscience of what is good is the conscience of the internal man, and the conscience of what is just is the conscience of the external man. The conscience of what is good consists in acting according to the precepts of faith, from internal affection; and the conscience of what is just consists in acting according to the civil and moral laws, from external affection. They who have a conscience of what is good have also a conscience of what is just; and they who have only a conscience of what is just are in the capability of receiving a conscience of what is good; and they also do receive it when they are instructed.

With those who are in charity towards the neighbour, the conscience is a conscience of truth, because it is formed by the faith of truth; but with those who are in love to the Lord it is a conscience of good, because it is formed by the love of truth. The conscience of these is a higher conscience, and is called the perception of truth from good. They who have a conscience of truth are of the Lord's spiritual kingdom; and they who have the higher conscience which is called perception are of the Lord's celestial kingdom. (H. D. n. 133-135.)

THE LORD'S FAVOUR TO MAN'S VARIED CONSCIENCE.

There is no pure intellectual truth, that is truth Divine, with man; but the truths of faith, which are with man, are appearances of truth, to which fallacies of the senses adjoin themselves, and to these the falsities which come of the lusts of self-love and the love of the world. Such are the truths which exist with man; and how impure these are may appear from the fact that they are adjoined to such things. Yet the Lord conjoins himself with man in these impurities; for He animates and quickens them with innocence and charity, and thus forms a conscience. The truths of conscience are various, being according to every one's religion; and these, provided they are not contrary to the goods of faith, the Lord is not willing to violate, because man is imbued with them, and attaches sanctity to them. The Lord never breaks any one, but bends him. This may appear from the consideration, that there are some of all denominations within the church who are endowed with conscience; though their conscience is more perfect in proportion as the truths which form it approach nearer to the genuine truths of faith. (A. C. n. 2053.)

The Pleasures of Life.

There is no pleasure existing in the body which does not arise and subsist from some interior affection ; and there is no interior affection which does not arise and subsist from one still more interior, in which is its use and end. These interior things, which proceed in order even from the inmost, man is not sensible of while he lives in the body, and most men scarcely know that they exist, much less that pleasures are thence derived. As however nothing can ever come forth in externals except in order from the interiors, pleasures are only ultimate effects. . . . . This may be evident to any one from the consideration of the sense of sight and its pleasures. Unless there were interior vision the eye could never see. The sight of the eye springs from an inner sight; and therefore a man sees equally well after death, nay, much better, than while he lived in the body,—not indeed worldly and corporeal objects, but those which are in the other life. They who were blind in the life of the body see in the other life equally well with those who were quick-sighted; for the same reason also a man sees while he sleeps and in his dreams, as well as when he is awake. By the internal sight it has been granted me to see the things that are in the other life more clearly than I see those that are in the world. From these considerations it is evident that external vision springs from interior vision, and this from a vision still more interior, and so on ; the case is the same with every other sense, and with every pleasure.

Some are of opinion that no one who wishes to be happy in the other life should ever live in the pleasures of the body and of the senses, but should renounce all such delights; saying, that these corporeal and worldly pleasures are what draw away and withhold a man from a spiritual and heavenly life. But they who thus believe, and therefore voluntarily reduce themselves to wretchedness while they live in the world, are not aware of the real truth. It is by no means forbidden any one to enjoy the pleasures of the body and of sensual things; that is to say, the pleasures of the possession of lands, and of wealth ; the pleasures of honours, and of offices of the state ; the pleasures of conjugial love, and of love towards infants and children; the pleasures of friendship, and of social intercourse ; the pleasures of hearing, or of the sweetness of singing and music ; the pleasures of sight, or of beauties, which are manifold,—as of becoming raiment, of well-furnished houses, of beautiful gardens, and the like, which from their harmonies are delightful; the pleasures of smell, or of agreeable odours ; the pleasures of taste, or of the sweetness and usefulness of meats and drinks ; and the pleasures of the touch ; for these, as was observed, are outermost or corporeal affections from interior affection. The interior affections, which are living, all derive their delight from good and truth; and good and truth derive their delight from charity and faith, and then from the Lord, thus from life itself ; and therefore the affections and pleasures which are from thence are alive. Because genuine pleasures derive their origin from this source they are never denied to any one. Nay more, when pleasures thence derive their origin the delight of them indefinitely exceeds the delight which is not from thence. This, comparatively, is filthy. Thus, for example, the pleasure of conjugial love ; when it derives its origin from true conjugial love, it indefinitely exceeds the delight which is not from thence; yea, so much that they who are in true conjugial love are in a kind of heavenly delight and happiness, for it comes down from heaven. This, too, they who were of the Most Ancient church confessed ; the delight of adulteries, which adulterers feel, was so abominable to them that they were struck with horror at the bare thought of it. From this it is evident what is the nature of delight which does not descend from the true Fountain of Life, or from the Lord. That the pleasures above mentioned are never denied to man, nay, that so far from being denied they first become real pleasures when they are from their true source, may also appear from the consideration, that very many who have lived in the world in power, dignity, and opulence, and have enjoyed abundantly all the pleasures of the body and of sense, are among the blessed and happy in heaven ; and with them the interior delights and felicities are now alive, because they derived their origin from the goods of charity and the truths of faith towards the Lord. And as they were thence derived, they regarded all their pleasures with a view to use, which was their end. Use was itself most delightful to them ; and from this they received the delight of their pleasures. (A. C. n. 994, 995.)

NATURALISM.

At this day naturalism has nearly inundated the church, and can only be shaken off by means of rational arguments whereby man may see that a thing is so. Naturalism arises from thinking of things Divine from things proper to nature only, such as matter, space, and time. The mind that clings to such things, and is not willing to believe anything that it does not understand, cannot but blind its understanding; and, from the darkness in which it immerses it, falls into a denial of the Divine Providence, and therefore of Omnipotence, Omnipresence, and Omniscience; when yet these, precisely as religion teaches, are within nature as well as above it. But they cannot be comprehended by the understanding unless spaces and times are removed from the ideas of its thought; for these are in some manner in every idea of thought, and unless they are removed a man can think no otherwise than that nature is all; that it is from itself; and that life is from it; and hence that the inmost principle of nature is what is called God, and that all beyond this is ideal. I know that such men will indeed wonder to hear that there is anything existing where there is neither time nor space; and that the Divine itself is without time and space; and that spiritual beings are not in time and space, but only in the appearances of them. And yet Divine spiritual things are the very essences of all things that have existed and that do exist, and natural things without them are as bodies without a soul, which become carcases. Every man who becomes a naturalist by thoughts from nature, remains such also after death; and calls all things natural that he sees in the spiritual world, because they are similar. They are however enlightened and taught by the angels that they are not natural, but that they are appearances of things natural; they are even convinced so that they affirm that it is so; but yet they relapse and worship nature, as in the world, and at length separate themselves from the angels and fall into hell; nor can they be taken out thence to eternity. The reason is, that they have not a spiritual soul, but only a natural, like that of beasts,—with the faculty however of thinking and speaking, because they were born men. Now, as the hells at this day are filled with such, more than before, it is of importance that so dense darkness arising from nature as at this day crowds and bars the threshold of men's understanding, should be removed by rational light derived from spiritual. (A. E. n. 1220.)

The Origin of Human Speech.

Human speech in its first origin is the end which a man wishes to manifest by speech. This end is his love; for what a man loves he regards as an end. From this flows the man's thought, and at length his speech. That this is so every one who reflects well may know and apperceive. That the end regarded is the first principle of speech, is manifest from the common rule that in all intelligence there is an end, and without an end there is no intelligence. And that thought is the second principle of speech, flowing from the first, is also manifest; for no one can speak without thought, or think without an end. That from this follows the language of words, and that this is the ultimate, which is properly called speech, is known. Because this is so a man who attends to the speech of another does not give his attention to the expressions or words of speech, but to the sense of them, which is that of the thought of him who speaks; and he who is wise attends to the end for which he so spake from thought, that is to what he intends, and what he loves. These three things are presented in the speech of man, to which things the language of words serves as the ultimate plane. (A. C. n. 9407.)

Four successive Solar Atmospheres.

There are four natural spheres which arise from the sun. The atmosphere which causes hearing is known. A purer atmosphere separate from the aërial is that which produces sight, or causes things to be seen, by the reflections of light (*nimbi*) from all objects. How far this atmosphere penetrates into the natural mind, and whether it presents material ideas, as they are called, or fantasies and imaginations, is not yet so evident; but it appears probable, from various considerations.[1] This, then, will be the first atmosphere that reigns in the natural mind. Another atmosphere, which is a still purer ether, is that which produces

---

[1] The reader will observe that this somewhat uncertain and conjectural manner,—so different from the author's way of speaking in his published works,—is in his posthumous Diary, and in fact in a very early part of it. The date attached to this note in the Diary is October 27, 1747. It was therefore in the preparatory and transition period, after the Divine call to his mission and the subsequent first opening of his spiritual vision, referred to above, p. 382, and before he began to publish. It is one of many passages in his Diary which evince the calmness and cautiousness of his judgment, at the time when, if ever, it might be expected to be over-confident, or unhinged,—whether one accepts his view and estimate of his experiences or not.

the magnetic forces (*vires magnetum*) which reign not only about the magnet in particular, but also around the whole globe; but to what extent it is not necessary to describe. It produces there the situation of the entire terraqueous globe, according to the poles of the world, and many things that are known respecting the elevations and inclinations of the magnet. This sphere, in the natural mind, appears to produce reasonings (*ratiocinia*); in which however, that they may be living, a spiritual principle must needs be present, as in the sight, and in every other sense, that they may perceive. The purest ethereal sphere is that universal sphere in the entire world which is presented [or is active] about the ratiocinations of the same mind. Hence that mind is called the natural mind; and its interior operations, when perverse, are called ratiocinations; but when according to order, they are called simply reason, and is a species of thoughts on account of [or arising from] spiritual influx. These spheres arise from the sun, and may be called solar, and are consequently natural. In the interior mind, however, there is nothing natural, but all is spiritual, and in the inmost mind is the celestial. (S. D. n. 222.)

A Prayer for Deliverance from Evil.

Man's state by creation is, that he may know that evil is from hell, and good is from the Lord; and that as of himself he may perceive this within him; and when he perceives it that he may reject the evil to hell, and receive the good, with the acknowledgment that it is from the Lord. When he does this he does not appropriate evil to himself, and does not do good for the sake of merit. But I know that there are many who do not comprehend this, and who are not willing to comprehend it. But yet let them pray thus:—

"That the Lord may be with them continually, and lift up and turn His countenance upon them. And, since of themselves they can do nothing of good, that He may teach, enlighten, and lead them; and grant unto them that they may live. Lest the devil seduce them, and instil evil into their hearts; knowing that when they are not led by the Lord he leads, and breathes into them evils of every kind,—such as hatred, revenge, cunning, deceit,—as a serpent infuses poison. For he is present, excites, and continually accuses; and wherever he meets with a heart that is turned away from God he enters in, dwells there, and drags the soul down to hell. O Lord deliver us." (A. E. n. 1148.)

THE CHURCH CANNOT BE RAISED UP ANEW IN ANY NATION UNTIL IT
IS ENTIRELY VASTATED.

The second Ancient Church[1] was degenerated and corrupted
until, from a kind of internal worship, it at last, in the family
of Terah, became idolatrous,—passing, as churches are wont to
do, from internal to the mere external things of worship, the
internal being blotted out of remembrance. . . . *Haran* (Gen.
xi. 28) signifies interior idolatrous worship; *Terah his father*,
signifies idolatrous worship in general; . . . *Haran died
before Terah his father*, signifies that interior worship was
blotted out of remembrance, and become merely idolatrous.
. . . As regards the fact that interior worship was blotted out
of remembrance, or had become none, the case is this :—The
church cannot arise anew among any nation, until it is so vastated that nothing of evil and falsity remains in its internal
worship. So long as there is evil in its internal worship, those
things, good and true, which constitute its internal worship are
prevented ; for while evils and falsities are present, goods and
truths cannot be received. This is evident from the fact that
they who are born into any heresy, and have so confirmed themselves in its falsities that they are entirely persuaded, can with
difficulty, if ever, be brought to receive the truths that are
contrary to their falsities ; but it is different with gentiles who
do not know what the truth of faith is, and yet live in charity.
This was the reason why the church of the Lord could not be
restored among the Jews, but among gentiles who had no
knowledges of faith. They entirely darkened and thus extinguished the light of truth, by their falsities ; but the gentiles
not so much, for they knew not what the truth of faith was,
and what they did not know they could not darken and extinguish. Now, as a new Church was to be restored, they were
chosen with whom goods and truths of faith might be implanted,
—with whom all knowledge of the good and truth of faith had
been obliterated, and who like gentiles were become external
idolaters. Respecting Terah and Abram, it was shown above [2]
that they were of such a character ; that is, that they worshipped other gods, and had no knowledge of Jehovah, nor
therefore of what the good and truth of faith were. They had
thus become better fitted to receive the seed of truth than
others in Syria, among whom knowledges still remained. That
they did remain with some, is evident from Balaam, who was
from Syria, and who not only worshipped Jehovah, but also
sacrificed, and was at the same time a prophet. (A. C. n. 1356,
1365, 1366.)

Organic Function the ground of Correspondence of Heaven with all things in Man.

The whole heaven is a Grand Man (*Maximus Homo*) ; and it is called a Grand Man because it corresponds to the Lord's Divine Human. For the Lord is the only Man ; and by so much as an angel or spirit or a man on earth has from the Lord, they also are men. . . . All things in the human body, in general and in particular, correspond most exactly to the Grand Man, and as it were to so many societies there. For, as in the human body there are members and organs, and these consist of parts, and parts of parts, so the Lord's heaven is distinguished into lesser heavens, and these into still less, and these into least, and finally into angels, each one of whom is a little heaven corresponding to the greatest. These heavens are most distinct from each other,—each one belonging to its general, and the general heavens to the most general or whole, which is the Grand Man.

But as regards the correspondence, the case is this : the heavens spoken of correspond, indeed, to the actual organic forms of the human body,—on which account it is said that societies, or angels, belong to the province of the brain, or to the province of the heart, or to the province of the lungs, or of the eye, and so on ; and yet they chiefly correspond to the functions of those viscera or organs. The case is like that of the organs or viscera themselves, in that the functions constitute one with their organic forms. For it is impossible to conceive of any function except by forms, that is by substances ; because substances are the subjects by which functions are performed. For example : one cannot conceive of sight without the eye, or of respiration without the lungs. The eye is the organic form from which and by which sight is produced ; and the lungs are the organic form from and by which respiration is effected ; and so with the other organs. The functions therefore are what the heavenly societies chiefly correspond to ; but because they correspond to the functions, they correspond also to the organic forms, for they are indivisible and inseparable from each other ; insomuch that whether we say function, or organic form by which and from which the function is, it is the same. Hence it is that the correspondence is with the organs, members and viscera because it is with the functions. When therefore a function is performed, the organ also is excited. Such in fact is the case in all and each particular thing that a man does. When he wills to do this or that, or to act thus or so, and determines it, then the organs move comfortably ; that is, they move in accordance with the purpose of the function or use ; for it is the use which governs in the forms. It is evident therefore, also, that the use existed before the organic forms of the body were extant; and that the use produced and adapted them to itself, not the contrary. But when the forms are produced, or the organs adapted, the uses proceed from them ; and it then appears as if the forms or organs were prior to the uses, although it is not so. For use flows in from the Lord,—and this through heaven, according to the order and according to the form in which heaven is disposed by the Lord, thus according to correspondences. Thus man comes into being, and thus he subsists. It is evident again from this whence it comes that man, as to each and all his parts, corresponds to the heavens. (A. C. n. 4219, 4222, 4223.)

The Church passes through the Stages of Life like an Individual.

The Church appears before the Lord as one man ; and this greatest man must pass through his ages, like the individual man, and finally to old age, and then when he dies he will rise again. The Lord says:—"*Except a corn of wheat fall into the ground and die, it abideth alone ; but if it die, it bringeth forth much fruit*" (John xii. 24.) (T. C. R. 762.)

A Man's Mind is the Man himself.

For the elementary texture of the human form, or the human form itself with all and each of its parts, is from the principles continued through the nerves from the brain. This is the form into which the man comes after death, and which is then called a spirit, and angel, and which is in all perfection a man, but spiritual. The material form which is added and superinduced in the world is not a human form of itself, but from the former, being added and superinduced that the man may perform uses in the natural world. (D. L. W. 388.)

Swedenborg's Rules of Life.

1. Often to read and meditate on the Word of God.
2. To submit everything to the will of Divine Providence.
3. To observe in everything a propriety of behaviour, and to keep the conscience clear.
4. To discharge with fidelity the functions of my employments, and to make myself in all things useful to society (*From a posthumous MS.*)

INDEX

venly church could not exist without a church on earth, *ib.*; when near its end a new church is always raised up, 325 ; four churches have in general existed on earth, *ib.*; four represented by Nebuchadnezzar's dream, *ib.*; sketch of history and character of the four, 325-327.

Church, Most Ancient, cause of the fall of, 27 ; manner of conversation of men of, 28 ; men of, had immediate revelation, 113 ; style of writing of, 124 ; men of, had revelation from perception, 132, 328 ; was celestial, 264 ; was from the Divine above all churches on the globe, 328 ; state of men of, like the state of the celestial angels, *ib.* ; the Word of, 328 ; worship of, 329 ; men of, performed worship in tents, 330 ; composed of several different churches, *ib.*; perception in, 331 ; dignities and riches among men of, 332.

Church, Ancient, was spiritual, 264 ; signified by Noah, 334 ; character of, *ib.*; the communication of men of, with heaven was external, 335 ; was a representative church, *ib.*; composed of churches differing as to doctrinals of faith, *ib.*; was in representatives and significatives, *ib.*; men of, accounted doctrinals of faith as relatively nothing, 336 ; worship of, *ib.*; doctrinals of, 337 ; style of writing of, *ib.*; decline of, 338 ; three churches of, *ib.*; second, 339, and *see* Hebrew church ; compared with the Christian, 372.

Church, Hebrew, origin, 339 ; name applied to all who used sacrificial worship, 342 ; abominated by others of the Ancient church because of their sacrifices, 342 ; descent of, into idolatry, 343.

Church, Israelitish, when begun, 352 ; representative, *ib.*; character of, *ib.*; representative of all things of the church in heaven and on earth, 356 ; *see* Jews.

Church, Apostolic, did not know the doctrine of imputation, 314.

Church, Christian, dies if the Divinity of the Lord Jesus Christ be denied, 314 ; primitive and subsequent condition of, 373 ; why not sooner established in the European world, *ib.*; present state of, 374 ; end of the first, 377 ; state of, after the Last Judgment, 716.

Church, New Christian, 385 ; foretold in the Revelation, *ib.*; primary doctrine of,

ib.; is signified by the New Jerusalem, *ib.*; is first established among a few, 407 ; to be the crown of all the churches and to endure for ever, 411 ; is at first external, 415.

Church, representative, *see* Representative church.

Circumcision, baptism instituted in place of, 417.

City, Holy, vision of the, meaning of, 390 ; Memorabilia concerning Temple and, 400.

Cognitions, what, 284, and *note*, and knowledges distinguished, *ib.*

Colours, correspondence of, 165.

Combat may be waged from truth not genuine, 299.

Coming of the Lord, *see* Advent.

Commandments, tables of ten, broken by Moses, 165 ; signification of tables, 165 ; why promulgated from Sinai, 192 ; natural, spiritual and celestial senses of, 194 ; he who offends in one offends in all, 213 ; were the first-fruits of the Word, 257, and *note ;* precepts of the, in every religion, 519.

Conception, or idea, difference between a spiritual and a natural, 4.

Concupiscences of evil, man cannot be purified from, in the internal except as he removes evils in the external, 492 ; innumerable in every evil, 494.

Confirmations, 236.

Confusion of tongues, signification of, 239.

Conjugial love, remains after death, 445 ; conjugial pair in heaven, 451 ; they who are in love truly conjugial feel themselves to be truly one, 457 ; is the treasury of all delights, 460 ; wisdom and intelligence are in proportion to conjugial love, 462 ; qualifications for receiving, 463 ; none can be in love truly conjugial but those who receive it from the Lord, *ib.*; obstacles to, 464 ; the love of domination entirely banishes conjugial love, 465 ; difference of religion incompatible with, 466 ; true conjugial love is scarcely known at this day, 468 ; semblances of, 469 ; the conjugial union of one man with one wife is the jewel of human life, 469 ; conjugial love accompanies religion in its steps, 470 ; it cannot be told from appearances who has and who has not conjugial love, *ib.*; the beauty of the angels originates from, 474 ; genuine conjugial love an image of heaven, 475 ; affections and thoughts of, imaged in heaven by brilliant auras,

Seasons, spiritual signification of the four, 647.

Secret things revealed, spiritual signification of, 596.

Seed, spiritual signification of, 245.

Self-examination, necessity of, 256.

Self-love, 523 ; and love of the world can only be removed by degrees, 510 ; surpasses other loves in its capacity for falsifying truths, 513 ; the thick darkness of those who are in, 667 ; the nature of, 692 ; has no limit, 693.

Serpent, spiritual signification of, 185.

Servants, correspondence of, 164.

Sensation, is an affection of the substance of the organs of sense, 6.

Sensual, the very, which is the ultimate of the natural, can with difficulty be regenerated, 297.

Seven, spiritual signification of, 186 ; years of famine, 283.

Sex, distinction of, is in the spirit, 443 ; love of, remains after death, 444.

Shaddai, a name of Jehovah as regards temptation, afterwards an idol, 345.

Sheep, Feed My, spiritual signification of, 437.

Shem, spiritual signification of, 341.

Shiloh, why a name of the Lord, 43.

Sight, *see* Sensation.

Silver, spiritual signification of, 188, 326 ; age of, *ib.*

Sins, to confess, is to see evil in one's self, 279.

Slavery, what it is, 277.

Sleep, the Lord's providential care of man during, 615 ; evil spirits seek to hurt man during, 615, 616.

Smell, *see* Sensation.

Solar systems, earths of other, 733.

Son of God, from eternity not acknowledged by the Apostolic church, 315.

Son of Man, meaning of the phrase, 72, 84 ; the Son, meaning of, 86.

Soul, the secret operations of the, in the body, 533 ; prevailing ignorance respecting the, 541 ; what it is, *ib.*, 542, and *note* ; origin of, 543 ; true influx, or the intercourse between the soul and the body, 549, 561, 562 ; is a spiritual substance, *ib.*

Sound, how the state and form of, are made in the lungs, 557 ; spiritual signification of, 558.

South, spiritual signification of, 645.

Space, God is not in, 4 ; spaces apparent in the spiritual world, *ib.*, 645 ; no spaces there, 593 ; spaces and distances in their origin are changes of state, 733.

Speech, origin of human, 743 ; *see* Language.

Sphere, meaning of, 603 ; character perceived in the other life from the, *ib.*

Spiral motions of the mind, 551.

Spirit, Holy, *see* Holy Spirit.

Spirits, world of, *see* World of spirits.

Spirits, angelic, 247 ; evil, excite evils and falsities, 299 ; all were once men, 579 ; conversation and language of, 604 ; changed according to man's affections, 609 ; danger of conscious intercourse with spirits, 616-619 ; speak with man from his memory, 619 ; man not enlightened by intercourse with, 622 ; what is meant by being in the spirit, 625 ; how spirits can be enabled to see into this world, 628 ; of every earth are near their own, 725 ; the quality of every spirit manifests itself by an influx, 726.

Spiritual world, spaces appear in the, as in the natural world, 4 ; all things in the, correspond to all things in man, 16 ; spiritual things proceed from love, 17 ; immensity of the, 577 ; extension of man's thought into, 627 ; no material earth visible to the inhabitants of, 725.

Spiritual sense of the Word, *see* Word.

Spiritual kingdom, the, and its correspondence, 636 ; government in the Lord's, 654.

Stars, spiritual signification of, 641.

State, final, *see* Final state,

Stealing, spiritual signification of, 207.

Stone, correspondence of, 310.

Sun, Divine sphere acts through, 10 ; there are two suns, a spiritual and a natural, 16 ; nature of the natural sun, 17 ; standing still at Joshua's command, 170 ; correspondence of sun, 183, 527, 640 ; the spiritual principle is from the, where the Lord is, 572 ; the sun in heaven, 639 ; the Lord appears as a sun to the angels, *ib.*

Swedenborg, all that he learned from angels or spirits was from the Lord alone, 383 ; Second Coming of the Lord effected through his instrumentality, 382 ; why introduced into the spiritual world, 383 ; permission given to Swedenborg to converse with the spirits of the other earths, 719 ; a prayer recommended by, 744 ; his rules of life, 745.

Tabernacle, spiritual signification of, 330 ; reason why the feast of tabernacles was instituted, *ib.*

INDEX

TO THE

EXTRACTS FROM THE WRITINGS OF SWEDENBORG.

———o———

APOCALYPSE REVEALED.